Dimensions of physical education

Edited by

Charles A. Bucher, A.B., M.A., Ed.D.

Professor of Education and Director of Physical Education,
School of Education, New York University,
New York, N. Y.

Myra Goldman, B.S., M.S.

The C. V. Mosby Company

Saint Louis   1969

Preface

Dimensions of Physical Education is intended as a source book for students in undergraduate and graduate professional programs. It is a concise anthology of readings that will prove to be of value to school and college physical education faculty members as well as to physical education leaders in youth agencies and other organizations in which such programs exist.

The readings in each division are grouped into several coordinated themes, each of which explores and defines the major emphasis of the entire division. The introductory section preceding each major division presents a brief summary of the readings in that division. Projects and thought questions based on the readings and a list of suggested references complete each of the seven major divisions.

The readings presented in this book have been drawn from textbooks, research journals, periodicals, magazines, and professional journals. Textbook chapters, research reports, philosophic discussions, and position papers are also represented. The selection of readings represents a desire for quality rather than quantity.

Each article has been selected on the basis of its depth of coverage in relation to a particular topic. Pertinence to contemporary thought in education and physical education or historical significance and interest also helped to form a rationale for selection. The reader will find each article highly readable and thought provoking. Not all of the selections are directly concerned with physical education, and not all of the authors are physical educators; yet each selection has definite implications for physical education. The reader will also find that some of the articles cut across the lines of several of the major divisions. Thus they may be utilized in any of several different contexts with pertinence to all of them.

Many authors and publishers have made the completion of this book possible. The recommendations of each author or publisher for proper documentation has been followed in crediting each selection.

Charles A. Bucher
Myra Goldman

v

Contents

Part one

Nature and scope of physical education

1. Making the most of your life (The Royal Bank of Canada), 3
2. Physical education: a new profession (Luther H. Gulick), 8
3. Physical education—an emerging profession (Charles A. Bucher), 11
4. Mental, social, maturity, and physical characteristics of underaged and normal-aged boys in elementary school grades (H. Harrison Clarke and John N. Drowatzky), 19
5. HPR with a difference (Joe B. Rushing), 23
6. A new and hard look at college physical education programs (Martin H. Rogers), 26
7. Athletics: ". . . . unquenchably the same"? (Byron R. White), 29
8. The ten most significant educational research findings in the past ten years (Daniel E. Griffiths), 34
9. The role of health, physical education, and recreation in the space age (Clifford Brownell), 42

Part two

Philosophy of physical education as part of general education

10. On the uses of philosophy (Will Durant), 51
11. Philosophical profiles for physical educators (Deobold B. Van Dalen), 54
12. A philosophical interpretation of the educational views held by seven leaders in American physical education (Richard B. Morland), 59
13. Identification of some philosophical beliefs of influential leaders in American physical education (Donn E. Bair), 63
14. Physical education—part of the general education program (Wilson W. Elkins), 67
15. What makes a champion? (A philosophy of sport) (Fred Russell), 69
16. The whole man, science, and physical education (Arthur H. Steinhaus), 72
17. The whole child: a fresh look (Harold Taylor), 79

Part three

Relationship of physical education to health, recreation, camping, and outdoor education

18. Vital ties between health and education (Delbert Oberteuffer), 87
19. School administrators must be safety-minded (Merrill Scott), 90
20. Nutrition and physical fitness (National Dairy Council), 93

21. The place of recreation in modern living (Joseph Prendergast), 97
22. The marks of a professional man in recreation (Howard G. Danford), 101
23. Education comes alive outdoors (Robert M. Isenberg), 103
24. Outdoor education for lifetime interests (Julian W. Smith), 106
25. A philosophical definition of leisure (Paul Weiss), 108
26. A tale of the times (Sebastian deGrazia), 113

Part four

Changing concepts of physical education

27. Sport, play, and physical education in cultural perspective (Franklin Parker), 119
28. The Greek tradition and today's physical education (Robert H. Beck), 123
29. Did the Greeks and the Romans play football? (Norma D. Young), 127
30. The impact of Edward Hitchcock on the history of physical education (J. Edmund Welch), 131
31. The confessions of a once strict formalist (Ethel Perrin), 134
32. Origins of contemporary sports (Marvin H. Eyler), 140
33. Are we losing the Olympic ideal? (Charles A. Bucher), 147
34. The significance of human movement: a phenomenological approach (Seymour Kleinman), 150
35. Learning about movement (Naomi Allenbaugh), 154
36. Moto ergo sum (Peter V. Karpovich), 157

Part five

Scientific foundations of physical education

Biological foundations of physical education

37. Learning to live with science (Emmanuel G. Mesthene), 163
38. Is physical fitness our most important objective? (Raymond A. Weiss), 168
39. Don't just sit there; walk, jog, run (Time magazine), 172
40. Exercise and weight control (Committee on Exercise and Physical Fitness of the American Medical Association, The President's Council on Physical Fitness, and the Lifetime Sports Foundation), 174
41. Physiology of training, including age and sex differences (Lucien Brouha, M.D.), 180
42. A comparison of isotonic and isometric exercises in the development of muscular strength (Stan Burnham), 189
43. Women and the medical aspects of sports (Evalyn S. Gendel, M.D.), 192

Psychological foundations of physical education

44. The contributions of physical activity to psychological development (M. Gladys Scott), 198
45. Somatopsychic education—a rationale for physical education (Dorothy V. Harris), 208
46. Body concept as it relates to self-concept (Leela C. Zion), 215
47. Health, physical education, and academic achievement (Charles A. Bucher), 219
48. Motor skills—foundation stone of progress (D. H. Radler with Newell C. Kephart), 222

49. The worth of physical skill (Charles A. Bucher), 227
50. Overview of educational innovation (Lawrence Balter and Emanuel Sanger), 230

Sociological foundations of physical education

51. The science of sport and sports sociology—questions related to development—problems of structure (Günter Erbach), 235
52. The function of sport in human relations (Michel Bouet), 245
53. Physical education and leisure (V. Artemov), 248
54. Basic understanding for teaching the disadvantaged (Allan C. Ornstein), 254
55. The contribution of school athletics to the growing boy (Ray O. Duncan), 260
56. Little League baseball can hurt your boy (Charles A. Bucher with Tim Cohane), 263

Part six
Leadership in physical education

57. Qualities related to success in women's physical education professional preparation program (Reuben B. Frost and Margery Servis Bulger), 271
58. Securing professional personnel (Waneen Wyrick), 277
59. Certain psychosocial and cultural characteristics unique to prospective teachers of physical education (Gerald S. Kenyon), 280
60. Problems of and competencies needed by men physical education teachers at the secondary level (Elmo Smith Roundy), 287
61. The role of the coach in American education (John D. Lawther), 293
62. Professional preparation of the athletic coach (Charles A. Bucher), 295
63. I'm a woman physical educator—not a coach (Gayle Dawley Moore), 298
64. Communicate or perish (Robert N. Singer), 300
65. The potential of physical education as an area of research and scholarly effort (Arthur S. Daniels), 302

Part seven
The profession

66. The American Association for Health and Physical Education: a department of the NEA (Charles H. McCloy), 309
67. The American Academy: its role in the profession (Rosalind Cassidy), 311
68. The Canadian Association for Health, Physical Education and Recreation, Inc. (Maxwell L. Howell), 312
69. Trends in certification (Robert Holland), 315
70. Implications for physical education in the current re-examination of American education (Ruth Abernathy), 316
71. The case for a bold, new physical education experience (Charles L. Mand), 319
72. Fundamental issues in our profession (Ray O. Duncan), 322
73. Vibrations in the ivory towers (Samuel Baskin), 327
74. What will physical education be like in 1977? (Reuben B. Frost), 330

Part one

Nature and scope of physical education

Physical education as a profession and as a curricular area is undergoing a slow and continual metamorphosis. The leaders of our profession and leaders in other academic areas as well are calling for us to become more of a profession and more of an academic discipline.

What *is* new about the present nature and scope of physical education? What changes in emphasis have taken place since World War II? What new considerations is the space age forcing upon us? What will physical education be like in the future?

The nature of today's physical education is one of an orientation toward science and toward a more scientific comprehension of the profession of physical education. The scope of physical education has broadened to include an emphasis on intellectual understandings as supplementary and complementary facets of physical skill development.

By becoming thoroughly acquainted with the nature and scope of physical education, the physical educator can better formulate and develop his own intellectual concept of his profession. This concept will be a significant part of his personal relationship with and contribution to the whole of education and physical education.

The readings presented in this book have been drawn from a large group of writings by outstanding educators and researchers. Each of the readings is either directly concerned with the nature and scope of physical education or has definite implications for physical education.

The opening selection, from The Royal Bank of Canada's *Monthly Letter,* is a summary of the "good life." This reading gives some explicit suggestions for attaining the most out of life by showing how each individual can learn to solve one problem at a time by simply living one day at a time. This article holds many implications for educators and physical educators by its advocacy of capitalizing on such human traits and needs as constructive thinking, the pursuit of happiness, character building, and creativity.

The profession of physical education itself is the concern of the article by Luther H. Gulick, who discusses his thesis of the nature of the profession of physical education. His views, first published in 1890, are not inconsistent with those of more contemporary writers. Gulick defends the right of physical education to call itself a profession, and he explores the worth of physical education to society.

Charles A. Bucher, in his article "Physical Education—An Emerging Profession," examines the criteria for professional status. He then scrutinizes physical education in light of each of the four criteria selected to ascertain whether or not it is a profession. The findings indicate that physical education is emerging as a profession but has yet to reach full-fledged professional maturity.

Physical educators serve their profession in a variety of settings. The following representative group of articles is concerned with teaching physical education on the four educational levels: elementary school, secondary school, junior college, and college.

H. Harrison Clarke and John N. Drowatzky studied selected mental, social, and physical characteristics of elementary school-age boys who were either of normal age for their grade level or slightly underage. The results of the study seem to indicate significant differences between the boys on certain strength and motor ability measures. Such research can aid the physical educator in developing a rationale for grouping his students, and can give him some concrete ideas for program planning.

The junior and community colleges are the most rapidly expanding type of educational institutions today. Joe B. Rushing describes the health, physical education, and recreation program at a junior college in Florida. The program emphasizes lifetime sports in its basic physical education instructional program while giving the student an opportunity to participate in team sports through the intramural program. At the time the article was written the college had no physical education facilities of its own. The article shows how full use was made of off-campus community and commercial facilities and how this unique arrangement helped to enhance the goals and objectives of the program.

College physical education programs are critically analyzed by Martin H. Rogers. Rogers says that changes in higher education and changes in the needs of today's college students demand greater flexibility and a new focus in basic instructional programs in physical education. The author calls for more relevant programs in physical education to parallel the new trends in higher education.

Physical educators also serve their profession through the school and college athletic programs in which they are involved. The address by Byron White gives a brief history of athletic competition, beginning with the period of the ancient Persians and Greeks, and shows how the idealistic concept of athletics and athletes gradually deteriorated. White goes on to demonstrate the educational nature of today's athletics and discusses some of the controversy surrounding athletic competition for young men and women.

Physical educators contribute to all of education through teaching, research, and various other services. General education contributes in turn to physical education. Daniel E. Griffiths reports on ten significant lines of educational research dating from 1959. Each of these lines of research has important implications for both education and physical education. Studies in human growth and development, the effect of computer technology on learning theory, school administrators, Project Talent, new curriculum projects, the Conant reports, and the biochemical aspects of learning and memory are outlined and discussed.

The effects of the space age on health, physical education, and recreation is the topic of Clifford Brownell. He explores the need for curriculum enrichment and coordination in these allied fields so that the schools can offer programs in these areas that are adequate to today's needs and reach out to the future as well.

1. Making the most of your life*

There is no easy way to make the most of your life. Even if you follow the Hedonists in believing that pleasure is the only good, you have to do some work to make the pleasure possible.

The Canadian way of life has as one of its principles the fact of work. One is expected to contribute economically, socially and culturally.

Having mastered the daily routine of living within this pattern, then we add grace notes and go on to fill our lives with personally rewarding projects. These may be in any of six areas: aesthetic, economic, political, social, religious and philosophical. Some persons are successful in linking three or four in their satisfying lives.

Of what does a full life consist? First of all, it requires that you be awake and active. It requires that you stretch your mind muscles so as to grasp and comprehend much that will not force itself upon you. It requires that you see and appreciate beauty. It requires you to stand on your own feet, measuring up to life's demands, while at the same time you bow in awe of life's unexplained mysteries. This adds up to seeing life steadily and seeing it whole.

Obviously then, there is more to making the most of your life than learning the plod and punctuality books by heart. You need to absorb their precepts into your own individuality, tailored to your environment and your purpose in life.

Here is where mottoes and slogans, autosuggestion and the association of ideas, principles and standards come in handy. This *Letter* is an attempt to pull together some of the precepts in capsule form.

*From Monthly Letter, Vol. 46, No. 4, Apr. 1, 1965, The Royal Bank of Canada. Used by permission.
This article will help to stimulate your thinking in regard to your goals and accomplishments as a physical educator.

As you progress from youth to adulthood you will learn to adjust yourself to the circumstances of your new life so that you fit into the total situation. Insofar as you adapt yourself intelligently, you are master of your fate.

The time has come to grow up, and growing up consists in the main of bringing random impulses under control and coordinating hit-or-miss activities. The mature world, whether business, professional or technical, has no use for youths who enter it glorifying infantilism . . . like a small child crying "look at me!" as he jumps off a six-inch-high step.

Do not be afraid to get wrinkles on your face in the process of developing maturity. There is nothing less interesting than a face on which life has written no story. In the ruins of Pompeii the visitor sees a wall painting of Narcissus, the young man who was so enamoured of himself that he could not tear himself away from a pool that reflected his good looks. He had thrown away his past, he ignored what was going on around him, and he gave no thought to the future. A myth-maker tells us that when Narcissus came to the end, and was being ferried over the River Styx, the River of Death, he passed the time gazing over the side of the boat at his reflection.

One needs a sense of proportion, and to learn to command the self one has to live with. Mind-set, whether on self-gratification or some other love, is a state that prevents your making the most of your life.

ABOUT BEING AMBITIOUS

When you are seeking personal fulfilment, that is true ambition. You take into account your talent, your tastes and your hopes, the demands of the business or professional or scientific career you want, and you move toward perfecting your ability to meet them.

3

It is remarkable what may be accomplished by plain, homespun capacities governed by an indomitable purpose and common sense.

What is your real, chief and foremost object in life? The vocation you choose will colour your relations with the world. The act of choosing will give you a miniature plan to stimulate and rouse you, to urge you on to desirable action, and to keep you from false paths.

Self-fulfilment does not always mean reaching a lofty height of perfection. The perfection of a tree on a rocky hillside is judged by this: in its environment of soil and climate and molestation by men and animals, it has done all that could be expected of it. The tree may be poverty-stricken, hunger-pinched, tempest-tortured, and stripped of bark, not at all an ideal tree of its species, but it has prevailed in being the best tree possible under the circumstances.

Ambition to succeed must take account of two things as you enter the world market-place: what have you to offer, and what are you prepared to do to improve the quality of what you offer? During the next thirty years you will sell about seventy thousand hours of your time and energy. What you get for it depends upon a constructive and determined answer to these questions.

How constructive are you? Instead of urging their imagination to produce a high and attainable goal, some people are content to struggle and whine through their days with a dull resentment of what they call their "bad breaks." They are the sort of people who, about to be cast away on a desert island, would select a packing-case full of light novels and cartoon books to keep them company. The constructive person would ask for some blank notebooks and a supply of pencils.

THE BEST IN LIFE

A perceptive person discriminates between what the herd approves and what he himself has set his mind upon as being valuable. To such a person most of the pleasures which are run after by mankind are superfluous, or even a trouble and a burden.

Discrimination means to prefer the best. It takes account of what may be, rather than what is. It looks for possibilities. It has learned to scorn mediocrity and things that are shoddy by becoming acquainted with the best. This is easy to do. Whether your interest is in poetry, science or business, there is available to you the opportunity to make yourself familiar with the first-rate of all time.

Everything else in your life is relative to the thing you choose as your measure of success, so let it be nothing small.

When you are striving for money, position, or power, you have many competitors, but when you are developing your own personality so as to get the most out of life you have no outside competition. The chief good you seek is something which is your own, not easily taken from you.

We can add very much to our happiness, said a great German philosopher, by a timely recognition of the simple truth that every man's chief and real existence is in his own skin and not in other people's opinions. We need the courage to be what we are, and to follow the course we have mapped out.

All of this presupposes activity of thought. This is different from gathering scraps of fact or amassing technical detail. It implies the possession of an ideal against which to measure critically the value of things.

A good question to ask once in a while is this: "How close am I to what I should expect to be at this stage?" It brings your thinking to a point. It reminds you that though there is no reason why every man cannot grasp all the happiness of which he is capable, he has to keep reaching.

THE SEARCH FOR HAPPINESS

Happiness is an individual thing, made up of work, interests, friendships, the pursuit of an ideal, and health.

A man does not have to go around oozing cheerfulness in order to be a happy man. He may be happy in depth, and that sort of happiness, in the words of Robert Frost, the United States poet, "Will bear some keeping still about." He is enjoying durable satisfactions.

To get the most out of life we need to do our best work, participate in the best sort of leisure activity, and solve our problems in the best way. "Best" in this context means the highest for which our talents equip us. It means more what we put into life than what we loot out of life.

A rich full life cannot be described in terms of money, power and prestige. It cannot be defined as winning notoriety, for glory is only an impassioned name for what is merely our itch to hear ourselves spoken of. John Ruskin, the nineteenth century essayist and lecturer, insisted that to live a full life we must have five qualities similar to those required in good architecture: Unity, the type of divine comprehensiveness; Repose, the type of divine permanence; Symmetry, the type of divine justice; Moderation, the type of government by law, and Infinity, the type of divine incomprehensibility.

There is no place for make-believe in such a life. You are not living through the day to please others or to put on a good show, but to meet your critical self at nightfall. That self takes little account of what the people around you during the day said about you. They are incompetent to judge your compulsions and your purposes, and if your standards are high you need pay no heed to their finicky criticisms.

One thing needed is to avoid the habit of mind in which a man is forever looking for something against which to defend himself, and to face your future with a positive spirit and a confident posture. You must step resolutely from the cloistered life of home and school into the hurly-burly of the working world. Having given your best thought to where the step will lead you, stride out boldly. When Caesar, with a small force of horse and foot, reached the banks of the River Rubicon, he halted to consider the greatness of his enterprise. Then, having weighed the difficulties against the gains, he said to his staff: "Let the die be cast," and led his army across the Rubicon to become master of Rome.

WHAT IS CHARACTER?

All the precepts looked at so far contribute to the building of character. A person of character is one who hates cruelty, despises softness, and detests those who climb on the shoulders of others. He recognizes the dignity of duty, fairness, sympathy, co-operation, and all the other things that make a decent society possible. He has taste, which is the instinctive and instant preferring of one material object to another without any obvious reason.

These are essential to making the most of life. They imply development of the whole man and the harmonizing of all his parts.

To live a full life you need to score heavily on interests, tapping your energies and your store of qualities through a great variety of outlets. A person who is not wise enough to seek diversity of interests leads a monotonous and thin life, and is subject to the evils of satiety and boredom.

Look around at people who are laggards in business: are they not people who have buried themselves in their immediate occupations? They never give a thought to what they need to know or do so as to ready themselves for the next stage of advancement. They see facts singly or in twos or threes, but their sight becomes blurred and dim when they try to grasp in their rough proportions all the multitude of facts that compose a future situation.

If you are "well-rounded" everything you do will be done with enthusiasm, a sense of values, imaginative thinking, and self-confidence.

Without enthusiasm you are living only half a life, merely "getting by." This most dynamic of human qualities can be pictured as the ideal descended on earth to battle with realities. It is the whole-heartedness that carries you through difficult tasks and routine activities.

Another word for it is "zest," defined by the dictionary as "gusto, something that gives a relish." Having zest means that you are so eager about living that you can hardly wait for morning to get started again. It makes life perpetually fascinating.

Should one of your enthusiasms run into an immovable barrier, call your sense of values to your aid. Here is a chance to test your standards, to put first things first, to give up the lesser good in favour of the greater good. So long as you have not lost the something in your life which is vital to you, continue with your usual zest to do the important things.

USE YOUR IMAGINATION

Imaginative thinking is necessary if you are not to be merely a plodder, but you must be able to dream without making dreams your master. Imagination is not a sedative to deaden life, but a force toward a more abundant life. It is the mind's ability to recall past experiences and relate them to new situations in combinations of infinite variety.

Your imagination needs limbering up once in a while. It cannot be ignored for long periods and then called upon in some crisis. The difference between on-going and routine men is simply this: the successful people have kept their imaginations at work. The flash of inspiration is important, without doubt, but the certainty that it will occur can be increased by enlarging the stock of ideas in your mind upon which imagination has a chance to work. The bright idea, the brainstorm, will come if you have been alert in observing, persevering in examining, and constructive in thinking, looking expectantly for a link between something present and something not yet thought of.

Hold your mind's door open to new ideas, all kinds of them. When a new idea enters, it may seem timid and rough hewn, it needs to be encouraged and to have its jagged edges smoothed. It may be only a small idea, but don't despise it. Look back over the past year and you will find that your truly significant ideas started in a small way, perhaps just as some new slant on something already in your mind.

The highest, most varied and most lasting pleasures are those of the intellect, toying with ideas and building them into new forms such as no one has seen before.

It is said that people who give free scope to this sort of creativity are not conformists, but their difference from other people lies in the realm of the mind and not necessarily of outward appearance. If a man seems out of step with his fellows it may be because, as the social rebel Henry David Thoreau said, "he hears a different drummer. Let him step to the music which he hears, however measured or far away."

This is quite different from indulging in extravagances of appearance or behaviour thought up in some joyous hour. Being strange in your manner or clothes may make you distinguished, but distinguished for what? To cultivate idiosyncrasies may give the impression that you are striving to convey something. Why not strive to *be* something?

Instead of working to increase their individual knowledge and understanding so as to make the most of their lives, some young people attend congresses and parades where they find fault with the lack of attention they are accorded. How can self-indulgence,

self-preoccupation and exhibitionism contribute to a full life?

This kind of behaviour is far removed from the self-confidence of the constructive seeker after goodness in life. He knows the difficulties but does not shrink from them; he is not one who leans on others; he is not afraid to face facts; he is not one who has to be pampered at every turn. Our happiness in our endeavour to make the most of our lives depends on what we back ourselves to be and do.

ON MAKING FRIENDS

Be fastidious in adopting new modes and new friends. They must fit your personality and your ambition.

Everyone needs friends. Joy is empty unless it is shared with someone. Success is valueless unless friends participate in it. The friendless man recalls the plight of the grand army of Napoleon entering Moscow—for the first time, entering a capital, they found none but themselves to be witnesses of their glory.

The company you keep should be no less worthy than yourself. It should be made up of people who make you feel the roominess of life. Even if you feel more at ease with third-raters, you must not repose there: people of a higher intellectual order must be your companions if you are to fulfil your potentiality.

This is not to say that you must be a climber, a detestable sort of person, but you need to protect your good name and your future against the disrepute of bad or inferior company. And when you have made friends of whose affection and devotion you can be sure, take Shakespeare's advice to heart: "Grapple them to thy soul with hoops of steel."

THE STRENUOUS LIFE

The person in search of a satisfying life does not ask for comfort, but for an opportunity to exercise his abilities. Not everyone is born with a longing for strenuous discomfort in remote places, but everyone who is trying to accomplish something knows that you cannot make the most of your life if you try to exist as a non-participating unit in the life around you.

Indolence is a distressing state. We must be doing something to be happy. Effort and struggle with difficulties are as natural to a man as grubbing in the ground is to a gopher. To have all his wants gratified is intolerable. It is a denial of the abundant life.

We recall the address by Theodore Roosevelt in the closing year of the nineteenth century. It was called "The Strenuous Life," and even then, when the affluent century had not yet dawned, it was derided. Now, after sixty years, it seems to thoughtful people that a return is needed to Roosevelt's principles if we are to make life rewarding. A life of ease, lived by those who are slow in thought and slugglish in action, is shabby and worthless.

Roosevelt summed up his principles in this way: "I wish to preach not the doctrine of ignoble ease but the doctrine of the strenuous life; the life of toil and effort; of labour and strife; to preach that highest form of success which comes not to the man who desires mere easy peace but to the man who does not shrink from danger, from hardship, or from bitter toil, and who out of these wins the splendid ultimate triumph."

Absorption in ease or passing pleasure is one of the most common signs of present or impending decay. There is a phrase: "To rest on your laurels," meaning to quit trying after winning a crown or a gold medal or a promotion. A prize does nothing else but reward past achievement. To abandon ambition upon reaching a plateau is to suffer diminution of our essential manhood.

"Comfort," said Kahlil Gibran, the Lebanese poet, "is a stealthy thing that enters the house as a guest, and then becomes a host, and then a master." We should be alert to unmask its nature before we learn to love it too greatly.

DON'T SIT DOWN TOO SOON

The problems accompanying success are more agreeable than those contingent upon failure, but they are no less challenging. To handle any sort of problem successfully, we need to weigh possibilities, discard details that are irrelevant, divine the general rules according to which events occur, and test our decision by experiment.

You can't treat all facts as being of equal value. Some have validity in your circumstances, and some have not. The problem must be tidied up and its dimensions learned. Get inside it and feel its contours. This approach avoids rushing toward an answer and then retracing your steps to check. By working more deliberately, marshalling facts and resources, you move with an air of certainty.

Do not be easily discouraged in your search for a satisfying life. Some people sit down too soon. They remind us of the Lotus Eaters, people told about in Homer's *Odyssey,* who lay lazily on their beach eating a fruit which caused them to lose all interest in work and all desire to reach their native country. The worst thing in life is not to fail, but not to try to succeed; to live in the gray twilight that knows neither brightness nor shadow, neither victory nor defeat.

You may not always be able to play the game gleefully; you may, indeed, be glad to think sometimes that because an unhappiness has not befallen you that is your happiness. Like Robert Louis Stevenson, writer of remarkable poetry and still-living prose, you may rise above self-pity. He was so frail in health that he had to leave the home he loved and go into far countries: and he wrote an essay called "On the Enjoyment of Unpleasant Places."

Let your preparations for making the most of your life be suitable to your hopes and the greatness of your enterprise. Of this be sure, there is no free pass that will admit you to a full life. But if the effort you make appears to be tedious or irksome, recall your purpose and your quest, then the vexations of daily life will seem trivial.

These are some parts of a well-rounded life, but so dismembered life loses its attractiveness and its joy. You will not find your desired life in shrivelled abstractness and formally stated precepts, but you will find it clothed in the living form of your own personality when all these principles are made part of you.

Then, every day, you can look forward to tomorrow with calmness and anticipation, because you have lived fully today.

2. Physical education: a new profession*

Luther H. Gulick

One of the foremost leaders in physical education during the late nineteenth and early twentieth centuries

There seems to be a very general misapprehension, even among intelligent men, as to the nature of the work in which we are engaged. By many it is regarded simply as a speciality in medicine; others think it merely a department in athletics; others still, with more gross ideas, regard us as men who devote our time and energy to the building up of muscular tissue.

Perhaps I can best define the profession by stating its objects. It is difficult to formulate any classification that is at once logical and complete. The following, therefore, is presented, not without feelings of diffidence, as in some respects at least, it differs from any that have been hitherto presented.

I will make three grand divisions of exercises, according to their purpose: namely, Educative, Curative, and Recreative gymnastics. Hard and fast lines cannot be drawn, assigning each exercise to a particular one of these classes, as frequently it will be found that one exercise belongs to two or more classes at once, as in medicine, opium is a hypnotic, cardiac stimulant, antispasmodic, cerebral stimulant, anodyne, etc. This is a division of the objects of exercise, and not of exercises themselves. I will now take up the divisions somewhat in detail.

1. Educative Exercises, or Physical Education. We adopt the following definition for the object of educative exercises: "To lead out and train the physical powers; to prepare and fit the body for any calling or

business, or for activity and usefulness in life." This may be divided as follows:

a. Muscular Strength. This includes strength of the heart and respiratory muscles, as well as the arms, legs, and body.

b. Endurance, a matter of the heart, lungs, and nervous system as well as of the extrinsic muscles.

c. Agility or quickness of action, being largely an affair of the central nervous system.

d. Muscular Control. Excellence in almost any art or trade involves accurate control or discipline of certain parts of the body. In playing the violin, a great deal is demanded in this direction; first as to the co-ordination of the fingers of the left hand, being able to place them rapidly, independently, and with absolute precision, both as to time and locality upon the finger board of the violin, in a position that is naturally awkward; second, to be able to use the right and left arms with entire independence, the muscles of the wrist being used principally in one case and of the fingers in the other. In piano playing there is similar training. The hands have to learn to work independently, and even the fingers independently of each other. They have to learn to act with extreme rapidity, with absolute certainty, with automatic regularity. And so on with all the musical instruments, there is a large amount of work to be done which is primarily, fundamentally, and essentially physical training.

In the trades there is a similar state of affairs. Perfect control is fundamental and is usually secured only by years of practice on the thing to be done. . . .

There are numerous departments in the

*From Proceedings of the American Association for the Advancement of Physical Education, Ithaca, N. Y., 1890, The Association, pp. 59-66. Used by permission.

trades, the arts, and daily life where the excellence of work depends largely upon physical training in some branch. Today these are manned by specialists,—specialists, not in physical training, but in the end for which the training exists. To make my meaning plainer, let me refer to the violin player again. The music teacher teaches the violin, and gives finger exercises, and a large portion of the time of the music teacher is spent, not in teaching music, but in physical training. Now, the music teacher, unless exceptionally qualified, as music teachers are not ordinarily in this direction, is not as competent in physical training as a man of equal abilities would be who gave his whole time to the subject. Thus the physical-training part of learning to play the violin or piano could be better by a man who made a specialty of physical training than by a man who was primarily a very fine musician, and who took up this physical training as an incidental matter. Flexibility of the wrist, perfect control and co-ordination of the muscles, independent action of the hands, action and quickness of the fingers, can all be gained better by other means than by mere finger exercises on the violin or piano; but in general it is not the teacher of music who is best qualified to take up this work, for the questions are primarily those of physiology rather than of music. Let each do what he can do best: physical trainer, physical training—music teacher, music and not physical training.

e. Physical Judgment. This may be called a correlative of muscular control, this the intelligence telling when and where. "It is a sort of psychic trigonometry by which the trained mind calculates the distance, position, and motion of objects." None of the important points already considered can take the place of this, nor can we get along without it. A man wishes to jump a ditch; he has no time to measure it and calculates how much muscular effort will be required to clear it, but physical judgment enables him to do all this at once. There seems to be confusion as to the difference between muscular control and physical judgment. Take a catcher behind a baseball bat; physical judgment tells him where to put his hands and the exact instant that the ball will reach them; muscular control enables him to put his hand where he chooses. One

might be able to put his hand where he chose, but not know where; or he might know where without being able to place his hands there.

f. Self-Control. This may be described as the power of the mind over itself. It is the power which gives self-possession, allowing a man to act naturally in time of excitement and danger.

g. Physical Courage, that which renders a person willing to undertake, that quality which comes to one naturally, from a knowledge of his ability, gained through experience. "There is sometimes a constitutional timidity, or lack of what we may call physical faith, that has to be overcome." A presumptuous daring is not physical courage, being born usually of ignorance of the real dangers rather than a calm meeting of them.

h. Symmetry, harmonious, or all-round development of the body. The strength of a chain is represented by the weakest link, and this is not untrue of the body.

i. Grace, which is fundamentally economy of action. It differs from muscular strength and from muscular control. A man may have both these and not be graceful. Comparing grace and symmetry, grace is beauty of action, while symmetry is beauty of form.

j. Expression. In this country we do not know very much about these special exercises. The Delsarte gymnastics, perhaps, are the best example of this type, their aim being primarily to enable the body to express the thoughts, ideas, emotions of the mind in the most intelligible way to other minds through their eyes and ears, thus including much of gesture, elocution, etc.

2. We now come to the second division, Curative Exercises. It is not designed to trench upon the field of the medical profession; but it is well known that some disturbances of the system can be cured, and many prevented, by the correct use of exercise. The same is true in relation to some bodily deformities. Certain cardiac, spinal, and nervous diseases and disorders of the nutritive system are peculiarly susceptible to gymnastic treatment. I will not speak further of this branch, as its importance is already coming to be understood.

3. Recreative Exercises. There is a real and fundamental difference between recreative or play exercises and educative gym-

nastics. It consists primarily in the attitude of the will, and it matters little so far as this is concerned whether it has to exercise itself in confining the mind to a difficult task in arithmetic, or to keeping a fixed and sustained attention on the leader of a calisthenic drill. . . .

I wish next to speak of the opportunities that are offered for scientific work in the profession. It is hardly possible at the present day for a man to look forward to adding materially to the sum total of knowledge in any one of the older professions. A man who goes into physical education with fair abilities and preparation expects in the course of a few years to have acquired all that has been known up to his time (the scientific side of the subject is as yet young) and to add materially to the sum total of knowledge on this subject. In this respect, then, does this profession differ from others, in that it is new, and every man may expect to do that scientific work which will be not merely original with him, but original to the world. In fact, each man will have to depend to a considerable extent on the results of his own investigations, for he has not as in medicine, reliable and elaborate treatises on which to rely. The science is as yet too young to have developed them. He must expect to assist in the development of such works for the use of those who come afterward. An oak tree during the first year of its existence is susceptible to slight influences which would be entirely unfelt a few years later, even if multiplied a thousandfold. This profession has still to be defined, it has not yet crystallized, and thus it is possible to stamp it with one's own character as it will never be possible again.

. . . There are few scientific fields today which offer opportunities for the study of problems of greater value to the human race, or more fundamental in regard to its ultimate success, than does that of physical education. It is a factor in modern life, that is as yet unappreciated. It deals with life on a broad side, is in line with the most thorough modern physiological psychology in its appreciation of the intimate relations of body and mind, is in line with our modern conception of evolution, as it works to develop a superior race. This profession offers to its students a large and broad field for intellectual activity, involving for its fullest appreciation a profound knowledge of man through psychology, anatomy, physiology, history, and philosophy. To sum up this part of the argument, I would say that physical education offers a greater field for original work than almost any other. Second, on account of its youth and plasticity, it offers the possibility of a permanent influence that is never offered except in the youth of such profession. Third, this work is intrinsically of great value. Fourth, it offers a great field for intellectual activity.

This profession, then, differs from any that now exists. It is readily seen that it is not merely a department of medicine, which relates primarily to the prevention and cure of disease. The mere fact that a man is an excellent medical practitioner will not qualify him to take hold of educative gymnastics, although it would qualify him to understand curative gymnastics. On the other hand, the study of psychology and pedagogy will not qualify a man to take hold of curative gymnastics, although it might qualify him to understand educative exercises.

I take it that there is no other factor which is as prominent in the development of any profession as the kind of men who take upon themselves the functions of that profession. The advance of physical education will depend more upon the kind of men who take up this work as their profession, than upon any other one factor. If it is largely taken up by men of little education and small abilities, the work will never become of the greatest value, nor will it be favorably known to the general public. If, however, on the contrary, men of collegiate training, philosophic minds, of broad purposes and earnest hearts, are induced to enter this field, the profession will show that it is intrinsically a broad, scientific, philosophic field, and it will be recognized by thinking men as one of the departments in education, fundamental in the upbuilding of the nation.

I have endeavored in this paper to show: First, that this is a profession, and in the rough to define its aims. Second, to show that opportunities for valuable work are abundant. Third, that great importance is to be attached to the kind of men who enter this profession.

3. Physical education—an emerging profession*

Charles A. Bucher

Professor of Education and Director of Physical Education, School of Education, New York University

Eero Saarinen's majestic work of art, the 630-foot-high Gateway Arch in St. Louis, symbolizes man's desire to surmount his obstacles, to reach greater heights, and to achieve his destiny. Our aspiration as physical educators is to become a mature and respected profession. We desire to be respected for our expertise in physical education in a way analogous to the manner in which doctors and lawyers are respected for their skill, training, and experience. The Gateway Arch reflects the spirit to which each of us should be committed if we are to gain this professional goal. In the days and months ahead we need to explore, to reach, and to achieve.

The word "profession" is a common term in our language. It is as characteristic of our world today as was the term "craft" in ancient times. In the language of the man on the street most fields of endeavor, whether selling, insurance management, or banking, are frequently labeled "professions." To the more knowledgeable person the term is limited to such fields of specialization as medicine, law, the ministry, architecture, psychiatry, and social work. Those who have traced the origin of the term "profession" cite the fact that the three classic professions were theology, law, and medicine.

Many of our illustrious leaders of the past referred to their field of endeavor as being a profession. Luther Halsey Gulick, who contributed so much to Springfield College and to the Playground Association of America, to mention only two items,

*From an address to the Physical Education Division, American Association for Health, Physical Education, and Recreation, St. Louis, Apr. 1, 1968.

wrote an article in 1890 entitled "Physical Education: A New Profession." George L. Meylan, president of our national association from 1907 to 1911, in his presidential address in 1911 referred to the physical education profession. James Edward Rogers, who gave the initial impetus for starting the Society of State Directors of Health, Physical Education, and Recreation, wrote an article that was published in the *American Physical Education Review* entitled "Physical Education—A Profession." William Gilbert Anderson, who provided the spark for the founding of our Association, writing in our national journal, entitled his article "The Founding of the American Physical Education Profession."

These early leaders used the term "profession" because of reasons advanced at that time: the philosophical and psychological foundations upon which physical education rests, and the general cultural and specialized education that characterizes our professional preparation programs. Is physical education considered a profession today?

WHAT DIFFERENCE DOES IT MAKE WHETHER PHYSICAL EDUCATION IS LABELED AS A PROFESSION?

One way to answer the question "What difference does it make whether physical education is labeled as a profession?" is to think back to the time of World War II and ask a question in return: "Who were the persons selected to head our national armed services programs designed to physically train and educate the cream of the country's manhood?" Do you recall such names as Hank Greenberg (a baseball player), who was head of the Air Force Program, and Gene Tunney (a boxer), who was head of the Navy Program? Do you recall the time in the middle 1950's when President Eisenhower was concerned with the fitness of American youth and called together a group of persons for consultation purposes, thinking he had the nation's experts on physical fitness? Among those present were Joe Louis (a boxer), "Big" Bill Mikan (a basketball player), Willie Mays (a baseball player), and Sammy Lee (a diver). Why were these sports heroes selected rather than physical educators? Would this have happened if physical education was labeled a profession in the public's thinking and in the mind of the President of the United States?

It makes a great difference whether or not physical education is labeled a profession. There are many reasons, but I list only three: (1) *It means public recognition.* The doctor and lawyer, members of recognized professions, are highly respected. The public trusts their judgment and skill and seeks their advice. (2) *In an occupational sense, the professional is placed above the rank and file of workers who do not posssess specialized knowledge and skill.* The true professional, · according to the traditional idealogy of professions, is never in a position, like the rank and file, where he is hired. Instead, the doctor is consulted; the lawyer is retained. (3) *It identifies an individual with a group that has such special qualifications as knowledge, skill, and intellectual competency for rendering a particular specialized service.* It yields a feeling of self-respect, of achievement. It separates the fit from the unfit, the qualified from the unqualified, the respected practitioner from the quack.

WHAT IS A PROFESSION?

Alfred North Whitehead, in his book *Adventures of Ideas,* distinguishes between a craft and a profession. A craft is based, he says, on "customary activities and modified by trial and error." A profession, he continues, "is subject to theoretical analysis and modified by theoretical conclusions derived from that analysis."

Everett C. Hughes, Professor of Sociology at Brandeis University and former President of the American Sociological Association, cites the role of the profession in society: "A profession considers itself the proper body to set the terms in which some aspect of society, life or nature is to be thought of and to define the general lines or even the details of public policy concerning it." "Lawyers," he points out, "not only give advice to clients and plead their cases for them; they also develop a philosophy of law, of its nature and functions, and of the proper way to administer justice." "Physicians," he continues, "consider it their prerogative to define the nature of disease and of health, and to determine how medical services ought to be distributed and paid for."

Myron Lieberman, in his book *Education As a Profession,* explains the roles of the "physical" and the "intellectual" as they apply to professional status. "Proficiency in physical techniques may or may not be required," he points out. For example, in legal work the physical is minimal, but in surgery the exercise of skill and dexterity is very important. Today, in the age of heart transplants and delicate brain surgery, the need for physical skill is essential. The important point to remember is that the physical activities of professional workers are guided by a high level of intellectual control—it's not just physical activity without rationale—it's not just arms and legs and good intentions. Instead, a body of knowledge undergirds how the physical activity is best performed, under what conditions it is best performed, when it should be performed, and the results achieved when it is performed correctly.

CRITERIA FOR PROFESSIONAL STATUS

One way to better understand what constitutes the requirements for professional status is to look at what the experts say constitute the criteria for a profession. Many persons have written upon this subject. Some of the more respected individuals include Abraham Flexner, Bernard Barber, and Myron Lieberman. I studied the listing of perhaps 20 authorities and came to the conclusion that the criteria could be stated under four headings. In order to achieve full professional status a field of endeavor must:

1. Render a unique and essential social service
2. Establish high standards for the selection of members

3. Provide a rigorous training program to prepare its practitioners
4. Achieve self-regulatory status for both the group and the individual

If physical education can lay claim to professional status, perhaps it falls into the classification of an emerging profession. An emerging profession is one where we have leaders who are dedicated to the field of endeavor, try to upgrade standards, get public recognition, develop strong professional associations, strengthen professional schools, and undertake other responsibilities that will move their field into the ranks of a mature profession. Many of the practitioners, however, are apathetic and do not seek to improve themselves or their service in the same way their leaders do.

WHAT MUST PHYSICAL EDUCATION DO?

The question that now must be answered in light of these criteria is "What is the current status of physical education, and what are some things that it must do in order to become a mature and full-fledged profession?"

First, if physical education desires full-fledged professional status, it must render a unique and essential social service

What is a unique and essential social service? Webster's dictionary says the word "unique" means that it is something without a like or equal, it is matchless. In other words, physical educators are the only persons who perform this service in the scientific manner that sets them apart from the rank and file. The term "unique" also means that the nature and scope of the service is clear in the minds of the group and also in the minds of the public. The public clearly understands the function of the group, and the group is recognized for this service. For example, in respect to medicine and law, for all practical purposes it can be said that only medical doctors perform surgery or prescribe drugs for persons who are sick and only lawyers practice law.

What then is physical education's unique and essential social service? Students of history, like Dr. Bruce Bennett and his colleagues in their book *A World History of Physical Education,* have traced the services rendered by physical educators since early times. They have pointed out that "physical education. . . has been utilized for worthwhile and ennobling aims and conversely it has been employed for brutal and degrading purposes." They have cited the fact that since the time of primitive man physical educators have rendered such services as developing physical efficiency, providing recreation, and encouraging participation in physical activities.

History also tells us that the service we render has been increasingly based on scientific grounds. Scientific advances in physiology, for example, started us on the road to placing physical education in a more respected position. This made it possible to render our service on a much sounder educational footing and provided us with a basis for training our practitioners in a way that would enable them to render their service in a more scientific manner, as contrasted with those persons who were untrained. Other scientific advances have also made it possible for us to better adapt exercise to age and sex and to have a better understanding of such things as motor learning, body mechanics, tests and measurements, and movement education.

Our field of endeavor has advanced until today, as Dr. Bennett and his colleagues point out, "Physical education is both a science and an art—the laws of movement, the reaction of the organs of the body to exercise and the effects of motor response make it a science; the skillful execution of movement in sport, dance, or gymnastics, make it an art."

As the public looks at physical education programs today, what do they deduce as being our unique and essential social service? Is it one that is scientifically based? Do they view physical education as a science and an art capable of being rendered only by persons trained in the foundational sciences? Let's take a look at a physical education class I observed recently. A tall, muscular-looking young man was in charge of the class. After taking roll he had the students snap to attention, marched them around the gymnasium a couple of times, gave a series of warm-up exercises, and then ran them through an obstacle course. Then the pupils chose up sides and played racehorse basketball the rest of the period, with the teacher acting as referee. Finally the boys went dripping with perspiration to the showers. *Is this our unique and essential social service?* That was the service rendered in the ninth grade. Then I observed the service rendered in the tenth, eleventh, and twelfth grades to see how it differed. I was confused to find it was the same thing: exercise, basketball, perspiration. *Is this our unique and essential social service? Is this the physical education that is both a science and an art?*

There are, of course, examples of another kind. The best teachers of physical education are providing sound educational experiences for their students, are teaching motor skills in a scientific manner, are providing for progression in their activities from grade to grade, and are providing for theory as well as physical activity in their classes. *This is the physical education that is both a science and an art.*

If the service physical educators render is unique with us, we who are trained in the foundational sciences of physiology and anatomy, the behaviorial sciences of psychology and sociology, and in various learning theories, especially as they relate to motor learning, then how does our service differ from that performed by Debbie Drake, who poses seductively in her leotard on TV, or Jack LaLanne or Ed Allen, who tell their audiences to smile and kick? Is our service the same as theirs or is ours unique with us? If unique with us, how do we make this clear in the public's mind? How do we become recognized for our expertise? How do we separate ourselves from the untrained and the services rendered by the shapely ladies, muscle men, and drill sergeants?

Perhaps in order to become a more mature profession we must be more concerned than we have been in the past with the intellectual controls that provide the rationale, understanding, and scientific foundations for what we do and the intellectual controls that make it possible for us to teach and utilize physical activity in a most effective manner. Perhaps we need to be more concerned with the participant than with the spectator. Perhaps we should go beyond physical activity and try to get our students to do some thinking—to get at the "why" of the activity as well as the activity itself.

Second, if physical education desires full-fledged professional status, it must be very selective about whom it permits to perform this service

The profession of medicine is highly selective about whom it permits to enter its ranks. It is very difficult to be admitted, to be tapped on the shoulder and told you can be one of the select group. One person describes it as "the inner fraternity" of medicine—a profession that uses very potent mechanisms to repel the intruder. The minute the young man files an application with a medical school the selective machinery begins to work, with the medical hierarchy standing guard at the controls. The unfit are cast aside without fear or trepidation.

Myron Lieberman, an astute observer of what constitutes professional status, has said, "A profession cannot in good conscience or in good faith with the public gain respect and have full-fledged status unless it is willing and is able to undertake the onerous task of weeding out the unethical and incompetent practitioner, who in some numbers get admitted to practice."

Arthur Corey's words still haunt us: "To the teaching profession, the most devastating canard ever invented is the oft-repeated assertion, 'He who can does, and he who can't teaches.' " Our goal as physical educators should be to try to turn this phrase around and direct our organized efforts toward the end that those who can teach physical education will teach and those who can't teach physical education will be guided into business or some other career.

Historically, it seems, we in physical education have attempted to become more selective primarily by upgrading our professional preparing programs in institutions of higher learning. If we go back in history to when the first class of teachers was graduated from the Normal Institute of Physical Education in 1861, we find they had only a 10-week course at this institution that was founded by Dio Lewis. We have made outstanding progress over the years. The length of training has been increased, degrees are now awarded, affiliation with colleges and universities of distinction has taken place, more general education is required, and recently there is more stress on graduate study and research. But does this mean we are really selective about whom we permit to render this service?

Are we selective in respect to the quality of intellect and academic achievement of our practitioners? Certainly we have made progress since the Peik and Fitzgerald study, reported in the December, 1934, *Research Quarterly,* indicating that physical education majors stood at the bottom of all teaching fields studied in the range and depth of their general academic training. We have come a long way, but we still need to stretch, recruit the scholar into our ranks, appeal to the brain power of our youth: young people who rank high on College Board scores and National Merit Scholarship Honors and who are the valedictorians and salutatorians of their high school senior classes.

Are we selective in regard to licensure? Certification requirements for teaching physical education vary from state to state, ranging anywhere from as little as 16 semester hours to 40 credit hours. Coaches have few if any requirements in many states other than a teaching certificate. Private schools and colleges to a large degree establish their own standards for faculty members (governed somewhat by the standards or criteria of the accrediting bodies to which they belong), but unfortunately they are frequently very lenient in the area of physical education.

Emergency certificates are quite common in physical education. I had a girl in one class last year who had been teaching physical education for 2 years in the state of New Jersey. She was taking her first professional course in physical education. There are no emergency certificates for medical students. None of us would want a surgeon with an emergency certificate to operate on us. A question can be raised as to whether there should be any emergency certificates in physical education.

Are we selective in regard to members who make a full-time commitment to physical education? Professor Everett Hughes points out that, once the medical schools select their students, they watch over them very carefully and are very much disturbed if a sheep is lost from the fold. The medical profession wonders what they have done wrong. As Professor Hughes states, "The medical profession and schools make it clear

to the professional recruit that he owes it to himself, the profession, and the school to stick with his choice. The theme is mutual commitment—one owes allegiance for life to the profession."

How about the full-time commitment of physical educators to their field of endeavor? Why is it so many of our people have changed into the fields of administration and guidance? I once heard a major student say he wanted a job in an elementary school. The reason he gave was that since he was a man he would have a better chance of being selected as a principal over a woman—and that he was interested, he assured me, in administration as a career—*not* physical education.

Third, if physical education desires full-fledged professional status, it must provide rigorous training programs for those who are to perform this unique and essential social service

Elbert Hubbard once said: "Education is a conquest, not a bequest. It cannot · be given, it must be achieved. The value of education lies not in its possession but in the struggle to secure it."

There are very few worthwhile accomplishments in this world that are possible except through much toil and effort. The best things in life are *not* free. There is no substitute for hard work, and this goes for students who desire to major in physical education.

While visiting an eastern university recently, I noticed the following motto over a student's bed: Do not let your studies interfere with your college education." A college is, or at least should be, first and foremost an institution for education, and the departments, divisions, and schools that make it up should be likewise. This should be particularly true of physical education, where sometimes the play of the sideshows seems to take over.

In respect to quality of training, John Gardner captured the idea in his book *Excellence.* "Excellence," he says, "implies more than competence—it implies striving for the highest standards." A question can be raised as to whether we can achieve this excellence and quality of training when we allow such practices as dual majors and minors in physical education, or when students seek just to "get by," and some professors help to pave an easy road for them. Master's degree students—in New York State, for example—whom we call "coupon snatchers," often receive their permanent teaching certificates, not by taking work to become more competent in their special field but, instead, by taking a variety of courses that may or may not have any relationship to improving their performance or service but frequently are taken because they are "snap" courses.

We should insist upon our students' stretching a little, rather than just being satisfied with getting by—receiving a gentlemanly "C." We should expose our students to the best minds on the faculty—to general sociologists, general psychologists—as well as to educationists. We need to follow an interdisciplinary approach. We need to do away with much of the inbreeding of faculty, a practice that seems to have infested many of our institutions of higher learning.

In training our practitioners, we need a longer period of formal education. The student of medicine follows a 7-year course, the student of theology 7 years, and students in law and dentistry 6 years. The period of preparation at the undergraduate level should be increased for our students. Although many of our practitioners take graduate work, there is need for an extended period of preparation before any teaching is done.

As one observer has said: "There is a world of tragedy for all of us found in the fact that it takes six years of college training for a veterinarian to work on a sick pig, while a very large percentage of our teachers can work on a child's mind and body with less than four years of training."

Fourth, if physical education desires full-fledged professional status, the individual and the group must be self-regulatory in nature

Lawyers have the sole power to decide such things as the requirements for admission to the bar, rules in regard to the suspension or exclusion of a member from practice, and standards for ethical and unethical conduct. Physical educators should also be self-regulatory.

In achieving this autonomy the profession must have some recognized organization that can and will speak for it with an authority that springs from and is granted to it by its membership. According to sociologists, the recognized organization must have a quality called *completeness*. This means that the organization must be representative of the members in the field, provide for two-way communication, and have sufficient consensus to be able to speak authoritatively in behalf of the profession.

Since the AAHPER is probably our most representative organization, let's examine it for a moment. A common interest in physical education led to its founding in 1885, under the impetus of Dr. William G. Anderson, a youthful instructor in gymnastics at Adelphi Academy in Brooklyn. Forty-nine people attended the first meeting on November 27, 1885, at Adelphi Academy, and Dr. Edward Hitchcock of Amherst was elected president.

The AAHPER has grown until today it has approximately 50,000 members. But more important than size from a professional viewpoint, the question must be asked as to whether this organization speaks for all the physical educators in this country, such as the elementary school, high school, and college teachers; the coaches; the physical educators in YMCA's and other organizations and agencies; and the young people who are majors in physical education in our colleges and universities. Does this organization have "completeness"? Does this organization speak out authoritatively on the great issues of the day in a manner comparable to the way the medical profession speaks out on Medicare? Has this organization taken effective steps to cast out the intruders, the charlatans, the unfit? And does this organization speak for our young people who represent nearly one-fourth of the membership? Our young people want a respected profession, a recognized profession, and I would suggest to those of us who are older that we listen to them very attentively. Our young people have the courage and the fortitude to be standard-bearers for their convictions. Along with many of you, I have admired and have been greatly impressed with the great outpouring of youth and their efforts in the presidential campaign this year. Youth represents a significant and potent force throughout the world today and also in our field of endeavor. They should play an active role in determining which officers should lead them and what issues the Association should speak out authoritatively and convincingly about. The young person has much at stake—his destiny, his hopes, his self-respect, his future.

In addition to having an organization with "completeness," to achieve autonomy the individual practitioner himself has to assume some responsibility. The professional worker is confronted with a wide variety of problems that requires the application of a high degree of intelligence and specialized training. Therefore he must be free to exercise his own best judgment. But in order to have this freedom he must accept responsibility for acting in an informed and intelligent manner.

Do we, the practitioners of physical education, accept the responsibility that goes with such autonomy, for judgments made and acts performed within the scope of professional autonomy? For example, do we keep up with the latest trends, read the latest professional literature, keep abreast of what is new in such areas as learning theory, and understand the scientific foundations underlying our field of work?

Do we, the practitioners of physical education, accept the responsibility for our professional behavior? We need to police ourselves. This is essential in light of our obligations to our clients and to society. To guide our behavior, there must be a code of ethics that has been clarified and interpreted at ambiguous and doubtful points by concrete cases.

Does physical education have a code of ethics? If so, are we, the practitioners, familiar with it? Has it been clarified at ambiguous and doubtful points by concrete cases? Has machinery been established to enforce high standards of professional conduct? What penalties can the group levy against an offending member? Is the power of expulsion available if necessary? What happens to the coach, for example, like the one just outside New York City who told one of his basketball players who fouled out of the game to go down in the locker room and switch jerseys with different numerals with another player and go back into the game under an assumed name?

The answer—In this case *nothing happened*. What happens if one of our researchers knowingly manipulates data in order to get what he considers to be desired results? The answer—*Nothing* happens. What happens to the teacher who breaks a contract? The answer—Usually *nothing* happens. What happens to the physical educator turned faddist who advertises in newspapers and magazines advocating some miracle way for removing fat from human bodies, charging a fabulous price, and thereby bilking the public out of thousands of dollars? The answer—*Nothing* happens.

A FULL-FLEDGED PROFESSION?

We would all agree, I suspect, in light of this discussion, that physical education at this time is not yet clearly established or fully accepted as a mature profession. We have not yet arrived. We are emerging as a profession, and there are many difficult tasks that lie ahead. Down deep in our hearts, however, we yearn for the day that we will have full-fledged status as a profession.

We yearn for this day because it will enable us to better exercise our powers—powers that we have spent years developing in the form of knowledge, understanding, and skill. We yearn for this day because it will enable us to render a greater service to our fellow human beings. We yearn for this day because we will be able to live more abundantly in loyalty to a growing brotherhood. Being a member of a profession means that each of us is no longer merely an individual person, but instead belongs to a group. As a group we possess a common stock of knowledge, common purpose, and common standards, which are continually growing and to which each member of the group contributes. Knowledge of our science and art accumulates from generation to generation and furnishes the common stock from which we all grow. To have this day arrive for which we all yearn, we need a dynamic quest for truth and excellence among our membership.

The great threat to our future is apathy. We need more satirists, more persons who will stand up and be counted, more persons who do not accept the status quo, more vigorous stands by our Association on issues where we provide the expertise, more critical abrasiveness among our students and colleagues to test our ideas and thoughts.

Unfortunately we have too many members among us who are noninvolved, nonparticipating, and, most devastating of all, noncommittal. The ambition of this group, our enemy within, is a quiet life, a regular paycheck, freedom from controversy, and an absence of stress and unpleasantries. Such burning issues as determining our unique and essential social service, gaining greater selectivity in our ranks, providing for more rigorous training programs, and becoming more self-regulatory are not important as far as they are concerned. Such members contribute to a dying field of endeavor that never will achieve its destiny, make progress, or be a mature profession—a field of endeavor that is no longer nourished by perspectives and values of informed judgment. Rather, it will starve to death in its own aimlessness and inertia.

To gain the professional label is not an easy road. It is a rough journey. It is full of bumps, pressures, and uncertainties. One thing is certain. Full-fledged professional status cannot be bought, forced, or legislated. It must be earned. It is up to physical educators themselves whether their occupation is ever recognized as a profession. As Lieberman pointed out, it is the physicians who have created the profession of medicine by constantly advancing its standards; it is the lawyers who have converted the practice of law into a profession by continually striving for excellence. So must it be the physical educators who establish their vocation upon a strong professional footing.

To gain full professional status is physical education's priority for progress. This is what Eero Saarinen's Gateway Arch symbolizes for us: our desire to reach, to explore, and to achieve full-fledged professional status.

4. Mental, social, maturity, and physical characteristics of underaged and normal-aged boys in elementary school grades*[1]

H. Harrison Clarke

Research Professor of Physical Education, University of Oregon

John N. Drowatzky

Department of Physical Education, University of Toledo

This study was conducted to compare intelligence, scholastic achievement, interest, aspiration, peer status, maturity, body size, physique type, strength, and motor ability elements of boys seven to twelve years of age who were underaged and normal-aged for their respective grades.[2]

PROCEDURE

Subjects. The subjects involved in this study consisted of 79 boys in grades 1 through 6 and ages seven through twelve years. Forty-five subjects were tested annually from age seven years and 34 subjects were tested annually from age nine years. The subjects tested annually from age seven years are known herein as the original sevens and those tested annually from age nine years are called the original nines.

Formation of groups. Two groups of sub-

jects were formed for this investigation; one group was underage for their grade placement and the other group was normal in age for their grade placement. The seven-year-old underage group had birth dates from January 1950 through May 1950, while the normal-age group had birth dates from August 1949 through December 1949. The nine-year-old underage group had birth dates from January 1948 through May 1948, while the normal-age group had birth dates from August 1947 through December 1947. The distribution of boys comprising these groups is shown in the following tabulation:

	Underaged	Normal-aged	Total
Original sevens	13	32	45
Original nines	10	24	34
	23	56	79

The following arrangement of subjects was formed to facilitate the statistical treatment utilized in the study:

grade 2: age 7 vs. age 8 years
grade 3: age 8 vs. age 9 years
grade 4: age 9 vs. age 10 years
grade 5: age 10 vs. age 11 years
grade 6: age 11 vs. age 12 years

All subjects were tested within two months of their birthdays. This practice ensured reasonable homogeneity with regard to chronological age.

Experimental variables. The following ex-

*From Proceedings, 1965, p. 103, National College Physical Education Association for Men. Used by permission.

[1]Bibliography may be obtained from the author on request. Summaries of significant t ratios for the differences between the means of underaged and normal-aged boys on the experimental variables accompanied the original paper.

[2]This study was conducted as a part of the Medford, Oregon, Boys' Growth Project. Support for the project was provided by Medford public schools, Southern Oregon College, the Athletic Institute, the Curriculum Development Fund of the Oregon State Education Department, and the Office of Scientific and Scholarly Research of the University of Oregon.

perimental variables were selected for use in this study:

Intelligence. California Mental Maturity, Form S: Otis Quick Scoring Mental Abilities, Form A, B, E, or M.

Scholastic achievement. Gates Primary and Advanced Reading Tests; Stanford Achievement Test; Grade-point averages.

Interests. Children's Interest Blank; Dreese-Mooney Interest Inventory for Elementary Grades; What I Like to Do Interest Inventory.

Peer status. Sociometric Questionnaire; Cowell Personal Distance Ballot; Cowell Social Behavior Trend Index, Forms A and B.

Aspiration. Grip Strength Level of Aspiration Test.

Maturity. Skeletal age from hand-wrist X-ray evaluated by the Gruelich-Pyle standards.

Physique type. Somatotype components of endomorphy, mesomorphy, and ectomorphy.

Body size. Anthropometric measurements of upper arm girth, abdominal girth, thigh girth, standing height, body weight, and the chest girth times height index.

Strength. Physical Fitness Index; push-ups performed on the parallel bars; and the average score of eleven cable-tension tests.

Motor ability elements. Speed and agility in the 60-yard shuttle run; explosive power in the standing broad jump.

Analysis of data. The mean scores on all tests were computed separately for the underage and normal-age boys. The difference between the means of the two groups were then computed and tested for significance at the .05 and .01 levels by application of the t ratio. Inasmuch as the number of subjects differed for the various comparisons of means, the t ratios needed for significance also varied; for the various degrees of freedom, these t ratios ranged from 1.99 to 2.04 at the .05 level and from 2.64 to 2.75 at the .01 level.

RESULTS

Intelligence. In the comparisons of the intelligence quotients obtained by underaged and normal-aged boys in grades 3 through 6, no significant differences between the means were found. The mean intelligence quotients obtained for these boys ranged from 107.85 to 114.25. Thus, all of the means obtained in these comparisons were above the national norm of 100.

Scholastic achievement. Of the 34 comparisons, 7, or 20 percent of the differences between means on the scholastic achievement measures were significant at or above the .05 level. To conserve space in this report, only the variables on which significant differences were obtained are presented.

The situation in the 4th grade was most noteworthy with four differences between means being significant; in all instances Stanford Achievement Test elements were involved and the older ten-year-old boys were superior to the younger nine-year-old boys in this grade. Two of the mean differences were significant between the .05 and .01 levels; the Stanford elements were word meaning and spelling with t ratios of 2.44 each. The other two Stanford measures were arithmetic reasoning and arithmetic comprehension; significance was beyond the .01 level with t ratios of 4.45 and 4.02 respectively.

Three other differences between means were significant between the .05 and .01 levels; again the older boys had the highest means. The scholastic measures and grades were as follows: paragraph meaning, Gates Reading Test, in grade 2; arithmetic comprehension, Stanford Achievement Test, in grade 5; paragraph meaning, Stanford Achievement Test, in grade 6.

All differences between the means of underaged and normal-aged boys on scholastic items without significant differences in any grade were grade point average, language and total achievement on the Stanford Achievement Test, and word meaning on the Gates Reading Test.

Interest. Of the 42 comparisons on the interest measures, 6, or 12 percent of the differences between means were significant at or above the .05 level.

The only significant differences between means on the interest inventories were obtained in the 6th grade; in all instances What I Like To Do Interest Inventory elements were involved. In this grade, the younger eleven-year-old boys obtained higher means than the older twelve-year-old boys in art, music, active play, and quiet play interests; the t ratios ranged from 2.02 to 2.77. However, the older 6th grade boys obtained higher means on home arts and science interest elements; the t ratios of 3.12 and 2.39 were significant at the .01 and .05 levels respectively.

All differences between the means of underaged and normal-aged boys on interest measures were insignificant in grades 2, 4, and 5; no comparisons were possible in grade 3, as comparable interest inventories were not administered in this grade. The interest items without significant differences in any grade were the Children's Interest Blank, the Dreese-Mooney Interest Inventory, and the social studies and manual arts elements of the What I Like to Do Inventory.

Peer status. Of the 26 comparisons on the peer status measures, 4, or 15 percent of the differences between means were significant at or above the .05 level.

The situations in the 2nd and 5th grades accounted for all significant differences; in all instances, sociometric questionnaire elements were involved and normal-aged boys obtained higher means than underaged boys in each grade. In the 2nd grade, two of the mean differences were significant between the .05 and .01 levels; the questionnaire elements were number of times chosen as a friend and number of times chosen to help with homework, with t ratios of 2.05 and 2.29. For the 5th grade, significant mean differences were observed in the number of times chosen as a friend and the number of times chosen for homework; significance was near or at the .01 levels, with t ratios of 2.84 and 2.61 respectively.

All differences between the means of underaged and normal-aged boys on peer status measurements were insignificant in grades 3, 4, and 6. The peer status items without significant differences in any grade were number of boys chosen for friends category of the sociometric questionnaire, the Cowell Personal Distance Scale, and the positive and negative forms of the Cowell Social Behavior Index.

Level of aspiration. In the comparison of the level of aspiration evaluations of the underaged and normal-aged boys in grades 4 through 6, no significant difference between the means was found.

PHYSICAL MEASURES

Skeletal age. For all grades, the normal-aged boys had significantly higher skeletal age means than did the underaged boys. The differences between the means were significant at and above the .01 level; the t ratios ranged from 2.86 to 4.94.

Somatotype. The differences between the means of the underaged and normal-aged boys in the various grades on the three somatotype components were not significant.

Body size. Of the 40 body-size comparisons, 30, or 75 percent of the differences between means were significant near or above the .05 level. With one exception (upper arm girth), the normal-aged boys in each grade had higher means than the underaged boys. The significant differences favoring the normal-aged boys were as follows: standing height, all grades; body weight, all grades but the 5th; chest girth × height, 2nd, 3rd, and 4th grades; abdominal girth and thigh girth, 4th and 6th grades. Of these significant differences, five were found at the 4th grade, four at the 5th grade. The upper arm girth mean of the underaged boys was higher than the mean of the normal-aged boys in the 3rd grade; this difference only approximated significance, however, since the t ratio was −2.

Strength. For all grades, normal-aged boys had significantly higher means for the average score of 11 cable tension tests than did underaged boys. The differences between these means were significant at and above the .05 level; the t ratios ranged from 2.53 to 4.29. However, in grade 3, the underaged boys obtained a significantly higher mean Physical Fitness Index; the t ratio of −2.16 was significant at the .05 level.

Motor ability elements. Of the 15 comparisons involving motor ability elements, 9, or 60 percent of the differences between means were significant at or above the .05 level. In all instances, the normal-aged boys in each grade had higher means than did the underaged boys. These significant differences were as follows: shuttle run, 2nd and 3rd grades; standing broad jump, 2nd, 4th, and 6th grades; standing broad jump × weight, all grades but the 3rd. Of these significant differences, three were found at the 2nd grade, two at the 4th and 6th grades, and one at the 3rd and 5th grades.

SUMMARY OF RESULTS

1. No significant differences between the means of boys who were underaged and

normal-aged in the same elementary school grades were obtained in the physique type and intelligence tests.

2. Significant differences between the means of underaged and normal-aged boys were obtained in scholastic achievement, interest, peer status, maturity, body size, strength, and motor ability elements; these differences were obtained in 25 percent of the scholastic achievement, 12 percent of the interest, 15 percent of the peer status, and 56 percent of the physical measure comparisons. The most noteworthy situations were found in the 4th grade for scholastic achievement and the 6th grade for interest elements. The relative superiority in maturity, body size, gross strength, and motor ability elements possessed by the normal-aged boys appeared to prevail throughout the elementary school grades.

5. HPR with a difference*

Joe B. Rushing

President, Tarrant County Junior College District, Fort Worth, Texas

The symbol HPR may have many meanings. Even within the Junior College of Broward County [Florida] it is understood in different ways.

HPR is a code to the mysterious mind of the computer. It and other three-letter characters help that electronic marvel to consume great quantities of cards and tape and spew out grade reports, permanent records, and a vast amount of other important information.

To a few members of the faculty HPR merely refers to another instructional department located on the perimeter of the campus where both faculty and students seem to devote most of their time to "non-academic" endeavors.

In a real sense, however, the meaning of HPR is far different and far more significant. For the students of the Junior College of Broward County it means health, physical education, recreation—improved health habits, better physical well-being, and valuable recreational skills which they will carry with them throughout their lives.

There is no place today in American education for the "country club" college. Despite cries of chronic critics, higher education in general is making giant strides toward greater intellectual development. The pressures of modern society are felt by the college student as perhaps they have never been felt before. The demands for scholastic achievement, of accelerated programs, and of the vast expansion of human knowledge are inevitable for today's collegian. Some who have studied this problem feel grave concern. Many believe we need to reemphasize the physical well-being of the student at the same time we accent

his intellectual growth. This need becomes more apparent as we observe the trends of our social and economic order. A democracy requires a healthy citizenry; and, as we see a constantly shortening work week, earlier retirement, and a trend toward America becoming a nation of old people, we readily recognize the increasing need for skills and leisure time activities.

The program of HPR—health, physical education, and recreation—in the Junior College of Broward County is not designed to detract from the rigorous academic curriculum; instead, it is intended to supplement and complement that phase of the student's educational career. The instruction is planned for the student of today and the citizen of tomorrow.

A MATTER OF PHILOSOPHY

From its beginning in 1960, the Junior College of Broward County has emphasized the importance of physical education and recreation. Courses in these areas are included in the general education requirements. Each student must have four semesters in the activity program. The faculty, however, feels that these four semesters must be more than activity for activity's sake. They must offer something which has meaning for the student now and in later years.

From the beginning the faculty has attempted to serve the individual student. Staffing of the department and the development of the curriculum have emphasized a wide range of student needs and desires. This has not been an easy thing to accomplish, especially since the college has had practically no physical education facilities in the four years of its operation.

The program emphasizes individual sports

*From Junior College Journal, Vol. 35, p. 14, May 1965. Used by permission.

23

and achievement. The college works on the assumption that, throughout secondary school, the student has had extensive activities in group games and team sports. Consequently, these are held to a minimum in the instructional program. Team sports, however, are encouraged in the intramural sports program. For the most part, the HPR activity curriculum is designed for personal achievement. In addition to the physical benefits gained from good instruction, the student also has the psychological value to be derived from becoming proficient in one or more sports.

A third point of emphasis in this program, and perhaps most important, is the carryover value. Every student has an opportunity to master one or more sports which will provide recreational outlets for many years. The value of such an approach is easily recognized, especially by those living in retirement areas such as those of the Florida "Gold Coast."

AGAINST MANY HANDICAPS

The Junior College of Broward County opened in 1960. Its first buildings consisted of half a dozen two-story barracks at the old Fort Lauderdale Naval Air Station. Although there were adequate classrooms for temporary use, the facilities for physical education were virtually nonexistent. One of the barracks buildings was converted to shower and dressing rooms. These, along with two asphalt tennis courts and three handball courts dating back to World War II, comprised the HPR facilities. There was no gymnasium available within reasonable distance of the campus. These shortcomings were not without advantages. For out of these limited resources came a curriculum of considerable variety and a concept of facility use which promises to have lasting value.

When the college occupied its first permanent building in 1963, the Department of Health, Physical Education, and Recreation realized only slight improvement. The faculty offices were air-conditioned and the shower and dressing rooms were new and modern, but the department still had little in the way of instructional space. A physical conditioning room and a dance classroom were the only indoor spaces available but the pattern had already been set and the

college was able to continue an excellent program despite limited space.

The unique feature of the instructional program is that it is conducted largely in community and commercial facilities.

OFF-CAMPUS INSTRUCTION

The use of off-campus facilities began in 1961. At that time the faculty decided that students should be allowed to elect bowling as a physical education activity. Two sections were scheduled with the instruction to be given at bowling lanes in Fort Lauderdale. This was on an experimental basis. A fee was charged each student to cover the exact charge made by the owners of the installation. To the surprise of the staff, both sections were soon filled and a third one was opened. When it was filled, students were placed on a waiting list for the second semester. Today bowling is regularly taught in some of the finest facilities to be found anywhere. This is done by college faculty members but without the necessity of heavy capital expenditures.

Golf is another sport taught off-campus. Though some of the instruction is given on the campus, the college is within a few minutes' drive of several fine golf courses. As in other sports, the owners of public and private facilities have been most cooperative with the college in giving reasonable rates to students.

The Junior College of Broward County does not have a pool. Yet swimming instruction is given each semester to many students who elect it. In 1962 scuba diving was added to the curriculum. In this case as in others, the department is able to secure part-time instructors who are specialists in their fields. The college has invested no money in diving equipment but finds it more economical to contract for it through agencies ideally equipped to give this service. It is only natural that in this center of water sports sailing is on the list of departmental offerings for the near future.

One of the most popular activities now taught in HPR is horsemanship. Again the faculty has turned to the community and contracts were signed with proprietors of riding stables to provide horses and equipment. All instruction is given by the regular faculty and is under the complete control of the college.

The fees necessary to cover the additional cost of these community-centered programs are paid by the students. Special fees range from $3 per semester for swimming to $20 for horsemanship. There are many other activities which the student may elect and for which there is no fee.

In 1964 a new course was started—one which has received much attention, despite the unexciting designation—HPR 250. For two years the faculty had discussed aviation training, both for its recreational value and as a business asset. Negotiations with owners of private flying schools revealed that the cost would be too high for most students. In September of 1963 a request was made of a philanthropic foundation for a special grant. The grant was received, and in February, 1964, the college purchased a new airplane and admitted twenty-one students to the first class. Since foundation funds pay for the airplane and all maintenance and operation costs, the student is charged only the cost of instruction. For a fee of $56 he receives twelve clock hours of ground training and ten hours of dual flight instruction. Fifteen students were selected from among many applicants to make up the summer class. Forty students were enrolled in the fall term in 1964. Evidence from the first class shows that a few may enter satisfying careers in aviation, and that many will continue training to the private pilot's license.

BETTER IN THE FUTURE

The Department of HPR in the Junior College of Broward County has many things in its favor. One is the weather. There are few days during the year when outside activities cannot be conducted. A second is the availability of resources. There are many public and private facilities available to the college for a wide variety of sports either free or for a nominal cost. Third, and perhaps most important, is a philosophy which places the health and physical welfare of the student in a prominent place among the purposes of the institution.

College-owned facilities will be added. Enrollment is expected to reach 10,000 by 1972. As the student body grows, the program will be improved and expanded. Plans are already on the drawing board for a gymnasium and other physical education facilities. Continued use will be made, however, of community resources. There will be a constant effort to resist the pressures toward "mass activity" and to always emphasize the individual and his educational needs, both now and in his future.

6. A new and hard look at college physical education programs*

Martin H. Rogers

Chairman, Department of Health and Physical Education, State University of New York, College at Brockport

The traditional rallying cry of those with high aspirations, seeking ever higher achievements, was "Excelsior." In higher education at the moment, and certainly in physical education, the battle cry now seems to be "Change." If there is one thing certain in this pragmatic society of ours, it is the constancy of change. This truth is apparent in all phases of our lives—government, economics, social structure, and, of course, education. It affects us at all levels and is equally true for youth, middle age, and adults. It is as true for college education as it is for elementary education. In a randomly selected sample of fifty-eight articles on education, eighteen of the articles stressed change. It is obvious to most of us that this is as true for college physical education as it is for all other phases of college education.

It is not only important for us to recognize the existence of change, but it is also essential that we recognize the directions in which changes are occurring. Education, and physical education, must not only keep pace with the changes, but must anticipate changes and prepare citizens for a new life in a new society. Education has a responsibility to provide opportunities for the development of intelligent citizenship. Education has the responsibility for reflecting changes in knowledge, value emphasis, societal attitudes, and individual responsibilities. With this in mind, it is necessary to take

a new and hard look at college physical education programs.

William F. Brazziel . . . wrote . . . : "Who would have thought in years gone by . . . that archery, tennis, and community health, scoffed at in the past as beneath the ken of solid academics, would come to be viewed more and more as experiences necessary for the new leisure and to provide leadership for helping communities where poverty and poor health conditions still grip a third of our population." This statement not only indicates that changes are taking place in college education, but it also implies that the direction of some of these changes is toward greater objective relevance of higher education to contemporary needs. Is college physical education keeping up with the world of changes? Is it changing in compatible directions? Is college physical education relevant to contemporary needs? Does it produce the changes within individuals which we have established as objectives of our programs?

The colleges and universities of the country, and the physical education programs which they organize and support, face a variety of changing ideas. In the first place, in spite of the generally accepted pragmatic view of education, there is a renewed interest and emphasis in the liberal arts in higher education. Partly in contrast with that shift, there is secondarily an increasing tendency to pass on to the student a greater responsibility for the determination of his own educational goals and educational programs. A third shift, arising from the greater stu-

---

*From Proceedings, 1966, p. 53, National College Physical Education Association for Men. Used by permission.

dent assumption of responsibility, is the need within the colleges and universities for a greater flexibility of program to meet the students' self-defined needs. Next, rapidly increasing stores of knowledge, both scientific and sociological, create new emphases in the curricular content of educational programs. Trends in the organization of society increase the need for new competencies and talents for individually directed self re-creation and self-realization. Finally, in the face of all these changes, there continues the university responsibility for providing quality instruction in quality programs.

Each of the six trends in education requires some closer examination as far as physical education is concerned. The first of these—the renewed interest and emphasis in the liberal arts—reflects a somewhat new and different interpretation of the term liberal. The liberal arts at one time meant those studies which led to freedom from the bonds of ignorance, those studies which were actually liberating. The term liberal now seems to mean free, flexible, nonrestrictive. It is a liberalness more of the political nature than the educational. As far as physical education is concerned, it means that our basic instruction programs must offer a variety of paths to the goals which we have set for them. It means a reduction in requirements as far as specificity of courses or skills is concerned, with more options appropriate to reaching certain goals. I think that it still means, also, that physical education must be liberating in the sense that the program does develop certain specific physical competencies and activities knowledges. It should be liberating in the sense that it provides students with skills which can be useful and with understandings of sports and skills which lead to a better comprehension of that segment of our culture which is related to sports.

The second trend relates to the increasing tendency for students to be given the right of self-determination in education. The student is expected to evaluate his own strengths and weaknesses and to design education programs which will, hopefully, lead to his own maximum development. In physical education the implication is that there must be sufficient basic instruction in a variety of activities to serve as a foundation from which such self-determination can

be intelligently made. It also means that there must be a wide variety of activities available to the students to enable them to reach levels of excellence in certain selected activities.

The third change is very closely related to the second. If the student is to be given the responsibility for self-determination, the lockstep curriculum of the past must become obsolete. The college must provide a variety of routes toward the goal of self-realization. Physical education programs must adjust to this by providing basic and elementary instruction in some activities; opportunities for advancement in skill to the level of expertness; and participation (as a part of physical education) in higher level activities customarily organized as intramural athletics, athletic clubs, and intercollegiate teams. It is necessary that we recognize the need for this flexibility and the need for students to determine some of their own goals. The student body now exists as a "fourth estate" —involved in governance, housing, extra-class activities, and recreation as related to their lives on the college or university campus. About one-third of the articles on new developments in colleges and universities are currently devoted to student personnel problems. The change exists now and must be dealt with.

The fourth trend is the rapidly increasing store of knowledge. This affects the entire college or university program and does not leave physical education untouched. Increased understanding of the function of the human body requires us to examine our physical education programs to see whether or not we actually do meet certain physiological objectives, provide both interesting and safe activities, and contribute to the overall physical development of the students. Knowing about how much exercise is required to build increments of strength or fitness, do we actually organize programs that contribute positively to this development? And from the sociological viewpoint, are the skills we teach and the activities we organize really relevant to the social situation today? A new emphasis in lifetime sports is developing, with a decreasing emphasis in college level instruction in highly organized team sports. We must scrutinize closely the degree to which the programs we offer are compatible with the physiological and psychological demands which society places upon persons and the opportunities society provides for people to recreate.

The fifth trend is the increasing realization that education must exhibit greater relevance to contemporary needs. If educated individuals are to strive for goals of full self-realization, opportunities must be provided in colleges and universities for them to achieve superior physical development and physical fitness. Conceivably, physical education requirements should be in terms of standards of development rather than in hours of participation. It must also provide opportunities for students to achieve a level of expertness in perhaps two or three sport activities which may be continued into adult life. It should also recognize the fact that the population in general devotes approximately one-fifth of its leisure time to participation in sports, individual and family recreation, and spectator participation in athletic events. The educated person in today's society should have a good understanding of what is going on in the field or on the television screen as he watches professional football, NCAA football, televised ice hockey, the world series, and other sports spectaculars.

Finally, as a sixth point, there is the continuation of a university responsibility. Though I have viewed the changes with some excitement, I may seem to be dragging my heels when I express the feeling that adequate programs of physical education can adjust to these changes only when the university meets its responsibility for providing quality instruction. Many physical education basic instruction programs across the country have continually reinforced the feeling that the success of the programs has been due in large part to the fact that instruction has been professional, experienced, and thorough. The skills and understandings of physical education and sport activities should receive attention from quality instructors just as much as the basic skills in languages and sciences. It is a questionable practice to relegate instruction in physical education skills to inexperienced and incompletely educated graduate assistants. While the youth and energy of the younger teachers are important, the overall responsibility for instruction and the development of high quality programs should be in the hands of well-educated, mature, and experienced instructors.

Though the call to arms may be "Excelsior" or "Change," our aspirations must be high. Change there will be, and change we will. We may never reach the point when we can cap off the process with the cry of "Eureka," but we will be well on the way toward that goal if we constantly analyze the trends and scrutinize our programs critically to determine whether or not they actually are achieving the goals which we set for ourselves.

7. Athletics: " . . . . unquenchably the same"?*

Byron R. White

Associate Justice of the Supreme Court of the United States

Speakers normally either entertain or they educate, educate in the sense that they review the old or instruct in the new, arouse or reassure, criticize or reaffirm. But sometimes the speaker's main function is merely to satisfy a curiosity by appearing, showing himself and making a noise or two. A college dean told me a short while ago that the students probably didn't care at all what I said; they were simply curious to see and make sure that people from the bench were human too.

What all this does to clarify my mission here is difficult to tell. Entertainment is not my line and I cannot hope to educate you experts and specialists in the areas with which you are concerned at this annual meeting. Nor am I so sure that many of you are so very curious about Justices of the Supreme Court.

Nevertheless, here I am; in any event you have the comfort of knowing that I have only a one night stand and the truth is that in accepting your invitation I acted rather impulsively. A moment of reflection would have suggested that I should not preempt this podium and deny it to others who might contribute more to your meeting. But organizations like yours, to say nothing of Williamsburg, have an hydraulic attraction for me. I knew my family and I would have a good time and we truly have.

. . . it is said in the books that Darius, the Persian king in the sixth and fifth centuries B.C., determined to conquer the Greeks, considering them to be an inferior race. He accordingly sent a spy among them to see how they trained for battle and to determine their capabilities. This spy disguised himself as a merchant and infiltrated

the Greek army. What he saw was Greek soldiers, their bodies naked and oiled, practicing a variety of athletics. They did much dancing, too, clad only in a bronze shield. And they walked together, arm in arm, hand in hand. These soldiers seemed strong enough, but they sat and paid close attention when Greek poets were read aloud to them. The spy reported to Darius that the Greeks spent their time cavorting around in the nude or sitting, partially clothed, while listening to idiots propound ridiculous ideas about freedom and equality for the individual citizen.

Darius and his luxurious court were greatly amused and thought conquest of Greece would be a terribly easy job. What a rude shock it was when at Marathon the Persian army was driven out to sea. All of this was beyond the comprehension of the powerful emperor.

The same can be said of his son Xerxes, who succeeded his father and also tried to conquer Greece. The night before his naval forces were to battle the Greeks at Salamis, word came to Xerxes that Themistocles, aboard his flagship, was in a deep discussion about certain passages in a Pindar ode. Xerxes, like his father had been, was amused. But the next day he wept when he saw his naval forces routed by the art loving Greeks whose only weapons were their virile bodies and steel minds.

I don't know how much fact or myth these stories contain but they do express a basic idea about the Greeks: For them, intellectual power and physical vigor were not incompatible but were natural allies; together they counted for much more than either one alone and even more than the sum of the individual parts.

The ancient Greeks made what were probably history's greatest contributions to philos-

---

*From an address to the National Federation of State High School Athletic Associations, Williamsburg, Va., June 27, 1965. Used by permission.

ophy, government and the arts. But at the same time, athletics were an essential part of education and training, and no other nation has ever produced so high an average of physical development as the Greeks did in the classic period. The result was a standard of athletic excellence perhaps never again equaled.

The historian Isocrates expressed the idea well when he said this: ". . . certain of our ancestors, long before our time, invented and bequeathed to us two disciplines: physical training for the body, of which gymnastics is a part, and for the mind, philosophy. These twin arts are parallel and complementary, by which their masters prepare the mind to become more intelligent and the body to become more serviceable, nor separating sharply the two kinds of education, but using similar methods of instruction, exercise and discipline."

For the Greeks, a strong body was not only of great utility for simple survival. Athletics were a joy in themselves. Strong and graceful performance was inherently satisfying. A vigorous body did much for personality and much for the mind. Moreover, physical training and competitive sports were thought productive of that sound character and noble vision so essential to wise government which was a central concern of the serious minded Greek.

The representative nature of the Panhellenic athlete and the connection of the games with the national religion perhaps explain the great honor which came to winning athletes. Whole cities turned out to welcome the returning heroes. Songs were composed and their exploits recorded on pillars of stone. Athletic poetry and art were common. Statues were raised in some public places. It became common to give substantial prizes to winning athletes, and they also enjoyed important public privileges. They were even exempted from taxation at a later date. It is probably true that the victorious athlete in Greece enjoyed a distinction such as he has never had, before or since.

But the sad story is that Greek athletes destroyed themselves. Even in those ancient days, sports without serious competition became meaningless. Competition begat specialization, trainers, coaches and winners who had time for little else. Professionalism

followed, with excessive prizes and the accompanying corruption.

Even in Socrates' day, many youths were turning away from sport. He once lectured a young man for his poor physical condition. The youth haughtily said he was not competing because he was an amateur. Socrates replied that there was no such thing as an amateur as far as physical condition was concerned and that it was the young man's duty to be strong and healthy.

Plato and Aristotle decried the trend. Euripides, himself fond of athletics, said, "Of all the countless evils throughout Hellas, there is none worse than the race of athletes. . . . In youth they strut about in splendor, the pride of their city, but when bitter old age comes upon them, they are cast aside like threadbare garments."

Xenophanes added these words about the athlete: "Yet he is not so worthy as I, and my wisdom is better than the strength of men and horse. Nay, this is a foolish custom, nor is it right to honor strength more than wisdom."

The historian Isocrates, whom I have quoted before, lucidly posed the problem, and he might well have written some of the speeches which are given today. "Many times," he said, "have I wondered at those who first convoked the national assemblies and established the athletic games, amazed that they should have thought the powers of men's bodies to be deserving of so great bounties, while to those who had toiled in private for the public good and trained their own minds so as to be able to help also their fellowmen, they apportioned no reward whatsoever, when in all reason they ought rather to have made provision for the latter, for if all the athletes would acquire twice the strength they now possess, the rest of the world would not be better off, but let a single man attain to wisdom and all men will reap the benefit who are willing to share his insight."

The first case of bribery in Greek athletics was reported in 388 B.C., when one boxer bribed another to give the match away. Other instances followed. It took some time, but in a span of 100 years athletics had fallen into a corrupt and deplorable state, and the country had developed into an unathletic nation of spectators. The glory and value of athletics were dead.

All of this has a familiar ring. Neither the fascination with athletics nor the problems which beset them are unique to the Greeks. Many other countries in many other periods have become heavily involved with sports, which in some instances have entered into the very social fabric of the community. The British, for example, have an old and solid commitment to athletics. Indeed, among their most valuable exports in the eighteenth and nineteenth centuries were their athletic games and all that the idea of sports implied. This tradition is very much alive today. On July 17, 1956, at the Guildhall in London in the presence of Her Majesty the Queen, the Lord Mayor interrupted the city's reception for King Faisal of Iraq to announce the score in the cricket match with Australia. And in January, 1957, there was widespread surprise, disappointment and anger that the famous bootball player, Stanley Matthews, had not been knighted. The New Statesman went so far as to say that Sir Anthony Eden would lose more votes over this than over the Suez Canal or petrol rationing. English athletics, of course, have their problems but their rather firm tradition of amateurism has not yet been seriously eroded by the overlay of their immensely popular professional sports.

As for ourselves, massive involvement in athletics is an obvious aspect of our culture. Our investments in facilities and manpower are astronomical at both the amateur and professional levels. Millions are engaged in some form of athletic recreation each week and millions more are spectators. Interschool and intercollege competitions are of consuming interest to large groups of people. The current group of heroes always includes a number of athletes. The professional games have grown enormously and promise great financial return. Professional football has even revolutionized family life on Sundays.

I would hesitate to assess the total picture in America. Others have tried and I refer you to them. A much narrower focus is the situation in the high schools and colleges, indeed in the handing of athletics and sports in any of our schools as part of the educational process. Here the debate has been intense and continues to be so.

The basic question, I suppose, is why we put up with physical training or athletics in any form in any of our schools or colleges.

But I think this is primarily a rhetorical inquiry, for I doubt that any significant number of thinking people would advocate excising from the schools any and all forms of physical education and training. This is so for a number of reasons.

In the first place, athletic games are immense fun. Young people, given a little room, the opportunity and a minimum of intelligent supervision, can easily have an exhilarating time. And this, I must confess, I consider to be a worthy end in itself, at least for those children who live in the predominantly gray atmosphere of our great cities. Secondly, there is the matter of health and physical fitness, which are also seminal values and which need no further justification. Our gigantic health programs aimed at curing disease are perhaps limited only by the preventive measures which the young should learn at an early age, including as a primary matter the whole process of physical training and conditioning. The immediate and practical benefits of a strong and healthy body— and I am not talking here of those who make a fetish of their physiques—are very great indeed. There is a considerable difference between health on the one hand and strength and vigor on the other. I am sure you can count among your friends many who are perfectly healthy but not very energetic; who are seldom sick but tire easily; who don't seem to need a doctor but who do seem to need a rest, a nap or a coffee break; or who appear perfectly normal but wear out in the middle of that sustained, emergency effort which everyone of us has from time to time, whatever our line of work.

Appearance, demeanor and personality are equally basic considerations in pleasant and effective living and each, more often than not, is subject to measurable improvement by significant involvement in some form of vigorous athletic or recreational activity.

It is also said, and I am one of those who believe it, that our athletics afford one of the few opportunities for our youth to nourish and develop those important qualities of character which are absolutely essential to the great performances required of this nation in the next few decades. Native ability plus formal education may be an inadequate formula to produce the excellence we so urgently require. We need those mysterious and elusive qualities of courage, determination, presence of mind, self-control and concentration upon a given task—these are the traits which we hope will be inevitably developed when the athlete is repeatedly confronted with situations demanding them and which he will carry with him to his other endeavors.

The late President Kennedy said all this in these few well chosen words which I will quote: ". . . the physical vigor of our citizens is one of America's most precious resources . . . [It] is not only one of the most important keys to a healthy body; it is the basis of dynamic and creative intellectual activity. The relationship between the soundness of the body and the activities of the mind is subtle and complex. Much is not yet understood. But we do know what the Greeks knew; that intelligence and skill can only function at the peak of their capacity when the body is healthy and strong; that hardy spirits and tough minds usually inhabit sound bodies.

"In this sense," he went on, "physical fitness is the basis of all the activities of our society. And if our bodies grow soft and inactive, if we fail to encourage physical development and prowess, we will undermine our capacity for thought, for work and for the use of those skills vital to an expanding and complex America.

"Thus," he concluded, "the physical fitness of our citizens is a vital prerequisite to America's realization of its full potential as a nation, and to the opportunity of each individual citizen to make full and fruitful use of his capacities."

But with all this undergirding for our athletic programs, there are troublesome areas left to consider. Of course, the schools should concern themselves with the body as well as the mind, for it is the schools who have the only really consistent access to our youth and, if room for recreation is not available in the schools, it will not be available at all. But all this may be admitted without accepting the validity of our existing athletic system. Perceptive critics argue that a physical fitness program can produce a strong and healthy youth without the elaborate overlay of competitive athletics on an interscholastic basis. The system of school against school, it is said, inevitably has unfortunate consequences for a truly comprehensive program; energy and effort are concentrated upon producing the school team; it is an exclusive system which leaves all but the chosen few sitting in the grandstands to cheer; the participants themselves are so pressured into peak performance and pushed to such limits that they neglect their minds and overtax their bodies, the very antithesis of a sound program. Moreover, if these unfortunate conditions exist in the high schools, it is said that the colleges are even worse, much worse.

To what extent these criticisms are true, you know better than I. Certainly, in some schools and in some areas they have considerable validity. And wherever valid, they prove what history has taught before—that athletics carry the seeds of their own destruction and without sound direction the suicide will most surely occur.

No one can justify a school program which benefits only the few and neglects the many. No one can defend a system which discourages the many who cannot compete with the best and see no reason, therefore, to compete at all. No one can fairly close his eyes to those many young people who do not put athletic skill high on their priority list, but who urgently need and would enjoy athletic participation, given more inviting conditions. Is it really necessary for the schools to choose between the school team on the one hand and no athletics and no physical fitness programs on the other?

The answer is clearly in the negative. There is no incompatibility between a broadly focused physical education program and the team sports. There is no necessity to discard either. On the contrary, there is ample justification for both. Such a program presents few problems that able management and direction cannot cure, particularly when it is tied to the schools, which have the responsibility of producing whole men and women who are stunted in neither mind nor body, who are neither mental nor physical cripples and who must be willing and able to face the rigors of the future.

This is familiar territory to all of you and to your organization. The basic criteria under which you operate reveal your awareness of these problems and of the goals for which you strive. Your handbook says that athletics are to be an integral part of the secondary school program; that athletics are for the benefit of all youths; that the aim is maximum participation in a well balanced intramural and interscholastic program with emphasis on safe and healthful standards of competition; and that your task is concerned primarily with extending benefits of athletics to all participants and to spreading these benefits to constantly increasing numbers.

There is, as I have said, no mystery about what your problems are; and your goals are reasonably clear. The difficulties lie more in day-to-day performance and in closing the gap between principle and practice, between theory and reality in everyday life. I have no illusions, and I am sure you don't either, about the difficulties which you consistently encounter in implementing admittedly sound ideas. Solving public problems in a democracy is not an easy task, nor should it be. It is a job for the patient and the hardy and a job that deserves doing, not for some impersonal notions about athletics, but for the generation of the young.

There is not a shadow of a doubt these days as to our need for men and women of intellect, energy and character. Since its very beginning, this country, along with others, has been in constant change and flux. The rate of change has been steadily increasing and there is every indication that the trend will continue. Change in our country has ridden on an unfolding technology which has left nothing untouched, on a rapidly growing population and on a socio-economic system which has emphasized shared values. With rapid change has come a vast complexity and the imposition of almost an absolute demand for not only an adequate but an extended education. Whatever the unemployment figures seem to indicate, there is today, and there will be, an almost inexhaustible demand for talent to manage the private business world, to man essential government positions and to devote itself to solving the critical problems swirling around our position in what we sometimes call the family of nations.

But this kind of talent must prove itself and this process of proof which goes on in our schools all across the land can be an unnerving thing to the average young person who has begun to think and ask questions about his future. There seems to be that rather awesome necessity to shape up and measure up, and the entrance requirements to any kind of meaningful life are constantly on the rise. Energy, brains, character and motivation seem basic ingredients for a successful formula.

Unquestionably, difficult demands are imposed on the young. But the rate of obsolescence of their elders is very high indeed and for the young who want it, there is almost unlimited opportunity in the challenges which lie ahead.

Herein, I suppose, lies the importance of organizations like yours, which are tied to the overall academic institution but are dedicated to producing those nonacademic consequences which bear so heavily on achievement and the way a young man makes his peace with the world.

Substantially, you are dealing with human nature in a specialized context. This, as was said by Dr. George Norlin, long-time president of the University of Colorado, is a very old problem. Using his words, "Lo, all these centuries human nature remains unchanged . . . Perhaps we had better accept this unflattering fact and make the best of it. Perhaps the time may come when college students will hold pep meetings to stir the philosophy department to do or die or will root with enthusiasm when the department of chemistry discovers a new element, but that time has not come nor will the Carnegie report on athletics (or others like it) bring it about in our day or our generation."

Human nature and athletics, as Shelley said about another subject, are "through time and change, unquenchably the same."

We have our peculiar problems in the judiciary, ladies and gentlemen, but your distinctive tasks involve the management of the young and their athletics. Fortunately, I can leave these tasks with you during the forthcoming week and I wish you the very best of things.

8. The ten most significant educational research findings in the past ten years*

Daniel E. Griffiths

Dean, School of Education, New York University

The writer has rarely undertaken a task as interesting and rewarding as this paper has proved to be. The assignment was accepted as an act of professional and organizational loyalty, but the background work and writing proved to be a unique educational experience.

PROCEDURES

When the magnitude, difficulty, and the sheer arrogance of determining a list of the ten most significant educational research findings in the past ten years was revealed last fall, that standard administration technique, asking one's professional peers what they thought the findings might be, was selected as a data-gathering and evaluational technique. Twenty-five people considered to be the most knowledgeable in the country were selected, and each was sent a letter posing the question and containing a form for his responses. Of the 25, 13 made nominations and several others made useful comments. Similar letters were then sent to 25 school administrators, 22 of whom were superintendents and their responses were computed with the above.

GROUND RULES

One of the first problems in handling this topic was, how should the word "findings" be defined? If one chooses to define the word to mean a definitive conclusion of a single study, then the topic has little meaning. Several of the respondents went to great lengths to point out that a single finding is

*From Executive Action Letter, Vol. 6, No. 10, p. 73, May 1967, Croft Educational Services, New London, Conn. Used by permission.

rarely important in itself, but acquires importance because it fits a system of findings. Another way of saying the same thing is that a single study never produces significant findings, with rare exceptions, and that major contributions are usually series of interconnected studies conducted by a number of investigators. This will be illustrated several times in this paper. It may also be said that when a single study produces significant findings, it is the culmination of a number of related researches. (I acknowledge the contributions of Drs. Fred Kerlinger and Glen Heathers, School of Education, New York University, and Dr. R. M. W. Travers, School of Education, Western Michigan University, for thoughts on the meaning of "findings.")

The second problem relating to ground rules for this paper was, What is the meaning of "significant"? In a sense, this raises the question of the criteria used in this paper. "Significant" was defined in the letter sent to the jury as "those [findings] which either have influenced or have the potential for influencing educational practice." Dr. Lawrence M. Stolurow of the Harvard Computing Center suggested several questions which could be asked to ascertain the significance of research in education:

1. To what extent has the behavior of individuals in education been changed?
2. How many articles have been written as a result of the findings?
3. To what extent do educators talk about or use the concepts generated by the research in discussing their own problems?

He also believes, as do many others, that

there must be a critical mass of research evidence which then triggers behavior change in educational practitioners. The size of the critical mass probably varies with a number of factors including the readiness of the field, the power of the findings, and the size of the groups to be affected by the study.

"Research" is used to mean applied research and development as well as fundamental, theory-testing research. A wide range of research methodologies was accepted for inclusion in this paper.

SIGNIFICANT LINES OF RESEARCH
I

The best example of what has been discussed above—i.e., that significant findings for education emerge from long lines of inquiry—is to be found in the work of Bloom published in *Stability and Change in Human Characteristics*. (1)

Bloom reviewed almost one thousand studies of selected human characteristics in an attempt to understand the development and change in these characteristics over a period of time. The studies, taken as a whole, summarize what is known about quantitative development of certain human characteristics from near birth to adulthood. Bloom's major hypothesis is that "the environment in which the individual develops will have its greatest effect on a specific characteristic in its most rapid period of change and will have least effect on the characteristic in its least rapid period of change."

The following table, from *Stability and Change in Human Characteristics,* is a good way to illustrate the differential rate of growth which exists for stable characteristics.

The table should be read as follows: "General intelligence appears to develop as much

Half-development of selected characteristics	
Height	Age 2½ years
General intelligence	Age 4 years
Aggressiveness in males*	Age 3 years
Dependence in females*	Age 4 years
Intellectuality in males and females*	Age 4 years
General school achievement	Grade 3

*Since we do not have an absolute scale for these characteristics, we have indicated the age at which one-half of the criterion variance can be predicted.

from conception to age 4 as it does during the 14 years from age 5 to age 18."

Bloom's second major hypothesis is that "change measurements are unrelated to initial measurements but they are highly related to the relevant environmental conditions in which individuals have lived during the change period."

It can be readily seen that Bloom's work points up the tremendous importance of early education. The significance of his work has been reflected in the Head Start Program, in the interest in nursery school and kindergarten education, and in a revival of concern for primary education.

Bloom has also written directly for school administrators, pointing out some of the implications of his work for the schools of the country. In "Stability and Change in Human Characteristics: Implications for School Reorganization," *Educational Administration Quarterly,* Winter, 1966, pp. 35-49, he urges that special nursery schools and kindergartens be established. The educational program should differ radically from the traditional preschool experiences which have been offered to middle-class children. The emphasis should be upon the intellectual development of the children. The child should be helped to perceive the world and to describe it through the use of language. In this way he learns to develop concepts and to express them. This should be accomplished by making learning exciting and by encouraging the child to spend larger and larger periods of calculated effort at learning.

Bloom recommends that a major reversal take place in the allocation of resources in schools. At the present time, more money is spent per child in the secondary school than in the elementary. He argues that more money should be spent in the first three years of schooling because:

1. Teachers in the initial years should be the best-trained in the system.
2. There should be a ratio of at least one adult for fifteen children.
3. There should be intensive in-service training for teachers.
4. There should be extensive diagnostic service for the children.
5. There should be reading and language specialists, school psychologists, and testing and evaluation specialists to help the teachers.

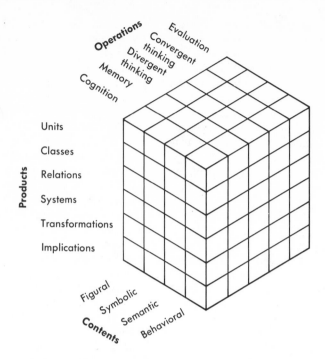

A cubical model representing the structure of intellect. (From Guilford, J. P.: Three faces of intellect, The American Psychologist, Vol. 14, 1959.)

Only a few of the implications of Bloom's work for education have been selected, because of the limitation on the length of this paper. The research on human characteristics is very probably the most significant line of inquiry in the past ten years, and it has implications for all aspects of the educational system.

II

The study of human intelligence is one of the most distinguished lines of inquiry. Beginning with Galton, and his two-factor theory, moving through Binet and Terman with their development of tests, then L. C. Thurstone and his explorations of factors in intelligence, the line has now been fed by the unified theory of human intellect developed by Guilford. The work of the Aptitudes Project which he directs at the University of Southern California has organized the known, unique, or primary intellectual abilities into a single system called the "structure of intellect." (2) The method of research was the administration of numerous especially constructed tests to different classes of people and factor analysis of the

scores. The factors which resulted were grouped in three ways and were pictured in a cubical model representing the structure of intellect (see diagram).

One basis for the classification was the basic process or operation performed. This classification produced five major groups of intellectual abilities: factors of cognition, memory, convergent thinking, divergent thinking, and evaluation. Briefly, cognition means discovery or rediscovery of recognition, while memory, of course, means retention of what is cognized. Divergent thinking means thinking in different directions, while convergent thinking leads to one right answer, these being two ways of generating new information from known information. Evaluation refers to reaching decisions as to goodness, correctness, suitability, and the like.

A second way in which Guilford classified intellectual factors was according to the kind of material or content involved. These are figural, symbolic, semantic, and social.

The third way of classifying was according to products involved. These are units, classes, relations, systems, transformations, and implications. In other words, as a result of the way in which a person deals with content he produces a transformation, sees relations, or develops a system; his thought process brings forth a product. Guilford contends that the above six are the "only fundamental kinds of products we can know."

What are the implications of the structure of intellect? Only two are dealt with in this paper: Vocational testing and education.

The model predicts as many as 120 distinct abilities, and at least 50 are now known. Depending on one's point of view, it can be said that there are at least 50 ways of being intelligent, or 50 ways of being stupid. The major implication for vocational testing and counselling is that a large number of scores is necessary if the counsellor is to know the range of an individual's intellectual resources.

When contemplating the implications of Guilford's work for vocational testing it is most useful to consider the content dimension of the model. All four groups on this dimension have particular significance; only the behavioral or social group is discussed here. The theory suggests as many as 30 abilities, such as understanding, evaluation of behavior, and productive thinking about behavior. Abilities in the area of social intelligence are of importance to those who deal with other people: teachers, law officials, social workers, politicians, statesmen, and leaders in general.

The implications for education are numerous, and only two are here discussed. There is great interest nowadays in creative thinking. Guilford tells us that the ". . . more conspicuously creative abilities appear to be concentrated in the divergent-thinking category, and also to some extent in the transformation category. . . ." If one were to exercise this ability (divergent thinking), he would concentrate on the production of a variety of responses to a problem. Guilford suggests that in education a better balance is needed between training in divergent thinking as contrasted with training in convergent thinking and in critical thinking or evaluation.

Guilford believes that the most important implication of his work for education is that it changes the conception of the learner and the learning process. He characterized the prevailing concept of the learner as a kind of stimulus-response device much like a vending machine. The learner is taught to give out a certain response when a particular stimulus is administered, just as a vending machine emits a given product for a coin. According to the structure of intellect model, the learner should be conceptualized as an electronic computer. The computer is fed information, it stores the information, uses it to generate new information by either divergent or convergent thinking, and evaluates its own results. In addition, the learner has an advantage over a computer in that he can seek and discover new information outside himself.

This conception of the learner leads to the idea that learning is the discovery of information, not merely the formation of associations. The great acceptance of this idea and its introduction into the schools in the past seven or eight years is evidence of the significance of Guilford's work.

III

The application of computer technology to research in learning theory might well be considered as a research breakthrough. There has been a long line of studies of learning. The modern era started with James and Thorndike, moved through Hull, Guthrie, Gates, and others to such present-day workers as Bruner. A second line of inquiry has a much shorter history; that is the work in teaching machines by such men as Pressy and Skinner. These two lines have now merged, and the new line is the study of learning in computer-based laboratories. It can be said that neither learning theory research nor teaching machines constituted powerful lines of inquiry, and that the hope held earlier for them has largely been dissipated. The reason is largely technological. It is virtually impossible to handle the empirical data generated by a study of learning in a classroom, and a non-computerized teaching machine can deal only with learning processes which are too simple to be of much value. The computer changes both of these conditions.

The work discussed in this paper is that of Suppes, the Stanford philosopher, in which he describes research on five principles of learning in a computer-based laboratory.(3) The laboratory is a simulation of a teaching environment created by a tutor working with an individual child. The computer provides not only visual information on a television-like screen, but also provides auditory information through speakers or earphones.

It is apparent that in the computer-based laboratory teaching proceeds at a rate appropriate to the needs of each learner; therefore, research on individual differences in learning rates can be done readily. The computer provides instant feedback, therefore there is immediate reinforcement and correction for each student, something that is highly desirable but is impossible in conventional classrooms. The third principle being studied is transfer of training; the computer makes possible the collection of data and permits the analysis of transfer among concepts over a long period of time. The fourth principle deals with the optimal organization of stimulus material. For instance, in teaching vocabulary in a foreign language, what is the optimal size of a block of words to be presented to students? In a preliminary study blocks of 6, 18, 36, and 108 words were used, with best results obtained by using 108 words; the worst results were obtained with the block of 6 words. The unique value of the computer in learning research comes when the fifth problem is studied by Suppes. This is the attempt to apply response latency, the time between a stimulus and the onset of a response, as a criterion of learning. Presumably, the shorter the time, the better the student is learning. Measurements of response latency in ordinary classrooms are impossible; in computer-based classrooms they are feasible.

The potential for influencing education of the line of inquiry described above is great, but it has not yet been fully realized. It is, however, one of the most promising of the present ventures.

IV

Another line of inquiry, now many years old, which has been significant for education is the study of the effects of environment on the development of individuals. Probably most emphasis is now being concentrated on what has been termed cultural deprivation. Typical of the type of inquiry is the work of the Deutsches and their as-

sociates in the Institute for Developmental Studies, now located at New York University.(4) In a study called "The Verbal Survey," the verbal and conceptual performance of lower- and middle-class, first- and fifth-grade, white and Negro children was investigated. Among the significant findings which have emerged is that: The more deprived group shows a significantly greater decrement on factors of intelligence, conceptual relatedness, contextual understanding, and formal language than the less deprived group, with some exceptions. For instance the more highly deprived children generally have lower factorial scores, except for boys with a relatively favorable self-concept.

The educational implications of the Verbal Survey are numerous, among them being the finding that four-year-old lower-class children who do not receive specialized programs reveal patterns of slow, but steady loss in their intellectual performance, compared with more advantaged populations.

V

Inquiries into the development of the individual have constituted a line of study for a considerable period of time. The work of Gesell has been most influential in this country, but recently has been overshadowed by that of Piaget, the Swiss psychologist.

As stated by Eleanor Duckworth, Piaget's theory is that the "development of intellectual capacity goes through a number of stages whose order is constant, but whose time of appearance may vary both with the individual and with the society. Each new level of development is a new coherence, a new structuring of elements which until that time have not been systematically related to each other."(5) Four factors are related to the development of individuals: nervous maturation, experience, social transmission, and auto-regulation. The last is seen as more important than the first three.

The chief implication for education in Piaget's work is "a plea that children be allowed to do their own learning." Further, "Good pedagogy must involve presenting the child with situations in which he himself experiments, in the broadest sense of that term—trying things out to see what happens, manipulating things, manipulating symbols, posing questions and seeking his own answers, reconciling what he finds one time with what he finds at another, comparing his findings with that of other children."

Piaget is apparently having an impact on the education of young children. He is very popular among elementary school educators, psychologists, and specialists in child development. He is referred to constantly, his experiments discussed widely, and his developmental stages are common currency in educational parlance. His influence on school practice has not been, in the opinion of the writer, as significant as has been his influence on conversation.

VI

The publication of *Administrative Performance and Personality*(6) capped a long line of inquiry into characteristics and styles of administrators. The methodology of this study was the creation of a simulated school in which 232 elementary school principals worked. Their administrative activities were scored and factor-analyzed, and the resulting factors were related to a large number of variables. Eight styles of administration and of the personalities that tended to accompany each style resulted from the study. Each style was related to measures of basic mental ability, basic personality factors, interests, job performance values, group interaction, superiors' ratings, teacher ratings, professional and general knowledge, and biographical data. The result was a detailing and explanation of the style through description of the people who perform in accordance with it. Following is an operational definition of one style and a description of those principals whose performance was best characterized by that style.

When confronted with in-basket items, certain principals tended to: ask for information, opinions, advice, or permission from subordinates; give information to subordinates; require further information; give information to outsiders; and involve a number of subordinate groups. Consequently, members of this group were characterized as "exchanging information."

These principals had high verbal knowledge and facility, they knew elementary ed-

ucation, school administration, and facts about the general culture. They were sociable, sensitive, trusting, confident, and relaxed and had interests like superintendents, lawyers or psychologists, but unlike policemen. They were concerned with teacher and pupil personnel problems, especially with the reaction of pupils to the educational program. This style is more characteristic of women than of men. Such principals elicit very positive responses from superiors and positive responses from teachers.

The study has had a rather peculiar impact upon the educational world. The report of research has not been widely distributed nor, apparently, read by many people. The materials used in the study have, however, had wide use. The in-baskets, as they are called, the kinescopes, tape recordings, and other printed materials have been used in graduate courses in over 100 universities. Thousands of administrators have been trained on the in-baskets developed in this study, yet a recent doctoral research indicated that only two universities used the written report in their instructional program.

VII

High hopes are held for Project Talent. This project was designed to find out about students' interests, their career plans, and the relation of their high school courses to their life objectives. It is also an attempt to determine why so much potential is lost and what can be done to reduce the loss. A sample was drawn consisting of 5% of the public and private high schools of the country, and a large battery of tests was administered; some 2,000 questions were asked of 440,000 students. In addition, a questionnaire on school characteristics was answered for each of the 1,353 secondary schools. Obviously, a great deal of information has been collected, but the major value of Project Talent is that follow-up studies of the students are planned for one, five, ten, and twenty years after they are graduated from high school. The long-range outcomes are thought to be:

. . . to provide a comprehensive inventory of the talents of our youth; to develop a set of standards for improving educational and psychological measurement; to develop a comprehensive counseling guide; to gain a better understanding of how young people choose their life work; and to gain a better understanding of the educational experiences which prepare students for their life work.(7)

VIII

At this point the writer was left on his own to nominate the remaining significant research findings, since all of those receiving substantial support have been reported.

It would seem that any listing of findings significant to education would have to include the results of the numerous curriculum revision projects. While most of these are not researches in the usual sense of the word, they are highly significant and influential developmental projects. The "new math," for example, is a household phrase and is even the subject matter of a popular song. The characteristics of these programs are: they generally involve academic scholars, they emphasize modern learning concepts such as the structure of knowledge and the discovery method, they emphasize the laboratory approach in the sciences, and they have "caught on" well in the public schools.(8)

IX

No list of ten findings would be complete if it did not include the name of James Bryant Conant. While the preceding sentence may sound incorrect grammatically, it is correct in actuality. Conant's reports on the American high school, the junior high school, teacher education, and educational policy-making may not meet most people's criteria for research, but no one can say that his pronouncements have not profoundly affected the behavior of educators, school board members, lay citizens, and even the students. Without arguing the merits of Conant's recommendations, suffice it to say that his work, taken as a whole, certainly has been significant.(9)

X

The last line of research to be presented in this paper is included more for potential than current significance. A number of studies have attempted to determine biological bases for learning and memory. This work has largely employed neurological and biochemical approaches. Probably the work best known to educators is that of K. S. Lashley, reported in his *Brain Mechanisms and Intelligence* (Chicago: University of Chicago Press, 1929). Biochemical studies now appear to be more popular than neurological ones, and some exciting research has been done which bears on the possible involvement of DNA (deoxyribonucleic acid) and RNA (ribonucleic acid) in memory functions.(10) In reviewing the research on DNA and RNA in relation to memory, Gaito concluded that while there was no conclusive direct evidence to indicate that either was the memory molecule, there was inferential evidence. He expressed the belief that the next decade should see important research results from psychologists and biological scientists in the biochemical approach to learning and memory.

CONCLUSION

This has been an attempt to name ten lines of educational research which have been significant in the past decade. No doubt much important work has been omitted, but if so the oversight has not been intentional. It is also hoped that the studies selected to illustrate certain of the lines of inquiry will not raise the hackles of those not selected or of their supporters. This has been a sincere effort to present lines of research thought by many to be significant for American education.

FOOTNOTES AND SUMMARY:

Lines of inquiry	*References*
(1) Studies of the quantitative development of human characteristics.	Benjamin S. Bloom, *Stability and Change in Human Characteristics* (New York: John Wiley, 1964).
(2) Studies of the nature of intelligence; the structure of intellect.	J. P. Guilford, "Three Faces of Intellect," *The American Psychologist*, Vol. 14, 1959, pp. 469-479.
(3) Application of computer technology to studies in learning theory.	Patrick Suppes, "Modern Learning Theory and the Elementary School Curriculum," *American Educational Research Journal*, Vol. 1, No. 2, March 1964.
(4) Effects of environment on the development of individuals.	*Annual Report 1965*, Institute for Developmental Studies, School of Education, New York University, pp. 13-27.
(5) The development of the individual.	Richard E. Ripple and Verne N. Rockcastle (eds.), *Piaget Rediscovered* (School of Education, Cornell University, 1964).
(6) Characteristics and styles of administrators.	John Hemphill, Daniel E. Griffiths, and Norman Frederiksen, *Administrative Performance and Personality* (New York: Teachers College Press, 1962).
(7) Talents of young people—Project Talent.	John C. Flanagan, "Maximizing Human Talents," *The Journal of Teacher Education*, Vol. XIII, No. 2, June 1962, pp. 209-215; John C. Flanagan, et al., *The Identification, Development, and Utilization of Human Talents: The American High School Student.* Cooperative Research Project No. 635, University of Pittsburgh, 1964.
(8) Curriculum revision projects.	Richard E. Ripple and Verne N. Rockcastle (eds.), *Piaget Rediscovered* (School of Education, Cornell University, 1964).
(9) James Bryant Conant.	*The American High School Today* (New York: McGraw-Hill, 1959); *Education in the Junior High School Years* (Princeton: Educational Testing Service, 1960); *Slums and Suburbs* (New York: McGraw-Hill, 1961); *The Education of American Teachers* (New York: McGraw-Hill, 1963).
(10) Biochemical approaches to learning and memory.	John Gaito, "DNA and RNA as Memory Molecules," *Psychological Review*, 1963, Vol. 70, No. 5, pp. 471-480.

9. The role of health, physical education, and recreation in the space age*

Clifford Brownell

Former President, American Association for Health, Physical Education, and Recreation

Americans greet the space age with mixed emotions. On the one hand human wisdom and fortitude, coupled with an abundance of natural resources, can fashion a better culture than man has enjoyed in previous generations. On the other hand, failure of persons in key positions to utilize properly scientific and social developments can impoverish and restrict the lives of the American people. There is no doubt that *education* plays the most significant role in the resulting success or failure.

But education—and especially secondary education—occupies a strange position, with strong pressure groups voicing different views concerning the school's ultimate purpose and program content. Some critics emphasize training the mind and abolishing so-called frills. Others follow the basic principle that public education should remain free to accept into its curriculum broad areas of learning experiences designed to enrich the lives of people. The comprehensive high school represents a middle ground, with strict attention given to academic subjects, classification of students according to scholastic ability, and provisions made for socialization among various groups through the avenues of physical education, home-room activities, and other programs. This confusion places grave responsibilities upon the secondary-school principal.

His duties become no easier when he recognizes the unique forces operating to-

day. He knows that schools belong to the people who support them; that communities can have the kinds of schools they want and are willing to pay for, and that most communities find a way to finance the kinds of schools they want. But, oftentimes, he doesn't know which pressure groups speak for the majority. He knows, further, that his position of leadership compels him to make decisions on the implementation of school policy, decisions frequently accompanied by unfavorable criticism. He knows that research on child growth and development over the past quarter-century places great emphasis on educating the "whole" child—not merely giving attention to youth's intellectual capacities. He knows that the complexities of modern culture, occasioned by remarkable discovery and invention, demand a broader and richer curriculum than has existed in previous generations. And he usually agrees with recently accepted practices in educational administration that make him primarily accountable for the curriculum—with such customary duties as discipline and child accounting delegated to other authority.

What is the role of secondary-school principals in the space age as curriculum coordinators and consultants with reference to health and safety education, physical education and athletics, and recreation? This document attempts to highlight these functions in broad perspective. Authors agree that noteworthy achievements of the present generation suggest only the beginnings of vast gains anticipated in future years. Man is making great strides in the control of his environment, but human nature and the bi-

*From The Bulletin, Vol. 44, No. 256, pp. 3-9, May 1960, National Association of Secondary School Principals, 1960, Copyright: Washington, D. C. Used by permission.

ological organism remain about the same. Sound education constitutes the focal point in enabling man to cope with and utilize effectively the changes that lie ahead.

HEALTH AND SAFETY EDUCATION

The World Health Organization defines health as a state of complete physical, mental, and social well-being—not merely the absence of disease or infirmity. Another definition states that health education means putting into practice the scientific knowledge available for optimum human growth and development. Health education, properly taught, has few deferred values; the youth lives his health every day. As a student in secondary school, he becomes increasingly responsible for his own health and must learn to assume rightful obligations for the welfare of his family and community.

What are some of these responsibilities? Take nutrition, for example. Not more than one person in ten now follows an adequate diet, despite the known facts and the surplus of food in this country. Skilled nutritionists contend that most families could have better diets at a saving of at least one third the present cost. Wars often occur largely because of lack of food and sky-rocketing population in a country. As another example, take appearance. Grooming and peer status bulk large in the minds of adolescent youths. Most of them have personal problems of dress, cleanliness, cosmetics, changing biology, making friends, and similar problems about which they need sympathetic guidance.

Scientific advances in health emerge by leaps and bounds. Some concern nutrition, alcoholism, narcotics, polio, tuberculosis, heart disease, fluoridation, colds, emotional disturbances, health and hospital insurance, and there are scores of others. Opportunities for worthy learning experiences about health in secondary schools can be organized around seven areas: *personal regimen* (activities for which the individual is responsible); *professional health services* (the work of doctors, dentists, nurses, clinics, and hospitals); *public health* (duties performed by official and voluntary health agencies); *mental health* (happiness, and control of the emotions); *social health* (boy-girl relationships, family life, and getting along with people); *temperance* (alcohol, tobacco, and narcotics); and *safety* (protecting oneself and others against accident and injury, and first aid).

Perhaps safety education deserves special mention here. Few life experiences exceed in importance the avoidance of accidents. The mechanization of industry and home appliances, increased leisure, and crowded traffic conditions give rise to more need for safety education. The mounting toll of injuries makes safety almost a "must" in any functional curriculum. Recent trends in secondary education favoring re-emphasis on academic subjects has led to the exclusion of driver education in a few schools, yet evidence produced by safety engineers clearly indicates the importance of this subject. Besides operation of motor vehicles, driver education contains many elements pertinent to the social sciences.

Health education and safety education belong to the secondary-school curriculum. Both of these areas bear specific relationships to American culture in the space age. Neither the home nor other community agencies can do the job without concerted efforts by schools in effecting a healthier, happier, and safer citizenry. And one more item—these subjects deserve positive credit toward promotion, graduation, and college entrance. Possibly they should be termed "health science" and "safety science" for better public sanction.

The occasional trend to substitute science for health education in secondary schools, with the brighter students taking science while those with lesser ability elect health education, appears unrealistic. To be sure, students should know the essentials of atomic energy and mathematical formulas, and *a few* of these youths will become productive scientists and engineers. But *all* of them will live in a generation where sound health and protective safety represent necessary attributes to personal and social welfare.

PHYSICAL EDUCATION AND ATHLETICS

The increasing number of secondary-school principals, whose earlier preparation and experience encompassed certain aspects of physical education or athletics, helps to ensure a significant place for these programs in the curriculum. Community pressures, however, sometimes cause the principal to neglect his obligations in these important matters.

One might raise the question, "What does the principal, as curriculum coordinator and consultant, have a right to expect from a well-organized and properly conducted program of physical education and athletics?"

Since other parts of this document contain detailed accounts of the subject, only four brief and general statements are appropriate here. *First,* physical education and athletics comprise the *instructional program* (required of all enrolled students); the *intramural program* (planned on an elective basis for students to satisfy individual interests); and the *interscholastic* program (designed for those with superior skills and competitive interests). *Second,* the classification of activities in a sound program usually includes games and sports; rhythmic activities; gymnastics, stunts, and tumbling, and aquatics. *Third,* the above activities serve as the *medium* through which education takes place; thus, physical education and athletics use physical activity for the identical purpose that mathematics, for example, employs numbers, symbols, and formulas. *Fourth,* the true function of physical education and athletics deals with realistic contributions made by these programs to the over-all and avowed purposes sought by the school in its total curriculum.

In keeping with the above four general statements, certain objectives emerge as broadly outlined below.

HEALTH

This objective has appeared in every acceptable list of desired educational outcomes for nearly a century. Medical scientists emphasize the abiding need for exercise as related to human welfare. Today's mechanized environment reduces opportunities for the development and maintenance of strong bodies. Biologists point out that normal growth among children and adolescents requires exercise, even family physicians recommend additional activity for most older persons who are free of restricting defect or disease. Physical education and athletic programs should stress the value of exercise for health reasons, and equip youths with neuromuscular skills and habits that can be practiced with satisfaction in later years.

[The] Council on Youth Fitness[1] [now called the President's Council on Physical Fitness and Sports] has aroused national interest in this matter. Some uninformed persons view this movement as belonging only to the schools and only to physical education. Such is not the case for several reasons. In the *first* place, the President's original proclamation clearly specified "total fitness"—with its competent adjectives, "physical," "emotional," "social," and "spiritual." *Second,* while schools can play a prominent role in establishing total fitness (largely because of their captive audience), other community agencies and the home must assume appropriate responsibilities. *Third,* physical education and athletics alone cannot effectively do the complete job assigned to the schools; all subjects have potentials in total fitness. Thus the principal, as curriculum coordinator and consultant, has an opportunity to articulate the various facets of fitness within the curriculum, and to coordinate the school fitness program with programs conducted by out-of-school agencies.

The health objective should remain constant throughout planned activities in physical education and athletics. Corrective and adaptive classes serve the needs of students unable to profit by programs established for "normal" youths.

Since more injuries occur in physical education and athletics than elsewhere in the schools, safety education (including first aid) becomes important here as youths learn to protect themselves and others in pursuits that challenge the adventurous spirit of young adults.

CHARACTER VALUES

The space age seems destined to reflect the true character values exemplified by Americans. Recent years have produced alarming increases in juvenile delinquency, accounts of rigged entertainment programs, and a shocking lack of moral fiber in Congressional investigations of individuals occupying high and important places. The years ahead could bring prolonged evidence of these dubious qualities, and create others with threats to world peace, more broken homes, economic disaster, and social dis-

---

[1]Established in 1956 by President Eisenhower.

order of various kinds. While schools alone cannot guarantee the production of solid citizens, character education has enjoyed a prominent role in scholastic literature even before the publication of McGuffy Readers.

Physical education and athletics strive to engender the principles of courage, fair-play, sportsmanship, tolerance, and other traits of the good citizen. The youth here learns that certain rules are necessary and learns to abide by them. He learns to respect the rights of others. He learns to win with grace and humility, and to accept defeat with poise and dignity. Physical education and athletics serve as an excellent laboratory for acquiring these noble and virtuous traits because of youth's inherent interest in play and competition. Psychologists and experts in growth and development readily acclaim these values. Physical educators and athletic coaches should emphasize the carry-over worth of the programs they represent. And principals should regard interscholastic competition as an integral part of the total curriculum.

RECREATIONAL ATTITUDES AND SKILLS

The import of this objective becomes apparent to everyone. Shorter working hours and more leisure signify an intensified function for education in this area. The sale of athletic and sports equipment increases each year, even beyond expectation, owing to an expanding population. Further, authorities state that a person's enduring recreational attitudes are best formed during the years of childhood and adolescence.

Physical education and athletics represent prized avenues for the evolution of recreational attitudes and skills. Motor activity is held in high esteem by the average youth, and his attitude toward play (playfulness) constitutes the best assurance that he will continue the process. Again, skill in a given activity adds to satisfaction gained through participation—another reason favoring a wide range of events in physical education. The years ahead may well see courses in such activities as fishing and scuba diving, to keep pace with the direction of cultural and recreational interests.

PEER STATUS

One seldom finds this objective listed for physical education and athletics. But peer status or the sense of belonging ranks high among the desires of everyone, especially among adolescents. Students in high school attain status in various ways: some excel in academic pursuits; others perform admirably in art or music; still others become leaders in clubs or other organizations. Physical education and athletics present wholesome opportunities for youths to gain esteem as athletes, as gymnasts, or as members of a dance group.

It seems relatively obvious that the driving force behind leaders in any field starts with a desire to attain peer status. This great urge, coupled with education which helps an individual improve his knowledge and skill, suggests the wisdom of a diversified program in secondary schools—including physical education and athletics.

In summary, the principal can insure a sound program of physical education and athletics if he keeps in mind that this field requires competent leadership, a program that shows progression from year to year rather than a repetition of the same activities semester after semester, allotted time in the daily or weekly schedule, a student-teacher ratio comparable to other subjects, adequate equipment and facilities to conduct the program, and equitable student credit for successful achievement.

RECREATION

The section on recreation has a two-fold purpose in terms of secondary-school responsibility: to indicate the school's function in developing recreational attitudes, interests, knowledge, and skills; and to suggest types of cooperation (both ways) that should exist between the school and other community agencies.

With reference to the school's role in this matter, practically all acceptable lists of objectives stress the value of education for leisure. Most secondary schools provide recreational opportunities for students. These opportunities may exist as integral parts of specific courses. But recreation covers a much broader field than physical education alone. Arts and crafts, music and dramatics help to swell the list of activities in this area, along with numerous organized clubs, forums, societies, and the like. Increased attention to leisure as a significant cultural force may suggest change in teacher education whereby subject matter specialists will have two strings to their professional bows: (1) helping youths to master the essentials of a given subject—and this means educating youth through the media of subjects; and (2) guiding youths in the use of these essentials for recreational purposes. The wide range of leisure interests expressed by students, or remaining as latent phenomena, indicates the need for concerted efforts in education to satisfy these interests. Many school principals now assume the task of organizing and coordinating such programs.

On the matter of cooperation with out-of-school groups current educational publications often contain statements urging better intercommunication between the schools, homes, and other community agencies. Recreation provides a splendid avenue through which this goal may be accomplished. Emphasis on family recreation has skyrocketed and most communities now vigorously support this activity in such forms as commissions, departments of government, church programs, police athletic leagues, and YMCA's, and there are scores of others. Besides these official and voluntary groups, all sorts of private agencies offer recreational programs. Bowling alleys, skating rinks, and social clubs become more popular in each decade.

Most principals and superintendents seek new and improved ways to bring the schools and community closer together. Not only is this process educationally sound but rising costs and population growths favor efficient utilization of all community resources. Wise planning in the exchange of recreational facilities and leadership between the schools and out-of-school organizations represents sound practice; this must be a two-way exchange to insure success, with each type of organization understanding that it has cooperative functions to perform and understanding the nature of these obligations. Many administrators and executives have found that such mutual relationships serve as excellent public relations for schools. In fact, all of the programs described above have excellent potential public-relations value because of their proximity to goals identified with good home and family living, and because of their association with activities pursued by numerous community agencies—official, voluntary, and private.

CONCLUSION

The over-all program, accompanied by sound administrative leadership, contains many functional elements designed to enrich the lives of young people and brighten their future, and to help produce a fitter and happier generation of young adults capable of protecting and furthering the tenets of American democracy.

Projects and thought questions for part one

1. Assess your own life to see if you have made the most of it to date. Develop a personal program for achievement of your goals as an individual and as a physical educator.

2. What criteria must physical education meet in order to be fully accepted as an academic discipline?

3. Develop your own definition of physical education. Show how your definition is based on realistic goals and objectives.

4. Tell how you would explain the profession of physical education to someone who is not familiar with the field.

5. Survey at least five leaders in the field of physical education to determine their definitions of the nature of physical education.

6. Read and summarize two research reports written since 1965 that in whole or in part agree with or present results different from those of the research done by Clarke and Drowatzky.

7. Based on the presentation by Rushing, draw a series of implications for physical education programs, facilities, and staffs in the junior and community colleges of the future.

8. Detail how you as a physical educator in a liberal arts college would alter your programs to better meet the needs of the college student.

9. Write a factual essay that shows how athletics help education to meet its objectives. Document your statements.

10. Defend or refute the statement, "Interscholastic athletics should not be conducted on the junior high school level." Justify your argument with factual evidence.

11. Select two recent lines of research that have significance for education and/or physical education. Discuss them according to the logic followed by Griffiths.

12. Critique at least three recent research studies concerned with technologic advances directly related to or having implications for the future of physical education.

13. Write an essay concerned with the changing role of the physical educator in the space age.

14. Outline the steps you would advise a field of endeavor to take if it wished to align itself more closely with other academic disciplines.

Selected readings

Abernathy, R., and Waltz, M.: Toward a discipline: first steps first, Quest, Monograph II (Spring Issue), Apr. 1964.

Esslinger, A.: Physical education's contributions to healthful living, Professional Contributions No. 1, 1951, American Academy of Physical Education.

Frankena, W. K.: Public education and the good life, Harvard Education Review 31:413, Fall 1961.

Michael, D. N.: The next generation: the prospects ahead for the youth of today and tomorrow, New York, 1965, Random House, Inc.

National Congress of Parents and Teachers: PTA guide to what's happening in education, New York, 1965, Scholastic Book Services.

Oberteuffer, D.: The years ahead, Journal of Health, Physical Education, and Recreation 30:36, Sept. 1959.

Piel, G.: Science in the cause of man, New York, 1961, Alfred A. Knopf, Inc.

Reynolds, J. W.: The junior college: what next? In American Association for Higher Education: In Search of Leaders, 1967, The Association.

Part two

Philosophy of physical education as part of general education

Physical education must be concerned with the mind of the individual as well as with his body. Physical education cannot educate one exclusively while ignoring or paying little heed to the other. Although we are practitioners of the educational field called *physical* education, we must also be conscious of our commitment to the *social, emotional,* and *mental* growth of the individuals we influence through our programs. Our chosen commitments and professional conduct as teachers arise from our philosophies of life and education.

Philosophy is a discipline through which individuals attempt to evaluate their personal relationship to the world in which they live. The various philosophies attempt to give each individual a basis on which to evaluate himself and the world. The key concepts of the philosophies vary because each philosophy looks at man and his world from a different position. The philosophies of education and physical education that have prevailed through the years have emerged from the larger bodies of philosophic thought.

Each educator and each physical educator has a philosophy of education, although it may be true that for many educators a particular philosophy has never been fully articulated. Nevertheless, the minute-by-minute behavior of each teacher in all matters involving the school and its students is a reflection of some educational philosophy. It is important for each teacher to understand why he is a teacher and for him to be able to make a contribution to his students both in and away from the classroom. Understanding educational philosophy helps a teacher to understand himself, his profession, and the implications for himself as an individual within his profession.

The readings in this division are of two types. The first group of readings is directly concerned with exploring various philosophies. Educational philosophy forms the basis of each of the readings in the second group, but in a larger sense each selection shows the integration of individuals within the educative process. Each provides deeper insights into physical education as a part of general education.

The introductory article is taken from the writings of Will Durant, the famed historian of philosophic thought. Durant provides us with some insights into the discipline of philosophy and shows how philosophy and humanity are inextricably bound together.

The separate schools of philosophy are the topic of Deobold B. Van Dalen, who presents a synthesis of four of the major philosophies. Van Dalen contrasts each of these philosophies and shows how each relates to education, to the student, to the curriculum in physical education, and to the teacher.

A doctoral dissertation by Richard B. Morland investigates the educational philosophies of leading professional physical educators. Morland first defines the differing philosophies commonly associated with education and then selects a series of quotations from the writings of noted educators known to support a particular philosophy.

The writings of the physical educators who were subjects for this study are also analyzed in the light of the selected philosophies. Morland is able to classify the physical educators by philosophy through a comparison of their writings with those of the educators whose positions are known.

A research study conducted by Donn E. Bair explores the philosophic beliefs of selected professional physical educators who are members of the American Academy for Health, Physical Education, and Recreation and a group of influential physical educators who are not members of the Academy. Conclusions concerning the predominant beliefs of these educators and the effect of these beliefs on physical education are drawn by Bair.

In an article primarily concerned with physical education programs, Wilson W. Elkins emphasizes the need for programs of health and physical education within programs of general education, particularly on the college level. Elkins writes that physical educators must demonstrate a more positive approach in communicating the worth of physical education to other members of the academic community.

Fred Russell, a newspaperman, discusses the philosophy of sport and the championship aspect of sports. Russell says that a man who participates in sports finds happiness of a sort not attained by other means. The author states that other personal gains to be made from sports participation include equality of opportunity to compete, the opportunity to succeed, and increases in emotional maturity.

Arthur H. Steinhaus and Harold Taylor are concerned with the individual within the educative process. Steinhaus, through Platonic parable and descriptive physiology, explores the contributions of physical education to the mind, body, and spirit of man. He points out that parental and teacher guidance play important roles in the development of each individual. Taylor discusses liberal, conservative, and progressive educational philosophies and shows where and why each has succeeded or failed in adapting education to the needs of the child.

10. On the uses of philosophy*

Will Durant

America's foremost contemporary philosopher

There is a pleasure in philosophy, and a lure even in the mirages of metaphysics, which every student feels until the coarse necessities of physical existence drag him from the heights of thought into the mart of economic strife and gain. Most of us have known some golden days in the June of life when philosophy was in fact what Plato calls it, "that dear delight"; when the love of a modestly elusive Truth seemed more glorious, incomparably, than the lust for the ways of the flesh and the dross of the world. And there is always some wistful remnant in us of that early wooing of wisdom. "Life has meaning," we feel with Browning—"to find its meaning is my meat and drink." So much of our lives is meaningless, a self-cancelling vacillation and futility; we strive with the chaos about us and within; but we would believe all the while that there is something vital and significant in us, could we but decipher our own souls. We want to understand; "life means for us constantly to transform into light and flame all that we are or meet with"[1]; we are like Mitya in *The Brothers Karamazov*—"one of those who don't want millions, but an answer to their questions"; we want to seize the value and perspective of passing things, and so to pull ourselves up out of the maelstrom of daily circumstance. We want to know that the little things are little, and the big things big, before it is too late; we want to see things now as they will seem forever—"in the light of eternity." We want to learn to laugh in the face of the inevitable, to smile even at the looming of death.

We want to be whole, to coordinate our energies by criticizing and harmonizing our desires; for coordinated energy is the last word in ethics and politics, and perhaps in logic and metaphysics too.

"To be a philosopher," said Thoreau, "is not merely to have subtle thoughts, nor even to found a school, but so to love wisdom as to live, according to its dictates, a life of simplicity, independence, magnanimity, and trust." We may be sure that if we can but find wisdom, all things else will be added unto us. "Seek ye first the good things of the mind," Bacon admonishes us, "and the rest will either be supplied or its loss will not be felt."[2] Truth will not make us rich, but it will make us free.

Some ungentle reader will check us here by informing us that philosophy is as useless as chess, as obscure as ignorance, and as stagnant as content. "There is nothing so absurd," said Cicero, "but that it may be found in the books of the philosophers." Doubtless some philosophers have had all sorts of wisdom except common sense; and many a philosophic flight has been due to the elevating power of thin air. Let us resolve, on this voyage of ours, to put in only at the ports of light, to keep out of the muddy streams of metaphysics and the "many-sounding seas" of theological dispute. But is philosophy stagnant? Science seems always to advance, while philosophy seems always to lose ground. Yet this is only because philosophy accepts the hard and hazardous task of dealing with problems not yet open to the methods of science—problems like good and evil, beauty and ugliness, order and freedom, life and death; so soon as a field of inquiry yields knowledge

*From Durant, W.: The story of philosophy, New York, 1933, Simon & Schuster, Inc. Used by permission.
[1]Nietzsche, *The Joyful Wisdom*, pref.

[2]*De Augmentis Scientiarum*, VIII, 2.

susceptible of exact formulation it is called science. Every science begins as philosophy and ends as art; it arises in hypothesis and flows into achievement. Philosophy is a hypothetical interpretation of the unknown (as in metaphysics), or of the inexactly known (as in ethics or political philosophy); it is the front trench in the siege of truth. Science is the captured territory; and behind it are those secure regions in which knowledge and art build our imperfect and marvelous world. Philosophy seems to stand still, perplexed; but only because she leaves the fruits of victory to her daughters the sciences, and herself passes on, divinely discontent, to the uncertain and unexplored.

Shall we be more technical? Science is analytical description, philosophy is synthetic interpretation. Science wishes to resolve the whole into parts, the organism into organs, the obscure into the known. It does not inquire into the values and ideal possibilities of things, nor into their total and final significance; it is content to show their present actuality and operation, it narrows its gaze resolutely to the nature and process of things as they are. The scientist is as impartial as Nature in Turgenev's poem: he is as interested in the leg of a flea as in the creative throes of a genius. But the philosopher is not content to describe the fact; he wishes to ascertain its relation to experience in general, and thereby to get at its meaning and its worth; he combines things in interpretive synthesis; he tries to put together, better than before, that great universe-watch which the inquisitive scientist has analytically taken apart. Science tells us how to heal and how to kill; it reduces the death rate in retail and then kills us wholesale in war; but only wisdom—desire coordinated in the light of all experience—can tell us when to heal and when to kill. To observe processes and to construct means is science; to criticize and coordinate ends is philosophy: and because in these days our means and instruments have multiplied beyond our interpretation and synthesis of ideals and ends, our life is full of sound and fury, signifying nothing. For a fact is nothing except in relation to desire; it is not complete except in relation to a purpose and a whole. Science without philosophy, facts without perspective and valuation, cannot save us from havoc and

despair. Science gives us knowledge, but only philosophy can give us wisdom.

Specifically, philosophy means and includes five fields of study and discourse: logic, esthetics, ethics, politics, and metaphysics. *Logic* is the study of ideal method in thought and research: observation and introspection, deduction and induction, hypothesis and experiment, analysis and synthesis—such are the forms of human activity which logic tries to understand and guide; it is a dull study for most of us, and yet the great events in the history of thought are the improvements men have made in their methods of thinking and research. *Esthetics* is the study of ideal form, or beauty; it is the philosophy of art. *Ethics* is the study of ideal conduct; the highest knowledge, said Socrates, is the knowledge of good and evil, the knowledge of the wisdom of life. *Politics* is the study of ideal social organization (it is not, as one might suppose, the art and science of capturing and keeping office); monarchy, aristocracy, democracy, socialism, anarchism, feminism—these are the *dramatis personae* of political philosophy. And lastly, *Metaphysics* (which gets into so much trouble because it is not, like the other forms of philosophy, an attempt to coordinate the real in the light of the ideal) is the study of the "ultimate reality" of all things: of the real and final nature of "matter" (ontology), of "mind" (philosophical psychology), and of the interrelation of "mind" and "matter" in the processes of perception and knowledge (epistemology).

These are the parts of philosophy; but so dismembered it loses its beauty and its joy. We shall seek it not in its shrivelled abstractness and formality, but clothed in the living form of genius; we shall study not merely philosophies, but philosophers; we shall spend our time with the saints and martyrs of thought, letting their radiant spirit play about us until perhaps we too, in some measure, shall partake of what Leonardo called "the noblest pleasure, the joy of understanding." Each of these philosophers has some lesson for us, if we approach him properly. "Do you know," asks Emerson, "the secret of the true scholar? In every man there is something wherein I may learn of him; and in that I am his pupil." Well, surely we may take this attitude to the master minds of history without hurt to our pride! And we may flatter ourselves with that other thought of Emerson's, that when genius speaks to us we feel a ghostly reminiscence of having ourselves, in our distant youth, had vaguely this self-same thought which genius now speaks, but which we had not art or courage to clothe with form and utterance. And indeed, great men speak to us only so far as we have ears and souls to hear them; only so far as we have in us the roots, at least, of that which flowers out in them. We too have had the experiences they had, but we did not suck those experiences dry of their secret and subtle meanings: we were not sensitive to the overtones of the reality that hummed about us.

Genius hears the overtones, and the music of the spheres; genius knows what Pythagoras meant when he said that philosophy is the highest music.

So let us listen to these men, ready to forgive them their passing errors, and eager to learn the lessons which they are so eager to teach. "Do you then be reasonable," said old Socrates to Crito, "and do not mind whether the teachers of philosophy are good or bad, but think only of Philosophy herself. Try to examine her well and truly; and if she be evil, seek to turn away all men from her; but if she be what I believe she is, then follow her and serve her, and be of good cheer."

11. Philosophical profiles for physical educators*

Deobold B. Van Dalen

Chairman, Department of Physical Education, University of California, Berkeley

To many physical educators, philosophy is a province for professional speculation, and is of little practical value to a teacher. When dealing with the urgencies of daily life in the classroom, they contend that one must apply good common sense, for there is no time to mull over abstract theories. But what is the nature of their "common sense"? Not uncommonly it is a haphazard collection of concepts that they have unconsciously or uncritically acquired from varied cultural contacts. Many of their practices may be surprisingly sound, but some of them may be directed toward the achievement of objectives that are philosophically incompatible. All too frequently when common sense is the criterion for determining what to do in the classroom, it boils down to doing that which requires the least effort, or that which is professionally chic at the moment, or that which current pressures for conformity demand.

Rare is the physical educator who does not long for a better sense of direction, who does not ask: "What is my purpose here? What should I be doing with and for these students?" To answer these and other related questions, he must first critically examine his basic beliefs. Not until after asking what is life all about, what is the real nature of the world, and what is of greatest significance in life, can he make discriminating decisions about what and how to teach. All of us hold certain beliefs about life, of course, but many of us may not be able to state them explicitly and may never have submitted them to sharp scrutiny. A physical educator who wishes to burst out of this cocoon of complacency can profit from examining philosophical explanations

that endeavor to make our existence intelligible and meaningful and to give direction and purpose to our activities.

Philosophers are concerned with three basic problems: What is reality? What is truth? What is of value? The problem of reality (ontology) forces them to decide what is fundamental, real—what is the ultimate nature of being or existence. The problem of truth or knowledge (epistemology) makes them probe into how man arrives at knowledge and how he can be certain that it is true. The problem of value (axiology) causes them to consider the worth of things. They may, for example, give attention to ethical, aesthetic, religious, social, educational, recreational, or health values. Their basic concern is to ascertain what is good in human conduct, in social organization, and in art.

Adherents of various philosophical schools have come to somewhat different conclusions about the nature of reality, truth, and value. The *idealist* believes that ultimate reality lies in a "thinking being"—a self, mind, spirit—rather than in "physical things"—matter. Men live in a world of ideas; what they know of the physical world is what their minds have created. In contrast, the *realist* believes that reality is independent of human experience; it exists in the laws and order of nature which are neither subject to the human will nor dependent upon a human mind for their existence. The *pragmatist* contends that the only reality we know is that which we actually experience each day. He does not believe in an all-inclusive reality, an unchanging order. Reality is not something that is static or everlasting—it is an ever-changing flow of experience. The *existentialist* contends that ultimate reality resides within the individual

*From The Physical Educator, Vol. 21, No. 3, p. 113, Oct. 1964. Used by permission.

human person. Reality is a man's own experience of being: the awareness of his moral self and his irrevocable responsibility for making choices that will fashion his essence.

How do the various philosophies differ in regard to the nature of truth or knowledge? The *idealist* believes that true knowledge consists of universals or ideals that are eternal and purposeful. Man discovers them through mental activity, insight, and intuition. The *realist* believes that true knowledge consists of the real things in the physical world—the laws and order of nature. These laws exist by themselves; they are independent of the mind and self. Man discovers them through sense perception, through scientific reasoning, through objective means that are free of any personal, emotional or subjective approach. The *pragmatist* believes that knowledge is discovered through experience, and he questions the possible absoluteness of truth. To him, truth is a matter of consequences. If a suggested solution to a problem works in a given set of circumstances, it can be considered as truth for the time being. But, to the pragmatist, truth may change as circumstances change; what is true today may not necessarily be true tomorrow. As men gain greater insight into the world through experience, they will continue to revise and correct their knowledge. The *existentialist* does not believe that truth is forced upon him by an external or objective reality, but rather that the individual is the final court of truth. He contends that all knowledge, all intuiting, all experiencing, arise within the heart and mind of the individual and receive certification by him. Knowledge—truth—is what exists in man's consciousness and feelings as a result of his experiences and the meaning he has given to them.

How do the various philosophies differ in regard to the nature of value? To the *idealist*, the essential values of life are eternal, fixed, and man discovers them through his intellect. Sometimes man imperfectly interprets or perceives what is good or bad, beautiful or ugly, right or wrong, but the values themselves do not change. The *realist* believes that a thing is good, right, or beautiful if it conforms to the laws and order of nature, that it is evil, wrong, or ugly if it does not, and that these values are not variable. The *pragmatist* is skeptical of fixed and immutable values. He contends that value is based on human judgment. Man creates his own values through purposeful action and the interpretation of his experience. Good is that which the group discovers, works out satisfactorily in practice—not in a selfish sense, but in a social sense. To the *existentialist*, the final arbiter of what is good or beautiful is the individual. He rejects the uncritical acceptance of value systems that have been established by social, political, scientific, or theological groups, because he does not want to forfeit his essential existence—his freedom to choose. The *existentialist* looks within himself for an understanding of what is good and beautiful, and establishes his own value system. He assumes full responsibility for contributing to the moral and aesthetic essence of man, through personally deliberating about and practicing what he decides is best for himself and mankind.

The *idealist, realist, pragmatist,* and *existentialist* look upon education in light of their particular beliefs concerning reality, knowledge, and value. Consequently, they develop different, but not mutually exclusive, philosophies of education. It is rather difficult to generalize concerning their beliefs because adherents of each philosophy express various shades of opinion, and members of different schools embrace similar as well as different views. In bold outline, however, eliciting answers to the following questions will tend to set these philosophies apart.[1]

First, let us ask: What is the objective of education?

The *idealist* encourages a vigorous, full development of the individual's creative powers in a manner that will bring him into harmony with the highest ideals. Seeking ever greater individual perfectability includes the development of the body and good health. This objective is placed at the bottom of the hierarchy of values, but it is considered basic for the realization of the social, moral and spiritual aims.

The *realist* does not emphasize the "self" —the individual—for he believes that reality exists in the laws and order of nature.

---

[1]For a more detailed discussion of the relations of these philosophies to physical education, see E. C. Davis, *Philosophies Fashion Physical Education,* Dubuque, Iowa: William C. Brown Company, Publishers, 1963.

Hence, the objective of education is to acquire verified knowledge of these laws and to mold youths so that they will live in conformity with them. The educator is to build competencies in youths that will enable them to understand and make an adequate adjustment to the real, external world.

The *pragmatist* is not interested in "absolute ideas and inexorable laws," but in the obvious realities of life—the here and now. His objective is to have students solve successfully the problems of life as they arise. He strives to stimulate a desire for continuous growth and helps students become functional members of society by providing opportunities for ever-changing experiences. In brief, he seeks many sided social efficiency.

The *existentialist* elevates the individual to a position of central prominence, for he contends that self-determination is the ultimate objective of pedagogical attention. Education is to awaken the student to a knowledge of his moral self. It is to make him understand that the responsibility for choosing what he will become and for living with what happens as a result of his decisions rests with him alone.

Secondly, let us ask: What is the nature of the student?

To the *idealist*, the student is not merely a biological organism that is shaped by the physical environment; he is a "mind, personality, soul"—a "self" whose body is responsive to his will. As Horne explains, "It is not so much the stimulus shaping the individual, as the individual responding to the stimulus."

To the *realist*, the student is a biological organism with a highly developed nervous system that interacts with the physical environment. The physical stimuli within and without the student determine his behavior —not his personal whim, his will, or blind chance.

To the *pragmatist*, the student is an active, doing organism who grows through effective interaction with the ever-changing, social-physical environment. Upon meeting problems in life situations, he proposes hypotheses and tests them to find workable solutions.

To the *existentialist*, the learner is a unique, autonomous individual who independently makes the commitments and takes the action that determines what he will be.

Third, let us ask: What is the nature of the curriculum?

The *idealist* is primarily concerned with content that consists of ideas—the humanities, but he includes physical education in the curriculum as a means of providing for the full development of the individual and the realization of an ideal society. To him, any content or activity is acceptable that acquaints students with the accumulated wisdom of the race and permits them to re-create truth, goodness, and beauty in their own thoughts, feelings, and actions.

The *realist* believes in a rigorous, systematically organized curriculum that places emphasis on the transmission and mastery of content—particularly scientific facts and principles. The contents and sequence of the curriculum are scientifically determined. The realist is primarily interested in quantitative subject matter, and the idealist is interested in qualitative subject matter.

The *pragmatist* utilizes any activity that gives students experience in applying the scientific method of solving problems. The curriculum is not a systematic structure consisting of rigid work units that are presented in a particular sequence. It may consist of related or disparate units of work and may utilize any content that will help the problem at hand. The curriculum is closely related to pupils' interests and to community and current problems; new activities are added whenever there is a need for them. Emphasis is placed on "group activities," "cooperation," "doing," "problem solving"; hence, sports and games provide an excellent medium for instruction.

The *existentialist* believes that the curriculum cannot be prefabricated for the child. Rather the child is made aware of his moral self and of a wide variety of alternatives, activities, and tools. He is absolutely free to appropriate those that will help him fulfill his unique purposes. In the existentialist curriculum, individualized activities would probably predominate. Group activities would be self-chosen. A deep conviction of the need to be with others to become the person that the individual wants to be would cause him to join or organize group activities. The objective of the group would not be to impose the will of the majority on members, but rather to help one another bring about a realization of their individual essence and develop a genuine relationship with society. The curriculum would not shield the child from the wholeness of life—it would make him aware of evil and good, the ugly and the beautiful, joy and tragedy, pain and pleasure, so that he could prepare himself to meet them squarely as a part of life.

Fourth, let us ask: What is the nature of the teacher and his methods?

To the *idealist,* the teacher is more important than facilities, equipment, or any physical "thing." He is a firm, friendly individual who thoroughly understands his subject and pupils. His personal example of wholesome, vigorous living and the attention he focuses on personalities and works of inspiring greatness stimulate students to develop their full creative powers. His pupils are surrounded with positive influences and are shielded from deleterious ones. They are provided with inviting opportunities for creative effort; challenged to put all of their powers into their performance; and given ample opportunity for discussion, self-initiative, and self-direction. Students learn—fashion their character—through making decisions, judgments, and analyses. Whenever possible interest is utilized to evoke effort, but external discipline may be employed to stimulate enough effort to cultivate interest and establish the habit of self-discipline. When evaluating pupils, the idealist is not especially concerned with quantitative assessments of the mechanics of an activity and the reproduction of specific knowledge, but rather in the changes in "self."

The *realist* rejects the idealist's subjective, personal approach to teaching. In his classes, pupils are brought into contact with the real world through demonstration, experiments, field trips, and audio-visual aids. They are exposed to clear, distinct facts in an objective and logically ordered manner and are drilled in the mastery and application of scientific principles. External discipline is utilized, if necessary. Learning proceeds inductively; it starts with elements and details and builds toward a systematic whole. When selecting equipment, grouping students, choosing teaching and administrative techniques, the realist makes decisions upon the basis of scientifically demonstrated facts. When evaluating students, he employs objective rather than subjective tests and seeks quantitative measures of achievement.

The *pragmatist* guides students so that they can find successful solutions to problems as they arise. The emphasis is placed on "how" to think rather than on "what" to think. The teacher serves as a "co-worker and co-learner" who helps students identify problems and apply the scientific method of solving them. In this socialized approach to learning, group decision making is stressed. Ample opportunity is given for the free interchange of ideas and continuous evaluation of progress. Little emphasis is placed on systematic lectures, terminal tests, and traditional coverage and organization of subject matter. The learning environment is often extended beyond the walls of the classroom. The pragmatist believes that if students tackle problems that intensely interest them, they will spontaneously put forth the effort required to seek solutions. Consequently, the teacher will neither have to lure them with external rewards or have to serve as a drill master or moralizer.

The *existential* teacher is not a transmitter of information, nor a director of projects, nor a model to imitate. He is a provocateur of thought who awakens the child to the moral dimensions of life. Through posing moral and intellectual questions, he causes a student to think seriously about who he is, what he is in the world for, and what he should make of his life. The existential teacher establishes an intimate, exploratory communion with the student in which an atmosphere of free association prevails. After getting the student authentically concerned about moral issues and encouraging him to search for facts, to examine alternatives, and to consider probable consequences, he strictly refrains from prescribing a course of action. The student is required to make his own choices in light of what he thinks man ought to be and is held strictly accountable for what happens as a result of his decisions. The existentialist sees little value in traditional testing procedures that are based on group norms and that measure prescribed subject matter.

This brief summary of selected philosophical concepts and their relationship to education suggests how some of the most profound and productive minds of the past two thousand years have grappled with the problem of helping man understand the awesome cosmos. By delving more deeply into this invaluable intellectual heritage, a physical educator can start on a long, rigorous, and rewarding pilgrimage of thought and criticism. As he re-examines his beliefs and teaching practices and strives to clarify his philosophy of life and education, many questions will arise: "How did he come to accept a belief? Is it ambiguous? Is it defensible? Does it conflict with other of his beliefs? Are some of his basic beliefs and teaching practices inconsistent? How can he eliminate contradictions and conflicts?" By applying philosophical methods, the physical educator can remove some of the perplexities that arise when he attempts to say systematically and clearly what he is doing in education and why.

Inquiring into the nature of his beliefs, appraising his teaching practices in light of what they imply about his beliefs, weighing whether his beliefs and practices are worth retaining or need to be revised will be a disturbing but an exhilarating experience. The physical educator may decide that one school of philosophical thought is most compatible with his beliefs and provides the most meaningful insights for clarifying his educational problems and directing his professional life. On the other hand, he may find that his beliefs do not fit into the straight jacket fashioned by any of the existing philosophical approaches. Becoming familiar with views of the world and concepts of the purpose of education that others have developed in detail and have submitted to rigorous examination should sharpen his critical consciousness, but blindly accepting beliefs, standards, and practices that others impose upon him cannot be condoned. A physical educator must engage in a never ending personal quest to clarify and to coordinate the concepts that constitute his personal act of commitments. Building, broadening, and deepening his own philosophy of physical education, eliminating inconsistencies, and developing the capacity to articulate his ideas to others is a professional responsibility of the highest order.

12. A philosophical interpretation of the educational views held by seven leaders in American physical education*

Richard B. Morland

Chairman, The Graduate Council, Stetson University

The growth and rapid expansion of the physical education movement is without parallel in the history of American education. A half century ago it was rare indeed for academic credit to be offered by accredited institutions for courses in this area. Today physical education and its related fields occupy places of prominence in programs of learning at every educational level.

This paper is concerned with the educational philosophies of seven professional leaders who were instrumental in shaping the direction of the field during the crucial period when physical education was fighting for recognition as an educational subject. It is confined to a selected group who were still active in the movement during the second quarter of this century for this was the period of its greatest expansion and acceptance. Prior to World War I only five states had required programs in its schools,[1] and even as late as 1927 only four state universities offered graduate work in physical education.[2]

The assumption was made that physical educators are educators; that, whereas they have been engaged professionally in a highly specialized area and have directed their thoughts to its improvement, each has a total view of education and it is possible to identify and classify his beliefs according to systematic schools of educational philosophy. To show this relationship, it was necessary to compare the views of the physical educators with those of exponents of the various positions in educational philosophy. The comparative approach to the study of philosophy was adopted, and after reviewing several different classifications, four philosophies—progressivism, reconstructionism, essentialism, and perennialism—were selected as the basis for interpretation. These positions were chosen because it was felt that they were representative of contemporary educational thought.[3] The attempt was made to substantiate the fact that while there is considerable overlapping in the practices that all philosophies advocate, the differences in emphases and basic beliefs were sufficient to justify the four demarcations. The point was stressed also that the particular labels were only operational concepts that were used to clarify the emphases that educators place upon different aspects of the educational process. The danger arises when these classifications are mistaken for concrete entities, or when the reader allows himself to fall into what Whitehead calls, "The Fallacy of

*From a synopsis of a Doctor of Philosophy dissertation sponsored by Professors Leonard A. Larson, Theodore Brameld, and William W. Brickman of the School of Education of New York University, 1958, 540 pp. Used by permission.

[1]Thomas A. Storey, et al., *Recent State Legislation for Physical Training*. Washington: U. S. Government Printing Office, Bureau of Education Bulletin No. 1, 1922, p. 3.

[2]Ruth Elliott, *The Organization of Professional Training in State Universities*. New York: Bureau of Publications, Teachers College, Columbia University, 1927, p. 50.

[3]See John S. Brubacher, *Modern Philosophies of Education*, second edition. New York: McGraw-Hill Book Company, Inc., 1950, pp. 296-325.

Misplaced Concreteness."[4] The constructed types served as the means through which philosophical delineations could be made and through which a study of this design could proceed.

Owing to their recent introduction into the literature, these terms may not be as familiar as some of the more traditional classifications. Limitations of space preclude a detailed description of these positions. In brief, the progressivists, or experimentalists, hold that man is continuous with nature with his growth and development contingent upon the interaction of the self with the environment. They conceive reality as empirical, knowledge as operational, and values as relative, assessed by their influence upon and their benefits for society. Truth is more than conformity to fact; it is the instrument for the verification of ideas.

The progressive contend that education is inherently social, a continual search for the more qualitative experiences that enrich living. Their concept of learning is based upon organismic psychology with the individual participating actively in shared experiences that have meaning for him. The progressivists believe in the scientific method as the key to learning, integrated curriculum experiences that emphasize problem-solving under conditions where the needs and interests of the child are paramount, cooperative planning, the teacher as a motivator and leader, discipline through group control, and that democratic living is fostered best in a climate where all who are affected share in the planning and execution of policies and decisions.

Essentialism is an outgrowth of the venerable philosophies of idealism and realism. In metaphysics, the essentialist believes that there is an antecedent order standing in back of human experience that reflects permanence and stability. The epistemological challenge for the essentialists is found in the attempt to discover this true nature of reality and in the ability to become relationally identified with it. Hence, truth is the conformity of the concept held in the mind to the facts as they exist in reality or with judgments established as valid. Values are

objective, based upon fixed standards drawn from the wealth of funded experience.

In education, the essentialists hold that the purpose of the educative process is to transmit the enduring aspects of our social heritage and the lessons learned from the accumulated wisdom of the race. This will call for proper attention to the fundamentals or essentials—the information, skills, and aptitudes which are necessary for the individual to become a contributing member of society. He believes in positive teacher control, that the learning effort need not be intrinsically appealing or attractive, systematic presentation of subject matter, a prescribed curriculum, logical organization of course materials, imposed discipline as the necessary means of self-discipline, respect for authority and authoritative procedures, objective standards for grading, and in the line-staff pattern of control as the most effective administrative procedure. The essentialist is not to be confused with the old-fashioned traditionalist—the prototype of the iron-fisted schoolmaster. He is a moderate who proceeds cautiously and with discretion. He is sensitive to the welfare of the individual, but he feels that it is not his job to appease the desires of the immature but to see that measures are taken so that they will grasp the truth.

Since none of the physical educators was found to be reconstructionists or perennialists, a description of these positions is omitted in this presentation. In essence, reconstructionism is an extension of progressivism. It is the philosophy of culture that would use the manifest possibilities of group experience to re-make the culture according to a specific design where the ideals of democracy become factual realities on a global scale. Perennialism is the educational counterpart of the general philosophies of rational humanism as found in the writings of Adler and Hutchins, for example, and the views of the neo-scholastics or Thomists as portrayed in the writings of Roman Catholic educators.

Extended quotations were gathered from the works of ninety-six educators and philosophers who were chosen as exponents of these differing positions. Among others, the following were included: Progressivism—Boyd H. Bode, John L. Childs, John Dewey, William James, and William H. Kilpatrick; Reconstructionism—I. B. Berkson, Theodore

[4]Alfred North Whitehead, *Science and the Modern World* (1925). New York: The New American Library, 1948, p. 52.

Brameld, Kurt Lewin, Karl Mannheim, and Lewis Mumford; Essentialism—William C. Bagley, J. Donald Butler, Frederick S. Breed, Henry S. Broudy, Michael Demiashkevich, Herman H. Horne, and Rupert C. Lodge; and Perennialism—Mortimer J. Adler, William F. Cunningham, Robert M. Hutchins, William J. McGucken, Jacques Maritain, John D. Redden, and Francis A. Ryan. The technique of generalization was employed to formulate four points of view toward each of six general areas with twenty sub-areas that were used for the basis of the comparative analysis of the ideas of the physical educators with those of the educational philosophers. These areas included the general philosophic orientation, views on specific aspects of the educative process, the type of curriculum, administration, the role of the school in society, and aims.

Using the same frame of reference, quotations were collected from the writings of seven professional physical educators, and a synopsis of their beliefs in each of these areas, when expressed explicitly or inferentially, was presented under the same topical headings. These leaders were Thomas D. Wood, Clark W. Hetherington, Jesse Feiring Williams, Jay B. Nash, Charles H. McCloy, Mabel Lee and Elmer D. Mitchell. Although each is a recipient of the Gulick Award and all are recognized for their signal contributions to the field, no claim was advanced that these persons are the most outstanding that the profession has produced. The effort was made to select individuals with varied backgrounds in their professional preparations as well as in their teaching careers. For this reason, many persons with established reputations were not chosen because of their close association with one of the earlier leaders or because they represented the same institution.

By comparing the ideas expressed by the physical educators with the general position as determined from the expositions of the representatives of the four schools of educational philosophy, the physical educators were classified in accordance with the point of view most harmonious with their own thinking. Upon this basis, Wood, Hetherington, Williams, Nash, and Mitchell were determined to be progressivists, while McCloy and Lee were found to support essentialism.

The fact that these physical educators

were classified as adherents of a particular school of thought in educational philosophy does not mean that there were no deviations from the basic point of view in any of these areas. When a person philosophizes, he is making a concerted attempt to understand himself and his role in society in order to give coherence and direction to his everyday affairs. Applied to institutional settings, the philosopher in education endeavors to relate in a meaningful fashion the contributions of his own field to what he thinks the process of education should accomplish. Originality of thought does not lend itself to rigid compartmentalization. Numerous instances were cited to show how philosophers who support a particular position sometimes differ among themselves. A study of the history of ideas demonstrates conclusively that philosophers are not at all reluctant to point out what they consider to be conceptual errors and inconsistencies in the thinking of their adversaries. Still, philosophers are classified by scholars as embracing a specific position in educational philosophy because of the overall consistency with which they adhere to the basic beliefs of a systematic school of thought. The same technique was adopted in this study.

Only a quick overview is permitted at this time to justify the classifications assigned to the physical educators. Wood, who was the first health educator and who directed most of his thoughts to this area, still set the keynote for the progressive philosophy of physical education with his "naturalized program" of activity. Although Hetherington developed his philosophy of play independently of the ideas of John Dewey,[5] there is a remarkable similarity in their theories. Hetherington's four objectives of physical education, for example, are permeated with pragmatic thought, and his insistence for the educational effort to be placed on the basis of "practical living experience"[6] is a cardinal principle of progressivism. Williams

[5]Both started their initial experiments in 1896; Dewey with his Laboratory School at the University of Chicago and Hetherington at the juvenile reformatory at Whittier, California. Hetherington, incidentally, does not refer to Dewey in any of his writings.

[6]Clark W. Hetherington, *The Demonstration Play School of 1913*. University of California Publications in Education, Vol. V. No. 2. Berkeley: University of California Press, July 30, 1914, p. 244.

is the most articulate spokesman for the progressive philosophy of physical education and is the person who extended its base to cover every aspect of the school program. Emphasizing that physical education must be a social experience if its full potential is to be realized, he built a workable philosophy upon this basis. Nash does not fit neatly and conveniently into any category, but there is a strong undercurrent of progressivism that forms the core of his thinking. His progressivist inclinations are revealed in his stress upon functional subjects, skill as knowledge, play as education, organismic approach to mind-body relationships, and the techniques he would use to draw forth the creativeness that he believes to be within every person.

Although McCloy supports what he calls "the saner and more intelligent practices"[7] of progressivism, his basic philosophy points toward essentialism. His essentialistic beliefs are shown principally in his emphases and in the practices he advocates such as effort over interest, positive teacher control, the manner in which he would implement the "forgotten objectives," his appraisal of the student as the immature person who needs firm guidance, the need for a thoroughly systematized curricula, and his staunch plea for objective standards of measurement and evaluation. Mabel Lee is closer to McCloy in

her thinking than to any of the others discussed.[8] Her views toward the prescribed curriculum, transfer of training, formal discipline, testing, the use of drill, teacher-pupil relationships, and, especially, the role of the administrator mark her as an essentialist. Mitchell's writings, particularly his numerous editorials and his brilliant treatise on the theory of play, are consistent with progressivism. This is especially discernible in his general philosophic orientation, his operational philosophy of activity, and in his developmental treatment of aims.

In conclusion, the findings indicate that while no single philosophy of education can be said to be representative of these physical educators, the philosophy of progressivism is the most predominant. Additional research is needed to determine if the favorable ratio to progressivism would hold as well for the other leaders in the profession. The study by Bair[9] is a notable contribution in this area, and more research of this nature should be undertaken.

---

[7]C. H. McCloy, "A Planned Physical Exercise Program? or 'What Would You Like to Do Today?'" *The Physical Educator* 10:38 (May, 1953).

[8]Her two books, for example, carry more references to McCloy than to all of the others combined.

[9]Donn E. Bair, *An Identification of Some Philosophical Beliefs Held by Influential Professional Leaders in American Physical Education.* Doctor of Philosophy dissertation, University of Southern California, 956. (Health and Physical Education Microcard No. PE 343, University of Oregon, Eugene, Oregon.)

13. Identification of some philosophical beliefs of influential leaders in American physical education*[1]

Donn E. Bair

Assistant Superintendent of Professional Services, Unified School District, Covina, California

ABSTRACT

The purpose of the study was to determine with what eminent educational philosophies the beliefs of contemporary professional leaders in American physical education are identified, and from the identification determine philosophical directions which seem to be indicated for American physical education. Data for the study were secured from responses to a checklist of philosophical-professional beliefs sent to a highly selected group of leaders in American physical education. The responses were tabulated with relation to the philosophical identity and intensity of beliefs, as well as the age, sex, and geographical location of the respondents. On the basis of present indicated beliefs, professional leaders are providing a predominantly naturalistic direction to American physical education, with evidences of spiritualistic beliefs exerting an influence in certain professional areas.

Beliefs may represent guides which determine the direction of things to come. The beliefs of individuals, like those of a profession or nation, are significant as a body of concepts which provide the basis for a working philosophy. The identification of these beliefs should reveal the present status of thought and perhaps indicate directions of action for the future.

The purpose of the study was to determine with what eminent educational philosophies the beliefs of contemporary professional leaders in American physical education are identified, and from such identification determine the philosophical directions which seem to be indicated for American physical education.

REVIEW OF RELATED LITERATURE

The study was approached through an examination of numerous publications that described the philosophical systems underlying present-day education and the forces which have shaped American physical education. Most of the literature related to his study was devoted to an analysis of philosophical differences in educational thought and practice.

Several authors have investigated the influence of social, cultural, and economic forces upon programs of physical education (1, 7, 10). In spite of an early recognition of differences of belief within American physical education, it appears that there has been no previous attempt to identify beliefs in physical education with respect to philosophical position—namely, Pragmatism, Realism, Idealism, and Aritomism.[2]

---

*From Research Quarterly, Vol. 28, p. 315, Dec. 1957. Used by permission.
[1]This report is taken from the findings of a study, made under the direction of Dr. Elwood C. Davis, and presented in partial fulfillment of the requirements for the Doctor of Philosophy degree at the University of Southern California.

[2]The fourth philosophical position covered in this study represents a combination of Aristotelian and Scholastic philosophy. Since the two philosophies are quite similar educationally, and differ primarily in theology, considerable difficulty was encountered in formulating statements of belief relating to physical education that differentiated clearly between the two positions. For purposes of this study, it was decided that Aristotelianism and Scholasticism be combined and referred to as Aritomism.

Of the literature reviewed, none has provided physical education with any precise data concerning the educational beliefs of its professional leaders. Nor was there any evidence of earlier attempts to identify philosophically, with a view toward determining professional directions, the beliefs of American physical educators.

PROCEDURE

In attempting to arrive at the educational philosophy of professional leaders in physical education, it was necessary to formulate an instrument suitable for determining the beliefs of contemporary physical educators, and to secure responses from a highly selected group of professional leaders.

Development of the instrument. The instrument developed to focus upon the beliefs of contemporary physical educators was comprised of 12 categories selected from background reading indicating areas from which rather basic beliefs could be drawn. The following categories were included: the universe, man, values, education, program building, program content, the administrator, the teacher, the learner, learning, teaching methods, and evaluation. Each category contained statements representative of four eminent philosophical positions—Idealism, Realism, Pragmatism, and Aritomism.

In addition to checking the belief which most nearly coincided with his own, each respondent was asked to indicate the intensity with which the belief was held—namely, strongly, moderately, or slightly. This differentiation appeared workable and was meant to augment the findings and interpretations of the study.

Method of selecting leaders. A two-way approach was used in selecting professional leaders in physical education who might be considered to be exerting a profound influence upon thinking in the field of physical education today. The initial approach was to utilize a screening device intended to identify those members of the American Academy who seem to be exerting the most profound influence in the profession. Since a well-defined list of professional criteria is operative in determining membership in the American Academy for Health, Physical Education, and Recreation, it was decided to use some of this group as the type of respondent desired. The degree of selectivity in the

Academy membership is indicated by the fact that there are currently about 23,000 members in the American Association for Health, Physical Education, and Recreation and the Academy maintains an active membership of about 70 Fellows.

Three staff members of the Department of Health, Physical Education, and Recreation at the University of Southern California who were active members of the Academy, were consulted concerning active Fellows in the Academy who were currently exerting profound influences upon professional directions in American physical education, and who thus might be selected as qualified respondents. Independently-made selections by the three staff members were undertaken with some thought as to each candidate's professional leadership responsibilities, contributions to the professional literature, and honors and awards received.

The lists of names from each of the three staff members revealed considerable similarity, but only those names were selected which were mentioned by at least two of the three consultants. This procedure yielded 35 names of Academy members who were regarded as exerting a profound influence upon professional directions.

The second phase in the selection of leaders attempted to take into account non-members of the Academy who might be considered as very influential in determining professional directions in American physical education. Each of the initial 35 professional leaders was asked to return, in addition to the checklist, the name of a person or two who they considered should be included in a study involving influential professional leaders in American physical education.

The returns from this supplementary selection provided 86 different names, 51 of which were "new" names. However, only those persons receiving mention from two or more of the initial 35 were used as respondents in the investigation. This accounted for the selection of 17 additional individuals and extended the list of influential leaders to a total of 52.

Tabulation of the data. Of the 52 checklists distributed to leaders in American physical education, 49 were returned. The process of tabulating the returns included the tallying of the responses according to philosophical positions and the intensity of the belief as indicated by the respondent. The total response was then tabulated to determine the extent of eclecticism and the relationship of philosophical positions to factors of belief intensity, age, sex, and geographical distribution.

Analysis and interpretation of the data. Following the tabulation of the data, interpretations of the responses were made within each category in the checklist. The checklist responses, having been tabulated and interpreted, were then analyzed and grouped, on the basis of common elements, into what seemed to indicate two basic educational philosophies—Naturalism and Spiritualism.

Naturalistic philosophy includes Realism and Pragmatism and holds that the universe requires no supernatural explanation. According to Naturalism, the universe is self-directing and constitutes the whole of reality. Spiritualistic philosophy, on the other hand, is a general doctrine which includes Idealism and Aritomism and holds that ultimate reality in the universe is Spirit. The one major position, Naturalism, stems from a view of nature as dynamic and characterized by change. The other major position, Spiritualism, emerges from the view of a changeless universe comprised of primarily stable factors which stem from a supernatural source. The first mentioned major position views human nature as more materialistic and regards values as never more than relatively constant. Such a position can be seen as a continuation of the

more general naturalistic concept of the universe. The spiritualistic position continues with a view of man as a spiritual being and considers values as absolute and enduring.

FINDINGS

It was in the area of "program building" that leaders in American physical education indicated the greatest unanimity of belief. On the basis of the naturalistic response in this area, it seems reasonable to expect that professional leaders are emphasizing the scientific bases for programs of physical education. It is likely, too, that programs of physical education are reflecting national, cultural, and economic changes in an attempt to equip students with physical-recreational skills to meet the problems of life.

In three of the checklist areas—Evaluation, The Administrator, and Education, the majority of naturalistic or spiritualistic beliefs was less than 60 percent. There appeared, therefore, to be evidence of a dual influence in these three areas.

The extent of eclecticism. Among the most striking characteristics of the total tabulated responses was the extent of eclecticism indicated by the respondents. Generally defined as "the practice of choosing beliefs from various or diverse systems of thought," eclecticism, as used in the present study refers to the extent which respondents checked beliefs from various philosophical positions.

In order to more sharply determine the consistency of naturalistic or spiritualistic responses on an individual respondent basis an interpretation of the data for this eclectic factor was limited to those 39 respondents who checked one belief in all 12 of the checklist categories. Since an accurate tabulation for this particular interpretation could be made only on the basis of the same number of responses by each individual, the ten respondents who checked more than one statement within a single category, or failed to check a statement in one or more of the categories, were not included.

Twenty-one respondents, 54 percent of those who completed the checklist according to instructions, indicated naturalistic beliefs in at least two-thirds of the checklist categories. Five respondents (13%) indicated spiritualistic beliefs in at least two-

Table I. Percentage of responses showing extent of naturalistic and spiritualistic beliefs according to categories in the checklist

Categories of the checklist	Percentage of naturalistic responses	Percentage of spiritualistic responses
The universe	76	24
Man	64	36
Values	73	27
Education	54	46
Program building	89	11
Program content	75	25
The administrator	42	58
The teacher	65	35
The learner	60	40
Learning	69	31
Teaching methods	73	27
Evaluation	56	44

thirds of the checklist categories. Thirteen respondents (33%) were eclectic to the extent that they indicated naturalistic or spiritualistic beliefs in seven, and the alternate position in five categories. According to the accepted view of eclecticism, 13 respondents appeared to hold essentially eclectic beliefs.

The responses to the checklist indicated that, when considered individually, about twice as many of the respondents appeared to hold essentially naturalistic beliefs as either spiritualistic or eclectic. However, those who held an essentially spiritualistic view indicated somewhat more strongly-held beliefs.

The factor of "advanced maturity." Seven of the 49 respondents who participated in the study were either in or approaching retirement. This did not constitute a sufficient number from which to draw a conclusion. However, considered from the standpoint of two major philosophies, there was virtually no difference between the responses of this group and others participating in the study.

The geographical factor. The checklist responses indicated a predominance of naturalistic beliefs checked by the respondents from all four sections of the United States —eastern, central, southern, and western. The largest percentage of checklist responses identifiable with naturalistic philosophy (68%) was checked by respondents from the West, and the largest percentage of spiritualistic responses to statements in the checklist (45%) was indicated by respondents from the South.

The sex factor. A tabulation of responses with respect to the sex of the respondent revealed no significant difference from that of the total group. The male respondents, however, indicated a majority of moderately-held beliefs, whereas the female respondents indicated a majority of strongly-held beliefs.

CONCLUSION

On the basis of present indicated beliefs, it was concluded that most professional leaders appear to be providing a predominantly naturalistic direction to American physical education. The study revealed some evidences of strong spiritualistic beliefs which suggested a dual influence and lack of general agreement in some areas of physical education.

REFERENCES

1. Brownell, Clifford L., and E. Patricia Hagman, *Physical Education—Foundations and Principles.* New York: McGraw-Hill Book Co., 1951. 397 pp.
2. Brubacher, John S. *Modern Philosophies of Education.* New York: McGraw-Hill Book Co., 1950. 340 pp.
3. Enlow, E. R. Identify your educational philosophy, *Peabody Journal of Education,* 17:18-23 (July 1939).
4. Hocking, William Ernest. *Types of Philosophy.* New York: Charles Scribner's Sons, 1939. 508 pp.
5. Leonard, Fred E., and George B. Affleck, *The History of Physical Education.* Philadelphia: Lea and Febiger, 1947. 476 pp.
6. Lodge, Rupert C. *Philosophy of Education.* New York: Harper and Bros., 1937. 341 pp.
7. Lynn, Minnie L. *Major Emphases in Physical Education in the United States.* Unpublished Ph.D. dissertation, University of Pittsburgh, 1944.
8. McCloy, Charles Harold. *The Philosophical Bases of Physical Education.* New York: F. S. Crofts and Company, 1947. 311 pp.
9. National Society for the Study of Education, *Philosophies of Education.* 41st yearbook, Part I. Chicago: 1942. 321 pp.
10. Van Dalen, Debold, Elmer Mitchell, and Robert Bennett. *A World History of Physical Education.* New York: Prentice-Hall Inc., 1953. 599 pp.
11. Wegener, Frank C. *The Philosophical Beliefs of Leaders in American Education.* Unpublished Doctor's dissertation, University of Southern California, 1946. 386 pp.
12. Williams, Jesse F. *The Principles of Physical Education.* Philadelphia: W. B. Saunders Co., 1939. 436 pp.

14. Physical education—part of the general education program*

Wilson W. Elkins

President, University of Maryland

The purpose of education is to develop the potentialities of the individual. A complex variety of factors and agencies are involved in this development, and the schools and colleges have the primary responsibility of promoting intellectual growth. While carrying out this responsibility, proper consideration must be given to the interdependent parts which, taken together in sum total, constitute the personality. These parts cannot be separated, nor do they grow independently of each other. The intellect develops within the structure of the human body, and it depends upon a proper climate. In a large measure, that climate is good health. The extent to which the individual, and ultimately society, will profit by the development of potentialities depends upon the fitness of the individual to fulfill his objectives. It is exceedingly important, therefore, that physical education be included in any general program designed to improve our human resources.

Health is more important than anything else. It is not the sole or the primary responsibility of the school or college, but the general welfare of society demands that it be given a place which will attract attention, assure interest, and command respect. However strongly one may feel about the responsibility of the home for physical fitness, the educational institutions must support and strengthen what is done on the outside. It is a well-known fact that if the general curriculum does not include a program of physical development and the es-

*From Journal of Health, Physical Education, and Recreation, Vol. 32, p. 25, Feb. 1961. Used by permission.

sentials of good health, these will be neglected by the student and will not be adequately supplied by the home or other agencies.

There is a continuing discussion among educators today about what courses should be required of all students, particularly at the college and university level. The professionals in almost every discipline can make a good case for their courses. Only a limited number of subjects can be required of every student. The choice becomes more debatable and more difficult as knowledge increases and our perspective of man changes. Unfortunately, the discussions which occupy the time of curriculum committees often "bog down" in the deep ruts of vested interest. It is extremely difficult to get a cross section of a faculty to look at the changing picture with objectivity and vision and to emerge with recommendations which reflect the changes that have taken place and that may be anticipated in the near future. This regrettable situation offers little hope for achieving sharp departures from the past. We cannot reasonably expect revolutionary changes outside the existing pattern.

There is hope, however, for desirable changes within the accepted patterns, and this imposes a special responsibility upon those who are teaching and revising courses now included in general education. If the responsibilities are not accepted, the status quo will fall prey to the "heretics" who would seek to overhaul our antiquated general programs.

Some of the advocates of reform, who would give the general curriculum a new look, have been critical of physical education. To them it has been a soft spot in education, hardly worthy of collegiate recognition. Although the criticism has been aimed at professional programs, it has brought into focus the content of the required courses. Regardless of the validity of this criticism, the attitude has spread beyond our campuses. It cannot be ignored; there is too much at stake.

The physical educators know that their curriculums have been strengthened in recent years, but they have failed to communicate this change to their colleagues in other fields and to the consumers. If communication does not repair the damage, there is a real danger that physical education, as a part of the general program, will suffer.

There is a strong case for physical education as an integral part of the general program. The case must rest on content of lasting value to the individual—on content which looks to the future as it continues to serve present needs. If it is to compete for the limited time of the student, it cannot rely on past practices or be considered as just a modest amount of exercise which may or may not be useful. It must be associated with solid information and the development of habits and skills that will contribute to health and happiness throughout life.

The planners of the general program are hard pressed to include a little of what every student should know. They have an increasingly difficult task. The final test of selection should be based on questions which concern lasting values. These values are inherent in physical education courses which are properly designed to improve physical fitness and promote better health through increased knowledge and wholesome recreation. Arguments and achievements can be persuasive, but they will not be taken for granted. Physical education, as a part of the general curriculum, is under skeptical scrutiny. It is exceedingly important that it maintain a respectable place in the education of the individual. It will do so if quality and good judgment prevail.

15. What makes a champion?

(A philosophy of sport)*

Fred Russell

Vice President and Sports Editor, Nashville Banner, Nashville, Tennessee

To be your keynote speaker is a rare privilege. You gentlemen, as leaders of state high school athletic associations, are fortunate to be close to competitive sports. I, as a sportswriter, am equally lucky. I say that not because all of us are in on a lot of excitement and thrills; that part's fine. But I believe there's an even more appealing factor.

According to my reading of the Bible, the game we call Life got off to an unusual start. The Referee explained the rules; the rules got broken right off the bat; a penalty was inflicted. You may ask what was unusual about that? Well, it was the severity of the penalty—banishment forever from the Garden, and the guilty man would henceforth have to work for a living.

I start off this way only to try to set up the fact that sport is the opposite of work.

Sport has been with us for a long time, but I'm not yet sure of its full meaning. You can look up the word *sport* in the dictionary and find two meanings. One is "to carry away from work." It means enjoyment, relaxation. It's the abbreviation of *disport,* which means to divert, to amuse, to make merry. Another, and more serious meaning, is "competition for a prize, discipline, effort for self-improvement." I think these two definitions make for the greatest combination in the world.

I think there are probably higher degrees of happiness in some things other than sport. But, I say that happiness is found most readily in sport, and more predictably—by plan—than in almost anything one does. I once heard a very learned man say: "Man's greatest moment of happiness is to be tested beyond what he thought might be his breaking point—and not fail."

Out of this comes the life of self-improvement, the striving for greater achievement. In other words, the continuous effort to put into actual practice man's limitless potentialities. In this way, records are broken year in and year out; the impossible of today becomes the average of tomorrow.

Effort in sport is a matter of character, rather than reward. It is an end in itself and not a means to an end. That's why, in defeat, one can rest on his character and keep a stout heart.

I make the claim that sport offers the highest-grade happiness to man on the most convenient terms available anywhere.

Now to get down to another of its great values—and virtues.

The field of sport is a place where people can succeed—beyond their success anywhere else—in behaving themselves while having fun. I'm talking about *fairness.*

Where else do we always give everybody an even start and an equal number of times at bat?

Sport is quick to outlaw any piece of unfairness that can be covered or controlled by a rule. But sportsmanship is more than mere observance of the letter of the law. Sportsmanship means obedience to the unenforceable. Yet, even the true meaning of sportsmanship fails to cover another aspect of the fairness that pervades sport. I refer to the kindly workings of the Law of Average, and to the fair distribution of talents that commonly occurs between teams and

---

*From an address to the National Federation of State High School Athletic Associations, French Lick, Ind., June 26, 1966. Used by permission.

individuals. Great size and great speed are very seldom found together in one person; the greatest size and the greatest speed— never!

There is a balance, which, to me, somehow, seems not totally unrelated to fairness.

To surpass others is a common aspiration among human beings. Sport offers the opportunity, and some can succeed.

To surpass ourselves is even better, and is also a common aspiration. Here, sport offers opportunity wherein all can succeed.

Those who succeed to the highest degree are the champions.

What makes a champion in competitive sports?

Certainly physical ability is an essential ingredient. But how many times have you seen the young man of exceptional physical ability fail to develop into any kind of champion?

Calisthenics can build up the body. Courses of study can train the mind. But the real champion is the person whose heart can be educated?

How?

There are many ways, but I think one stands out. It might be called "The Experience of Having Failed." Not failing just once, but many times. What I mean is, failing in something, and finding out that it wasn't the end of the world.

I believe that a prime factor in the making of a champion is this conquering of the fear of making a mistake. Later, there comes the realization that without errors, there could be no competitive sports—just like there could be no living.

In practically every moment of competitive athletics, there's a mistake, a failure of some kind. We think a baseball player with a .300 average is a pretty good hitter. Yet that average shows that in 7 out of 10 times, he has failed. Or in football, a runner gains 20 yards; somebody missed a tackle. A runner is thrown for a 10-yard loss; somebody failed to block.

When a mistake happens, the potential champion is the person who doesn't tuck his tail or blow his top. He is developing a feel for pressure; he is becoming clutchworthy; he is gaining the championship attitude.

I like the story about the hill in China, where two gangs of coolies, one on each side

of the hill, were digging a tunnel. The idea of the engineers was that they would meet in the middle. Someone asked the foreman: "Suppose they don't meet?" He replied: "In that case, we'll have two tunnels."

So the time comes when an athlete gains that confidence, that emotional maturity, of being at his best when the going is roughest, when he experiences that tremendous satisfaction of keeping his presence of mind in the deepest difficulty, that genuine joy of being able to function in disaster—and finish in style. That's the true champion.

I have been asked: Why does our society give such adulation to sports champions? Why do athletes seem to be admired the most—more than the successful businessman, professional man or politician?

I think we are always eager to pay tribute to excellence, but in our modern industrial society it becomes increasingly harder to identify excellence. The world has grown so complex that we don't know whom to admire, or for what reasons. With the successful politician and businessman and professional man, nobody really knows how much of their success comes from talent and how much from low cunning, from self-serving, from politics and publicity and all the other highly organized strategies of today.

But with the athlete it remains clear. He cannot fake. He cannot cheat. He cannot use others, or hide behind them, or blame them. His excellence is out in the open, for everyone to see. We need personal heroes, and the champion in athletics is one who cannot fool us. He exists on merit, and that's what makes it so refreshing.

In distilling the qualities that make a champion, there is skill, of course—a special kind of skill, polished by practice and fully harnessed through understanding. And there are the common denominators of determination and pride. But above all, I think, is that quality of emotional balance which enables a person to operate at his optimum level, regardless of the tenseness of the situation.

In athletics, tension is the No. 1 enemy of top performance. A competitor in sports has to be loose, has to be relaxed, in order to put all his energy and strength into his muscles when the brain commands. It's my belief that nothing can relieve tension quicker than humor—that quality that makes something seem funny.

The person with the best chance to become a champion—I think—not only has a backbone and a wishbone—he also has a funny bone.

Just a smidgen of humor helps, but blessed is he who can laugh. Laughter cheers the soul. I regard it as the lubrication of the human spirit. Most of the champions I've known could laugh.

I think of you men of the National Federation of State High School Athletic Associations as champions in your endeavor. I treasure my association with Foster Bridges in Tennessee. Throughout the nation, there is genuine respect for the vital leadership all of you demonstrate, for your splendid contribution in the way you help to make athletics a pattern for living.

I wish to conclude with some lines which the late Grantland Rice, were he writing them today, might have dedicated to you men:

> If somebody whispered to me,
> You can have your pick,
> If kind fortune came to woo me
> Where the gold is thick,
> I would still, by hill and hollow,
> Round the world away,
> Stirring deeds of contest follow
> 'Til I'm bent and gray.
>
> Sport is youth and youth's eternal
> Where the flame is bright,
> And our hearts will still be vernal
> When our hair is white.
> And tho' wealth may never love us,
> Say that we have seen,
> That the sky is blue above us,
> And the turf is green.

16. The whole man, science, and physical education*

Arthur H. Steinhaus

Dean Emeritus, George Williams College

To participate in this pilgrimage to the cradle of sport in Olympia is in itself the event of a lifetime. That this event celebrates a newly revitalized Olympia makes it a most joyous occasion. The presence here of peoples from many lands who feel themselves united in the spirit of the new Olympic tradition is for all of us an inspiring experience of the first magnitude.

All of us know that were it not for the herculean efforts of one man this historic week in the annals of sport would not have come to pass and none of us would be here today.

For more than 50 years Carl Diem† has breathed Olympia and has hoped, worked, and prayed for the fulfillment that you and I are privileged to live out in these days. Diem has with the ancient fathers of Olympia and with Baron de Coubertin of the modern era, seen Olympia as more than sport. He has as he demonstrated 25 years ago in Berlin seen it as a Festival of Youth in which the feats of the body are coupled with those of the mind and together these are dedicated to the God of peace and greater understanding in a spiritual experience even as our predecessors of old dedicated themselves here in this holy place.

You will all be happy to learn that this most highly respected and beloved physical educator, Carl Diem, will this year become the first European physical educator to be

*From Steinhaus, Arthur H.: Toward an Understanding of Health and Physical Education, Dubuque, Iowa: William C. Brown Company. Publishers, 1963, pp. 6-11. Used by permission.
As presented to the First Olympic Academy at Olympia, Greece, June 20, 1961.
†Carl Diem is deceased, but the remarks concerning him will be of interest to the reader.

awarded an honorary doctor's degree in the United States.

With your consent, I now declare him to be today's Hercules of world Physical Education.

May the Academy that this week climaxes the dreams and labors of Carl Diem continue through the years as the immortality of the spirit of Olympia made manifest by the life of Carl Diem.

The thoughts that I have collected under my title, "The Whole Man, Science, and Physical Education" are as old as the wisdom of ancient Greece where civilization flourished two thousand years before Columbus discovered my homeland. They are also as new as the great neurological institute of our generation. Both old and new they give to physical education greater responsibilities for helping to maintain modern man fit in body, in mind, and in spirit.

Plato's concept of the soul or total personality is pictured by him to be a charioteer driving a pair of winged steeds. Whereas in a god soul both of the horses are good and of good extraction, in the human soul only one horse is such a modest, honorable, and chivalrous thoroughbred, whereas the other one, which by the way has lost its wings, balks and bolts to fulfill its lust in carnal delights.

In this classic parable, the charioteer represents wisdom or judgment, the thoroughbred horse rational thought and the other one, the baser animal, traits ruled by appetites. These baser traits, Plato tells us, require man to have a body which the gods do not need. Thus encumbered, mankind is earth bound. Only the best can for a time keep pace with the gods to secure glimpses of the real existences. "But the common herd follow at a distance, all of them indeed burning with desire for the upper world, but, failing to reach it, they make a revolution in the moisture of the lower element, trampling on one another, and striking against one another in their efforts to rush one before the other." (Plato's apparent preview of today's world then continues) "Hence, ensues the extremest turmoil and struggling and sweating; and herein, by the awkwardness of the drivers, many souls are maimed, and many lose many feathers in the crush; and all after painful labor go away without being blessed by admission to the spectacle of truth, and thenceforth live on the food of mere opinion." (From J. Wright's translation of Phaedrus as reproduced in #456 of Everymans Library, New York, Dutton, 1910.)

Neurologists have now discovered Plato's charioteer and two horses inside the cranium and spinal column and there with electrical stimulation, surgery, and brain waves, they have localized and analysed the characters of this trinity.

In the limbic system, composed of the primitive cortex and its related nerve centers in the brain stem, and the hypothalamus they have identified the bolting, appetite driven, wingless horse that holds man earth bound. Here it is that electric stimulation evokes overeating, fighting, and a host of activities related to self-preservation. Here also stimulation produces behavior related to procreation and race preservation. One electrode will evoke the brooding reaction in a hen causing her to crouch and with spread wings cluck for chicks to get under her, whereas another nearby electrode will stimulate the alarm cry, a backward look over the shoulder, and escape as from a chicken hawk. When stimulated simultaneously with both electrodes the hen remains brooding, but with evident signs of conflict, only to fly off the more violently when excitation to brooding is suddenly terminated.[1]

Here also Professor Olds[2] found the cell masses that animals, given access to an electric circuit for self-stimulation, elect to activate more than two thousand times an hour for 24 consecutive hours until they fall exhausted for lack of food. Even though food is present throughout the experiment

they ignore it in their eagerness to experience the electrically induced feeling of gratification. Some isolated observations on man indicate that he also has such centers of wonderful feeling. These so-called motivation centers, be it noted for later reference, make connections with regions of the brain where will be identified both the nobler horse and the charioteer.

These older portions of the brain together with the cerebellum and spinal cord are shared alike by pigeon, dog, and man. When in experimental animals the higher cortical centers are removed leaving only those parts that correspond to Plato's baser steed, the animal shows perfect coordination for walking, running, fighting, mating, and flying. Its behavior is instinctive and predictable as that of a robot. It possesses no great storehouse of previous experiences that give individuality to animal and man, and to man the stuff out of which his thoughts are composed and his intelligence arises. I can demonstrate this, though somewhat imperfectly, with these pigeons from which we removed the cerebral hemispheres nine days ago. You will note that they possess perfect coordination for walking, balancing, and flying but they have no memory of friends or enemies and are quite incapable of learning. They preen themselves periodically and when they become hungry they perform pecking movements with head and neck but they will not feed themselves. This experiment shows us that no cortex is needed for mere physical activity. For physical education, however, the cortex is essential.

Plato's second horse of rational action and intellect undoubtedly resides in the neocortex of higher animals and man. Because this cortex is only poorly developed in experimental animals it has thus far eluded full exposure. Beginning with Fritz and Hitzig who in 1870 stimulated the brains of soldiers suffering head wounds in the Franco-Prussian War, a number of brain surgeons have stimulated the cortex of conscious patients to explore its character. Today the activity of this outer mantle of gray matter, composed of some ten billion nerve cells, is identified as the human mind with powers that we call memory; discrimination; symbol, word, language, and idea formation; the capacity of reasoning; and voluntary activity. Here Professor Penfield's electrodes[3] evoke not only bodily movements but cause also the conscious patient to relive, vividly, long forgotten experiences with their complete agenda of music, conversations, location, and associated feelings. Destruction of portions of the cortex results in predictable losses of mental functions.

It would no doubt surprise Plato to learn that his nobler horse is neurologically an offspring of the baser one since the neocortex actually arises by repeated multiplication of a few nerve cells that early in embryonic development wander away from the old cortex but continue in two way communication with it over a very rich set of intercommunicating pathways.

Bulging into the forehead of man is that special mass of gray matter comprising the prefrontal lobes which have been variously called the seat of wisdom, of conscience, of values, of worry, and of judgment. Nearly absent in animal forms below man and, judging from skull contours, also poorly developed in early human forms such as Sinanthropus pekinensis, these lobes are probably the last to become functional in each of us. They do not attain their optimum efficiency until the end of the second

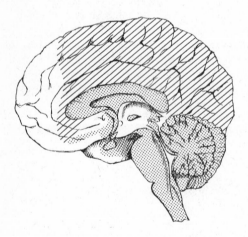

Midsagittal section of human brain and upper cord

Cord, brain stem, cerebellum, and old cortex or limbic system—the baser steed of Plato

New cortex—the nobler steed of Plato

Prefrontal lobe—the charioteer of Plato

decade of life when their connections with the brain stem are fully perfected.[4] When in 1850 Phineas Gage, a New England Yankee, accidentally set off the explosion that drove a powder tamping rod into his prefrontal lobes, he recovered consciousness within an hour and lived another twelve years; but no longer was he the honest, homeloving, conscientious Puritanistic New Englander of his preaccident days. Other accidents, the removal of prefrontal tumors, and the practice of psychosurgery, all indicate that this area of cortex in some special way integrates the activities of the new and the old brain. Over multifarious two way nerve paths between them and the reasoning cortex on the one hand and the brain of feelings, fights, and appetites on the other, these lobes connect feelings with ideas and reason with baser drives.

In the accompanying figure of the nervous system of man I have roughly designated these three divisions of the nervous system. In heavy black is shown the cord, cerebellum, brain stem, and related portions of the cerebral hemispheres that house the baser appetite-driven nature of man. This is Plato's baser steed.

Stippled with small dots are the portions of the cerebral hemispheres in which reside the capacity for sensory discrimination, memory, concept or idea formation, learned activities, and voluntary actions, also speech and the power to use it and other tools of mind in rational thinking. This corresponds to the nobler steed in Plato's parable.

In clear white are the prefrontal lobes where thoughts become associated with feelings and drives in ways that are determined by standards of the home, society, and civilization. It is here that values are placed on experiences to develop conscience and wisdom, i.e., the desirable use of knowledge and power is born. This is the charioteer of Plato who must wisely couple the powerful drives of the baser horse and the rational knowledge of the nobler one to the end that the whole man "attain admission to the spectacle of truth."

It remains now for us to examine how physical education can help to perfect this whole man so that he may be more successful in the great contest that is life.

Seventy years ago Luther Halsey Gulick, the father of American Physical Education, pondered a similar question. He invented the triangle to symbolize man as a unity of body, mind, and spirit. Whether Dr. Gulick was influenced by Plato's parable we do not know; but we are certain that he shared the great philosopher's conviction that man is a closely knit integration of higher and lower ingredients and that each is important to the effective functioning of the whole. He was convinced that in the conduct of physical activities and all other activities designed to develop man, this unity must always be recognized and respected.

Comparing Plato's parable and Gulick's symbol one realizes that Plato makes no mention of the chariot itself, which should in reality be the body of man, and Gulick fails to distinguish between the baser drives and nobler thoughts in his expression of mind. But one must not expect too much of any analogy.

Much has been learned and written about the effect of physical activity on the body or shall we say the chariot. Thus it is common knowledge that whenever muscles, heart, blood vessels, and lungs are caused to operate at intensities above normal, i.e., when they are overloaded, they respond by becoming larger, stronger, and more efficient in their ability to withstand the stresses imposed on them by exercise. We know also that with the cessation of such overloading these changes are reversed so that muscles, heart, and lungs again become smaller and weaker. Extra capillaries that developed under strenuous training in heart and muscles, disappear and the more efficient regulations of the circulatory system that mark the trained state are lost soon after training is ended.

Every use of the body involves related portions of the nervous system. Voluntary movements and especially the learning of new skills are functions of the newer cortex where also are left the memory traces of what has been learned. The unconscious adjustments of circulatory and endocrine functions that mark the trained state are regulated by nerve centers in the brain stem, hypothalamus, and the limbic lobes that compose Plato's baser animal. With or without interference or direction from the "thinking cortex," repeated use of these centers improves the effectiveness with which they mobilize the inner organs and circu-

latory system to support better functioning of the whole man.

The recently identified intimate connections of hypothalamic nerve centers with the posterior and anterior lobes of the pituitary gland provide an anatomic basis for the long suspected connections between neural and hormonal regulation of the body. Today we know the nerve centers in the hypothalamus produce various neurohumors that find their way via the axon surfaces of neurones and via special connecting blood vessels into the posterior and anterior lobes respectively. Here they induce formation of hormones that stimulate kidneys, smooth muscles, thyroid, ovary or testes, growth centers in bones, adrenal cortex and other organs.

In turn the reproductive and adrenal glands excite activity in other parts of the body. Thus we should really include these slower acting chemical regulators of body function with the brain stem and limbic systems as part of Plato's steed of lowly origin.

Recent studies by Raab[5] give reason to believe that strenuous physical training through its influence on this interacting neurohelp protect man from the threat of heart failure. The explanation seems to be as follows: By action of the vagus nerve (cholinergic activity) the heart is caused to beat more slowly and in other ways to find itself in position to recuperate its powers between beats. On the other hand sympathetic discharges (adrenergic activity) speeds up its action in every way. Such augmented action is useful and necessary to cope with the stresses placed upon the body by the struggle for existence in the jungle, in strenuous labor, and in athletic competition. But after the struggle in which the sympathetic system must dominate, there should come a quick return to the resting state under rule of the vagus. This appears to be the case in the well-trained athlete but not in the untrained person. Not only is there a stronger resting vagus tone in the trained person but very likely also an active inhibition of sympathetic tone. This means that in the trained person at rest, the heart is more fully bathed in quieting acetylcholine (vagus Stoff of Loewi) and through inhibition of sympathetic discharges there is reduced formation not only of adrenalin and noradrenalin from sympathetic endings in the heart and everywhere in the body but also less of the corticosteroids from the adrenal cortex.

These substances which are necessary to mobilize the body's resources for survival in crises are virtually useless and even harmful when continued through the resting state. Inability to shut down their production when the need is over, subjects the heart to dangers resulting from their continued action.

Unfortunately, in our present day world many stresses caused by unhygienic ways of people and nations arouse man's sympathetic nerves to place such strain on his heart. Add to this the fact that substances released by stimulation of the sympathetic nerves cause blood to clot more rapidly and you have the ingredients that make a cardiac thrombosis. This is why some observers are convinced that the stresses of many occupations and the lack of regular exercise should be matters of graver concern than dietary cholesterol, as possible causes of the mounting death rate from heart disease in so-called civilized man.

What more can we do for this horse of lowly ancestry whose ways of acting have passed the test of natural selection through hundreds of millions of years in the struggle for survival. These ways are the driving forces of pain, fear, hunger, sex, and rage; the elemental struggles for food, for mate, and for existence. Without them there would be no existence for man or animal. They can never be ignored. They must never be repudiated. They cannot be changed but they can be brought under domination of the charioteer and harnessed to team up with the nobler horse as when anger becomes righteous indignation; the struggle for existence, enlightened self-interest; and the care of young, love for mankind.

Although we cannot change this animal nature in man, we could slow its coming of age even as we have in recent generations hastened its maturing. Studies reported by Mills[6] show that since 1795 the age of the onset of sexual maturity has dropped from approximately 16.6 years to 13.0 years and even lower. This accelerated sexual maturation that distinguishes recent generations from their forerunners, is undoubtedly due to the higher nutritional levels attained by the more prosperous civilizations.

The wife of an Innsbruck professor, after a year in the United States, last summer, expressed to me her astonishment over the early and plentiful feeding of meat and eggs to very young children in my country.

In recent studies Slovenian girls that reived meat once a week[7] were found to mature at age 14.1 whereas girls that ate 14 servings of meat per week matured on the average at 11.7 years.

Bigger babies may not always be better babies. The nutritional pressurizing of sexual maturation by the present hysterical emphasis on high protein diets may well be reflected in the staggering increase of unwed child mothers and other sex related forms of delinquency that mark today's families of both high and low culture in the more prosperous countries. In a small German village the Pastor told me last summer that by actual count 54% of the girls that came to be married by him were already pregnant. A high protein diet may bring earlier maturity to the animal in man but it cannot bring to his educable cortex the endless succession of experiences through which alone this cortex can become an effective guide to behavior. The development of discriminating thought patterns and strong habitual controls of conduct takes time. Have we inadvertently placed man-sized instinctive drives into the custody of child-sized cortical learnings?

Physical education that is interested in the whole person cannot overlook such facts.

The neocortex contains nerve centers that make possible seeing, hearing, and localization of touch; speaking, and delicate movements of face, hands, and other body parts; memory, reasoning, and awareness of self. It is because of these abilities that Plato's horse of noble heritage knows the way. Here are stored memories of the past, here are learned the rules and skills of sports that cause one person to differ from another, here are correlated the sensory experiences that acquaint us with objects and events in the world about us, thus to give meaning to our concepts and ideas. Here also is located the least understood yet most important of our senses, namely, the muscle sense.

Approximately 40% of the nerve fibers in

the motor nerve to a muscle are actually sensory fibers that carry nerve impulses from muscles, tendons, and related joint structures into the cord and brain. More important to life than vision and hearing, this proprioception, kinesthesia, or muscle sense provides the mind with its understanding of stretch, tension, movement, and the third dimension. Observed by the eyes alone, a sphere is but a circle. Only after the hand has closed around it does the concept of a sphere become "true to life." How incorrect would be the concept of the sun to a person whose hands had never clutched a ball? What is the meaning of "tension" to a man who has never strained his muscles to pull a rope or lift a heavy object? Without the sensations that arise from activity in muscles and joints our "inner world" of concepts would be flat and completely unreal.

Herein lies the most important contribution of physical activity to the mind of man. Every movement, every body position, every tension in muscle, tendon, and joint structure contributes to the formation of concepts or ideas that form the building stones with which we construct our thought life. How important then it is, that each concept represent as truly as possible that object or event of the external world for which it is the thought world's counterpart.

It is probably safe to guess that many unlearned persons who work much with their hands often exhibit a high grade of "common sense" because their concepts are richly supplied with this "muscle sense" ingredient. On the other hand the unexpectedly naive judgment often displayed by persons educated too much in the rarefied air of books and abstract ideas may well be due to a shortage of this ingredient in their mental life. For modern man whose occupation keeps him in a world of abstractions, sports and other physical activities may be among the few retreats into reality and therefore sanity, readily available to him.

There are many other ways in which the practice of sports and other activities involves the neocortex but time permits the mention of only one. Largely because of the work of Pavlov and his successors in Russia we have come to realize that many of the adjustments in the circulatory, respiratory, and probably the endocrine systems that serve to prepare the organism for perform-

ance in competition are in reality learned, conditional reflexes that undoubtedly are formed in the neocortex. Thus the memory trace left by an often repeated activity includes in addition to the nerve patterns for the practiced movements also the nerve paths that govern the associated visceral adjustments. Most recently Gutman and Jakoubek[8] found that the blood sugar level and liver glycogen stores of rats rose considerably soon after they were placed in the environment in which they had previously been trained to run.

Now we must turn to Plato's charioteer, the prefrontal lobes. It is through these centers that the differing talents of the older and newer centers are wisely or unwisely coordinated. It is here that the ideas and other activities of the rational cortex are brought together with the pleasures, pains, drives, and appetites of the older centers.

The kinds and amounts of such feeling tones that become associated with each thought or voluntary act depend upon how these components are brought together in the life experience of the child and adult. Thus if a boy in his early experiences with basketball is wisely guided to experience pleasure when his play is that of an honest sportsman and pain when his actions are unfair and unsportsmanlike, corresponding connections are made through the prefrontal lobes. Subsequently, the persistence of these associations of thoughts and acts with feelings will determine the athlete's conduct.

It is only through many such experiences and much practice that the charioteer of the prefrontal lobes stores up the wisdom needed to integrate the thought life and baser feelings and appetites to assure victory in the race of life.

Always in life the horses and charioteer must function together. Sports and other physical activities are life speeded up. In a game of football the body moves much faster and the mind must make decisions much faster than in ordinary life. Thus in competition hundreds of decisions are made and executed in the time that ordinary life allows for ten. Even more important, these decisions must be made in the heat of emotion, engendered by the competition, and they must be made fairly and efficiently. In this sense competition places a terrific overload on the body to perform efficiently, on the mind to make quick and accurate decisions, and on the spirit to make these decisions with the right control over the emotions. Thus the chariot, the two horses and the charioteer, in other words the whole man is given a tremendous work-out in athletic competition.

The degree of success that is attained by whole man depends on how well he learns to perform—on how well his parents and other teachers have succeeded in leading him to accept their guidance. The most perfect says Plato, "follows a god most closely and resembles him most nearly, succeeds in raising the head of its charioteer into the outer regions, and is carried round with the immortals in their revolution, though sore encumbered by its horses, and barely able to contemplate the real existence; while another rises and sinks by turns, his horses plunging so violently that he can discern no more than a part of these existences. But the common herd follow at a distance . . . without being blessed by admission to the spectacle of truth, and thenceforth live on the food of mere opinion."

REFERENCES

1. Reported by Fremont-Smith as a personal communication from Konrad Lorenz on p. 94 *The Central Nervous System and Behavior, Trans. of the Second Conference, Feb. 22, 23, 24, and 25, 1959*. Princeton, New Jersey. Edited by Mary A. B. Brazier. New York, Josiah Macy, Jr. Foundation (1959).
2. Olds, James, *ibid* p. 47
————, *Pleasure Centers in the Brain*, Scientific American, October 1956.
3. Penfield, W. *The Excitable Cortex*, Springfield, Ill. Thomas (1958).
4. Burr, H. S., *The Anatomy of Anxiety*, Conn. Med. Jour. 24:21-26 (1960).
5. Raab, W. *Metabolic Protection and Reconditioning of the Heart Muscle through Habitual Physical Exercise*. Ann. of Int. Med. 53:87-105 (1960).
6. Mills, C. A. *Geographic and Time Variations in Body Growth and Age of Menarche*. Human Biol. 9:43-56 (1937) and Eskimo Sexual Function, Science 89:II (1939).
7. Kralj-Cercek, Lea. *The influence of Food, Body Build, and Social Origin On The Age of Menarche*. Human Biol. 28:393-406 (1956).
8. Gutman, E. and B. Jakoubek. *Preparatory Reactions to Muscular Work*. Physiol. Bohemosl. 10:275-282 (1961).

17. The whole child: a fresh look*

Harold Taylor

Former President, Sarah Lawrence College

The real quarrel between the conservatives and the liberals in education is about the kind of society they wish to live in. The conservatives want more control over children and more stability in the society; the liberals want more freedom and more change.

But the issue between them is seldom put in these terms. Instead, each is inclined to attack and defend abstractions. Attacks are made on "progressive education" and the "philosophy of John Dewey," which is equated with "life adjustment," "doorbell ringing," "play projects," "citizenship courses," and the "child-centered school" where it is said precious time is wasted on the child's psyche while he gropes for his own conclusions and his own identity. He should be taught the hard subjects under strong discipline.

On the other hand, progressive ideas and programs are too often defended by their proponents as if critics had no right to raise questions, as if the ideas and practices on which their theories rest were valid for all time. The progressives must again become progressive.

For example, there is merit in the criticism of the kind of false liberalism that tries to overcome intellectual and social inequality by smothering it in sentiment. There are differences in the capacities of children and there are differences in their social status. They know it, their parents know it, their teachers know it. The task of the educator, liberal or otherwise, is to deal directly with these differences and to take the children where they are. If children are slow learn-

ers, it is no kindness to them to act as if they weren't. Nor does it help them to hold the others back in order not to damage the confidence of the slow. This may have the opposite effect if what they really need is to learn how to learn. If children are culturally undernourished, have little vocabulary, come from poor and broken homes, what they need is not merely liberal sentiment but direct action by teachers who understand how to deal with their deficiencies.

The conservative's program of higher academic standards and more subject matter misses the entire point; the problem of the slum child is a total problem. If the slum child is also a Negro, Puerto Rican, a Mexican, in America he is segregated socially, economically, physically and mentally, all at once. The problem is poverty, poverty of every kind—cultural, intellectual, economic, and emotional.

The educator must go to the root of the matter, and he must deal with the whole child. The root is in the social and economic conditions in which the child exists. The educator must deal bluntly with those who support the residential segregation of the colored people and the poor. He must fight those who wish to profit in real estate at the expense of the children. He must think of education as a total process, in which the conditions of society deeply affect the child's mind, the level of his achievement, and the range of his possibilities. The curriculum, the classroom, the guidance office are instruments for dealing with one part of the child's life. But they do not and cannot function in a social vacuum.

Nor is it permissible any longer to say that the social environment of the child is not the problem of the educator, that it be-

*From Saturday Review, Dec. 16, 1961, p. 42. Used by permission.

longs to city planners, social workers, economists, housing experts, or society. It belongs to everyone, but most of all to the educator. The educator is not a personnel manager, an administrator, an organization man, although his work involves organizing, managing, and administering. He is a social and intellectual leader, and he begins to exercise his leadership when he recognizes the conditions of his society and brings to bear upon them the force of a humanitarian philosophy.

It is in exactly this matter that the conservatives and the liberals alike have failed; the conservatives by turning their backs on it and concerning themselves with the "gifted," the intellectually well-to-do, and cultivation of an elite; the liberals by failing to extend into practice the implications of their own philosophy. The conservatives have been quite clear in their view that education is a stabilizing force, concerned with the transmission of the culture from generation to generation, and acting as a sorting device for the social classes. The liberals have been equally clear that education is an instrument of social change, through which a society may reform itself upon the initiative of its citizens.

But in practice, the liberals and the progressives have addressed themselves of late, not to the deeper questions of social and cultural change, but to a fairly narrow range of emotional problems to be found in the young, and to the development of new techniques for learning. They have tended to equate democracy with tolerance and good feeling, while the real questions have to do with the radical extension of democracy itself. The work of the progressives has for the most part been carried out in the suburbs where they have been content to accept the *status quo* of a segregated, white, and affluent society while they adapt their methods and ideas to the needs of a suburban clientele.

These community needs have become more and more directed to the improvement of status and are expressed in the desire, sometimes mounting to compulsion, to have children attend schools, colleges, and universities that confer that status. The tendency of the progressives has been to accept without a struggle the legitimacy of all such values, provided they are held by a suitable number of people of respectable means and appropriate social position. The educators have joined the establishment.

At a time when conservatives are becoming more conservative, and often turning into radical reactionaries, the liberals have thus lost their initiative and have been drawn along in the wake of their adversaries. The progressives, that educational wing of the liberal movement, have stayed behind the line of battle.

There are many reasons for this, among them a national confusion about where the line of battle really is. It is too often put at that point where the antagonisms between the United States and the Soviet Union intersect, and educators have been pressed into the role of civilian-soldiers on our side of the line. We are at present so absorbed in competition with the Russians that Americans are now using the Russian arguments for a controlled educational system, including the argument that more scientific and technical subject matter applied more stringently to all will produce high school and college graduates who will strengthen the national security.

At a time when education is publicly regarded as an instrument of national policy (in itself a dangerous and misleading assumption), it follows that we place our main emphasis on classifying and selecting for special treatment those students who are already scholastically able, rather than tackling the bigger question of how to correct the social and economic conditions that stunt children's intellectual growth in the first place. There is no more dramatic instance of this neglect of the main issue than in our failure to provide even a minimal basis for financing the American educational system through federal aid. We have put the money into a $50 billion military budget, because that is where we think the national interest lies.

In fact, our national interest lies in the construction of a strong and vigorous educational system, reaching into the entire range of the country's population for the discovery and encouragement of every kind of talent that exists there. Some of the most promising of the young are to be found in the city slums, in the Negro ghettos of the Southern states, in the industrial areas of the north where only half the children finish high school. Some of the most talented are not in school at all. We have the money and we must spend it in massive amounts to clear out the educational slums, to take the action that will give us schools and communities across the country which are truly integrated in a racial, economic, and social democracy. Once we tackle the educational question head-on we are on the way to solving the social problem.

At the present time our policies are constructing a class system, not a democracy. We lack a social dimension in our educational planning, and we work almost exclusively in terms of the academic curriculum, the measurement of I.Q., the pressure for academic achievement. An education has come to be considered as a way of moving into a higher social class than the one into which a person is born; it is a means of increasing personal income.

The time has come for a new progressive movement that can push once more to the front edge of educational and social change. There are some who are already there, educators like those who began their pioneer work at the George Washington High School in New York, where the education of the child in a depressed area was considered a total problem, not merely a lack of high I.Q. levels in the student body.

The main effort was to enrich the child's total experience by using the whole of New York City and its arts and culture as the educational environment, by extending the range of possibility for all the children beyond the limits of their local streets, by reaching out to the children and their parents with sympathetic guidance and improved instruction in every segment of the curriculum. The success of that project, now grown to the Higher Horizons program and spreading through similar efforts around the country, is a clear sign of the direction we must go. The success is to be measured, not simply by how many children who were formerly deprived of good education are now able to attend universities, but by how all of the children in school have been educated up to the limits of their particular talent, and how the community itself has been enriched and changed by the increase in knowledge and the lift in attitude. The recruitment, on a national scale, of hundreds of young college graduates to teach in these communities, and

to enter into the life of the community itself, would have an immediate effect on the improvement of these areas. We need a Peace Corps for our own educational system.

There are others who form the vanguard for a new progressive movement to be found among those who are pressing toward a new conception of the child's mind and his capacity to learn. These are men and women who, like Jerome Bruner is his experimental work at Harvard, are dealing directly with children to find the best ways in which they can learn, and who collaborate actively with scholars from the university and teachers from the schools to infuse the subject-matter of the school curriculum with ideas drawn from modern discoveries in science, mathematics, literature and the arts.

Too often in the past, those progressives who worked with the concept of the whole child made their own separation of the intellect from the emotions, and the child from his society, by placing primary emphasis on the child's psychic security and emotional comfort. The particular contribution of the "whole child" concept to education in this century has been to turn the educator's attention to the psychic development of the child and to the way in which his personal relations, his emotions, his ability to learn and to build a character are directly affected by the social and psychological environment of the classroom and the school. In part this was a reaction against the rigidity and insensitivity of traditional school practices. In part it was a new and fascinating theory of learning and of personality development which has dominated modern thought since the century began.

But the original concept of the whole child has become corrupted by use and misuse into something no longer recognizable in the original. There are many who have accepted modern ideas without understanding them, and have developed a simple-minded psychology which holds that as long as there is good feeling and "warm" relationships there is healthy emotional development. Or, conversely, that in order to preserve the sense of worth and the feeling of confidence in the child it is necessary never to express or convey negative judgments or to carry out direct instruction.

What may very well happen here is that

you get neither emotional nor intellectual maturity, but instead sloppy work, under-achievement, and unstable emotions. Freud's point was that neuroses in later life could be traced back to traumatic experiences in childhood. He did not argue that all negative experiences and prohibitions in childhood are traumatic. In fact, the removal of authority and of critical judgment on the part of the teacher may leave the child to wallow in a mass of indecision, or, in the case of the adolescent, to spend so much time in self-concern, question-raising and in rationalizing his indolence that there is no longer any inclination toward responsibility. The child may begin to feel that he must be forgiven everything, and failure to meet sensible standards may be called by dozens of forgiving psychological names.

The conservatives are now legitimate in their criticism of that kind of "adjustment" which adjusts moral and intellectual scruples right out of the educational situation. It is wise for a child to know that there are certain things to which a teacher and a society should not be expected to adjust. A recent statement from a group of psychiatrists describes an effort on their part to develop drugs which will, they hope, lead to the control of disgust, pique, resentment and other emotions, and in the long run instill "altruism, brotherly love and scientific creativity." For certain situations and certain actions there can be no more healthy emotion than that of disgust, and I would hate to see it done away with.

Some of those who equate modernism in education to the necessity of being permissive in every situation are using their personal response to children as a kind of drug in exactly this sense. True learning comes from engaged effort in the right circumstances. It does not spring full-blown from the unconscious, nor should it be overly protected from the reality into which it goes. The necessity for meeting clear criteria of achievement is one of the spurs to creative effort. The student who is not measuring himself against a set of standards appropriate to himself and his situation cannot gain the strength he needs no matter how desperately friendly everyone is. He will gain in personal stature and emotional size more from engaging in serious intellectual tasks to meet the expectations of a sensitive and discerning teacher than he will from undiluted tender loving care.

On the other hand, the conservatives who argue for more discipline, harder subjects and more of them, seldom pause to think about actual consequences as far as the children are concerned. What they are likely to get is the elimination of a large number of children who simply can't do the work. This converts the subjects into testing devices to screen out those who can't do them well. It may also assure that these subjects will contain little nourishment for the intellectual life of the children who can.

As a result there are extraordinary pressures on the child from all sides—from his parents who urge him to work harder and "get good grades," from the community where his status is involved, from the testing program of the school, that mechanical monster which decides his fate. But such pressures do little more than to destroy the possibility of his genuine intellectual growth, since the necessities of test-passing inhibit the enjoyment of ideas and the deeper consideration of their meaning.

The child gains no benefit from constant admonition unless the urging is accompanied by sensitive help in learning. The stance is wrong. The child who is unable to do well in mathematics or in English does not need goading or the threat of a bad grade. He needs good teaching and a curriculum of the kind which does not badger him with difficulties but helps him to overcome them.

The conservatives, after calling for more discipline, denounce the progressives for wanting the opposite, for wanting to pamper children, cater to their interests, and leave them undisciplined. The denunciations are valid in those cases where teachers assume that anything which is not exciting and interesting to the child is therefore bad for him. This kind of teaching is not particularly progressive, it is simply bad teaching, and there are many kinds of bad teaching.

Progressive theory does not call for sacrificing intellectual achievement to emotional well-being or to superficial game-playing. It calls for intellectual activity to which the child can commit himself, it calls for practical experience with the arts, sciences and society, it calls for consideration of the child's capacity to learn and of the stage of learning which he has presently reached. It holds that the subject-matter of the curriculum must be designed in such a way that it nourishes the intellectual growth of the child and gives him a chance to handle ideas for himself.

The trouble with much of the elementary and high school curriculum is not that it has been constructed by progressives, but that it has not kept pace with the child's ability to learn. It has fallen behind that ability, partly because too little attention has been paid to the child as an individual, thus striking an average of standard material which has neither lifted the slow nor challenged the fast, and partly because too little attention has been paid to the intellectual content of the curriculum itself.

Beneath this is a deeper cause—the lack of sustained attention by scholars in the sciences and the arts to the intellectual quality of the entire public school curriculum. This is also true of the college curriculum, an apparatus consisting mostly of standard textbooks, a pre-arranged syllabus and a content which goes unrevised from year to year except for occasional changes in the textbooks. The scholars in the universities have been interested almost exclusively in their own subject-matter and not in education. Therefore the content of the curriculum in the schools and in the colleges has seldom been refreshed by the contributions of first-rate minds in contemporary scholarship.

The establishment of a strong curriculum with serious intellectual content is not a question of adding more subject-matter in order to give children more to do, or to make the curriculum "harder," so that the mind will be trained. It is a question of holding in one's mind a double image of what the curriculum must be and what it must do, just as the composer writes down what he is composing and hears his own sounds as he writes. A curriculum is a composition in just this sense, and it consists not merely in textbooks and readings, but in questions, experiences, atmosphere, attitudes, remarks, interests. A true curriculum can only be made by one who knows intuitively what his plan of education will be like in action, what kind of response it can evoke in the learner.

The educator must therefore have an image of the child in the reality of his school and his society, at a particular stage in the child's life, and in relation to all the parts of that life. Once endowed with this empathy, the educator must then be a scholar who is deeply educated in a field of knowledge he has mastered, and must be concerned that the learner be enabled to come to terms with that field. Progressive theory calls for experimental work of the kind now being done in mathematics by those scholars who are finding new ways to overcome the unnecessary difficulties standing between the child and mathematical concepts. The problem of these educators is not simply to make things easy for the child, but rather to build a curriculum in such a way that the child is able to learn from it, to enjoy it, to work with it. Out of such work comes intellectual discipline.

We must be very clear about this. It is the deepest point of difference between liberal and conservative ideas, and it goes to ultimate questions of social and moral philosophy. In effect, the conservatives say, teach the sciences, foreign languages, mathematics, history, literature, teach them straight, teach them early. There are facts, ideas and subjects which everyone must know; the children who grasp these readily should be recognized and rewarded, should be assigned to the best teachers, while the rest should be recognized for what they are—inferior in mental ability.

What the conservative is really arguing against is the compassion of the liberal, who wishes to shield the child from punitive devices, from the strictures of authority and the destructive effects of competition, both intellectual and social, until the child is strong enough to establish a true character of his own. He may then be discovered to have become tough-minded, disciplined in independence, while retaining his sensitivity.

To this end, the curriculum must be a means through which each child may become engaged in serious intellectual action; the curriculum is the substance on which his growth is nourished.

Serious intellectual effort is a joy to the child, the discovery of facts and the creation of one's own conclusions are the ultimate joys of learning. The kind of society which makes this possible is one which respects the child for what he can do and does all that can be done to help him to do it.

Projects and thought questions for part two

1. Write an essay on "Value, perspective, and philosophy in the space age."

2. Using the article by Van Dalen as a guide, write a paper concerned with the philosophy of naturalism.

3. Prepare a chart or other graphic device that shows the contrasts and interrelationships within physical education of the philosophies of idealism, realism, and pragmatism.

4. Prepare, administer, and evaluate the results of a questionnaire you have designed to identify the philosophic beliefs of a selected group of physical educators known to you.

5. Develop and give an oral report that explains your own philosophy of sport and athletic competition.

6. Write an editorial concerned with the present philosophy of physical education.

7. Define and explain the differences between a conservative, a liberal, and a progressive approach to physical education.

8. Show how physical education can help man to relate better to his world.

9. Defend Elkin's statement that physical education is an integral part of the general education program. Justify your position through references to current literature.

10. Lead a discussion concerned with physical education's contributions to the whole child.

Selected readings

Allport, G.: Becoming, New Haven, 1955, Yale University Press.

Brameld, T.: Education for the emerging age, New York, 1965, Harper & Row, Publishers.

Davis, E. C.: Philosophies fashion physical education, Dubuque, Ia., 1963, William C. Brown Co., Publishers.

Educational Policies Commission: An essay on quality in public education, Washington, D. C., 1959, National Education Association and the American Association of School Administrators.

Ehlers, H. and Gordon, C. L.: Crucial issues in education, New York, 1966, Holt, Rinehart & Winston.

Frankena, W. K.: Three historical philosophies of education, Chicago, 1965, Scott, Foresman and Co.

Hook, S.: Does philosophy have a future? Saturday Review, Nov. 11, 1967.

Kerber, A., and Smith, W.: Educational issues in a changing society, Detroit, 1962, Wayne State University Press.

Kirk, H. H.: A superintendent looks at physical education, Journal of Health, Physical Education, and Recreation 9:586, Nov. 1938.

Pullias, E. V.: The education of the whole man, Quest, Monograph I (Winter Issue), Dec. 1963.

Spencer, H.: Education: intellectual, moral, and physical, New York, 1889, Appleton-Century-Crofts.

Tanner, D.: Schools for youth, New York, 1965, The Macmillan Co.

Wolfbein, S. L.: Automation, education, and individual liberty, Teachers College Record, Oct. 1964.

Relationship of physical education to health, recreation, camping, and outdoor education

Physical education, health, and recreation have been closely allied educational fields. Undergraduate curriculums concerned with preparing physical education specialists generally require that the student take courses that will acquaint him with the other two fields. The same is true for those students preparing to be specialists in health education or recreation education. Teachers of physical education must have a comprehensive knowledge of their own field, but they must also be able to impart the fundamentals of sound health practices to their students. Likewise they must be able to give their students a background of lifetime sports—one of the essential elements in the worthwhile use of leisure time.

The health educator is concerned with instructing his students in sound health practices, with instilling proper health attitudes, and with helping them to gain health knowledge. He is also concerned with showing his students how physical activity and health are inseparable. The recreation specialist has similar responsibilities. Although physical education, health education, and recreation education are often separate and distinct areas of specialization in the college curriculum, they are not truly independent facets of the educational process.

Advances in science and technology within recent years have had far-reaching implications for physical education, health, and recreation. In the area of recreation alone, increases in the amount of leisure time has dictated the need for the recreational reeducation of many adults. Recognizing the need for expanded recreational facilities, the federal government has passed several pieces of legislation that guarantee to the public the continuing availability of vast reaches of recreational lands that might otherwise have been commercially exploited. But despite national and local measures to provide public recreational facilities, this is still the age of the spectator. Many individuals obtain their physical activity vicariously while seated in a stadium or in front of a television set. Too many spectators have lost the habit of engaging regularly in physical activity.

Many public school systems recognize the need to educate their students both inside and outside the classroom. Outdoor education is not an extension of academic subjects into a different environment. Rather, outdoor education has as one of its goals educating the young about the wonders of nature. Concomitantly, some school systems have developed extensive school camping and outdoor education programs and have found these innovations to be a vital contribution to the entire curriculum. The physical educator, the health educator, and the recreation specialist all lend their special knowledge and skill to these special programs.

The first readings in this division are concerned with health education and with the interrelationship of health education and physical education. The remaining readings are concerned with recreation, outdoor education, and leisure.

Delbert Oberteuffer discusses the relationship between health education and general education. Oberteuffer examines the reasons why health education is not stressed in school curriculums and develops a rationale for health education. Further, the author shows how opposition to health education programs can be met successfully.

Merrill Scott delineates six areas concerned with safety that are the responsibility of school administrators. Scott also identifies the need for every faculty member to realize individual responsibilities in regard to the safety of the students. Of Scott's six areas, the school playground and school athletics and physical activities are of primary importance and interest to physical educators.

The National Dairy Council provides an interesting discussion of the relationship of nutrition to physical fitness. The article shows the importance of both exercise and nutrition to physical fitness and shows why both are necessary for the athlete who desires to perform at his best.

Joseph Prendergast projects the need for educating for leisure into the future. Prendergast says that a philosophy of leisure must be developed in the present so that we can develop a nation of individuals who are adequately educated and prepared to make the best recreational use of their leisure hours. Prendergast shows the need for trained recreation specialists. The reading by Howard G. Danford, which follows that by Prendergast, gives eight of the criteria that these recreation specialists should fulfill.

Outdoor education is the topic of the article by Robert M. Isenberg. This presentation highlights the educational value of outdoor education programs and provides a description of how these programs are conducted. Physical educators often play a vital role in staffing and conducting school outdoor education programs.

Julian W. Smith, a leader in the field of school camping and outdoor education, discusses the current trend toward programs of outdoor education. Smith defines outdoor education and illustrates the numerous ways in which it is available to people of all ages. Further, the author discusses the importance of outdoor education programs for children and shows how these programs can contribute to the total educational program.

The discussion on the philosophy of leisure by Paul Weiss shows how leisure has a single definition for all people but a multiplicity of applications among individuals. Weiss points out that work and leisure are interrelated and gives examples of the many ways in which leisure time can be put to active use.

Sebastian deGrazia contends that the shorter workweek does not really increase the time given to recreation since most individuals tend to devote this time to non-recreational uses. The writer describes how the average person abuses rather than exploits his free hours.

18. Vital ties between health and education*

Delbert Oberteuffer

Editor, Journal of School Health; Former Chairman, Division of Physical Education for Men, The Ohio State University

Apparently it takes a great deal of time to develop the integrated relationship between health and education that is so vital to both. For centuries wise people have been saying that a definable relationship exists between the two which makes the contribution of each an absolute necessity to the effective development of the other.

To express this relationship in simple terms: One needs to be educated in order to develop fully one's health, and one needs abundant health to make full use of one's education. This being so, why then, in this land of literate people, do we have so much ignorance about health, so much wastage of human potential, and so much preventable distress? Why do so few live to their fullest capacity? Why do the curriculums and requirements in our education structure pay so little attention to education in and about health?

One general reply will answer all three questions: Educators have not as yet fully comprehended the situation and therefore have not as yet constructed the educational program to give full play to this reciprocal relationship.

Let's examine this thesis. But as we do so, let it be clear at the outset that the case presented can be but fragmentary with scant documentation. My credentials in health education in particular and education in general must sustain, for the most part, the positions taken.

Man has forever sought the answers to the riddles of birth, life, and death. He has never been content to be baffled or misinformed.

Always there have been those who have sought the truth and who, step by step, have made the truth available. Books are filled with the findings of those great names of yesteryear—Harvey, Jenner, Pasteur, Semmelweis, Roentgen—and those of our day—Waksman, Salk, Sabin, Enders, and others.

But people do not learn about these findings by chance. If the scientist in biology has something to say, if the physician has come upon something he wants others to know about, if the geneticist discovers a new factor in heredity, if the pathologist can save a million lives by telling people what he knows, if cancer deaths among women can be reduced by having women do something or other, then somehow people must be taught these things. The only way to get the job done in anything but a haphazard way is for society to demand that its educational system rise to meet the need—and the opportunity.

The transmission of knowledge and understanding requires teaching. This all seems so obvious, but it is at this point that the simplicity ends.

Even if we all agree that it is well for a man to enjoy good health, to conserve and develop his resources, to enjoy his marriage, to raise fine children, to escape debilitating illness, to achieve mental and physical well-being which extends over his span of years, how is he to accomplish this?

Well, for one thing, he needs to learn a great deal. He is not born thoroughly equipped with effective knowledge about desirable personal and public health practice, about human reproduction, the effects of radiation, or means of attaining emotional orientation.

He has to *learn* these and many other things. He has to *know* that he can order a

*From NEA Journal, Vol. 53, p. 57, Mar. 1964. Used by permission.

life, given a fair break from circumstance, which will be rewarding and which will bring out his potential.

In order to learn and know, he has to read and study and listen. Since he cannot recapitulate every scientific advance himself, he has to be given the synopsis or the conclusions of books, talk, and experience. And this means education—organized, planned education.

It is at this point that education as now set up in school and college has *not* accepted its responsibility to the degree the cultural influence of health education demands.

Our schools have not granted the time, the dignity, or the quality of teaching personnel needed to transmit knowledge and experience of healthful living. Our educational programs have been heavily weighted with the study about man's environment rather than about man himself. From elementary grades through college, the health education of most students remains impoverished because health education has not yet been accorded the status of academic respectability and is not yet thought of generally as an academic discipline worthy of full standing in the curriculum family.

Evolutionary change in curriculum matters is a slow process. Physical science struggled for years to gain full acceptance; so did engineering, pharmacy, and medicine itself. Home economics, agriculture, health education, and physical education have not yet fully gained it.

Reform not only comes slowly in education, but when it does come, the public or the legislature is likely to cry, "Away with the frills and newfangled ideas."

Education aimed to make people healthier has been caught up in this resistance to change. I know that some progress has been made in the development of school health education. I know that courses in health were offered even back in the nineteenth century.

I know of the heroic efforts since 1911 of the Joint Committee on Health Problems in Education of the NEA and the American Medical Association. But I also know that in thousands of schools scattered over the land health programs go barely beyond an annual lecture on temperance or an arrangement whereby students can receive the education necessary to be certified as food handlers.

I know also of required courses in health

education at the college level. Most of them are courses where the staff, with great heroism, tries to deal with 40 or 4,000 freshmen on a lecture or lecture-discussion basis. In most instances these courses carry one or two credits while the general education requirements of the first two years of many college curriculums will require ten to fifteen hours of science or social studies.

To claim a broad and liberal education without including quite a bit about one's own physical, emotional, and mental mechanisms and their care is nonsense. Despite this, however, the applications of biological science to the professional problems of living are virtually nonexistent in the curriculums of many of our prominent Eastern colleges. It is as if these faculties were actually afraid to study man himself for fear such a study might not be academically respectable!

As I see it, there are two reasons for such an attitude: Tradition stands in the way and internal institutional competition is too keen.

We inherited most of our format for education from the ancient European universities—the system of degrees, ranks, tenure, and academic prerogative; the format of curriculum; and most significant, our sense of what is academic and what is not.

Literature, mathematics, and philosophy were originally accredited, but in the last century the bars have been let down a bit to admit physics, chemistry, physiology, and a few others. Today, the gradations of respectability are clear, inflexible, obstructive, and indefensible.

Dr. Conant's report, *The Education of American Teachers*, makes no recommendation for preparation of classroom teachers in health education even though study after study has shown the paucity of preparation currently given teachers in the area of child health. Traditions born in antiquity are strong indeed.

The competitive situation within education, particularly higher education, is clear enough. Who wants to give up advantage gained? For centuries, and particularly in the last century, we have been assured that the academic subjects contained within the liberal arts and sciences represented the epitome, if not the only worthwhile kind, of education.

Early in this century, when other disciplines such as commerce, agriculture, and engineering arose to challenge this claim, the advocates of the arts struck back with violence and have succeeded fairly well in preserving the integrity of the traditional arts and science curriculum as the only respectable road to education. At every sound of the campus chimes, one hears that some things are "academic" and thus untouchable and some things are not—although in forty years of university teaching, I have not had an intelligent distinction drawn for me.

At the level of secondary education, commission after commission has sought to solve the riddle of how to deal with the millions of American youngsters in our high schools. What shall be the common denominators, if any, in secondary education? The system of evaluating high school graduation requirements by Carnegie units and the use of the College Entrance Examination Board tests have made it most difficult for a newcomer such as health education to gain any sort of prestige.

But I hope this criticism of academic practice will not be regarded as another instance of anti-intellectualism on the part of a specialist in education. It should not be so construed because *studies to enhance personal health contribute to intellectual power rather than detract from it.*

We said in the beginning that one needs abundant health to get the most out of one's education. The uninformed are likely to disagree. They take the position that intellectual activity goes on without any particular dependence upon any other aspect of the organism. They are unimpressed with the implications of psychosomatic relationships; in fact, they may deny their existence. They see no relation of physiological states to the intellect, and think of the mind or intellect as the medieval poets and philosophers did— as an independent entity to be cultivated by a rigorous schooling.

This point of view regards medical guidance, health counseling, and physical education programs as necessary nuisances that have no relation to the basic purposes of education. This point of view takes a heavy toll in student health and is responsible for much wastage of teaching effort because students may simply not be fit enough to receive the education intended for them! For example, it is really difficult for a student to learn if he is exhausted or if he has mononucleosis.

Intellectual, physical, and emotional de-

velopment all originate in and are dependent upon the nature and nurture of the cell. What influences cells influences life and learning. Furthermore and perhaps most important, all cells wherever they are bear a relationship to all other cells, are influenced by the same metabolic factors, and react to each other in very complex interrelationships.

Learning, although thought of by many as a purely intellectual process quite unrelated to fatigue, anemia, or nutrition, is *very much* related to these. The same is true of motivation. It can as easily be affected by a better functioning thyroid gland as by a stimulating teacher.

No matter how you add it up, the health of the student has a profound effect on his educational progress. Learning is the product of *all* the organisms, *all* the physiology, and *all* the structure as well as all the stimuli imposed in the classroom and community.

My point is that the individual's capacity to learn is conditioned by the quality of the cells doing the learning. Whatever learning takes place depends upon the receptivity of the organism involved. Actually, I believe the opponents of health education and physical education programs in education are the anti-intellectuals because they refuse to face or accept the truth about man.

Programs of health education and of physical education, aimed as they are toward improving the organism, are not only contributing to learning about life itself but are fundamental to any learning because they improve receptivity.

There are bright spots, of course. Dozens of large and small cities have good programs. Educators in these places have been endeavoring to give children awareness of the health problems of mankind. But only if both educational personnel and the general public are aware of the needs that such a program can meet and only if such a program arouses the same enthusiasm that now exists for the physical sciences and mathematics can education *about* man reach its full and deserved development.

That day will come. It *has* to come. To quote Norman Cousins, "There can be no more important education today than education for personal effectiveness. . . ." Education in health is at the center of such a quality.

19. School administrators must be safety-minded*

Merrill Scott

Superintendent, Scott County School District Number Two, Scottsburg, Indiana

Of all the responsibilities a public school administrator bears, one of the most worrisome is safety. This is so mainly because of two basic human feelings:

1. *Care for others.* He desires that all those under his supervision be safe.
2. *Fear.* He thinks about the dire consequences which may be his in the event of a fatality or a near fatality.

He fears the thought of being partially responsible from the purely humanitarian viewpoint, and he fears the possible results of law suits which may arise out of legal actions taken against the school district, the school board, and the superintendent.

As a public school superintendent, I see six major areas of safety consciousness to be concerned about:

1. school transportation
2. school street crossings
3. school buildings
4. school playgrounds
5. school athletics and physical activities
6. school administration and faculty

Let us consider each separately and briefly.

SCHOOL TRANSPORTATION

In an issue of the *Louisville Courier Journal,* Paul Sisco, in an article entitled "How Safe Is the School Bus?" stated that the odds are that one in 19 will be in an accident . . . . His article recounted recent school bus accidents and their causes. As state director of the School Traffic Safety Division for the State of Indiana in 1959 and 1960, I viewed with constant alarm the rising number of

*From Annual Safety Education Review, 1966, p. 1, American Association for Health, Physical Education, and Recreation. Used by permission.

school bus accidents. All of us are alarmed by these accidents and read about them with regret—but are secure in the knowledge that "it won't happen to us."

I am sure that many of you read, as I did, about the lady school bus driver in Orland Park, a suburb of Chicago, who, when her brakes failed, slammed into a loaded cement truck. Fortunately, the 46 children aboard survived. . . .One student was killed in Madison County, North Carolina, when a school bus went tumbling down a 50-foot embankment. . . . Near Flemington, New Jersey, a bus load of high school students had a wild ride down a mile long hill when the brakes on their bus failed. . . .Near Dumas, Texas, a school bus loaded with 25 students skidded 200 feet and overturned in a ditch when a set of dual wheels fell off.

However, none of these approached the Prestonburg, Kentucky, bus disaster of February 28, 1958, when a school bus smashed head-on into a wrecker, caromed over an embankment, and plunged 50 feet into a flood-swollen river. The driver and 26 children were killed in perhaps the worst school bus disaster in our country's history.

How can we avoid these accidents? The answer is not so simple. I view with favor some of the tests now being made by the National Safety Council, such as those on seat belts for school buses. We all agree, I am sure, that buses should be made of high strength steel, have special stop and signal lights, have high-visibility safety windows, and other special safety features. However, school bus operations are local operations, and standards are nonexistent or vary too widely to be an effective safety force.

As a school superintendent I submit these questions to you:

1. Should all buses be safety inspected regularly?
2. Should state and/or local police make spot checks on school buses?
3. Should all bus drivers have physical examinations each year?
4. Should standards be set on age, mental aptitude, and physical fitness for drivers?

I shall leave this area with the observation that of the 6,454 school bus drivers who operated either publicly owned, privately owned, or mixed ownership vehicles during the 1959-60 school year in Indiana, over 20 were past the age of 72!

SCHOOL STREET CROSSINGS

What a helpless and empty feeling it is to learn that a student has been killed at a school crossing. Many school superintendents have experienced that awful feeling. I shall never be able to forget one traffic accident which wiped out a car load while I was serving as a high school principal. School administrators should take every step possible to avoid these horrible tragedies. In our own city of Scottsburg, Indiana, we have recently cooperated with our mayor in assisting a governor's traffic survey team to help us with our school street crossing problems. We have initiated every recommendation made by this team of experts at a most minimal cost in dollars and cents.

I almost hesitate to use the word "expert" as it relates to safety, because the very day the first draft of this paper was written a governor was quoted in the newspapers as observing that there were more "experts" in safety than in any other field of endeavor, but the tally sheets showed the most disappointing results. Perhaps this indictment of our record is correct.

As a school superintendent I submit these questions to you:

1. How far should we go in having planned street crossing safety programs?
2. Should we heed every hue and cry about unsafe street crossings?
3. Is it possible to take advantage of every group who promotes street crossing safety?
4. Must we be concerned for *every* child who crosses the street on his way to and from school?

Permit me to leave this area by observing that some people feel that parental responsibility has not been explored and sufficiently encouraged to assist schools in this vital operation. Perhaps we, as administrators, have not even scratched the surface in planning effective, safe street crossing programs.

SCHOOL BUILDINGS

Many people consider school buildings as very safe places for students and teachers alike. Those of us who are on the scene know better. We all know that thousands of accidents—preventable accidents—happen each year in school buildings and on school property. One of the hardest jobs I have ever had in my entire life was that of state director of the Schoolhouse Planning Division for the State of Indiana in 1960 and 1961 when I worked with architects, superintendents, school boards, faculties, and others to encourage the safety angle in school plant planning. It often seemed that safety was forgotten in the hustle and bustle of preparing to build a "grand new school building."

In Indiana last year two school corporations were taken into court over school accidents. One school corporation was sued for imposing a three-day expulsion of a student who broke parking lot safety regulations. Yes, we are seeing the time-honored court admonition that "the king can do no wrong" tested in our courts today relative to schools. We cannot expect in the future to escape from liability in court cases involving schools.

I suppose nearly every classroom teacher in the United States has in his or her room each school year at least one accident which could have been avoided. Safety, like everything else worthwhile, requires planning on the part of all of us.

As a school superintendent I submit these questions to you:

1. Are we, as school personnel, responsible for classroom safety programs which will assure safety daily?
2. Are we making sure that all new school buildings being constructed have incorporated within them the latest safety features?
3. Are we afraid to enforce safety rules and regulations in buildings or around

buildings for fear of personal or physical abuse or for fear of law suits?

Allow me to repeat a comment I made in Indianapolis on April 4, 1965, while speaking to a safety-minded gathering at the Claypool Hotel. "We must, as school people, do what we think is just and prudent in each and every safety predicament, and let the people who are anxious to sue 'have their day in court' if that is what it takes to protect the lives of children—our most valuable asset in this country!"

SCHOOL PLAYGROUNDS

Simple injuries such as skinned knees we expect, even though we recognize that most of them could be avoided. But, as you well know, some not so simple injuries happen on the school playground. Why? These answers are not easy and often have many ramifications. Many authorities do not agree on what to do *after* the accident happens, to say nothing of what to do to *prevent* the accident from occurring.

As a school superintendent I submit these questions to you:

1. Can we cut down the number of playground injuries?
2. Do we play playground activities so as to avoid accident-producing situations?
3. Do we give enough thought to and have sufficient control over school playgrounds and equipment thereon?
4. Is there adequate school playground supervision at all times?

Suffice it to say that some of the real lessons of life are learned on school playgrounds and such areas deserve the best planning, execution, and supervision that is humanly possible for school personnel to give. The school administrator should give his full support to carefully planned, well equipped, and supervised playground activities.

SCHOOL ATHLETICS AND PHYSICAL ACTIVITIES

Each of us hears constant rumblings of "win at all costs" in athletics with safety and other important factors neglected. But most of us are aware that any coach worthy of the name is cognizant of safety limits within his own area. Physical education instructors are prepared today to cope with problems in their areas. Yet, human judgment is involved, and mistakes are made. Let us all hope that these mistakes of judgment are minimal in number and not due to poor planning, poor supervision, or poor equipment.

As a school superintendent I submit these questions to you:

1. Do we plan safe physical education activities for boys and girls? Are they supervised adequately?
2. Do we take the necessary precautions in intramural and interscholastic athletics?
3. Do we still have coaches who would rather win at any cost and let safety be damned?

Permit me to observe that we in public school administration have a great responsibility and opportunity to inculcate the safety-above-all thought in the minds of our teachers of health, physical education, and safety and in our athletic coaches. We must not fail a single athlete for a victory bought at the price of safety. Likewise, we must not fail any student by having inadequate safety procedures for his activity.

SCHOOL ADMINISTRATION AND FACULTY

How mindful are administrators and faculty members of safety? Are we each so hidden away in our own little closet of work that we fail to see safety in the big picture? Do we have the ability to formulate and execute plans which show the world that we are safety-minded and conscious of the needs of all the charges under our direction, control, and supervision?

As school administrators and faculty members, we would like to think that we are. Yet I am constantly haunted by the charge reportedly made by a very distinguished gentleman in the Congress when Public Law 89-10 was being passed, funded, and left to school personnel to plan, direct, and supervise. His famous or infamous—take your choice—question was, "Do we dare let educators plan such an important undertaking as this?"

20. Nutrition and physical fitness*

National Dairy Council

An interpretive review of recent nutrition research

SUMMARY

Adequate nutrition and exercise are important in achieving and maintaining fitness. Physical inactivity, improper eating habits and obesity are interrelated factors in today's health problems. The principles of good nutrition for the athlete are the same as for all persons: to eat a variety of foods—meat, milk, eggs, cheese, fish, fruits, vegetables, cereals and breads—every day and to maintain weight at the desired level. If, as the evidence suggests, a certain amount of physical activity is needed to maintain metabolic functions in a state necessary for health and to prevent degenerative processes, opportunities and education for active recreation and sports which can be engaged in over the entire lifespan are a basic physiological need.

Physical fitness is an inseparable component of total fitness for effective living. Fitness involves interrelationships between intellectual and emotional as well as physical factors. Good health, a basic component of fitness, implies in addition to freedom from disease, sufficient strength, agility and endurance to meet the demands of daily living and sufficient reserves to withstand ordinary stresses. Adequate nutrition and exercise, sufficient rest and relaxation, suitable work, and appropriate medical and dental care are important in maintaining fitness.[1]

CHANGES IN AMOUNT OF PHYSICAL ACTIVITY

In the past, when the chief source of power available for all work was muscle, physical fitness was a natural by-product of daily living.[2] The technology which has developed in the U. S., however, now deprives most people of the activity necessary for healthy physical development. In recrea-

tion as well as in work, there has been a strong trend toward the sedentary. "There are already signs of the presence of a new type of man and woman, *homo sedentarius* . . . in North America and Western Europe . . ."[3] Because of the significant reduction in muscular effort, less food is required for maintenance of desirable body weight. The lowering of the calorie allowance in the 1964 revision of the Recommended Dietary Allowances[4] was an attempt to help *homo sedentarius* balance his caloric intake with his energy output. A better solution to the problem, however, might well be the attainment of energy balance by increasing physical activity instead of, or in addition to, reducing food intake.

PHYSICAL ACTIVITY AND HEALTH

Physical activity enhances physical and mental well-being and improves physiological efficiency, as evidenced by increased endurance, strength and agility. The more demand placed on the normal heart and circulatory system to move blood to active regions of the body, the more efficient they become. Protracted exercise also increases the ability of the lungs to take in more air and to utilize a greater proportion of the oxygen in the air.[1]

Evidence from research is accumulating to show that physical inactivity is a factor in today's health problems.[1] Although the causes of obesity are numerous, and in any one individual several may be operative, there is no doubt that in many persons lack of adequate exercise is contributory.[5] Many obese subjects do not eat more, but are much less active than non-obese controls. In a group of obese men, pedometer readings averaged 3.7 miles a day, whereas the average for a control group of the same age and

*From Dairy Council Digest, Vol. 36, No. 5, Sept.-Oct. 1965, National Dairy Council. Used by permission.

occupation was 6.0 miles a day. Similarly, for obese women the average was 2.0 miles a day and for the controls, 4.9.[6] Unfortunately, as an individual becomes more obese he is likely to become increasingly inactive as his bulk and weight make exercise difficult for him, both physically and physiologically.[7] The high mortality rate associated with obesity suggests that obesity contributes to organic degeneration. A large part of this excess mortality can be attributed to coronary artery disease, vascular lesions of the central nervous system and diabetes mellitus.[2]

As requirements for physical activity in modern living have decreased, deaths and disability from cardiovascular diseases have increased. Although a causal relationship has not yet been established, a number of studies indicate that physical inactivity may be one of possibly many factors involved in the increasing prominence of coronary heart disease.[8] A study of 355 former (1901-1930) Harvard football players was made in 1958. Those who died of coronary heart disease had a greater family history of the disease and had gained more weight. Those who maintained even moderate habits of exercise were less prone to coronary heart disease. None of the 38 who continued to exercise heavily had a myocardial infarct in the 25 to 50 year period, while 25 infarcts had occurred among those who were less active.[9]

In a group of professional men who participated in 6 months of progressively more strenuous physical conditioning, there was no change in mean serum cholesterol or phospholipid levels, but a significant reduction in serum triglycerides occurred within a few hours after exercise and lasted about 2 days. The effect appeared to be cumulative. Lowering serum triglyceride levels may be a mechanism by which exercise protects against coronary heart disease.[10]

The importance of regular physical activity throughout adulthood as well as in youth should be emphasized. Finnish champion skiers who continue to exercise have a life expectancy 7 years longer than that of the general male population of Finland.[11] In another longevity study, 16 of the 18 surviving individuals over 80 years of age were regularly active.[12] Possibly because the majority of college athletes do not continue to be active after their college years, no effect on longevity has been seen in those who have participated in strenuous sports.[11]

NUTRITION OF ATHLETES

The coordination and controlled expenditure of energy required in athletic performance are matters of endowment and training and are not significantly influenced by variations in the normal diet.[13] The principles of good nutrition are the same for the athlete as for the non-athlete. The same meat, milk, eggs, vegetables, fruits, enriched and whole grain breads and cereals that are fundamental to the health of every person are needed by athletes. Larger amounts of food, of course, must be consumed so the energy intake will balance the athlete's higher energy expenditure so that he will reach or maintain the body weight which he and his coach consider will provide maximum efficiency for a given sport.[14]

There is great variation in energy expenditure in various types of athletic performance and it may be that the sources of energy differ somewhat. In types of contests requiring prolonged expenditure of energy, the intensity cannot be as great as in those of a few minutes' duration. With lessened intensity, the oxygen debt mechanism is of less relative importance. In running moderate distances, for example, the athlete may depend in part on his "recovery" period, but for long distances he must run in a "steady state" (the condition in which the intake of oxygen meets the metabolic needs of muscle).[13] The capacity for prolonged muscular work may be greater if there are ample carbohydrate stores prior to the exercise period. Athletes have been maintained for several days prior to exercise on extremely high fat diets, on high carbohydrate diets, and on mixed diets. When tested in the post-absorptive state, endurance of the athletes was greatest after the high carbohydrate diet. The investigators concluded that although carbohydrate and fat can be utilized equally well during rest and light work, an increased percentage of carbohydrate is used by athletes performing heavy work if such carbohydrate is available.[15]

The traditional practice of providing athletes during training season with large quantities of meat probably is of more value psychologically than physiologically. It has been demonstrated that protein is not metabolized in significant amounts during muscular exercise in well-nourished individuals and that athletic performance *per se* does not increase protein requirements. However, during the period of training in which muscle mass is increasing larger amounts of high quality protein are needed. Nitrogen balance studies have shown that in subjects undergoing strenuous physical training, but who had formerly been sedentary, nitrogen retention was greater on a diet providing 2 grams of protein per kilogram body weight daily than on a diet providing 1 to 1.5 grams.[13] Young athletes who are still growing require extra protein to meet these demands just as do their non-athlete peers.[14]

For the average athlete, vitamin and mineral supplements are unnecessary. All the vitamins, minerals and other nutrients he needs are assured when his meals are planned to include a good variety of foods.[14] The effect of a vitamin-mineral supplement on performance of gross motor tests by college football players and physical education majors has been investigated. The supplement or a placebo was given for a 12-week period and tests were conducted at 5 different times. No statistically significant differences were found in the performance of the experimental and control groups.[16] There has been no convincing evidence that supplements of additional vitamins of the B complex, or vitamins C or E can enhance the physical performance of well-nourished individuals.[17] During hot weather adequate amounts of salt and water should be given to replace sweat losses.[13]

MILK IN THE DIET OF ATHLETES

Milk is an important source of nutrients in the diet of athletes, just as it is for all individuals. It is one of the foods enthusiastically recommended for athletes by secondary school coaches, according to a recent national study.[18] However, several unfounded beliefs have caused some coaches to eliminate milk consumption during training and particularly on the day of competition. One of these beliefs is that milk increases the secretion of mucus in the respiratory system.[16] Increased mucus secretion during athletic performance due to the ingestion of milk has not been substantiated in any scientific study. It has been suggested that the stress of competition causes the mouth to become dry and that

activity itself causes increased mucus secretion. Further study of the relation of stress and excitement to these physiological changes is needed.[19]

Lack of endurance in athletes is sometimes attributed to "cotton mouth." This condition of dryness and discomfort in the mouth is believed by some to be caused by the inclusion of milk in the pregame meal. Studies have indicated that saliva flow and the condition of the saliva are related to the amount of perspiration and reduction in water content of the body and are not affected by the kind of food eaten prior to exercise.[20]

In a study of the effect of milk in the diet of athletes 3 levels of milk (0, 1 and 2 qt./day) and 3 levels of protein were used.[21] When milk was included in the diet, it was consumed within one hour of testing. Gross motor tests, given the last 3 days of each diet period, were selected to measure such basic components as speed and reaction time, power (vertical), strength and endurance. There were no significant differences in results on any of the diets. The author concluded that a diet adequate in every respect contributes the necessary fuel for the body to perform well in big muscle activity.[19]

The effect of eating a 500-calorie meal consisting of cereal, milk, sugar, toast and butter 1/2, 1 or 2 hours before swimming, or omitting this meal, has been studied. The subjects were experienced swimmers each of whom competed against his or her own best swimming time. It was found that the eating of a cereal and milk meal at any of the times tested prior to swimming had no adverse effects on swimming times nor in the form of nausea or stomach cramps during or after the swims.[22]

Trained trackmen participated in an investigation of the effect of milk consumption on endurance performance. During the 8 weeks of training one group consumed a minimum of 3 pints of milk a day and about 2 pints of ice cream a week. The experimental group was not permitted any milk, cheese or ice cream except in those dishes in which milk was used in cooking. While there were no differences in the training response or in all-out performance when dairy products were excluded from the diet, the intake of calcium and riboflavin fell below recommended levels.[23] Since milk is an excellent source of these as well as other required nutrients, it should be recommended in the diet of athletes.[19]

THE PREGAME MEAL

The muscular efficiency of the subject in brief periods of very strenuous exercise is dependent on energy reserves and training and not on the composition of the pre-exercise meal. Athletes frequently are under considerable emotional stress on the day of the contest and the time required for the digestion of food may be greatly prolonged. Simultaneous demands on the general blood pool by digestion and muscular activity compromise either one or both functions. X-ray studies done on days of competition have shown that a solid pregame meal may still be in the process of digestion 4 hours after ingestion, whereas a calorie-rich liquid meal has left the stomach 2 hours after ingestion.[24] Replacement of the solid food pregame meal with a liquid meal has been tried and found to be physiologically and practically sound. Muscular cramps and pregame and game time vomiting were eliminated, and strength and endurance improved.[24,25] As a general rule, the pregame meal should consist of highly digestible foods and should be consumed not less than 3 hours before the contest. Individual food preferences should be respected, as the athlete knows from experience which foods he can eat without subsequent discomfort.[15]

BIBLIOGRAPHY

1. Special Report. Exercise and Fitness. J. Amer. Med. Assoc. **188**:433, 1964.
2. Davies, C. T. M., Drysdale, H. C. and Passmore, R. Lancet **2**:930, 1963.
3. Passmore, R. Lancet **2**:853, 1964.
4. *Recommended Dietary Allowances, Revised 1964*, Pub. 1146, Nat. Acad. Sci., Nat. Res. Council, Wash., D. C.
5. Dairy Council Digest **36**(3):13, 1965.
6. Chirico, A. M. and Stunkard, A. J. New Eng. J. Med. **263**:935, 1960.
7. Auchincloss, J. H., Jr., Sipple, J. and Gilbert R. J. Applied Physiol. **18**:19, 1963.
8. Fox, S. M., III, and Skinner, J. S. Amer. J. Cardiol. **14**:731, 1964.
9. Pomeroy, W. and White, P. D. J. Amer. Med. Assoc. **167**:711, 1958.
10. Holloszy, J. O., Skinner, J. S., Toro, G. and Cureton, T. K. Amer. J. Cardiol. **14**:753, 1964.
11. Karvonen, M. J. In: Rosenbaum, F. F. and Belknap, E. L. (eds.), *Work and the Heart*, Paul B. Hoeber, Inc. Med. Book Dept. of Harper & Brothers, New York, 1959.
12. Montoye, H. J., Van Huss, W. D. and Nevai, J. W. J. Sports Med. **2**(3):133, 1962.
13. Van Itallie, T. B., Sinisterra, L. and Stare, F. J. In: Johnson, W. R., *Science and Medicine of Exercise and Sports*. Harper & Brothers, New York, 1960.
14. Upjohn, H. L., Shea, J. A., Stare, F. J. and Little, L. J. Amer. Med. Assoc. **151**:818, 1953.
15. Christensen, E. H. and Hansen, O. Skand. Arch. Physiol. **81**:160, 1939.
16. Nelson, D. O. Scholastic Coach. May, 1961, p. 32.
17. Keys, A. Fed. Proc. **2**:164, 1943.
18. Horwood, W. A. *A National Study of the Current Practices of Secondary Coaches in Recommending Diets for Athletes*, thesis, Michigan State University, 1964.
19. Nelson, D. O. The Research Quarterly. **31**(2):181, 1960.
20. Fait, H. F. *What Research Shows About the Effects of Milk in the Athlete's Diet*. School Physical Education, University of Connecticut (No date.)
21. Wilcox, E. B., Galloway, L. S. and Taylor, F. J. Amer. Diet. Assoc. **44**:95, 1964.
22. Asprey, G. M., Alley L. E. and Tuttle, W. W. J. Amer. Diet. Assoc. **47**:198, 1965.
23. Van Huss, W. D., Mikles, G., Jones, E. M., Montoye, H. J., Cederquist, D. C. and Smedley, L. The Research Quarterly. **33**(1) 120, 1962.
24. Rose, K. D., Schneider, P. J. and Sullivan, G. F. J. Amer. Med. Assoc. **178**:30, 1961.
25. Cooper, D. L., Bird, B. and Blair, J. Oklahoma State Med. Assoc. J. **55**:484, 1962.

21. The place of recreation in modern living*

Joseph Prendergast

Executive Director, National Trust for Historic Preservation, Washington, D. C.

To talk about the place of recreation in modern living is, in effect, to preview the twenty-first century. It is my belief that in the next century the central fact in the life of every individual and of the nation will be the immense amount of free time available to everyone.

The average American already has more leisure hours than working hours in a year . . . .

This is a stupendous fact, the significance of which is still hardly realized. So long as we could consider leisure only as time in which to refresh ourselves for more work, it was a manageable concept. Now we must think of leisure as the greater part of life—no longer a side show but the main event. It may well be the greatest challenge the human race has ever been called upon to face in all its 1,750,000 years.

If we can develop an ethic of leisure to guide our free use of time, we may, in fact, be well on the way to solving all our other problems. It will mean adaptation of our educational system, plus development of more and better recreation leadership, plus facilities and opportunities for lifelong activities. Given these, and a philosophy for their use, we may indeed look forward to the twenty-first century as a golden age of health, happiness, and creativity. Nor is it too much to say that if we fail in this, we fail as free men—and we may ultimately fail as a free nation.

Our first need is to develop an ethic of leisure and a philosophy which will take into account the significance of our new leisure. A leisure society *can* have high ethical values, the word "recreation" *can* include all creative and constructive activities engaged in for their own sake, but we cannot assume that the mass of our fellow citizens starts from these premises or agrees with our conclusions.

In fact, we know that many of them do not. The ethics of work—the belief that Satan finds mischief for idle hands to do—served us well when we were an expanding nation with few machines and low individual output. The concept that only work has merit is deeply ingrained in our national thinking. It will not change overnight. But change it can and must.

What will be the most potent factors bringing about that change?

I can envisage the day when our schools, down through the elementary level, will think it important to have on each staff not only teachers for its academic subjects but full time recreation leaders. They will be in charge of recreation education, including the school's extracurricular program, and will help students get acquainted with all the community resources that will provide the basis for life-long interests. "Education for leisure," which has for years been one of the stated educational goals of the National Education Association, must take on added stature and will require new emphasis in the years ahead. Education for leisure is now education for the greater part of a man's life. Educators are already devoting much time and thought to the implications of this fact.

The need for a philosophy of leisure is here and now, however. Today's adults need it as well as tomorrow's children. Recreation in modern living is already expanding to meet our increased leisure—not widely enough, not fast enough, but it is expanding;

*From Journal of Health, Physical Education, and Recreation, Vol. 33, p. 22, Sept. 1962. Used by permission.

and this in turn is reacting on our entire society. Ideas are changing, almost without our noticing, and action goes along with the ideas.

MORE LAND FOR RECREATION

For example, increased leisure is creating tremendous pressures for more recreation areas, better access to them, more effective use of the areas we have. Recreation is a job inducement, a population builder, a civic asset, a national concern.

We are now seeing a settlement of the much argued question of regional planning versus state or local planning in the river basins of our nation. Great plans are now being developed, river basin by river basin. The interesting aspect is that these are multiple-use plans. All the natural resources of each river basin are to be developed not just for industry but also for recreation. Read any plan and you will find that recreation needs have helped to shape it; recreation is now considered one of the most important uses of the land and water which make up the basins.

Recreation in today's living is anticipating and shaping tomorrow's world. And, at the same time, these physical developments are helping to reorient our thinking about leisure and recreation. As recreation looms larger in our physical planning, a philosophy of leisure and recreation may seem more important to us.

There are examples that indicate this change in thinking may already be occurring. The Outdoor Recreation Resources Review Commission was charged with determining what the American people will need in outdoor recreation opportunities in the year 2000, and how they can get them. Among other things, the Commission mended the substantial investment of federal and state funds in the purchase of land for parks and other recreational areas. The effect of the Commission's thinking was apparent even before its final report. Things are happening on the state level. New York State, for example, passed a bond issue to buy open space, parks, and recreation areas; New Jersey passed a bond issue for the same purposes; Wisconsin has a [similar] plan. Other states, including Pennsylvania and Michigan, are giving serious consideration to expansion of their outdoor recreation areas.

These land purchases already are affecting recreation in today's living. In addition, however, a pattern of action is beginning to appear which will shape the recreation of our children and our children's children.

Thinking about recreation is not limited to nonurban areas or even just to the out-of-doors. The Federal Housing Act of 1961 had a very significant section on open space, which provided funds for the acquisition of space in metropolitan and other urban areas. The Act also placed special emphasis on the provision of recreation areas in urban renewal developments and on the construction of public recreation facilities. Above all, the Act stimulated further thinking, and the development of a point of view, for it made aid for open space, urban renewal, and public recreation facilities provisional upon planning—well-thought-out, long-r a n g e planning.

Thus the tremendous new leisure of the American people is already causing physical changes through the purchase, development, and use of land for recreation purposes.

THOUGHTFUL USE OF FREE TIME

We are also beginning to realize that the social setting of our lives as well as the physical environment requires more thought, more awareness of the implications of what we do with our expanding free time.

It was natural for a nation with millions of automobiles and thousands of miles of good roads to ride rather than walk. It was natural for families who had worked hard to use a large part of their increasing income for comforts, for luxuries, and for giving their children an easier time than the parents had had. But the relentless pressures of increasing leisure have brought an increasing and uneasy sense that all this is not enough.

The high proportion of boys and girls who fail simple physical fitness tests has been accepted, and rightly, as a challenge by physical educators to teach new skills and attitudes toward physical activity. But it is also a challenge to recreation leaders. No program of fitness can be successful unless it is a program that is voluntarily carried on in leisure hours and in the years after school days have ended. Here recreation and education must work hand in hand so that American young people will not only get fit but will want to keep fit and will have available plenty of recreation opportunities where they can practice skills learned in class. Ours is a society based on free choice. The recreational approach—recognition of the joy of doing something for its own sake—is an indispensable part of a free citizen's preparation for living in today's world.

This recreational approach, so important in its relation to development of physical fitness, will be increasingly important in helping our citizens adjust to their growing purchasing power and increased leisure. Already we are seeing resistance to a shorter work week, not by industry but by workers who don't know what to do with their time when there is no boss and no personal necessity to determine what must be done. Yet, assuming we have no fighting war, the work week will inevitably get shorter.

If we can overcome inertia, we can utilize some of our leisure to develop physical fitness. Physical exercise as part of both school and recreation is a concept that is at least understood even though it may be more honored in the breach than in the observance. But creative use of our remaining free time is another matter. Here we have an education and reeducation job of stupendous proportions. If fitness is primarily a problem of the young, creativity is a problem usually associated with adults and especially with older adults.

The average older person has had a lifetime of conditioning to get his sense of satisfaction and fulfillment from paid work, or, if a woman at home, fulfillment from raising a family. Neither of these undertakings can be counted on any longer to bring a lifelong sense of purpose and importance.

How then can we help these men and women see that our affluent society must do more than supply them with an abundance of things? Educators will surely wish to increase their emphasis and refind their techniques of educating for leisure, but the field of recreation must also do something to aid those who have leisure now but no philosophy of leisure to guide them.

Here, too, a philosophy can grow out of experience. Just as Americans today are more aware of the need to preserve our national heritage of the great out-of-doors, so Americans can become aware of the joys of creativity if they have more opportunity to experience those joys or to see others experience them.

The recreational response to the need for creative use of leisure is apparent in the growing number of community art councils and art centers, in the expansion of museum programs to include the performing arts and to make displays increasingly dramatic, varied, and informative. These are hopeful developments but they are just a beginning. They must be far more widespread. Ways of bringing them to the attention of more people must be devised.

The President of the United States gave his full backing to a national movement for greater cultural and creative development.

Specifically, he urged rapid completion of the National Cultural Center, as established by Congress in 1958. The Center has responsibility for developing programs in music, drama, poetry, dance, and opera for the education, participation, and recreation of all age groups. As a national center, it will be a stimulus for the entire nation and will be concerned with the performing arts as recreation for all American communities.

The challenge of today's unprecedented leisure, however, goes beyond even the creative and cultural arts. The citizen may come to accept his role as patron and participator in the arts, but in our free society he must do more.

It has been said that democracy is government by amateurs. The remark was not meant to be complimentary, but it is true. The ultimate power in our country resides in those who are not trained in the art of government and who do not hold office for a living. The average citizen is the voter, the committee member, the force that makes or unmakes national policy; he strengthens the fabric of the state by his vigorous participation or allows it to decay through his ignorance and carelessness.

If government by amateurs is not to be a joke, we must rediscover the meaning of the word amateur—one who does something for the love of it and not for financial reward. The amateur knows what true recreation is. "Amateur" need not connote lack of skill or low performance but should connote just the opposite. The pursuit of excellence is the main part of an amateur's satisfaction.

Our Founding Fathers—Washington, Jefferson, Madison, Adams, Hamilton—were all amateurs in politics. Benjamin Franklin, for example, was a successful businessman and an amateur in government. He retired in his forty-fourth year in order to devote himself to public life. How many men in our time have stopped to think what Franklin's philosophy could mean if it were applied today to all men and not just to the few. And how precarious would our national survival have been if Franklin and others had not been joyous amateurs of statecraft, politics, and diplomacy?

The challenge of our new leisure is the challenge that Franklin boldly sought. The challenge has come to a whole generation, not merely to a few exceptional men. The measure of this challenge is the distance between the expanding boundaries of our leisure and our ability to fill the space thus provided. We might call it the leisure gap— a gap that will be with us for some time. How can we help our nation to fill it? How can we prevent leisure from being the major problem rather than the major blessing of the next century?

First of all, we must recognize the leisure gap for what it is—a challenge to both education and recreation. We must agree on the dimensions of the problem—physical, social, intellectual, spiritual—and recognize that our solution must be broad enough to encompass all.

Secondly, we must take a lesson from the experience of the planners who are saving our open space and rebuilding new cities.

Education and recreation must not be afraid to plan, and to plan together. Multiple-use schools that are also community centers; community colleges deeply rooted in the leisure needs as well as the job needs of a town or a county; recreation centers, parks, and sports areas that challenge the citizen to use what he has learned and to expand his horizons still further—all these increasingly should be the subjects of consultation and joint planning.

Third, we must use all our resources to help American citizens develop a new awareness of what recreation in their new leisure can mean, in short, a new philosophy of leisure.

I personally hope that the National Education Association, through the American Association for Health, Physical Education, and Recreation, and the National Recreation and Park Association can spearhead this undertaking. The Fourth Yearbook of the AAHPER, *Leisure and the Schools,* had some important things to say about the problems. NRPA's reports and studies provide information that is pertinent. Both organizations have always shared information, but I believe the times call for even closer cooperation. With that cooperation, we can close the leisure gap and make it the stepping stone to America's golden age—when every citizen is educated to use his leisure wisely and creatively and there are challenging, recreative opportunities for Americans of all ages, to meet all interests and all needs.

22. The marks of a professional man in recreation*

Howard G. Danford†

Former faculty member, Colorado State College

1. He is motivated primarily by ideals of service rather than by money. He is in recreation because he loves it and he would not be in any other type of work even if he could be. He believes that people, not activities or facilities, are the most important thing in the world and that the basic purpose of recreation is to enrich the lives of people. He judges the worth of an activity and everything he does in terms of what it does to people. If it hurts people the activity is bad; if it enriches the lives of people it is good. Since people are the most important thing in the world, the professional man respects all human beings and is interested in their welfare. In all his relationships with people, on his staff and elsewhere, he treats them as he would like to be treated. He is friendly and he likes people.

2. He is an educated man who has undergone a prolonged period of preparation for his work. He has a high regard for education and the educated person; he does not ridicule or belittle education. Not only is he educated with respect to *what* should be done in recreation and *how* to do it, he also knows the *why*. He knows the values which should be sought through recreation in a democracy, and he is deeply committed to democratic ideals and values. He seeks constantly to improve himself professionally. He knows that education is a continuous process which is never ended, so he reads constantly and attends professional meetings in an attempt to keep abreast of new discoveries in the sciences which underlie his field of work. He knows that no man is well educated in his particular field unless he is conversant with the fields that are closely related to his own. Therefore, he seeks to understand and appreciate the work of his professional colleagues in education, health, physical education, sociology, psychology, and others. Not only does the professional man attempt to master a body of knowledge, he also seeks to contribute what he can to this body of knowledge through research, writing articles or books, and in any other way he can.

3. He voluntarily joins his professional societies or associations, pays his dues, attends meetings, and contributes both time and energy to furthering the work of his profession and elevating its standards. When he accepts membership on a professional committee he contributes to the work of this committee to the best of his ability.

4. He conducts himself at all times in such a manner as to enhance the prestige and dignity of his profession. He knows that people judge a profession by the individuals who are in it and that undignified conduct on his part will hurt his profession in the eyes of the public. His professional life and conduct are regulated by a code of behavior based on moral and ethical principles. He is an ethical man. He is an honest, truthful, decent human being. He doesn't have to sprout wings, but he is a square shooter. He spreads no malicious gossip about his professional colleagues nor does he engage in the practice of attacking persons in related areas of work.

*From Journal of Health, Physical Education, and Recreation, Vol. 31, p. 31, Nov. 1960. Used by permission.
†Deceased.

5. The professional man seeks to exclude from the profession those who are not qualified to enter it. He is interested in the exercise by the state, or by the profession itself, or by both, of some form of control over who may enter into at least the most responsible recreation positions. He wants no quacks, frauds, or unfit individuals in the profession.

6. He is a team player, not a prima donna. He prefers cooperation as a way of life. He works with all agencies and individuals in the community on matters of common concern. He recognizes that many groups or agencies in a community have a stake in recreation and that he holds no divine charter from above granting him an exclusive monopoly on public recreation. He is not characterized by professional jealousy nor by an all-absorbing desire for credit. He is motivated primarily by the idea of public service and he understands that credit for what he does is much more likely to come as a by-product of good work than when it is sought directly.

7. He insists on high standards of excellence in his work; he is not satisfied with mediocrity but is constantly working to upgrade his professional performance. A professional person is curious, welcomes new ideas, experiments, creates, originates, and is never quite satisfied with things as they are. He is motivated by a spark of divine discontent with what has been and what is now. He seeks perfection although he never quite achieves it, for when a person believes he has achieved perfection and rests on his oars he no longer possesses this important quality of the professional man. He does not ridicule new ideas but welcomes them, studies them, and, if they are good, adopts them whenever possible.

8. And finally, the professional man in recreation enjoys life. He has fun; he is no sour-puss, no stuffed shirt, no kill-joy. For how can he lead others in joyous living if he doesn't live joyously himself? But he does not forget that the public will respect his profession and accord to it the dignity and status it should have only when its members conduct themselves in such a manner as to merit respect.

23. Education comes alive outdoors*

Robert M. Isenberg

National Education Associaton Center, Washington, D. C.

"When we studied water, we waded in it." Sixth grader Rose Anne and her classmates had just returned from a week at the Outdoor School, a regular part of the curriculum for many sixth grade children in Los Angeles County. Enthusiasm bubbled as the children described their experiences.

"We used a can and funnel to measure the rain." "We learned about things I never even heard of before."

In every school which has outdoor education as part of its regular program, children show the same honest excitement about learning. They not only discover that learning can be fun but that they learn more quickly in an outdoor setting and retain what they learn longer.

Every school is surrounded by an outdoor laboratory that offers a perennial invitation to teachers searching for ways to motivate reluctant learners, a laboratory that provides a wealth of enriching experiences for all kinds of students and an almost limitless variety of instructional materials at virtually no cost.

Providing children with opportunities to learn through firsthand outdoor experience has been part of the school program in Los Angeles, Riverside, and San Diego Counties and other counties and cities in California for nearly 20 years; individual school systems in New Jersey, Maryland, Ohio, Michigan, Illinois, Wisconsin, Washington, and Oregon have had programs in operation for at least as long. Outdoor experiences are contagious. They can find their way into various courses and classrooms.

The number of schools now including outdoor experiences in their programs of instruction is still relatively limited, but in the past year the educational potential of such activities seems to have been rediscovered. A number of Elementary and Secondary Education Act Title III projects are initiating outdoor education programs. Some communities are providing outdoor experiences as part of the local Head Start program. Some are providing them for the educationally disadvantaged under Title I. Still other schools are developing programs on their own without financial help.

What a school's outdoor education program includes and the way it is conducted depend largely upon how people locally conceive its potential and what resources or facilities are available.

Some school systems transport class groups to a park or other nature center where the regular teacher or a specialized staff directs children's activities. In Kittery, Maine, the Robert W. Traip Academy is developing an ocean center to provide experiences with marine biology and oceanography. Children in Middletown Township, New Jersey, study some of the mysteries of the ocean and the beach at the Spermaceti Cove Interpretive Center in Sandy Hook State Park. New York City children can learn about photosynthesis, soil composition, and water pollution at the High Rock Park Nature Conservation Center on the City's Staten Island.

No special laboratory is necessary, however. A nearby swamp, pond, primitive area, beach, or the school grounds are rich with possibilities for capitalizing on children's interest in nature. A rock quarry, an ant hill, a fallen tree, or a clump of grass struggling through asphalt offers opportunities for gaining insight and understanding.

*From NEA Journal, Vol. 56, p. 34, Apr. 1967. Used by permission.

One of the most stimulating instructional programs to be found anywhere—the natural science and conservation course offered to junior high students in McPherson, Kansas—operates without a special outdoor laboratory. Supplemented by occasional field trips, this program consists largely of bringing the outdoors into the classroom. Films, slides, models, collections, live specimens, and a host of books, charts, and other items fill the classroom where children work. The youngsters have a chance to observe, examine, handle, read, study, and raise questions. Resource specialists—those involved with wildlife for example—are frequent guest instructors.

An outdoor laboratory offers such an intriguing approach to science that it is difficult to understand a classroom-and-textbook-centered program in biology, geology, astronomy, botany, horticulture, or any of the aspects of conservation without one. To follow a traditional approach is simply to turn away from the kinds of teaching materials and resources that can make learning in these various subject fields a true adventure of exploration, observation, and discovery.

Using the out-of-doors gives children an opportunity to deal with real things—planting hatchery-reared trout in a river; watching the operation of a turbine as it generates hydroelectric power; discovering that some plants grow better in the shade, others, in the sunshine; observing a demonstration of the equipment used in fighting forest fires; and feeding birds in winter. In an outdoor setting, science comes alive.

Sometimes a school district develops a resource area as part of the school itself. The Southwest Licking School District in Pataskala, Ohio, has its junior and senior high buildings on an 83-acre site, 30 acres of which are woods used as a forest-land laboratory. Foreign language, home economics, art, and other class groups use this woodland area in various ways. The agriculture classes, which have planted windbreaks, built diversion ditches, and completed other conservation projects, manage the woodlot according to the best forestry management practices. The forest-land laboratory is also utilized during the summer as part of a day camp program which includes gardening, soil conservation, and biological sciences.

The Jefferson County School District in Colorado has developed an Outdoor Education Laboratory School on a 550-acre site at the foot of Mt. Evans. During the school year sixth grade classes spend a week there along with their regular teacher to study conservation, astronomy, biology, botany, creative writing, music, and art. A retired forester and a retired geologist are available as "specialists in residence."

The Highline School District in Seattle operates a camp facility in the Cascades; Frederick County, Maryland, schools utilize a camp in the Appalachian foothills near Camp David; similar facilities are being developed for the 10-county area of northern Idaho. In Snohomish County, Washington, schools have access to both Camp Silverton in the mountains and a marine laboratory on Puget Sound.

Schools which provide a camping experience for children usually give just as much emphasis to the personal and social development of individual youngsters as they do to the science-related activities. For many children, attending school camp is their first experience in group living outside the family. For some, everything about attending camp proper rest, balanced diet, fresh air, happy surroundings—may be a new experience.

By sharing responsibilities in the camp setting, children are involved in a type of democratic living and cooperation that frequently produces observable behavior improvement after they return to home and school. Teachers who accompany their classes to camp are often amazed by how a week of camp activities can draw out the withdrawn, enlist the cooperation of the uncooperative, and broaden the interests of the self-centered.

Perhaps the greatest contributions the outdoor environment can make are in the development of aesthetic values. Children develop a perceptiveness that can bring the sounds and beauty of nature to life in their expressions of art, music, and drama. They respond in paint and color, sound and play, each in his own way.

Children also appear to be able to express themselves more easily when they describe real things. All experiences become background for reading, for understanding literature, and for writing.

Outdoor learning experiences are appropriate for all children. A third grader uncovering a nest of turtle eggs is no more excited than is a blind student who "sees" a plant through touch and his teacher's description. In a camp situation, severely mentally retarded children have demonstrated that they can adjust, feel comfortable, and respond even with a strange new teacher; fear and uncertainty disappear. The same camp situation can fit the needs of a science honors group whose members can pursue individual research projects.

To capsulize descriptions of programs is to trim away their color and disguise their depth. A more detailed accounting of what teachers and children actually do in any of the programs mentioned above, how they work together, and how these experiences relate to broad educational goals would emphasize a most important reality: *Outdoor education is not a specific course or separate area of study; it is a method of teaching.* The rich resources of nature and outdoor activities can apply to all levels in all subject matter areas.

24. Outdoor education for lifetime interests*

Julian W. Smith

Professor, College of Education, Michigan State University; Director, AAHPER Outdoor Education Project

Children are attracted to the outdoors as ducks to water. Today millions of children are being deprived of living close to the land as their forebears did. The only way they will have their heritage of learning and living in the outdoors is to make outdoor experiences a part of the educative process. In response to this need there is an emerging emphasis in education currently termed *outdoor education.* In the broadest sense it means education in the outdoors for curriculum improvement and enrichment, as well as education for the outdoors with reference to acquisition of interests and skills for understanding and enjoying outdoor resources. While these two aspects of outdoor education cannot be separated any more than learning and play, it is the purpose to identify here some of the outdoor experiences that contribute to one of education's major objectives—the wise use of leisure time or, more appropriately in today's living, the constructive use of time.

Much has been said but too little done in the implementation of this increasingly important objective. An article in the *NEA Journal*[1] substantiates this statement and places the results of the survey at the bottom of the list in terms of achievement. The yearbook of the American Association of School Administrators[2] lists *education for leisure* as one of the imperatives of education.

A glance at the current recreation scene in the United States shows that millions of Americans are turning to the outdoors for adventure, relaxation and escape from tension. The Outdoor Recreation Resources Review Commission predicts that the number of people seeking outdoor recreation will increase sharply in the next few years.[3] Many people lack appreciations and skills necessary for gaining maximum satisfactions in outdoor recreational ventures and thus outdoor education is not only timely but urgent. The quality of leisure may well determine the rise or fall of our democracy and culture.

Outdoor education experiences are within reach of nearly every community. There are a wide variety of learning opportunities or "teachable moments" in the elementary school curriculum whereby children may acquire lifelong interests that contribute to the constructive use of time. Beginning with outdoor-related classroom experiences and extending to education beyond the four walls into nature's laboratories, the imaginations of children can be stimulated and learning enhanced with new horizons for creative recreational living. Appreciation of natural beauty, conservation concepts, lifelong interests in plant and animal life, and outdoor sports and their component skills can be learned during the early years.

Some of the activities and outdoor settings which have great potential for developing outdoor interests and skills for the constructive use of time are briefly described.

*From Childhood Education, Journal of the Association for Childhood Education International, Washington, D. C., Vol. 44, p. 79, Oct. 1967. Used by permission.

[1]"A New Look at the Cardinal Objectives of Education." *NEA Journal* (January, 1967), pp. 53-4.
[2]American Association of School Administrators, *Imperatives in Education* (Washington, D. C.: AASA, 1966.)

[3]Outdoor Recreation Resources Review Commission, *Outdoor Recreation for America* (Washington, D. C.: U. S. Government Printing Office, 1962.)

ADVENTURES IN OUTDOOR SETTINGS

Beginning with short trips on the school site and extending into the community, many of the basic skills leading to enjoyment of scenic beauty, hiking, picnicking, outings, family camping, and outdoor skills can be learned by children. Some special types of settings include:

School gardens and farms. Planting seeds and shrubs and watching them grow are of great interest to children. Gardening and landscaping are among outdoor education programs which have lifelong values and are activities which can be conducted by schools and recreation departments. In Battle Creek, Michigan, gardening and farming are among the popular activities in the elementary grades conducted at the Schools' Outdoor Education Center. Flower gardening and landscaping are other examples of outdoor activities which have recreational value. Farming and rural living—pioneer and modern—hold great fascination for children and increasing numbers of school systems are acquiring farms for outdoor laboratories. Many outdoor education activities can be conducted in these settings, including observation and care of farm animals and participation in simple farm operations.

Parks and nature centers. In many communities there are outdoor areas and facilities, such as local parks, nature centers, zoos, museums and wildlife sanctuaries, which can be used for outdoor education by schools and recreation agencies. In the larger cities particularly, such resources make it possible to provide outdoor experiences for large numbers of children who otherwise would not have opportunities to get outside the cities in which nearly three-fourths of them live.

Outdoor schools. The use of camp settings, whereby children and their teachers spend a period in an "outdoor school," provides a wide variety of recreational living experiences. For younger elementary groups, a one- or two-day period is often possible, while the later elementary grades usually spend a school week in the camp. There are more than 1,000 school districts in the United States which provide this type of outdoor education experiences. Hiking and exploring, cookouts, rock collecting, nature arts and crafts, fishing, archery, compass games are examples of outdoor activities appropriate in the camp setting.

PHYSICAL EDUCATION AND RECREATION PROGRAMS

Many of the simple, but basic, outdoor recreation skills can be taught in physical education classes, after school, and in recreation. They range from hiking on trails, outdoor cooking and nature games for the young to fishing, archery, marksmanship and gun safety through the use of air rifles, skiing, tobogganing, boating and other activities for the later elementary grades. Outdoor clubs are particularly effective in after-school and recreation programs, including cane pole clubs, air rifle clubs, outing clubs, and junior conservation organizations. Such activities often involve parent participation which helps stimulate family interest in the outdoors.

NATURAL PLAY AREAS

Many of the opportunities for nature-related play activities can be an important part of outdoor education for children. In the past little imagination has been shown in the development of school sites and park areas that would help develop outdoor interests and skills as well as contribute to physical growth of children. Some fine activities are: simple nature trails; trees to climb; bridges to cross; swinging ropes that resemble natural vines; small caves; shallow streams and pools for wading and floating toy boats; fishing ponds; cement or plastic models of animals of the area; and tree houses. A small area for a "rumpus room," where children may construct simple shelters and work on camp crafts, could be planned. With rotation and plantings, nature will quickly restore the area. These and similar facilities would excel and be more popular with children than most of the mechanical gadgets and apparatus usually found in city playgrounds and parks and would stimulate outdoor interests and appreciations.

Outdoor experiences are important components in the "growing up" process. It can no longer be taken for granted that, somehow, today's children will have opportunities for outdoor learning and living. Outdoor education must be planned and be a part of the process of education. While such programs as described are not a panacea for the ills of society, outdoor education can add a dimension to the education of this generation of children and youth who, like their forbears, may find "great good places" close to the land and under open skies.

25. A philosophical definition of leisure*

Paul Weiss

Sterling Professor of Philosophy, Yale University

Leisure time is that portion of the day not used for meeting the exigencies of existence. No one has leisure who has no time he can dispose of as he will. Infants, the seriously ill, and those just managing to live on a subsistence level therefore have no leisure time. All their energies are devoted to the task of living. Slaves of the life they live, their rest and play are only occasions for recuperation and preparation, pauses in a single activity.

Leisure time is made possible by work, not a time in which work is made possible. It is therefore distinct from recreational time. Recreational time is useful time, a period when men are to be made ready, through relaxation and rest, for work which is to follow.

Leisure time is a free time subject to two restrictions. It should not preclude the performance of necessary work. If it did, it would be self-defeating, for work makes it possible. It must not be used for the sake of work; it is not a means for work, itself a means to some other end. It is a separate period in which no work is done.

The rich and the uninstitutionalized recipients of public charity have maximum leisure time. They need spend only a minimum period on tasks essential for the continuation of a healthy existence. Most of their day is unrequisitioned by nature or society. It is theirs to waste in idleness or to spend in some enriching activity.

Most men have leisure time somewhat below the maximum. Its amount depends on two factors—what they accept as necessities and the circumstances in which those necessities are to be provided. An unnecessary luxury for one is indispensable for another. Because men differ on what it is to be a man, they differ on what they accept as necessities.

We all live in a society, in various subdivisions of it, and in terms of some peer group—which may not be our own but one superior to it. Depending on the place we are or aspire to, existence makes different demands on us. These demands might be easily met, even when they are multiple and beyond those which the majority attends to or can satisfy. And, when few and minimal, they may, if the times are unpropitious, take up all one's thoughts and energies. In periods of peace and ease, the demands men feel called upon to meet increase in range and number without a necessary shortening of their leisure time. In war, in crises, when cataclysms overwhelm, it may take an entire day to meet the minimal needs that a day's bare living defines.

It is sometimes thought that maximum leisure time can be made available by providing the most favorable conditions for satisfying bodily needs. Such an approach has the advantage of making use of a single, universally applicable idea of man (that is, a biological being), of a useful conception of the exigencies of existence, of what is needed in order that men may live in health, and of a comprehensive and flexible meaning for leisure time (that is, the time that remains after bodily needs have been provided for). It also allows one to recognize the fact that, no matter how precious the goods of civilization are, they are not as necessary for man's being as are food and drink, shelter and rest. Still, it would be foolish to overlook the fact

*From The Annals of The American Academy of Political and Social Science, Leisure in America: Blessing or Curse? Monograph 4, Apr. 1964, (Philadelphia, Pennsylvania) p. 21. Used by permission.

that man has a mind and a will as well as a body; that he has emotions, drives, ambitions, hopes; that he has a personality which needs development and direction and a promise that he ought to fulfill if he is to be a whole man.

There is more justice in taking a man to be essentially one who ought to meet intellectual, spiritual, and emotional demands as well as biological demands. If we take that view, we will then have to say that leisure time is available only after one has satisfied the minimal conditions for having and using a genuine human mind, personality, self, and body. Unfortunately, no one knows just what these minima are, and, because so few people do anything to see to it that they have and use not only a body but a mind, personality, and self as well, comparatively few could be said to have any leisure time at all. Men set different values on what is available after the bare means of subsistence have been provided. They have different minima which they think must be met before they can take themselves to have any leisure time. However, they differ on these questions not as individuals but, rather, as members of different classes.

Men, by virtue of a similarity in age and education, financial condition and interest, make up distinct classes in which there is a concern for rather common values. Most laborers have a common set of necessities they feel it incumbent on them to meet; their ages, education, financial state, and interest, and therefore their necessities, have somewhat the same range. Most executives are older, have more education, are financially more secure, and have wider interests than the laborers. Many things that the laborers ignore are, for the executives, essential parts of a minimal standard of decency. Only after these have been accounted for do the executives feel they have leisure time. The amount of leisure time for both classes might be more or less equal precisely because each acknowledges distinctive necessities above the bodily which must be met before leisure time is available. In the same amount of leisure time, they will do quite different things. Evidently no program or policy will have much value or effect which ignores the different classes men constitute and instead tries to concern itself with the leisure time common to all.

The problem of obtaining leisure time is, in root, the problem of the allocation of only part of one's day to necessary work. This each individual can determine for himself, once he escapes from circumstances which require him to devote all his time to providing necessities for his type of life.

With the abolishment of slavery, child labor, and peonage, with the increase in protective devices, the destruction of the sweatshop, the introduction of a shorter work week, social security, annuities, and pensions, almost all working men have a greater leisure time available to them than their parents did. Some, without appreciable gain in ability or opportunity, set their sights higher than their parents had and, as a consequence, have less rather than more leisure time at their disposal; some of them spend their energies trying to meet the minimum conditions of a life beyond their capacities and are therefore without any leisure time. Others are in a somewhat similar state because they are less gifted than their parents were, and a few others, having settled for a life more limited than their parents', may find themselves with a great deal of leisure time, even though circumstances may not be much different for them than they were for their parents. The children of moderately successful immigrants sometimes take this last alternative. They abandon the ambitions of their parents to settle for their achievements, thereby making possible a greater leisure time.

AVAILABLE LEISURE

It is possible to be freed from the pressures of daily life and still not have a leisure time. This occurs when one has no interest in leisure, no ability to make use of the free time, is subject to conditions which are not propitious, or lacks the facilities which enable him to express his interests, make use of his abilities, and take advantage of the conditions.

There are some men so absorbed in the activities of daily practical life, that they have no interest in anything else. They have no hobbies and no curiosity. They want to keep themselves occupied in what they always do. Given a shorter work day or work week, vacations, release from duties, they become depressed, forlorn, unhappy, awaiting the passage of time so that they can return to their work. Leisure time for them is a burden, something to be disdained, feared, and denied.

There are others who have sufficient interest in matters which can be pursued only in a leisure time but who lack the capacity or ability to engage in these. Interested in reading, they are comparatively illiterate; interested in the arts, they are rather uncultivated or insensitive; interested in new experiences, they are somewhat timid or unimaginative. As a result, they become frustrated. Leisure time for them is a period of exposure, and sometimes of self-discovery, when they are anxious, anguished, and defeated, gaining little except an awareness of their limitations and comparative inferiority.

It is possible to have both the interest and the ability to make use of leisure time and yet be prevented by circumstance. Interested and able to fish, the weather may not be suitable or there may be no lake or river nearby. Interested and able to enjoy the theater, one may be too far from any playhouse or theater group.

Interest, abilities, and conditions may all be adequate and still no leisure time may in fact be available because there are no facilities making possible its use. The fisherman needs his rod and net; the musician needs his score and instrument. It is foolish, of course, to provide these facilities for men who have neither an interest nor an ability to make use of them or under conditions where their use is difficult or impossible, but it is cruel to refuse to provide facilities for men interested and able to make more than a minimal use of their surplus energies.

A realistic program regarding the use of leisure time takes account of the nature of man's interests and abilities, what it is that the conditions permit, and what facilities can and will be provided. But, because it is true that not all interests are equally valid, all men fully developed, all conditions equally desirable, or all facilities readily obtainable, it is essential that such a program be guided by an idea of the proper objective to be obtained through the best use of leisure time. It is not a time when men should be occupied with or encouraged to engage in trivialities.

Leisure time, paradoxically, can be best used only if some leisure time is used up in the preparation of a man for leisure. The awareness, for example, that men's interests need awakening, refinement, expansion, and direction points up the necessity for an educational program. That program involves an incursion into available leisure time. Similarly, men need training and opportunity to exercise their powers before they are able to have abilities for making profitable use of a leisure time. Men are then once again required to use up some of their leisure time getting ready to use leisure time. Such preparation is work; it serves to meet necessary demands for a life of a certain kind. If the preparations are extensive, one will end with the paradox that all one's leisure time will be used up in getting ready for a more effective use of leisure time. The escape from this difficulty is, obviously, to have a good deal of the educating and training provided early in life and to envisage ways of making use of leisure time which will require little education and training beyond that provided during school days.

The enterprise of making use of leisure time requires not only those who will participate in it but those who make it possible through work. The altering of conditions and, particularly, the provision of facilities require the concentrated thought and energy of men who are interested in making maximal leisure time available to others. They must be supplemented by men who see to it that the time is used most advantageously. The former work to reduce the time and energy which the work of others consumes— thereby leaving a larger period for leisure. The latter work at seeing that the time and energy thus made available are used well. Both types of work, to be most successful, should produce the desired results with maximum efficiency—that is, with the least amount of time and effort. Their work involves knowledge of what men want and ought to want, what they can do and what they can be taught to do, no less than it involves a concern for the conditions and the facilities for the use of the time. No one can claim to have this knowledge. Moreover, those who are primarily involved in the work of making this knowledge have practical importance are in no position to know just what the ultimate outcome of a leisured life is or ought to be. All workmen have goals beyond themselves and their work, set by someone else. In industry, it is the executive branch and the market that decide what the workman is to do; in the world of leisure, one must turn instead to those who make it their task to understand what a man is, ought to do, and ought to become.

THE USE OF LEISURE TIME

Leisure time has no "use" if by "use" one intends to refer to what is only a means to some external end. It does not have a use so far as it is spent in harmless pleasure, card games, spectator sports, amateur theatricals, light reading, and the like. These may even enable a man to do better work subsequently, but they need not be engaged in for that purpose. They are to be pursued in leisure time because they are good in themselves. They are simple joys, yielding some self-knowledge and insight. One's grasp of oneself and other is sometimes deepened then. But, usually, they offer only pleasant moments set over against the rest of the day. Leisure time is better used when it promotes an end which is then and there being realized. A life is no mosiac of periods of leisure and work but a unity in which there should be moments in terms of which the rest gains meaning and value. In leisure time, one ought to engage in activities that are good in themselves and good for what is good in itself. What are such goods? How many are there? How can we discover them?

The questions are best answered in reverse order. We can discover the goods by noting the nature of man's promise, then isolating the activities which are complete in themselves because they are fulfillments of that promise, and finally selecting from these the activities which promote further fulfillment because they are internally variable and have an extended field of operation. There are as many of these activities as there are basic subdivisions of man, diverse channels through which he makes himself manifest. Among these goods we must surely number health, knowledge, self-expression, character formation, personality, and self-adjustment.

(a) When in health, we act without impediment in the use of our energies and in the selection of our goals. The having of health is a good in itself; it gives tonality to the entire life and all one does. But a vital health goes beyond this. It is not only enjoyed but employed to make its continuance and increase possible. The result is promoted by engaging in participational sports and salubrious exercise.

(b) Knowledge is itself a good. He who knows has laid hold of what is not himself and thereby has added other realities to his own, so as to become more perfect, more complete. When the knowledge is merely factual, a tissue of items of information, it is merely good in itself; when it is guided and controlled by principles of inquiry, a lively curiosity, general rules, it becomes a stronger form of knowledge, grounding the possibility of further knowledge. It is the function of galleries, museums, libraries to · help men share in this kind of knowledge in their leisure time.

(c) The arts offer us final goods, to be enjoyed for what they are. Without losing this value, they can be engaged in actively, to make possible a greater range and sensitivity in the arts. No one knows what capacities one has in these directions until one has experimented with multiple media, techniques, instruments. A leisure time is well used if men will not only enjoy the arts but pursue them.

(d) We rarely have an opportunity to put ourselves to the test. We exercise our wills occasionally and then in limited and somewhat familiar circumstances. But virtue is a habit, achieved through the repetition of acts of virtue. Many virtues intertwined constitute a good character. This is a good in itself. It could be made to ground the achievement of still other virtues, still better character. This is done in leisure time by giving men the opportunity to test themselves in adventures with nature, with one another, and in themselves. Hikes, climbs, contests, explorations, endurance trials, and the like are ways of achieving the double end of having and producing character in leisure time.

(e) The personality is the person made manifest. It is not a matter of agreeableness or charm but rather of a self-acceptance with an acceptance of others as being of equal significance. It is to be oneself in oneself together with others who are then and there helped to be themselves. The result is excellent men severally and together. Celebrations, rituals, communal activities, and, above all, the living in the light of what one takes to be a final assessment by God not only sustain and enrich the personality but guide one toward its enrichment. All religion, with the exception of that which is practiced by the "professional" religious, is for leisure time. We turn it into work when we engage in magic or convert our prayers into petitions.

(f) Religion is also one of the avenues through which men find themselves and learn how to adjust to themselves and to one another. This outcome is also promoted by engaging in common enterprises. But it is most readily promoted by activities which make for the concretionalization of the common myths and ideologies. When men sing and dance together, when they tell stories and exercise their imaginations, they provide frames in which each one can find a place. When their self-adjustment serves as a spur to a deeper and firmer mastery of themselves by themselves and in relation to others, self-adjustment becomes a good in itself which is also good for itself.

In each one of these ways, leisure time becomes a time when men are at their best, making it possible for them to maintain that state in the future. When they return to work, the level of maturity and control that they have managed to reach in leisure will affect the tone of what they then do. Though the enhancement of one's work is not the objective of leisure time, work is an inevitable beneficiary, but only because and so far as it is being engaged in by a more complete man.

The excellence of the activities engaged in during a rich life of leisure makes it desirable to continue them at other times. It is for this reason that some men reverse the usual attitudes toward work and leisure and work mainly at that which is a continuation of what they do when they have leisure. And so we get athletes, scientists and philosophers, artists, saints and ethical leaders. These men live unitary lives in which the excellence obtainable during leisure characterizes the work in which they engage. That work is primarily occupied with the same ends that concern them during leisure, but, even when these men are forced to attend to the exigencies of bare existence, they do so in a spirit which leisure time alone made possible. These men offer us models of what we are to do with our lives. In their different ways, they tell us to find that kind of work which continues the activities that it is desirable to carry out in leisure time and to make everything else we do be permeated by the greatest values achieved during that time.

Leisure, then, is the time when men can be at their best, making it possible for them to make the rest of their day as excellent as possible—not by enabling them to work with more zest or more efficiency but by enabling them to give a new value and perhaps a new objective to whatever is done. The good life is a life in which a rich leisure gives direction and meaning to all else we do.

26. A tale of the times*

Sebastian deGrazia

Research Director, The Leisure Study Research Staff, The Twentieth Century Fund

The great and touted gains in free time since the 1850s . . . are largely myth. We could have approached the problem at the other end, by questioning the figure of a 70-hour work week in the 1850s. The compilers of that figure, when they published it, were careful to state its problematical aspects. It has been a popular figure; no one has raised a doubt about it, not even those the authors themselves raised. Besides clutching to our bosom the pretty statistic, we have made other mistakes. I have pointed out that we calculate free time by the decline in the work week. This is a strange way to keep books. It is like counting each year that medical science snatches from death not just as another year of life, but as a year of happiness. Death is so much feared that the mere sparing of life is regarded as beatitude. And work, it seems, is so oppressive that any time saved from it is regarded as freedom. The figures here, too, work out comfortably for those who wish to see or portray the United States as a lush playground.

Why should free time be calculated this way? Instead of considering it the opposite of time on the job why not first decide what it is and then add it up? Had we done so, we would not have needed a shaky figure for 1850. When Americans are asked why they would like a few hours, a half day, a day more of free time, they answer typically that they could then get the shopping done, or take the children to the dentist, or replace that worn-out weather stripping on the back door. They mention such unfree things because they assume "free" means "off-the-job." The word leisure has turned into the

phrase free time, and the two are now almost interchangeable. We have slipped backward to the level of ancient Greece before Plato, when *scholē,* too, meant either leisure, time or free time. It was through the efforts of the philosophers that leisure found its identity. Today the benefit of their thinking is largely lost to us.

Why should this confusion in terminology continue to exist? Does anyone benefit from it? In a way everyone benefits from it. The confusion helps us to think of our life as the best of existing or possible worlds. Industrialization gives us not only work and many other good things; it gives us the gift of leisure, that is, free time, more free time than ever this hitherto backward old world has seen. It is the signal for a new era, a new way of life, a tribute to freedom and democracy and the fruits they have borne us. Only industrialism and democracy could ever have produced such a marvel. If people somehow feel that this leisure is not passing their way, it is easy to show them how wrong they are. Cite the facts, in leisure hours gained; compare today's leisure with 1850 or 1900. They can go on thinking they have lots of free time and wondering why they do not. Perhaps this makes each person feel petulantly virtuous; he believes all his fellow Americans are having a gay old snap of it while he works like a dog and never has a moment's free time.

We have seen where most of these hours have gone. Free time can perhaps be converted into leisure, but this is only a chance, though an important chance. We should also have pointed out that the country or century or group used for comparison with today's free time makes a lot of difference.

Steelworkers a hundred years ago worked

*From Sebastian deGrazia, Of Time, Work and Leisure, A Twentieth Century Fund Study (New York, 1962). Used by permission.

a 12-hour shift, 7 days a week; miners rarely saw the sun in winter. So far we have made our chief comparisons with this one earlier setting. The time was 1850, the place the United States. It was a point from which we had some statistics to go by. Marking a century's distance, it also lent an ample perspective. Moreover, since we were not citing Greece or Rome or some other foreign country, we did not have a patriotic bias to contend with. The only bias we might have had was a progressive one: we might have wanted to show how much progress has taken place since then in these United States. Having skirted that danger, we can now choose other times and places for comparison.

Instead of ancient Greece, let us consider modern Greece for a change, a country not yet fully industrialized. Most of the population is agrarian, living in villages. The intense work of cultivating and harvesting takes only a few weeks. Outside of these periods Greek farmers have an evening with ample spare time. They pass it sitting in the village *cafeneion,* reading papers, talking politics, gossiping, playing backgammon, and just leaning back watching the passers go by and the evening close in on the square. By custom the women cannot hang around the *cafeneia,* though they can stop in to buy something to take out. Their time of talk and gossip is while drawing water from the fountain, while working in the village laundering pool, while marketing, and in and around church. Except at the market, the men are conspicuously absent from these feminine gatherings. They usually do not go to church unless it is a holiday.

In the more populated towns the schedule is not much different. People rise with the sun, the streets bustle with women buying food and men on their way to work. As the morning goes on, the streets empty. In early afternoon, there is a briefer flurry; then the shops close, everyone goes home to eat and sleep. Another brief flurry in late afternoon. Some of those who went to work in the morning return to their labors; some do not; the government offices close in the early afternoon. Between seven and eight o'clock in the evening the streets and squares repopulate themselves. The cool of the day or the relaxation of twilight brings everyone out. The promenade is on. Crowds move through the town, from one end to the other and

back and back again, walking, talking, stopping, in motion once more. Children play, boys and girls divide off, tease and flirt. By nine-thirty or ten the lights go out, everyone is back home, and the town drifts to sleep until the light of rosy-fingered aurora touches on house walls. As in the villages, the coffee houses are numerous and well-frequented. No business presses on the men who sit there. Those who cannot afford the tariff sit on curbs, benches, and monuments. A few cents for coffee rents a table at least for half a day.

Do we have such leisureliness here? Some may say we do, that one can find, specially in the rural South, the kind of front-porch life we all once had fifty or one hundred years ago. Undoubtedly, today one could find places in the United States where life still moves at a pace similar to that of the 1850s, but they are isolated instances of something that was once general.

If instead of to the 1850s we go farther back into the Middle Ages, a long period of ten varied centuries, what do we find? The amount of free time would be even more difficult to estimate than that of a century ago, were it not for the fact that the years typically went by according to a calendar of holidays. It varied from place to place. The number of holidays during the year seems commonly to have been about 115, to which the inviolable 52 Sundays had to be added, making a total of 167 days. Even serfs and slaves had many of the same holidays. One hundred and sixty-seven days a year amounts to over three days a week. Converted to a week with work days 12 hours long, longer even than in the frontier days of 1850, the hours come to 45.6 a week—worked at a tempo closer to that of the 1850s than to the present. The average does not include market days, which usually were also days of no work. Not bad for dark medieval times. And we are talking about peasants, not just about nobles, kings, and patrons.

In Rome working and nonworking days went in the ratio of about 2 to 1. Much depended on the number of public games. At the end of the republican period, there were seven sets of games occupying 65 days. In Greece at about the same time, the late first century B.C., according to Strabo the geographer, the Greek calendar had developed into a complicated catalogue whose fêtes and holidays exceeded its working days. Rome's own calendar within a century or two began to resemble the Greek. By the middle of the second century A.D., Roman games took 135 days, and by the middle of the fourth century as many as 175 days. In republican times the games lasted only part of the day; they gradually began to take up the whole day from early morning onward. At the later period they went on into the night in many cases, requiring artificial illumination.

Apart from exceptional periods of brutal transition, each community weaves its work and nonwork fabric together. Comparisons in our favor are delusive. Since 1850 free time has not appreciably increased. It is greater when compared with the days of Manchesterism or of the sweatshops of New York. Put alongside modern rural Greece or ancient Greece, though, or medieval Europe and ancient Rome, free time today suffers by comparison, and leisure even more.

Projects and thought questions for part three

1. Develop three key concepts for a co-ordinated elementary or secondary school program in physical education and health education. Show how each concept is of value to the student.

2. How would you suggest that health education become a more vital part of general education?

3. Chair a debate on the statement, "Resolved: Physical educators should be responsible for health instruction on the secondary school level."

4. Survey a local community to determine to what extent the safety of schoolchildren is a concern. Draw up suggestions to improve or modify any questionable conditions you may discover.

5. Survey the public school system in your community to determine to what extent education for leisure is taking place.

6. Using Danford's eight criteria, develop your own qualifications for professionals in physical education.

7. Develop and deliver an oral report that explains how a camping experience contributes to the education of the child.

8. Develop a course outline on a selected level for a school program in outdoor education.

9. Explain how you as a physical educator can heighten your students' awareness of nature and the world outdoors. Show the goals and objectives you would propose for your program, and describe the methods you would use to achieve them.

10. List the responsibilities of the physical educator, the health educator, and the recreation specialist in a school camping and outdoor education program.

11. Write an essay that refutes deGrazia's hypothesis. Justify your argument by reference to current research and literature.

12. Tell how you use your leisure time at present. Project your personal use of leisure 5 years into the future, taking into account the technologic discoveries that may emerge.

Selected readings

Dulles, F. R.: A history of recreation, New York, 1965, Appleton-Century-Crofts.

Erickson, E. H., editor: Youth: change and challenge, New York, 1963, Basic Books, Inc., Publishers.

National Collegiate Athletic Association: The relation of physical and health activities to the academic program, Round Table Conference, 1935, National Collegiate Athletic Association Proceedings.

Phenix, P. H.: Values in the emerging American civilization, Teachers College Record 61:335, Apr., 1960.

School Health Education Study: Synthesis of research in selected areas of health instruction, Washington, D. C., 1963, National Education Association.

Williams, J. F.: The high school curriculum, New York, 1956, The Ronald Press Co.

Ziegler, E. F.: A philosophical analysis of recreation and leisure, Quest, Monograph V (Winter Issue), Dec. 1965.

Changing concepts of physical education

Physical education has a long and fascinating history within which there have been many shifts of emphasis. Some of these changes have been startling, while others have been more subtle and thus have evolved almost unrecognized by the vast majority of physical educators.

From the quest of early man for survival, to the militarism of later years, and more recently to the emphasis on physical fitness, physical education has constantly been adding new pages to its history. Presently there are several new chapters being written. One of these chapters is the growing emphasis on movement education.

While it is undeniably essential that the physical educator understand the history of his profession and that he relate this history to the educational system in his own country, it must be remembered that physical education is not a national but an international process. One of the predominant international features of physical education is Olympic competition. Further, many of the new ideas in physical education, such as movement education, received their initial impetus in the schools of Europe.

The readings in this division cover a broad range of topics concerned with the changing concepts of physical education and with the new trend toward movement education programs. Each of these readings has been selected for its scope and depth of coverage in one of these important areas.

Franklin Parker traces the history of sport and play in relation to cultural and social customs beginning with the time of the Puritans. Parker shows how early technologic advances are often directly related to sports. The article concludes by considering man's need for the activities of physical education.

Robert H. Beck, an educational historian, compares Greek education and physical education with health, physical education, and recreation today. Beck points out the similarities and divergencies between the Greek and the modern era.

An historical research study by Norma D. Young attempts to discover if football was played by the early Greeks and Romans. This report is based on a survey of the literature and a comprehensive study of etymology. The researcher could not find conclusive evidence concerning the playing of football, but she did discover several references to games of the soccer type.

J. Edmund Welch discusses the impact of Edward Hitchcock, one of the physical education leaders in the late nineteenth and early twentieth centuries, upon the history of his field of endeavor. His work in anthropometrics and his contributions to the college service and health programs stand out as milestones.

Ethel Perrin relates her personal experiences as a physical educator. Specifically, the author discusses the curricular emphases in early programs of teacher training and tells how these emphases influenced her own teaching and growth as a teacher of physical education.

Marvin H. Eyler presents a research study that traces the orgin of many sports. Eyler gives the date and geographic origin for as many sports as could be documented.

Further, the researcher presents information concerned with the evolution of certain sports and games.

Charles A. Bucher's article is a plea for a reassessment of the spirit and aims of the Olympic games. While this article was written in 1955, the criticisms and suggestions made are no less valid for the current conduct of Olympic competition.

Human movement is the theme of readings by Seymour Kleinman, Naomi Allenbaugh, and Peter V. Karpovich. A view of the significance of human movement is developed in the article by Kleinman, who uses philosophic inference to describe ways in which physical educators misuse the human body in physical education classes and programs. The author develops and discusses six movement objectives for physical education and suggests that physical education stress movement activities rather than emphasize sports and games.

Naomi Allenbaugh discusses the nature of human movement in relation to the elementary school-age child. This article explains the conceptual approach on which movement education is based and demonstrates the methodology used by movement educators.

Karpovich deplores muscular inactivity and proposes that all individuals be encouraged to engage in activity to enhance their physical fitness. He writes that it is physical movement rather than the choice of activity that is of prime importance.

27. Sport, play, and physical education in cultural perspective*

Franklin Parker

Benedum Professor of Education, College of Human Resources and Education, West Virginia University

My big question is: Why does man play and engage in sport and dignify his theory and practice as physical education? This is a large question and though I will fall short of a full answer I have benefited from searching through the literature in quest of the answer. Let me start with what we know best, with sport and play in our own America.

In the beginning, Puritans frowned on sport in general and on Sunday sport in particular. In the language of the New England Primer, "Your deeds to mend, God attend." In the North, the sporting seed was lost on rocky Puritan ground. In the West, sport, play, and dancing to the fiddle were restricted to house-raising festivities. In the South, Virginians copied English cavaliers in fencing, horse racing, and fox hunting. Early American sport was at first not of the common people or of the frontier. In the Middle Atlantic states and elsewhere boxing, card playing—even baseball—were an upper-class prerogative. In 1845, when members of the exclusive Knickerbocker Club in Manhattan played baseball, it was a genteel game for gentlemen.

But times were changing and between 1840 and 1880 America leaped from fifth to first place among industrial nations. Immigrants poured in by the tens of millions, half of them Germans and Irishmen accustomed to the relaxed European Sunday. The Puritan Sabbath retreated before the labor-ing man's taste for Sunday picnics and ball games in small towns, and beer gardens and saloons in big cities. With the frontier closed, rural agrarianism in decline, and urban industrialism triumphant, sport rose swiftly. One historian, Frederic Logan Paxon, has suggested that sport was the safety valve that replaced the closed frontier. Surely in 1885, when the International Young Men's Christian Association founded Springfield College in Massachusetts as a training school for physical education teachers, sport in America had reached the age of consent. And by the turn of the century as it enlarged to include every known game, sport was already feeding back ideas to serve the American drive for speed and efficiency.

Sport had a marked effect on social custom and technological advance in late nineteenth century America. Frederick W. Taylor was a doubles tennis champion in 1881. Not long afterwards he established the time and motion study movement and fathered the scientific management revolution. It was in golf and tennis that he first saw the value of analysis of motion, the importance of methodical training, and the worth of time study.

Leland Stanford, president of the Central Pacific Railroad and benefactor of Stanford University, bet a friend $25,000 that a trotter in gait lifted all four hoofs off the ground. He hired a photographer to prove his point. Photographer Muybridge set up trip wires for a 24-camera-shot sequence. He proved Stanford correct and laid the basis for motion picture photography. The first commercial motion picture ever shown on a

*From Journal of Health, Physical Education, and Recreation, Vol. 36, p. 29, Apr. 1965. Used by permission.

screen was a six-round boxing bout in May, 1895. It was the filming of boxing events that took motion pictures out of the peep show and into big time.

Radio, too, received impetus from sports. As early as 1899, when Marconi desperately needed money to perfect his wireless, the *New York Herald* paid him $5,000 to transmit via radio the finish of the American Cup yacht race.

Above all, the bicycle had large influence. The cycling craze took hold after improved English bicycles appeared in the Philadelphia Centennial of 1876. Lady riders shortened their skirts and feminists had new support.

The League of American Wheelmen, a million strong at its peak, campaigned for better roads. By 1900 half the states had passed legislation for better highways. From improved bicycles came the ball bearing, wire wheels, hub-braking, the pneumatic tire, and variable speed transmission from which came automatic gear shift in cars.

The bicycle industry developed tubular nickel steel and played a key role in developing the motor boat, the motorcycle, and the automobile. Orville Wright was a bicycle racer and with his brother Wilbur ran a bicycle repair shop in Dayton, Ohio.

Henry Ford's first cars were racers. He needed financial backing; to get moneyed people interested he needed publicity. Racing car winners gave him the public attention he sought. The man Ford got to race his 80 horse-power "999" engine was a professional bicycle rider named Barney Oldfield.

After the turn of the century sport hit America with a bang. Teddy Roosevelt's Cabinet was often called the "Tennis Cabinet." By 1919 sport represented an annual expenditure of $73 million. By the 1920's, aided by radio, the spectator boom was on. Baseball, football, and boxing drew enormous crowds. During the Depression in the 1930's the trend turned toward participant sports. The Works Progress Administration alone built 10,000 tennis courts, 3,026 athletic fields, 2,261 horseshoe courts, 1,817 handball courts, 805 swimming pools 318 ski trails, and 254 golf courses. National and state parks and fish and game sanctuaries helped extol the outdoor life.

As direct participation rose, personal attendance declined. Radio and television in our time have aided this trend. Big-time sport has become an entertainment spectacle, set up and arranged for home listening and viewing. Gate receipts have dropped; the crowds just do not come any more; advertising has become the moneyed middleman. Wrestling, boxing, baseball, and football have been turned into parlor sports.

Conversely, swimming, boating, skiing, camping, bowling, skating—in short, most participant sports, whether private, school, or company sponsored—are on the rise. If, as I think, it is a healthy trend, then how can participant sports be encouraged? How can we make creative use of the participant trend to produce physically stronger and more mentally alert Americans? We are back to my original question—why does man play and engage in sport and dignify the theory and practice of sport as physical education? Let me approach some theoretical answers through a brief historical survey.

In the beginning the amoeba stirred and all its descendants moved and crawled and ran and roamed the face of the earth to find favorable life conditions. For man, from the beginning, the bodily development was imperative since efficient movement meant survival. The more efficient man, physically and mentally, led others out of danger. The root meaning of the word education is "to lead forth."

When danger was for the moment averted and food enough was at hand, prudence may have directed the channeling of surplus energy into preparation for tomorrow's challenges. From this surplus energy during earliest times of brief leisure, in imitation of previous battles, and in exultant hope for future achievement, youth may have learned to engage in sport and to play. Whatever the origin in the dim past, sport, play, and physical development are part of man's heritage and the necessary complement to his mind's search for understanding and meaning.

The richest blending of physical and mental activity occurred in ancient Greece. It was a rare and balanced blend. Can you remove the dance and not limit Greek drama? Can you take away running, jumping, and wrestling and not weaken Greek education? Can you subtract military training and not undercut Greek citizenship?

Physical movement and intellectual ideas

were interrelated. Socrates hammered mallet to chisel on stone before he looked for virtue. Aristotle trained Alexander's body in the Lyceum before he taught him philosophy.

It is a challenge that prompts response; there is physical-emotive stirring that coincides with thought. No people, no civilizations rise except against adversity. In the desert Moses gained his insight into the Ten Commandments. Along the overflowing rivers man first controlled floods and developed agriculture.

Great as Rome was, it was surpassed by Greece. Rome's overemphasis on military training and underemphasis on intellectual concern led to wanton luxury and eventually to decline. Where mental wonder is barren and the future holds no promise for improvement, then people feed on circuses, then brute force satisfies base appetites for grim spectacle.

Unexpected good often comes out of supposed evil. With Rome in decay the barbaric hordes broke through. It took several centuries, but the Teutons who swamped the Mediterranean into the Dark Ages fused their virility into the Greco-Roman world. Physically strong and vigorous, with large families of sturdy children, these northmen assimilated and ultimately surpassed the culture they had first smothered.

Much has been said in criticism of bodily neglect implicit in the early Christian search for man's eternal soul. But monastics' cloistered walks that accompanied holy prayer and St. Benedict-inspired field labor surely aided spiritual insight. Even in ivory-towered medieval universities young scholars found physical outlets in exuberant pranks, boisterous tavern sport, and unfortunate town-gown conflicts.

When knighthood was in flower, it married feudal obligation to religious idealism. After battle, page, squire, and knight all enjoyed sport, play, and falconry.

Renaissance man turned from faith to reason, darkness to light, otherworldliness to this world. The blanket of ignorance that had hidden Greece and Rome was lifted and the humanists proclaimed man's uniqueness. In the new spirit, Vittorino Da Feltre's court school at Mantua was called "The Pleasant House." Sport, play, health, and physical development were vigorously revived.

The Reformation that split Christendom may briefly have eclipsed this revival as Protestant groups disciplined themselves in finding ways to God through Holy Writ. Out of this reform came three thinkers whose ideas had profound impact on sport and play. First, John Locke, the English Puritan, whose *tabula rasa* theory held that the mind is like a blank tablet on which experience writes. In his *Essay Concerning Human Understanding* Locke denied innate ideas. He threw doubt on the existence of Plato's divine truths, supposedly imbedded in rational thought, which proper education could nurture to fruition in some individuals. Locke's empiricism had several implications. If experience is everything, then all men are born with equal potential; human depravity is disproved; and man at birth is neither good nor bad but neutral, a being to be shaped by environment and experience. Locke's ideas formed a large basis for the English Enlightenment, the French Age of Reason, and the American and French Revolutions. From Locke flowed religious deism and philosophical skepticism.

Locke reopened an age-old philosophical problem: Does knowledge come from the rational mind or from the objective world? This problem was examined by a frail and small man, Immanual Kant (1724-1804), a German professor at the University of Konigsburg, in three books: *The Critique of Pure Reason* (1781), *The Critique of Practical Reason* (1788), and *The Critique of Judgment* (1790). The objective world, said Kant, is indeed the source of much of our knowledge—but not all. Space and time do not exist as realities outside of the mind— neither does the concept of God or religion or morality, or the sense of duty, or the sense of beauty. These the mind of man alone supplies. The senses may transmit the crude materials of knowledge but the mind has categories and structure which give meaning and understanding to complex impressions. In reinstating idealism Kant pointed to a connecting link between the physical world of things and the mental world of ideas.

It is with Schiller that I end this trilogy of great thinkers; Johann Christoph Friedrich Schiller (1759-1805), German poet, dramatist, historian, and philosopher who died in his 46th year. It was Schiller, following Kant, who gave us an aesthetic theory of play. His *Letters on the Aesthetic Education of Man* deserves to be studied by physical educators. It is profound and beautiful. Locke had said that the mind was passive and that sense impression was all. Kant had said that sense experience transmits crude impressions to the mind which through categories of its own provides meaning and substance. Schiller said that in giving meaning and substance to sense impressions, the mind does so in imagination. Schiller found the connecting link between mind and matter to be creative imagination. Aesthetics unites the sensory and the rational nature of man. It is this aesthetic link that evokes surplus energy, physical movement, and spontaneous play: it is an inborn desire to create form out of impressions. Aesthetics feeds the emotions, controls instinct, excites and relaxes the soul, awakens beauty, and sublimates passion. It explains the spirit of romance. It is the heart of the creative act. It is the sublime in education on which Pestalozzi, Froebel, and Herbart sought to build a better mankind.

It is easy to wax eloquent about Schiller's aesthetic theory of play. Philosophers have not dwelt sufficiently on it—nor have physical educators or their doctoral candidates. More research is needed on why man plays and engages in sport. Perhaps he does so to recapitulate the cultural history of his species, relive his ancestors' times of danger and victory, feel anew the trials of old, and gird himself for battle. That is one theory. Let us call it the *Recapitulation* theory.

Perhaps he does so because from infancy he has will to power, to master his environment, to be aggressive and to win, to prove his superiority by competitiveness, to emulate and to match adult strength. Let us call this the *Will to Power* theory.

Perhaps it is because he needs a catharsis, to let loose his animal instincts, to yell and push and kick and shove and snarl away his animal nature. Let us call this the *Catharsis* theory.

Perhaps, as Schiller has said, man plays and engages in sport to give satisfaction to his creative imagination. He plays and moves and strives somehow in some way to build and create beauty. Let us call this the *Aesthetic* theory.

Why does man play and engage in sport? Probably for all these reasons. All our theories may be but variations of one theme. Man may be an unfinished creature placed on an unfinished planet in an unfinished galaxy of an unfinished universe. Even man's concept of God is unfinished. What man learns today he must relearn and redefine in tomorrow's context. Man moves because he has to move, like the amoeba, to find the best conditions for life. He must move efficiently for survival.

In this anxious age we need to strengthen both body and mind. We need release to soar into space, fresh air to overcome mental torpor, insight to move in new directions. Inner form and beauty may help dispel outer dross and disarray. Whatever makes for play in man also offers you, the physical educator, unusual opportunity. More than other teachers, you touch a deep well of interest. This taproot is there, rich and vibrant, awaiting only your nourishing direction.

28. The Greek tradition and today's physical education*

Robert H. Beck

Professor of History and Philosophy of Education, College of Education, University of Minnesota

The . . . upsurge of national interest in physical fitness, in maintenance of good health, and in the recreation of men whose leisure will steadily be increased by automation, prompts a historian of education to remember that education for good health, for physical and mental well-being, and for the worthy use of leisure have been important educational objectives in the West since Homeric times some thirty-two or -three hundred years ago.

The history of education in the West runs back beyond the Hellenic Bronze Age of 1400 to 1200 B.C. But the older tradition, that of ancient Egypt and of the Mesopotamian civilizations of Sumer, Babylon, and Assyria, had no place for education and training leading to sound health, physical fitness, and prowess, or for recreation. The older civilizations were preoccupied either with training scribes who could write and keep accounts, or preparing priests and rulers. There appeared to be no call in Egypt or in Mesopotamia, in those centuries, for such warriors as Homer's Achilles, "fleet of foot," Achilles of "giant might." Whereas the Greeks, *our* intellectual ancestors, memorized the tales of strength and courage that made up Homer's *Iliad,* the ancient Egyptians turned their back on life and showed their preoccupation with life after death by taking as their text the *Book of the Dead.* As for Mesopotamia, its great epic told of the wanderings of Gilgamesh and his friend,

Enkindu. Whereas Achilles sought *arete*—that is, the honor that comes to a brave, powerful soldier—Gilgamesh wandered in search of the secret of immortal life.

To understand the Homeric view of education, in contrast to the Egyptian and Mesopotamian desire to learn to write, compute, and divine, one needs only read of the contests and games underwritten by Achilles in honor of the memory of his dear friend and comrade in arms, Petroculos, slain by Hector. The whole twenty-third chapter of the *Iliad* is a recital of recreation based on physical fitness. In that chapter we read of the "fleet chariot-racers," of the boxers, wrestlers, runners, archers, and others. I think no contest ever has been described that out paces in excitement the account of the chariot race between the competing Achaean tribes.

Homer wrote in the ninth century B.C. The times described in the *Iliad* had passed half a millenium earlier. But for five hundred years after Homer every Greek schoolboy recited the *Iliad*. In the *Iliad* were the examples of manhood Greek youth was to adopt.

By the seventh century B.C., the physical training that Homer describes as given noble, aristocratic youth was available to all free men. The vitality that we find missing in Egypt and in ancient Mesopotamia filled the life of Hellas. Every Greek city of the seventh, sixth, and fifth centuries—and for centuries later—had its gymnasium or palaestra, as well as its teachers of dance for boys and for girls. Many of the odes of Pindar were written for those who triumphed

*From Journal of Health, Physical Education, and Recreation, Vol. 34, No. 6, p. 19, June 1963. Used by permission.

at the games at Olympus. Unhappily the time came when city-states so coveted the honor that came with Olympic prizes that professional athletes were hired. All historians of ancient Greece record that sports, games, and physical education all were corrupted by the zeal for prizes and the professionalization of the Olympic and other competition. We would have done well to have remembered the fate that overtook physical education and recreation in Greek times.

We only dimly remember how seriously the ancient Greeks took physical education. Plato has been incorrectly thought more or less contemptuous of anything but rigorous intellectual discipline. Granted that dialectic—what we would term logic and the analysis of philosophic issues—was the study Plato esteemed for the very few who continued their education until suited to be philosopher-kings. Plato was equally concerned that the education of the ordinary citizen, especially those who would guard the state, be sound. To glimpse Plato's views on the education of the guardians of the state, it is only necessary to read the short Platonic dialogue named *Laches*. In that dialogue, Lysimachus and Melasias discussed with two renowned generals, Nicias and Laches, the education of their sons. The subject of the dialogue reduces to opinion of the value of gymnastics practiced in the palaestra. Nicias was very much in favor of gymnastics; Laches opposed it.

The dialogue *Laches* becomes an arena in which Socrates, or Plato, lays out alternative views of the meaning of courage. Plato was anxious to convince his audience that courage is a matter of intelligence and moral strength as much as it is of endurance. Nevertheless, it is clear that Socrates and Plato sided with Nicias, who recommended gymnastic training not only for its advantages as preparation for war. "There is an advantage," said Nicias, "in their (the young men) being employed during their leisure hours in a way that tends to improve their bodily constitution, and not in the way in which young men are too apt to be employed." Moreover, Nicias went on to explain, training in gymnastics "inclines a man to other noble lessons."

It is said that Rome went to school in Greece. Surely a portion of what Rome took from the Hellenic philosophy of education was a belief in the importance of physical education, whether for sports and games to be played in one's leisure time, or for the cultivation of a handsome and healthy physique, or for the development of strength and courage needed in battle.

And when Europe emerged from the Medieval world into Renaissance of the fourteenth, fifteenth, and sixteenth centuries, Greek and Roman confidence in the importance of physical education in the education of the young also was reborn. True, for centuries, really until the late eighteenth century, physical education, as secular education generally, was thought primarily for those who either would constitute the aristocracy or would serve the aristocracy as scribes and accountants. That was so simply because the scholars of the Renaissance knew Homer but did not know that physical training, sports, and games had become popular, and for all freemen, not only for the aristocracy.

Although nothing new was added by the Renaissance to Greek thought on physical education, the Renaissance did not downgrade the role of physical education. The famed intellectual humanists, notably John Milton, found a place in general education for physical education, and in typically Hellenic terms.

Moving to early modern times, to the eve of the French revolution, physical education received a tremendous boost in the educational writings of Rousseau. Looking into Rousseau's treatise on the education of boys, the *Emile,* the reader is left in no doubt that Rousseau believed in physical fitness for youth. The development of the body, after all, fitted Rousseau's conviction that education could not be reduced simply to the three R's. Development of all the physical potentialities of men, including their abilities to invent and use tools, commanded Rousseau's philosophy of education and became his principal dowry for succeeding generations of educational thinkers.

Educators in the area of health, physical education, and recreation should reserve a place of honor for the German educator, Basedow, much influenced by Rousseau. Basedow, who founded a boarding school in Dessau in 1774, included any number of sports and physical activities beyond gymnastics. His reputation was such that other schoolmen accepted Basedow's philosophy of education. Among these was Guts Muths, who wrote *Gymnastik fur die Jugend,* the first educational treatise on gymnastics.

It was just at this point in time that European monarchs awakened to the national importance of physical fitness programs. As in our own day, that Greek-like thought that a nation's sinews are in part those of its men and women boosted the reputation of physical education for physical fitness. The preparation of special teachers of physical education dates from 1799 when Franz Nachtegall of Denmark, opened an institute for training teachers of physical education.

The first attempts at scientific research on physical education appeared at about the same time. In no other field of education was the special preparation of teachers of a subject so rapidly associated with research. It was one of Nachtegall's own students, a Swedish student by the name of Pehr Henrik Ling who disciplined himself to make an extensive study of the anatomical and physiological bases for gymnastics. Ling's Royal Central Institute of Gymnastics, located in Stockholm, developed a most enviable reputation.

By the middle of the nineteenth century it seemed as though the future of physical education, and its twin collaborators, health education and education for recreation was fully accepted and on the way to becoming one of the most thoroughly studied, carefully developed studies in the schools.

Research by staff in physical education, in school health programs, and in the field of recreation could be remarked at formidable length. The fact is that despite the thoughtful manner in which the curriculum in health, physical education, and recreation has been built, schooling on this continent, in Latin America, and in most of Europe has permitted the appearance of a gulf between academic studies and those in physical education, in recreation, and in health.

Inquiry into the origin of the barrier between academic studies and all that is lumped into the nonacademic—be it vocational training, driver training, extracurricular activities of all types, or physical education, recreation, and health programs —points to the mischief that was done in ancient Greece when the city-states exaggerated the importance of winning in the Olympic games and invested in professional athletes. The poor repute in which they have been held might have been distinguished from the excellent results being achieved by men and women teaching and coaching in physical education, in programs preparing leaders and participants in recreation and health programs.

The effect of the cold war plus the accelerating transformation of knowledge produced by modern science and technology has unbalanced American education. Our nation's leaders grant the importance of physical fitness but there is danger that all of health, physical education, and recreation will be reduced to attain strength needed in the days of cold war. Surely physical fitness is not to be undersold. Grant that and a very great deal remains to be admitted about the potentiality of health programs, as well as those in physical education and recreation.

Think first of recreation. Everyone knows that the work-week will be reduced, that automation will cause a good deal of physical work to disappear, and there will be more leisure. One hopes that this leisure will permit many more to read, to become caught up in the arts, in learning of all forms. But there will be time to learn to enjoy the out-of-doors. Is there a more effective alternative to complete urbanization and life lived in the rhythm of the machine than outdoor recreation in our parks far and near, in camping, in boating, fishing, and all that recreational programs touch upon?

And what of education for healthful living? There is no need to spell out the portions of a full-blown curriculum in health education. The very most tentative contact with the field quickens us to its values. But I think that those professionally concerned with health programs in our schools should help their colleagues in biology and in chemistry understand that the topic of physical, and indeed, mental health, affords excellent opportunities for units of study in the biological sciences and in chemistry.

In physical education of men and women there are just as many bridges that can be built with academic departments. Think only of the history of physical education.

Any student of that history becomes a student of general history. One could not adequately study the social and cultural history of the West without becoming acquainted with the history of physical education.

Physical education instruction that looks forward to enhanced health and recreation can win recognition today equal to that accorded by the Hellenes. But the laurel will not be awarded without ambition and effort.

If leaders in these fields accept the status of second-class educators, we will have turned our back on our Greek progenitors. There is no necessity of unseemly modesty. The better stance is one that shows leaders in physical education, health education, and recreation reflecting on their fields and clearly intending that these contribute to education of undeniable worth.

29. Did the Greeks and the Romans play football?*

Norma D. Young†

Former faculty member, State University of Iowa

This investigation was prompted by a statement in Coyer's *The Coaching of Soccer* that *harpastum,* a handball game of the Greeks, was developed by the Romans into a game in which the ball was kicked, thus becoming one of the forerunners of soccer. Coyer states that the Greek word *harpaston* is derived from a word meaning *to hurl forward.* The latest edition of the Liddell and Scott Greek Dictionary does not recognize such an etymological explanation. The word comes from the Greek word meaning *to seize* or *to grasp.* The dictionary mentioned immediately above gives the word as a neuter substantive of an adjective *harpastos,* meaning *carried-away.*[1]

Scholars have, from time to time, attempted to find evidence as to whether or not the ancients played football. Two notable illustrations are Koch's *Die Geschichte des Fussballs im Altertum und in der Neuzeit,* which Keller finds to offer highly problematical positive evidence; and Becq de Fouquieres, in *Les Jeux des Anciens,* who, however, cites no authority for his statement. In this paper I have not endeavored to survey all Greek and Latin literature for references to ball games or even to look up all references to ball games as indicated in existing *Indices* and *Concordances.* I have, however, in an effort to clarify our conception of *harpastum,* studied in the original sources the references listed in the two chief ency-

clopedias of antiquities, the *Real-encyclopädie classischen Alterumswissenschaft* and the *Dictionnaire des antiquités grecques et romaines.*

The word *harpastum,* in addition to the conjecturable etymology referred to above, offers another problem. The dictionaries, both Greek and Latin, define it as a handball. References in literature refer to it both as a handball and as a ball game. Whether the ball derived its appellation from the game or whether the game derived its appellation from the ball is a moot point. It is known, however, that the Greeks not only did have a "word for it" but even had "two words for it." Athenaeus, a Greek scholar of the second and third centuries, A.D., tells us that *harpastum* was originally called *phaininda;* Clemens of Alexandria, a Father of the Church at the same time, that it was originally called *pheninda;* Eustathius, an archbishop of Thessalonica in the twelfth century, that it was originally called *phaininda.* Evidence to support the fact that *harpastum* and *phaininda* were the same game is that both Athenaeus and Pollux so identified the games and that no writer mentions the games as being distinct from each other. In addition, Athenaeus refers to the ball game, which was then called *harpastum* and which formerly had been called *phaininda,* as being the kind of ball game he liked best of all, which statement would seem to indicate that he had more than an academic interest in the game and that the identification of the two games was trustworthy.

Now if *harpastum* was originally called *phaininda,* an interesting point, etymologically, is added to our hazy concept of the game, for the *Etymologicum Magnum,* of

*From Research Quarterly, Vol. 15, p. 310, Dec. 1944. Used by permission.
†Deceased.

[1]Coyer further states in this connection that the word *harpoon* has the same root as *harpastum.* This explanation is erroneous, for the word *harpoon* is derived from a French noun and verb meaning *claw* and *to grapple.*

the tenth century, the oldest Greek lexicon, derives *pheninda* from *phennis,* which means *trickery,* which etymology, it will be seen later in this paper, has a direct bearing on as much as we know of the way the game was played. Athenaeus, however, tells us that the game may have been called *phaininda* because the players "shot"[2] the ball or because, according to Juba, the Mauretanian, the inventor was Phainestius, a trainer.

The reconstruction of the games of the ancients is an arduous task, usually with equivocal results. In the *Deipnosophists*[3] of Athenaeus, however, Antiphanes specifically describes the game of *phaininda* as follows:

> One player seized the ball, and rejoiced to give it to another, at the same time avoiding still another. He lifted another player to his feet, in the midst of shouts of "out-of-bounds."

He refers, also, to the violent twistings and turnings of the neck incurred in this game.

The grammarian, Julius Pollux, of the second century, A.D., who is the most authoritative writer on ball games of the ancients, gives us the following information about *phaininda*:

> It was so named either by a trainer of similar name or from the verb meaning *to deceive.* He explains the latter derivation by saying that the players pretend to throw the ball in one direction and then throw it in another.

Archaeological evidence to date has offered little help in the reconstruction of the game in question. In February, 1922, among the sculptured reliefs found in the Themistoclean circuit wall in Athens was one relief showing six players, three on each side, lined up at intervals behind one another, engaged in playing with a small ball.[4]

Those scholars who are certain that they have reproduced *harpastum* base much of their evidence on a treatise on *The Small Ball,*[5] written by Galen, a physician of the second century, A.D. This writer, however, is interested in different kinds of exercise through ball playing, and there is no conclusive evidence that he is describing only one game and that being *harpastum.* Galen does, however, offer us evidence that the ball was not kicked, for he refers to the exercise gained by the arms in throwing and by the legs in running. If the players had kicked the ball, Galen, in such a complete treatise on exercise by means of ball playing, would certainly have referred to the exercise gained by the legs in kicking.

The positive information we have concerning *harpastum* is thus seen to be scanty and may be summarized as follows: *Harpastum,* originally *phaininda,* was a game in which two or more players threw the ball to one another in such a way as to avoid a player between them.

Further information advanced concerning *harpastum* is largely conjectural. The fact that the ball could be caught either on a volley or on the first rebound is deduced from the adjective *pulverulenta* (dusty) and *arenaria* (sandy) applied, by transferred epithet, to the ball by Martial. Obviously, the ball might have landed on the ground, thus becoming dusty or sandy, without the implication that a point would be counted if the ball were caught on a rebound.

The players may have stood in a circle if we are to accept a passage from Isidorus—the circle of players standing by and waiting —yet this passage is corrupt, and can offer no positive evidence.

A passage from Sidonius Apollinaris may or may not be describing *harpastum.* It refers to a middle player (*medicurrens*) constantly losing his balance as he tried to return to his area of play, and of finally retiring breathlessly from the game. However, in the game so described, similar to our game, *Keep the Ball,* the players seemed to enter and to retire at will. Hence *harpastum* would not have been a team game.

---

[2]If this derivation is correct, *harpastum* is derived from *aphesis,* meaning *a sending away,* or *shooting* (as translated by Gulick in the *Loeb Classical Library* edition of Athenaeus)—a very doubtful etymological explanation.

[3]*The Deipnosophists,* or "The Sophists at Dinner" or "The Gastronomers" is the oldest cookery book extant. It might be called a philosophical treatise on dining: the "Sophists" engage in a heterogeneity of discussions.

[4]The *harpastum,* which was made of strips of leather and stuffed with hair, was the smallest ball of the ancients. Larger balls were filled with feathers or with air.

[5]The writer has thought it worth while to include as an appendix to this article a translation of this treatise because she believes that it negates beyond doubt the assumption concerning the ancestry of football derived therefrom, *and* because she believes that there is an intrinsic interest in the pertinence of many of the items therein presented eighteen centuries ago!

Scholars have apparently confused the game of *harpastum* with that of *episkyros*. While there is no evidence of kicking the ball in the latter game, there is some evidence, at least in the marking of the ground, that *episkyros* might have been a forerunner of soccer. Pollux explains the game thus:

> *Episkyros,* a game of youths, was played with the member of one team matched with those of another. There was a middle line, the *skyros,* upon which the ball was placed. There were two other lines, apparently goal lines. Those who had been chosen first sent the ball to the others whose task it was to throw the ball back. This performance continued until one team succeeded in throwing the ball beyond the goal line of the other team.

While this discussion presents but few facts concerning either *harpastum* or *episkyros,* the facts presented are those for which there is evidence, and many fanciful deductions have been ironed out. This game of *episkyros* is familiar to the game of handball played in Germany, called in this country *German handball* or *field handball.*

Did the Greeks and the Romans play football? There seems to be no positive evidence to date that they did engage in pedal action with a ball. Perhaps the ancients, good runners as they were, were still not expert enough to meet a flying ball with their feet. Perhaps, too, many were like Epictetus who said that he could not catch a ball even if he spread out his coat to catch it in, let alone with his hands.

APPENDIX
(A translation of Galen's treatise *The Small Ball*)

Ancient authorities, both philosophers and physicians, have presented adequate treatises concerning the contribution of exercise to health, but they have failed to write concerning the superiority of exercise with the small ball over other forms of exercise. The purpose here, therefore, is to set forth some of these advantages gained from exercise with the small ball. Your criticism of this treatise, Epigenes, will be awaited, for you are expert in this form of exercise, and the hope is expressed that the treatise will be useful to any readers with whom you may share it.

That form of exercise is best which not only exercises the body but also is a source of joy to the participant. Men who engage in hunting with dogs are wise and understand human nature; they pleasantly modify their toil with a competitive element. The essential need of the soul for joyful outlet is corroborated by the fact that many men have avoided disease by the feeling of joy alone and, on the other hand, that many have become ill because of grief. No feeling of the body is strong enough to overcome the feeling of the soul, which must, therefore, be considered to be of prime importance. This advantage, then, is common to all exercises which provide an outlet for pleasurable expression, but there are some advantages peculiar to exercise with the small ball.

The accessibility of the exercise should be considered. When the amount of time that is needed for hunting is taken into account, it becomes obvious that busy men cannot engage in this form of exercise. When the equipment—nets, arms, horses, and hunting dogs—is considered, it becomes obvious that this form of exercise is prohibitive in the case of poor men. Exercise with the small ball requires little time and little equipment, and is, therefore, generally accessible. It does not cause any other activities to be neglected; indeed, what could be more advantageous than an activity which partakes of every human fortune and action? It is readily seen that this form of exercise in its flexibility of adaptation to the needs of the individual is more effective than all other forms. It provides for strenuous or moderate movement; it provides for movement up or down; it provides for the movement of some parts of the body—loins, head, hands, thorax—more than of others; it provides for an equal movement of all parts of the body, requiring a maximum or a minimum of motion. No other exercise, except this with the small ball, exists which can be so well adapted to the current needs of the participant. A great expenditure of effort is required, for example, on the part of the players who strive to prevent the ball from being caught; indeed, many twistings of the neck are experienced, and use is made of many holds learned in wrestling. The loins and the legs, the foundation of the walking apparatus, are taxed by such activity.

The fact that this exercise, if the player plays in every position, is the only one which exercises all parts of the body should be stressed; also that there are equal periods of rest and of activity so that the player is not permitted to become sluggish, on the one hand, or unduly tired on the other. It also exercises the eyes, for the player must make adequate use of his peripheral vision to catch the ball. He must not throw the ball aimlessly; he must prevent another player from catching it; or he must catch the thrown ball. Being on the alert constantly may itself weaken the body; but when it is a product of exercise and of emulation, it tends toward joyful expression and contributes not only strength to the body but also wisdom to the mind, both of which qualities leaders wish to develop in their soldiers for the preservation of the laws. For the best leader must be both a guardian and a thief; he must attack the enemy opportunely, be in ambush when he is on the defensive, make an attack on a moment's notice, capture by strength or by strategy, and defend what has been taken. Is there any exercise, then, more suitable than exercise with the small ball for gaining or defending spoils, or for recovering stolen possessions, or for foreseeing the strategy of the enemy? Indeed this exercise even causes the sluggish and the dull to be revived. Many men who exercise only in wrestling develop muscles and bulk to the neglect of skill; to be sure, many have developed so much bulk that they can scarcely breathe, and, consequently, are not more fit than swine either for civil or for martial duties. Lest it be thought, however, that there is approval for any exercise which debilitates the body, it should be said that what is immoderate is condemned, and that anything which lacks measure is not beautiful. Races, therefore, that weaken the body and do not increase fortitude are not endorsed. Victory is not deserved by those soldiers who flee quickly but by those who have the fortitude to endure in close contest. The Lacedaemonians were powerful, not because they fled quickly, but because they persisted in killing the enemy. But if the question is asked to what extent running is beneficial to the body, the answer is that it is not beneficial insofar as it causes the parts of the body to be exercised unequally; in causing some parts to be exercised excessively and in leaving other parts inactive, it weakens the person and may even be the source of illness.

Therefore that form of exercise is recommended which contributes to the health of the body and to the harmonious functioning of the parts and to the strength of the soul—exercise like that derived from playing with the small ball, suitable for men needing development in strength or in speed. It is flexible in that it may be adapted both to the young and to the old, to the out-of-condition, or to the convalescent; the player who wishes to limit himself to moderate movement should take the middle position; after the exercise the player should take advantage of a rubdown with oil and a bath—a relaxing procedure to revive strength.

Those who wish to profit most from this form of exercise must recognize which movements require more exertion, which less, and which movements affect the different parts of the body so that if they have become unduly tired in certain parts of their body because of their occupations they will know how to exercise with the small ball to bring the requisite amount of exercise to the various parts of the body. If a player standing in place throws a ball a great distance, he taxes the upper parts of his body more than the lower. But if a player runs quickly for a great distance, throwing a ball now and then, he will tire the lower parts of his body more than the upper; the speed of the exertion will tax the breathing. Throwing and catching without speed, however, increase the exertion and the consequent strengthening of the body. Throwing and catching with speed, the most violent of all exercises, tires the body and taxes the breathing. Although it is impossible to state the requisite quantity of exercise, it can be stated, however, that the intensity of the exercise is of no avail unless the dosage is sufficient, the determining of which is the task of the coach.

In conclusion, attention is called to the fact that in addition to the advantages of exercise with the small ball already named, this activity is not beset with danger. Races in which runners carry vases have resulted in broken vases and injured runners. The perils of horseback riding, jumping, and discus throwing are numerous. Participants in the gymnasium and on the athletic field are fre-

quently injured. Just as Homer referred to those crippled, wrinkled, and with deformed eyes, so the participants in the gymnasium and on the athletic field become crippled, with distorted or broken bones. Thus to the advantages which have already been elaborated concerning exercise with the small ball, this supreme advantage—namely that it is not fraught with peril—is added.

BIBLIOGRAPHY
Greek and Latin sources
Athenaeus. *Deipnosophistae* (edited by George Kaibel). Leipzig: Teubner, 1887.

Athenaeus. *Deipnosophistae* (with an English translation by Charles B. Gulick, Loeb Classical Library). New York: G. P. Putnam's Sons, 1928.

Epictetus. *Dissertationes* (edited by Henry Schenkl). Leipzig: Teubner, 1894.

Galen, *De Parvae Pilae Exercitio* (Greek text in *Claudii Galeni Scripta Minora,* edited by John Marquardt). Leipzig: Teubner, 1884.

Isidorus. *Etymologiae sive Origines* (edited by W. M. Lindsay). Oxford: Clarendon Press, 1911.

Martial. *Epigrammata* (edited by W. M. Lindsay). Oxford: Clarendon Press, 1902.

Pollux. *Onomasticon* (edited by Ericius Bethe). Leipzig: Teubner, 1900-37.

Sidonius Apollinaris. *Epistulae* (edited by O. M. Dalton). Oxford: Clarendon Press, 1915.

Dictionaries and encyclopedias
Daremberg, C., and E. Saglio. *Dictionnaire des antiquités grecques et romaines.* Paris: Librairie Hachette et Compagnie, 1877.

Lewis, Charles T., and Charles Short. *A new Latin Dictionary.* Chicago: American Book Company, 1907.

Liddell, Henry G., and Robert Scott: *A Greek-English Lexicon.* Oxford: Clarendon Press.

Pauly-Wissowa. *Real-encyclopädie der classischen Alterumswissenschaft.* Stuttgart: J. B. Metzlersche Buchhandlung, 1912.

Peck, Harry T. *Harper's Dictionary of Classical Literature and Antiquities.* Chicago: American Book Company, 1896.

Nettleship, Henry, and J. E. Sandys. *A Dictionary of Classical Antiquities.* New York: Macmillan and Company, 1895.

Webster, Noah. *New International Dictionary of the English Language.* Springfield, Massachusetts: G. and C. Merriam Company, 1943.

General
Becq de Fouquieres. *Les Jeux des Anciens.* Paris: Didier, 1873.

Coyer, Hubert E. *The Coaching of Soccer.* Philadelphia: W. B. Saunders Company, 1937.

Gardiner, E. N. *Athletics of the Ancient World.* Oxford: Clarendon Press, 1930.

Koch, K. "Die Geschichte des Fussballs im Alterum und in der Neuzeit" (Keller), *Berliner Philologische Wochenschrift,* XVI:4 (January 25, 1896).

Marindin, G. E. "The Game of 'Harpastum' or 'Pheninda'," *The Classical Review,* IV (April, 1890).

Wright, F. A. *Greek Athletics.* London: Jonathan Cape Limited, 1925.

30. The impact of Edward Hitchcock on the history of physical education*

J. Edmund Welch

Professor, Department of Physical Education, West Virginia Institute of Technology; Chairman, Historical Records Committee, NCPEAM

Edward Hitchcock was professor of hygiene and physical education at Amherst College, Amherst, Massachusetts, from 1861 until his death in 1911. As director of the first successful program of physical education in any American college, Hitchcock was in fact the "founder of physical education in the college curriculum." The example he set was followed by many colleges and universities in America, as well as in Japan. Amherst College was the first institution of higher learning to make physical education an integral part of the college curriculum.

There had been sporadic attempts by other colleges and universities to start physical education programs during the period 1826-1830 and later during the 1850's, but in no case did the institution provide adequate facilities and competent instructors. President William A. Stearns of Amherst College pointed out the need for physical education in college in his inaugural address of 1854. From the very beginning of his administration, Stearns was plagued with problems of student health. He urged the trustees to build a gymnasium and appoint a competent professor of hygiene and physical education. Stearns was successful in his efforts. Barrett Gymnasium was begun in 1859, and John W. Hooker, a physician and gymnast, was appointed as the professor in 1860. Hooker served effectively, but his

health broke and he resigned at the end of his initial year. In 1861 Hitchcock was appointed to the professorship, and he served Amherst College and the cause of physical education with great distinction for the next half century.

Hitchcock was born in Amherst, Massachusetts, on May 23, 1828, where his father was the third president of Amherst College and an eminent geologist. From his father Hitchcock gained many insights into science and teaching. Hitchcock was superbly educated for a man of his day. His preparatory work was done at Amherst Academy and Williston Seminary, and he graduated from Amherst College with a bachelor of arts degree in 1849. He also held a master of arts degree from Amherst. His medical degree was from Harvard University, and he spent four months in Paris and London studying medicine, natural history, and comparative anatomy. In London he was the private pupil of Sir Richard Owen, the outstanding comparative anatomist of the British Museum. Hitchcock's work under Owen was the high point of his professional preparation, for comparative anatomy was his favorite subject.

After graduating from Amherst, Hitchcock taught natural history at Williston Seminary from 1850 to 1860. During the early 1850's he took leave to secure his medical degree from Harvard. When he became professor of hygiene and physical education at Amherst, he was especially prepared to direct a program of student health. He lacked training in gymnastics, but he overcame this weakness while on the job.

---

*From an abstract of the author's book entitled, *Edward Hitchcock, M.D., Founder of Physical Education in the College Curriculum,* published in cooperation with the East Carolina College Library, 1966. Used by permission.

THE PROGRAM

The program which Hitchcock developed at Amherst comprised required exercises for all students; extensive health care, supervision, and instruction; and scientific measurement. It became known nationally and internationally as the "Amherst Plan" of physical education. Each of the four college classes was required to meet four times per week for thirty minutes of exercise under the direction of the professor. The students dressed in uniforms and elected their own class and platoon captains. These captains were trained by Hitchcock in the art of giving calisthenics and maneuvering the class in the gymnasium. The exercises consisted of calisthenics with light wooden dumbbells, and the students repeated the drills in unison in time to piano music. A portion of every class was given over to free exercise during which the students ran, used the heavy apparatus, sang, danced, or turned somersaults. Hitchcock felt this recreational portion of the class was important to allow students an opportunity to work off their boisterous instincts.

The trustees of Amherst were particularly desirous that the health of the students be a primary concern of the new professor of hygiene and physical education. Hitchcock carried out this mandate with the utmost skill and success. He gave regular medical examinations to the students, and he kept detailed health records. Each student could call on him for health care and counsel, and he made daily visits to the rooms of sick students. His dream of a student infirmary finally materialized in 1897 when the Pratt Health Cottage was built and endowed.

Health instruction was a vital phase of the Amherst Plan. Hitchcock gave regular lectures in hygiene to the freshman class. He covered such subjects as diet, exercise, care of the muscles, care of the eyes, alcohol, tobacco, and reproductive organs. A course in anatomy and physiology was given to sophomores.

BODY MEASUREMENTS

One of Hitchcock's most original contributions was his work in anthropometrics, or the science of bodily measurements. He desired to put his physical education program on a scientific basis. By keeping accurate measurements on all students, he was able to show that regular exercise and proper health supervision improved the growth and health of college students. Hitchcock was the first American physical educator to apply the science of anthropometry to problems of the profession. Through his efforts and those of Dudley A. Sargent, anthropometrics became the central foundation for the entire profession of physical education in America during the latter half of the nineteenth century. Hitchcock knew that detailed physical measurements over a period of years would be invaluable to anthropometrics in general. His work helped determine the average measurements of college students, and these statistics have been used in studies of human growth.

PUBLICATIONS

Hitchcock contributed only one book to the profession. This was a textbook in anatomy and physiology. However, a list of his published articles, papers, manuals, and reports covered eight pages in the *American Physical Education Review*. He ranks as one of the important writers in physical education in the nineteenth century, along with Sargent, Anderson, Hartwell, and Gulick.

Through his papers and news stories describing the Amherst Plan, Hitchcock influenced the development of physical education in many other American colleges. Three of his students, Edward Mussey Hartwell, Watson L. Savage, and Paul C. Phillips, made national contributions to American physical education. The Japanese government requested Amherst College to send a teacher to Japan to install the Amherst Plan. George A. Leland, another of Hitchcock's students, was selected for the assignment, and he spent three years in Japan. He is credited as being the founder of modern physical education in that country.

NATIONAL LEADERSHIP

Hitchcock was a prominent member of the two principal professional organizations of his time. He was the first president of the American Association for the Advancement of Physical Education, and he was chairman *pro tem* of the meeting at which the Society for College Gymnasium Directors was founded. Hitchcock was a charter member of both organizations and was particularly active in the affairs of the Association. In addition to being president for the first two years, he was vice president for six years, a member of the National Council or executive committee for ten years, and, as a member of the committee on statistics and measurements, he presented important papers on anthropometry at the national meetings. Of equal importance was the fact that Hitchcock served as a harmonizing agent during the critical, formative era of the Association. He never dodged a debate, but he was friendly to all, especially to the younger men in the profession, and he was successful in holding dissident elements together for the advancement of the profession.

HONORS

Many honors and recognitions were bestowed upon Hitchcock. He was granted an honorary doctor of laws degree from Amherst College and an honorary master of physical education degree from Springfield College. A special dinner was given in his honor by the American Association for the Advancement of Physical Education. This dinner, held at a national convention in New York City, was in commemoration of Hitchcock's fortieth anniversary as professor at Amherst College and as leader in the profession. Later, the same organization made Hitchcock an honorary member, and this was his most prized recognition. Hitchcock is a fellow in memoriam of the American Academy of Physical Education. Hitchcock Memorial Field and Hitchcock Memorial Room at Amherst College were dedicated in his memory. In 1932 Amherst College was awarded the first certificate of high merit of the American Student Health Association. This award was in recognition of the pioneer work of President Stearns and Hitchcock.

SUMMARY

Prior to 1860 there were no planned physical education programs in American colleges and universities. As a result of the outstanding work of Hitchcock at Amherst College, the way was opened for physical education to become an integral part of the college curriculum throughout the United States.

31. The confessions of a once strict formalist*

Ethel Perrin†

*An early leader in public school physical education, the author held positions at
Smith College, the University of Michigan, the Detroit public schools, and
the American Child Health Association*

I know it is dangerous to reminisce, give
me credit for that much, but I'm not going
to begin with an apology, for that is even
worse—that is poor psychology. I am giving
you some personal experiences, which is
almost as boring as telling one's dreams at
the breakfast table, but it is with the hope
that you of my generation who read this will
at least find some amusement in hearing
experiences laid bare which resemble your
own, and that the youth of the Association
will see a bit more clearly how to meet some
of their difficulties, and will also decide it is
wiser in the long run not to take yourself too
seriously.

In 1892—yes, do your own figuring—I
graduated from the Boston Normal School
of Gymnastics, and have held some sort of a
professional job without a break till 1936.
The pathetic part is the downward trend in
the mental caliber of my pupils. I began
with the highest, the students of the Boston
Normal School of Gymnastics, where I
taught as soon as I graduated, for fifteen
years. From there I descended to the college
level, thence to high school, from there to
elementary, and now I am in full charge of
the day-old chicks on my farm.

Going back to the beginning of things
when I was a student forty-six years ago, we
find the graduates of the Boston Normal
School of Gymnastics firmly believing this
school to be the best school of physical education in the world. It was founded and
grounded in the Swedish system of gymnas-

tics and no other system or mixture of systems could be mentioned in the same breath.
I remember speaking in disparaging terms,
after I had attended this school for a few
months, of a fine teacher in a nearby high
school because she ran in a few dumbbells
and clubs with her Swedish work. I claimed
that her Swedish gymnastics were not pure—
a terrible thing—and got myself greatly
disliked by the lady, and no wonder—but I
stuck to it. It seems impossible now that we
could have been so narrow-minded, but on
the other hand it was wonderful to be cock-
sure that we alone were on the right track.
It gave us a great sense of responsibility and
we felt it was our mission to spread pure
Swedish gymnastics from Maine to California. I suppose many of you never heard of
the Swedish Days Order, but I assure you,
after going through one under the skilled
leadership of Dr. Enebuske or Dr. Collin,
for sixty minutes, there was a satisfied feeling
of exhilaration and well-being. Just so much
time for waking-up exercises: right face, one
step forward, side step to the right and
about—*march*. Then just so much exercise
for head and chest; for arms, legs, trunk.
Then the great climax, the jump and run,
followed by the quieting down exercises and
the deep, deep breathing to be heard all
over the room. It was the perfect example
of the "I yell, you jump" method and this I
taught for fifteen years and never dreamed
I could do anything else.

We all gave our commands as nearly like
Dr. Collin as we could. He would stand at
one end of the gymnasium and say, "With
right hip and left neck firm and trunk
twisting to the right, left outward fall—out,"
while we would stand in line at the other

*From Journal of Health, Physical Education, and
Recreation, Vol. 9, p. 533, Nov. 1938. Used by
permission.
†Deceased.

end of the room and in concert imitate his inflection over and over again. We were taught that in order to make our pupils put the right amount of energy into their exercises, we should exaggerate in all of our demonstrations when teaching—work much harder than we expected them to work. We practiced being a split second ahead in response to our own commands in order to get them there on time. When we said "At-tention!" every pair of heels had to click and every head come up at least two inches.

Professional formality surrounded me and this included not only formal and stereotyped teaching but all matters of behavior and of dress. After seventeen years of this I was sent as a substitute for a year as Director of the Women's Gymnasium at the University of Michigan. It was a far cry from Boston and I shall never forget my astonishment when a freshman looked me over and said "What a pretty dress you have on." A personal remark from a student to a member of the faculty was a new one to me, but I liked the friendliness of it. Then a wild idea came into my head. Why not take these girls out for hikes instead of staying in the gymnasium on nice autumn days—my first really original act in my teaching. I had always before done just what I had been taught to do, and there was no place for a walk in the woods in the Swedish Days Order.

A Middle West college group was a wonderful one to try my wings on, and while they were perfectly willing to conform to some of my Boston idiosyncracies, such as no gum chewing in the gymnasium and keeping both feet on the floor in my office, still I learned more from them than they from me. Anyway, we had a happy year even if the Senior Basketball Team and I did have some rough sledding. Their methods and manners were terrible and I was wickedly glad when my freshmen beat them. The janitress and I retired to my dressing room and shook hands on it.

Then came the next step in my downward path when I was asked to interview the Superintendent of Schools and the Principal of Central High School regarding the directorship of the work in the first girls' gymnasium in the Detroit public schools. I had never been interviewed in my life and had never even seen, much less spoken to, a Su-

perintendent of Schools. I brushed up on my physiology, anatomy, and kinesiology, read over seventeen-year-old notebooks—anyone knows how discouraging and futile that is—bought a new pair of gloves, the only point I could remember from my training in regard to interviews, and took the train to Detroit in fear and trembling. I had no knowledge of public high schools, having been to a private school only, and no particular interest in them. I went as I had done everything else professionally, because my school asked me to go.

The Superintendent, the Principal, and I sat solemnly looking at each other, my mind a blank, when the Superintendent burst out with "Can you swim?" Aghast, for I had never even heard of a high school with a pool, I said "Yes, I can swim" and thereupon they hired me. If they had asked me to describe my method of teaching swimming, I might not have been hired.

Here was my first opportunity to build something of my own, for my experience had all been in carrying out work planned by others. I had no educational philosophy—had never heard of one, and doubt if many of us in physical education had heard of one in 1908. I had many strong convictions and prejudices but no methodology. One conviction was that friction and success did not go hand in hand and that I must have the respect and willing cooperation of those high school girls and of the faculty, whether I got my way in all matters or not. This was very daring of me because in the Boston Normal School of Gymnastics there was but one way of doing things and we did as we were told, whether we liked it or not, because someone else knew what was best for us. I had always followed this regime willingly because I believed that the one in authority always was right, but somehow where I had a chance to be the dictator, I wanted to try out other methods. I was not quite so sure that I was always right.

My first problem was in basketball, which game I thoroughly enjoyed and had taught ever since it was originated by Mr. Naismith. I had a very strong prejudice against interscholastic basketball competition, although I had had no experience with it in the past. I found this to be well organized between the three high schools of Detroit in 1908. It had been started and gratuitously coached and run by enthusiastic graduates of the University of Michigan. Some were teachers of other subjects and some were entirely outside the school system. Each school had its coach. The schedule for the school year was made at the close of the preceding season and the referees engaged. My principal was against it but public opinion and the newspapers had forced him into it. When he found that I too was against it, he jumped at the chance of saying there should be no Central High Girls' Team, but I would not agree. We cancelled out-of-town games, but played the schedule between Detroit high schools as already planned for that year. I knew I was right. The games were well played and the sportsmanship of the players was pretty good, except for the spirit of "getting by" which would crop up. But the audiences were terrible—just a screaming mass of maniacs. I shall never forget my astonishment when I first saw it. We managed to improve the behavior of the audiences at the games held in Central's gymnasium by inviting the boys in. Previously they had only been allowed to see by climbing and peeking from the outside— more fun for them perhaps but not so good for us to contend with. I visited one of their games and saw a well-behaved mixed audience of boys and girls. I corralled a few of the leaders among the boys and got them interested in helping us out of our difficulties. At our next game they scattered through the audience and we had no more screaming girls; a girl intuitively knows that she does not look her best when screaming.

I have told you that I had no educational principles or practical guides to follow but we might draw a few out of these experiences. After all, I suppose experiences did come before principles. From the success which these boys had with my school girl audiences, we might say *coeducation has its place in physical education*—a long way from what we now mean by this, but it was a start. With basketball came my old enemy, gum chewing. My team all indulged in it during our first practice. I had a talk with the captain—a real leader, not only of her team but in the whole school. I simply told her how I felt about gum chewing and left it up to her without making any suggestion. I can see her leading the team down the winding stairs from the dressing rooms to the gymnasium, every girl chewing her hardest. She halted at an open window at the foot of the stairs and, saying "One of the new rules girls—out goes your gum," she threw hers out of the window. Every girl followed suit and never a shot missed. That was that, and think of the time and words I would have spent had I attempted to argue them into it myself. Shall we say as a principle, *never do yourself what a pupil may be able to do better.*

At the end of an unsuccessful season as far as winning goes, Central decided to give up its girls' team, and this ended the league. There were so many activities going on, there was not much time for the team to practice, and I guess I wasn't a particularly good coach. It seemed to die a natural death. Nobody cared much, not even the team. But I am sure there would have been a rumpus if we had killed it before they had learned through experience that a gymnasium was good for other things than basketball games. So, shall we say as another guide that it is well to *build up before you break down.*

I still clung to much of my formal work that year and I filled the gymnasium with Swedish booms and window ladders and horses and bucks and boxes and all sorts of truck. I did know enough to get plenty of balls and everybody had a chance to play. I gave every girl an examination and wrote to all mothers of narrow chests, round shoulders, and crooked backs for permission to give their children special exercises. Please note the following very important item. In this group fell the favorite daughter of the Superintendent of Schools and as luck would have it, this procedure both astonished and pleased the Superintendent for he thought only the strong received special training in physical education, and instead of being peeved at my saying his daughter was crooked, he was gratified with the attention. The girl liked to take her exercises and she and I got on together famously. I tell you this because I have always felt I never would have been a supervisor in the Detroit public schools if her back had been straight. The Superintendent did not pay me a visit the whole year through but on the day schools opened the next fall he suddenly appeared before me with the following, "The Board of Education will vote tonight for a Supervisor of Physical Culture. We have had two and they were both dead failures. Somebody is going to present the name of another candidate whom I do not want. May I propose your name?" I had never thought of being a supervisor, but that Superintendent had a forceful personality and a steely blue eye. I seemed to feel him saying to himself "Has she got the nerve?" and I said "Yes" but felt terrified. He always had his way with his Board, so of course I was elected. One member said he would have liked to see me, as he voted for my predecessor because of her fine "fizzykew."

I had no knowledge of elementary schools in general or in Detroit. I had never supervised anything or anybody, nor had I taken a course or read a book on supervision. School principals, teachers, and school children were unknown quantities. I have always felt that it was the confidence of the Superintendent's daughter and his steely blue eye that drove me to it. So I say to you young people, *never be afraid to take a chance even if the opportunity comes by chance.*

All that the Superintendent asked of me for the first year was to make teachers and children like it, for in 1908 one and all hated it. I made a few trial visits to discover what was left by my predecessor with the fine "fizzykew." I found black looks from teachers and disgust from children when they stood up and clapped their hands eight times on the right and eight times on the left—all they could remember.

There must have been about eighty schools in Detroit at that time and I knew that my success or failure depended upon the principals and the teachers, and I shall add the janitors, for if they reported me "downtown"—as our headquarters were familiarly called—as a nuisance in their building, there was the devil to pay. And so, I laid my plans for friendliness first and foremost. Shall we say then, *gain friendliness before you ask for cooperation.*

The first thing I did was to open the Central High pool for free use of principals and teachers every evening. The comradeship we established lasted me during my fourteen years of service in Detroit, and these few teachers formed a nucleus of friendliness. Next I held those bugbears called teachers' meetings to put across my "subject" as this seemed the way of all super-

visors, *but* I never asked a teacher to take an exercise. They sat after a hard day's work, while I, in a gymnasium suit, stood on a table, gave myself commands and did the exercises, much like a monkey on a string. It seems that my predecessor had stood them up in rows and kept them till six o'clock clapping their hands and what not. Anyway, I scored a hit, and shall we say, *if you cannot make your co-workers happy, make them as happy as you can.*

I advised them not to demonstrate to the children but to follow the simple directions I was sending them in mimeographed form and to let the children help them work it out and to use children as demonstrators.

Next I selected simple exercises that brought big muscles into play but took little skill and could not easily go wrong. I threw away complicated demands and made short cuts, all of which probably made the founders of Swedish gymnastics turn in their graves. I showed the teachers what I wanted the children to do and said that they, the teachers, could use any method they found worked best to get results. Another guide then might be, *be willing to throw past practices to the winds if they do not fit the situation,* or shall we put it, *separate essentials from nonessentials.*

I soon yielded my place on the demonstration platform to children who were delighted to be selected and become part of a lesson to teachers. As I visited classrooms I was astonished at the excellent results of untrained people, I mean untrained in physical education. They violated all hard and fast rules I had always thought essential to success. They followed with joy my request that they never demonstrate and that eliminated one great chance for error. I remember one very lame teacher who sat at her desk during the lesson and she had the peppiest sort of response from her huge eighth-grade class and exactly the sort of work I wanted. Of course there were funny mistakes. I was still a believer in deep breathing, and we called it West Point Breathing—rolling our hands and arms backward and puffing out our chests like soldiers. In one room I saw the children in perfect unison and with great pride turn and point to the west, but the breaths were very deep and the teacher had no sense of humor so I praised them highly and let it go—a case of relative importance—of essentials versus nonessentials.

When I waxed enthusiastic over a room to a principal, she would say "Why not, she is the best teacher I have." I learned from hundreds of best teachers that perfect rapport between teacher and pupils, which only comes with character, intelligence, and a sense of humor, counts more than methods of teaching.

You remember that the Superintendent required me to make them like it the first year, and I never shall forget my joy the first day the children rubbed their stomachs when I entered the door. That was the Detroit method of expressing perfect satisfaction. It seemed, however, that there was a limit to enthusiasm in the mind of the Superintendent for one day with fire in his eye he told me that staying after school to dance had to stop—the doors must close at four o'clock and the children should go home. I found out that a complaint had come over the dance idea so for a while we did "rhythms" instead, without changing the activities, and all was well. What's in a name anyway?

As for games, we had a terrible enemy in the Supervisor of Buildings. We probably did make some of those old school houses rock, for we played hard, so we made compromises and in some of the worst places the children used a sort of shuffling run that didn't shake the floor. That supervisor one day saw the children sitting on their desks to do some exercises and after that every scratch was laid to me. He said it was their buttons, and my assertion that they didn't have buttons where they sat was of no avail. One of the nicest uses for desks came as a surprise in a third-grade room when on command every boy slowly uncurled in his seat and stood on his head on top of his desk and slowly curled up again and sat down. We had chinning bars in the doorways and when children got restless they would work it off on those bars. I have seen boys turning cart wheels on their way up to the teacher's desk, rather than walk. I remember taking visitors to one room where games were a great success and on leaving I foolishly said "We would like to stay and play with you all day but we must go." Up jumped a little girl and leaning toward me hopefully with both hands on her desk, she said "Oh hey—

come on." I want you to get the idea that out of my formal gymnastic background came a program enriched by a corps of the finest teachers and children a greenhorn ever met.

The contrast between our rather haphazard methods and what I saw in another city not long ago will show you into what I might have grown. There was a supervisor who knew what he wanted and got it. He could go into any school, jump up onto the teacher's platform, and say "Monday— *Begin*, 1, 2, 3, 4" and away they went. He could do that for any day of the week and not a mistake or a variation in the whole city. That was truly wonderful organization and both he and the city were proud of it.

By the end of the first year I had not satisfactorily covered every school and I asked for four assistants. No other supervisor had any, and the Superintendent said I was crazy and extravagant, but he would ask the Board for two. Another principle might be, *it is sometimes wise to ask for more than you expect*. But this demands caution and careful study of your superiors. It was quite an issue because it set a policy and I had to interview Board members. The last one came the day the Board met and I was pretty nervous. He shot the question "How many minutes do you plan that each assistant supervisor will spend in each room?" I had been so busy trying to get them that I had made no plans like that—besides it seemed like a waste of time till I got them. But something told me that with this businessman I must be quick and definite so I looked him in the eye and said "Thirteen minutes." I don't know why thirteen unless I thought it would bring me luck. He took out a notebook and began to figure. My knees shook, but the mahogany board table hid them. I didn't know if he would discover that we three would reach each school once a month or once in ten years. He finally closed his book with a snap and said "I can see that you have worked this out very carefully and I shall vote for your two assistants." His bluff was as good as mine for I don't believe he knew how many rooms there were either. I'm afraid I can drag out no educational principle from this, unless we say *it sometimes is better to be quick on the trigger than cautious*.

Next morning the *Free Press* announced

in big front page letters "Miss Perrin Gets Her Two Assistants," and the department began to grow. When I left in 1923 there were over three hundred of us. Now that has doubled and it is still growing. For several years my elementary supervisors were women, but there came a lucky year when I appointed Mr. Pearl and Mr. Post in charge of athletics for boys. About this time my old school sent out a scout to discover if I had gone crazy. I was appointing graduates from physical education schools and college departments of physical education from all over the country. That was bad enough, but these two men had never attended a physical education school in their lives. They were just plain elementary school principals from Butte, Montana—of all places!

The men members of the department who taught in our high schools protested, but things were going my way in those days. *Select your assistants for what they can do, not only for their training.* These two men knew schools far better than I did and they knew and loved children. They had a philosophy of real education, what we now call Progressive Education; they had lived in the big open spaces and were athletes of the finest type. The enthusiasm, the new ideas, and the hard work of these two were never ending. The happiness of the children and the good of the department were always uppermost with them and they put new life into our work. The Decathlon for boys and Pentathlon for girls, old-time stunts for all, and the Belle Isle Field Day with its huge clock by which events were run, are outstanding results of those days.

Our program grew more and more informal because we seemed able to accomplish more that way and the more we tried informality the more we liked it. Then came a period of great growth when the platoon schools were started, each with one and many with two gymnasiums, and children in them and on the playground every period, necessitating from three to six special teachers in a building. At the same time came the intermediate or junior high schools, each with two gymnasiums and two swimming pools and special teachers to man them. Everywhere the classes were large and we found that the informal small squad work with much pupil responsibility produced the best results. . . .

32. Origins of contemporary sports*

Marvin H. Eyler

*Professor and Head of the Department of Physical Education, College of Physical
Education, Recreation, and Health, University of Maryland*

ABSTRACT

The central purpose of this study was to determine the origin of sports extant in English-speaking countries. The method of research utilized was principally historical-bibliographical and was concerned with the collection, criticism, and synthesis of source material in an effort to establish past actuality. Specific documentary evidence concerning the date, place, and significant circumstances asociated with the origins of 95 sports was synthesized. In most instances, establishing the date and place of origin was possible. Often, however, determining the personnel and circumstances connected with the origins was not possible. Charts show the dates of the origins chronologically, the origins attributed to various countries, and the activities from which the 95 sports evolved.

Approximately 12 years ago certain graduate requirements led the writer to explore, quite superficially at first, the beginnings of some of our more popular and universally practiced sports. It soon became evident that the sources for such information were widely diverse and in many instances not generally known or readily available. By diversity of sources is meant the immense range of extant artifacts and documents which reveal information relative to the origins of sports. It also became quite evident that within the literature there was considerable variance, confusion, and, in some instances, contradiction.

PURPOSE

The purpose of the original study,[1] therefore, was to determine, as far as was practicable, the origins of sports. More specifically, the study attempted to specify: (a) the date of origin or the earliest refer-

ence in the literature when a date could not be ascertained with any real degree of accuracy, (b) the geographic location of the sport's origin, and (c) certain activities from which the sports reported upon evolved.

Originally the writer intended to study and report upon the origins of all currently practiced sports in English-speaking countries. However, it soon became evident that this could not be accomplished at present due to the immensity of the problem, the unavailability of credible sources, and the factor of time. After an extensive search for evidence, the material collected was collated, analyzed, and synthesized. As a result, information relative to the origins of 95 of the sports extant in English-speaking countries is being reported. This information is based on the resources available in the New York Public Library, the Library of Congress, the University of Illinois Library, the Huntington Library, and, in film form, the Bodleian Library and the British Museum.

LIMITATIONS OF THE STUDY

In considering the "firsts" in any area of knowledge, problems immediately become apparent. In a study of the origin of sports, problems pertain to those sports which were previously a method of protection, a means of livelihood, or a preparation for military pursuits. A point had to be determined when an activity ceased to be chiefly utilitarian and became primarily a sport or an amusement. Such sporting activities as angling, archery, boxing, swimming, and wrestling fall into these categories.

Another problem is the question of how far back one should go in searching for the genuine origin. To be specific, when did such activities as rounders, one-o-cat, and town ball coalesce into the sport of baseball? It was obvious that there could be no set rule

---

*From *Research Quarterly*, Vol. 32, p. 480, Dec. 1961. Used by permission.
[1] The study was a doctoral dissertation completed under the guidance of S. C. Staley, dean, College of Physical Education, University of Illinois, Urbana.

to follow in synthesizing such material; the solution depended upon the circumstances of each individual case. The general rule followed was that for highly controversial origins, a date was designated only at the point in the sport's development when the sport became easily recognizable with the modern concept of method of play, and/or when the sport was governed by a body of recognizable rules.

Certain limitations were imposed on the scope of the study. Sports that are practiced largely or exclusively in non-English-speaking countries were eliminated except for cases in which mention of such a sport was necessary to a full understanding. For example, a statement explaining the relationship of *jeu de paume* and the origin of tennis is relevant. Extinct sports such as bull, bear, and badger baiting, jousting, cudgeling, and tournament were not included. Children's play activities, that is, games or sports such as hopscotch, blindman's buff, and battledore and shuttlecock, were excluded. The study did not include games or pastimes which require little or no gross muscular movement, such as card games, chess, and checkers. Sport-work activities or contests such as woodchopping, plowing, axe throwing, and tree climbing were not investigated. Excluded also were miscellaneous sporting activities such as dog and horse shows. Omitted were some sports currently practiced in English-speaking countries for which there was insufficient source material available to warrant a valid statement. Finally, no attempt was made to present techniques, rules, or the development of the sports included.

The term *sport* is derived from the word disport (spelled dysporte, in the fourteenth century). According to *A New English Dictionary on Historical Principles*[32] disport meant sport, pastime, recreation, pleasure and was first used in the literature in 1303. This work stated that Cotgrave had used the French term *se desporter*. Skeat[36] traced the same word to du Cange.[2] A search of

Cotgrave's *A Dictionaire of the French and English Tongves,* published in 1611, showed no evidence of the existence of the term *se desporter*. However, Cotgrave did use the term *se deporter* which, among other things, meant "to disport, play, recreate himselfe, passe away the time."

The modern term *sports* has been defined as: (a) "that which diverts, and makes mirth, pastime . . . game or mode of amusement . . . diversion of the field . . ."[41]; (b) "any play, pastime, game or contest involving a reasonable degree of individual skill and physical prowess . . ."[12]; (c) "that which makes with pastime, amusement . . . play or game . . . such as rowing games, hunting and fishing . . . contest . . . involving physical prowess and individual skill . . ."[13]; (d) "sports specifically connotes those activities which require certain patterns of athletic executions which must be performed with some skill and which often must conform to prescribed rules . . ."[4]; and (e) "Pleasant pastime; entertainment or amusement; recreation, diversion in participation in games or exercise, especially those of an athletic character.[36]

For this investigation the term *sports* is interpreted in a broad general sense and embraces all those activities which require physical performance (movement), involve some degree of skill and/or conditioning, and embody a pattern of performance and/or a set of recognizable rules. No one particular sport necessarily qualified under all of the requirements listed above.

METHODOLOGY

This study involved principally the use of the historical-bibliographical method of research. Contrary to the historiography concept of Fling,[17] Nevins,[18] and Garraghan[19] where the observer (researcher) neither controls nor evaluates the data, a provisional attempt was made to interpret some of the findings in the light of chronological and social implications.

Critical valid historical research embodies the concept of the unique circumstance[17] or the significant phenomenon.[1] In any such historical study of man three basic factors must be considered. They are: (a) past facts, sometimes referred to as past actuality; (b) remains of the past left by society, often referred to as documents and/or artifacts; and (c) a synthetic re-creation of the

---

[2]Charles du Fresne Sieur du Cange's, *Glossarium Mediae et Infimae Latinitatis*, in five volumes, was first published in 1678. In it, the following phrase may be found: "De porter praeterea resurparunt, pro Oblectari, recreare, vulgo Se divirtir, se rejouir," which loosely means among other things, to divert or delight oneself, to restore or recreate oneself openly, or to exercise for enjoyment.

past, often referred to as historiography. For the most part, historiography is merely the vehicle utilized to recreate as accurately as possible past actuality. Such a method necessitates extensive use of artifacts and documents. Inasmuch as the historical researcher is at least once removed from past actuality, he must rely almost entirely upon credible documents and genuine artifacts.

One of the most difficult problems in the search for historical truth is, of course, the establishment of fact. A particular event which occurred can never again be repeated or reconstructed exactly in the same way. Even the account of eyewitnesses, which is considered a primary source under certain circumstances, is difficult to accept at times because it is essentially a record of the impression made upon the witness.[17] The witness recorded what he thought he saw or heard, not necessarily what actually happened or was said. One suggested method which might help at this juncture is the affirmation of two or more independent witnesses.[23] In order to establish evidence in this way, the statements should not differ in important points nor agree in every detail.[40] Collusion should certainly be suspected if the latter was the case.

No attempt will be made here to relate the use and function of historical criticism. For those interested in a detailed analysis of the use of external (authenticating) and internal (credibility) criticism refer to Gottschalk,[22] Nevins,[33] and Garraghan.[19]

Some of the richest sources for the early beginnings of sports in England were legal documents in such compilations as *Rotuli Parliamentorum*,[35] *Statutes at Large from the Magna Charta*,[8] *A Collection in English of the Statutes now in force, continued from the beginning of the Magna Charta*,[8] *and the Lavves and Acts of Parliament, Maid Be King Iames the First. . . .*[27] Other early sources pertain to the techniques of how the sports were played as well as to their origin and development. Some such sources are Nichols' *Progresses of Queen Elizabeth*,[34] James I's *Basilikon Doron*,[24] Cleland's *The Institvtion of a Yovng Nobleman*,[7] and Burton's *Anatomy of Melancholy*.[5]

Another notable early source is Stow's *Survey of London*,[39] first published in 1603, which included a translation of the very valuable document of William Fitzstephen called *Descripto Nobilissimae Civitatis Londonniae,* which, in turn, was found in the preface of Fitzstephen's *Life of Thomas Becket* written in 1174. Gaston de Foix's *Livre de Chasse,* published in 1387, probably the earliest comprehensive treatise on the sport of the field, is devoted especially to hunting and has been almost literally translated in *The Master of Game* by Edward, Second Duke of York.[16] This work is considered the oldest treatise on the subject of the chase in the English language. *The Boke of Saint Albans,*[3] attributed to Dame Juliana Berners and published in 1486, is an important source of information on early hunting, falconry, and heraldry. Frederick II's *De Arte Venandi Cum Avibus,*[18] written sometime between 1244 and 1250, is a masterly and comprehensive treatise on falconry and hawking as the sport was known during the Middle Ages.

Some dates of origins could be definitely fixed; some could not. In some cases, it was only possible to fix a date *ante quem* and *post quem*. The critical point to be determined was the date before which time it was reasonably certain that the sport did not exist and after which time it was certain to have been in existence. For the most part, only when a date could be established beyond reasonable doubt was it included. The writer may have erred, in some instances, on the side of conservatism; quite probably, some of the sports included have an older history than that indicated but reasonable proof thereof is lacking. The sport of archery is a case in point. It is probable that for many years the bow and arrow played a triple role, of warfare, livelihood, and recreation, and the problem was to determine a point after which time archery was definitely practiced as a recreational activity, that is, as a sport.

CONCLUSIONS

1. The evidence shows that there was a substantial increase in the number of sports introduced during the nineteenth century (see Table 1). A close relationship seems to exist between the increase of leisure time, in part induced by the Industrial Revolution, and this development. Of the 95 sports covered, 49 or 52 percent came into being during the nineteenth century. A combination of the figures for the nineteenth and the

Table 1. Chronological distribution of established dates of origins*

Sport	Date of origin
Wrestling	(2160) 1788 B.C.
Boxing	(2160?) 850 B.C.
Field events	(900 B.C.?) 776 B.C.
Track events	(900 B.C.?) 776 B.C.
Hunting	(2357) 400 B.C.
Kite flying	(1121) 221 B.C.
Coursing	7 A.D.
Cock fighting	77
Angling	200
Falconry	350
Horse racing	(648 B.C.) 1174
Tennis	1230
Lawn bowls	1366
Quoits	(450 B.C.) 1409
Golf	(1380?) 1457
Target rifle shooting	1498
Fencing	1517
Hurling	1527
Shuffleboard	1532
Archery (target)	(1530) 1585
Billiards	(1520?) 1590
Fowling	(2475 B.C.) 1596
Polo	(475?) 1596
Curling	1607
Ice skating	(500) 1659
Cricket	(1600) 1744
Fives	1746
Yacht racing	(1675) 1775
Pedestrianism	(1610) 1792
Racquets	(1555) 1799
Horseshoes	(1750?) 1801
Coaching	(1590) 1807
Steeplechasing	(1740) 1810
Mountaineering	(1780?) 1811
Gymnastics	(1790) 1816
Pigeon racing	(1800) 1818
Harness racing	1825
Sculling	(1715) 1839
Lacrosse	(1400) 1839
Rowing	1839
Bowling (ten pins)	(1600) 1840
Croquet	1840
Handball	(1500?) 1840
Baseball	(1750) 1846
Rugby	1846
Iceboating	(1720) 1850
Weight lifting	(1720) 1854
Canoe racing	(1790?) 1859
Soccer	1859
Squash racquets	1859
Swimming	(1530) 1859
Roller skating	1863
Trap shooting	1866

*The date given after each sport is that of the earliest documented evidence of its origin in organized form. Dates shown in parentheses are those of documented evidence of previous existence, as unorganized or noncompetitive activity. A date in parentheses with a question mark indicates that reputed evidence previous to this date may not actually refer to this specific sport.

Table 1. Chronological distribution of established dates of origins—cont'd

Sport	Date of origin
Field trials	1866
Bicycle racing	1868
Badminton	1870
Skiing	(1750) 1870
Target pistol shooting	1871
Model sailboat racing	1872
Lawn tennis	1873
Football (American)	1874
Dog racing	(1810?) 1876
Roque	1879
Ice hockey	(1810) 1880
Rodeo	(1830) 1880
Judo	1882
Tobogganing	(1837?) 1883
Water polo	1885
Field hockey	(B.C.?) 1886
Birling	1888
Table tennis	1889
Darts	(1850?) 1890
Rope spinning	(1850?) 1890
Squash tennis	1890
Basketball	1891
Automobile racing	1895
Volleyball	1895
Jai alai	1896
Paddle tennis	1898
Motorcycle racing	1902
Corkball	1904
Motorboat racing	1904
Model airplane flying	1905
Airplane flying	1907
Soaring	1909
Speedball	1920
Softball	(1890) 1923
Miniature golf	(1860) 1927
Soapbox racing	1927
Six man football	1933
Skin diving	1934
Miniature auto racing	1936
Water skiing	1939
Skish	(1880?) 1939
Flickerball	1948

twentieth centuries reveals that 65 or 68 percent of the sports reported originated during this period.

2. England and the United States are the sites of origin for 56 or 59% of the sports covered (see Figure I). When considered from a world-wide sports viewpoint, this is interesting. One of the limitations imposed upon the study was to include only those sports practiced principally in English-speaking countries, and under such limitations, one would normally expect a large percentage of the sports' origins to have been attrib-

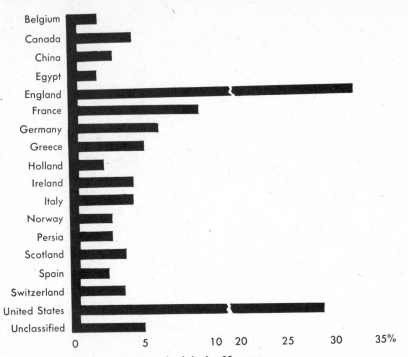

Fig. I. Percentage distribution of place of origin for 95 sports.

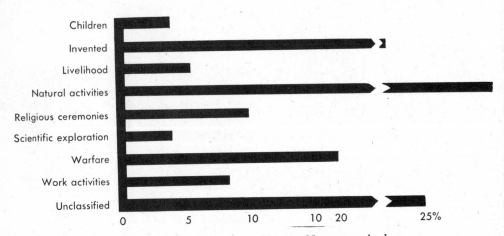

Fig. II. Percentage distribution of activities from which the 95 sports evolved.

uted to England and/or the United States. If the study could have included the origins of all known sports, the percentage reflecting the origins traced to England and/or the United States would no doubt have been reduced.

3. Of those origins attributed to the United States (a total of 24), 17 or 71 percent occurred since the relatively late date of 1890. Many of these sports are not particularly popular or universally practiced.

This finding implies a rather late sports awakening for the United States compared to that of older European cultures. This may be because the results of the Industrial Revolution may not have affected the sporting life of the people of this country until late in the nineteenth century. It has been rather well established that the Industrial Revolution did not fully develop here until after the Civil War.

4. In a general sense, it appears that of

the 95 sports covered (see Figure II), three emanated from children's play activities (examples: basketball and volleyball), four came out of a search for food or livelihood (examples: hunting and fishing), 26 evolved from what might be termed natural activities such as transportation and communication (examples: skiing and pedestrianism), eight were originally affiliated with religious or ceremonial activities (examples: tennis and lacrosse), two emerged from scientific exploration (examples: mountaineering and soaring), 13 resulted from activities primarily used in warfare (examples: archery and target rifle shooting), six came from work activities (examples: rodeo and birling), and finally, 22 of the original 95 sports were left unclassified because of lack of supporting evidence.

REFERENCES

1. Abelson, H. H. *The Art of Educational Research*. New York: World Book, 1933.
2. Ainsworth, Dorothy S., and others. "Historical Research Methods." *Research Methods Applied to Health, Physical Education, and Recreation*. Washington, D. C.: American Association for Health, Physical Education, and Recreation, 1949.
3. Berners, Dame Juliana (?). *The Boke of Saint Albans*. London: Elliot Stock, 1901.
4. Bridgewater, William, and Sherwood, Elizabeth J., editors. *The Columbia Encyclopedia*. New York: Columbia University Press, 1946.
5. Burton, Robert. *Anatomy of Melancholy*. Oxford: John Lichfield and James Short for Henry Cripps, 1621.
6. Catlin, George. *Letters and Notes on the Manners, Customs and Condition of the North American Indians*. Volumes I and II. Henry G. Bohn, 1851.
7. Cleland, James. *The Institvtion of a Yovng Nobleman*. Oxford: Joseph Barnes, 1607.
8. *A Collection in English of the Statues Now in Force, Continued from the Beginning of Magna Charta. . . .* Imprinted at London: by the Deputies of Christopher Baker, 1588.
9. Comenii, John Amos. *Orbis Sensualium Pictus*. Translated by Charles Hoole. London: Printed by S. Leacroft, 1777.
10. Cotgrave, Randle, compiler. *A Dictionaire of the French and English Tongves*. London: Printed by Adam Islip, 1611.
11. Culin, Stewart. "Games of the North American Indians." *Twenty-fourth Annual Report of the Bureau of American Ethnology*. Washington: Government Printing Office, 1907.
12. Cummings, Parke, editor. *The Dictionary of Sports*. New York: A. S. Barnes and Company, 1949.
13. Cummings, Parke. "Sports, Athletic." *Encyclopedia Americana* **25**:434-43; 1955. pp. 434-443.
14. Cureton, Thomas K. "Library Research Methods." *Research Methods Applied to Health, Physical Education, and Recreation*. Washington, D. C.: American Association for Health, Physical Education, and Recreation, 1949.
15. Cushing, Frank H.: "Outlines of Zuni Creation Myths." *Thirteenth Annual Report of the Bureau of Ethnology*. Washington: Government Printing Office, 1896.
16. *Edward, Duke of York, The Master of Game*. Edited by William A. and F. Baillie-Grohman. London: Chatto & Windus, 1909.
17. Fling, Fred M. *The Writing of History*. New Haven: Yale University Press, 1920.
18. Frederick II. *De Arte Venandi Cum Avibus*. Translated by Casey A. Wood and F. Marjorie Fyfe. Stanford, California: Stanford University Press, 1943.
19. Garraghan, G. J. *A Guide to Historical Method*. New York: Fordham University Press, 1946.
20. Giles, Herbert A. *Adversaria Sinica*. Shanghai: Messrs Kelly and Walsh, Ltd., 1914.
21. Gini, Corrado. "Rural Ritual Games in Libya." *Rural Sociology* **4**:283-99; 1939.
22. Gottschalk, L. *Understanding History*. New York: Alfred Knopf, Inc., 1950.
23. Hockett, Homer C. *Introduction to Research in American History*. New York: The Macmillan Company, 1949.
24. James I. *Basilikon Doran, or His Maiesties Instrvctions to His Dearest Sonne, Henry the Prince*. Edinburgh: Printed by Robert VValdegrave, 1603.
25. Johnson, Leighton H. "Education Needs Historical Studies." *The Phi Beta Kappan*. **36**: 157-59; January 1955.
26. Keble, Joseph. *The Statutes at Large from Magna Charta Until This Time*. London: The assigns of John Bill, Thomas Newcomb and Henry Hills, the assigns of Richard Atkins and Edward Atkins, 1681.
27. *Lavves and Acts of Parliament, Maid Be King Iames the First and His Svcessors Kinges of Scot*. Edinburgh: Imprinted by Robert, 1597.
28. Maigaard, J. "Battingball Games." *Genus* **1-2**:57-72; December 1941.
29. Markham, Garvase. *Country Contentments, or the Husbandmans Recreations*. London: William Wilson for Iohn Harison, 1649.
30. Massingham, H. J. *The Heritage of Man*. London: Jonathan Caps, 1929.
31. Mooney, James. "The Cherokee Ball Play." *The American Anthropologist* **3**:105-32; April 1896.
32. Murray, James A., editor. *A New English Dictionary on Historical Principles*. Volumes I-X. New York: Macmillan and Company, 1888-1926. (Supp. 1933.)
33. Nevins, Allan. *The Gateway to History*. New York: C. Appleton-Century Company, 1938.
34. Nichols, John. *The Progresses of Queen Elizabeth*. Volumes I-III. London: Printed by and for John Nichols and Sons, 1823.
35. *Rotuli Parliamentorum;* et petitiones, et

placita, in Parliamento Tempore Edward R. I finem Henrichi VII, 6 vols. London: 1767-77.

36. Skeat, Walter W. *An Etymological Dictionary of the English Language*. Oxford: Clarendon Press, 1898.

37. Staley, S. C. *The World of Sport*. Champaign, Illinois: Stipes Publishing Company, 1955.

38. Stern, Theodore. "The Rubber-ball Games of the Americas." *Monographs of the American Ethnological Society* No. 18, 1948.

39. Stow, John. *A Survey of London*. Volumes I-II. Oxford: Clarendon Press, 1908.

40. Vincent, J. M. *Historical Research*. New York: Peter Smith, 1929.

33. Are we losing the Olympic ideal?*

Charles A. Bucher

*Professor of Education and Director of Physical Education, School of Education,
New York University*

The Olympic ideal is dying. It will not permeate the games unless Americans and the rest of the world demand a change in emphasis. This great international festival is becoming cannon fodder in the cold war, with major stress on national pride, winning, scoring points and beating Russia at all costs. The drive to produce champions and to win is traditional in America and must be preserved. However, in the Olympic Games the emphasis is supposed to be placed on the individual athlete rather than the nation, on making friends rather than making points. As Eddie Eagan, former chairman of our National Olympic Finance Committee, says, "The true purpose of the Olympics is to bring about world sportsmanship and goodwill. It is not an event to bring athletes together in competition to foster nationalism. The Olympic ideal of sports for sports' sake, regardless of race, color or creed, must continue or the Olympics should be canceled as an international event."

As now conducted, the games are hampering the achievement of international goodwill. Countries are confusing the winning of sports with national prestige. The honor of the flag is not involved in the winning or losing of a race or game, in the fact that a foreign contestant may finish a tenth of a second ahead of an American in the 100-meter dash. The honor of the flag *is* involved in the success or failure to promote the brotherhood of man and world peace.

Baron Pierre de Coubertin, the French-

man responsible for the revival of the Olympic Games in 1896, said: "The important thing is not winning, but taking part; the essential thing in life is not conquering, but fighting well." All nations, large or small, strong or weak, are encouraged to participate, not for the purpose of gaining national honors, but in the spirit of friendly rivalry and respect for the ability of the individual athlete.

These principles represented the Olympic spirit of the Greeks many years before the birth of Christ. Officially recorded as first being held in 776 B.C., the games were held in honor of the god Zeus. The victorious athlete received only a garland of wild olive branches, of no material value but held in the highest esteem. The games were held for the next 1,100 years. Emperor Theodosius I of Rome banned them in 394 A.D., but the Olympic ideal did not die with the decree. Some 1,500 years later de Coubertin brought about its revival. He formed an International Olympic Committee, whose members owed their allegiance in the field of sports to all nations rather than to just their own, to further the ideal and spirit of the games.

In order to insure recognition of the individual athlete, de Coubertin felt strongly that no point score should be used. The point score was purposely disallowed to prevent the larger nations and their hordes of athletes from monopolizing the games by sheer weight of statistics. It was felt that regardless of how many points a large country might tally, a single victory by a lone representative of a smaller country should be considered of equal importance.

But sportswriters at the Olympics in 1952

*From Sports Illustrated (Vol. 3, Aug. 8, 1955). Copyright 1955 by The Reader's Digest Assn., Inc. Condensed in the Sept. 1955 Reader's Digest. Used by permission.

147

at Helsinki played up the cold war in sports and used point scores as bait to attract readers. To read the American press, anyone would think the only participants were the Soviet Union and the United States— although 69 nations took part. Newspapers ran such headlines as these:

RUSSIA AND UNITED STATES SET FOR OLYMPIC FEUD

RUSSIA EXULTS OVER UNITED STATES' DEFEAT IN SOCCER

UNITED STATES CLOSES POINT GAP WITH RUSSIA IN OLYMPIC RACE

The many competing nations used a variety of scoring systems in order to grab an advantage and gain scoring honors. Some systems awarded 10 points for first place, others seven, still others six. The end result was a potpourri of figures adding up to more confusion and ill will.

Actually, as Brutus Hamilton, coach of the 1952 U. S. track and field team, pointed out, "There is no way to score the overall Olympic results. You can score the individual contests, such as track and field, of course, but it seems ridiculous to me to score as many points for the winner of the 135-pound Greco-Roman wrestling bout as for the winner of the men's 1,500-meter run." Yet sportswriters solemnly tot up imaginary "points" not only for the winner but for the first three, four, five or six contestants in everything from the hop, step and jump to the women's shotput.

The fair sex has not been able to escape the pressure to insure an American Olympic victory. Eleanor Metheny, professor of Physical Education at the University of Southern California, is a national leader in women's sports. She says: "In the 1952 Olympic Games, American girls excelled in swimming and diving, and most of them responded with indifference to the scathing comments of some sportswriters about the poor showing made in gymnastics and track and field. Practices which may have value for the women of Russia may not interest girls in the United States, who are—and want to be—essentially feminine human beings."

In addition to forgetting the nonexistent "point system," we must keep the games out of politics. Douglas F. Roby of Detroit, former vice president of the U. S. Olympic Committee, says that several congressmen have wanted to introduce bills to pay the entire cost of sending our athletes to Melbourne. "We turned them down," Roby says, "because we didn't want our amateur sports to get involved in politics. The money to support these athletes should come freely and spontaneously from the people." Eddie Eagan says: "The reason we appeal for private contributions is because we want the people in the grass roots and in the large cities to feel that they are a part of this great movement. And the U. S. Olympic Committee wants all Americans to give their donations, not for victory, but for the encouragement of sportsmanship."

The armed services are also trying to get their fingers into the pie. The Pentagon is making available to every soldier, sailor and airman who shows promise, the chance of winning a gold medal. This effort has Congressional backing. The 84th Congress passed Public Law 11, which gives the top brass authority to get their athletes in shape. Last September the Department of Defense accented the Olympic effort with an order to provide for contestants who wanted to compete on an international basis. The main objective in the minds of these military men is, apparently, to prove their might and strength in the sports stadium as they do on the field of battle.

Avery Brundage, president of the International Olympic Committee, has warned the armed services that special concentrations of athletes for competitive sports training might jeopardize their amateur standing.

Daniel J. Ferris, secretary-treasurer of the Amateur Athletic Union of the United States, despite widespread criticism, voted for admission of an all-China federation at the International Amateur Athletic Federation meetings recently held in Bern, Switzerland. This would permit both the defenders of Formosa and the Reds to compete in Olympic track and field events. As Ferris said, "I still believe it beneficial to the cause of international friendship to have athletes from all sides of the political fence get together in sports competition."

The Olympic spirit expressed by Brundage, Roby and Ferris has not penetrated the prejudices which cloak many American minds. Some persons do not seem to understand that our athletes are competing against the boys and girls who are the champions of track and field in Russia—not the leaders in the Kremlin. They have forgotten that in the Olympics, official team championships have purposely been eliminated to encourage every country, regardless of size, to participate.

The Russians may be violating amateur regulations and engaging in overzealous athletic promotion to make Americans lose face when they meet down under. There is evidence they are buying their athletes, working them full time and making mockery of the Olympic ideal. But let's not let Russia push us into doing likewise.

Although the nonthinking, flag-waving politicians and journalists in many countries have become involved in the cold war of sports, we can be thankful the athletes on the field have not yet enlisted. At Helsinki, spectators and participants could not understand the incompatibility of the battle raging in the press and the sportsmanship and fair play that were actually expressed throughout the games. Americans can be especially proud that the hates and jealousies were not reflected by their athletes. Braven Dyer, writing from Stockholm for the Los Angeles *Times,* said: "After the fine spirit of sportsmanship which all competitors displayed at Helsinki, I am firmly convinced that the main hope for peace in the world is through athletic competition and not through political channels. . . ."

Dick Hamilton, a University of California student who was wounded in Korea, went to the Olympic Games with anger in his heart. He was greatly impressed by the sportsmanship displayed by contestants. He says:

"In April of 1951 I was wounded while on duty with the U. S. Marine Corps in Korea. So naturally, when the Russians marched on the field I saw an arrogant, hardened group of athletes. At least, that's what I thought I saw.

"But I was sadly mistaken. On the following day, the first day of actual competition, I saw a Russian turn and shake the hand of the American who had just beaten him. As the games progressed this happened not once, not twice, but every time a similar situation arose. There never was any dislike shown by any of the athletes on the field, and I never saw a display of poor sportsmanship by anyone."

Brutus Hamilton reports: "There was not a single unpleasant incident to mar the competition. We found the Russians to be good sportsmen and their showing, of course, was impressive. In all the six games I have attended as competitor or coach, I have never seen any really bad feelings between the athletes themselves. Such unpleasant incidents as have occurred have arisen largely from the older people who are followers of the teams."

How long can the athletes uphold this fine tradition under the strain of pressures to get the scalps of their opponents?

Our athletes should be encouraged to win, to compete to the very limits of their abilities, but an equally important objective should be to better understand their fellow contestants and the countries they represent.

For the true tradition

The Olympic Games must reflect their true Greek tradition and ideal. In order to accomplish this, the following I suggest as musts:

1) *The unofficial point system must be eliminated.* Scoring points stresses the nation instead of the individual athlete.

2) *The Olympics must not become involved in politics.* Government subsidization should not be allowed.

3) *The games must be strictly amateur.* No professionalism can be tolerated.

4) *All Olympic contestants should be schooled in becoming ambassadors of goodwill among the nations of the world in addition to being champion athletes.*

5) *Tributes, praise and publicity should be awarded for excellence of individual performance, regardless of national origin.*

If the people of the United States and the rest of the world will put these principles into practice, the games will take on new significance. The contestants will march into the great stadium with the Olympic spirit in their hearts. There will be new meaning in the Olympic oath which they will recite in unison. A greater love of sport will prevail as the Olympic flame is lighted.

As de Coubertin so aptly phrased it, "May joy and fellowship reign and may the Olympic torch pursue its way through the ages, increasing friendly understanding among nations for the good of humanity."

34. The significance of human movement: a phenomenological approach*

Seymour Kleinman

The Ohio State University

It is rather ironic that those activities which are most intimately concerned with body are precisely the ones which physical educators choose to ignore or pay only a minimal amount of attention to. Those activities which explore movement with great scope and depth appear to be studiously avoided. For a long period of time gymnastics was almost a dirty word in this profession. And the discipline which encompasses all aspects of movement, the dance, is almost completely alienated from physical education. In men's physical education, dance is practically nonexistent. It appears that in our pursuit of and subservience to game and sport, the body almost acts as an obstacle which must be overcome in order that the ends of sport and games be achieved. The body and its movement is viewed as the means to attain the ends of a game. We seek neither significance nor meaning to human movement. The game has become the thing. We have become uneasy about body and movement. Witness our testy attitude toward the emphasis on fitness and our embrace of the impersonal scientific analysis of human activity. We have divorced the body from experience and we do not attempt to understand it as it operates in the life world. Rather, we attempt to explain it as a physiological organism. We don't look at it as it is but as we conceptualize it scientifically.

To understand one's body as one lives with it is foreign to us, but not to the phenom-enologist. For the phenomenologist, to understand the body is to understand its existential being in the world. This is different from viewing the body as an object for study the way one would study a thing. Merleau-Ponty held that such a view of the body is a secondary meaning of bodily being. He wanted to penetrate into a primordial meaning of the human body. Probably the best and most widely noted illustration of this is Jean Paul Sartre's description of the three dimensions of the human body. An understanding and awareness of these dimensions will help us understand from whence human movement derives its significance. I will use Sartre's example as described by Van Den Berg in an essay from the book *Psychoanalysis and Existential Philosophy.*[1]

A mountaineer about to set out to achieve a difficult peak makes careful plans and pays careful attention to things like his ropes, his shoes, his pitons, and other items of equipment. He concerns himself with the preparation of his body for the task. He is cognizant and actively aware of his body. However, as soon as he begins the climb, all these thoughts vanish. "He no longer thinks of his shoes to which a short time ago he gave such great attention; he forgets the stick that supports him while he climbs . . . he 'ignores his body' which he trained for days beforehand. . . . For only by forgetting, in a certain sense, his body, will he be able to devote himself to the laborious task that has to be performed." What remains, what *is,* is only the mountain. He is absorbed in it, his thoughts are completely given to it. And it is *because* he forgets his body that the

*From Selected Papers: Aesthetics and Human Movement, 1964 Ruby Anniversary Workshop Report, National Association for Physical Education of College Women. Used by permission.

body can realize itself as a living body. "The body is realized as *landscape*"; its length is demonstrated by the difficulties which must be faced from hand hold to hand hold. "Fatigue shows itself first as the changed aspect of the landscape, as the changed physiognomy of the objects." The rocks, the snowfields, the summit appear more hostile.

"The qualities of the body: its measurements, its efficiency and vulnerability can only become apparent when the body itself is forgotten, passed over in silence for the landscape." *It is only the behavior, the act, the movement that explains the body.* In this dimension the landscape is where the significance lies. It is to the landscape that the movement is directed and there in the landscape is where the movement is furnished with significance. Knowing one's body is not revealed by scientific analysis or observation. We just do not come to know our bodies in this way. Wolff discovered that on the average only one out of ten persons can recognize his hand when shown a series of photographs which includes a likeness of his own hand. And yet in fact we *do* know our bodies. It "is that which is most our *own* of all conceivable things, which is least opposed to us, least foreign and so, least antagonistic."[2]

"The second dimension of the body comes into being under the eyes of his fellow man. In the first dimension, remember, the mountaineer in order to accomplish his task transcended his body, 'passed beyond' it in silence." The only change introduced into the second dimension is that the mountaineer unknown to him is being watched by another. The viewer in this dimension concentrates on the very thing that the climber has transcended. He sees the boots, the movements, the bruises. He sees the *body*. The viewer's landscape is centered in this moving body—this object. That which holds least significance to the climber contains the most significance for the hidden viewer. It is this recognition of another as a functioning organism which makes anatomical and physiological analysis possible. And it has been with this dissectable thing—the body—that psychology has been until recently solely concerned. Also physical education has been content to limit its study of movement to this dimension. We have embraced physiological and anatomical analysis with such

vigor and tenacity that it has become the only dimension of being in the world which we recognize. We regard man as a moving organismic thing—an object, capable of being completely understood by means of stimulus-response conditioning, laws of learning, transfer of training, and neurological brain wave analysis. But I shall return to this point later.

The third dimension of the body comes into being when the mountaineer becomes aware that he is being watched. For Sartre, this dimension of being is destructive. It destroys the "passing beyond." The climber becomes annoyed, uncomfortable. He feels vulnerable and defenseless. He miscalculates, he stumbles, he becomes ashamed. For Sartre, the look of the other always results in alienation. Van Den Berg disagrees. "Sartre's look is the look from behind, the malicious look of an unknown person. There is (on the other hand) the look of understanding, of sympathy, of friendship, of love. It may impart a happiness far exceeding in value any solipsistic satisfaction."

The significance of the movements on this dimension lies *in the look*. The somewhere where the movements take place also lies in the look. Under the gaze of the other, whether it be one of approval or disapproval, my body, my movements, my being is out there at the gaze, at the look. This dimension has great meaning and implication for teachers.

Now it is important to note that only one of these three dimensions of being attributes and suggests significance to movement as we physical educators generally regard it. Our profession's approach to movement has been by means of the mechanical, the kinesiological, the physiological, and the anatomical. The psychologically and sociologically oriented people in our field who attempt to study and predict cultural patterns and behavior strive to operate on this same kind of scientific level. During the course of experimentation and observation the individual comes to be regarded as an organism capable of being manipulated. He becomes a thing or an object in the eyes of the other. Analysis and explanation of human movement result but not real understanding.

To the phenomenologist, to understand the body is to see the body not in terms of kinesiological analysis but in the awareness and meaning of movement. It's to be open to gestures and action; it's the grasping of being and acting and living in one's world. Thus movement becomes significant not by a knowledge about the body but through an awareness of the self—a much more accurate term.

What are the implications of this view for physical education? From the phenomenological view it becomes the purpose of the physical educator to develop, encourage, and nurture this awareness of and openness to self—this understanding of self.

I suggest that this will not be accomplished if we continue to equate physical education with sports and games. Games provide satisfactions and fulfill a need to play and compete, but I contend that it is not the function of physical education to take as its responsibility the teaching and playing of games, especially when there is so much more that can be done in the way of enhancing fulfillment and realization through movement.

Thus the objectives of physical education become the following:

1. To develop an awareness of bodily being in the world.
2. To gain understanding of self and consciousness.
3. To grasp the significations of movements.
4. To become sensitive of one's encounters and acts.
5. To discover the heretofore hidden perspectives of acts and uncover the deeper meaning of one's being as it explores movement experiences.
6. To enable one, ultimately, to create on his own an experience through movement which culminates in meaningful, purposeful realization of the self.

This last I feel is the stage of true freedom, ultimate existence, and being. Its result is the attainment of the truly independent spirit, and this should be the goal of all education.

Needless to say this is not the purpose or function of sports and games. Nor should it be! I am not here to deprecate games. But somehow back in its earlier days this profession reacted against the stultifying discipline of gymnastics and equated play with democracy and freedom. Our readiness to accept and encourage the concept of sport and physical education as being one and the

same has brought us to this present state of uneasiness and dissatisfaction—a profession in search of a discipline. Nothing could be more shattering to a dedicated group of people such as we have in this field. It has resulted in a fantastic race to justify our existence and gain respectability by publishing nonbooks, nonarticles, and *non*sensical data by the score. This attempt to convert a field such as ours which operates on a human experiential level into a science would be absurd were it not so tragically close to being accomplished. Physical education is an art, not a science. In our attempts to exhaustively analyze movement, exercise, fatigue, and the like we have moved farther and farther away from the experience as it is acted out—as it *actually* occurs.

This flight to science for respectability has turned many of our best people toward research in this area. But might I point out that whatever these people do in the sciences be they behavioral or physical, they are not doing physical education. If they study muscle fatigue, they are doing physiology. If they study mechanics of movement, they are doing physics. If they study behavior, they are doing psychology. If they study games and sports, they are doing sociology. But these fields are disciplines in their own right. They are certainly not the discipline of physical education. In fact, I don't believe this profession knows what it means to do physical education.

How does one go about *doing* physical education? It is, I believe, our job to deal with the experience of the movement, and it is our role to make this movement experience as highly significant as possible. The student must "enter into" the movement as completely as possible. And I am convinced that no other area in our field fills this need as successfully as the dance. Dance points toward this objective specifically and directly. The interesting thing about this is that most of the dancers and choreographers don't intellectualize and verbalize the experience to death. They just do it and it comes. The objective is attained in the experiencing of it.

Dance is the most demanding of all movement activities. It requires almost complete submissiveness to an iron discipline. And teachers of dance aren't known usually for the democratic spirit that exudes from their studio. Yet despite all of the "wrong" educational techniques the results are astonishing. Out of this experience emerges, not a slave, but a truly free individual—one who has such knowledge and command of his body that he is capable of experiencing movement at its highest and most significant level.

Although all participants in a dance may be performing exactly the same movements, the individual, if he is truly engaged in the act, knows nothing of others. He is completely absorbed in his landscape. He is acting only as *he* can act. He is deriving meaning and significance only in the way *he* is capable. He is aware of his movements as a creative art. It almost doesn't matter that he didn't design the move. He brings to it what he has to offer and what emerges is a noble experience, an enriching experience, a rewarding experience. Even the gaze of the other is transcended at this point. The audience becomes part of the landscape too. The spectators gain their rewards by what they as individuals bring to the experience.

Of course, all this happens if these movements—the dance—are good. So much of dance is extraordinarily poor. On these occasions both audience and dancers suffer. But dance, even when it fails, is by its nature concerned with significant movement.

Of the three dimensions of being outlined in this paper, those two, the first and third, which are most intimately related to physical education still await investigation and description. This is most unfortunate because it is here, in the phenomenological realm, where most of the work needs to be done. Gaining greater sensitivity and awareness of landscapes and their importance in contributing to significant movement is a task with which physical education must become intricately involved.

"Existence as a giver of meaning, manifests itself in all human phenomena, in the gestures of our hands, the mimicry of our face, the smile of the child, the creation of the artist, speech and work. . . . The body is this power of expression. It gives rise to meaning; it makes meaning arise on different levels. . . ."[3] My contention is that for physical education the goal should be meaning and significance on the highest level of existence. I don't believe this can be achieved by a physical education as we know it today. Games and sports by their inherent nature do little toward achieving this goal at best and, in fact, often do much to keep us from it.

REFERENCE NOTES

1. J. H. Van Den Berg, "The Human Body and the Significance of Human Movement," *Psychoanalysis and Existential Philosophy*, H. M. Ruitenbeek, editor (F. P. Dutton & Co., New York, 1962, pp. 90-129).
2. F. J. J. Buytendijk, *General Theory of Human Carriage and Movement* (Utrecht, Spectrum, 1948).
3. R. C. Kwant, *The Phenomenological Philosophy of Merleau-Ponty* (Duquesne University Press, Pittsburgh, Pa., 1963, p. 57).

35. Learning about movement*

Naomi Allenbaugh

Professor, Division of Physical Education for Women
The Ohio State University

Through the decades, elementary physical education has progressed through three major stages, the major emphases of these stages being participation, socialization, and physical fitness. A rapidly developing fourth stage, one of greater sophistication, combines these three earlier stages and adds an emphasis on understanding the environment, movement, and man. It focuses on education for efficiency of movement and for self-discovery, self-direction, and self-realization while incorporating from the earlier emphases such specifics as understanding of and improvement in fundamental and specialized motor skills.

The great increase in knowledge has brought sharply into focus the need for each child to have a broad understanding of many areas and how they relate to each other. Physical education, like every other discipline, can be organized so each child can gradually develop the main ideas of the discipline through the accumulation, comprehension, and synthesis of the related subject matter. Let us examine three of many broad concepts around which it can be organized: Man moves to survive; man moves to discover and understand his environment; man moves to control and adjust to his environment.

The first concept, *man moves to survive,* recognizes the anatomical and physiological nature of man and his need to acquire physiological understanding and readiness for efficient movement. The individual must develop, maintain, and value muscular strength, endurance, flexibility, agility, and balance if he is to survive without unusual dependency on others.

Young children force parents and nursery school teachers to recognize the second concept—*man moves to discover and understand his environment.* Yet when the elementary school child enters the gymnasium to participate in physical education, his drive to examine and explore is frequently destroyed or destructively limited rather than released, encouraged, and guided. As a child comes to understand his environment and use it successfully in movement, he acquires a more realistic body image and a more wholesome self-concept. With the resulting sense of power, he can then accept the task of developing his individual potential rather than wastefully trying to imitate other people.

As the understanding of self and environment evolves, the third concept—*man moves to control and adjust to his environment*—takes on deeper meaning for the individual. He begins to recognize that control of and adjustment to the environment is dependent upon efficiency of movement. Thus he begins to work for the advantageous use of the elements of movement—space, time, force, and flow.

For example, he works to develop the ability to apply appropriate force in his movements in relation to the space and time available to him. He works to develop a smoothness, a flow, a unity of all parts of the body involved in movement. He acquires the ability to understand his movement and he learns ways of improving it.

This ability involves the development of a comprehension of the mechanics of motion. His movement leads him to ask:

*From NEA Journal, Vol. 56, p. 48, Mar. 1967. Used by permission.

What is the center of gravity in my body? How does it influence equilibrium? How do I use my body to maintain balance?

How can my arms, my legs, my whole body serve as levers to increase the force and speed with which I move?

To gain an understanding of the principles of movement, he begins to ask: How can I distribute my weight to gain accuracy, force, and speed, yet maintain my balance? Why does continuing movement in the direction of projected or received force increase my efficiency? Why is my whole body involved in effective movement?

In seeking and finding the answers to these questions, he increases the vocabulary from which he can select the movements most effective in meeting specific demands of the moment. In order to choose which movements are appropriate for various activities, he must develop an understanding of efficient performance of locomotor skills (how to walk, run, hop, leap, slide, skip, and perform combinations of these), non-locomotor skills (turn, twist, stretch, bend, and swing), and manipulative skills (throw, hit, and catch).

Finally he becomes proficient in the *instant organization* of any combination of these skills, demanded for an efficient response to a given situation. He uses his movement vocabulary purposefully.

What experiences can the teacher provide to help the child grasp the meaning of the movement concepts just discussed, to develop movement proficiency, and to become a self-accepting, productive individual?

One answer is to have all children working independently but simultaneously to discover the many different ways in which each child can move *within, through,* and *with* his environment and to establish the requisites for effective movement. The teacher can base problems on the elements of movement (space, time, force, and flow) and their various dimensions so the child moves alone or with others or he moves upon, through, around, and with moving or stationary objects.

In solving these problems, the child uses many fundamental motor skills. Sometimes, at a very young age, he will discover and use combinations of movements which in reality are specialized motor skills normally used in the complex organization of a dance,

a sport, or a game. The important factor in the use of problems is the emphasis on body movement as it relates to space, time, force, and flow.

The direct teaching of an exact skill may follow these earlier experiences or the problems may be deliberately designed so the exact skill will gradually emerge. Such

---

ELEMENTS AND DIMENSIONS OF MOVEMENT

Space	*Levels:* high, medium, low. *Ranges:* wide-narrow, far-near. *Directions:* forward-backward, upward-downward, sideward, circle, diagonal. *Shapes:* round, straight, angular, twisted.
Force	Heavy-light, strong-weak, tight-loose.
Time	Slow, medium, fast.
Flow	Free, bound, sequential.

BODY FOCUS

Body relationships	Head or feet above, level with, or below torso, and combinations.
Body leads	Shoulder, hip, head, knee, foot, etc., combinations.
Body supports	Feet, knees, hands, back, shoulders, head, etc., combinations.
Body control	Starts-stops.

---

movement experience allows each child to progress at his own rate and to feel comfortable with the way he moves rather than to be blocked in his initial learning by the necessity to move exactly as the teacher says he must.

Some specific examples of problems developed around the elements and dimensions of space will serve to illustrate the above ideas:

In what different directions can you move (forward, backward, and the like)?

At how many different levels (high, low, medium) can you move: through space, in your own space, in space with an object, through space with an object, with a partner through space, with a partner in your own small space, sending an object through space to a partner, moving yourself through space as you send an object through space to a partner?

How many different ways can you change the width and length of your body (wide to narrow, long to short, and the like)?

What different shapes can you make with your body (round, straight, angular, curled, twisted)?

Problems using the elements of force and time can be developed in a similar manner. Following these experiences, the children can deal with increasingly complex problems, such as combinations of dimensions within an element (high, backward, wide), combinations of dimensions selected from the different elements (high, forward, fast; high, forward, slow; high, backward, fast; high, backward, slow).

In experimenting with such problems, the child experiences contrasts in dimensions and discovers the ease or difficulty of movement inherent in certain combinations. Throughout these experiences the teacher can raise questions to direct pupils' attention to *what* they are doing, *why* some combinations of movements are more difficult than others, *what* is valuable in the movements, and *how* pupils can become more proficient.

Such movement experiences, which lead into fundamental motor skills and then into specialized motor skills, should lead the student to value the concepts of survival, of discovery and control of the environment, and of self.

36. Moto ergo sum*

Peter V. Karpovich

Research Professor of Physiology, Springfield College

An ancient philosopher who strongly believed that motion is the most essential characteristic of life coined a phrase: "Moto ergo sum" or "I move, therefore I exist." He must have been a somewhat odd if dedicated man. When he became hoarse and could not talk, he would raise his hand and move his index finger as a symbol of his existence.

I heard this story from my high school teacher of history, and I have forgotten the name of the philosopher, but I think he was a Greek. My library searchings for his identity invariably have led me to a French philosopher, Descartes, who paraphrased this motto as "Cogito ergo sum" or "I think, therefore I exist."

I have no quarrel with Descartes' motto. As a matter of fact, these two mottos should be combined into "Cogito et moto, ergo sum" meaning "I think and I act, therefore I live." Today I will limit my remarks only to movements and actions.

You all have read about the poor Gulliver made motionless by the tiny Liliputians; and you probably have sympathized with him. Some of you probably also have read books by Lagrange, a French father of the physiology of exercise. Lagrange mentioned a prisoner who, upon being captured, was hogtied so that he could not move any limb. This, according to the prisoner, was the worst torture he had ever had.

However, besides Liliputians, illness and accidents, there is another and even more powerful factor which enforces muscular inactivity. It is our progressing civilization with its concomitant substitution of machines for muscles.

Since the progress of mechanization is inevitable and we can neither run away nor stop the clock, the outcome should be considered inevitable. Thus it follows that, in the near future, it will be normal for man to have flabby weak muscles since he will not need strong muscles anymore. If now-a-days automobiles are blamed for weak legs, what will happen when we have moving sidewalks in business centers?

There is, however, a certain fallacy in accepting weak muscles as normal. Braus, in his *Anatomy*, gives a very interesting illustration showing certain changes of the human foot. He compared the relative position of the heel bone in a chimpanzee, Neanderthal man and in our normal contemporary man. The human foot shows the unmistakable evidence of evolution. The vertex of the angle formed by the tibia and calcaneus in man points inward instead of outward. On this basis, then, we should accept the flat feet of a floor walker or of a policeman as normal feet, since eventually all men will have seemingly flat feet.

We would hardly agree with this. Firstly, because there is no reason to believe that the foot of the future will be flat; secondly, because if it becomes flat, it will take many thousands of years, and during that period some additional anatomical adjustment may develop which will strengthen the foot. Jumping, as it were overnight, into the future constitutes a pathological phenomenon, and therefore such an untimely "foot of the future" should be treated and its further appearance should be prevented.

The same attitude should be maintained toward muscles. There is one point which

*From Journal of Sport Medicine and Physical Fitness, Vol. 1, No. 2, Sept. 1961. Used by permission.

frequently is forgotten. We may deplore the ever progressing muscular weakness, and we may look back to the cave man as a symbol of superman; but what about the muscles of men who live now outside of civilization? One may find enough of them even now. Some of them still live at the Stone Age level. Are they supermen? A series of illustrations carried recently in Life magazine showed that Australian aborigines do not have excessively developed musculature. Most of them would not be a match for civilization tainted American varsity wrestlers. The life of these aborigines does not depend so much on excessive strength as on good muscular endurance which makes them fit for their environment. A student of Anthropology cannot find any evidence that the salvation of our weakening generation lies in hefting heavy bar bells and developing huge muscles. Common sense also would indicate that salvation will not be found in endless running, or swimming or in eating miracle foods. Then what should be done? Where should salvation be looked for?

This brings us to the responsibility of the American College of Sports Medicine and other similar organizations. Our primary task is the pursuit of physical fitness. This is such an important function that it should have been included in the Constitution of the United States, although it probably is implied in the "pursuit of happiness."

The pursuit of physical fitness means achieving and maintaining a desired level of fitness. We know how to develop and how to maintain physical fitness, but we do not know how much of fitness we need.

Our duty is to find the answer. The search will not be limited to just testing the muscles. It will involve a diversified research in physiology and medicine. One should only read the titles of contemporary studies pertaining to physical fitness to see that an investigator of physical fitness has to delve into both physiology and medicine. The laboratories carrying research in physical fitness look more and more like "physiology" laboratories, and there is no clear cut borderline indicating where physiological research ends and medical research begins.

We should develop tables showing relationship between the functions of various organs at various levels of muscular exertion. We should establish how these relation-ships are affected by ambient temperature, atmospheric pressure, humidity and diet.

We should find the optimum and the limits of a desirable fitness in relation to sex, age, body size and type.

We should campaign for less lip service and more actual help in research in physical fitness. Funds should be provided for research, and a National Institute for Research in Physical Fitness should be established. This Institute should have all the modern facilities and a well trained staff.

All this will take some time. What should we do in the meantime? Meantime and afterwards we should work. Work more and harder. The fellows of the American College of Sports Medicine should be more active in research pertaining to physical fitness.

Now what else can we do? We should cooperate and assist in the promotion of physical fitness by either governmental or private organizations. We may prevent an overemphasis of just one activity for growing boys and girls. It is true that playing basketball, riding a bicycle or even playing baseball does contribute to fitness and sometimes one of these activities is all that an individual needs; but it cannot be considered as the only activity needed by all. Especially by growing children.

However, no matter in what physical activity an adult participates, we should encourage this, instead of forcing him into an activity which he dislikes and in which he would not participate whole heartedly. Something is better than nothing, especially when we are not sure how much a man needs. Many people seem to derive all their needed exercise just from walking.

We may deplore an overemphasis on interscholastic varsity teams because they benefit a few at the expense of many. If we want to remedy this situation, we have to deal not so much with the school administration as with the alumni, and this often means with ourselves. And when it comes to the defense of athletics in the alma mater, we, the alumni, become dragons with many heads. And where is that modern St. George who can slay the dragon? Probably it is not slaying that is needed, because the alumnus mysteriously can turn into a goose who lays golden eggs, and who wants to destroy this biological mint?

I don't want to complete my notes in the

spirit of Jeremiah. I want to assure you that I am very optimistic. When I think about physical education forty-five years ago and make a comparison with present conditions, I feel elated. Men and women engaged in physical education now are often considered to be educators. We are doing research, and we have strong organizations backing us. And what is forty-five years in the life of a nation or race? We should pave the way for the succeeding generation. Remember, physical education is a profession for tomorrow; and tomorrow is just one day ahead.

REFERENCES

1. Lagrange, Fernand. L'hygiene de l'exercise chez les enfants et les jeunes gens. 9me Ed., p. 1, Felix Alcan, Paris, 1910.
2. Braus, H. Anatomie des Menschen. Vol. 1, p. 604, Julius Springer, Berlin, 1921.
3. Anonymous. Man at His Most Primitive. Life Magazine, p. 52, May 19, 1958.

Projects and thought questions for part four

1. Read the Platonic dialogue *Laches*. Using your own words and thoughts, refute Laches' criticisms of physical education. Justify your arguments with references to current literature.

2. Develop an essay concerned with increasing sports participation and reducing the trend toward spectatorism.

3. Using the type of logic demonstrated in the research by Young, develop a brief report entitled "Did the North American Indians play lacrosse?"

4. Write a paper concerned with the contributions to physical education and athletics of Per Henrik Ling, Dudley Sargent, Amy Morris Homans, or Delphine Hanna.

5. Give an oral report on the history of American physical education during the period 1920-1945.

6. Defend the use of the Swedish Days Order in physical education classes in 1900. Show why the Swedish Days Order is or is not appropriate in modern physical education programs.

7. Trace the origins of sports introduced after the publication of the research by Eyler.

8. Write an editorial based on recent developments in the conduct of the Olympic games.

9. Develop your own definition of movement education, and justify the place of a movement education program within the physical education curriculum.

10. Explain why man needs physical activity in his daily life.

Selected readings

Broer, M. R.: Movement education: wherein the disagreement? Quest, Monograph II (Spring Issue), Apr. 1964.

deCoubertin, P.: The re-establishment of the Olympic games, The Chautauquan, Sept. 1894.

Hamilton, E.: The echo of Greece, New York, 1957, W. W. Norton & Co., Inc.

Hanson, J. W., and Brembeck, C. S.: Education and the development of nations, New York, 1966, Holt, Rinehart & Winston.

Kieran, J., and Daley, A.: The story of the Olympic games, Philadelphia, 1961, J. B. Lippincott Co.

King, E. J.: Other schools and ours, New York, 1963, Holt, Rinehart & Winston.

Van Dalen, D. B., Mitchell, E., and Bennett, B. L.: A world history of physical education, Englewood Cliffs, N. J., 1964, Prentice-Hall Inc.

Part five

Scientific foundations of physical education

Physical education is rapidly increasing its orientation toward science. Although physical education as a field of endeavor has traditionally been based on scientific principles, it is only recently that writers and researchers in the profession have begun to concentrate so extensively on understanding modern science and scientific thought and the implications they have for physical education.

The four major objectives of physical education are frequently listed as organic development, neuromuscular development, mental development, and social development. Physical educators have often been well prepared in their professional programs in the scientific concepts of the first two objectives. The latter two objectives have frequently suffered from lack of interpretation. The behavioral scientists are at present contributing much valid new knowledge to the psychological and sociological foundations of physical education. Research directly concerned with physical education is helping to create a balance of knowledge based on scientific interpretations.

The readings in this division cover a diverse range of scientific thinking in three areas of understanding. This entire section is subdivided in order to reflect the newest thinking in physical education. Prefaces to the individual articles are at the beginning of each subdivision, while projects and thought questions and suggested readings immediately follow each subdivision. The readings in the first subdivision are concerned with the biological foundations of physical education. The second subdivision concentrates on the psychological foundations of physical education, while the sociological foundations of physical education comprise the final subdivision.

Biological foundations of physical education

What implications does the future have for physical education? Emmanuel G. Mesthene points out the effect of new scientific developments on modern life and projects them into the future. He shows the results of these technological explosions on the scope of all of education and, by implication, on physical education.

Raymond A. Weiss asks the physical educator if physical fitness is or should be the most important program objective. The author points out that physical and mental well-being depend in part on physical activity and that lack of activity is often detrimental to the state of well-being. Weiss explores the concept of physical fitness and

161

discusses the value of placing a stronger emphasis on fitness.

Time magazine has frequently explored concepts related to physical education. The topic of the essay is the physiological and psychological value of exercise, with emphasis on the former. The essay suggests that a regular program of exercise is a requirement for the maintenance of the health and welfare of individuals.

The Committee on Exercise and Physical Fitness of the American Medical Association and the President's Council on Physical Fitness cooperated with the Lifetime Sports Foundation to develop a brief but comprehensive statement concerning exercise and weight control. The value to the individual's health of a regular program of physical activity, common fallacies concerned with the relationship of exercise to caloric intake and utilization, and the overall advantages of exercise are considered. Also included is information concerned with diet, recreation, and occupational considerations.

Dr. Lucien Brouha explains how the trained individual is better able to maintain a higher level of physiological fitness than the untrained individual. In a comprehensive discussion, Dr. Brouha shows the effect of regular training periods on muscle strength and on the cardiovascular and respiratory systems. Training for a specific kind of work and individual differences affecting a training program are also topics of this article.

Training programs are also discussed in the research report by Stan Burnham. This study investigates the relative effect of isometric and isotonic exercises on the development of muscular strength. The researcher finds both exercise systems effective, but states that isometric exercises may help the individual to reach the ultimate achievement level more quickly.

Evalyn S. Gendel discusses the medical folklore surrounding the effects of vigorous exercise on the physiology of women. The author does not attempt to prove beyond a doubt that there are no harmful effects but instead points out the misconceptions that must be dispelled and indicates those areas in which research is needed.

37. Learning to live with science*

Emmanuel G. Mesthene

*Executive Director, Harvard University Program on Technology and Society,
Harvard University*

It was Gilbert Murray who first used the celebrated phrase "the failure of nerve." Writing about ancient Greek religions, Murray characterized as a failure of nerve the change of temper that occurred in Hellenistic civilization around the turn of the era. The Greeks of the fifth and fourth centuries B.C. believed in the ultimate intelligibility of the universe. There was nothing in the nature of existence or of man that was inherently unknowable. They accordingly believed also in the power of the human intelligence to know all there was to know about the world, and to guide man's career in it.

The wars, increased commerce, and infiltration of Oriental cultures that marked the subsequent period brought with them viscissitude and uncertainty that shook this classic faith in the intelligibility of the world and in the capacity of men to know and to do. There was henceforth to be a realm of knowledge available only to God, not achievable by human reason. Men, in other words, more and more turned to God to do for them what they no longer felt confident to do for themselves. That was the failure of nerve.

I think things are changing, I doubt that there are many men today who would question that life will be produced in the laboratory, that psychologists and their personality drugs will soon reveal what really makes men tick, that scientific prediction is a far more promising guide to the future then divination, and that the heavens cannot long remain mysterious in the face of our ability

to hit the moon today and the stars tomorrow. In a recent article, Daniel Bell characterized this new-found faith as follows: "Today we feel that there are no inherent secrets in the universe . . . and this is one of the significant changes in the modern moral temper." I would say, indeed, that this is a major implication of our new world of science and technology. We are witnessing a widespread recovery of nerve.

Paradoxically, this taking on of new courage is tending at the same time to produce an opposite reaction, vague but disturbingly widespread. At the same time that we admire the new machines we build—the ones that play chess, and translate Russian, and catch and correct their own mistakes, and tend each other—we also begin to fear them. We fear them in two ways—one that we talk about, and one that we joke about.

We talk quite openly about our fear that machines may take away jobs, deprive people of work. But we dare only to joke about our fear that machines will replace people, not only as workers, but as people. Already they do arithmetic better than any of us. How much longer can it be before they make people obsolete? This fear is part of our technological world, but I see it only as derivative. I think it has its roots in a deeper, moral implication.

Some who have seen farthest and most clearly in recent decades have warned of a growing imbalance between man's capabilities in the physical and in the social realms. John Dewey, for example, said: "We have displayed enough intelligence in the physical field to create the new and powerful instrument of science and technology. We have not as yet had enough intelligence to use this

---

*From Saturday Review, July 17, 1965. Used by permission.

instrument deliberately and systematically to control its social operations and consequences." Dewey said this more than thirty years ago, before television, before atomic power, before electronic computers, before space satellites. He had been saying it, moreover, for at least thirty years before that. He saw early the problems that would arise when man learned to do anything he wanted before he learned what he wanted.

I think the time Dewey warned about is here. My more thoughtful scientific friends tell me that we now have, or know how to acquire, the technical capability to do very nearly anything we want. Can we transplant human hearts, control personality, order the weather that suits us, travel to Mars or to Venus? Of course we can, if not now or in five or ten years, then certainly in twenty-five, or in fifty or a hundred. If each of us examined the extent of his own restored faith in the essential intelligibility of the world, we might find that we have recovered our nerve to the point that we are becoming almost nervy. (I think, incidentally, that this recovery of nerve largely explains the current crisis of the churches. After twenty centuries of doing man's work, they are now having to learn how to do God's. The Ecumenical Council is evidence that the long but false war between religion and science is ended, and that we are once more facing Augustine's problem, to distinguish what is God's and what is man's.)

If the answer to the question "What can we do?" is "Anything," then the emphasis shifts far more heavily than before onto the question "What should we do?" The commitment to universal intelligibility entails moral responsibility. Abandonment of the belief in intelligibility 2,000 years ago was justly described as a failure of nerve because it was the prelude to moral surrender. Men gave up the effort to be wise because they found it too hard. Renewed belief in intelligibility 2,000 years later means that men must take up again the hard work of becoming wise. And it is much harder work now, because we have so much more power than the Greeks. On the other hand, the benefits of wisdom are potentially greater, too, because we have the means at hand to *make* the good life, right here and now, rather than just to go on contemplating it in Plato's heaven.

The question "What should we do?" is thus no idle one but challenges each one of us. That, I think, is the principal moral implication of our new world. It is what all the shouting is about in the mounting concern about the relations of science and public policy, and about the impact of technology on society. Our almost total mastery of the physical world entails a challenge to the public intelligence of a degree heretofore unknown in history.

But how do we come to grips with the challenge? How do we pull together and learn to use the knowledge we already have, and in using it learn the other things we need to know? What do the implications of our great contemporary scientific and technical spurt forward add up to? I do not have the answers, but I should like to propose some hypotheses.

My first hypothesis is that the time will come when machines will put most people permanently out of work. What will happen to people when there is no longer work for them to do? Consider the foreman in a steel plant. He brings thirty years' experience to one of the half-dozen really crucial jobs in the mill. At the critical point in the process, it is his trained eye that tells him the molten metal is ready to pour, and it is his well-developed sense of timing and steady hand that tip the cauldron synchronously with the processes that precede and follow. For this he is well paid, and can provide for his family perhaps better than the average. For this, too, he is looked up to by his fellows. They seek him out as a friend. He has prestige at his work, status in the town, and the respect of his children. He belongs. He contributes. He is needed.

Then you move in a machine that takes his job away, and does it better. What happens to this man? What happens to his many juniors at the mill whose aspiration was to an achievement like his? One of the pervasive characteristics of our civilization has been the identification of life's meaning with life's work. The evidence is strong in the problem of the aged: how do they fight the conviction that their life is done, that the world could do very well, perhaps better, without them? Are we heading toward a time when society will be burdened with a problem of the aged beginning in most cases at age twenty, because there will no longer be work to enter upon, let alone retire from, at the age of sixty-five?

Among the suggestions for banishing this specter are two that do not impress me much. The first is essentially a cry of anguish. Stop automation! Stop making more and more complicated machines! What business have we going to the moon, or tampering with life and heredity? Life is difficult enough without going out of our way to make it more so.

All the odds are against the success of that kind of solution. The technologies of the atom bomb, the automobile, the industrial revolution, gunpowder, all provoked social dislocations accompanied by similar demands that they be stopped. But there is clearly no stopping. Aristotle said a long time ago that "man by nature desires to know." He will probe and learn all that his curiosity leads him to and his brain makes possible, until he is dead. The cry of "stop" is the fear reaction I talked about earlier. It comes from those who have not yet recovered their nerve.

A second suggestion, specifically aimed at the prospect of loss of work, is that we find better ways to employ leisure. There is a whole literature growing up on this theme, and I think it should be encouraged. Other things being equal, and given my own biases, it is better to read a good book than to watch television, or to play a Beethoven quartet than listen to the Beatles. But leisure activity, no matter how uplifting and educational, is not a substitute for work. The very concept loses meaning in the absence of the correlative concept of "work." No, I do not think that is the happiest solution.

But then that may not be the problem either. My second hypothesis is that my first hypothesis is wrong. Machines might not in fact put a significant number of people out of work permanently. It might just be that machines will simply take over the kinds of work that people have done up to now, and that people will then be freed, not to become problems to themselves and to society, but to do entirely new kinds of work that have hardly been thought about seriously because there has not yet been a serious possibility that they could be done.

It is often said, for example, that as work in agriculture and industry is progressively mechanized, job opportunities in the service sector of the economy will increase and absorb released manpower. I assume that production processes will not be mechanized except as machines prove more efficient than human labor. There should then follow a significant increment in wealth, which, adequately distributed, could buy more of the services already available, from baby-sitting to education and government and from better waiters to art and religion. The structure of the work force might thus be altered significantly.

Even more exciting is the possibility that the nature of service itself might be altered. I suggest a trivial, perhaps ridiculous example. Doubled police forces and quadrupled sanitation forces could give us, for the first time, really safe and really clean cities. Put 20,000 people into the streets every day to catch the cigarette butts before they even hit the ground, and you might have a clean city.

Inherently, there is nothing ridiculous about a clean city. If the suggestion makes one smile, it is rather because such use of people, by today's standards, is ridiculously uneconomical. People are more efficiently employed to produce the goods we consume. But if machines will be doing most of that, then maybe people can be employed to produce the services, such as street-cleaning or teaching, that we would like to have more of if we could.

Consider another example. One of the genuinely new and exciting ideas of the Kennedy Administration, I think, was the Peace Corps, the idea that young Americans in large numbers could, by example, help less favored peoples to help themselves. Imagine a Peace Corps 50,000,000 strong in Africa, released by machines to pour the kind of sweat that machines will never pour. This is the kind of service that can anticipate, peacefully and constructively, the ugly danger that the have-nots of the world will resort to uncontrollable violence as the gap between their expectations and reality widens. It is also the kind of service that might provide to individuals a satisfaction and a goal to life undreamed of by today's assembly-line worker in Detroit, however fully employed. From such a perspective, the new machines and the new technologies may spell, not the end of the world, but the beginning of a new one. We might begin to see, for the first time, what God meant when he said that the meek shall inherit the earth.

There has been a long tradition that divides work into creative and intellectual for the few, and routine and mechanical for the many. There has grown up around that distinction (although we are told that that was not yet true in the time of the Greeks) a moral judgment: that the first kind of work was for superior people, and the second for inferior people. There then occurred, I think, one of those curious inversions of history whereby an effect is later seen as cause. The reason the majority of people did routine and mechanical work, we were told, was that that was the only kind of work they were fit to do, because they were inferior.

It seems to me much more plausible, however, that the reason the majority of people have done routine and mechanical work is that there has been a very great deal of routine and mechanical work to do. I am not denying that some people are more gifted than other people. But it seems to me that we have not yet been motivated to inquire sufficiently into how many people of what kinds can do what, because there has up to now been so much routine and mechanical work to do that most people have necessarily been impressed into doing it.

I suggest also that it is this same imperative of a great deal of routine and mechanical work to do that has led to the ivory-tower syndrome on the part of creative, intellectual workers. I doubt that artists and scientists have typically detached themselves from the world because they liked it that way. The cry for application of knowledge, at least since Francis Bacon, and the essential need of the artist to communicate preclude that view. I suspect, rather, that there may be another reversal of cause and effect here: that the ivory tower may be symptomatic of a world by necessity too preoccupied with the routine and mechanical to generate a real demand for the product of the artist and the scholar. It is no accident that art and philosophy were the exclusive province of the freemen, not the slaves, in Greece, or that science, even in our own age, has for most of its history been indulged in by the gifted amateur who was rich in fact or by philanthropy.

And now machines will do the routine and mechanical work of the world. Very large numbers of human resources will be released and available for services to mankind beyond those required for subsistence. The need to discover the nature of this new kind of work, to plan it and to do it, just might overcome the traditional gap between the creative and the routine. The many will be challenged, as they have not been before, to rise to their maximum potentialities. The few—the scholars and the artists—may find that there is a new demand for them in the world, to muster, to shape, and to guide this new force. The two historical judgments that I have criticized as inverted, in other words, might become true from now on in: work could finally become the measure of man, and efficacy the measure of ideas.

What will be the nature of this new work? What goals will it serve? How will it be done? What talents will be needed for it? I do not know the answers to these questions, either. Each, I think, provides an opportunity for imaginative inquiry still to be done. I have undertaken only to state a hypothesis, or, more accurately, to indicate a hunch that precedes hypothesis. My hunch is that man may have finally expiated his original sin, and might now aspire to bliss. I think also that my hunch may hang together historically. Original sin was invented after, and to account for, the failure of nerve. With the recovery of nerve, we do not need the concept any more, and the advance of technology frees us from the drudgery it has imposed.

But freedom from drudgery, as I have suggested, entails a commitment to wisdom. Consider, as one example, the staggering implications for education. Education (in foot-high letters on public billboards) has become a panacean word. But education for what? For whom? What kind of education? And when? There is very little small print on the billboards to answer those questions.

The response of education to the new world of science and technology up to now has taken the form of five principal proposals or goals: 1) more education for more people, 2) educational booster shots in some form of continuing adult education, 3) increased production of scientists and engineers, 4) expanded vocational training, and 5) mid-career refresher training or retraining for a different specialty.

It is hard to quarrel with more education, or with continuing education. With respect to the other three goals, however, one can raise the question "For how long?" To be sure, we need more scientists and engineers than we have now, but we already hear warnings that the demand will level off, and it is perhaps not too early to start thinking about a massive effort in the social sciences and the humanities.

Similarly with vocational education. Training in a trade is desirable and useful. But in which trade? Certainly not in those doomed to extinction in the next ten to twenty years. The informal experience of the young people who have recently been crusading in Mississippi and Alabama might prove a much more relevant vocational education for the future that lies ahead of us.

Today's best educational judgments, in other words, might turn into tomorrow's worst mistakes, because they depend on forecasting successfully the shape of what is coming. Of course, the judgments must still be made today, despite the risk, despite the increased uncertainties of a world that changes shape rapidly and radically. This is a measure of the difficulty of the modern educator's task. Yet in this very change may lie a relative certainty, with a particular further implication for the job of education. I add a word about that.

There were two ancient Greek philosophers, long before even Socrates haunted the streets of Athens, who had diametrically opposed views about reality. There was Parmenides, who argued that all change is illusory, transitory, imperfect, unreal. And later there was Heraclitus, who saw reality as a flowing river, apparently the same but never the same, to whom all was constant flux and change, and who dismissed the permanent as unreal, as evidence of human imperfection, as a distortion of reality.

I go back to those ancient thinkers, because each gave his name to a major and persistent theme in Western intellectual history. Parmenides, the apostle of the eternal, has had his emulators in Christian theology, in romantic idealism, and in twentieth-century mathematics and logic. The followers of Heraclitus, who saw the world as flux, include the medieval nominalists, the nineteenth-century evolutionary philosophers, and today's existentialists.

Are we Parmenidians or Heracliteans? In our social attitudes, we certainly lean to Parmenides. In our concept of work, the real is the career that holds together, makes sense, and lasts a lifetime. If a man changes jobs too often, we consider him a drifter, or, if we like him, we say he has not yet found his proper work. We see the change as un-natural, unreal, unwanted, and feel much more comfortable with the permanent, the stable.

Similarly with our social institutions. Democracy, capitalism, socialism, the organized faiths—these are the real, the cherished, and any change is transitional, accidental, to be avoided, or dealt with as quickly as possible, to return to the stable, the familiar, the true.

The evidence is becoming compelling that we are going to have to change these attitudes and comfortable habits. Careers are increasingly becoming shorter-lived than people. The complexities of national existence lead to an increasing and inevitable mixing-up of the public and the private. State's rights, that honored mark of eighteenth-century federalism, has become a slogan of those who would have us return to the eighteenth century. The profit motive is being introduced into the Soviet economy, and the world's religions are beginning to talk to each other. All our familiar institutions, in other words, are changing so rapidly and so constantly that the change is becoming more familiar now than the institutions that are changing. The change is the new reality. We are entering an era that might aptly be called Social Heracliteanism.

The challenge to education is indeed staggering. Teachers who have been brought up to cherish the stable must take the children of parents who have been brought up to cherish the stable, and try to teach them that the stable, the unchanging, is unreal, constraining, a false goal, and that they will survive in an age of change to the degree that they become familiar with change, feel comfortable with it, understand it, master and control it.

When that task is done, the recovery of nerve will be complete, because our new technical mastery will have been supplemented by the wisdom necessary to harness it to human ends. John Dewey's dream will have been realized. We will be the masters of our techniques instead of their slaves, and we might just become the first civilization since 500 B.C. to be able to look the Greeks in the face with pride, instead of just with wonder. I do not like to think of the alternative, which is that the people of a century from now will say of us: "Look at the trouble and woe they had with their technology, and look what ours has done for us."

38. Is physical fitness our most important objective?*

Raymond A. Weiss

Professor of Education and Chairman, Division of Physical Education, Health, and Recreation, School of Education, New York University

There is a growing awareness in America that Americans are doing themselves harm by becoming progressively less physically active. The late President John F. Kennedy summed it up in his Presidential Message to the schools when he stated: "The softening process of our civilization continues to carry on its persistent erosion."

Can it be true that inactivity is a factor in today's health problems? The answer appears to be "yes." The belief is growing among knowledgeable persons that physical inactivity may be harmful and that activity enhances physical and mental well-being.

A number of studies suggest a relationship between the extent of physical activity and a tendency toward certain nonspecific diseases such as degenerative heart disease. Two medical specialists, Hans Kraus and Wilhelm Raab, in their book entitled *Hypokinetic Disease,* have drawn upon their rich clinical experience to describe to the medical profession the role that physical inactivity plays in the origin of a variety of diseases. (Dr. Kraus coined the word "hypokinetic," which is a Greek term meaning "caused by insufficient motion.")

Apparently the danger of physical inactivity is real. If the danger exists, what can we do about it?

The answer, starting first as a whisper and gradually swelling in volume, has been: "We must change a nation of softies to a nation that is physically fit." The profession of physical education was grateful to President

Eisenhower for urging people to be more physically active. President Kennedy urged the physical education programs in the schools to place more stress upon physical fitness.

The effects of the current emphasis can be seen everywhere. Turn on your television set in the morning and build your biceps with TV exercisers. Pick up the daily paper and read about a physical fitness contest sponsored by the local community recreation department. Examine your professional journals and notice the number of research reports on the topic of exercises for building strength. Study the printed programs of state, district, and national conventions and note the number of sessions devoted to methods of developing strength and endurance.

From all this emphasis on physical fitness, one is likely to get the impression that physical fitness is in some way responsible for physical and mental well-being. But, is physical fitness really responsible? I have some doubts. From what I have read, and in the absence of conclusive evidence to the contrary, I am beginning to believe that it is the stimulation of physical activity rather than the strength and endurance of muscle building exercises that promotes physical and mental well-being. I have noticed that members of our profession and others often interchange the terms "physical activity" and "physical fitness" when discussing the values of exercise. I would suggest that these terms are not equivalent and should not be equated. Instead they should be used to connote different meanings.

According to a variety of definitions used

*From *Journal of Health, Physical Education, and Recreation,* Vol. 35, p. 17, Feb. 1964. Used by permission.

in our profession, and according to our tests of physical fitness, a person grows more physically fit as he increases his strength and endurance. Harrison Clarke has stated that physical education can improve three fundamental fitness components: muscular strength, muscular endurance, and circulatory endurance.

Physical activity, on the other hand, is motion. Walking is motion so it must be physical activity. It is true that walking is relatively mild exercise which would not produce much strength and endurance, but if we are speaking of the value of exercise to help attain physical well-being, should we care whether walking develops strength and endurance? There is evidence that a person must engage in strenuous exercise to develop strength, but where is the evidence that such exertion is needed for physical well-being?

Medical authorities recommend walking, golfing, bowling, and bicycling as excellent forms of exercise for mental and physical well-being. Dr. Paul Dudley White includes walking as one of the activities he recommends to benefit the nervous system.

In our profession, proponents of physical fitness have suggested that we discard such activities as softball, golfing, volleyball, badminton, and bowling. They say these activities are not strenuous enough to develop strength and endurance, just as walking is not strenuous enough to develop strength and endurance. But, medical experts say these activities offer all the exercise that is needed to promote sound medical health and emotional well-being.

In a physical fitness program, these milder sports would be omitted. Yet according to respected authorities they have value in a program to promote physical and mental well-being. So long as this contradiction exists we will be unable to agree upon the place of moderate exercise in the school physical education program. However, until there is evidence to the contrary, I will argue for the notion that physical activity is more important than high levels of physical fitness as a factor for human well-being.

Does this mean that we should drop physical fitness as an objective in our programs? Not at all. Physical fitness can be useful in our programs in at least three ways. First, fitness helps us enjoy physical activity. We have all seen the person who starts enthusiastically to play badminton and then quits when he runs out of gas prematurely. It is no fun to be active when the body lacks stamina for the sport. Second, fitness sustains skill learning. A person who tires easily will not learn as rapidly or as effectively as a physically fit person. For one thing, skill learning requires concentration, and studies have shown that the ability to concentrate is lessened when fatigue sets in. For another thing, the ability to coordinate movements is the very essence of skill learning. Yet one of the first visible signs of fatigue is a loss of muscular coordination.

Third, fitness enhances excellence in performance on the athletic field. That remark is probably the safest statement in this presentation. If anyone doubts it, read Lucien Brouha's chapter on "Training" in the book *Science and Medicine of Exercise and Sports.*

These three uses of physical fitness suggest the role that the school should play in helping youth achieve physical fitness. In physical education the teacher should assist youngsters to attain physical fitness at levels needed to enjoy physical activity and to sustain skill learning. In school athletics, the coach should encourage the athlete to develop as much strength and endurance as is possible in the time available.

It is not difficult to answer the question, "How much fitness?" The level of fitness needed for fun and for skill learning depends upon the activity. Shuffleboard requires less strength and endurance than badminton; badminton requires less fitness than tennis. The experienced physical education teacher should have little trouble recognizing the level of fitness needed to sustain the participant. He should set this level as the physical fitness standard for the physical education program. Then when he is asked, "How much fitness and for what?" he can reply, "The fitness it takes to learn and enjoy the activities of the physical education program."

If I were to offer one additional bit of advice, it would be to establish physical fitness as a prerequisite to the physical education program rather than as an ultimate goal around which the program revolves. At the beginning of the year, the teacher should assess each student's physical fitness. If fitness is satisfactory by the standards just mentioned, the teacher should turn to a program of skill learning, sports, and other physical activities. If the class lacks physical fitness, the teacher should conduct a remedial fitness program like that proposed by the President's Council on Physical Fitness. Vigorous physical activity will raise physical fitness to a desired level. Then the instructor should shift to sports and other worthwhile activities in the program. If the student participates regularly thereafter, he won't have to worry about his physical fitness. It is known that a person can maintain fitness more easily than he can raise it.

Turning very briefly to fitness for competition, I agree that a competitor cannot become *too* physically fit. We should make that belief perfectly clear to those who aspire to compete and then limit varsity membership to those who are willing to put in the time and effort required to train for competition.

By these remarks, I wish to make it clear that I believe in the importance of physical fitness. But I do not believe that because some physical fitness is good, more fitness is better.

Consider what we might have to sacrifice to gain high levels of fitness. First, we would sacrifice time. As we raise the standards of physical fitness, more time must be invested. Unfortunately, physical education time is at a premium.

Second, we would sacrifice instruction in activity skills. The process of skills instruction interferes with the development of fitness. The only way we know to develop fitness is to overload the body through intensive exercise. In contrast, during skills instruction the participants exert themselves relatively little. Skills instruction and fitness activity tend to be mutually exclusive—participation in one tends to exclude the other. Let us not underestimate the importance of skill learning. Youngsters are naturally inclined to engage in activities in which they excel. If we expect them to form the habit of being physically active we must give them the skills with which to enjoy activity.

A third sacrifice is incentive. It has been stated that raising the level of physical fitness is one way to stimulate a person to want to be physically active. With all respect to the persons who hold this opinion, I suggest that the opposite is more likely to be true.

The intensive physical conditioning programs I have seen were administered with strict discipline in a formal atmosphere. Such a concoction is hardly seasoned to the tastes of most Americans.

The list of sacrifices to the cause of physical fitness grows longer when we think about the ways in which the physical education program contributes to the general goals of education. These contributions include the development of personality, furthering the democratic way of life and integrating the individual into the community. These are worthy goals, but not just any kind of program will do the job. Some doctoral studies show the extent to which physical activities vary in their potential for achieving goals of physical education. Not surprisingly, sports show up as among the most valuable forms of physical activity. Sports demand cooperation and team spirit. Sports require that the participants subordinate their personal wishes to the welfare of the group effort. Sports require that the individual learn to get along with others in an emotionally charged group situation. Individual sports have real social value.

Whereas sports and other types of enjoyable physical activities serve the goals of education, physical conditioning exercises, especially calisthenics, are not nearly so valuable. There is, of course, a place for calisthenics and other types of physical conditioning exercises because there is a place for physical fitness in the physical education program. But if we make physical fitness the center of the program we may destroy physical education, and there will remain only a program of physical conditioning.

I'm sure we want more than this. We want our youngsters to learn the values of being physically active. We want them to taste the nectar of enjoyable physical activity and to develop an appetite for its pleasures. By giving them physical skills we can reinforce their interest in physical activity and encourage them to be active throughout life.

Naturally youngsters need the stamina to engage in physical activity and we should help them build that stamina. Of course, they would not attain the high levels of strength and endurance many people believe is called for. To achieve that level of fitness, every minute of physical education would have to be devoted to conditioning exercises.

I am not yet convinced that the results are worth the investment.

If a sacrifice is to be made, I would prefer less physical fitness and more learning. We need physical education more than we need physical training.

In summary, let us take another look at the importance of physical fitness in the physical education program. The schools have been asked to stress physical fitness because of a belief that Americans are doing themselves harm by becoming progressively less physically active. As evidence accumulates for the beneficial effects of exercise, medical authorities increasingly support the notion that physical activity is essential to physical and mental well-being. Somehow, the idea that physical activity is important to well-being has been translated to mean that physical fitness is important. This paper presents the notion that it is more important to develop the habit of being physically active than to develop high levels of physical fitness. It is quite possible that overemphasis on physical fitness in the school can lead to less interest in physical activity later in life. Also, overemphasis on conditioning exercises leaves little time for skill learning and may create a distaste for physical exertion. Rather than place major emphasis on high levels of physical fitness, it is suggested that we raise fitness to moderate levels and then proceed to more important objectives of skill learning and activity habit formation. Fitness at higher than moderate levels requires more time than can be spared from other important objectives of the physical education program.

39. Don't just sit there; walk, jog, run*

Editorial essay, Time magazine

Consider the human machine in middle age: atrociously maintained, rusty from disuse. None of its parts—the bellows, the tubes, the pump—function as efficiently as they once did. The muscles have degenerated into blancmange. If, in an emergency, the demand for air rises abruptly from the idling requirement of six to eight quarts a minute to 100 quarts or more, the maw gulps like that of a beached carp. The heart throbs about two to three times its customary rate, pumping blood through pipes thickened by sedimentary deposits and grown inelastic with age.

This gruesome image has been framed in the consciousness of a great many flabby, middle-aged Americans. And how have they reacted? They are skipping rope in a gym class, jogging around the reservoir, pedaling a pinioned and wheel-less bicycle, flailing arms before the bedroom mirror, doing push-ups on the office floor—in a tenth-hour campaign to redeem years of reprehensible physical neglect.

From yesterday's fad, the cult of physical fitness has developed into a national middle-aged obsession. Its manifestations are everywhere. Through numberless public parks, in every sort of weather, straggle the beflanneled registrants of Run for Your Life programs, jogging up to five miles a day, sometimes at the very respectable rate of seven minutes per mile. In thousands of gyms, yoga and dance studios, reducing emporiums and downtown athletic clubs, an uncomputed and possibly unprecedented tonnage of soft and mature flesh jiggles, bends, hops, kicks, creaks and groans. Washington's Governor Dan Evans organized the Six-Thirty Track Team, a club of state government executives who meet at that dawning hour

to exercise, and as a result he was recently given the Tired Tennis Shoe Award as the individual who has done the most in his state to advance the cause of regular jogging. U. S. Senator and Mrs. Mark Hatfield are often seen trotting around their home in Maryland in his and hers black nylon warm-up suits. *Dolly* Carol Channing has adopted a schedule of exercise—doing the boogaloo (good for muscles in the back, abdomen, knees and some other parts) three nights a week at The Factory, Hollywood's current In nightspot. Behind these scenes, the evidence indicates, hundreds of thousands of Americans are quietly—even furtively—exercising.

Bicycle riding has more than doubled in popularity since 1960. The annual bill for Exercycles, slant boards, Relax-A-Cisors and other muscle-toning devices exceeds $35 million. Sales of the Royal Canadian Air Force exercise book have passed eleven million. This bible of the physically insecure now shares its popularity with dozens of other references works, among them *Be Young with Yoga*, *Jogging* and *Sexercises* (which promises to refine the sexual performance of both genders). A U. S. Government pamphlet on *Adult Physical Fitness* has sold 750,000 copies, without benefit of advertising, since 1963. By the tens of millions, U. S. televiewers genuflect to the exercise programs of Jack LaLanne, Ed Allen and Richard and Diane Hittleman.

FROM LEGS TO BRAIN

Dwight Eisenhower's 1955 heart attack, the most highly publicized coronary occlusion in history, is usually cited as the trigger of this national impulse to perspire for the sake of health. Eisenhower's heart specialist, Paul Dudley White, seized his moment of national prominence to lecture the public

---

*From Time, Feb. 23, 1968. Used by permission.

repeatedly on its deplorable shape, suggesting that the tone of the body has much to do with pace of the mind. "The better the legs," said White, still bicycling today at 81, "the clearer the brain." There is little doubt that some triggering was necessary. For the first time in history, a society found itself so advanced materially that human beings no longer got enough exercise in the search for sustenance. Estimates suggest that 40 million Americans have a temperamental indisposition to any kind of hard physical work. Research by the University of California's Dr. Hardin Jones indicates that, if the circulatory system is any clue, the average U. S. male becomes middle-aged at 25. American women shape up no better, beneath their façade. "They have such beautiful hair, beautiful faces," says German Antoinette de Haass, who teaches dance at an Elizabeth Arden salon in Chicago. "But when they take off their clothing, what do you see? A calamity!"

The question that troubles the lazy, the suspicious, the cynical and even the practical is whether all this exercise really does any good. Some claims appear extravagant. Former Detroit Lions Back Dick Woit, who conducts a spartan exercise course for men at Chicago's Lawson Y.M.C.A., insists that his workouts relieve hangovers, nervous stomachs, bad tempers, potbellies, headaches and marital strife. A special exercise regimen for convicts, devised by Bonnie Prudden, is supposed to reduce recidivism, or criminal backsliding.

FOR LIFE

Whatever the claims, nearly all medical men who have given serious consideration to the matter agree that a regular program of exercise is not only good but also quite necessary for human well-being amid the tensions of contemporary society. By general agreement, the best exercise for most people is walking, then jogging, then running. These activities have the important side advantages of requiring no skill or equipment while offering endless opportunities for self-congratulation. Beyond this there are specialized programs of exercise under the careful direction of experts. Whatever

the exercise, the experts agree that it must be consistent—not just for weeks or months or years, but for life. In a familiar pattern, many Americans start by doing too much in the mistaken hope of doing better. Exercise should lead to exhilaration, not to exhaustion or pain. Back aches, slipped disks and lumbago can affect people who overdo the famous Royal Canadian Air Force exercises. Even joggers can ask for trouble. "The distance some of them go scares me," says Dr. Richard Morrison, who presides over a heart conditioning program for West Coast executives. "Long distances can make your knees arthritic or give you shin splints." Recent studies at the University of Saskatchewan confirm earlier suspicions that some of the so-called isometric exercises can impose dangerous demands on the heart.

Along with a considerable amount of overdoing, there are a great many misconceptions. A common one involves the benefits of popular sports and games, such as swimming, tennis and golf, which attract the week-end athlete. They are good exercise, but they are generally practiced in such an irregular and undisciplined way as to be of doubtful value. Says Manhattan's Dr. Hans Kraus, physical therapist, author (*Backache, Stress and Tension*), part-time mountain climber and the man who eased President Kennedy's aching back: "I'm very much for golf as a game, but don't assume that it's the exercise that you need. People think that they are doing something good for themselves and they are not. It doesn't burn off calories and it may even add to tension depending on how you play it."

Whatever form exercise takes, authorities agree that there are psychological as well as physiological benefits, giving the exerciser a gratifying sense of doing something virtuous, sensible and good about his condition. What all of the experts are wholeheartedly against is nonexercise. This leaves little comfort for the many who hold that the only good exercise is lifting a glass at the end of a tense day. For them, a word must be said about the tendency to overdo: after the last glass of Pommard with the blue cheese, it is not wise to rise too rapidly from the chair. That might be too strenuous.

40. Exercise and weight control*

Committee on Exercise and Physical Fitness of the American Medical Association, The President's Council on Physical Fitness, and the Lifetime Sports Foundation

The key to effective weight control is keeping energy intake (food) and activity energy output (physical activity) in balance. This is true at all ages for both sexes. When the calories consumed in food equal those used to meet the body's needs, weight will remain about the same. When one eats more than this amount, one will put on fat unless physical activity is increased proportionately.

For years physicians have talked about the varying caloric needs of differing occupations and physical recreations. Yet in their attempts to lose excess fat, weight-watchers have often concentrated on counting the calories in their diets and have neglected the role of exercise. For those who are too fat, increasing physical activity can be just as important as decreasing food intake.

Weight depends not only on how many calories are taken in during the day, but also on how many are used up in physical activity. The overly fat person who merely cuts down his intake of food to lose weight will make slow progress since the number of calories needed to maintain the body is much smaller than most people think.

In fact, lack of exercise has been cited as the most important cause of the "creeping" obesity found in modern mechanized societies. Few occupations now require vigorous physical activity. Although there is more time available for recreation, many persons fail to fill this gap by choosing leisure time activities that give them exercise. Even among those who do exercise, their activity is often neither vigorous nor sustained.

Authorities point out that adding 30 minutes per day of moderate exercise to one's schedule can result in a loss of about 25 pounds in one year, assuming food consumption remains constant. To put it another way—just one extra slice of bread a day—or a soft drink—or any other food item that contains about 100 calories—can add up to 10 extra pounds in a year if the amount of physical activity is not increased accordingly.

Recent studies seem to indicate that lack of physical activity is more often the cause of overweight than is overeating. These studies have compared the food intake and activity patterns of obese persons with those of normal weight. Several age levels—teenage, adults, and older persons—have been studied. In each instance, the findings showed that the obese people did not consume any more calories than their normal-weighted age-mates, but that they were very much less active.

The person who has a trim figure and wants to keep it should exercise regularly and eat a balanced, nutritious diet which provides sufficient calories to make up for the energy expended. The thin individual who wishes to gain weight should exercise regularly and increase the number of calories he consumes until the desired weight is reached. The overweight person should decrease the food intake and step up the amount of physical activity. Since a large proportion of the U.S. population is overweight, the latter group is a matter of concern to those who are interested in the nation's fitness and to many readers of this booklet.

Most people will exercise regularly only if it brings enjoyment and satisfaction.

---

*Used by permission of the Committee on Exercise and Physical Fitness of the American Medical Association, The President's Council on Physical Fitness, and the Lifetime Sports Foundation.

Walking, gardening, cycling, and swimming provide these values for some people. The lifetime sports such as tennis, bowling, golfing, badminton and archery satisfy the needs of many others and establish desirable exercise patterns that can be enjoyed by people of all ages. Active team sports such as basketball, volleyball or softball furnish similar benefits for still others, particularly the younger age groups. Calisthenics or weight training are a bore to some, but a pleasure to those who practice them regularly. Recently jogging has become a club activity in a number of places. Whichever are fun and are most accessible on a regular basis will be most helpful.

The exercise should be sufficiently vigorous to use up the required number of calories, and to some degree, it must be sustained. To the extent possible, one should meet one's needs for regular activity through sports and other forms of physical recreation that are enjoyable; otherwise the activity is likely to be abandoned or played only irregularly.

Exercising once a week yields only sore muscles; pick activities that can be done regularly. They needn't be the same ones every day; in fact variety adds spice to an exercise schedule.

WEIGHT CONTROL FALLACIES

Two basic fallacies have been widely held with respect to exercise and weight control. The first is that a great deal of time and effort is required to use up enough calories to affect weight materially. The second is that exercise increases the appetite and so will increase, not decrease, weight. Scientific experiments on animals and man have demonstrated the falsity of both of these assumptions.

Energy expenditure in exercise

If activity is not increased eating only a few more calories per day than are utilized can have a telling effect in a few years, since small gains tend to be cumulative. One physician who has studied the problems of obesity in great detail has said that a woman would need to eat an average of only 96 calories a day more than she expends to gain 50 pounds from the time of her marriage to the arrival of her third child five years later. Had she added only 25 minutes

of brisk walking to her daily activities, this weight gain would have been prevented.

The average adult man will burn up 2,400 to 4,500 calories a day depending on the amount and kind of exercise he gets. Active persons such as laborers, soldiers in the field and athletes may consume as many as 6,000 calories a day and yet not gain weight. This is a fact that has been well-known for many years.

In an experiment a few years ago, a group of university students increased their daily food intake (from 3,000 calories daily to 6,000) without gaining weight. This was accomplished merely by stepping up the amount of exercise they did each day.

The cost in calories of different types of exercise has been established and is shown in the chart. The number of calories expended depends on how strenuously these activities are undertaken. For example, canoeing upstream in quick water will use up more than the 230 calories per hour, as specified in the chart—and strolling along the street looking in shop windows will obviously use up many less than brisk walking.

The figures on energy expenditure through various activities are probably underestimates. They are usually derived by measuring the amount of oxygen consumed during a specific bout of exercise and then computing the equivalent number of calories burned. However, the effects of exercise continue after the actual time in which the exercise is performed. Body processes have been stepped-up and only gradually are lowered; this takes energy—sometimes for long periods after the exercise is stopped.

Energy expended is also affected by body weight since in those activities where the individual has to move his own weight, energy costs are increased for the heavier person and decreased for the lighter. To illustrate, a person walking 3 mph, weighing 100 pounds, will burn as few as 50 calories in 15 minutes, while someone weighing 200 pounds would use up as many as 80 calories in the same length of time.

Remember that although it takes an hour's jogging to use up 900 calories, one does not have to do it all in one stretch; a half-hour, for example, uses up 450 calories. It is a fact that one must walk 35 miles to lose one pound of fat but the 35 miles need not be walked at one time.

Energy expenditure by a 150 pound person in various activities*

Activity	Gross energy cost cal per hr.
A. Rest and light activity	**50-200**
Lying down or sleeping	80
Sitting	100
Driving an automobile	120
Standing	140
Domestic work	180
B. Moderate activity	**200-350**
Bicycling (5½ mph)	210
Walking (2½ mph)	210
Gardening	220
Canoeing (2½ mph)	230
Golf	250
Lawn mowing (power mower)	250
Bowling	270
Lawn mowing (hand mower)	270
Fencing	300
Rowboating (2½ mph)	300
Swimming (¼ mph)	300
Walking (3¾ mph)	300
Badminton	350
Horseback riding (trotting)	350
Square dancing	350
Volleyball	350
Roller skating	350
C. Vigorous activity over	**350**
Table tennis	360
Ditch digging (hand shovel)	400
Ice skating (10 mph)	400
Wood chopping or sawing	400
Tennis	420
Water skiing	480
Hill climbing (100 ft. per hr.)	490
Skiing (10 mph)	600
Squash and handball	600
Cycling (13 mph)	660
Scull rowing (race)	840
Running (10 mph)	900

*The standards represent a compromise between those proposed by the British Medical Association (1950), Christensen (1953) and Wells, Balke, and Van Fossan (1956). Where available, actual measured values have been used; for other values a "best guess" was made.

†Prepared by Robert E. Johnson, M.D., Ph.D., and colleagues, Department of Physiology and Biophysics, University of Illinois, August, 1967.

Walking an additional mile each day for 35 days also will take off that pound. This means one can lose 10 pounds in one year by walking an extra mile a day—providing, of course, that food intake and other physical activity remain the same. This really isn't an impractical amount of time or effort and to lose more or faster one needs only to increase the extent of activity.

Appetite and exercise

The idea that increased physical activity is useless as a means of losing weight because it always increases the appetite is equally fallacious.

It is true that a lean person in good condition may eat more following increased activity, but his exercise will burn up the extra calories he consumes. But the obese—the overly fat person—does not react the same way to exercise. Only when he exercises to excess will his appetite increase. Because he has large stores of fat, moderate exercise does not stimulate his appetite. This difference between the response to exercise of fat and lean people is important.

Laboratory tests on experimental animals have borne this out. When their exercise was moderate, food intake did not increase. In one experiment, animals exercised one hour a day, ate a smaller amount of food than those exercised less than an hour a day or not at all! On the other hand when the animals were exercised vigorously over longer periods they ate more, but the extra activity kept their weight constant.

In other experiments, when the animals' activity was decreased, they continued to eat the same amount of food and became obese.

Similarly, a study of overweight adults showed that the start of their obesity corresponded with their decline in activity. Although their activity decreased, their appetites didn't. This is a common observation. When people finish school and go to work (especially if the job is a sedentary one), they tend to exercise less but, through habit, eat as much as ever. Before long they are obese.

ADVANTAGES OF EXERCISE

If weight control can be achieved either through dieting or exercise, wouldn't it be simpler to concentrate on dieting and not worry about exercise? Remarkable claims are made for a variety of so-called crash or very restricted diets.

Some crash diets do achieve noticeable weight loss in a short time. Much of this may be due to a loss of body water, however, and such a loss is quickly restored when a normal food and liquid intake is resumed. Those dieters who fail to realize that fat is lost very slowly become discouraged and conclude that it is impossible for them to lose weight.

Furthermore, extreme diets carried out for an extended period, if they are not well-balanced and under medical supervision, may create nutritional problems. This is especially true among teen-age girls who may attempt self-prescribed diets to improve their figures and only make themselves ill by causing deficiencies of essential food substances. Recent studies indicate that weight reduction through near starvation may be at the expense of valuable body tissues rather than reduction of fat.

The person who gives proper attention to exercise derives benefits in addition to weight control and does not create nutritional problems for himself. Muscles which may have been weak and sagging become strong and firm. Feelings of listlessness and fatigue are replaced by sensations of alertness and energy. Sleep is better and more restful. With proper guidance, body posture can be improved, which, in addition to reduction of body fat and toning up the muscles, creates a more pleasing body profile.

Moveover, exercise can be fun, provide recreation, and offer opportunity for companionship. The exhilaration and emotional release of participating in sports or other activities are a boon to good mental, as well as physical health. Pent-up anxieties and frustrations seem to disappear as one concentrates on knocking over pins, returning a serve, or sinking a putt. Cutting the lawn, weeding the garden, or taking a brisk walk can be good tonics for both mind and body.

The man or woman who takes regular exercise will maintain a better state of physical fitness, will keep active longer, and is more apt to be resistant to the degenerative diseases of middle and later life, especially diseases of the heart and of the blood vessels.

IMPORTANCE OF DIET

The role of exercise in weight control . . . has only recently been given attention in the past. Many booklets and articles on weight control have stressed diet but have not recognized the dual role of exercise. This emphasis on exercise here should not minimize the need for proper nutrition in keeping fit and in maintaining a desirable weight. Both are valuable.

So remember, increasing exercise doesn't give license also to increase one's diet! Step up the exercise, but keep the diet well-balanced, the calorie intake the same—or a little less—for the best long-range results.

The reader is advised to choose his daily food requirements from the Basic Four—(1) Milk Group (2) Meat Group (3) Vegetable-Fruit Group (4) Bread-Cereal Group. Doing so he can follow a low calorie diet and yet make sure that his body receives the needed nutrients. . . .

EXERCISE AND MODERN LIVING

What kind of exercise does a given person need? Health authorities recommend regular activity that utilizes many parts of the body. The activity should be vigorous enough to tax the power of the muscles and should be done long enough and strenuously enough to produce a sense of healthful fatigue.

The exercise also should be suited to age, sex, and physical condition. It is wise to consult the personal physician before launching into a program of increased physical activity. Some persons have conditions that could be aggravated by the wrong kind of exercise.

One thing is certain. Most people do not get enough exercise in their ordinary routines. All of the advances of modern technology—from electric can openers to power steering—have made life easier, more comfortable, and much less demanding physically. Yet human bodies need activity. This requires a definite plan—and purposeful pursuit of that plan.

There are four main approaches to being adequately active:

1. A regular exercise schedule
2. Supplementary physical recreation
3. Stepped-up ordinary physical activity
4. Physical activity in the day's occupation

Each of these outlets for participating is important in keeping fit and in burning calories. The sum total activities for a day or a week should be sufficient and balanced.

Regular exercise schedule

Each individual should commit himself to a planned program of exercise and stick with it. This means setting aside 30 minutes to an hour a day about five times per week for physical activity. This schedule of exercise should be thought of as being as essential as a proper diet.

An exercise program should be balanced

just as a diet should be balanced. Some parts should be designed primarily to exercise the heart and lungs in a way that will develop endurance. Brisk walking, jogging, and swimming relatively long distances are good for this purpose.

Other parts of the program should be directed toward the improvement of strength, agility, flexibility, balance, and muscle tone.

Make this a personal keep-fit program. Start easily. Keep a record of what is done and how many times it is done. Gradually increase the amount of exercise until a reasonably good level is reached.

Of course, alternatives can be employed. If one can enroll in a keep-fit program at the Y, or the school, or the recreation center, or the club, the home routine can be skipped on the meeting days. On those days when there is no class, the do-it-yourself program can be followed. Those fortunate enough to have the time and facilities for sports should by all means take part.

One should swim when he can but should really swim; sunbathing doesn't use up many calories. A vigorous game of handball, or tennis, or badminton will meet activity needs for that day. Golf is fine if one walks fast between strokes—for eighteen holes—but not if he rides a cart. Likewise continuous, individual or dual bowling is more beneficial than interrupted team bowling. Hunting, snow skiing, skin diving, bicycling, water skiing, canoeing, hiking are all good for that day—that is, if one gets at least the equivalent in exercise of what he would otherwise do in his home exercise program.

Many people who engage in sports can do so only occasionally on weekends or in season. However, a home exercise program can help maintain good condition so that when one has the opportunity to engage in sports, he will not become stiff, sore, or overtired.

A person may follow the new program for several days and yet find no difference showing on the bathroom scale. Adjustments in metabolism take place and it may be some time before any reduction in weight can be seen.

When one exercises regularly some flabby tissue is changed to muscle. Muscle tissue takes much less space, hence a trimmer figure results even though weight may not drop markedly.

Supplementary recreation

Most people, especially those who wish to lose weight, should supplement the scheduled exercise with additional physical recreation. Gardening on weekends, a pleasant walk, bird watching, bowling in the office league, a family outing or fishing trip, an evening of social dancing, the square dance club's regular sessions; these and many more such activities provide recreational benefits and a bit of exercise as well. These should be looked upon as an extra bonus in the weight-watcher's campaign.

Stepped-up daily activities

To a scheduled program and supplementary recreation add a little more action each day. Walk to the neighborhood grocery instead of using the car. Park several blocks from the office and walk the rest of the way. Walk up a flight or more of stairs instead of using the elevator; start with a few steps and gradually increase. Stand up to put on and remove stockings and shoes; most people neglect to use their sense of balance. Get off the chair to get what is needed. Bend, stoop, stretch, squat, reach, move, lift, carry.

In today's sedentary world, people need to re-direct their whole approach to movement. Look for opportunities to use the body. Time-saving devices and gadgets that eliminate drudgery are boons to mankind, but when they substitute increasingly for physical activity they can demand a high cost in health and fitness.

These little bits of action, while not taxing, are cumulative in their good effects. A few calories used up by walking, going up steps, bending or otherwise moving can add up to a fair-sized total in the course of the day. And the contribution they make to muscle tone, flexibility, and balance are also significant.

The day's occupation

The amount of activity involved in one's job also is important. The suggestions above on daily activities of living apply also to on-the-job opportunities for exercise.

Within reason, one should look for ways of increasing his activity. It is a matter of outlook. Instead of considering an extra little walk, or trip to the files, or an errand downstairs as an annoyance, look upon it as an added fitness boost.

A PERSONAL WORD

We hope the information presented in this booklet has helped you gain a greater appreciation of the value of exercise in maintaining proper weight. More important, if you have a weight problem, we hope you have been motivated to do something about it.

Instead of sitting around worrying about why you are gaining weight, or cannot lose it, do something about it. With your doctor's advice, find some type of regular vigorous physical activity you can enjoy.

Each of us deep down inside has some feelings about his own self-image and what he wants it to be. Each person in these intimate aspects of life has to answer mainly to himself. So make up your mind to begin your program now and stay with it.

It won't be easy—especially at the start. But as you begin to feel better, look better, and enjoy a new zest for life, you will be rewarded manifold for your effort.

41. Physiology of training, including age and sex differences*

Lucien Brouha, M.D.

Haskell Laboratory for Toxicology and Industrial Medicine, E. I. duPont de Nemours and Co., Inc.

People performing regular muscular activity are capable of greater efforts and resist fatigue better than sedentary individuals. Repeated periods of exercise, or "training," produce changes in many physiological functions. During training, the homeostatic mechanisms become more efficient so that, in response to an equal amount of work, the displacement from the resting equilibrium is reduced and the speed of return to normal is increased. What happens during training is one of the fundamental problems of the physiology of muscular activity. Most information has been obtained by comparing the physiological reactions to exercise of trained and untrained individuals. This method shows how various degrees of efficiency are achieved by the human body, but it does not reveal the phenomena that take place during a training period. The following presentation is based upon experiments in which the same subjects were followed during a training program, and it is limited to the physiological functions showing the most important changes as a result of training. These changes all contribute to an increased capacity for muscular activity and include greater strength of the muscle; better neuromuscular co-ordination reducing the energy requirement for a given amount of external work; improved cardiovascular functions leading to a better supply of oxygen to the working muscles and to a greater amount of blood available for heat dissipa-

tion; and improved pulmonary ventilation permitting adequate oxygen and carbon dioxide exchanges for lower energy expenditure of the respiratory mechanisms.

1. EFFECT OF TRAINING ON THE MUSCLES

Repeated muscular work produces an *increase in the size of skeletal muscles.* Fibers that are small from lack of use are present in every muscle, and they develop to full size when regular exercise puts a greater demand upon the muscle. The increase in size is accompanied by the development of more capillaries in the trained muscle.[1] This change in the fibers and in the number of capillaries is accompanied by a gain in strength which is characterized by the ability to produce more powerful contractions, i.e. gain in power; to repeat contractions more rapidly, i.e. gain in speed and for a longer period of time, i.e. gain in endurance. The gain in strength is more striking than the hypertrophy of the muscle, and it is possible to increase the power of muscles three times or more without a proportional increase in volume.

The final result of training on the muscles varies with the kind of work performed, the degree of repetition, speed, duration, and intensity of contractions. Individual factors are also involved, and two subjects following the same training program may not necessarily develop their muscles in a similar manner. Increase in speed and endurance, which is out of proportion with the gain in size, suggests that the quality of muscular contraction is improving by train-

---

*From Journal of Sport Medicine and Physical Fitness, Vol. 2, No. 1, Mar. 1962. Used by permission.

ing. Better vascularization in the trained muscles makes more fuel and more oxygen available for the contraction processes and, furthermore, glycogen, phosphocreatine, and myoglobin are stored and available in larger quantities in the muscles themselves.

Another factor improved by training is the transmission of nerve impulses to the motor units. The result is that a given impulse produces the simultaneous contraction of a greater number of muscle fibers and the muscle can be used in its entirety without idle fibers and with maximum strength. Whether the greater muscular efficiency obtained by training is due primarily to chemical factors in the muscle, to an improved blood circulation, to a more efficient action of nervous impulses, or to other causes is still debatable. Further research is needed to elucidate the mechanisms which lead to increase in muscle power and endurance through training.

Training improves the *precision and economy of any motion* or sequence of motions involved in muscular activity. Unnecessary static and dynamic muscular contractions are progressively eliminated, more complete relaxation of the antagonist muscles is achieved, the motions become more simple and more automatic because reflexes replace in part voluntary action. The final result is that after training a decrease in energy expenditure may occur up to $\frac{1}{4}$ of the total energy needed before training. The greatest differences are found among beginners who must learn the motions involved in a particular activity and then acquire the skill to perform them efficiently.

Many problems in this field remain unsolved; and as yet few precise data are available on the best training methods to improve neuromuscular co-ordination and develop skill in the specific motions used in various occupations.

2. EFFECT OF TRAINING ON THE CARDIOVASCULAR SYSTEM

The heart becomes more efficient with training and, while beating less frequently, is able to circulate more blood[2]; it empties

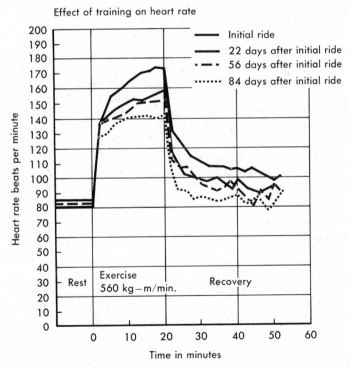

Fig. 1. Effect of training on heart rate for a standard amount of exercise: pedalling a bicycle ergometer for 20 minutes with a work load of 560 kg-m/min. Training was achieved by riding the bicycle four days a week with the same work load.

itself more completely at each systole, and stroke volume and cardiac output are increased. For a standard amount of work the heart rate becomes slower as training progresses (Fig. 1). Slower heart rates are observed even at rest and it is not exceptional for the resting pulse rate to be reduced by 10 to 20 beats per minute between the beginning and the end of a training period. This greater efficiency of the heart enables a larger blood flow to reach the muscles, insuring an increased supply of fuel and oxygen, and permitting the individual to reach higher levels of performance.[3]

Blood pressure also is influenced by training. Prolonged effort in an untrained subject leads to a progressive fall of the systolic pressure which indicates approaching exhaustion. The appearance of this phenomenon is greatly retarded by training so that heavy work can be maintained for a longer time without appreciable change in the blood pressure.[4]

The *cardiovascular recovery processes* after exercise improve: the better trained the individual the sooner his heart rate and his blood pressure return to the pre-exercise level (Fig. 1).

Blood distribution is modified by training which reduces the amount of oxygen needed by the working muscles, and consequently the necessary blood flow of these muscles. Under these conditions, for the same cardiac output, more blood remains available for the other organs of the body after training than before. For example, training improves in part, the capacity to exercise in heat because, as long as less blood is needed by the muscles for their work, more blood is available for heat dissipation in the skin and body temperature remains lower.

3. EFFECT OF TRAINING ON THE RESPIRATORY SYSTEM

Respiratory responses to exercise change during training. These changes are progressive and normally reach maximum efficiency in four to six weeks. Because of the improvement in neuromuscular functions, oxygen consumption and carbon dioxide production decrease progressively for the same work load to a minimum level as training progresses. As a result, for a standard amount of exercise, the pulmonary ventilation is reduced and the work of breathing decreases.

Thus, the amount of oxygen needed by the respiratory muscles and the blood flow to these muscles becomes smaller. The respiratory muscles themselves, like the other muscles, improve their efficiency during training. Per-minute changes in pulmonary ventilation are associated with a decrease in rate and an increase in depth of breathing. In the trained subject even at rest the depth of breathing is greater, and the respiratory rate may fall from about twenty to about eight breaths per minute. During heavy work the improvements due to training are quite striking and the diminution in respiratory minute volume can reach up to 25 per cent for a given work load.

Because of all these functional improvements, the amount of muscular work that can be performed with an adequate supply of oxygen becomes greater with training. Therefore, aerobic processes of muscular contraction are sufficient to perform higher levels of work with little accumulation of lactic acid, and anaerobic processes of muscular contractions are not necessary until heavier exercise is performed. A balance between aerobic and anaerobic processes can be maintained in a steady state at a higher level of work.

After a few weeks of training, improvement ceases and a constant level of training is reached which varies with the individual. At this point, if the *duration* of the daily training is increased, the work rate remaining the same, no additional improvement is achieved. On the other hand, if the *work rate* is increased, a standard exercise test can very rapidly be performed more efficiently as shown by lower heart and respiratory rates and by a reduced amount of blood lactic acid (Fig. 2). After a week or two the subjects reach a new steady level of training. This procedure can be repeated several times with a progressive increase in work rate until a state of maximum training is reached.[5]

When training involves a moderate level of activity, it can be interrupted for as long as a week or ten days without any sign of deterioration. On the contrary, when the work is heavy, interrupting training for no more than four to six days is immediately followed by a decrease in efficiency as indicated by faster heart rate and higher concentration of lactic acid in the blood. Here again many problems are unsolved, and

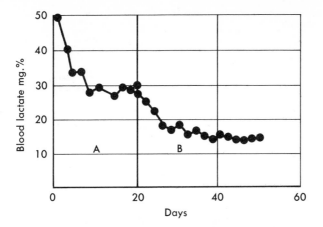

Fig. 2. Progressive decrease of blood lactate for a standard amount of exercise: running on a treadmill at 7 mph for ten minutes. During the first 20 days (Section A) training consisted in running daily on the treadmill for 20 minutes at 7 mph. A steady level of blood lactic acid is reached around 28 mg %. During the following 30 days, training is increased to running at 8.5 mph for 15 minutes daily (Section B). Blood lactic acid decreases further and a new steady level is reached around 15 mg % after the standard test.

more studies are needed to determine the best training methods for various kinds of physical activity.

4. SPECIFICITY OF TRAINING

General physical training increases the efficiency to perform any kind of muscular activity provided the work load is moderate. For heavy work, however, an individual trained for a specific activity is more efficient and capable of doing more work of that particular nature than any other kind. Experiments were undertaken in an attempt to elucidate this problem, and the performances of highly trained runners and oarsmen were studied.[6] A first test consisted of a treadmill run at 7 miles per hour, grade 8.6 per cent, for five minutes. The second test was made in a rowing tank at 22 strokes per minute for four minutes and 30 strokes per minute during the fifth minute. Heart rate was recorded and a blood sample was taken five minutes after the end of exercise for lactic acid determination. All subjects were able to complete the two tests, which for them was submaximal work. The results were remarkably constant and showed that for the two tests, running and rowing, the cardiovascular reactions were similar for all subjects. It seems that for these experimental conditions the responses of the circulatory system of an athlete to heavy muscular work remains the

same regardless of previous training and the nature of the exercise performed.

On the other hand, blood lactic acid varied markedly according to the kind of test performed and to the nature of the preceding training. It was found that for a practically identical cardiovascular reaction, a runner accumulates more lactic acid when he rows than when he runs, and an oarsman reaches a higher lactic acid level when he runs than when he rows. Therefore, physical training has a definite specific action in relation to lactic acid production during heavy muscular work. The final result is that the maximum lactic acid saturation is reached more rapidly, and exhaustion appears sooner when the subject performs an exercise for which he is not specifically trained compared with the type of exercise for which he is trained. Since in the above experiments the cardiovascular reactions were constant, it appears that the specific training process occurs at least partly in the muscles themselves.

The specificity of training can also be shown when the effects of performing various sports regularly are compared.[7] Four groups of young men were studied before and during an athletic season. The standard test consisted of pedalling a bicycle ergometer at the rate of 900 kg-m/min for five minutes. Heart rate was recorded through-

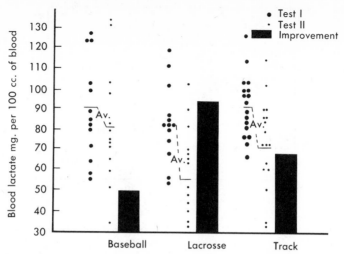

Fig. 3. Comparison of blood lactates of members of the baseball, lacrosse, and track squads at the beginning and end of 6 weeks of competition, together with averages and average improvement for each squad. The average improvement has been derived from the algebraic sum of the differences between the initial and final fitness indices of each individual.

out the test and blood lactate concentration was determined on a sample collected five minutes after the end of work. As soon as the first test had been performed, all the subjects started training for their own athletic specialty: 13 for baseball, 11 for lacrosse, and 17 for track. They were tested again after six weeks of training and competition. As expected, heart rates and blood lactates were definitely lower in the second test. The individual and average changes in blood lactate are shown in figure 3. It is seen that the improvement was greatest in the lacrosse group which was submitted to a more homogeneous and intense training than the others. Similar results were obtained in comparing the same varsity athletes before and after training. Physical efficiency as determined either by a bicycle ergometer or by a treadmill test was always highest after training in the men who were involved in strenuous and prolonged activities such as rowing or cross-country running. Therefore, the nature of training is a specific factor in determining the maximum efficiency that can be attained.

5. INFLUENCE OF INDIVIDUAL FACTORS ON TRAINING

Inborn capacity, sex, and age of the individual influence quantitatively the adaptation processes to muscular activity and the maximum improvement that can be achieved by training.

The ability to perform muscular work usually improves in all subjects submitted to training, but the physiological functions involved in muscular work have a considerable range of values. Therefore, an individual by appropriate training will progress to a certain maximum efficiency above which he cannot go and which is specific for that individual. Table 1 demonstrates that statement even within a small group of highly selected athletes.

Another example of differences in individual inborn capacity is given by studying the changes produced by training in neuromuscular coordination. In this experiment twelve subjects were studied while performing a test consisting of twelve deep knee bends performed on a force platform at the rate of a complete cycle, down and up, every 2 seconds. Two tests per week were made on each subject. The same exercise was used for training and was performed twice daily, morning and afternoon, for three weeks. The force platform is a device which permits registration in vertical, frontal and transverse axis of the complex forces produced by motions.[8] In an ideally performed knee bend most of the forces should be ap-

Table 1. Examples of variations in physiological measurements before and after physical training in a group of oarsmen*

	Treadmill test—5 min. run at 7 mph, grade 8.6%			
Number of subjects: 21			*Averages*	
Maximum pulse	Before training	191	Range	172-205
	After training	177	Range	158-195
Maximum blood	Before training	105	Range	53-166
lactate	After training	80	Range	41-142

	Individual values			
	Maximum pulse during run		*Maximum lactate mg./100 cc of blood*	
	Before	*After*	*Before*	*After*
Subject	*training*		*training*	
Cu.	172	158	68	41
Mar.	173	170	141	83
Er.	180	164	102	73
Gi.	185	172	112	64
No.	185	172	53	50
Ri.	190	170	84	70
La.	190	180	117	77
Cha.	190	178	77	77
Wh.	190	172	108	62
So.	192	174	130	95
Ch.	193	186	74	74
Ly.	195	180	78	75
Pr.	195	195	166	142
O.	195	176	149	90
Fi.	195	192	133	110
Eu.	196	182	91	59
J.	196	180	93	89
Br.	196	168	121	95
Ma.	200	180	74	68
Sn.	204	178	103	89
An.	205	186	122	106

*Data from "Variability of Physiological Measurements in Normal Young Men at Rest and During Muscular Work" by L. Brouha and B. M. Savage, *Revue canadienne de Biologie*, 4, 140, 1946. Courtesy of the Revue canadienne de Biologie.

plied in the vertical component, a certain amount in the frontal, but none in the transverse. In an untrained subject with comparatively poor coordination and balance the transverse component is expected to show a certain amount of forces needed to maintain the body balance while performing the knee bend. These forces should decrease with training if the coordination improves, and the body balance is more easily controlled. The subjects were tested morning and afternoon, and the number of displacements greater than 5 mm. was averaged for the two daily sessions. The preliminary study of the transverse displacement amplitudes suggests three types of training responses.

1. Some subjects showed a progressive training effect from the beginning to the end of the training period.
2. Others showed a delayed response and began to improve only after one or two weeks of daily practice.
3. The last group did not show any apparent effect of training after three weeks of practice.

Figure 4 gives the average curves for the three kinds of reactions. Curve I is the average for four subjects, Curve II includes five subjects, and Curve III the remaining three. Curve I shows that the subjects who were least coordinated at the beginning improved rapidly and regularly up to the end of the second week. They remained at that level

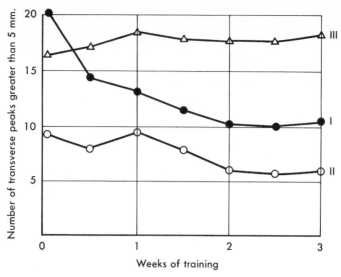

Fig. 4. Effect of training on coordination (see text).

during the third week of training. The subjects who were best coordinated at the start did not begin to show improvement until the latter part of the second week, and they remained at that level during the third week. The three subjects shown in Curve III started in between the two other groups, deteriorated slightly during the first week, and then remained at that high level until the end of the experiment in spite of regular training.

From experiments of this kind it is obvious that some individuals lack the possibility of significantly improving their neuromuscular coordination for certain motions. As a consequence when that motion is involved in any kind of activity, they will not be able to reach the level of efficiency achieved by others who show a definite improvement through training.

Sex influences training mostly due to the fact that men and women differ in their physiological capacity to perform exercise.[9, 10] At a given level of oxygen consumption the heart rate is higher in women than in men and, conversely, for a given heart rate, men can transport more oxygen than women during submaximal and maximal work. On the average the aerobic capacity is 25 to 30 per cent lower in women but trained subjects of both sexes seem to be able to utilize their anaerobic processes to the same extent. In both sexes the maximum heart rate during exercise is related linearly with increasing work load, but exhaustion is reached at a lower level of performance in women (Fig. 5).

The difference between boys and girls in their capacity to perform hard muscular work appears early in life as shown in figure 6. Nevertheless, the possibility to improve a given performance by training seems to be about the same for both sexes, taking into account that the females start at a lower level and reach a lower maximum. By computing the results on a per cent basis, it was found that after comparable training programs, high school and college girls and boys showed the same amount of improvement.[11, 12]

Age also influences training because of its relation to physical capabilities. In the older age range D. B. Dill has reported a series of investigations made on himself over a period of more than 20 years.[13] After thirty years of age, the maximum oxygen consumption diminishes progressively, associated with a decrease of cardiovascular and respiratory maximum capacity. Therefore the ability to withstand strenuous exercise is reduced and maximum performances of youth are no longer possible. But in the older as in the younger subjects, efficiency during submaximal work as well as maximum performance attainable are often related more to the fitness of the individual than to his chrono-

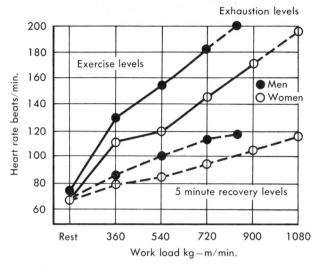

Fig. 5. Comparisons of heart rates of men and women.

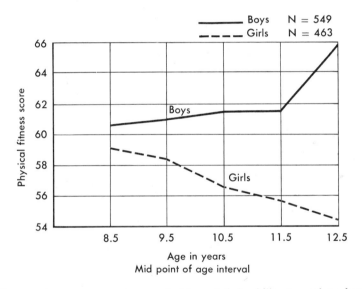

Fig. 6. Differences between young boys and girls and their ability to perform hard exercise.

logical age, and a number of examples are known of men of 60 or more who are still better than the majority of younger men. What is the effect of training on older individuals? Few data are available as yet but from recent experiments on a limited number of subjects above fifty years of age the picture seems to be as follows. As usual the gain in performance by training is determined by what the subject can do when he is not trained and the maximum he can achieve after adequate training. Since this

maximum is progressively reduced with advancing age, the margin of improvement diminishes accordingly. There is also an indication from results now at hand that the training period needed to reach maximum efficiency increases with age, but more research is necessary before a definite conclusion can be formulated.

In the younger age range, training increases the performance from childhood to young adulthood. Here again *physiological age* is the real factor which influences the capacity for muscular activity. In adolescents we have found a much higher correlation between the ability to perform hard exercise and the size of the individual than with his chronological age,[14] and similar results have been reported by Astrand.[15]

In summary, the training processes appear to be qualitatively similar for all, and the differences observed in the capability of adjusting to exercise are only quantitative. These differences are determined by individual characteristics, including sex, age, and inborn capacity which are not necessarily apparent in the untrained subject but are revealed by training. The wide individual differences in physiological functions and in physiological adaptability to training are striking. It should be fully realized that although anybody can improve his working capacity by training, outstanding athletic performances are attainable only by a comparatively small number of individuals whose physiological mechanisms are highly efficient and precisely integrated. To become a champion implies innate capabilities, mental and physical, that are developed to a superior level by adequate training and permit outstanding performances in a particular field of athletic activity. This is the exception. The variation in capacities and the limitations of any individual who goes into training should be known by those who are responsible for the physical education and the sports activities of man as well as by those who are in charge of the selection and control of workers involved in physical labor.

REFERENCES

1. Petrén, T., Sjostrand, T., and Sylvén, B. Arbeitsphysiologie, 9, 376, 1936.
2. Dill, D. B., and Brouha, L. Le Travail Humain, 5, 3, 1937.
3. Johnson, R. E., and Brouha, L. Revue Canadienne de Biologie, 1, 171, 1942.
4. Chailley-Bert, P. Sports, Education Physique, Leurs Reáctions sur l'Appareil Circulatoire. Paris, J. B. Baillière et F., 1946.
5. Edwards, H. T., Brouha, L., and Johnson, R. E. Le Travail Humain, 8, 1, 1939.
6. Brouha, L. Revue Canadienne de Biologie, 4, 144, 1945.
7. Gallagher, J. R., and Brouha, L. Yale Journal of Biology and Medicine, 15, 671, 1943.
8. Brouha, L., and Smith, P. E., Jr. Federation Proceedings, 17, 20, 1958.
9. Astrand, P. O. Physiological Reviews, 36, 307, 1956.
10. Metheny, E., Brouha, L., Johnson, R. E., and Forbes, W. H. American Journal of Physiology, 137, 318, 1942.
11. Gallagher, J. R., and Brouha, L. Revue Canadienne de Biologie, 2, 395, 1943.
12. Hardy, H. L., Clarke, H. L., and Brouha, L. Revue Canad. de Biologie, 2, 407, 1943.
13. Dill, D. B. Transactions of the 7th Annual Meeting of the American College of Sports Medicine, 1960.
14. Gallagher, J. R., and Brouha, L. Yale Journal of Biol. and Med., 15, 657, 1943.
15. Astrand, P. O. Experimental Studies of Physical Working Capacity in Relation to Sex and Age. Copenhagen, Ejnar Munksgaard, 1952.

42. A comparison of isotonic and isometric exercises in the development of muscular strength*

Stan Burnham

Physical Education Department, University of Texas at Austin

Heavy resistive exercises are used extensively in present-day training programs as a means of conditioning the muscles of individuals for participation in vigorous physical activities. This practice is based on the concept that muscle must be overloaded in order to improve strength and that an appropriate level of strength is fundamental to successful performance of physical activities. In the past decade both isotonic and isometric exercises have been used for the purpose of training muscle strength, and although much has been learned about strength development from research and practical experience, many questions remain unanswered as to the effectiveness of the two methods for improving strength. Physical educators and physiologists have continued in their search for conclusive evidence as to the most effective method of muscle training and to ways by which these methods can be adapted to practical situations for the training of man. Little attention, however, has been given to the degree and rate of strength development as it is related to initial strength, or strength present at the beginning of training, or to change of exercise treatment when increase ceases and the training contraction becomes ineffective.

PURPOSE

The purpose of this investigation was to determine the effectiveness of isotonic and isometric contractions as training stimuli in the development of muscular strength for individuals with different levels of strength. Specifically this study was concerned with—
1. The comparison of the two resistive exercise methods in the development of muscular strength of individuals with relatively low levels of strength.
2. The comparison of the two resistive exercise methods in the development of muscular strength of individuals with considerably high levels of strength.
3. The applicability of changing from one exercise method to the other as strength of an individual increases during a period of training. For example, would it be best to change to isotonic contractions for an individual whose strength status has changed from relatively little to a considerable amount during a training period in which isometric contractions were used?

SUBJECTS

Subjects for the study were 148 male students enrolled in the required physical education program at the University of Texas during the spring semester of 1964-65. Each subject volunteered to participate in the experiment and insofar as possible, individuals were assigned to one of four exercise groups on the basis of indicated interest in a particular training method. For the purpose of exercise training the subjects were placed in one of the following groups:

Group I   Trained by the isometric method for a period of ten weeks

*From Proceedings, Dec. 1966, p. 106, National College Physical Education Association for Men. Used by permission.

Group II Trained by the isometric method for five weeks and then changed to the isotonic method for five weeks

Group III Trained by the isotonic method for five weeks and then changed to the isometric method for five weeks

Group IV Trained by the isotonic method for a period of ten weeks

The subjects in each exercise group spent approximately forty-five minutes during each class period in the performance of the exercises. Each individual was encouraged to refrain from any other heavy physical activity outside the class during the course of the training period. The subjects in each group performed all exercises on Monday, Wednesday, and Friday of each week for a period of ten weeks. Each exercise group followed a training regimen designed to develop all muscle groups in the body. In both training regimens specific exercises were used for development of those muscles upon which measurements of strength were taken.

EXERCISE METHODS

For the purpose of training muscle strength in this study both isometric and isotonic contractions were used as a means of placing overload on the working muscles.

In the isotonic method the subject lifted heavy weights through a specified range of motion. All exercise movements were performed with a weight that could be lifted only five times through the complete range of motion for each exercise. The progressive resistive procedure was followed throughout the training period whereby additional weight was added to the lift as the muscle gained in strength. In this training program weight was added each time the subject was able to perform more than five repetitions of the exercise.

In the isometric method the subject exerted a maximum contraction for six seconds, against a resistance that did not allow movement or shortening of the muscle. The resistance in the isometric method was provided by a strap that furnished an immovable resistance at a specific position in the range of movement for the isotonic method. Each exercise was performed at this position with three six-second maximal contractions.

TESTS

The measures of muscle strength for this investigation were obtained before, at the middle, and at the end of exercise training through the use of an aircraft cable tensiometer. The tests used were selected for the purpose of determining the strength of muscles involved in the coordinated action of—

1. Arm flexion and forearm extension
2. Arm extension and forearm flexion
3. Thigh extension and leg extension
4. Trunk flexion

In this method of testing, the subject used the muscles involved in the specific movement to exert pressure against a cable. The tensiometer revealed the tension developed in the cable and thus the strength of the muscles involved in a specific movement at one point in the range of motion. The subject took two trials on each test with thirty seconds rest between trials. Both trials were recorded and the better of the two was used as the score.

STATISTICAL PROCEDURES

The major statistical task in this investigation was to discover whether or not significant differences in muscular strength existed in the various exercise groups as a result of having trained the subjects by different methods of muscular contraction. The results of training were interpreted on the basis of findings revealed by the multiple linear regression analysis and through an examination of changes in subjects' strength as related to initial status.

Regression models adapted for use on a Control Data Corporation 1604 computer were used for all the multiple linear regression analysis reported in this study. Regression analysis is an estimation or prediction of the value of one variable from the values of other given variables and this technique allows for the evaluation of all pertinent influences impinging upon the variable in question. Just as any variance analysis, the multiple linear regression technique is based on the concept of "error sum of squares" and indicates the relationship between a criterion or dependent variable and the predictor or independent variable.

In order to analyze the data in terms of the purpose stated for this investigation, certain problems involving categorical infor-nation with an underlying hypothesis were postulated. The data related to these questions at issue were interpreted on the basis of findings revealed through a comparison of applicable restricted regression models to full models related to mid-test and post-test scores. In this study two full models were constructed, one from post-test data and the other from mid-test data. Restricted models designed for specific questions were constructed by combining the variables containing scores of the groups in question, and these were compared with the appropriate full or unrestricted model. F-ratios computed from the obtained values of the error sum of squares for the full model and the appropriate restricted model were compared with tabled values of the F statistic to provide a basis for decisions concerning the various hypotheses.

ANALYSIS OF DATA AND INTERPRETATION OF FINDINGS

For the purpose of analysis, the data on each of the strength measures were grouped into first, second, third, and fourth quarter strength levels on the basis of the subject's initial status on the different strength tests. That is, each of the four exercise groups were divided into four subgroups on the basis of scores on the initial administration for each of the four tests of strength. Thus there were sixteen groups in the analysis for each strength test.

Treatment effects are reflected in the scores on the mid-test at the end of five weeks and those on the post-test at the end of ten weeks. The data examined by the multiple linear regression technique revealed no significant differences between isotonic and isometric contractions in the development of muscular strength either for the groups as a whole or for the different strength levels.

A tabular analysis was made to study individual responses to the different methods of training since the statistical technique of variance analysis did not reveal this kind of information. The information obtained through this analysis indicated that during the first five weeks of training more individuals gained strength through the isometric exercises than in the isotonic program. During the final five weeks most individuals who gained strength during the first five weeks continued to improve strength when they remained in the same program. Although an examination of individual changes within the various strength levels revealed no consistent pattern, it would appear that as individuals reached very high levels of strength, most continued to improve through the isotonic program.

From the findings revealed by the statistical technique used in this study it appears that there was no difference between the two methods of exercise employed to develop muscular strength. The analysis of individual responses indicates, however, in exercise programs where improvement in strength is a major objective that isometric exercises may be preferable inasmuch as this method of training apparently leads to maximum results in terms of individual improvement with a minimum of time and equipment involved.

On the basis of evidence revealed in this investigation and other related studies, it apears that trainability of muscular strength varies with individuals and that it is the strength of the training stimulus which is important in producing improvement in strength. There seemingly is no significant difference between the effectiveness of isotonic and isometric contractions as training stimuli. It may be assumed that as long as the training contraction is above the training threshold, strength improvement will result regardless of the kind of contraction used or the strength level of the individual. When the training contraction is below threshold value, either because of a weak contraction or because the strength level of the individual places the training threshold above the maximum strength of the training contraction, no improvement in strength results.

43. Women and the medical aspects of sports*

Evalyn S. Gendel, M.D.

Chief, School Health Section, Division of Maternal and Child Health, Kansas State Department of Health

"Women shouldn't be involved in sports —it's unladylike."—School board member.

"Girls aren't strong enough to excel anyway in sports, why try to attract them to such fields?"—Chairman of school bond committee.

"Girls are too unreliable physiologically to spend a lot of time developing their sports activity."—School principal.

"Girls don't need aggressive physical education and intramural sports—they're too interested in their polished fingernails and special sprayed hairdos."—Coach.

"Women are not supposed to be so strenuous—they'll shake up something."—A student's father.

"We can't really motivate women in these sports areas—they may permanently impair their chances of normal pregnancy."—School administrator.

The network of cultural, emotional, social, physical and psychological factors which have led to expressions like these are complex. They are the same factors affecting other facets of women's lives. The sexual, maternal, vocational and political roles of women are being and have been dissected and examined continually, but perhaps never more so than in our current culture. Speculation on why this is happening can lead to a rehash of the "battle of the sexes"; to an exploration of the theory of evolution or to almost any other related topic. Repeatedly, in the furor, information and misinformation are "legitimatized" with so-called "medical" reasons. The acceptance of these reasons without adequate study has significantly

helped to determine some of the past and present trends in girls' and women's sports.

The "unladylike" connotation frequently applied to physical exertion by the female is an historical and societal hangover from other times in certain cultures, and hopefully, is on its way out. If translated into gender influence, it has little scientific validity, since being female implies no inherent biological deterrent to physical activity.

Closely allied to this rationale is the one which decries the lack of strength in women. If health and endurance are any criteria of strength, women have special advantages, which might be cultivated to enhance their eligibility for better sports programs. (Morbidity and mortality rates in a majority of diseases are less in women than men.) Ulcers, coronary heart disease, cancer, respiratory diseases, diabetes, and many other conditions occur more often in men than women. Due to fewer illnesses and disabilities, aptitude for endurance could be developed further in girls and women.

The physiological disadvantages so frequently described as deterrents to women's physical activity, are the subject of many papers pro and con on the effect of the menstrual cycle on women in sports. Much of the recent literature and numbers of studies have indicated that we have been overprotective about this phenomenon for years. Facts about menstruation, though well documented and understood, have been colored by the folklore of the female subculture and the influence of women on men. Men of science have had to weigh their knowledge of scientific fact against living with women— their mothers, wives and daughters. Phy-

*From The Journal of School Health, Vol. 37, p. 427, Nov. 1967. Used by permission.

icians have been further influenced by patients' complaints and reactions about their
own menstrual styles. Science may have
come out on the short side considering that
most of the people weighing the evidence
have been men. Perhaps this accounts for
the language of state and local school regulations and recommendations on physical education and sports for women and girls.
Not only at the turn of the century, but as
late as 1960, some restrictive regulations are
explained with the phrase: "young women
being of such delicate physical nature are to
be excluded from these activities."

In the more recent literature, in a number of articles and studies, it is generally
concluded that participation in all sports
activities before, during, or after menstruation, causes no deleterious effect on the normal menstrual cycle. (1, 2) This is as far
as the conclusions may go. Very few of them
provide more fundamental analysis on long-
range beneficial or harmful effects.

The coach's comment on fingernails and
hairdos was included because it reflects the
readiness with which we invent excuses for
being indifferent to physical activity and
sports for girls. Perhaps these feminine gim-
micks were devised by the girls as a defense
against the indifference. There are parents
who request "excuses" for their daughters
for absence from intramural sports, swimming, and other team activities, who may
refer to "standing" or regular hair appointments. Some of the medical excuses have
been granted by a physician who may not
have a positive conviction about girls' physical activities and fitness and who has also
been worn down by an aggressive over-
solicitous parent. The medical excuse sometimes adds substance to an indifferent attitude.

The comment about "shaking up something" has surely arisen from the patient's
translation of gynecological jargon about
"tipped uteri" and the positioning of female
organs. Some sociological studies on what the
doctor thinks he told the patient—what the
patient thinks the doctor told her, and what
the patient tells her neighbor she thinks the
doctor told her, already reveal a lack of
understanding of what we learn about ourselves. If this is applied to gynecological discussions, the errors, exaggerations and fantasy, are compounded dangerously. Unfor-

tunately, this type of "medical information"
travels quickly—often picked up by the
popular press to become "medical fact"
before we know it. Both patients and doctor
contribute to this problem. Physicians seldom discuss among themselves their patients
who are "normal"—it is the case with
"findings" which receives all the discussion
and publication. The woman who had no
problem with her yearly pelvic check-up has
nothing to discuss with anyone as compared
to the girl or woman with a diagnosis of
mild anatomical disfunctioning or pathology.
She receives the attention as she tells her
story. The effect is one which would lead us
to believe that defects are common—that
normal uncomplicated female functioning is
rare. Realistically, there *are* patients with
menstrual disorders and with gynecological
pathology who do require medication, surgery or special prescriptions or precautions
pertaining to exertion, but these patients are
a very small segment of the general population.

Where pregnancy is concerned the slightest
implication that it might be influenced ad-
versely precipitates profound pronouncements
on both sides. Many studies conclude that
regular exertion and competitive athletics
will *not* have a harmful effect on pregnancy.(3) They demonstrate that women athletes experience no more complications than
non-athletes. Others have indicated that increased muscularity of the athlete increases
complications of pregnancy. None of these
studies, as with those on menstruation, has
provided analytical comparative data with
control groups to indicate a more accurate
picture.

The gamut of conditions needing special
"medical" consideration in women which
supposedly are more complicated or earth-
shaking than the general considerations for
men, are largely centered around the reproductive tract. The psychological and motiva-
tional disposition of women in sports is influenced from this same focal point, i.e. their
own attitudes toward sports activities shaped
by their perception of female physiological
functions. These fears, prejudices, and the
misinformation have been overcome only in
part. By publicizing the results of research
which demonstrates that strenuous activity
will not alter the menstrual cycle abnormally
or interfere with normal internal anatomy,

much could be done to alleviate the persistent myths.

In the debates about women and physical exertion, competitive sports, and Olympic participation, the emphasis has been chiefly on proving that no *harm* will be done. What is needed is more information on what *good* might be accomplished were these activities recommended. The "good" being more than the physical exuberance, camaraderie and well-being experienced by participants. The "medical" advantages which may be present should be explored more fully and explained.

As an example, a study reported by this writer (4) in 1965, showed that lack of physical activity and sports since childhood, leading to underdeveloped, poor tone abdominal musculature and weak fascial tissue, is a major contributing factor in chronic severe low backache following pregnancy in a group of 35 young women. These had been screened out of a group of 100 patients, 18-23 years of age, who were followed over a period of from one and a half to five years. All of the patients were seen by the same physician—supervised throughout pregnancy and the postpartum period. Others whose babies had been delivered elsewhere, came as patients when they moved into the area. Without reproducing the entire study in this paper, I will try to condense the essence of it in a Composite Case Study.

The typical patient was between 18 and 23 years of age; had one or two children, and had returned for a six months check-up following her last delivery. She gave a history of chronic backache, which had been moderate to severe ever since she returned home with the infant. She complained that pain was aggravated by many things: whenever she lifted the baby, made beds, carried heavy objects and following sexual intercourse. Orthopedic, pelvic, urinary and circulatory pathology were ruled out in this final group. (Those who appeared to have psychological complications were also excluded.) Detailed history further revealed that calisthenics, playground activity and other exercises or sports had not been encouraged at elementary school years. The patient had no courses in physical education or sports in junior or senior high school. None of these patients, for instance, had ever ridden a bicycle; only one or two of them cared about dancing. None were walkers; none had ever partici-

pated in a physical improvement program on an individual or group basis. None of the group were bowlers, skaters, golfers, or indulged in any active leisure exercise programs. These patients exhibited deficient abdominal muscle strength, postural abnormalities, and protuberant abdomens. None were obese. All of these patients responded to a selected prescribed series of exercises conducted individually over a $1\frac{1}{2}$ to 5 year period.

Recently, in some work in health education with high school and college students who had never been pregnant, the physical activity history was utilized on a small group of 50 girls. Twenty-two gave histories paralleling the post partal study. Although they did not complain of backache, when they were examined, 19 had similar physical findings also.(5) With the added physiological stress of pregnancy at a future date, will these young women be candidates for the same chronic condition of the study patients?

These findings have been interpreted by some people to mean that there are "magic" exercises which can be prescribed in the post pregnancy period which will alleviate this backache and chronic disability. This is not the point at all. The tremendous effort required by these patients—the motivation which finally led them to rehabilitation required the kind of heroics in which most of us would not indulge. The plea would be to devise a generally accepted preventive activity which would eliminate the physical findings in the first place. Why not discuss how physical activity of a regular nature begun in childhood provides better body mechanics, improves development of abdominal and spinal musculature which in turn may prove of benefit in the progress of pregnancy, and in prevention of postural complications of pregnancy. In the matter of the menstrual studies, I believe it can be shown that the occurrence of these same improvements enhances the integrity of the menstrual physiology. There are less of the hemorrhagic abnormalities, cramping and associated symptom when general muscle tone is maintained at an optimum level—providing other medical conditions do not exist.

There are other disabilities in women—idiopathic scoliosis, lordosis, chronic general fatigue, and fatigue related to vague backache which need similar controlled investigation. Where pathology can be ruled out, exercise histories should be taken. From orthopedic observation and experience, we have seen that in patients who demonstrate scoliosis of unknown origin, the ones who are regularly involved in individual and team activities, tolerate the disability with fewer complications than those who are underdeveloped and of a sedentary nature. The disfiguration for the former group is also much less and often barely noticeable. Since this is a condition found most often in young women, it cannot be attributed to aging or to a natural slowing down of physical activity. What I am suggesting is that scientific comprehensive studies be undertaken to determine the extent to which normal growth and development can be guided to increase each individual's understanding of his own body functioning. If he appreciates its capabilities and uses them to his own best advantage, the preventive aspects could be measured and appraised. Such studies to be reliable must be undertaken with "controls," with consideration of multifaceted environmental, physical and psychological modifying factors.

A re-examination of some of the material already available to us suggests that this kind of research could prove fruitful. Considering the cultural trends in this country to more spectacular activities, to increased television viewing, to added leisure periods and to a mounting number of psychosomatic complaints, the time to accelerate such study is yesterday.

SUMMARY

The emphasis on girls' and women's sports need not be centered on competition alone. There is need to dispel the medical folklore of women for their own benefit and for the furthering of scientific investigation.

This goal can be accomplished by publicizing the valid controlled studies, and initiating more of them, on the effects of strenuous activity on female reproductive functioning, and other medical conditions.

We must recognize that programs which promote understanding and participation in regular physical activity (without undue stress in early years on competition) will build up a reserve of girls and women who expect to be "fit."

Through these methods, the attitude of teachers, parents, physicians and students can be altered by creating a climate of acceptance of regular physical exertion for women.

This group of conditioned youngsters will produce some gifted athletes. Some girls inspired by the programs will make a special effort in athletics, but more important, *all* women will benefit in their roles as women—athletes or not!

REFERENCES

1. Erdelyi, G., Gynecological Survey of Female Athletes, *The Journal of Sports Medicine and Physical Fitness,* Vol. 2, pp. 174–179, (September) 1962.
2. Menstruation and Sport, *British Medical Journal,* No. 5372, p. 1548, (December 21) 1963.
3. Walde, J., Obstetrical and Gynecological Back and Pelvic Pain—Especially Those Contracted During Pregnancy: *Acta, Obstetrica and Gynecologica Scandinavia* Supplements Vol. XLI supp 2 from the Department of Gynecology and Obstetrics, University of Bergen, Norway, pp. 11–53.
4. "Pregnancy, Fitness and Sports" paper presented by Evalyn S. Gendel, M.D., Asst. Director, Maternal and Child Health Division, State Department of Health, Topeka, Kansas at the Seventh National Conference on the Medical Aspects of Sports, Philadelphia, Penn., November 28, 1965.
5. Gendel, E. S., Spring 1965 interviews with physical education teachers, student teachers and local attending physicians. Unpublished material.

Projects and thought questions for biological foundations of physical education

1. Write an article that, from your own viewpoint, discusses physical fitness as an important objective of physical education.

2. Begin a personal jogging or exercise program, and keep a daily log. After a minimum of 6 weeks, write an essay on your program. Tell whether or not you found your program to be of value.

3. Assess your weight status in relation to your own diet and exercise program. Tell in what ways you can improve your status to obtain optimum levels of health and biological fitness.

4. Read at least five articles and/or research reports that deal with the effect of training on the individual. Give an oral summation.

5. Write a documented report comparing isometric and isotonic exercise programs.

6. Prepare an outline for a research project that attempts to assess the biological status of women sports participants.

Selected readings

Alexander, J. F., et al.: Effects of a four-week training program on certain physical fitness components of conditioned male university students, Res. Quart. 39:16, Mar. 1968.

Chapman, C. B., and Mitchell, J. H.: The physiology of exercise, Sci. Amer. 212:88, May 1965.

Johnson, W. R., editor: Science and medicine of exercise and sport, New York, 1960, Harper & Row, Publishers.

Thorsen, M. A.: Body structure and design: factors in the motor performance of college women, Res. Quart. 35:418, Oct. 1964.

Wear, C. L., and Miller, K.: Relationship of physique and developmental level to physical performance, Res. Quart. 33:615, Dec. 1962.

Psychological foundations of physical education

M. Gladys Scott discusses physical activity from the viewpoint of a variety of professional and lay individuals and lists the commonly stated psychological results of physical activity. The author describes each outcome and briefly details the associated research and literature. In concluding the report, she states that physical educators need to increase their competencies in many areas of anthropology and psychology.

Dorothy V. Harris discusses the interrelationship of the functions of the mind and body. She points out that there has been much research concerned with the influence of the mind over the body, particularly when illness is concerned. Conversely, she says, there is relatively little research showing how the body influences the mind. Fatigue is used as an illustration of one possible somatopsychic condition. The author states that research is needed and that the professionals in health and physical education must take the responsibility and the leadership for education and research in this area.

Leela C. Zion investigates the attitudes of female college freshmen in regard to the relationship of body concept to self-concept. Paper and pencil attitude scales for each concept were completed by the subjects. The researcher states that in general body concept and self-concept show a positive relationship and that this relationship may have a bearing on mental health.

The relationship of health and physical education to academic achievement is illustrated in an article by Charles A. Bucher. The work of the Achievement Center for Children, a research facility engaged in investigating scholastic difficulties of children, is described. Bucher shows how research at the Achievement Center and research done by independent investigators seem to indicate that specially tailored motor-activity programs enhance perceptual–motor achievement levels in children.

D. H. Radler and Newell C. Kephart describe motor behavior as the only directly observable type of human behavior. The authors state that motor behavior of some type underlies almost every activity, including the thought process, and that this indicates that motor behavior is both overt and covert. The authors discuss the mental capacities upon which motor behavior depends, illustrating their thesis by reference to human posture, coordination, laterality, and motor discrimination. The article considers the child's motor development in light of the process of conceptualization and explains how concepts become externalized into movement patterns.

The article by Charles A. Bucher states that, while many people receive satisfaction by watching the performance of a physical skill, it is the participant who benefits most because of the psychological values he derives. The author writes that among these psychological values derived are recognition and a sense of belonging, increased self-confidence, an interest in a variety of things in life, and greater personal and social adjustment.

Lawrence Balter and Emanuel Sanger report on recent educational innovations that are of special interest to educational psychologists. The five broad major areas of innovation are discussed and evaluated by the writers. Each of the innovations has implications for physical education.

44. The contributions of physical activity to psychological development*

M. Gladys Scott

Professor, Department of Physical Education for Women, State University of Iowa

The parents, educators, recreation leaders, clinicians, and therapists who advocate activity, play, or exercise have in mind some benefit to be derived. The parent may assume it is an inevitable part of the child's growth. The teacher sees it as a means of modifying behavior and improving the individual's capacity to live more fully. Those from the medical profession see some preventive or remedial goal. But everyone consciously or unconsciously sees more than a physiological organism going through motor gyrations or having fun. Each recognizes that play and exercise have some effect on the behavior patterns of the person.

When one deals with the concepts of motor movement and physiological derivatives and concomitants, one is led to an entity which man everywhere recognizes as "play." Huisinga says:

This intensity of, and absorption in play finds no explanation in biological analysis. Yet in this intensity, this absorption, this power of maddening, lies the very essence, the primordial quality of play. Nature, so our reasoning mind tells us, could just as easily have given her children all those useful functions of discharging superabundant energy, of relaxing after exertion, of training for the demands of life, of compensating for unfulfilled longings, etc., in the form of purely mechanical exercises and reactions. But no, she gave us play, with its tensions, its mirth, and its fun.

Now this last-named element, the fun of playing, resists all analysis, all logical interpretation. As a concept, it cannot be reduced to any other mental category. . . . It is precisely this fun-element that characterizes the essence of play. Here we have to do with an absolutely primary

category of life, familiar to everybody at a glance right down to the animal level. We may well call play a "totality" in the modern sense of the word, and it is as a totality that we must try to understand and evaluate it.

Since the reality of play extends beyond the sphere of human life it cannot have its foundations in any rational nexus, because this could limit it to mankind. . . . Play cannot be denied. . . . In culture we find play as a given magnitude existing before culture itself existed, accompanying it and pervading it from the earliest beginnings right up to the phase of civilization we are now living in. We find play present everywhere as a well-defined quality of action which is different from "ordinary" (17:24).

In this interpretation of play, the educator, the sociologist and the anthropologist more or less agree. Mead (44:44), speaking from the anthropologist's view, says that all the elements of a game are quite deeply human and that therefore games can be easily communicated or transmitted. It is the process of the game that is important to the players. According to a saying, sometimes attributed to the Dutch, "It is not the marbles that matter, but the game." And as Huisinga (17:49) points out, "success gives the player a satisfaction that lasts a shorter or longer while as the case may be." Some of the fruits of that success are prestige, a sense of superiority, and satisfaction of that fundamental need to be honored and praised for one's excellence.

And so whether the physical educator is philosopher and anthropologist enough to visualize the human compulsion of the activities done freely, without work goals and objectives, he is nevertheless practical psychologist enough to observe the inherent elements which operate to mold the behavior

*From Research Quarterly, Vol. 31, No. 2, Part II, p. 307, May 1960. Used by permission.

of the individual and of the group. It is on this basis that we have stated our claims for psychological outcomes. And in these claims can be seen the close interrelationship of health, physical education, and recreation.

These claims may be summarized as follows:

1. Changing attitudes
2. Improving social efficiency
3. Improving sensory perception and responses
4. Developing sense of well-being—mental health
5. Promoting relaxation
6. Providing psychosomatic relief
7. Acquiring skill

For the past three or four decades the literature pertaining to play, to physical education, and to recreation has made assertions within the framework of the above points. Cowell, Daniels, and Kenney[11] give a report which more or less summarizes views. They include many of the above points in their study of values. The entire AAHPER yearbook, *Developing Democratic Human Relations*,[3] is based on the premise that health, physical education, and recreation contribute to personal and interpersonal relations and to the individual's attitudes.

These assertions are perhaps more profoundly believed today than ever before. Let us examine the evidence accumulated through the work and publications of those doing research.

ATTITUDES ARE CHANGED

Attitude is a feeling or mood relative to action. The professional concern is for attitudes which are relative to learning of motor skills, participation in physical education classes and in recreational use of the skills acquired, to physical activity as a way of recreation, to use of prescribed exercise for maintenance of fitness, or for therapeutic purposes, to development of appreciation of excellence in movement, and many others.

It is recognized that attitudes are frequently in flux. If they are not improving, they are apt to deteriorate before long. The factors considered to have a bearing on these attitudes include such diverse matters as appropriateness of the activity for the ability and maturation of the class, the method of instruction and class conduct, and the freedom of the individual to choose and determine his own activity and goals. It appears that this is an area in which comparatively little has been done to verify our observations and assumptions.

The tools for measuring attitudes are fairly numerous. Wear[63] constructed an effective attitude scale for the college man with respect to physical education classes, and Plummer[41] developed another for the college women. McGee,[31] Scott,[50] and McCue[30] developed scales for attitudes of parents and teachers toward athletic competition. Bowman[8] constructed scales both for the elementary school child and for measuring parent attitude toward the child's active play experiences. All these show individual differences ranging from "highly favorable toward" to "indifference" and "highly antagonistic."

Attitudes toward health have also had some study. Kent and Prentice[24] stated increased interest from use of motion pictures in classes. Turner and others[58] studied health attitudes, knowledge, and practice with apparent high interest in obtaining facts on health topics.

In the area of recreation, attitudes have been studied primarily through inquiries about the individual's interests or desires, or "what he would like to do" or "knows he should do." However, the reports on what he actually does show a wide discrepancy. Examples of this may be found in Adams,[1] Toogood,[60] and Wylie.[65] These leave the reader with the question as to whether attitudes are as effective in governing action as we are prone to think and also with the unanswered question of the effect of rapid change in attitudes.

There has been very little done in the study of modification of attitudes. If Smith's[57] "level of aspiration" can be considered as an expression of attitude, then we have evidence on effect of success and failure in an athletic situation. The level rose with success and dropped with failure. The failure group also tended by overt action to escape from the failure producing situation. This seems to be in accord with the observations of teachers, coaches, and recreation leaders and may largely account for the drop-outs in recreation programs.

Annett[2] hypothesized that skill determined level of interest and attitute toward participation. He found in the area of dance that the earlier the age at which dancing was started and the more frequent the experience the greater the skill and the interest. The most popular dance was the one best known.

Plummer[41] found several factors affecting attitudes of the college woman toward physical education. They were mostly personal problems such as competition of other interests, physical appearance, previous experience, finance, and response to the group, but also the facilities and general environment.

McAfee[28] reported on a test of sportsmanship attitudes for sixth, seventh, and eighth grade boys. Progressive deterioration of attitude seemed to call for some revision of teaching methods to alter this trend. This again emphasizes the assumption that attitudes can be modified and that changes can be a direct objective of teaching.

The evidence is far from adequate on questions such as relative importance of different factors in affecting attitudes; individual differences in response to these factors and in "fluidity" of attitudes; relationship of attitudes to actual overt response in the presence of group stimulation, and other motivating stimuli.

As to the value of attitudes, little doubt remains from educational research or experience that intent to learn, receptivity, and motivation toward learning and participation are conducive to accomplishment and lack thereof is inhibiting.

SOCIAL EFFICIENCY IS IMPROVED

This suggests a broad area of human functioning. Professional goals deal with the individual's capacity to be a part of a group and to accept and work with other individuals in the group. Likewise, the individual is expected to demonstrate characteristics of integrity and honesty, fair play, acceptance and understanding, generosity, reliability, and other characteristics considered to be indications of a mature and socially desirable personality. Allegations with respect to character and personality growth are broad, covering development through participation in learning situations, engaging in competition, and establishing patterns of recreation participation. This development is alleged to make the individual more mature and more socially acceptable in a moral and

ethical sense. At the same time that he emerges as a strong personality he also becomes an asset in the social groups of which he is a part.

Research, of course, deals with fragments of this problem. Our answers to the total must be built on a summation of evidence.

Probably the greatest amount of research to date has been in the area of social interaction and the development of the sociometric tools and methods of analyzing them. These are products also of the last 15 to 20 years. Breck and Skubic were among the first to adapt the work of Mareno,[32] Jennings,[21] and others to physical education groups. Breck[9] developed scoring methods. Skubic[50] used the test on classes which were taught as usual with the additional objective of trying to promote acquaintanceship within the class. Fewer social isolates were found and more social leaders emerged during a six-week period. They agreed with Jennings that leadership and isolation are products of interpersonal interaction rather than attributes of persons. Perhaps one of the important findings here is that change did occur, a fact substantiated by Yukie.[66]

Fulton and Prauge[13] used this technique for comparing motor learning of the chosen and unchosen class members. They found no significant difference for the college women. On the other hand, McCraw and Tolbert[29] found a relationship between sociometric status and athletic ability of boys.

This problem is discussed in more detail in the article by Cowell in this supplement. However, it is essential to relate interpersonal patterns to individual behavior responses, and so it is presented briefly here.

Almost as much interest has been shown in personality changes in the individual. Because of the nature of the personality scales, these are apt to be interpreted as indicating good or poor social adjustment. Biddulph[6] found such a high relationship between athletic achievement and social adjustment that he emphasized the importance of athletic experience for all. Bentson and Summerskill's[5] study of the entering college man seems to indicate a relationship between social adjustment and success in athletics. This is a point often ignored in studies or observations of outcomes and may have led to erroneous conclusions. However, Biddulph was studying the younger boy and at that age adjustment may be more readily occurring. When considering the participant versus the non-participant in Little League baseball play, Seymour[51] found no significant difference in terms of needs and problems or in personality traits except "leadership." Here the participant started higher and gained more. Seymour by hypothesis, measurement design, and conclusions does recognize that with regard to personality the participant starts at a higher level and maintains it. It is failure to recognize this higher starting point that has led some authors to attribute more marked gains from competitive athletic programs than are actually demonstrated in their measurements.

Closely associated with this matter of adjustment is the effect of method. Todd[58] experimented with the "democratic" method and through sociometric analysis found improved acquaintanceship, upward mobility of most students, fewer isolates, better group cohesion, and group approval and satisfaction. Similarly Walters[62] found that group cohesion and unity improved as well as motor performance under motivation of team organization and recognition. The same was found for dance experiences. Page[38] said that when groups are working together, rhythmic cooperation has the ability to synchronize the efforts of the many who are concerned with the common task and to increase the pleasure and efficiency of the participants.

The other aspect of this problem which has been studied is the immediate and temporary effect of competition in athletics upon tensions and emotional control. Johnson and Hutton[22] believed they had demonstrated that the projective test is suitable to identify the altered pattern of precompetition anxiety, body consciousness, and aggression, and the post-competition release whether or not subjects won their wrestling event. Husman[18] also used projective tests and differentiated athletes in boxing and in other sports and the changing characteristics before and after competitive seasons.

Ulrich[61] also found "prestress" effects which were greater for the inexperienced than the experienced group where sport competition was the stress variable. In the post-stress period the experienced group showed greater effects if they had not been permitted to play and the inexperienced group showed

highest stress evidence if they had participated. Ulrich used evidence of eosinophil in the blood. Skubic[52, 54] worked in a similar problem with boys in Little League by means of the galvanic skin response. Both agreed that competition in Little League play had no greater effect than competition in physical education classes.

All of this evidence seems a bit inconclusive as to meaningful changes. Seymour makes a conclusion which probably summarizes the situation in terms of present evidence.

As a final conclusion of this comparison of behavior characteristics of participant and non-participant boys in Little League Baseball, it would seem prudent to exercise caution in ascribing with any degree of certainty behavioral changes, whether desirable or undesirable, to Little League Baseball or to any comparable program for youth (51:345).

It is by uncritical quotation of certain findings that the total issue is obscured. Such an example is found in that of Hale.[14] He falls into the error sometimes made in statistical interpretation of talking about significant findings in the absence of statistical significance. On such erroneous interpretation he then goes on to say that competitive athletics are not detrimental but rather beneficial for pre-high school age children. He further quotes Skubic[53, 54] as confirming his case. But at another point he says that more studies need to be made before the final report can be prepared. Longitudinal studies are needed, as well as more study of emotional responses, on the effect of rejection from participation and on effect of athletic competition for girls.

Skubic's statement on the present status of information is very clear. It should be remembered that this study was concerned with only one phase of the total problem of competition—the immediate effects of competition on emotionality. In order to completely solve the problem of highly organized competition, data must be gathered relative to the physical, sociological, psychological, and economic aspect of competition. Furthermore, to resolve the specific controversy concerning emotional effects of competition, it is necessary that additional data be secured particularly in regard to the influence of emotion on personality now and later in life (52:351).

Since psychiatrists attribute most of the psychological problems of youth and adults to earlier experiences and their emotional impact on later behavior, it would seem that actual "value interpretations" must wait for more objective evidence on long-term behavior patterns and personality characteristics.

IMPROVED SENSORY PERCEPTION AND RESPONSES

Claims in this area are less frequent, at least in written form. Yet it is from isolated instances and studies based on such hypotheses that recognition seems desirable in this review. These cases range through reaction time, depth perception, visual perception, speed, kinesthetic awareness, and empathy.

Olsen[37] attempted to determine if relationships exist between degree of athletic success and reaction time, depth perception, and visual span of apprehension—and whether differences exist between athletes in various sports. In general, relationships were found, but sports differences were not. In a still broader series of psychomotor tests fencers and nonfencers were nondifferentiated.[40] Keller[23] studied athletic groups on "quickness of movement" and Slater-Hammel[55] studied balance in athletic groups of varying skill levels. Both found their groups differed but like Olsen refrained from attributing these increments to increased experience. In light of present knowledge, the hypothesis that possession of the trait contributes to athletic success is as plausible as the reverse, that is, that athletic experience produces a higher degree of the capacity.

The effect of activity on kinesthetic awareness is a debatable point, partly because of lack of evidence, but also because of lack of agreement on a precise definition of kinesthesis. Research to date does indicate a high degree of specificity in kinesthetic functioning.[46, 48, 64] This is partly responsible for the lack of clarity in definition.

Those who propose the concept of an improved kinesthetic awareness from physical activity are doing so on the premise that learning takes place here in the same way that musical training may improve the individual's perception of quality or tone differences, or that experience can help the discriminative capacity of the person in the sensations of taste or smell. The other basic hypothesis is that higher kinesthetic acuity is associated with greater achievement. At least a few studies have been conducted on these hypotheses. Typical of these are Roloff,[45] Honzik,[15] Lafuze,[25] Mumby,[36] and Phillips.[39]

Evidence in general does not support such hypotheses. However, the imperfections of measures on both learning and kinesthesis may be responsible for the apparent lack of evidence. It appears to this author that it is too early to draw conclusions.

Empathy is another of the human responses to what one sees going on. Physical educators have considered empathic capacity as the very basis of appreciation of quality in performance, of esthetics in movement in general or dance in particular; of ability to see detail in demonstrations or observations as one goes through the learning process. The difficulty here is similar to that in kinesthesis. The educator and the researcher are talking about an entity within another human being, an entity which has no check in the same way one can verify that the subject sees the same color as the investigator, or hears the same whistle another hears.

As to the values of these sensory capacities, we can conjecture that they may facilitate learning, provide capacity for better neuromuscular performance, and enrich living in general by making the person more sensitive and responsive to his environment. However, our research to date does not give us a basis for confidence in the outcomes or for building a premise of values.

IMPROVED SENSE OF WELL-BEING

Good mental health is sometimes defined as being comfortable with one's self and with others. This has very broad implications if considered carefully. The health and physical education teacher and recreation worker claim mental health outcomes from physical activities and affirm the claims of their colleagues in the related health fields. The physical activities considered are particularly those labeled play, that is, having a fun or diversionary function, and those serving to redirect effort or to afford emotional release or creative outlets. The educator and recreation worker are most prone to base such assertions on case studies, that is, an individual carefully observed in his work, or on the clinical records and conclusions of the psychiatrists and physicians.

Jackson and Todd write comprehensively of the outcomes and values of play, based on extensive research on and therapeutic treatment of the very young child. Their in-interpretation of play and its meaning is revealed in the following quotation.

It [play] has educative as well as enjoyment value, yet in a broader sense than either Gross or McDougall assigned to it. The child's learning through play is more subtle and more general than is implied in Gross's theory, and his acquisitions far less obvious. By playing the part of father, mother, engine-driver, or doctor, he acquires no knowledge of how to behave in these parts when he grows up. What he does achieve is the experience of imaginative identification and intuitive understanding; what he gains is not practical skills, but an inner balance on which depends his future emotional development and the success of his relationships with other human beings (19:12).

The goals of the physical educator and recreation leader are based on evidence and conclusions such as that cited in the quotation and source above. It is commonly conceded that these goals are logical for the school-age child and perhaps even for the younger ones of the teen-age level. There are many outside the professions of play leadership who doubt that there is any necessity or value other than a fun value for the adult in his play activities. Again the best evidence on mental health values come from the psychiatrist. William Menninger writes from experience in the clinic and on research associated with patients in the clinic. The following quotations represent his conclusions from this evidence.

Mentally healthy people participate in some form of volitional activity to supplement their required daily work. This is not merely because they wish something to do in their leisure time, for many persons with little leisure make time for play. Their satisfaction from these activities meet deep seated psychological demands, quite beyond the superficial rationalization of enjoyment.
Too many people do not know how to play. Others limit their recreation to being merely passive observers of the activity of others. There is considerable scientific evidence that the healthy personality is one who not only plays, but who takes his play seriously. Furthermore there is also evidence that the inability and unwillingness to play reveals an insecure or disordered aspect of personality (33:343).
Good mental health is directly related to the capacity and willingness of an individual to play. Regardless of his objections, resistances, or past practice, any individual will make a wise investment for himself if he does plan time for his play and take it seriously (33:345).

I also wish to point out the fact that the most constructive and beneficial play is something that has to be learned and is not likely to be an accidental ability or an inherited trait. For maximum satisfaction, one requires not only encouragement but almost always some instruction.
An effective community recreation program is just as important to mental health as sanitation is to physical health (33:346).

Surely these statements make it clear that every individual has need for participation in some type of play activity and that instruction in these play skills is very important.

The Josiah Macy, Jr., Foundation-sponsored Conference on Group Processes made an analytical study of games and their effect upon children's behavior. Chairman of the conference was Fritz Redl, of the Child Research Branch of the National Institute of Mental Health.[44] He attempted to guide the conference through a "mental hygiene assessment" of game ingredients. The record of the conference discussion represents a philosophical weighing of game structures by a most competent interdisciplinary group of scientists; it should be read by all who deal with games as a means of helping the individual and should be a basis of very careful selection of play activity. This is indicative of one kind of research which we could promote within our own profession and in collaboration with the psychiatrist and psychologist.

BETTER RELAXATION IS PROMOTED

Relaxation is here referred to as the capacity to release muscular tension from whatever cause derived and the capacity to adjust effort in amount and sequence for a smooth, efficient functioning of *all* aspects of motor response.

Hypertension and relaxation have been among the harder aspects of human behavior to study. One of the earliest comprehensive statements is that of Rathbone,[42] who also has a more recent volume.[43] These verify the possibility of modifying degrees of hypertensions and are in agreement with medical clinicians, such as Jacobsen[20] and Zeiter and Lufkin.[67] All agree that education has a responsibility in this aspect of health learnings.

Probably the greatest contribution of Bullen[10] is to emphasize the individual variations in response to stress and tension producing environments.

The effect of exercise directly on relaxation is open to some doubt, probably because it varies with types of exercise and conditions under which the exercising is done. Mitchem and Tuttle[35] found magnitude of hand tremor (indicating stress) to vary directly with intensity of arm exercise, leg exercise, and general fatigue from work on the ergometer. Slater-Hammel[55] failed to find the same results with respect to leg exercises. Scott and Matthews[49] also failed to find this relationship in strenuous exercise of various types, and unpublished research by this author failed to find this relationship. It appears probable that other stress factors are more important in exercise well below all-out effort.

It would appear more probable that exercise tends to relieve these other forms of stress. This would support a popular assertion of the health and physical educator. This seems to be supported by Michael,[34] who theorizes on the basis of his findings that regular daily exercise improves the organism's ability to withstand emotional stress through hormonal effects on the nervous system.

The value of a tension-releasing medium could not be denied in the present state of society and world affairs. However, the objective evidence is far from complete. This is an area in which those in health, physical education, and recreation could join efforts with the physiologist and psychologist.

It also appears likely that variations in the activity and its outcome affect the degree of tension or relief therefrom. That is certainly indicated in Bullen's[10] investigation of work by adults. Likewise, Baldwin and Lewin,[4] working with children in "success and failure" situations found emotional states resulting from exposure of ability. They also interpreted their results and others as indicating that test failure tends to produce increase in speed and decrease of accuracy in repetitive motor tasks.

RELIEF PROVIDED ON PSYCHOSOMATIC PROBLEMS

It has been medically demonstrated that certain physical states are at times at least partially of psychogenic origin. These states vary from hysterical paralysis to chronic fatigue, psychological limits of work output, discomfort from bodily function, and the like. We are therefore dealing with a condition not unrelated to the one discussed above, hypertension versus relaxation.

The health, physical education, and recreation claims in this area are concerned more with chronic fatigue, fatigue postures, dysmenorrhea, phobias, and the like than with the clinical cases more often seen by the physician and psychiatrist. While the statements are common that exercise and recreation are diverting, are a means of releasing tension, and are a means of improving one's sense of well-being, there is little on specific conditions.

Posture therapy and prevention are substantiated more on the basis of physiological and mechanical improvements. Nothing is presented in evidence on the psychological ramifications of postural deviations.

There is probably more objective evidence on effects of exercise on dysmenorrhea than on any of the other aspects. Lundquist[27] found regular exercise over a period of several weeks relieved dysmenorrhea in its various symptoms, except for the women known to have structural defects. Cessation of exercise tended to revive the dysmenorrhea. Hubbell[16] went further in study of exercise effects by introducing a placebo exercise series. This group on nonspecific exercises had as much relief as the other two groups, leading her to hypothesize that there might be a psychic factor in the relief oriented presentation of the series. Billig[7] and Dick and others[12] give too little actual data on which to evaluate conclusions, but the high incidence of favorable modification of work habits would lead one to hypothesize in line with Hubbell.

SKILLS ARE ACQUIRED

The problem of skill learning and how it occurs . . . is beyond the scope of this chapter but is mentioned here because it is believed important that we recognize the psychological implications of the learning process and not just the recognition of learning or its absence.

Physical education has suffered from the old adage "practice makes perfect." It has led to wasted time under the supposed tutelage of the educator and to frustration in those practicing both with and without the educator's supervision. We would do well to remember the importance of our instruction as cited by Menninger: "For maximum satisfaction one requires not only encouragement but almost always some instruction." This was a statement made to recreation leaders and should point to opportunities for instruction in recreation programs, not just a permissive program of participation and play. It would seem to be imperative to learn more about *how* learning takes place and all the conditions which affect learning.

SUMMARY

There is perhaps no area of our professional background that offers more challenge to us than psychological development. The challenge is multiple. We need a better background in general psychology, personality development, social psychology, and cultural anthropology. We need to develop research competencies in these areas and to pursue our understandings of prophylactic and therapeutic contributions of experiences in motor skills. As teachers and administrators, we must be ready to modify our practice in line with new evidence.

The 1954 yearbook of the American Association for Health, Physical Education, and Recreation, *Children in Focus,* has a concluding chapter by Dorothy LaSalle, entitled "Looking Ahead." Her words would seem to set the challenge for consideration not only of psychological development but of all areas represented in this 75th anniversary supplement.

To look ahead with any degree of hope implies that we know where we want to go and where we now are. The profession of physical education is in substantial agreement regarding where it wants physical education to go. . . . Where are we now in relation to these goals? Are we realizing them for the boys and girls of the nation? Indications in many instances are that we are not. . . . The problems in school health today are essentially the same as they were a generation ago. . . . Do these things happen because we do not yet believe that education for leisure is important? Do they happen because the school is not yet assuming responsibility for improving cooperation between agencies which promote recreation?

What then is the task? The job is difficult and has many facets: to study, to conduct research, to glean the facts from other disciplines which bear on health education, on physical education, and on recreation; to improve the education of teachers, to work unceasingly for improved facilities, instructional aids, and time allotment; to integrate our work in schools with community resources; to become expert in sound argumentation. These are the tasks for the next decade (26:276).

REFERENCES

1. Adams, L. Carroll. "Active Recreational Interests of Columbia College Alumni." *Research Quarterly* 19:43-47; March, 1948.
2. Annett, Thomas. "Study of Rhythmical Capacity and Performance in Motor Rhythm in Physical Education Majors." *Research Quarterly* 3:183-91; May, 1932.
3. American Association for Health, Physical Education, and Recreation. *Developing Democratic Human Relations.* Washington, D. C.: American Association for Health, Physical Education, and Recreation, 1951.
4. Baldwin, Alfred L., and Lewin, Harry. "Effects of Public and Private Success and Failure in Children's Repetitive Motor Behavior." *Child Development* 29:363-72; 1958.
5. Bentson, T. B., and Summerskill, John. "Relation of Personal Success in Intercollegiate Athletics to Certain Aspects of Personal Adjustment." *Research Quarterly* 26:8-14; March, 1955.
6. Biddulph, Lowell G. "Athletic Achievement vs. the Personal and Social Adjustment of High School Boys." *Research Quarterly* 25:1-7; March, 1954.
7. Billig, H. E., Jr. "Dysmenorrhea: The Result of a Postural Defect." *Archives of Surgery* 46:611-13; May, 1943.
8. Bowman, Mary O. *The Relationship Between Students and Parent Attitudes and Skills of Fifth Grade Children.* Doctoral dissertation. Iowa City: State University of Iowa, 1958.
9. Breck, Sabina June. "Measurement of Status in Physical Education Classes." *Research Quarterly* 21:75-82; May, 1950.
10. Bullen, Adelaide K. *New Answers to the Fatigue Problem.* Gainesville: University of Florida Press, 1956.
11. Cowell, Charles, Daniels, Arthur S., and Kenney, Harold E. "Purposes in Physical Education as Evaluated by Participants, Physical Education Supervisors and Educational Administrators." *Research Quarterly* 22:286-97; October, 1951.
12. Dick, A. C., Billig, Jr., H. E., and Macy (Mrs.), H. N. "Menstrual Exercises, Absenteeism Decrease and Work Efficiency Increase." *Industrial Medicine* 12:588-90; September, 1943.
13. Fulton, Ruth E., and Prauge, Elizabeth M. "Motor Learning of Highly Chosen and Unchosen Teammates." *Research Quarterly* 21:126-31; May, 1960.
14. Hale, Creighton J. "What Research Says About Athletics for Pre-High School Age Children." *Journal of Health, Physical Education, Recreation* 30:19; December, 1959.

15. Honzik, C. H. "Role of Kinesthetics in Maze Learning." *Science* 84:373; October, 1936.
16. Hubbell, Josephine W. "Specific and Non-specific Exercises for Relief of Dysmenorrhea." *Research Quarterly* 20:378-86; December, 1949.
17. Huisinga, Johan. *Homo Ludens, A Study of the Play Element in Culture.* Boston: The Beacon Press, 1950.
18. Husman, Burris T. "Aggression in Boxers and Wrestlers as Measured by Projective Techniques." *Research Quarterly* 26:421-25; December, 1955.
19. Jackson, Lydia, and Todd, Kathleen M. *Child Treatment and the Therapy of Play.* Second edition. New York, N. Y.: The Ronald Press, 1950.
20. Jacobsen, Edmund. *Progressive Relaxation.* Chicago: University of Chicago Press, 1948.
21. Jennings, Helen, *Leadership and Isolation.* New York: N. Y.: Longmans, Green and Company, Inc., 1943.
22. Johnson, Warren R., and Hutton, Daniel C. "Effects of a Combative Sport Upon Personality Dynamics as Measured by a Projective Test." *Research Quarterly* 26:49-53; March, 1955.
23. Keller, Louis F. "Relation of 'Quickness of Bodily Movement' to Success in Athletics." *Research Quarterly* 13:146-55; May, 1942.
24. Kent, F. S., and Prentice, H. A. "A Comparison of Two Methods of Teaching Hygiene to College Freshmen." *Research Quarterly* 10:133-36; May, 1939.
25. Lafuze, Marion. "Learning of Fundamental Skills by Women of Low Motor Ability." *Research Quarterly* 22:149-57; 1951.
26. LaSalle, Dorothy. "Looking Ahead." *Children in Focus*, Yearbook, Washington, D. C.: American Association for Health, Physical Education, and Recreation, 1954.
27. Lundquist, Cordelia. "Use of the Billig Exercise for Dysmenorrhea for College Women." *Research Quarterly* 18:44-53; March, 1947.
28. McAfee, Robert A. "Sportsmanship Attitudes of Sixth, Seventh and Eighth Grade Boys." *Research Quarterly* 26:120; March, 1955.
29. McCraw, L. W., and Tolbert, J. W.: "Sociometric Status and Athletic Ability of Junior High School Boys." *Research Quarterly* 24:72-80; March, 1953.
30. McCue, Betty F.: "Constructing an Instrument for Evaluating Attitudes Toward Intensive Competition in Team Games." *Research Quarterly* 24:205-209; May, 1953.
31. McGee, Rosemary. "Comparison of Attitudes Toward Intensive Competition for High School Girls." *Research Quarterly* 27:60-73; March, 1956.
32. Mareno, Jacob L. *Who Shall Survive?* Washington, D. C.: Nervous and Mental Disease Co., 1934.
33. Menninger, William C. "Recreation and Mental Health." *Recreation* 42:340-46; November, 1948.
34. Michael, Ernest D., Jr. "Stress Adaptation Through Exercise." *Research Quarterly* 28:50-54; March, 1957.
35. Mitchem, John C., and Tuttle, W. W. "Influence of Exercises, Emotional Stress and Age on Static Neuromuscular Tremor Magnitude." *Research Quarterly* 25:65-74; March, 1954.
36. Mumby, H. Hugh. "Kinesthetic Acuity and Balance Related to Wrestling Ability." *Research Quarterly* 24:327-34; October, 1953.
37. Olsen, Einar A. "Relationship Between Psychological Capacities and Success in College Athletics." *Research Quarterly* 27:79-89; March, 1956.
38. Page, Barbara. "The Philosophy of the Dance." *Research Quarterly* 4:5-49; May, 1933.
39. Phillips, Bernath E. "The Relationship Between Certain Phases of Kinesthesis and Performance during the Early Stages of Acquiring Two Perceptive Motor Skills." *Research Quarterly* 11:571-86; October, 1941.
40. Pierson, William R. "Comparison of Fencers and Non-Fencers by Psychomotor, Space Perception and Anthropometric Measures." *Research Quarterly* 27:90-96; March, 1956.
41. Plummer, Tomi C. *Factors Influencing the Attitudes and Interests of College Women in Physical Education.* Doctoral dissertation. Iowa City: State University of Iowa, 1952. Microcard PE 128.
42. Rathbone, Josephine L. *Residual Neuro-muscular Hypertension: Implications for Education.* New York, 1936.
43. Rathbone, Josephine L. *Teach Yourself to Relax.* Englewood Cliffs, New Jersey: Prentice-Hall, 1957.
44. Redl, Fritz. *The Impact of Game—Ingredients on Children's Play Behavior.* Fourth Conference on Group Processes, October, 1957. New York, N. Y.: Josiah Macy, Jr., Foundation, 1959.
45. Roloff, Louise L. "Kinesthesis in Relation to the Learning of Selected Motor Skills." *Research Quarterly* 24:210-17; May, 1953. Microcard PE 148.
46. Russell, Ruth I. *A Factor Analysis of the Components of Kinesthesis.* Doctoral dissertation. Iowa City: State University of Iowa, 1954. Microcard PH 36.
47. Schaffner, Bertram, editor. *Group Processes.* Transactions of the Fourth Conference. New York, N. Y.: Josiah Macy, Jr., Foundation, 1959.
48. Scott, M. Gladys, "Measurement of Kinesthesis." *Research Quarterly* 26:324-41; October, 1955.
49. Scott, M. Gladys, and Matthews, Helen. "A Study of Fatigue Effects Induced by an Efficiency Test for College Women." *Research Quarterly* 20:134-41; May, 1949.
50. Scott, Phebe M. "Comparative Study of Attitudes Toward Athletic Competition in the Elementary Schools." *Research Quarterly* 24:352-61; October, 1953.
51. Seymour, Emery W. "Comparative Study of Certain Behavior Characteristics of Participant

and Non-Participant Boys in Little League Baseball." *Research Quarterly* 27:338-46; October, 1956.

52. Skubic, Elvera. "A Study in Acquaintanceship and Social Status in Physical Education Classes." *Research Quarterly* 20:80-87; March, 1949.

53. Skubic, Elvera. "Emotional Responses of Boys to Little League and Middle League Competitive Baseball." *Research Quarterly* 26:342-52; October, 1955.

54. Skubic, Elvera. "Studies in Little League and and Middle League Baseball." *Research Quarterly* 27:97-110; March, 1956.

55. Slater-Hammel, A. T. "Influence of Order of Exercise Bouts Upon Neuromuscular Tremor." *Research Quarterly* 26:88-95; March, 1955.

56. Slater-Hammel, A. T. "Performance of Selected Groups of Male College Students on the Reynolds' Balance Test." *Research Quarterly* 27:347-51; October, 1956.

57. Smith, Carnie H. "Influence of Athletic Success and Failure on the Level of Aspiration." *Research Quarterly* 20:196-208; May, 1949.

58. Southward, Warren H., Latimer, Jean V., and Turner, Clair E. "Health Practices, Knowledge, Attitudes, and Interests of Senior High School Pupils." *Research Quarterly* 15:118-36; May, 1949.

59. Todd, Frances. "Democratic Methodology in Physical Education." *Research Quarterly* 23:106-10; March, 1952.

60. Toogood, Ruth. "A Survey of Recreational Interests and Pursuits of College Women." *Research Quarterly* 10:90-100; October, 1939.

61. Ulrich, Celeste, "Measurement of Stress Evidenced by College Situations Involving Competition." *Research Quarterly* 28:160-72; May, 1957.

62. Walters, C. Etta. "A Sociemetric Study of Motivated and Non-motivated Bowling Groups." *Research Quarterly* 26:107-12; March, 1955.

63. Wear, Carl. "Construction of Equivalent Forms of an Attitude Scale." *Research Quarterly* 26:113-19; March, 1955. Microcard PE 59.

64. Witte, Fae. *A Factorial Analysis of Measures of Kinesthesis.* Doctoral Dissertation. Bloomington: Indiana University, 1953. Microcard PH 20.

65. Wylie, James A. "A Survey of 504 Families to Determine the Relationships between Certain Factors and the Nature of the Family Recreation Program." *Research Quarterly* 24:229-43; May, 1953.

66. Yukie, Eleanor C. "Group Movement and Growth in a Physical Education Class." *Research Quarterly* 26:222-33; May, 1955.

67. Zeiter, Walter J., and Lukfkin, Bernardine. "Progressive Relaxation in Physical Therapy." *Archives of Physical Therapy* 24:211-14; April, 1943.

45. Somatopsychic education—a rationale for physical education*

Dorothy V. Harris

Postdoctoral Research Fellow, Laboratory for Human Performance Research,
The Pennsylvania State University

Mankind has been cognizant of the manifold interactions between somatic and psychic responses for centuries. A vast amount of research has been done to investigate bodily (somatic) changes that are produced by (mental) (psychic) attitude but almost no systematic research has been done conversely.

Plato and Aristotle gave it a philosophical form—Plato's dictum is unequivocal: "Any defect of psyche or soma is the occasion of the greatest discord and disproportion in the other." P. J. G. Cabania wrote in 1806: "The disordered or regular emotions of the body have the same origin as the diseases or health of the body."

It is interesting to note that the two terms (psychosomatic and somatopsychic) which are used to designate response patterns between the soma and the psyche were the outcome of a bitter argument between those who insisted on the prepotency of psychological factors in mental disorder and those who stressed the somatic pathology. These words connoted extreme views of the causes of disorders and served to hide the complexity of the relationship.

Contrary to a dichotomous point of view, the individual is conceived as a complex dynamic system in an unstable state of equilibrium, acting and reacting to changes in the environment and to changes within the system. In disorder, that is, disturbance of homeostasis, many aspects of the system are affected.

It is rather astounding to hear physicians state that over 80% of all out-patients being treated have an illness traced back to some psychic origin. Because of this, much attention has been given to the so-called psychosomatic illnesses. Evidence collected in the last decade has linked hypertension, ulcers, allergies, skin disorders, asthma, digestive disorders, coronary heart disease, and many other ailments to some influence of the mind over the body.

The separation of mind and body no longer exists for most individuals. As evidenced by the knowledge of psychosomatic illnesses, one has to reckon with the great influence the mind has over the body. Perhaps this could better be expressed in another manner by saying as Plato said, the mind-body relationship is so integrated that one affects the other continuously. One has only to witness a demonstration of hypnosis to appreciate the amazing relationship. What makes an individual shiver with teeth chattering while placed in a hypnotic trance in a room of 80 degrees, at the mere suggestion of the person who placed him in the trance? This can be frightening and/or reassuring, depending on how one looks at it. Perhaps we are more the masters of our souls and the captains of our fate than we dare realize or even want to realize.

Almost any bookstore will offer a selection of books concerned with a discussion of mind over matter: "the power of positive thinking," "lose weight through hypnosis,"

*From Forecast for the Future, Proceedings of the Fall Conference, Oct. 1967, p. 64, Eastern Association for Physical Education of College Women. Used by permission.

"the road to happiness," etc. with elaborate formulas for the basic underlying theme of influence of the psyche over the soma.

Research is piling up daily to support the concept of a coronary prone personality. The very outlook on life of the time pressured, hard driving perfectionist drives him to his early grave.

We have real evidence of the effects of mental illness and the resulting physical incapacitations of those individuals with mental and emotional breakdowns. We know what the emotions of fear, hate, love, etc. can do to the physiological functions of the body, and we have an understanding of how mental stress can produce muscular tension, stage fright, loss of words and inability to move. All of these reflect how the mental processes can alter or block muscular performance.

It could be asserted that psychic stressors, when adequately determined, could be dealt with by the psychiatrist with methods already in use. It could also be argued that some of the benefits derived from modern medical psychiatry might fall under the education umbrella. Guidance counselors, teachers, coaches, clergy, and friends often attempt to assist individuals toward adequate psycho-social adjustments.

Upon observation it appears that problems are evidenced whenever an imbalance occurs in the unstable state of equilibrium. One might view it as a breakdown of the integrity of mind-body relationship. When a psychosomatic illness erupts, the "mind-body homeostasis" or balance has been upset.

Support for structuring a somatopsychic concept can readily be found. There is no doubt of psychosomatic responses; why is it not plausible to consider somatopsychic responses? Such an approach may help to bridge the hiatus between physiological and psychological research and thinking.

It seems ironical that man first studied those things farthest away from him, namely the stars. Then he started studying the physical and chemical environment, and finally, in the last century or so, man has begun to study himself. In the investigation of man we have tended to look at those who were ill or were atypical in some way. Rarely have we looked at the good solid healthy person and asked him how he managed to stay that way. Consequently we know more about dis-

integration than integration of the human being.

Just what the role of physical activity is in maintaining this integration is not entirely clear. We have some understanding of the physiological benefits of activity but we have yet to clarify the psychological and sociological benefits. In addition, we do not have research to support all the idealistic outcomes we claim for our programs. If we approach our investigation of this area in much the same way one approaches any problem and go from the known to the unknown, we might get some sound direction from observation and research in fields other than our own. As an example: If we are talking about somatopsychic responses and if we feel that physical activity could well be included in that category but we need some real evidence before we can say this is the case, then where do we start? I suggest that first we start looking for other somatopsychic responses and see what we can learn from them.

Let's start with something with which we are all familiar: FATIGUE. Extreme bodily fatigue or exhaustion serves as a good example of the degree of influence the soma can have on the psyche. If you have allowed yourself this experience then you know of what I am speaking. Mental and emotional responses are altered considerably with fatigue.

Research on sleep deprivation has provided much evidence of the breakdown of behavior. Dr. Louis West of the University of Oklahoma Medical School says that any normal personality will begin to disintegrate after approximately 100 hours without sleep. Hallucinations are quite prominent, to the extent that sleep deprivation could well serve as a substitute for an LSD trip—without the side effects as a good night's sleep will return one to normal. U. S. prisoners of the Korean war confessed to participating in gas and germ warfare to the amazement of those who knew otherwise. When the facts were assembled it was discovered that brainwashing had been accomplished through fatigue and sleep deprivation.

Absence of stress or stimuli to the somatic can disturb the homeostatic state in a relatively short while. Without the input of stimuli to the brain the mind begins to hallucinate. When stable individuals are placed in a dark, sound-proof room they begin to have hallucinations in a matter of hours. This also occurs when they are immobile and protected from all tactile stimulation.

How much do we know about the kinesthetic satisfaction of physical activity? If I should ask any one of you why you exercise and participate in sports you would, in all probability say, "Because I enjoy it." And, if I were to ask you why you enjoy it you probably could not give me a definite answer. It is a sad day in Mudville when we cannot explain why we practice those things we preach! Just what is the real meaning of "It feels good!" or "I like the feel of the wind in my face," "I enjoy it," "I just like to run," etc? In 1931 Buehler wrote that we find what is called the "Pleasure function" in psychology. We might express it as "Doing something just for the pure joy of doing it." Kreitler states that children enjoy movement as such and move for the sake of moving; when they discover a new movement they repeat it until it loses its fascination. He describes this as a satiation of kinesthetic stimuli and that this becomes progressive. In other words, variations of stimuli, such as sports and dance may provide, are necessary to keep a kinesthetic awareness. If satiation does occur, then doing things for the fun of it decreases steadily until movement becomes inhibited—to the point that elderly people are reluctant to move. Kreitler, in his work with the aged, indicates that this reduction in movement, apart from leading to the known effect of muscular degeneration, also has many psychological results. One of the most interesting of these is the distortion in body image. His studies published in 1967 indicated that people who seldom engage in movement tend to have a more distorted body image than people who move considerably more. This means that people who are over 50 years of age and who, by force of age tend to move less, also perceive their bodies to be broader and heavier than they really are. Because of this distortion their experience in bodily activities becomes increasingly more strenuous. This establishes a vicious circle between movement and body image: less body movement, more distortion in body image; this may account for the greater clumsiness and increased fear of physical activity characteristic of the aging. This very

system of feedback may also operate in younger people who have had little experience in activity. Perhaps those individuals who grow up without variation in kinesthetic stimuli develop a distortion of body image at a very young age, therefore, they avoid physical activity because it appears too strenuous for them. We need more research in this area before we can make any guesses as to causal relationships.

Konrad Lorenz, in his book *On Aggression,* states that the main function of sport today lies in the cathartic discharge of aggressive urges in addition to keeping people healthy. He continues by identifying the value of sport as being greater than a simple outlet of aggression in its coarser and individualistic behavior patterns such as boxing with a punch-ball. He believes that sport educates man to a conscious and responsible control of his own fighting behavior due to the framework of the rules of sport where lapses of self-control are penalized. Lorenz claims that the most valuable outcome is the educational value of the restrictions imposed by the demands for fairness which must be respected even in the face of strongest aggression stimuli. He suggests further that some of the more difficult and dangerous forms of sports, especially those demanding team cooperation and effort such as mountain conquest, polar expeditions, and exploration of space allow nations to fight one another in hard dangerous competition without involving national or political hatred. Lorenz feels that the space race has helped to preserve peace and that of all the people on the two sides of the iron curtain, the space pilots are the least likely to hate one another.

Bertrand Russell stated that the savage in each of us must find some outlet not incompatible with civilized life and with the happiness of his equally savage neighbor. He suggested that sport might provide such outlets. Russell said one of the things wrong with our civilization was that such forms of competition played too small a part in the lives of ordinary men and women. Men must compete for superiority and it is best that they do so in contests which yield utterly useless results. This is not to say that the results do not matter, they matter supremely, and if they do not, they will not satisfy man or nation. In sport, victory is never for all time, nor is defeat irreparable. The individual, the team, the nation, all live to fight another day.

Kreitler, when discussing aggression, pointed out that young people have more opportunity to release accumulated energy, thus releasing aggressions. Because they are not as inhibited, they move a lot more and movement is a natural and most adequate way to consume unused aggressive energies. Thus, philosophers and scientists discuss the real possibility of bodily activity and physical competition in sports and games serving to release aggressions that may build to warfaring states.

Minc, a physician, has expressed the somatopsychic response pattern in yet another way. He feels that physical activity serves as a "safety valve." He divides experiences into two broad categories: "emotion without motion" and "motion without emotion." Either of these can be deleterious. The physiological systems of the body are geared to the "fight or flight" response pattern so well defined by Cannon. Minc uses this description of "emotion without motion" to explain responses like the "Wall Street Stomach." He feels that physical activity should serve as a counteraction to stress, in other words, one should have "motion with emotion." This could well be one of the reasons why the conductors were less prone than the drivers in the research Morris reported from England. The fact that the conductors moved between the two levels of the English buses making sure he collected fares from all passengers provided "motion" with his "emotion" or anxiety concerning the collection of fares. Meanwhile, the drivers had "emotion" or anxiety about traffic, etc. but no "motion" to counteract the stress. Minc also feels that "motion without emotion" is harmful in that you do not have the body functioning as an integrated being, thus you do not get full benefit of the motion. Explained in another way, "going through the motions is not enough."

Selye, a pioneer in stress research believes that physical activity can serve as real stress therapy; it can snap the integrated being out of that stereotyped, self-perpetuating response pattern which contributes heavily to the development of physical and mental illness. Selye feels that activities with intermediate goals serve a real purpose. One might say that a little success goes a long way; satisfaction of short term aims may "carry" an individual to bigger and better things. Acquiring confidence may develop a more secure self-concept and body-image.

Speaking of self-concept, this whole area of self-concept and body-image needs further exploration. We have already discussed research done with the aged and the effect of physical activity on body-image and self-concept. Jean Mayer reports that obese girls have a concept of self which follows the pattern of all groups discriminated against. They hate themselves and they hate the way they look. Dr. Myer Mendelson of the University of Pennsylvania quotes an obese young man as saying: "Just looking at myself in a store window makes me feel terrible. It's the feeling that people have a right to hate anyone who looks as bad as me. As soon as I see myself I feel an uncontrollable burst of hatred. I just look at myself and say, 'I hate you. You are loathsome.'"

In sharp contrast to this view is a remark by a fat man who noticed how fat he had become over the winter and said: "It made me feel it was time to get some of this weight off."

The difference between these two men was: one was obese since childhood and the second had become fat as an adult. It seems evident that, since adolescence is a time of extreme sensitivity, to be obese during these years and to be exposed to the contempt of adults and contemporaries alike causes permanent psychological scars. Physical activity should help to prevent this situation.

Mayer says when you see an obese girl observing other girls at play and you ask her why she is not playing she will say "They don't want me to play." When you see a normal or lean girl observing and ask her the same question she says "I don't want to play." We know that girls of extreme body types shy away from swimming and dance classes when a uniform is required. We also know that obese adolescent girls move significantly less than normal girls but we do not know which comes first, the chicken or the egg; that is, do girls become obese because they are less active or do they move less because they are obese? We know too, from observation, that when one is proud of the image he presents physically he acts in an entirely different manner from one who is disgusted and self-conscious with his image. When you read the reports from psychiatrists describing the self-concept and body-image and some of the concerns of criminals you have to stop and wonder if there is perhaps some way to direct a more desirable image. Perhaps physical activity can serve that need. We need longitudinal studies to assist us in our direction. It may be plausible to think of prescribing specific activities for certain individuals in much the same way a physical therapist selects activities for specific muscles.

At Penn State our Human Performance Lab is currently involved with a study investigating the effects of exercise on risk factors in coronary heart disease. We have one group of middle-aged men who have been exercising three times per week for about five months and we have just completed a testing session with them. Without exception they look better, they feel better, and they are doing things they never dreamed of doing six months ago. The plea from them now is to do something for their wives so they can keep up with them. These men have difficulty in describing what they think is happening to them. We may find that exercise does alter risk factors to a degree in coronary heart disease but if these men have a better self-concept, a better body-image, and a better outlook on life then perhaps physical activity is preventing heart disease in an entirely different manner. It may be that the physiological measures will not show the subtle changes that occur with a new lease on life because of physical activity. Exercise may not change risk factors once they are evidenced but it may prevent the triggering" action of coronary heart disease.

Jacobson, in *You Must Relax* suggests that individuals can be trained to relax neuromuscularly to the point that worry and other emotional over-activity disappears. When trained in this method of relaxation one can stop thought processes. So, if your thoughts keep you awake at night, learn to relax neuromuscularly and you can drop right off to sleep. This is explained by the fact that it takes words to express thought and it takes muscles to express words so if one learns to relax the muscles required in speaking then the thought process chain is broken. Since Jacobson's training in relaxation is neuromuscular, his approach is to train the large body muscles to become sensitive to tension, thus this tension can be controlled. It may or may not be significant, but he has discovered that people who do manual labor are the easiest to train and athletes are the next easiest to train. Jacobson is a firm believer of the fact that if one learns to relax he will never have a nervous breakdown.

Lately the research of Kephart and Delacato has been discussed, especially among parents of slow learners and retarded children. Taking youngsters back to the creeping-crawling stage and using these physical movements to activate neural responses which stimulate the brain and develop greater cortical capacities seems plausible. Whether physical activity enhances cognitive learning or not needs to be investigated further before definite statements can be made.

A recent book, *Man, Sport and Existence,* presents an excellent discussion of the role of sport in man's existence. Slusher discusses at length the purpose of sport and suggests that sport situations may provide the atmosphere, within limited boundaries for the attainment of self-realization. Man needs an outlet that is ego-gratifying, an experience that brings to man a sense of that which he is! Frequently sport provides for self-actualization through self-extension; it encourages man to test untried abilities. Each day he needs to prove again that he is capable, not with words but with action. To participate one accepts and is continuously challenged by the situation of uncertainty he faces over and over. When discussing this with a fellow skier the other day we decided that skiing did just that; one is on the brink of catastrophe all the time. This may well be one of the fascinations that skiing holds.

A recent report from the U. S. Naval Hospital at Bethesda, Maryland stated that 27 U. S. Naval officers experienced mental breakdowns while in battle areas. Upon investigation, it was discovered that 25 of these men had never participated in competitive athletics. They had elected to do their extracurricular activities in other areas. Is this significant? Or, is this just a coincidence?

It appears at this point that we need to identify, define, and classify concepts and constructs which may be fundamental to the social science of sport. Any conceptual frame of reference for a given physical activity is undoubtedly going to be a complex one since physical activity is so complex.

"Physical education is for the sake of mental and moral culture and not an end in itself" is quoted from G. Stanley Hall. "When we play ball we have no ill-will" is an old Indian chant that may hold meaning for us or our own oft quoted "It's not whether you win or lose but how you play the game." . . . All of these are variations on the theme to which patrons of exercise have been alluding for centuries. Thinking along these lines has given rise to such familiar concepts as "character development," "structure of a value system," proper attitude," "moral behavior," "emotional development," and other expressions which are commonly used in arguing for the rationale of physical activity being something greater than the acquisition of strength, fitness, endurance, or motor skills. Judging by statements made in professional literature one would assume there exists carefully structured, philosophically sound, and empirically supported research concerning the degree to which engaging in physical activity contributes to the development of various nonphysical qualities. Writers continue to make such statements without real support.

Over the years numerous authors: Hetherington, McCloy, Nash, Oberteuffer and Ulrich, etc. have alleged that participation in "properly conducted" physical activities provides one of the best means of social development. Clarke, in his recent book, *Muscular Strength and Endurance in Man,* 1966, states "a number of researchers support the contention that physical vigor is related to mental accomplishments, especially as affecting mental alertness. Thus, it may be contended that a person's general learning potential for a given level of intelligence is increased or decreased in accordance with his physical vitality." The nature and functioning of the nervous system and empirical evidence causes one to seriously question this statement of Clarke's. If such a relationship does exist, is it spurious or is there a causal relationship and if there is, what is it? A number of studies will have to be carried out to settle this question.

In the same book Clarke quotes H. E. Jones as saying ". . . boys high in strength tend to be well-adjusted socially and psychologically; boys low in strength show tendencies toward social difficulties, feelings of inferiority and other 'personal maladjustments.' " The question arises as to how much credence can be given to such a statement and the studies on which it is based. To what extent are the mores of society determinants of such a relationship?

What is the basic purpose of physical education? Where is the emphasis to be? Body mechanics? Physical fitness? Sports fundamentals? Movement exploration? If the truth be known, our choice will be predicated on our own beliefs and to some extent on our abilities rather than on facts. Research has not provided us with information that any one of the preceding is *the answer.* Just what is the rationale for physical education?

When human movement performance is studied, integrated, and applied in terms of movement activity of the body or a body part it becomes uniquely the province of physical education. Our concern is whether physical education is taking its proper place and making its potential contribution. When one considers the wide range in which the field can rise to this contribution and the many roads research can take the thought becomes awesome.

The possibilities remind me of the man in C. E. N. Joad's *Gertrude Governess* who, when moved to action, jumped off the porch, leaped on his horse and rode off in just any old direction. Our main consideration should be to plan and to coordinate the directions, not to go at random. A better approach is suggested by Socrates' "Know thyself." Considering the heritage of physical education and that which is its desirable future, we have no choice but to find the answers. A discipline is concerned with *what is* . . . and a profession with what ought to be. It appears that we have not been functioning as a discipline should. Human movement is complex . . . the knowledge of why people move, of what occurs within one psychologically when one moves, and what happens when one fails to move; why does one compete, why does one enjoy activity, in short, why do people play? All of these questions fall in the realm of the unknown. Just why do people engage in exercise and sport? Does participation in physical activity enhance our living effectiveness?

Can we support statements that our perceptions, our emotions, our attitudes, and our ethical conduct are changed for the better with participation in physical activity? Does our work capacity increase? What about our mental efficiency, our social effectiveness? What evidence do we have to support these desirable outcomes? Perhaps we need to find better ways of evaluating our programs; fitness batteries and performance on skills tests may not be telling the true story. Maybe we should evaluate the self-concept of our students instead of their motor ability and fitness levels. Classification according to the self-concept may produce more desirable outcomes than other means of classification.

Health and physical educators are failing to assume the responsibility they should in educating to maintain a homeostatic state of mind-body. Perhaps the real rationale of physical education should be somatopsychic education . . . to educate for an integrated mind-body relationship and all the implications therein.

Physical education is one of the human performance disciplines, possibly even a social science. The effects of stress, the image of self, the human requirement of movement, the influence of bodily movement upon developmental processes of personality, plus numerous other expanding concepts and areas of knowledge that are now with us are important aspects to consider as components of our discipline. Further research requires use of these in the pursuit of knowledge of physical education.

We at the college level will probably not only have to give the leadership but much of the work toward research in these areas. At the same time we need to pick the brains of those in other disciplines and invite them to join with us in our quest for knowledge. We have to take the initiative . . . no one has a more vested interest than we. We cannot afford to sit and wait for other disciplines to produce the answers. We need the instruments and the research designs now. Go seek help from your colleagues in other disciplines. Don't be surprised when you find they are very interested in these problems too!

When talking about doing research in such undefined areas with a psychology professor that I had at the University of Iowa, I asked him if trying to do research in this area wasn't somewhat like trying to catch a black cat in a dark room. You know the cat is there but you can't find him. His reply was, "But, if you have a dead fish in your hand, you are pretty sure of finding him." I for one, think we have the cat in that dark room. I am more sure than ever that we have the "fish" somewhere to tease him out. It will take time.

BIBLIOGRAPHY

Clarke, H. Harrison. *Muscular Strength and Endurance in Man.* Englewood Cliffs, N. J., Prentice-Hall, 1966.

Jacobson, Edmund. *You Must Relax.* New York: McGraw-Hill Book Company, Inc., 1957.

Kreitler, Hans and Shulamith, Krietler. "Movement and Aging—Psychologically Viewed." Speech presented at The International Symposium on Physical Activity and Aging. Tel Aviv, Oct. 1967.

Lorenz, Konrad. *On Aggression.* New York: Harcourt, Brace and World, 1966.

Mayer, Jean. "What Should be Done About Teenage Overweight—and What Shouldn't." *Ladies Home Journal.* January 1967.

McIntosh, Peter C. *Sport in Society.* London: C. A. Watts & Co., Ltd., 1963.

Mendelson, Meyer. "Psychological Aspects of Obesity." *The Medical Clinics of North America.* Philadelphia. W. B. Saunders Company, 1964.

Minc, Salek. "Emotions and Ischemic Heart Disease." *American Heart Journal.* Vol. 73, No. 5, May, 1967.

Psychosomatic Disorders. World Health Organization Technical Report Series, No. 275. Geneva: World Health Organization, 1965.

Selye, Hans. *The Stress of Life.* New York: McGraw-Hill Book Company, Inc., 1956.

Slusher, Howard. *Man, Sport and Existence.* Philadelphia: Lea & Febiger, 1967.

West, Louis, editor. *Hallucinations.* New York: Grune & Stratton, 1962.

46. Body concept as it relates to self-concept[*][1]

Leela C. Zion

Associate Professor of Health and Physical Education, Humboldt State College

ABSTRACT

The purpose of this study was to investigate some of the relationships between self-concept and body concept. Measurements of self-description, self-acceptance, ideal self, and self-description-ideal discrepancy were correlated with measurements of body description, body acceptance, ideal body, and body description-ideal discrepancy, using a sample of 200 college freshman women. The results of this study indicate that there is a significant linear relationship between self-description and body description, ideal self and ideal body, and self-description-ideal discrepancy and body description-ideal discrepancy. The relationship between self-acceptance and body acceptance was ambiguous.

Throughout history man has been intrigued with the possibility that the outward characteristics of the body might reveal somehow the inner structure or personality of man. It has been hypothesized by Jersild,[5, 6] Murphy,[8] and Diamond[3] that a person's attitudes concerning his conception of himself will influence and be influenced by his view of his physical appearance and physical abilities. The emphasis is on what a person thinks he is, regardless of what he is in reality.

In physical education it is particularly important to know how the body influences other aspects of a student's life, as well as what we are doing to the body concepts of our students.

REVIEW OF THE LITERATURE

A review of the literature reveals that although there has been considerable research bearing on the relationships of body structure, physiological functioning, body distortions, and body malfunctions with personality variables, there has been a limited amount of research dealing with the concept one has of one's body in relation to the concept one has of one's self. There has been considerable research dealing with "body image" that is usually defined as the subjective experiences and organization of experiences of the individual with his body, which are below the threshold of awareness and hence not useful in a study of one's conscious perceptions of one's body.

In an attempt to investigate the area of the degree of feeling of satisfaction with the parts or processes of the body, Secord and Jourard[10] developed a Body Cathexis Scale. The scale includes a number of body parts and functions, and subjects are asked to indicate their degree of satisfaction or dissatisfaction with them. In this study, the Body Cathexis Scale correlated significantly with a Self Cathexis Scale developed by the authors. Only Secord and Jourard have attempted to investigate the conscious body concept in relation to the conscious self-concept, although their study was limited.

PROCEDURES

Freshman women enrolled in Humboldt State College comprised the total group of 200 who were examined.

For the purposes of this study, self-concept was defined by the writer as all possible self-regarding attitudes, consisting of four primary facets: self-description, self-acceptance, ideal self, and self-description-ideal discrepancy. Body concept was defined as all possible body-regarding attitudes, consisting of four primary facets: body description, body acceptance, ideal body, and body description-ideal discrepancy.

The self-concept measure used for this study is the Index of Adjustment and Values, constructed by Robert E. Bills[1] and designed to measure self-description, self-acceptance, ideal self, and discrepancy between self-description and ideal self.

The facets of body concept were measured by a test developed by the writer for this study. This test consists of five different Guttman scales for each of the first three

*From Research Quarterly, Vol. 36, p. 490, Dec. 1965. Used by permission.

facets of body concept. Scores for the fourth facet (body description-ideal discrepancy) were determined by finding the difference between the first and third facets.

The body concept scale consists of 60 traits arranged alphabetically in a vertical column followed by three blank columns. The subjects are asked to use each of the words to complete the sentence, "I am a (an) _____ person," and to indicate on a five-point scale to what degree this statement is like them. This rating is placed in the blank opposite the word in Column I. The use of ratings is as follows: (a) not at all; (b) a little; (c) average; (d) moderately; (e) very much. Column I measures body description.

In Column II, the subjects are asked to indicate how they feel about themselves as described in Column I. The ratings are as follows: (a) I very much dislike being as I am in this respect; (b) I dislike being as I am in this respect; (c) I neither dislike being as I am nor like being as I am in this respect; (d) I like being as I am in this respect; (e) I very much like being as I am in this respect. Column II measures body acceptance.

In Column III, the subjects are asked to use each of the words to complete the sentence, "I would like to be a (an) _____ person," and to indicate to what degree they would like this trait to be characteristic of them. The same numerical ratings are used as in Column I. Column III measures ideal body. The difference between Column I and Column III is a measure of the discrepancy between body description and ideal body.

The scaling technique used is the Guttman Scale Program[7] resulting in a unidimensional rank order, a technique that measures one dimension of an attitude. According to Stouffer and Guttman,[11] when the items of a scale are arranged in the order of descending popularity and the respondents are ranked according to their replies, it is possible 90 percent of the time to tell by a person's rank score how he responded on each question. According to Schutz,[9] errors must be few enough to allow a coefficient of reproducibility of 86.5 or better to be obtained. The coefficient of reproducibility is found through the following formula:

$$CoR = 1 - \frac{\text{number of errors}}{\text{number of responses} \times \text{number of respond}}$$

In order to achieve unidimensionality, it was necessary to select body concept traits that fell into specific dimensions. They are are follows:

1. Attitudes as affected by the opposite sex, including physical qualities of attractiveness or the lack thereof to the opposite sex: attractive, beautiful, blemished, boyish, disfigured, feminine, graceful, homely, inconspicuous, masculine, plain, pretty, sexy, ugly, unattractive, well-proportioned.
2. Attitudes regarding movement, including physical qualities depicting the manner or style of body movement: agile, awkward, clumsy, coordinated, easily fatigued, energetic, free, graceful, healthy, inhibited, physically fit, relaxed, sickly, slow, tense, weak.
3. Attitudes regarding grooming, including physical characteristics indicative of the care one gives to appearance: attractive, blemished, clean, immaculate, neat, plain, poised, poorly dressed, sloppy, slumped, stylish, unattractive, untidy, well-dressed, well-groomed, well-proportioned.
4. Attitudes regarding expressiveness, including physical qualities indicative of the use of the body to convey feeling: aloof, awkward, confident, dependable, domineering, expressive, free, graceful, ill at ease, inhibited, poised, relaxed, severe, shy, tense, unpredictable.
5. Attitudes regarding masculinity-femininity, including physical qualities depicting womanliness and manliness: awkward, beautiful, boyish, broad-hipped, delicate, feminine, flatchested, frilly, graceful, horsey, masculine, motherly, muscular, petite, sloppy, tailored.

The replies of the respondents were combined into a cumulative distribution for each item, and cutting points were decided upon, creating a continuum along which items ran from high popularity to low popularity. Items producing excessive scale errors were eliminated, and scales were reduced to the nine items producing the highest coefficient of reproducibility (except for one scale, which was reduced to seven items). Each respondent was assigned a scale score ranging from 0 to 9.

The four basic criteria of this technique were met which relate to (a) the range of marginal distributions, (b) the pattern of errors, (c) the number of items, and (d) the number of response categories. The scales were developed on 150 of the subjects and were cross-validated with the remaining 50 subjects to ensure that the scales maintained the characteristics required for Guttman scaling.

According to Schutz,[9] the reliability has been determined by a coefficient of reproducibility of 86.5 or better for each scale, which is an approximate measure of internal consistency. According to Guttman,[11] the validity of this type of scale is basically content validity. If the items are unidimensionally scalable, they are seen as a sample of items from that dimension; hence content validity is a property of all legitimate scales.

The measure of association used for correlating the body concept scores and the Index of Adjustment and Values scores is the Gamma Program[2] developed for use with the 704 and 7090 computers. The gamma coefficient is practically equivalent to the Spearman Rho and the Pearson r.[4] Given 200 cases, the 0.5 level of significance allows correlations of .138 and above as significant. Correlations of .181 and above are significant at the .01 level.

RESULTS

All five body description scales show statistically significant degrees of correlation with the Index of Adjustment and Values, self-description scores, as is shown in Table 1. All have a coefficient significantly different from zero at less than the .01 level.

Only two of the five body acceptance scales show significant positive correlations with the Index of Adjustment and Values self-acceptance scores (Table 2). These two are the Grooming scale and the Expressiveness scale, which have a coefficient significantly different from zero at less than the .01 level. The Opposite Sex scale and the Masculinity-Femininity scale show negative, though not significant, coefficients. The Movement scale, however, shows a negative correlation significantly different from zero at less than the .01 level.

All five of the ideal body scales show a statistically significant degree of correlation with the Index of Adjustment and Values ideal self-scores, as is shown in Table 3. All have coefficients significantly different from zero at less than the .01 level.

The four body discrepancy scores used show a statistically significant degree of correlation with the self-discrepancy scores, as is shown in Table 4. The Movement, Grooming, Expressiveness, and Masculinity-

Table 1. Self-description—body description correlations

Body concept	Index of adjustment and values	Confidence limits 99% probability	
Opposite sex scale	.4981[a]	.33,	.69
Movement scale	.3271[a]	.18,	.49
Grooming scale	.5324[a]	.36,	.74
Expressiveness scale	.3542[a]	.20,	.52
M–F scale	.5186[a]	.35,	.72

[a]Positive correlation significantly different from zero at less than the .01 level.

Table 2. Self-acceptance—body acceptance correlations

Body concept	Index of adjustment and values	Confidence limits 99% probability	
Opposite sex scale	—.1346		
Movement scale	—.2476[a]	—.06,	—.46
Grooming scale	.2991[b]	.11,	.52
Expressiveness scale	.2199[b]	.03,	.42
M–F scale	—.0969		

[a]Negative correlation significantly different from zero at less than the .01 level.

[b]Positive correlation significantly different from zero at less than the .01 level.

Table 3. Ideal self-ideal body correlations

Body concept	Index of adjustment and values	Confidence limits 99% probability	
Opposite sex scale	.4686[a]	.26,	.73
Movement scale	.4719[a]	.26,	.73
Grooming scale	.5434[a]	.32,	.82
Expressiveness scale	.5943[a]	.36,	.90
M–F scale	.4830[a]	.27,	.74

[a]Positive correlation significantly different from zero at less than the .01 level.

Table 4. Self-discrepancy—body discrepancy correlations

Body concept	Index of adjustment and values	Confidence limits 99% probability	
Movement scale	.2060[a]	.02,	.41
Grooming scale	.4636[a]	.25,	.72
Expressiveness scale	.2112[a]	.02,	.54
M–F scale	.2110[a]	.02,	.54

[a]Positive correlation significantly different from zero at less than the .01 level.

Femininity discrepancy scores all have coefficients significantly different from zero at less than the .01 level. The Opposite Sex discrepancy score was not used because the Ideal Body-Opposite Sex scale was the one scale cut down to seven items in order to achieve a high coefficient of reproducibility, whereas the Body Description-Opposite Sex scale has nine items. There were no feasible means available to equate the seven-item scale with the nine-item scale in order to achieve a realistic discrepancy score.

CONCLUSIONS

The results of this study indicate that there is a significant linear relationship between self-concept and body concept in most of the dimensions measured. It appears that the security one has in one's body is related to the security with which one faces one's self and the world. The concept of body acceptance deserves the consideration of physical educators and others who may be concerned with mental health.

REFERENCES

1. Bills, Robert E. Manual, index of adjustment and values. Auburn: Department of Psychology, Alabama Polytechnic Institute, n.d.
2. Deuel, Phillip. Gamma program GI BC RPT. Berkeley: Computer Center, University of California, Nov., 1961.
3. Diamond, Solomon. Personality and temperament. New York: Harper & Brothers, 1957.
4. Goodman, Leo A., and Kruskal, William H. Measures of association for cross classifications. *J. Amer. stat. Assn.* 49:732-64, 1954.
5. Jersild, Arthur. *In search of self.* New York: Bureau of Publications, Teachers College, Columbia University, 1952.
6. Jersild, Arthur. The psychology of adolescence. New York: Macmillan Co., 1957.
7. Krasnow, Eleanor S. Guts, a program for guttman scaling. Berkeley: Computer Center, University of California, Aug., 1961.
8. Murphy, Gardner. Personality: a biosocial approach. New York: Harper & Brothers, 1947.
9. Schutz, Wiliam C. Studies of the effectiveness of administrative interaction. In progress. Berkeley: University of California.
10. Secord, Paul, and Jourard, Sidney. The appraisal of body-cathexis: body-cathexis and the self. *J. Consult. Psychol.* 17:343-47, 1953.
11. Stouffer, Samuel, and others. Measurement and prediction. Princeton, N. J.: Princeton University Press, 1950.

47. Health, physical education, and academic achievement*

Charles A. Bucher

Professor of Education and Director of Physical Education, School of Education, New York University

Although nine-year-old Susan has normal intelligence, she couldn't master the fundamentals of arithmetic, social studies, English, and writing, regardless of how hard she tried. Her academic difficulties were compounded by a partial paralysis of the right side of her body. After her parents and teachers had unsuccessfully tried everything they could think of to help her, she was referred to the Achievement Center for Children at Purdue University, where much research has been done on children with academic difficulties.

At the Center Susan spent two and a half years in a specially designed program of motor activity under skilled leadership. As a result, her academic and physical improvement was termed "miraculous" by her mother, the principal, and her classroom teacher. Her report card jumped two letter grades in every school subject, and for the first time she was able to participate in a full schedule of classroom activities.

Susan is just one of numerous boys and girls, most of whom do not have a physical handicap like hers, who have been helped to improve academically at the Center by taking part in a program of motor activities used as an integral part of a perceptual-motor training program.

More research is needed to establish and define the exact relationship of physical activity, motor skills, and health to academic achievement, but the evidence to date firmly establishes the fact that a close affinity exists.

Indeed, the kind of physical and health education programs which lead to improved physical and social fitness and health are vital to the education and academic achievement of every boy and girl.

This fact has been recognized throughout history by some of the world's most profound thinkers. For example, Socrates stressed that poor health can contribute to grave mistakes in thinking. Comenius noted, "Intellectual progress is conditioned at every step by bodily vigor. To attain the best results, physical exercise must accompany and condition mental training." Rousseau observed that "an enfeebled body enervates the mind" and included a rich program of physical activities for *Émile.*

More recently, such authorities as Arnold Gesell, Arthur T. Jersild, and the Swiss psychologist Jean Piaget found that a child's earliest learnings are motor (involving neuromuscular systems and resulting in movement such as running, jumping, reaching, etc.) in nature and form the foundation for subsequent learnings.

As D. H. Radler and Newell C. Kephart wrote in their authoritative book, *Success Through Play:* "Motor activity of some kind underlies all behavior including higher thought processes. In fact any behavior . . . can function no better than do the basic motor abilities upon which it is based."

Physical education, as defined in this article, refers to more than athletics for physically gifted boys and girls. It refers to an instructional program built around basic motor activities which help achieve the goal of physical, emotional, and mental well-

*From NEA Journal, Vol. 54, p. 38, May, 1965. Used by permission.

being for every student. School health programs are concerned with the modification of behavior and the imparting of scientific health knowledge leading to the same goals, together with provisions for health services and a healthful physical and emotional environment.

Academic achievement refers to the progress a child makes in school as measured by his scores on achievement tests, his grade-point averages, his promotion from grade to grade, and the development of proper attitudes. As any experienced teacher knows, academic achievement requires more than intellectual capacity. Nonintellectual factors, such as the will to achieve, health, and self-concept, are almost certain to play an important part in a student's ability to achieve academically.

Health and physical education programs are related to academic achievement in at least four ways: (a) through emphasis on the development of motor skills, (b) by promoting physical fitness, (c) by imparting knowledge and modifying behavior in regard to good health practices, and (d) by aiding in the process of social and emotional development which leads to a more positive self-concept.

Typical of the research studies confirming the relationship between motor skills and academic achievement is that of G. L. Rarick and Robert McKee who studied 20 third graders grouped according to whether they had high or low motor proficiency. The study showed that the group with high motor proficiency had a greater number who achieved "excellent" or "good" ratings in reading, writing, and comprehension than the group with low motor efficiency.

In another study, Jack Keogh and David Benson experimented with the motor characteristics of 43 underachieving boys, ages 10 to 14, enrolled in the Psychology Clinic School at UCLA. They found that as individuals, half of the boys from 10 to 12 years old exhibited poor motor performance.

A. H. Ismail, N. Kephart, and C. C. Cowell, utilizing motor aptitude tests, found that IQ and academic success could be predicted from these tests, with balance and coordination items the best predictors for estimating achievement.

Other studies indicate that the child's first learnings accrue from an interaction with his physical and social environment. Physical action provides the experience to clarify and make meaningful concepts of size, shape, direction, and other characteristics. In addition, through physical activities he experiences sensations, he has new feelings, and he develops new interests as well as satisfies old curiosities.

The importance of physical fitness was stressed by Lewis Terman more than twenty-five years ago. After working with gifted children he stated, "Results of physical measurements and medical examinations provide a striking contrast to the popular stereotype of the child prodigy, so commonly depicted as a pathetic creature, an overserious, undersized, sickly, bespectacled child." He went on to say that physical weakness was found nearly 30 percent fewer times in children of higher intelligence than in those of lower intelligence.

Many research studies since Terman have supported the contention that physical fitness is related to academic achievement.

H. H. Clarke and Boyd O. Jarman, in a study of boys, 9, 12, and 15 years old, found a consistent tendency for the high groups on various strength and growth measures to have higher means on both academic achievement tests and grade-point averages than low groups. Studies conducted at the universities of Oregon and Iowa and at Syracuse and West Point have shown a significant relationship between physical fitness and academic success and between physical fitness and leadership qualities. David Brace, F. R. Rogers, Clayton Shay, Marcia Hart, and others have done extensive research showing relationships between scholastic and academic success and physical fitness.

A good school health program, too, makes a definite contribution to good scholarship. In health education classes, students learn about the harmful effects of alcohol, smoking, and dangerous drugs; they obtain scientifically accurate information about such things as good nutrition, the requisites for good vision, the importance of exercise, and the ingredients for healthful personality development and mental health.

Through the development of desirable attitudes and the application of health knowledge, the student achieves his maximum strength, energy, endurance, recuperative power, and sensory acuity. Furthermore, the effective school health program helps boys and girls to understand and appreciate the value of good health as a means of achieving their greatest productivity, effectiveness, and happiness as individuals.

Some research has shown a relationship between scholastic success and the degree to which a student is accepted by his peer group. Similarly, the boy or girl who is well grounded in motor skills usually possesses social status among his or her peers.

For example, J. B. Merriman found that such qualities as poise, ascendancy, and self-assurance were significantly more developed in students of high motor ability than in those with low motor ability.

Other research shows that popularity in adolescent boys is more closely associated with physical and athletic ability than with intelligence; that leadership qualities are most prevalent among school boys (and West Point cadets) who score high on physical fitness tests; and that well-adjusted students tend to participate to a greater extent in sports than poorly adjusted students.

Physical education and health not only affect social development but emotional development as well. Games provide release from tension after long periods of study; furthermore, achievement in physical activities gives students a sense of pride which pays dividends in emotional satisfaction and well-being.

In this sense, the value of physical education and health may be greater for educationally subnormal students than for average boys and girls. James N. Oliver, lec-turer in education at the University of Birmingham, England, has done much research on educationally subnormal boys and has found that systematic and progressive physical conditioning yields marked mental and physical improvement. He believes such improvement resulted from the boys' feelings of achievement and of consequent improved adjustment.

The value of physical education and health programs will depend largely upon whether or not they meet the following criteria:

• The physical education program includes a variety of daily movement experiences and instruction in many basic motor activities, aimed not at making the student a superior performer in one or two, but stressing a modest performance in all, consistent with his developmental level. It also helps each student to achieve physically according to desirable standards.

• The health program provides boys and girls with accurate and significant health knowledge related to their individual needs and interests. There is also concern for health services and a healthful physical and emotional environment.

• Physical education and health programs are accorded educational respectability so that students and parents will more readily appreciate their value and seek the benefits they offer.

By providing these essentials, the school will help to ensure a high standard of academic achievement on the part of all boys and girls.

48. Motor skills—foundation stone of progress*

D. H. Radler with
Newell C. Kephart

Executive Director, Achievement Center for Children, Purdue University

The very first thing that any child does is move. Even before birth the infant is shifting his position, pushing and kicking, a phenomenon that intrigues proud young first-time patrents. Immediately after birth he breathes, cries and wriggles—all of which are, of course, muscular movements.

Motor behavior is fundamental for another reason: it is the only behavior that we can directly observe. Thus we can see or hear a man walking, talking, etc., but we have no way of knowing directly whether he is thinking, planning or dreaming. This has led many psychologists, particularly those of the so-called "behaviorist school," to deny that there is *any* behavior in the absence of movement. We do not need to go quite so far, but it is certainly logical to assume that all behavior is basically motor behavior. Thus we find statements such as that by Charles Sherrington in his book, *Man on His Nature,* "As we look along the scale of life . . . muscle is there before nerve and nerve is there before mind. . . . The great collateral branch of life, the plants . . . has never, in any event, developed an animal-like locomotor reaction, nor a muscle, nor a nerve. It has likewise remained without recognizable mind."

There are, of course, many activities in which a human being sits quietly and appears motionless. If you are thinking or planning or worrying or dreaming, you are certainly *behaving,* despite appearances. But psychologists Krech and Crutchfield in *Elements of Psychology,* a recent textbook, tell us that research has revealed a general increase in muscular tension throughout the body during thinking and other "invisible behavior." You have often seen such an increase in tension in yourself and others during heavy thought. It betrays itself in drumming of fingers, tapping of feet, pacing the floor. In addition to this generalized tension, psychologists have discovered localized increases of tension in particular muscle groups. Sensitive electrodes placed over individual muscles and groups of muscles reveal that while you are thinking, you are sending nervous messages. Your muscles contract in response. Suppose, for instance, you recall an insult you have just suffered. If then you think angrily that it would be satisfying to slap the offender, the muscles of your hand and arm will tense as the thought crosses your mind. In some cases this tension is so great that others notice it; in other cases, only enough for you yourself to be aware of this "half-action"; and in some instances, so slight that even *you* don't feel it—but a sensitive electrode can.

Whether covert or overt, motor activity of some kind underlies all behavior, including higher thought processes. In fact, any behavior in which you indulge can function no better than do the basic motor abilities upon which it is based. This chapter will deal with these fundamental skills and their development in the child.

The underlying movement pattern out of which all motor behavior flows is posture. Unfortunately, the charts and diagrams rep-

*From Radler, D. H., and Kephart, Newell C.: Success Through Play, New York: Harper & Row, Publishers, 1960. Used by permission.

resenting "good posture" which we all saw in grade school have created the impression that posture is rigid and stationary. Nothing could be further from the truth. In order to maintain any posture at all—good or bad— we must balance the forces exerted by muscles on one side of the body against those exerted by their opposite numbers. In turn, our nervous systems sense this balance, or lack of it, and hasten to make adjustments so that we maintain a chosen position and don't fall flat on our faces. The zero point of this nerve-muscle balance—the center of the scales, as it were—is the mid-line of the body: one's own center of gravity.

We feel "right" when this mid-line is at right angles to the earth; we're off-balance when the mid-line varies from this perpendicular position. Thus we're comfortable standing up, sitting or lying down in these positions—

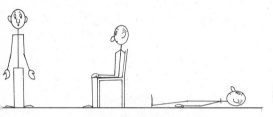

and we're strained in these positions:

One's posture, then, is a dynamic, changing position maintained by muscles and nerves in reaction to the shifting locations of the body's center of gravity.

From this fluid over-all response we derive all our ideas of up and down, right and left, in and out, etc. In other words, directions outside ourselves have meaning to us only in terms of directions within ourselves. For both, the point of reference is the body's center of gravity. It is this point of reference which we lose when we become "dizzy" through illness, injury, overexertion, overindulgence, etc. Anyone who has ever momentarily lost his zero point for any reason

knows that without it the world is a strange and unmanageable place.

Our safety—even our survival—depends upon posture. If we cannot maintain our relationship to the center of gravity (and therefore to the earth itself) we cannot be ready to move quickly and efficiently when danger threatens. For instance, to dodge out of the way of an oncoming automobile, we must know what direction to jump in. The only way we can know this is to know where we are in the first place. Just as we must have a zero point to establish directions in space, we must have a reference point for all movements.

Fortunately, posture is controlled not by the cerebral cortex, the higher brain center which requires conscious thought, but by the cerebellum, the lower brain center which operates constantly and without need of voluntary thought.

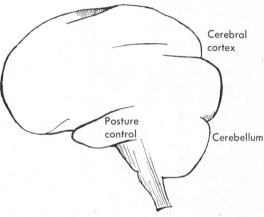

The cerebellum is a mass of brain tissue connecting directly with the spinal cord and the nerve tracts leading to the major muscle groups. In this commanding position between the higher brain and the body's movement system it sits as a censor. When the cerebral cortex works out an elaborate behavior pattern such as that involved in reading or writing, it passes the message along to the muscles through the cerebellum. If the planned behavior is something you can do without physical harm or major discomfort the cerebellum ratifies the message and permits it to pass. But if the planned behavior would hurt you in any way (such as kicking both feet at once) the cerebellum casts a veto.

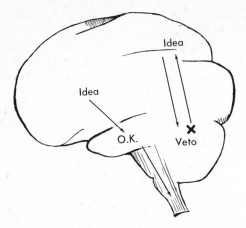

You might think of this veto as a short circuit that returns the behavior patterns to the cerebral cortex to be reworked. By this means nature makes sure that no behavior will result in action that is contrary to the body's structure or to the basic postural mechanisms. Thus we are prevented from injuring ourselves, from losing our orientation and from sacrificing our zero point, to and from which all behavior flows.

Since posture serves as the core of behavior, you want the postural adjustments you can make to be as flexible as possible. If the postural mechanism is stiff and inflexible, the range of action open to you before the cerebellum casts its veto is severely limited. But if your posture is flexible, it permits a wide range of activities. In general, if only a few sets of muscles move to maintain your posture, that posture will be rigid. But if most of your muscles work together, your posture will be free and easy—and so will all your behavior.

This intimate relationship between posture and behavior was demonstrated clearly in a recent study by Dr. Kephart and graduate student Rudolph Kagerer. They rated the posture of a group of first grade children along a scale ranging from "very rigid" to "very flexible." Then they compared these ratings with the children's school achievement. They found that the children with rigid posture were at the bottom of the class, while those with loose, comfortable posture were at the top.

There was no constitutional difference between the high achievers with flexible posture and the low achievers with rigid posture—they all had good bones, muscles and nerves. The differences lay in how well they had learned to use their bodies. Since this postural flexibility, commonly called "grace," "poise" or "co-ordination," is learned, it can be taught. . . . Of course we are not concerned with teaching parlor tricks, nor are we attempting to produce a set of bulging muscles. Instead we want to develop the basic grace and ease of movement—co-ordination—that underlies successful performance in *all* areas of behavior.

Co-ordination is essentially composed of two ingredients, known as "laterality" and "directionality." "Laterality" is the inner sense of one's own symmetry: "leftness" and "rightness," or "two-sidedness." We might call it the map of internal space. This map enables the child to operate smoothly with either hand or leg or with both hands or legs. . . .

Directionality is the projection into space of laterality—the awareness of left and right (and up and down, before and behind, etc.) in the world around you. We can call this the map of external space. There are, after all, no "real" directions in space; to everyone on earth the sky is "up" and the ground "down," although people in China are hanging down from the earth when we are standing up on it (and vice versa).

This fancy highlights the often unnoticed fact that space has direction only in relation to the person who is looking at it. Thus directionality is the counterpart in the world *outside* your skin of the sensations you feel *within* your skin—one man's up is another man's down; my left is your right when we are facing each other.

Both maps, the internal and external, depend upon learned postural adjustments and other movement patterns. They are, then, "the knowledge of the muscles." And again, you learn from the inside out. Laterality comes before directionality; the internal map precedes the external.

Our bodies are designed to be excellent

right-left detectors. We are bilaterally symmetrical—that is, we have two eyes, two ears, two arms, two legs, etc. Each pair of organs or appendages serves as a sensing device. It sends messages to the brain telling whether a signal comes from the left side or from the right. The nerve systems controlling the left side of the body pass up the spinal cord, cross in the brain stem and enter the right half of the cortex, or higher brain. Similarly, the separate systems for the right side enter the left half of the cortex. Although there is some relationship between the two nerve systems, essentially they are independent of one another. This independence is what makes our bodies such fine left-right detectors.

But even this relatively simple discrimination must be learned. Only by experimenting with the two sides of the body do we come to know which is which. After trying such movements, observing the results, comparing the results with inner sensory impressions, then re-experimenting—only after he has done this a number of times does the child sort out left from right within himself. It is this end product of learning that we call the internal map, or laterality.

There are several stages in the process of learning laterality at which the child can fail and can still make responses which *appear* adequate. Two of these stages are of particular importance. The first is that in which the child learns that as long as he responds equally from both sides he can avoid the problem of distinguishing lateral position. Thus, his movements and his responses will be organized so that both sides of the body are performing the same act at the same time: he will reach for a toy with his right hand, simultaneously making a useless reaching movement with his left. Such a child is avoiding the problem of creating a good internal map by maintaining, as nearly as possible, complete bilateral symmetry. The opposite problem is one in which the child becomes almost completely one-sided. In every activity he performs with one side and merely drags the other side along. Frequently, where he must use both sides of his body, one side will lead and the other side will only follow along without taking an active, constructive part in the performance. In either of these two cases, the child restricts his movement patterns and thereby restricts his learning. He does not

gain an adequate appreciation of right and left within himself. Confronted with problems of right and left in external space, he will reflect his difficulty through reversals, inaccuracies and failures; he will read *d* as *b, saw* as *was,* etc.

What we have been calling the internal map must be distinguished from "handedness" and from *naming* right and left. Laterality is a feeling of awareness of the two sides of the body and the difference between them. It is probable that for most of us, even after laterality is established, there remains the problem of keeping these relationships straight. Most probably we solve the problem by developing one side as the leading side—we become "right-handed" or "left-handed." (Only a very few people become truly ambidextrous, operating equally well with either hand.) In this connection, it is significant that studies of young children by Gesell and others have shown that "handedness" develops gradually, usually appearing somewhere around the age of two years. Prior to this time the child uses both hands alternately. "Handedness," then, is probably an indication that an internal map has been created, although it can appear in some cases as the result of *inadequate* laterality. Handedness and laterality are linked, but they are not one and the same thing.

In like manner, laterality must be differentiated from *naming* of sides. To ask the child, "Which is your right hand?" is not a test of his laterality. The recognition of the right hand as opposed to the left can be based, after all, on external characteristics of the two parts. Thus, the left hand may be the hand on which you wear a ring, etc. The child's differentiation is then not based on any internal map, but on the observation of superficial characteristics of the external parts themselves.

The development of laterality is extremely important, since it permits us to keep things straight in the world around us. As we have pointed out before, the only difference between a *b* and a *d* is one of laterality. If there is no left and right inside the organism, there can be no projection of this left and right outside the organism; consequently, the differences between *b* and *d* disappear. In this connection psychologist Lotts says, "If we had *only* visual impressions, the words up, down, left, right and so on could have no meaning. One cannot ascribe erectness, inverseness, or slantwise orientation to the universe. 'Upper' in the visual field is what appears nearer the head and could be reached by a tactile member of the head, such as an insect's antenna, if we had one; 'lower' is what appears nearer the feet and could be reached by lower tactile members." Similarly, "left" is to the side we *feel* as left and "right" is to the side we feel as right.

Once the child has developed an internal map and is aware of the right and left sides of his own body, he is ready to build a map of the space outside his body. By experimenting with movement patterns directed toward objects in space, he learns that to reach an object he must make a movement, say, to the right. From this deduction he develops the concept of an object *to the right of himself*. Through a number of such experiences he learns to translate the right-left discrimination *within* himself into a right-left discrimination among objects *outside* himself.

Research workers in the field of child development have consistently noted that appreciation of points in space develops first in relationship to the child himself. Only later do these points develop relationships *between each other*. Thus, early in his development a child locates two objects, each independently, in relation to himself: "That one is to my right; that one is to my left." This has been called "egocentric localization." Later in development the child is able to conceive of one object in relationship to another: "That one is to the right of this one." This later development has been called "objective localization." Piaget, Gesell and others have outlined this developmental sequence: first the child relates each object to *himself;* later he relates objects *to one another*.

One very important factor in the development of directionality is the control of the eyes. Since almost all of our information concerning space and the location of objects in space comes to us through our eyes, it is necessary for us to develop a series of clues by which this visual information can give us the same sense of direction as we formerly received through actually touching something. As young children we do this by comparing *the feeling of where our eyes are pointed* with the physical sensation of touching an object. This is how we learn

that when our eyes are pointed in a given direction, this means that the object lies in that direction. In order to learn this lesson well as young children, we must have many experiences in which we make a complicated series of matches between the position of our eyes and the position of our hands in touching objects of all kinds.

The eyes are moved by six voluntary muscles which must be controlled in patterns. The area on which the visual image is projected is quite narrow (about 2 millimeters in diameter). In order to focus the image on this tiny area, the eye must be moved with extreme precision. Given the small "screen" and the six muscles to co-ordinate the eye, learning to focus sharply is very difficult. When the child has learned this control, he matches the movement of his eye to the movement of his hand and thus transfers the directionality information—the external map—from the feeling in his hand and arm to the feeling in his eye. This complex matching procedure requires a great deal of learning to perfect. Only after it has been perfected can the child use his eyes to tell him exactly how far away are the objects that he can't reach with his hand.

One further difficulty is encountered in this matching exercise. . . . When the child is experimenting with basic movement patterns, he refers all movement to the center of his body as the zero point. Thus the young infant in his crib moves both arms at once toward or away from the center of his body. These movement patterns, for the most part, do not overlap. They come to the child as separate directions on each side of the mid-line. If we move a visual target such as a fingertip from left to right, the infant interprets the initial movement as one coming *toward* him. Then, when the target crosses the midline, the movement becomes one going *away* from him. Ultimately, the child must learn that the visual movement is *the same left-to-right movement* even though the direction he felt became switched when the mid-line was crossed. In other words, the child must learn to reverse his kinesthetic-visual matches every time he crosses the mid-line of his own body. This is the price we pay for being such fine right-left detection devices! And it is a high price for many children, whose problems can be seen in indecision and loss of control when movements cross the midline of their bodies.

49. The worth of physical skill*

Charles A. Bucher

Professor of Education and Director of Physical Education, School of Education, New York University

One of the great classics of history tells about the wanderings of Odysseus on his return from the Trojan war. His travels took him to such places as Ismarus, Sicily, and finally to the island of the Phaeacians. Here the emperor, King Alcinous, was so impressed with his adventurous guest that it was decided to hold a spectacular sports celebration in his honor. The ruler summoned the best athletes in the kingdom and bade them put forth their best efforts. There followed such a superb and exciting display of physical feats that roars of applause engulfed the athletic field and could be heard far and wide. Then Alcinous, with a "Can You Top This?" attitude, turned to Odysseus and asked if he, too, would like to perform. Much to the King's surprise, his challenge was accepted. Grabbing a discus larger than had been used by any of his competitors and dashing on the field with a heavy cloak restricting his movements, Odysseus astounded the spectators with a tremendous throw that smashed all records.

Ever since man first learned to coordinate his muscular and nervous systems for physical action there has been popular interest in acts of human skill. David casting the deadly stone accurately with his slingshot, William Tell splitting the apple on his son's head with his bow and arrow, Pheidippides racing to announce the Greek victory at Marathon, and Ben Hur driving his chariot at break-neck speed down the stretch to victory—all are a part of the world's literature that inspire young and old alike.

TEACHING PHYSICAL SKILLS

Physical skill plays an important role in the cultures of all peoples. It packs stadiums, crowds palestras, and usurps television screens. It emblazons the names of champions on printed programs, newspaper scareheads, and advertising billboards. It captivates men's thoughts, holds them spellbound, and receives their plaudits.

We, as coaches and physical educators, should be proud to be the teachers and the nurturers of skill. We help to shape men's lives, build a strong people, and further international peace. Our services are sought by schools, colleges, boys' clubs, girl scouts, hospitals, Peace Corps, churches, country clubs and other organizations. Yes, ours is an important business in this world in which we live.

The role we play in the skill education of boys and girls is probably our most important responsibility. Here we have an opportunity to apply our art in a manner that will influence a young person's life for the better. Just as a sculptor takes clay and with his hands molds a lifelike image of a person, so we through expert skill instruction mold human bodies which possess aesthetically beautiful qualities. As Aristotle once said, *"The body is the temple of the soul and to reach harmony of body, mind, and spirit it is important to develop physical as well as mental and spiritual qualities."* The development of the total person—to become all that he is capable of becoming—is what makes for the Good Life. To show a young person how to hit a backhand shot effectively, to execute a flying camel spin, or send the arrow straight into the gold circle, are contributions

*From The Coach, Vol. 39, pp. 3-5, (Mar.-Apr.) 1963. Used by permission.

to human betterment well worth our time, efforts, and energies.

When won and lost records have been buried in dust, headlines have faded, and loving cups have rusted, the coach and teacher can still see their work living on in youngsters who have grown into adulthood, because skill endures a lifetime. A skill that is overlearned is never lost and will provide enjoyable, interesting, and healthful experiences for its possessor throughout his years. A young boy who learns how to swim and then fails to get into the water for many years will still know how to swim. A girl who has imprinted upon her nervous system the way to hit a tennis ball correctly will always know how to perform this physical feat. Absence from the pool and court for a long period of time may require some polishing of strokes and improving of stamina—but the learned skills will stick.

Physical skill has values for many persons. The *spectator* thrills to the chase, struggle, competition, and challenge. The *sports writer* prospers as his copy spells out the exciting action. *The keeper of the coffers* smiles as the coins trinkle into the treasury. *Mothers and father* brag as they bask in the glory of their children's achievements. And *coaches* are imbued with a sense of pride as their charges gain fame. BUT great as these values may be for the people who vicariously profit from human skill, *non can compare to the worth it has for the PARTICIPANT*. Here are a few:

RECOGNITION AND BELONGING

One of the basic psychological needs of every human being on this earth is to be recognized and possess a feeling of belonging. To have a sense of worth is a must for good mental health. Not to possess it can result in feelings of despair, frustration, and failure.

The skilled person is a somebody—a person who is known, talked about, and emulated. He is recognized. He belongs. And one of the most wonderful things about physical skill is that it may be the only way for some underprivileged young men and women to achieve their basic psychological need. As a result of this skill they surge to the top, gain an education, and find a career. Andy Robustelli, Gary Gubner, Althea Gibson, Luis Aparicio, and Ted Kluszewski will attest to that.

HEALTH AND FITNESS

Mental research indicates the need of physical activity for health. Studies show that the chances of coronary heart disease may be greater for the inactive than for the active individual. Hippocrates, the father of medicine, said in respect to muscular development—that which is used develops and that which is not used atrophies or wastes away. Activity is essential to life and skill is the catalyst that propels human bodies into action.

Throughout life activity is a self-energizing process. Businessmen, lawyers, and others can spend all their free time drinking martinis, watching television, or sinking deeper into their living room chairs. Or, they can devote some of their leisure to exhilarating sport and thus enhance their well-being. Thorndike, the psychologist, pointed out that humans tend to repeat those things which give them satisfaction. Skill yields satisfaction and that is why those persons who have it will live a much more active life—and other things being equal will be healthier.

CONFIDENCE

As a result of skill a person has a feeling of readiness to meet the challenge. I can remember seeing Ben Hogan in his prime take a caddy and a bag of balls out on the fairway and spend hour after hour mastering every shot in the book—in the rough, buried in the sand, under the trees, and in a hundred other challenging lies. He developed skill which gave him confidence to meet any situation that developed and as a result he became one of the world's greatest golfers.

With skill the cup looks larger when putting on the green, the hoop has greater circumference when shooting for the basket, and the clay pigeon seems to hang in the air longer when firing a gun. The training, practice, and resulting coordination and accuracy have paid off—there is confidence that one can be successful in the game.

SAFETY

The skilled and conditioned athlete is not the player who usually gets hurt. It is the unskilled, poorly conditioned participant who finds himself on the stretcher and spending time in a cast. And the skill developed on the athletic field, gymnasium floor, or swimming pool also helps to promote safety in everyday life whether it's the agility which helps one to get out of the way of a speeding car or the ability to swim 100 yards from shore and save a person's life.

CONSTRUCTIVE USE OF LEISURE

The boy who has mastered the slalom doesn't have to be forced to hit the trails. The girl who can do a full gainer doesn't need her mother to encourage her to get into the water during her leisure hours. The man who can land a four pound bass with a fly rod will be on his way at 6 A.M. on Saturday morning although he got in bed late the night before. Why? Because it's fun and exciting. In addition to the thrills, there is always the challenge—setting a new record on the slopes, excelling in competition at the pool, catching the largest fish in the lake. Skill gives zest to living—living a more interesting and vigorous life.

A BRIGHTER WORLD

Several years ago, William Menninger, the famous psychiatrist, reported a study in which he compared a group of well-adjusted normal individuals to a group of maladjusted neurotic persons. He noticed that the maladjusted group did not possess hobbies. These people did not know how to play.

Skill is an excellent antidote for tension, worries, or sorrow. When a man is pitching the softball over the plate for an out and a woman is rolling the ball down the alley for a strike, they forget how the stock market slipped a fraction of a point, the fight they had with the neighbors, and the bills coming due the first of the month. The world looks rosy. Life is worth living.

Coaches and physical educators can and should be proud of the contribution they can make to humanity. It is within their power to give each boy and girl physical skills and thus help them to lead healthier, happier, and more worthwhile and productive lives. The world is a better place in which to live as a result of their work because PHYSICAL SKILL HAS WORTH.

50. Overview of educational innovation*

Lawrence Balter

Instructor, Department of Educational Psychology, School of Education, New York University

Emanuel Sanger

School Psychologist, Farmingdale Public Schools, Farmingdale, New York

Several factors seem to be responsible for the recent rise in educational research. The single most significant variable appears to be the 1957 launching of Sputnik. In 1958, legislation established State Aid for Experimental Programs. At first, attention focused upon mathematics, science, and the gifted. By 1960 the scope broadened to include English and foreign languages to the list of subjects for investigation. In 1964 the program was further extended to social studies and programs for disadvantaged children. Furthermore, the population explosion coupled with the growing popularity of the "excellence" notion, added impetus to the expansion of educational innovation and research during the past decade (Brickell, 1961; Miles, 1964).

Heathers (1965) has delineated five major areas of educational innovation. These areas are:

A. NEW CURRICULA—Science, mathematics, reading, and social studies;

B. NEW TEACHER EDUCATION—Internships, 5th-year programs, and liberal arts emphasis;

C. EDUCATIONAL TECHNOLOGY—Educational television, programmed instruction tapes, language labs, and instruction via computer;

D. SCHOOL REORGANIZATION—Nongrading, pupil-team learning, dual progress, and team teaching;

E. SCHOOL INTEGRATION AND COMPENSATORY EDUCATION—School redistricting, school consolidation, programs for disadvantaged children.

For illustrative purposes, five specific innovations which fall within the broad framework presented above will be outlined.

Innovation I: process in education

The current emphasis on process in education is that students should acquire certain skills which can be applied to all areas of knowledge long after they have left the formal school situation. Toward this end, new skills and concepts must be introduced which will help the learner (and teacher) to organize and structure knowledge (Bruner, 1960; Dewey, 1959). In this connection, it is the emphasis placed upon teaching all students competence in self instruction and independent study which sets apart the process approach from traditional methods (Heathers, 1965). The process approach embodies several *tool skills:* inquiry training, self-initiated learning, interpretation, evaluation, and utilization of knowledge (Wertham, 1963). Thus, the student is required to develop open-mindedness and tolerance for ambiguity.

Innovation II: educational television (ETV)

In 1952 The Federal Communciations Commission set aside 242 channels for educational purposes. Among the pioneers in the use of television as a medium of instruc-

*From Education Synopsis, Winter 1967-1968, p. 22. Used by permission.

tion were Iowa State and Western Reserve which offered courses for credit in the early 1950's. Medical and Dental schools soon found that television provided students with front row seats in observing surgery. It was estimated that by 1960 at least three million students in elementary and secondary schools were receiving part of their daily instruction by television (Scanlon, 1963). In 1963 it was estimated that ETV was viewed, in and out of school, by thirteen million occasional viewers and about 4.5 million regularly (Schramm, Lyle and Pool, 1963).

A number of advantages of ETV as a medium for instruction have been advanced. For instance, more students can be exposed to some of the nation's leading scholars. Furthermore, teachers may be able to learn along with their pupils. In addition to content, teachers may be able to incorporate new teaching methods. Finally, ETV may relieve the regular teacher of planning and presenting certain materials of the course leaving time for other phases such as eliciting student participation and discussion groups. It may also provide time for additional remedial instruction. Classroom space need and amount of teachers may also be lessened (Scanlon, 1963).

Innovation III: team teaching

Miles (1964) defines team teaching as that in which ". . . a small group of teachers jointly plans and carries out learning experiences for a larger than usual group of students (p. 6)." This approach seems to have grown out of two conditions: (1) limited leadership opportunities for career teachers, and (2) the impossibility of teachers being all things to all people (Goodlad, 1965). Thus, the team teaching approach attempts to provide an opportunity for the most talented teachers to influence a large group of students, while other teachers may concentrate and focus their attention on students who manifest educational difficulties. Also, team teaching allows for the establishment of large and small groupings within a flexible framework. Some examples of how this may be made operational have been suggested by Goodlad (1965). At a relatively uncomplicated level of arrangement, two teachers, for instance, who would normally teach independently of one another would pool their resources, students, and curriculum. In going up the scale of complexity there are instances where two self-contained classrooms come together for planning and teaching. The most complex levels of team teaching involve team leaders and coordinators, master teachers devising the curriculum, while regular teachers, interns, student teachers and clerks work towards educating the students who before were isolated in self-contained classrooms.

Innovation IV: the dual progress plan

In 1956 George D. Stoddard, then Dean of New York University's School of Education, first proposed the dual progress plan. He felt that the self-contained classroom was not effective in meeting the instructional needs of our school children. Several salient features of the self-contained classroom including the general purpose classroom, the general elementary teacher, grade level placement, and grade level curriculum, require modification under the dual progress plan (Heathers, 1964).

Stoddard describes the program as a plan which is "designed to end the concept of average pupils doing average work under average teaching conditions (1958, p. 352)." In a general sense, the plan calls for a combination of graded and ungraded instruction. Social studies and the language arts are provided by "core" teachers while math and science as well as physical education and the creative arts are ungraded and taught by specialist teachers. He proposed that instruction in the *cultural imperatives*—English and Social Studies—be in the conventional fashion consisting of grade-level curriculum, grouping and promotion. Students would be grouped according to ability in these areas and belong to a grade level. In the area of the *cultural electives*—mathematics, science, art, and music—nongraded grouping is instituted. In this plan, children move along at their own rate of accomplishment and promotion is dependent upon the imperatives rather than on the so-called electives. Electives are taken by all children and are elective only in the sense that the rate of advancement is not held constant for all pupils. A youngster proceeds from one level in the curriculum to the next as he masters each succeeding step in the curriculum sequence (Heathers, 1965).

Thus, in this program, the school is organized into two parts. One half, either morning or afternoon, is devoted to core and physical education while the other half is used for cultural electives.

Innovation V: programmed instruction

The emergence of programmed instruction as an educational innovation converges with the growth of ETV as aspects of the general area of mass communication and educational media. While ETV generally refers to mass communication, programmed instruction is thought of as an individualized learning medium. One of the most important features of programmed instruction is that it lends itself to the scientific method. That is, it consists of repeated measures under controlled conditions; it is possible to make continual changes in the program until it produces the desired result—learning. There are a number of salient aspects regarding how a program "teaches."

Markle (1963) outlines a number of such factors: the program (1) tells the pupil what he should know; (2) leads the student through steps of discovery; (3) fractionates subject matter into digestible bits; (4) provides forward steps which are logical and in accordance with the student's level; (5) asks the pupil to put knowledge to work immediately—at the moment of acquisition the pupil must finish sentences, answer questions, do problems; (6) compels the student to take each step on his own; (7) permits the pupil to know immediately whether he is right or wrong; (8) is paced at an appropriate rate for each pupil as it is the pupil who regulates the amount of time spent on each step. It is significant that unlike textbooks, flaws and difficulties can be precisely found and adjusted. Thus, the programmer may find it necessary to clarify in some places, give more examples in others, and provide more practice in still other areas, and so forth.

Projects and thought questions for psychological foundations of physical education

1. Observe a young child who is beginning to explore movement patterns. Attempt to evaluate and understand the mental and physical relationships involved.

2. Write a documented report on the contributions of physical education to the academic achievement of children and youth.

3. Develop a unique test of coordination or balance that might be used as a predictor of scholastic achievement. Give a complete rationale for your choice.

4. What psychological needs do sports and physical activities answer for you as an individual? For your friends and classmates?

5. Develop your own definition of somatopsychic physical education. Draw implications for your use of this aspect of physical education.

6. How can an understanding of the psychology of body concept affect the planning of physical education curriculums and programs?

7. Read and review several research reports dealing with the personality traits of female college athletic competitors. How do these reports compare with your own observations?

8. List the implications of educational innovations for physical education on a selected school level.

9. By what methods would you suggest that maladjusted people be helped through physical activities and sports participation?

Selected readings

Caillois, R.: Man, play and games, New York, 1961, The Free Press.

Lakie, W. L.: Expressed attitudes of various groups of athletes toward athletic competition, Res. Quart. 35:497, Dec. 1964.

Lawther, J. D.: Directing motor skill learning, Quest, Monograph VI (Spring Issue), May 1966.

Nash, J. B.: Physical education: interpretations and objectives, New York, 1948, A. S. Barnes & Co., Inc.

Piaget, J.: Play, dreams and imitation in childhood, London, 1951, William Heineman, Ltd.

Pines, M.: Can children think harder? The PTA Magazine 62:16, Feb. 1968.

Sociological foundations of physical education

In the domain of the sociological foundations of physical education, Günter Erbach demonstrates the ways in which sport affects culture. Erbach lists the various disciplines that relate directly to sport and discusses the objectives of a sociology of sport. The author also points out the need for research on the sociology of sport and suggests some of the finer points of research methodology in this area.

Michel Bouet discusses the humanizing aspect and potential of sports and games. Bouet shows why sportsmen compete, how sports draw competitors into closer human relationships, and briefly points out how sports can be used to help explain some of the conclusions made by behavioral scientists.

A Russian author, V. Artemov, investigates the effect of greater amounts of leisure time on physical education and on participation in physical activity. Artemov's research was conducted in Russia but his findings draw implications for other countries as well. Artemov gives suggestions on how free time can be more effectively used for physical activity.

Disadvantaged children are the topic of an article by Allan C. Ornstein, who shows how teachers can make a significant contribution to the lives of these children. Many implications may be drawn from this article for physical education, particularly in regard to educating for healthful living, in providing opportunities for success through the activities of the program, and in educating for future recreational needs.

School athletics and their place in education are discussed by Ray O. Duncan. Duncan shows how school athletics help to answer the competitive play needs of youth when the athletic program is an outgrowth of the skills learned in the basic instructional program. Duncan points out that youngsters should first improve their skills in an intramural program before engaging in the more highly competitive programs.

Charles A. Bucher discusses some of the dangers associated with Little League baseball competition. This article deplores the air of professionalism with which Little League contests are conducted and suggests that the entire concept, philosophy, leadership, and conduct of such leagues come under comprehensive scrutiny and revision.

51. The science of sport and sports sociology—questions related to development—problems of structure*

Günter Erbach

German Democratic Republic

ENLARGEMENT OF THE SPHERE OF SOCIAL INFLUENCE OF PHYSICAL CULTURE

As a result of the deep and most significant socio-economic changes which took place during the course of the past 100 years physical culture and sport[1] has been transformed from more or less regionally or nationally limited forms to a world-wide phenomenon. The external outlines of this development are thrown into relief by the setting up of national unions and associations, of international sports federations, the organization of national and international championships, by the crowning highlight: the Olympic Games—and the mass aspect of physical culture and sport in the various social systems, together with their economic,

political and cultural results. The development of the productive forces and the socialization of the working and living conditions, following in its wake, create for physical culture and sport in our times completely new conditions which change the attitude of the human being towards physical culture, and as a result the entire social relationship towards physical culture and sport appears in a different light. New aims set for physical culture and sport, due to the changed production conditions and more leisure time, participation of growing numbers of people in organized sports activity as well as in not organized forms, the markedly higher level of achievement in sport, the efficiency of the entire system of sports institutions, the growing public interest and the activity of the mass media of communication in the field of sports propaganda and information—just to quote only a few of the most striking aspects—point to the whole complex of social problems which are facing us in connection with this. Therefore it is fully justified and of theoretical as well as practical significance that in recent publications[2] the actual requirements,

---

*From International Review of Sport Sociology, Vol. 1, p. 59, 1966, Committee of Sport Sociology of The International Council of Sport and Physical Education (UNESCO).

[1] The customarily used combination of the two terms "physical culture and sport" signifies the total aspect of the social achievements and measures connected with the physical perfection of man. Physical culture serves as the main and guiding concept and includes: planned physical education, sport, physical exercises and all forms of active leisure pursuits. Sport is the dominating form of expression of physical culture (that is why it is as a rule used as a synonym for physical culture in general) and signifies the striving to succeed in physical efficiency, on the basis of the norms and rules in contests of all types. One may approach sport as a system of top-class performance as physical culture training based on scientific foundation—(generalizations in the entire social field of physical culture).

[2] See among others such publications as: E. Buggel [3, 4], R. Florl [8]. F. Gras [9], J. Kukuschkin [18], A. D. Novikov [11], G. Röblitz [12], H. Schwidtmann [16], H. Schnürpel [13], R. Schultz [15], F. Trogsch [21, 22], G. Erbach [6, 7] as well as the contributions published in the special issue *Über philosophische und soziologische Probleme der Körperkultur* (Philosophical and Sociological Problems of Physical Culture of the magazine "Theorie und Praxis der Körperkultur". Berlin, September, 1964.

which are the outcome of the new socio-economic conditions, are being taken into consideration, since they are in a decisive way shaped by the technical and cultural revolution and make it necessary to establish qualitatively new criteria for the further development of the system of physical education. This desire finds its expression in the passing over to a scientifically founded long-term development planning system as an always effective means and principle to bring about a planned development of physical culture. This requires theoretical thinking with foresight and an analytical examination of the state of development [3, 6, 17].[3]

From research and discussions so far, one can draw one important conclusion that our present-day system of physical culture must be substantially perfected, so that it could fully satisfy the growing requirements of the citizens for many-sided physical culture and education. Quite new requirements are the result of this process of development addressed to the science of physical culture (science of sport).[4]

In the process of social relations between people, taking place on various levels, in the individual and collective development, in school, in one's professional work and during the entire leisure time, physical culture and sport are accepted parts of an all-round formation of personality and are more and more highly valued, more and more attention is paid to it and growing numbers of people

practice it. The problem of top-class performances in sport is today not only the concern of the active and proper sports institutions and organizations, but of wide strata of the population and to some extent of the entire society. Should one ask for the reasons of this exceptionally high social and political evaluation of physical culture and sport, which can today be noticed everywhere in the international arena, one relatively quickly finds the answer; it is based on the significance to teach people to live a healthy life, to obtain high physical efficiency in one's profession as well as in life in general on the importance to develop valuable traits of character, to utilize one's spare time in a sensible way and finally (as one of the most important factors) it gives pleasure and joy and with the same teaches people to adopt an optimistic attitude towards life. All these factors that were mentioned (by no means are these all of them) play their role in social reality, in the social process of development and the spreading of physical culture and sport. And precisely this gives rise to new problems for the science of sport, especially for research connected with the social conditions, relations and requirements as a starting point for the establishment of trends of development [6, 16, 17]. For a prognostic determination of the trends of development as well as for a concrete analysis of the social conditions and circumstances regarding the development of physical culture, it is necessary to establish specialized philosophical and sociological as well as scientific organizational research in the science of sport (theory of physical culture, sport sociology, the science of organization of physical culture [7]). Thus there has been found a wide field for social research, and the aims and structure of sports sicence will, due to the establishment of a proper profile of tasks, set for the social science branches, gain a more complete aspect.

SPORT AS A COMPONENT OF CULTURE

The basic stimulae for the development of physical culture and sport stem from those spheres of life where the true activity and expressions of life of the human being actually take place, such as economy, politics, science and culture. These forms of activity exert their influence in other spheres of life and have already turned into relatively im-

---

[3]See also: *Outdoor Recreation for America.* The Report of the Outdoor Recreation Resources Review Commission to the President and to the Congress, Washington, 1962; *Friluftlivet in Nveringe* (Outdoor Recreation in Sweden), Part I and II, Stockholm, 1964; *Sport and Community.* The Report of the Wolfenden Committee for Sport, London, 1960; *(Soovenzioni per lo sport in Europe.* Subvention for Sport in Europe) Traguardi, Roma 7 (1963) 6.

[4]The conception science of sport is gradually also being accepted in the international field as a main term for the various specialized scientific disciplines which concentrate on the discovery of general and special laws and rules in physical culture and sport as a social phenomenon. We understand this as the combination of all the scientific branches, specializing in lecturing and research on physical culture (institutionally arranged into academic training facilities and research centres) which in this process have developed a relative independence.

portant components of the conscious shaping of the life of the individual as well as society as a whole. The objective connection, which can be understood only from the dialectical point of view, is of basic significance for the determination of the social functions of physical culture and sport and of their scientific reflection. As is generally known, the creative and productive activity of man is a presupposition of culture. Marxist philosophy considers culture to be the material and intellectual result of the creative ability of the human being, a process of physical and intellectual perfection of man, his upbringing and education, the ideological, artistic and scientific reflection of these processes as well as the achieved level in cooperation between human activity in practical life and the objective rules of nature and society. In this sense culture is the expression and measure of the humane aspects of life, the mastering of nature and society, order and the conscious shaping of social relations [10]. As social phenomena and as a social process, physical culture and sport are an integral part of culture. They reflect the achievements of physical perfection and the development of the physical prowess of man, which in the practical process of life find their expression in the aspirations to lead a life in which there is place for healthy cultural and sports activity.

Without such an aim a humanistic culture and physical culture would be unthinkable and always socially determined. As a product of nature and as a social being man is in this sense the final product of the cultural development and at the same time the most important productive force (22, p. 935 ff.).

The Marxist-Leninist ideology and science considers it as one of its most important tasks to bring about an all-round physical and intellectual development and education of man which would reach such a level where he would in a conscious way make use of the laws of nature and society for the benefit of the individual and society as a whole. In the social process of work man changes nature and shapes it according to his requirements. In this process he changes (as was proved by Marx and Engels in a most comprehensive way) his own nature as well and in the historical course of social development there takes place a steady change of his physical and intellectual forces. This aspect of the psychophysical unity of man in the process of social development leads us to the question, why physical culture and sport has to be accepted as man's expression of life and as a social phenomenon of a relatively independent character.

The physical qualities of man were in the past and are to this day one of the fundamental conditions of material production. However, during the process of the physical and mental interrelations in the field of material production and during the creation of intellectual and cultural values, changes are today taking place, in the existing conditions of our times, in other relations than in the past. The main purpose of physical culture and its specific forms (sport, gymnastic, games, tourism, etc.) is always the perfection of physical efficiency and in the broadest sense the preservation and and strengthening of health. The great variety of phenomena, experiences, achievements and skill, which are the outcome of the efforts made to achieve physical health and efficiency within the social development process, and which can be approached only in connection with all the forms and results of the intellectual and psychic development, point to the inseparable connection between physical culture and culture. That is why man as the creative producer of material and spiritual values and his all-round physical and intellectual development are the very centre of the science specializing in physical culture (the science of sport).

SPHERE OF ACTIVITY OF THE SCIENCE OF SPORT AND REVIEW OF THE STRUCTURE

The science of sport has already gathered quite a substantial amount of knowledge. But one could not yet state that we have already sufficient experience and can master the laws governing this many-sided social process and which are the basis of the appearance of new biological capacities of performance. Establishment of order as regards knowledge, systematizing of experiences, determination of the mutual relation between the various branches and of the entire system of the science of sport have therefore become a necessity in order to understand in a scientific way the biological and social function of physical culture, the important role it plays in the cultural life with its complex radiation and influence. In this sense the following explanations are to help to answer these questions. The starting point is the fact that physical culture and sport are a social process which in a purposeful and systematic way brings about the perfection of the physical qualities and efficiency of people, as an integral part of the rising cultural level of society. Employed in a conscious way they make their contribution to turn man into a creative producer of material and spiritual values. The object on which the science of sport should concentrate could therefore be defined in the following way: the science of sport examines the biological and social laws existing in the sphere of physical perfection of man as a psychophysical unit in the process of development, it reveals the basic features and causal connections of these processes, it examines them in practical social life and presents them in the form of conceptions, categories and theories.

"Physical perfection" signifies the process of all social efforts, the purpose of which is achievement of physical perfection. In this connection the term "physical perfection" [11] means a system of experiences of the biological and social development of social norms of health and physical efficiency that are worth to aspire to and in this sense it is a concrete historical category.

The science of sport is a type of science that has many various layers and is of a most complex nature; its object matter makes it necessary to give up the so far obliging division lines and to adopt the principle of units of science. In such a way it will be possible to provide proof of the independence of the science of sport as well as of its connections with kindred or principal branches of science.

Already a rough survey of the various branches of science that deal with the social process of physical perfection, reveals their great variety and complexity. This is knowledge gained in the following fields:

Philosophy and philosophical sciences. Dialectical materialism, natural, society and cognitive theory (Erkenntnistheorie), logics, aesthetics, ethics.

Social sciences. Sociology, history, pedagogics, psychology, political economy, law, culture, art.

Natural sciences. Medicine (including anatomy, physiology, social hygiene), biology (anthropology), physics, chemistry, mathematics.

All these sciences teach the most fundamental knowledge, but often they also provide detailed knowledge regarding the physical efficiency of man. However, this aspect is not the central item of these sciences, though it would certainly be a good thing and would be fully justified to pay more attention to this. Putting things together, generalizations, concrete application and exploring of the general processes of physical perfection exclusively from the point of view of sport is, after all the task of the science of sport. Research and teaching (on the university level) led to the taking shape of special scientific branches of the science of sport, which taken all together form the system of the science of sport [7, 20].

The process of the differentiation and integration of the sciences, which is still in the stage of formation, will therefore, out of necessity, also in the science of sport lead to new fields of work, to divisions and the establishment of certain profiles. Therefore, scientific and theoretical dissertations, in the form of a prognosis as well as those related to existing facts, will become more important for the science of sport, in order to be able to recognize in time trends of development and to draw from this the proper structural conclusions, also regarding personnel. One of the branches of science that shows very rapid development recently is Marxist sociology and we should examine what the results of this are.

SPORTS SOCIOLOGICAL RESEARCH—A NECESSARY AND TOPICAL TASK

As regards works in the field of the history of culture, Mr. Wohl and Mr. Trogsch [24, 22] deal above all with the development of physical culture and its forms of organization, in dependence on the socioeconomic class relations. They emphasized the social or rather political aspects regarding the efficacy of and the aims set in the past for the large associations of physical culture and certain individual personalities as well, and in such a way they gave a fundamentally new, historical and materialistic evaluation of the historical development of physical culture. However, this does not yet cover all the laws of a social nature existing in a concrete, historical formation of society. It suffices to point to the fact that side by side with the history of physical culture, inclusive historical research, one needs a discipline which would examine the social problems of physical culture together with all the interrelations with other social phenomena in the past as well as in our times.

One should consider this as the starting point for research in the field of sports sociology and such research embraces the historical, logical as well as empirical approach.

The fact that the social sciences develop more and more into sciences directing all social processes and that in such a way the habit to stick to once accepted laws, has been overcome, and the fact that the various parts of the social structure as a whole as well as the interrelations of the social associations and groups have to be approached on the basis of the various separate scientific findings—has made it clear, precisely in the field of the science of sport, how important the development of philosophical disciplines is, such as the theory of physical culture and also of the corresponding sociological disciplines, such as sports sociology. This task can be solved only through collective work, because despite all the division lines and differentiation of purposes, there nevertheless exists in the case of the various separate disciplines an overlapping due to the complexity of the social domain.

This becomes already obvious when decisions are made as to the objects to be dealt with and the tasks to be tackled (and all the specialists are unanimous as to that).

Braunreuther was absolutely right when he declared that "the exploration of the problems of the life of society cannot be squeezed into the narrow school frames of traditional disciplines" [1]. The same is true as regards research connected with the social problems of physical culture and shows at the same time how important it is to embark upon the social questions related to physical culture, in order to obtain knowledge and learn about the law governing this field, which would make it possible to direct this social field in a scientific way and to draw the proper conclusions.

SOCIAL RESEARCH AND THE SOCIOLOGICAL ASPECT

The manifold social processes in the sphere of physical culture are the expression of the efficacy of the general rules of social development as well as of the existence of specific laws. These are above all: the effectiveness of material and ideological factors to win over people to indulge in regular sports activity, the development of an attitude where sports activity is a need in life, where it serves to protect health and improve the efficiency of people in all spheres of life as well as the effectiveness of educational, moral and aesthetic factors in the many-sided social process of sports and cultural activity.

Regional research, the collection of objective values of the various sides of these complex processes are the general components of this Marxist social research. F. Trogsch gave in 1962 a most instructive review about their application in the field of physical culture and sport dealing simultaneously also with methodological basic problems [21].

The final results of the social research serve Marxist sociology as the material for generalizations, for the exploration of general and special laws ruling social life. Concrete social research is only in that case of any deeper scientific significance, if it is combined with this sociological aspect, with the sense of possible and necessary generalization. Thus it can, as a branch of science, make its contribution to the discovery of universally valid laws of society, or can provide concrete proof of the efficacy of these laws in that field of social life which is the subject of this branch of science. Several disciplines of the science of sport conduct research whose purpose is the discovery of the special laws of social processes in the field of physical culture. Concrete social research is conducted by teachers and psychologists in the sphere of school, mass and top-level sports; the entire sport literature is marked, like with a red thread by philosophical and sociological questions. It is getting evident everywhere, that there arise new aspects and connections and that we are witnessing the process of a scientific approach to and penetration of physical culture as a whole, with emphasis on the interrelation of all its various parts. But we should not overlook the danger caused by such a deep penetration, namely that one may forget about the connections with the fundamental and general laws.

And this precisely is the task facing sports sociology, which bases itself on the achievements of general sociology, and examines the specific laws governing physical culture as a whole and its relation to other social phenomena. Inside the scientific system of physical culture it develops into an independent discipline, just like the history of physical culture, sports pedagogics and sports psychology.

This is in accordance with the growing process of differentiation and integration in science as a whole and makes it possible for Marxist social sciences to examine the concrete social processes of physical culture in detail, as well as to make sociological generalizations, needed for a scientifically founded guidance and direction.

THE TASKS AND OBJECTIVES OF SPORTS SOCIOLOGY

Dependence, relationship, interrelations and mutual influence of physical culture in regard to other large spheres of society, such as economy, politics, culture and science, exert a stronger influence than ever before in the practical field of social management. One objective consequence of these problems embracing society as a whole, finds its expression in socialist conditions in the purposeful way of shaping the science of sport as a relatively independent system of science. Since physical culture and sport, according to their nature, are an expression of human life and in this sense an integral part of the mode of life, they are bound to be also an expression of the entire social cooperation—which according to Braunreuther and Steiner should be understood as cooperation and coexistence of a large number of different people with a great variety of presuppositions and functions and which effect all spheres of social life [2]. To the forms of expression of this type belongs the fact that people with different traits and features (age, sex, experience gained in life, professional qualifications, education, family and living conditions, personal interest) unite in sport groups and clubs jointly to practice sport. They meet in their work establishments, the area where they live, in their

spare time in the evenings, on Sundays and during their holidays to indulge in sports activity, to participate in contests, to observe rules, to travel and to establish new relations between people, that often are of long duration.

In such a way could be established many most instructive interrelations, which not only exert their influence on the social relations in general, but also exert a quite clearly visible influence on the personal course of life and the attitude of the individual towards society. Inside the organized sports movement there exist attitudes, typical of the various groups, which stem from the already mentioned characteristic features as well as from the character of the specific sports branch. These social processes provide the objective justifications for the necessity of the formation and relative independence of sports sociology as a scientific discipline within the framework of the science of sport.

CHARACTERIZATION OF THE OBJECTIVES OF SPORTS SOCIOLOGY

We do not consider it useful to continue the controversy conducted inside the bourgeois sociological trends, whether the so-called "Bindestrichsoziologien" (hyphenated sociologies) have any sense or not. The objectively existing social problems of sports have themselves given the answer to it. If one would try not to recognize them or to pay any attention to them this would mean to close one's eyes to the real processes taking place inside society, processes embracing today millions of people. Knowledge, theories and laws regarding the function of physical culture in society, its role in personal life and inside groups, clubs and social units, are not the outcome of the construction and schematic combination of separate facts, but can be obtained only with the help of research of the entire great variety of empirical facts and the reality of social interrelations. One of the tasks of research in the field of sports sociology is to reveal the inner mechanism of the socially-determined behaviour of people in the process of physical culture (in its various fields). Only in close and direct contact with the requirements of the entire social practice is it possible to examine the concrete processes of physical culture as a social phenomenon and to make the proper generalizations.

The range of social questions that arise is very broad in such a social field as physical culture and sport. It embraces such personally determined motives as proof of efficiency, prestige, confirmation of one's own value and glory to basic problems of a socio-political nature, such as furtherance of health by means of regular practicing of sport, questions connected with education and upbringing, top-class achievements in sport as the expression of the level of development of the entire society—sport as a political factor in the competition and contest of different social systems. Not all the above-mentioned factors can be directly related to socio-economic foundations, though we actually are aware of the fact that they are the highest authority and the decisive element for the social behaviour of society as a whole. A remarkably important role in sport is played by psychological stimulae and experiences. Sports sociology will in such a way with the help of socio-psychological knowledge be able to contribute substantially to the discovery of social laws governing the behaviour of individuals, teams and sports groups of the various branches. Questions from the fields of sports sociology and socio-psychological ones are closely interrelated. Other disciplines of the science of sport, such as sports pedagogics (dealing among others with the specific aspect of training and educating various age-groups of people who practice sport) and the theory of physical education (the pedagogical and methodological process of physical perfection in regard to various age-groups) as well as theory and methodology of sport in various, relatively independent spheres (school, top-class performance in sport, sport for adults), finally the history of physical culture, the science of organization and also sports medicine examine certain aspects of the entire social process of physical culture and supply answers to some quite detailed questions. Only the thorough evaluation of such detailed knowledge resulting from large-scale social research conducted in many individual disciplines of the science of sport permits the establishment of general trends and laws governing physical culture as a whole. Generalizations needed to direct the entire process have to be based on social detailed research and also on sociological complex research.

Special social research is to proceed side by side with general and complex sociological fundamental research. This principle should also be binding in connection with the various disciplines of the science of sport which conduct social research and consider sports sociology as a relatively independent discipline of science.

From this point of view and summing up what was said above we want to add a definition of the subject of sports sociology:

Sports sociology examines the dialectics of general and specific social development in the field of physical culture and sport, the interrelations to other social phenomena, the behaviour of people, influenced by physical culture and sport, people who belong to organized sports associations and groups and who individually and regularly indulge in sports activity; it examines the concrete behaviour of social groups and units in their attitude towards physical culture and sport, in order to discover in such a way laws which play their role in determining the social general behaviour of people under relevant social conditions in the process of their development.

By gathering comprehensive empirical material and with the help of the proper generalizations conditions are created for the social direction of all the processes of physical culture.

This definition is to make it possible to find the general trend for research work and to select and arrange the proper subject for investigation. Taking into consideration the present stage of development of sports sociology this can only serve as a means for orientation. However, that has always been the rule in the history of science, because: generally accepted definitions of the subject matter of a discipline make their appearance only after all-round research of a most general character has already taken place and even in this case it is constantly necessary to look for the proper profile.

It seems that for our specialized scientific orientations, on the basis of the temporary definition, the aspects for concrete sociological research mentioned by Braunreuther, are most purposeful and significant:

1. Without the need to yield hastily to generalizations, there should, nevertheless, be undertaken any kind of sociological research in practical life and any theoretical

discussion in this connection, in order to discover the laws and their effect.

2. Social relations ultimately determined by political and economic factors, have to be examined from the point of view of behaviour and the connections of modes of behaviour of people.

3. Taken into consideration should be socio-relevant states and modes of behaviour, for which categories have to be established in the case of each concrete investigation.

4. Attempts should be made to find the possibilities, implicit in the existing social conditions and modes of behaviour, to turn them into explicit ones, and, if possible to develop them in a planned way, sometimes in variants.

5. Existing conditions and behaviour are not to be described as something static, but have to be understood in their entire dynamic aspect, taking into consideration the laws determining this dynamic aspect [1].

MODE OF PROCEDURE OF SPORTS SOCIOLOGICAL RESEARCH

The practical application of these aspects requires at the same time the drawing of clear outlines in the organizational scientific manner of carrying out the intention to conduct sociological research. There actually exist two fundamental starting points which have to be taken into consideration, first: the precise theoretical definition of the aim to be pursued (taken from sociological theory), and second: the exact definition of the methodological and technological manner in which it is to be carried out (manner of selection, choice of method, system of evaluation).

On the basis of experiences gained during the carrying out of a representative, complex, territorial survey, conducted in the spring of 1965, according to the sample method, about the role of physical education in connection with leisure persuits of the citizens of the German Democratic Republic [3, 6], the following methods of work should be observed:

First of all there should be laid down a central, complex or guiding subject for research stemming from the requirements of social practical life. This is to be succeeded by a clearly defined conception for research and general outlines of the undertaking—taking its starting point from the historical

laws and concrete social purposes in the given social field. This includes a concrete determination of the aim of the research, most precise hypotheses and statements in the form of theses, destined for the programming of the general analysis (a programme of questions, trends and types of the elaborations of the subject matter for research).

Though no "encyclopaedia-like completeness" is required, because constantly new problems make their appearance and there take place enlargements and a deepening of the problems (greater precision), much depends on the most thorough preparation of the first fundamental conception (scope, media, forces). The latter is also to some extent a measure for the obtained degree of theoretical and ideological clarity in a research collective. Side by side with the conception there must be prepared as well a plan regarding organization and instructions for the practical implementation (training of assistants, sphere of responsibility, system of control, long-term development plan, detailed organizational problems, etc.). This has to be accompanied by the preparation of a bibliographic review (knowledge of the state of development in the international field), decision regarding proceedings according to the sample method, the method (questionnaire, interview, analysis of documents, etc.).

Proceedings according to the sample method and the methods to be adopted for research (starting point and the order in which one proceeds) have to be prepared with special attention, taking into consideration data obtained later and the general evaluation (monographs, individual reviews and general reviews), because this is of decisive significance for the achievement of the ultimate aim.

Already this short review points to the fact that fundamental and purposeful research in the field of sports sociology can only be a success if one adheres to the principle of collective work and if groups are set up of specialized research workers from the various disciplines, such as representatives of philosophical and theoretical branches, from psychology—if possible social psychology—from the sphere of mathematical statistics, the science of organization, social hygiene and finally the proper specialists, namely, representatives of sports sociology, as far as they have specialized in this field of education or have developed, coming from various disciplines.

REFERENCES

1. Braunreuther, K., *Die marxistische Soziologie und die Pädagogen* (Marxist Sociology and Pedagogues). In "Pädagogik," Berlin 19 (1964) 2.
2. Braunreuther, K. and Steiner,H., *Soziologische Probleme der sozialistischen Wissenschaftsführung* (Sociological Problems of the Socialist Economy). In: "Wirtschaftswissenschaft" Berlin (1964) 10.
3. Buggel, E., *Über eine repräsentative komplexterritoriale Stichprobenerhebung in der DDR für den Bereich der Körperkultur* (A Representative, Complex, Territorial Survey on the Basis of the Sample Method in the G.D.R. in the Field of Physical Culture). In "Theorie und Praxis der Körperkultur", Berlin 14 (1965) 4.
4. Buggel, E. and others, *Sport und Touristik im Urlaub an der Ostsee und im Mittelgebirge —Methoden und Ergebnisse einer Untersuchung im Juli 1963 in Heringsdorf und Friedrichroda* (Sport and Tourism During the Holidays at the Baltic Sea and in the Mountains—Methods and Results of a Survey Conducted in July 1963 in Heringsdorf and Friedrichroda). In "Wiss. Zeitschrift der DHfK". Leipzig 6 (1964) 2.
5. Erbach, G., *Internationaler Kongreß der Sportwissenschaften in Tokio vom 3-8.10.1964.* (International Congress of the Sciences of Sport in Tokyo, Oct. 3-8.10.1964). In "Theorie und Praxis der Körperkultur". Berlin 14 (1965) 3.
6. Erbach, G., *Über die Bedeutung der wissenschaftlichen Perspektivplanung auf dem Gebiet der Körperkultur, unter Berücksichtigung sportsoziologischer Grundlagenforschung* (The Significance of Long-term Development Planning in the Field of Physical Culture, from the Point of View of Research on Sports Sociological Foundations). In "Theorie und Praxis der Körperkultur". Berlin 14 (1965) 4.
7. Erbach G., *Gedanken zur Einordnung der Theorie der Körperkultur als Lehr- und Forschungsdisziplin in das System der Sportwissenschaft* (Ideas Regarding Inclusion of the Theory of Physical Culture As One of the Branches and Research Fields of the System of the Science of Sport). In "Theorie und Praxis der Körperkultur". Berlin. September 1964. Sonderheft: Über philosophische und soziologische Probleme der Körperkultur.
8. Florl, R., *Volkssport im soziolistischen Dorf. Versuch einer komplex-territorialen Analyse als Beitrag zur Leistungtätigkeit sportlicher Führungsorgane, dargestellt am Beispiel einer Untersuchung in der Landgemeinde Kyhna* (Sport in a Socialist Village. Attempt to Give a Complex, Territorial Analysis as a Contribution to the Work of Leading Sports Bodies, Presented With the Help of a Survey Conducted in a Rural Community in Kyhma). Dissertation an der DHfK Leipzig, 1964.
9. Gras, F., *Die Beziehungen zwischen dem Belastungsverlauf bei landwirtschaftlichen Arbeiten und der Gestaltung einer regelmäßigen sportlich-kulturellen Betätigung für die Beschäftigten in der sozialistischen Landwirtschaft—dargestellt am Beispiel der Gemeinde Machern, Krs. Wurzen* (Interrelations Between the Burden of Agricultural Labour and the Taking Shape of a Regular Sports and Cultural Activity for People Employed in Socialist Agriculture. Example: Community Machern).
10. John, E., *Der wissenschaftliche Kulturbegriff* (The Scientific Conception of Culture). In "Deutsche Zeitschrift für Philosophie". Berlin 6 (1958) 4.
11. Nowikow, A. D., *Über das Problem der Kategorien der körperlichen Erziehung— "Körperliche Entwicklung", "Körperliche Erziehung", "Körperliche Vollkommenheit"— und ihre wechselseitige Beziehung* (The Problem of Categories of Physical Education— "Physical Development", "Physical Education", "Physical Perfection"—and their Interrelations). In "Theorie und Praxis d. Körperkultur". Berlin, Sonderheft 1964.
12. Röblitz, G., *Freizeitnutzung und sportliche Betätigung der lernenden Jugend. Versuch einer pädagogischen Grundlegung* (Leisure Pursuits and Sports Activity of Studying Youth). Habilschrift an der DHfK. Leipzig, 1964.
13. Schnürpel, H., *Analyse dermateriell-technischen Bedingungen für Körperkultur und Sport im Bezirk Leipzig 1962, unter besonderer Berücksichtigung von Problemen der komplexterritorialen Perspektivplanung* (Analysis of the Material and Technical Conditions for Physical Culture and Sport in the Region of Leipzig). Dissertation an der DHfK. Leipzig, 1964.
14. Schnürpel, H., *Zu einigen volkswirtschaftlichen Aspekten der Materiell-technischen Bedingungen für Körperkultur und Sport* (Some Aspects of the Material and Technical Conditions for Physical Culture and Sport from the Point of View of the National Economy). In "Theorie und Praxis der Körperkultur". Berlin 14 (1965) 4.
15. Schulz, R., *Über Wesen und Methoden wissenschaftlicher Soziologie* (The Nature and Methods of Scientific Sociology). In "Theorie und Praxis der Körperkultur". Berlin 10 (1961) 2.
16. Schwidtmann, H. and Siegér, W., *Wissenschaftlich-technische Revolution und sozialistische Körperkultur* (Scientific and Technical Revolution and Socialist Physical Culture). In Einheit. Berlin 19 (1964) 12.
17. Sieger, W., *Zur wissenschaftlichen Planung und Leitung im Bereich der Körperkultur* (Scientific Planning and Direction of Physical Culture). In "Theorie und Praxis der Körperkultur". Berlin 13 (1964) 4.

18. Sonderheft der Zeitschrift "Theorie und Praxis der Körperkultur". Berlin, September 1964 (hrsg. von G. Erbach). *Über philosophische und soziologische Probleme der Körperkultur* (Philosophical and Sociological Problems of Physical Culture).

19. Stajkov, Z., *Sektion der Sportsoziologie* (Section of Sports Sociology). In "Vupr. fizic. kult." Sofija 9 (1964) 5.

20. Stranai, K., *Über die Notwendigkeit, die Theorie der Körpererziehung als selbständige wissenschaftliche Fachdisziplin auszubilden* (The Necessity to Shape the Theory of Physical Culture into an Independent Specialized Discipline). In "Theorie und Praxis der Körperkultur". Berlin 11 (1963) 9.

21. Trogsch, F., *Marxistische Sozialforschung auf dem Gebiet von Körperkultur und Sport* (Marxist Social Research in the Field of Physical Culture and Sport). In Wissenschaftl. Zeitschrift der DHfK. Leipzig 4 (1962) 2.

22. Trogsch, F., *Körperübungen als menschliche Lebensäußerung und kultureller Entwicklungsfaktor* (Physical Exercises as an Expression of Life and Factor of Cultural Development). In "Deutsche Zeitschrift für Philosophie". Berlin 12 (1964) 8.

23. Trogsch, F., *Entwicklungsdeterminanten und -tendenzen im Bereich von Körperkultur und Sport* (Determinants and Trends of Development in the field of Physical Culture and Sport). In "Theorie und Praxis der Körperkultur" 14 (1965) 8.

24. Wohl, A., *Die gesellschaftlich-historischen Grundlagen des bürgerlichen Sports* (The Socio-Historical Foundations of Bourgeois Sport). In Wiss. Zeitschrifft der DHfK 6 (1964) 1.

52. The function of sport in human relations*

Michel Bouet

France

Sport is one of the factors which bring people together. Sportsmen, either as partners or rivals, establish contacts between themselves and stay together thanks to the various opportunities offered by sport. Human relations are an organic characteristic feature of sport to such an extent that it seems queer if somebody practises sport alone. This practice is always very rare, anyway. Moreover, in numerous domains of sport it is out of the question as they are based on the principle of rivalry.

Although one praises sporting comradeship and the spirit of mutual assistance, as well as the union binding "true colleagues," competition is one of the inseparable attributes of sport. The function of sport plays the role of a lasting factor, is very widely popularized and is of basic importance, even though this importance is not emphasized in so many words as the aim of sport. What, however, would be left of sport if it were deprived of that characteristic of community and friendship?

Investigations carried out by us concerning the motives for the practice of sport have shown that many people look through sport for contacts with other humans.[1] Many persons among those investigated say that while at first they were not interested in the acquisition of colleagues, yet later, after having chosen a concrete sport field, they began to be directly interested in it. They maintain their ties with those colleagues even when they no longer practice sport actively.

The following statement made by one of the polled gives a particularly apt picture of this phenomenon: "For myself sport is above all play thanks to which I can always have friends." Such a real sportsmen as Roger Bannister expressed this in the following manner: "One wants to find in sport the comradeship of brotherly souls. Friendship established in the fire of sporting competition is exceptionally durable."

Frequently it is precisely through a colleague that one finds one's way into a sporting group. We know of the case of a footballer who had changed his club (misunderstandings with the management) but continued to pay visits to it, for he felt the need of contact with his "chums," comrades of long years of sporting competition.

Human relations in which sport abounds are of many kinds. We have in mind above all team competitions. "Even the very size of the teams alone facilitate mutual adjustment and brotherhood"—points out J. Prevost. The establishment of closer human ties is also favoured by the circumstance that the members of a team perform solidarily different functions, every one of them being responsible for the rest. We find the same nature of relations in a group of mountain climbers protecting mutually one another and in a relay team. The majority of sport disciplines puts the team to trial (team classification of victories, for example in fencing). The attitude towards a rival in sport is not antagonistic in character, but is a specific form of cooperation. To be a partner in a tennis match or in a race is frequently the manifestation of friendship linking two people. This does not prevent a

*From International Review of Sport Sociology, Vol. 1, p. 137, 1966, Committee of Sport Sociology of The International Council of Sport and Physical Education (UNESCO).
[1]One of the questions in the poll ran: "When you began to practice sport did you want to end your isolation and find colleagues?" Out of 294 sportsmen 56% answered "yes" and 40% "no."

tennis match or a race from having the character of hard-fought contest. A competitor who has a "personal" interest within the team not only disturbs the harmony in the team but violates the very spirit of sport.

Numerous rites customary in sport reflect the weight of human relations in this field, for example the handshake between team captains, exchange of shirts and badges between rivals, etc.

Besides the relations between sportsmen themselves which are dictated by the requirements of their sport discipline, it is also necessary to examine other forms of human relations in sport. They are relations with the coach or the team manager, men who are not only teachers but also guides, friends, trustees; the relations linking managers and coaches with competitors are for the latter a form of personal support, strongly differing from the impersonal prompting from the crowd.

Human relations among sportsmen are lively manifested in the clubs, in training camps where personal sympathies are established and where the discovery of unfamiliar comrades becomes a source of emotional experience. The stay in an Olympic Village every four years is such an opportunity for a chosen few. Sport relations have many marks of distinction: the establishment of relations between sportsmen is rather easy, they have a sort of straightforwardness in them. It is generally a simple matter in most sport disciplines to start calling each other by his or her Christian name. The seeming coarseness covers not infrequently an emotional character, and outbursts of joy or despair are also not infrequent. The effort required for the practice of sport, and the suffering which is sometimes connected with it, introduces an accent of spontaneous compassion. Let us point out that sport relations reveal the personal value of a man, his personality and freedom. The best side of an individual comes frequently out in these relations.

How to explain the fact that human relations in sport are marked by such a depth and that sport becomes a factor of variegated relations between people?

It would seem that the basic role played in sport by corporality brings together particularly people practising physical exercises. It creates a plane of equality between people, strengthens the realization of existence "for somebody" and "together with somebody." A physical exercise cuts down the "physical distance." Humans no longer preen themselves and they lose their false shame. A certain straightforwardness, certain intimacy, is being born. In many fields of sport where risk exists people are joined together by common danger. This constitutes a factor which binds people more strongly in sporting life.

Sport offers a man the possibility of revealing himself in things he likes, which has a disinterested character, offers a man the possibility of liberating himself, facilitates a more natural way of life. This is why sportsmen are more frank in their coexistence with their fellows, more communicative, more given to confidences.

The sporting value is measured by the exploit, with the rejection of differences which do not count in a given case, such as, for example, class differences or differences in culture. Many barriers impeding human relations disappear in sport. Sport constitutes also a factor conducive to the breaking through the tendency of human nature for solitude, for this side of human nature disappears to a certain extent during competition.

Here is a statement by one of the persons participating in our poll, which describes very aptly the role sport can play in the establishment of closer relations between humans:

"I was not particularly interested in colleagues. They came themselves (to a certain extent). Common sufferings (during mountain climbing expeditions, for example), experienced in silence for many long hours tie people up more strongly than long conversations, for the true value of a friend is revealed in an obvious manner. And as soon as he appears in your eyes as a rather exceptional man, you begin to want to be friends with him."

And finally, if it is true that all factors conducive to human relations are to be found in sport, these relations become at the same time stronger because of the requirement of comradeship which is inseparable from sport. "To be a sportsman assumes after all the necessity of good comradeship," said one of the participants in our poll, not unreasonably.

Sport develops human relations the need of which it feels itself. These relations constitute, therefore, a function of sport which it fulfils in its own interest, but also in the wider social interest. This function creates a certain style which reveals even a tendency to penetrate into other fields of life. This style is organically marked by such traits as simplicity, straightforwardness, mutual respect, sincerity.

53. Physical education and leisure*

V. Artemov

Union of Soviet Socialist Republics

Sociological treatment of physical education is becoming ever more indispensable. A large number of problems is closely connected with the place of physical education in the development of the society, with its interconnections with other social phenomena.

There are many roads in research into the sociological aspect of physical education. Let us dwell on some of them.

The working people in a socialist society have ever more leisure at their disposal. They utilize it in a more or less rational way. The quantity of leisure and the degree of its rational utilization depends on many factors, of both social and individual nature. On the initiative of the Labour Research Institute (Moscow) and the Institute of Economy and Organization of Industrial Production (Nowossibirsk), the Soviet Union resumed in 1958 research into time budget which had been started and developed as far back as the nineteen twenties and the beginning of nineteen thirties. Several important investigations were made into problems of the utilization of the entire time reserve, as well as into factors influencing the distribution of time. The investigations were carried out in a number of Siberian regions (in the Krasnoyarsk Territory under G. A. Prudensky, in Omsk under Z. L. Zhelezovskaya, in Irkutsk under Y. P. Tumanov). The analysis of the materials obtained during these investigations, as well as their comparison with the results of research conducted at other times in other places permits the drawing of a number of conclusions pertaining to the practice of sport. A study of the time budget may show what proportion of people participates in sport, how much time is devoted to this, what factors affect the participation in sport, etc.

The element of physical activity during leisure is sometimes underestimated. It is considered that if a man who does no manual work devotes much time to self-tuition, cinema, theatre, etc., then his time budget is shaped very rationally. While in fact this budget has very considerable minuses which affect health and fitness for work, which affect the results of a man's work. An examination of graduates of an evening school showed that sport is a favorite leisure occupation of manual workers. What is still more interesting is the fact that the harder a young man is working the more time does he devote to sport. Girls are apparently overburdened by manual work and practice sport less willingly. We do not say that this phenomenon appears everywhere. But even this fact alone faces us with a number of problems: While the division into mental and manual work is maintained even during leisure, what must one do to divide the distribution of the load of physical effort more uniformly between manual and brain workers in their own interests? Does not leisure serve today by any chance first of all for preparing oneself for professional work? To what extent is leisure conducive to an all-round development of personality? One cannot speak after all of an all-round development if one of its important elements, the physical development, is, to put it mildly, inadequate.

Of very great importance is the investi-

*From International Review of Sport Sociology, Vol. 1, 1966, Committee of Sport Sociology of The International Council of Sport and Physical Education (UNESCO).

gation into the sequence of occupations in the course of a day, a week, a month. A thorough analysis of the sequence of occupations, as well as the determination of the entire quantity of physical occupations in the course of a day and a week (taking into account all kinds of occupations) will be an essential contribution to the working out of an optimum system of work and rest. The investigation into the sequence of occupations is also important for the determination of the norms and forms of physical culture in different kinds of work. The problem involves also the question of changed activities within the time framework of a day or a week.

This is why one of the most important directions in the research on physical education is the investigation into the volume of time devoted to sport and other healthy occupations within the framework of a daily or weekly time budget, depending on various objective factors. Such an investigation would help to determine the optimum system of work and rest, particularly the most effective volume of time for the practice of sport for various groups of men.

The time used for sport has considerably lengthened in recent years, as may be seen in the results of time budget investigations. The share of time devoted to sport in the overall volume of leisure was increasing much faster than the leisure itself. The average length of time devoted to sport by Krasnoyarsk workers increased in 1963 one and a half times for men and ten times for women in comparison to 1959, and amounted to 2.66 and 0.70 hours per week respectively. The overall volume of leisure during that time increased by 36%.

If we take into account the spending of time for physical education, sport, rest and pastimes and calculate in it the share of active forms (walks, physical exercises, practice of sport, etc.), we note that it increased during 6 working days from 14% to 26.4% for men and from 17.9% to 18.9% for women. On days off it increased from 30% to 36.5% and from 21.7% to 33.2% respectively. We note an interesting symptom here: while for men the increase in the amount of time spent on active rest, on sport, takes place on working days, for women it increases on free days. This shows that free days are used by women ever more frequently for rest. Its

activeness, that it is to say also its effectiveness, increases. This is due most probably to the fact that a certain part of household chores executed before on free days decreases at present and is performed on working days. With the decrease of the proportion of rest and recreation during leisure (particularly as regards women) the overall activeness of leisure has increased. This is an important phenomenon characterizing the process of an ever more rational utilization of leisure.

According to data obtained by Z. L. Zhelezovskaya (Omsk), in the years 1960—1962 the time for occupations devoted to physical education and sport increased by 36% for men and doubled for women, while the overall leisure increased by 8% and 16% respectively. Worth noting is the fact that apart from the time for educating and bringing up children, the increase in the time devoted to physical education is highest in the entire leisure budget, particularly for women. The data quoted below indicate that active rest has increased and that ever better conditions are being created for strengthening and preserving health.

The Central Statistical Office of the Russian Socialist Federative Republic carried out in the summer of 1963 an investigation of leisure budgets in the family time budgets in the regions of Gorky, Rostov, Sverdlovsk and Ivanovsk showed that morning gymnastic exercises are practised by 6.5% of men and 1.7% of women, individual sport is practised by 8.3% of men and 1% of women, section training is performed by 0.3% of men and 0.13% of women (the percentages were calculated from the overall number of persons investigated; the time spending in each family was registered during a single day only). The highest proportion of workers practising sport was found in the Sverdlovsk region. The average amount of time for morning exercises amounted to 13.2 minutes for men and 11.8 minutes for women, while the average amount of time for individual sport practice amounted to 138 and 202 minutes respectively.

A survey of various age groups of workers has shown that the highest number of persons practising active sport is found in the group below 24 years: morning exercises are practised by 15.2% and individual sport by 21.6%. The lowest number of persons was found in the group between 35 and 49 years: 4.1% and 3.6% respectively. If we arrange the groups in the order of the proportion of persons practising morning exercises, the second place goes to the group between 50 and 59 years and the third place to the group between 25 and 34 years. A number of other data indicates that the amount of time devoted to sport decreases tremendously with age, although in principle the change should really affect the type of performance (intensive training should be replaced by occupations preserving fitness). Thus middle-aged workers are least engaged in sport occupations. This could be explained psychologically that youth seems to be passing already, while old age does not give any sign of itself. But it is precisely at this age that it is decided how a man will feel in 10 or 15 years' time, on what example will his children be brought up. After all, the way of life of the parents, their attitude towards the practice of sport, have frequently a decisive influence on their children.

Interesting results were obtained from a comparison of two groups of male workers from Krasnoyarsk. Group A included workers who practised as a minimum morning exercises or two—three times a week individual sport of trained in sections. Group B included the rest. The average budgets were calculated according to groups A and B. The average budgets were compared for two reasons. The comparison was to explain first of all at what cost can group A devote more time to sport. Secondly, it was to determine the mutual relation of the two groups as regards their leisure, which after all does characterize in some way or another a certain personality. The comparison of the characteristics determining the general structure of time budget revealed that a significant difference in groups depends on the family situation (group A contained 37% of unmarried men, group B only 13.5%). Since the difference in per capita incomes and housing conditions was very small, and in age also not great, it may be stated that the existence of one's own family is an important, if not the most important, factor affecting participation in sport occupations.

Group A has 4.5 hours of leisure per week more. This difference results above all from the amount of time devoted to household chores (3.74 hours). On weekdays the difference in the load of household chores (2.76 hours) proved almost equal to the difference between these two groups pertaining to leisure (2.65 hours).

The expense of leisure is affected also by age, education, studies, etc. Group A is younger. It contains 36.8% of workers aged 21—25 years, while the corresponding figure in group B is 17.1%. Group A has 21.1% of workers aged over 30, while group B has 30.9% of them. The level on education is higher in group A (29% have higher or secondary education, while the same figure for group B is 26%.

As regards educational schemes of various sorts, the participation in both groups is more or less equal. More members of group

The weekly time budget (in hours)

Basic elements of time budget	6 working days		Free day	
	Group A	Group B	Group A	Group B
Working time and time connected with work (commuting, etc.)	52.94	53.83	0.01	0.21
Household chores	8.2	10.96	2.33	3.31
Time for physiological needs—	52.43	51.43	9.92	10.58
including sleep	43.86	43.6	8.08	8.84
Free time including:				
Study and self-tuition	10.61	11.36	2.29	2.34
Social activity	1.67	1.9	0.06	0.21
Children's upbringing	1.4	1.45	0.49	0.51
Rest and pastimes	11.36	9.62	5.76	5.88
Creative and amateur work	0.61	0.74	0.44	0.19
Physical education and sport	4.15	0.73	2.51	0.53
Other forms of leisure spending	0.63	1.98	0.2	0.24
Total	144.00	144.00	24.00	24.00

A attend technical schools and institutes, while more members of group B attend ideological studies.

The leisure spending during the six weekdays is rather different in the two groups (see table). Particularly visible is the difference in the outlay of time for study and self-tuition, rest and pastimes. But the most important difference consists in the outlay of time for physical education and sport (3.42 hours).[1] This situation was brought about by the expansion of leisure. The comparison of the utilization of a day free from work gives a different result. Larger differences between groups may be noted here in two kinds of time outlay only: for creative and amateur work and for physical education and sport. The entire difference in the amount of leisure on a free day (1.84) is spent for sport occupations. This means that group A spends free days more actively, both physically and intellectually (creative work). Its rest is more effective, which is reflected in the length of sleep too. Staying within the limits of physiological norm the sleep length in group A is 0.76 hours shorter than in group B. The free day of group A is closer to the fulfillment of its fundamental function—to liquidate physical and psychic fatique after a week of work, to prepare the organism for new working load.

The calculation of the correlation coefficient proves that the relation between the amount of time for physical education and sport on the one hand, other categories of leisure (study, self-tuition, social activity, etc.) on the other is of little significance. Only in case of women may one note a barely visible relation with the time outlay for study. Significant, on the other hand, is the relation with the amount of time devoted to household chores and with the overall amount of leisure, both for men and women. The effect of household chores on the time budget consists both in the expenditure of a considerable amount of time for these chores (there is little or not time at all left for sport) and in physical fatigue which, together with the fatique due to professional

work, requires first of all rest and not physical exercises.

This shows that the family situation has considerable influence on the practice of sport. A cutting down of the time needed for household chores through the development of services, rationalization, mechanization and socialization of living conditions is the main source of an increase in the time which could be devoted to the practice of sport. Considerable possibilities are latent in the five-day working week. Time budget investigations conducted by L. S. Kolobov (Novossibirsk) showed that the overall amount of leisure in such a week increases. But most important is the fact that one of the free days is usually devoted to household chores, while the other day is devoted almost entirely to rest. In the case of a single free day, on the other hand, family-burdened women workers devote it as a rule to household work. The concentration and redistribution of leisure permits its more rational utilization.

A correlation analysis of the use of time shows also that the frequency of the practice of physical education and sport and the amount of time used for this purpose depend also to a considerable extent on factors which are not expressed directly in the time budget.

The investigation results indicate that engineers and technicians practice more morning exercises, while workers practice more sport and train in sections. It seems that morning exercises are to a greater extent an indicator of care for physical fitness than all the other remaining exercises. This is shown also to some extent by the fact that the proportion of people performing morning exercises in large cultural centres (Moscow, Sverdlovsk, Rostov) is higher than in the other regions of the country (according to data from time budget investigations). A greater regularity in exercises according to season is noted among engineers and technicians. In the period between winter and summer there is almost no difference between the categories of engineers and technicians. Among workers, on the other hand, this difference is quite considerable (according to materials of Y. P. Tumanov, Irkutsk). Our data have been obtained from investigations whose aim was to obtain average time budgets of the basic

---

[1]Time outlay for physical education and sport included time for morning exercises, training in sections and participation in competitions, hunting and fishing, ball playing, skiing and skating, etc. It is worth noting that only a few persons in group A had a high sport class.

categories of the population. These data are far from sufficient for the determination of indispensable norms of occupations in the field of physical culture for the various categories of the population. One must point out also that even if we succeeded in the determination of such norms, they would be to a great extent conventional. But work in this direction is indispensable and should be conducted by way of directional and more accurate complex investigations. The analysis of the problem of the social and particularly economic effectiveness of leisure is of tremendous importance in social planning. However, this problem is seldom taken up and is therefore not investigated properly. The effectiveness of leisure from the point of view of its utilization for physical exercises can be calculated with considerable accuracy.

The following investigation was carried out in a Novossibirsk factory: a list of sportsmen was drawn up in two departments (11.1% of the overall number of working departments). The losses of working time due to incapacity for work among sportsmen amounted in 1963 to 3.1% of the overall losses, that is were 3.6 times lower than the average. In 1963 sportsmen of one department (also 11.1% of the entire personnel of the department) accounted for 2.8% of absenteeism due to incapacity for work, while the number of working days lost amounted to 1.9%. In the first quarter of 1964 sportsmen of this department accounted for 2.4% of the total number of sickness cases, and for 0.9% of days lost due to incapacity for work. In the case of common colds the figures amounted to 3.3% and 2.4% respectively. It is also an interesting fact that the number of cases of unjustified absenteeism was three times lower among sportsmen. This shows that the loss of working time calculated in full days is approximately three times lower among sportsmen. Even if we asssme that the losses are not three but two times lower, we could surmise that with a maximum popularization of sport among workers the factory could increase its production by 0.5 million roubles and earmark 60,000 roubles out if its sickness allowance fund for other purposes. It is worthwhile to add in this connection that the cost of a tourist shelter for 100 persons amounts to 61,000 roubles. Physical culture

is also after all a very effective means of education. which in the final result is also reflected in the economic indices.

If, of course, all workers of the factory were attracted to the practice of occupations in the field of physical culture, it would obviously require an increase in funds (in 1963 the factory in question had spent over 21,000 roubles) to be used for wages for extra personnel, the purchase of sport equipment, the construction of sport facilities. The difficulty consists, therefore, in the selection of a variant of such a utilization of funds, which would enable the highest number of employees and members of their families to practice sport regularly.

Investigations concerning the incidence of diseases among persons practising physical exercises and not practising them, conducted in Leningrad (K. A. Maloletko), Sverdlovsk (I. P. Mokerov, K. G. Makhnutina, A. A. Rudayeva), Moscow (V. I. Zholdak) and Novossibirsk gave convincing results. The average quantitative disease incidence among persons practising sport is twice lower. And as regards the number of working days lost it is three times lower than among persons who do not practise sport. What does this mean? According to data of the N. A. Semashko Institute of the Organization and Protection of Health and the History of Medicine in Moscow every patient's visit to a polyclinic costs the state 60 kopeks, daily sickness allowance amounts on the average to 2 roubles 52 kopeks (data of the All-Soviet Trade Union Council), the treatment of influenza costs 19 roubles 44 kopeks ("Ogoniok", No. 8, 1963, p. 129, according to calculations made by A. M. Izutkin of Gorky), every day lost by a worker represents for the state the loss of 12 roubles in material losses, not counting the drop in ready production, and every industrial worker in the Soviet Union loses 13 days because of illness or injuries. This loss is tantamount to the stopping of the entire national industry for 13 days ("Economicheskaya Gazeta", No. 3, 1961). It is also necessary to take into account the losses in working time and material losses inflicted on the state in connection with premature retirement due to disability or illness. It becomes at once apparent what would mean even a fifty per cent reduction in the incidence of disease.

The investigations carried out indicate that the analysis of time budgets is one of the most rational methods for the determination of social, and particularly economic, effectiveness of physical culture. If we take daily, monthly and yearly time budgets and link them with a number of production indices, we shall be able to determine with a high degree of accuracy the degree of the effect of physical culture on the life span of production capacity (or the reduction of the loss of time due to illness or injuries, etc.). We shall be also able to determine the optimum utilization of the working time for the reduction of idleness caused by a worker), the labour productivity and the quality of production (thanks to a proper state of health, coordination, accuracy, economy and speed of movements).

During investigations into the time budgets of working people in the Krasnoyarsk Territory, the subjects themselves made proposals concerning the shortening of the irrational utilization of leisure and its better use. A part of the proposals pertained to physical culture. One of them suggested the expansion of the network of sports installations. A certain part pertained to the organization of local sections and interesting sport tournaments. Remarks were made concerning the serious shortage of sports equipment and trained cadres. It must be emphasized that all persons who drew marked attention to production gymnastics were over 36 years old.

We have a huge number of workers' towns and settlements built in recent years with no attention at all to needs of rational rest. What we need is a carefully worked out system of mass media connected with the organization of a rational active rest in industry, in science, in daily life, on free days and during holidays and leave. All this on the basis of a widest possible utilization of the natural factors of nature and their maximum combination with physical culture and tourism suitably organized for people of various sex, profession, age, etc. It is also indispensable to work out a system of complex research in the field of rest and physical culture. It is necessary to find an answer to the question of how to utilize best the expert knowledge and experience of leading sportsmen who no longer practise sport actively. Why does a man who systematically practises physical exercises over a period of 20 years (kindergarten, school, higher school) discontinue them later. How to improve the unsatisfactory situation with regard to playing fields in a tremendous majority of new residential districts. How to improve the standard of physical culture of the population and eliminate the negative effects of sport from the pedagogical point of view. These and a number of other questions require answers. They can be found only as the result of a serious sociological approach to physical culture as a social phenomenon.

54. Basic understanding for teaching the disadvantaged*

Allan C. Ornstein

Fordham University

This paper examines eight broad areas of deprivation that cause a boy or girl, through no fault of his own, to be disadvantaged: self-deprivation, social, environmental, parental, hygenic, racial, experiential, and educational deprivation.[1] It also considers how each of these influences the learning process, and how the teacher can work toward the child's adjustment.

SELF-DEPRIVATION

In a society which attributes a second-class status to a group, as in the case of most disadvantaged minorities, the group will tend to conform to its definition. Consequently, a self-fulfilling prophecy tends to set up feelings which become part of the child's personality, as indicated by his lack of self-esteem.

The teacher has an opportunity to influence the child's self-image, either confirming the feeling that the child is worthless or giving him hope and self-respect. A child's perceptions of his teacher's feelings toward him is directly related to his self-perception, and in turn to his academic achievement and classroom behavior. An understanding teacher will accept the children as individuals. He will build trust and win their confidence; he will assure them that they are worthwhile human beings. During his instruction, or in a private conversation, he helps them think about themselves; he offers suggestions; he rarely criticizes; he often praises; he accepts, but does not condone.

Not only do traditional stereotypes give way to present facts but traditional pictures of famous Negro men and women give way to pictures of middle-class minorities working in the larger society. The purpose is not to minimize the value of, for example, Jackie Robinson or Sammy Davis, Jr., but overemphasis upon outstanding figures from the world of sports and arts is a kind of stereotyping. It suggests that only a privileged few from disadvantaged groups can be successful, and it reduces the importance of an education. A wise approach is to point out less spectacular, but significant achievements of local men and women, perhaps even of former graduates from the particular school, whose success depended on working hard in school. Theirs are the pictures that should be displayed on bulletin boards; they are the people who should speak during school assemblies.

It is important to add that some Negro children have newly gained confidence, as expressed in the civil rights revolution sweeping across the country. Some see themselves as leaders, and not as helpless, inferior youngsters. This new pride is evidenced by their tendency to challenge authority. The teacher should expect, encourage, and be able to cope with this energy and channel it toward constructive goals. Classroom discussions about this movement can be helpful for stimulating instruction and clearing the atmosphere of any tension that might exist.

SOCIAL DEPRIVATION

The disadvantaged child is sophisticated about his environment and about the people he comes in contact with. He senses the discrepancies between what we "preach" and

*From Kappa Delta Pi Record, Vol. 4, p. 35, Dec., 1967. Used by permission.
[1]Allan C. Ornstein, "Who Are The Disadvantaged?" *Journal of Secondary Education,* April 1966, pp. 154-163.

our everyday conduct. He is disenchanted with the larger society, the phony world that Paul Goodman and Edgar Friedenberg write about, the world that is described in Salinger's *The Catcher in the Rye;* he is alienated by members of the larger society, who make it clear that they do not want or have any place except dead ends for youngsters who come from slums. The dope or sex party, the drinking spree, the easily observed rootlessness, all illustrate that the child feels unwanted and unattached; the knifing or rape of an innocent child, the vicious gang fights are manifestations of his hatred and alienation; it is the only time someone recognizes, takes notice of, or tries to help him.

Can the teacher help? Many teachers might argue that what the child does outside of school is not of their concern, that teaching these children is more than enough to worry about. The trouble is, however, that what the child does after school, or during the time when he should have been in school, affects his learning.

The teacher combats drinking, gambling, precocious sexual activity, smoking, sniffing glue, stealing, etc., with frank discussions— by allowing the children to voice their opinions and commenting on what is said. These discussions can and should be worked into the curriculum, especially since the home and street usually encourage deviant values. A teacher who works directly by the book and avoids such discussions is avoiding the real problem; he is nothing more than a file clerk. If the school was burning, and the appropriate stairway blocked, surely he would not feel that finding another exit was "not his concern."

Disadvantaged children spend a great deal of their money on clothing, in an effort to gain recognition and status among their peer group. It is a good practice for the teacher to take notice and comment when pupils are smartly dressed or wearing what they call new "vines" (clothing). There are many pupils, of course, who wear sunglasses or hats in the school, especially in schools where morale is low, and cooperation among teachers is minimal. They must be made to conform, at least when they enter the classroom. This should not be construed that a teacher wage war with these children, but in this case he is dealing with a subtle form of rebellion. The teacher is being tested, too, and the children are anxiously awaiting the outcome. The teacher can mention the rules of the class, perhaps even compliment the glasses or hat, but he should insist on their removal and at the same time allow the child to remove them himself. The disadvantaged are very sensitive about these two articles— "shades" and a "brimmer." They are signs of status; the type of hat, for example, and the way it is worn indicates the child's peer group and what he thinks of himself. An explosive situation is likely to occur if the teacher removes them or even touches the child in order to take them away. He should be equally discreet about other unpermissible items of clothing.

ENVIRONMENTAL DEPRIVATION

The disadvantaged child is a victim of an environment that is hostile and damaging from his birth. Sometimes he is unwanted at home so he takes to the street. To survive, he learns that brawn is more important than books. Despair and hopelessness are pervasive. You cannot remain long in a slum area and not sense them in the air. Young men and old are "hanging out" on street corners or on stoops near the local liquor store—of which there are so many—with nothing but time on their hands. Perhaps his father or an older brother is one of them. This is what the child has to look forward to; this is what life means to him.

The teacher must recognize that his students have lives that go on before and after school, and these lives are significant. As a result of a limited and uncertain future, the children are oriented toward the present, not the future. The teacher should make it clear that he has not given up on these children, and that they must not give up. Since many of the pupils do not know anyone who has a good job or perhaps any job, the teacher ought to take these children to places where members of their own ethnic group successfully work. Since the peer group will often poke fun and put pressure on those who perform well in school, the teacher should not assume that just because a child is scoring high in his academic work he has no problems, or that he is college-bound. Among those doing poorly, many are reluctant to show their intellectual capabilities because of the fear of ostracism. The teacher should be aware that such children are frequently labeled "slow"; they must be recognized or recommended for interschool, advanced-class transfers. The usual practice is for teachers to call the parents of "problem" children or to refer them to the guidance counselor. Good. But the teacher should consult the parents and counselor about the gifted children, too.

The disadvantaged child is often reared in a matriarchal family and feminine culture. When he enters elementary school, he finds that here too he is dominated by women, both teachers and administrators. Thus, the gang serves as a means for the male to prove himself as a "man." Instead of passively permitting him to engage in antisocial activities, the teacher ought to encourage a youngster to assert his masculinity in positive ways—doing well in school athletic teams or in shop; and most important, the teacher should try to instill in him the idea that by getting a good education he will be able to get a good job and be able to support himself and, therefore, be a real man and not have to depend on others.

PARENTAL DEPRIVATION

The meaninglessness of a threat to call the parent to school will often cause a child to laugh, inwardly or even to the teacher's face, because he knows that the teacher may call to his heart's content and no one will come. This youngster has been independent of his parents for many years and for many reasons. He may be dependent on an older sibling, but just as likely he is his own master. If he had a parent who would respond to a call from school, the call would probably not be necessary.

While the children are often independent of their parents, at the same time they generally have great pride in their family. They learn to stick together and to take care of each other, as well as to contribute to the support of the family. This family loyalty, to be sure, limits individual mobility; furthermore, individual success sometimes disrupts family unity. A child, for example, gets a job in order to help support his family. He earns one dollar an hour—below the minimum wage—on a milk truck which starts its rounds at 3 A.M. Of course this is not condonable, but on the other hand, he cannot buy himself or his younger brother a pair

of shoes by learning that "fog is like cat." After ten minutes in class the student is sitting, head resting on his hands, fast asleep. At this point the teacher might question the other students, who generally know the reason and will be truthful in this situation. The teacher should not disturb the child; the other children will understand, and will not think that the teacher condones lazy behavior, or just does not care. On the contrary, the teacher shows that he does care, and the children appreciate this concern, even though they will rarely admit it. At the end of the period or day, the child should be referred to the guidance counselor.

This situation, although depressing, is not hopeless. Every so often there comes into the life of a child—a child who has never had an adult to whom he could look for affection and guidance—a teacher with whom he enjoys the kind of relationship that more fortunate children find at home. This person can and does exert a great influence on the child, effecting a change in the child's attitudes and outlook on life. He can serve as the adult model who is so conspicuous by his absence in the home. To a child blessed with such a teacher, the school can become an oasis to which he runs without prodding.

Every teacher should at least be able to relate and build trust and rapport with one student. A "big-brother" or "big-sister" school program would be ideal, to aid the student in making a normal adjustment in the school and real life situation. The lack of such a program, however, should not prevent individual teachers from undertaking this project themselves. Their warmth and concern must be discernible; they must be willing to listen to a student's problems and help in any way possible; they must consult the guidance counselor, dean, and other teachers of the student who might help in understanding the child. The teacher could take the child on a tour of the city, go bowling, invite the child and/or his parent to dinner, keep abreast of the child's school work, and advise and counsel in a tactful manner. Perhaps some day every student will have the feeling that there is at least one person in the school who cares very much what happens, and to whom he can talk when he has a problem.

Of course, by no means is the author trying to dismiss the importance of the parent;

in fact, rarely will a child achieve marked success unless the interest and cooperation of the parent is present. Even if the parents are not often preoccupied with their children, the teacher should try to work with and communicate with them, and not only when the child is in some sort of trouble. A friendly telephone call, if there is a telephone at home, or a letter, or an invitation to accompany the class on a field trip is suitable for breaking the ice. Good qualities about the child should always be discussed first before problems concerning the child's school work and/or behavior are mentioned.

The author is not so naive to think that what he has just suggested is easily accomplished. But the teacher can devote some of the precious free time that he has in school to some of these activities. Hopefully, the day will come when the school will periodically dismiss classes early so that teachers will have the time to engage in such activities—even the time to visit each parent and talk about the child—for example, to discuss how the child is doing in school and what the parent can do to help the child learn. Parents should be urged to encourage their children to read certain prescribed books or watch certain prescribed television programs, as well as to set up, if it is possible, time and space where it will be quiet, where pencils and paper will be provided to do homework.

HYGIENIC DEPRIVATION

Many disadvantaged children come to school with untreated physical ills. Often when they are supposed to wear glasses, they do not because of embarrassment. Lack of a well-balanced diet, coupled with their popular eating habits—Coke and candy between meals, or instead of breakfast and lunch—is why many are undernourished and in great need of dental care. Nevertheless, when the school does arrange a clinic appointment, many children do not show up because no one is at home to see that they do go, or the family is too large for the mother to keep track of her older children.

A check with the school nurse or health records might amaze the teacher. There are students sitting in the back of the classroom who are reported to have severe cases of myopia but are not wearing glasses, never have worn them, and have not told the

teacher so. Some students, who are scheduled to visit the health clinic after school is dismissed, are playing basketball instead in the school center in the afternoon. Certainly a teacher can at least remind and check students to see that they keep their clinic appointments, seat children in the front who cannot see from the back of the room, and explain why glasses are important.

Many children come to school with poor health habits and with inadequate clothing. Although every teacher in every school should be a model of cleanliness and good health habits, it is even more important in teaching the disadvantaged. Good health habits should be stressed in the curriculum. Because of inadequate clothing, one child may stay at home on days which require white blouses or shirts; another, on days which require the student to have sneakers and a gym suit. Rarely, if ever, will the child voice his economic plight. A teacher, therefore, should look for such patterns in examining class attendance. A tactful discussion and referral to the proper school agency can correct the situation. Indeed, a child may be absent for a number of other reasons, and for a long duration. A teacher who notices a great number of absences should have a class monitor make an extra set of notes (this job can be rotated daily) so that when absentees do return to school they can at least make up the work.

RACIAL DEPRIVATION

Non-white groups suffer from discrimination and prejudice which is perhaps the most relentless and detrimental disadvantage, and which intensifies the other disadvantages. Disadvantaged white groups have greater economic mobility and more chance of being assimilated into the larger society. The obstacles against such assimilation are more formidable for non-white groups and are further complicated because everyone can see their ethnic identity. If society says it is better to be white, not only white people but non-whites come to believe it.

Without being accused of stereotyping, the teacher should realize that some minority group children react to their rejection and isolation with apathy, slowness, clumsiness, boasting, clowning, joking, hostility, and offensive and antisocial behavior. If the teacher can make the child understand why he is behaving the way he is, the teacher may help the child understand himself and establish more realistic and acceptable patterns of behavior.

An additional problem of classroom behavior is sometimes manifested by Spanish-speaking children. A knowing teacher investigates to see if these children are quiet or withdrawn because they do not understand English, and not because they are "dumb" or "slow." These children usually will not inform the teacher of their communication problem, because they are shy about their language barrier and because they are taught at home to be polite to teachers, and this is interpreted as not annoying their teachers with any personal problems. Hopefully, the school has a non-English-speaking class. However, if the school does not have such a class, the teacher can arrange a "buddy" system with the Spanish-speaking child and with a couple of bilingual students for the remaining academic year, to explain classroom and school routines, as well as to try to improve the language skills of the non-English-speaking child.

Once—with the best of intentions—it was considered proper to discourage children from certain vocations or studies because of race; now this would be senseless. Recently, job opportunities have been made available in all fields for non-white groups; in fact, unions, management, industry, and the professions are searching for qualified non-whites. Therefore, the teacher should encourage minority group members to seek any field of endeavor which they realistically have the ability to study. However, to believe in the possibility of self-improvement, these children need to have intercultural lessons that stress their heritage and culture, and enhance their self-esteem and feelings of belonging in context of national life. As previously mentioned, they should be exposed to pictures, speeches by guests and field trips that point out that people from all minority groups can achieve status and economic security, as well as work with white people as equals and in the larger society.

The issue of bussing should also be considered. Large numbers of minority group children may soon be entering our middle-class schools. The theme of brotherhood and cooperation among different races will certainly be stressed. Nevertheless, the author fears that teachers, subconsciously or consciously, may compare the academic achievement and classroom behavior of these newcomers with that of their middle-class students. In-service education is needed in order to help teachers gain insights into the socio-psychological problems of non-white, as well as white disadvantaged groups. Without this understanding, it will be impossible to promote brotherhood or to be objective, or to teach or maintain order in the classroom.

EXPERIENTIAL DEPRIVATION

Because of their impoverished environment, the disadvantaged have inhibited auditory and visual discrimination, as well as limited language, memory, and cognitive ability to meet the demands of school when they first enter. Hopefully, preschool programs will help the disadvantaged counteract their limited experiences. Nonetheless, elementary school teachers must continuously reinforce and increase the learning experiences of the disadvantaged; for example, by providing opportunity for them to manipulate and organize the perceptual aspects of the classroom environment, and by allowing them to listen, speak, and observe the multiple attributes to sounds and words. By promoting a social period or discussion, the teacher can find out what children already know and can use this as a guide for developing further experiences which they need to know to learn basic skills.

By the same token, it is the teacher's job to accept test scores only as a valid measure of the child's present academic achievement and of what needs still to be accomplished, not as a measure of his intelligence or his future academic achievement. Because of their limited experiences, many of these children do poorly on tests. For this reason, only the teacher who is sensitive and aware of the problems of the disadvantaged can discover the gifted under-achiever. There are many cases of people in our history who failed to pass a number of subjects and who were considered dull by their teachers, but became giants in their adulthood. Edison, Einstein, and Churchill are among them. But how many hundreds of thousands never developed their true potential because their teachers could not distinguish between test grades and potential? In nearly every class there is a student doing superior work in comparison with other members of his class. The teacher, nevertheless, feels his academic achievement is below the norm, not thinking that if the child were transferred to a "better" class or given extra work to do on his own, he would attain the norm. Another student may be bored or not really trying because he thinks that school is for "squares," or because every time he is teased or challenged by something that he reads, the teacher has no time to discuss the topic because too much valuable class time will be lost. There are many disadvantaged children who have the potential, but will respond only to a particular teacher. It is the duty of that teacher, and every teacher, to see that these children are not lost in our mass-scale, middle-class education, and that they are referred for counseling and retesting.

EDUCATIONAL DEPRIVATION

The school that the disadvantaged attends usually has no marauding rats, falling plaster or broken windows; it is often a new building. Although it is probably the most stable social institution they encounter, and the only one that can help them, many are unable to cope with it and unlikely will not benefit from it.

At school they are forced to fit a mold which does not fit them and which they do not need to prepare them for the life which they envision for themselves. Yet it is not as if the school was totally to blame. The children come to school neat and clean the first day, but they are victims of their culture and deprivation; they often lack the self-control and the ability to be "good" in the classroom, as well as to understand the verbal and abstract behavior which they need for learning.

By the time these children reach junior high school, many are alienated, withdrawn, angry, and apathetic. Some are unable to read street names on a sign. Some are unable to do simple addition problems. Their teachers protest, but room must be made for the next incoming class. As for the youngsters, they usually are no longer interested in school. They remain only because they have no place to go, because it is the proper thing to do until they are old enough to leave. Thus, the school, instead of providing assistance, merely becomes the latest in a series of social institutions transmitting to them the idea that they are doomed to failure, that they will produce the next generation of disadvantaged Americans.

Although it is the job of the school system to provide equal opportunities for its less fortunate, the teacher must continue to do the best job that he possibly can, even though many factors work against the learning process. Expectations should be reasonable and in line with the present academic level of the children. On the other hand, we must guard against a tendency to scapegoat the classroom teacher for having lower expectations for these children. It is often said that if expectations are too low, they reinforce the child's low esteem and expectations of himself. The solution is, perhaps, to draw a balanced picture of what should be taught, and on what level, and thereby improving the present learning situation for the disadvantaged, as well as giving them the skills they need to know.

SUMMARY

We have read about some problems of the disadvantaged, and how the teacher can provide adjustment. It is the opinion of the author that effective teaching and basic understanding of the disadvantaged go hand-in-hand with helping the disadvantaged child overcome his deprivation and implementing the learning process.

55. The contribution of school athletics to the growing boy*

Ray O. Duncan†

Former Dean, College of Health, Physical Education, and Recreation, University of West Virginia

School athletics are based upon the inherent need of children and youth for play. Sociologists have always recognized the value of play in the development of a strong social order. Davie expresses very well the sociologist's viewpoint in regard to the importance of play:

> Play is a biological and social necessity for children. It is the most fundamental thing about a child . . . Play for the child is one of the most serious facts of life; it is a form of work for the young and the basis for all natural education.[1]

The need of children for play has long been recognized by school authorities although methods for meeting the need have changed considerably. The play need of children gives birth to the sports and athletic urge which becomes so strong about the eleventh or twelfth year. This sports interest has resulted in school recognition and acceptance of responsibility as evidenced by the athletic programs of various types in practically all junior and senior high schools.

Let us look at the problem of athletics in relation to the growing boy. In the first place, athletics should be defined. The definition of the Educational Policies Commission seems to be quite adequate:

> School athletics . . . include all school-sponsored physical activities in the form of competitive games or sports in which students participate.[2]

The EPC definition continues with the statement that athletics are considered a part of physical education,[3] and recognition is made of the fact that athletics may be part of the required classes or on a voluntary basis.

Athletics have tremendous social significance in the life of a normal boy. Moody makes a very strong statement in this regard:

> The highest degree of peer esteem among boys is reserved for those who excel in sports. The rare individual who achieves adolescent popularity alongside ineptitude in sports—and such a one occasionally appears—ought to be called a 'social genius'.[4]

The entire concept of play and athletics being of tremendous importance to the growth and development of a normal boy implies certain school responsibility. It is not enough for a school to provide suitable playground and gymnasium facilities with the opportunity for students to participate during their leisure time. The acceptance by the school of the principle that children and youth need to play points up a chain of responsibility. The athletic and sports urge grows out of the play need. The old theory that children know how to play without instruction and direction because of their inherent interest is an absolutely false dictum. The play situation is a natural one in which the child is released from compulsion and

*From The Journal of Educational Sociology, Vol. 28, p. 271, Feb. 1955. Used by permission.
†Deceased.
[1]Davie, Maurice R., *Problem of City Life*, New York: John Wiley Sons, Inc., 1932, pp. 678-679.
[2]Education Policies Commission, School Athletics, NEA, 1954, p. IX.
[3]Education Policies Commission, *School Athletics*, NEA, 1954, p. IX.
[4]Moody, Caesar B., "Physical Education and Neurotic Behavior Disorders," *Understanding the Child*, January 1952, p. 21.

restraint. In such a situation, the emotions may range from vicious examples of misbehavior to the highest manifestations of sportsmanship. The greatest learning opportunity in the life of a child is likely to present itself during play; consequently, the highest type of leadership and guidance should be provided.

School athletics should be made available to all boys in the following manner:

1. Regular physical education classes. Instruction in basic athletic skills in the sports common to our culture should be provided for all boys. This instruction should include some competition between class groups. Physical education should be scheduled in all grades 1-12 with athletic sports entering the program about the 5th to 6th grade.

2. Intramural sports. Many students merely have their interest aroused in the basic physical education program and desire more competition and opportunity for more participation in athletics. The school should meet this need through intramural sports. The intramural sports program may be considered the laboratory where pupils who desire participation and competition beyond the regular physical education program may secure it. This program is usually seasonal and involves the sports which have interest and appeal to the boys. The program should be as broad as student interest indicates and school facilities will permit. The intramural sports program may begin on a small scale in the 5th or 6th grade and extend through the 12th grade. The activities in the program should be suited to the maturity level of the boys and be conducted in a manner compatible with sound educational principles.

3. Interscholastic athletics. This program is highly selective and provides an opportunity for the students with superior physical skill to participate in competitive sports beyond the limits of the basic physical education and the intramural programs. The interscholastic program has great appeal, not only to the participants, but also to the total student body and entire community. There is considered diversity of opinion about the range of the interscholastic program. No one objects to its application to high school boys, but there is disagreement in regard to grades below the senior high

school. The Educational Policies Commission's recommendation is that there should be "no inter-scholastic program below senior high school."[5] However, the Commission does make a very strong statement in regard to the importance of athletics in the school program:

We believe that the experience of playing athletic games should be a part of the education of all children and youth.[6]

The Commission recognizes that athletics make a contribution to "health and happiness, physical skill and emotional competences, and moral values."[7] Other outcomes are listed as character and learning to "take it"—to experience "defeat without whimpering and victory without gloating, and disciplining one's self to comply with the rules of the game and good sportsmanship."[8] Working with others for group goals, democratic processes and fair play are also stated as contributions made by athletics to the growing boy. The EPC report is an excellent publication and although all persons may not agree with the entire report, it is certainly worthy of being a basic guide for school athletic programs.

Anyone who has seen the expression on the faces of players as they listen to the coach's instructions before the game must realize what a powerful influence is moulding the minds and bodies of boys through athletics. Schools should provide a sound athletic program for all boys. Whether the program be a part of basic physical education, intramurals, interscholastic, or all three, should depend upon many factors, including the age, maturity, interest and readiness of the boys. Student welfare must always be the deciding factor in determining the type of athletic program for each individual participant. It must be kept constantly in mind that a school athletic program is for the students. It should be fun and contribute to the general educational goals. Likewise, it is highly essential that school athletics be kept at the maturity level of the boys who play. Jersild's caution should be brought to the attention of all coaches

---

[5] Educational Policies Commission, *School Athletics,* p. 55.
[6] Ibid, p. 3.
[7] Ibid, p. 3.
[8] Ibid, p. 4.

and physical educators who work with children:

> The child-development approach assumes a child's right to be a child. Nature has decreed that a human creature should be a child a long time before he becomes a man . . . one of the greatest temptations which confront an adult in dealing with a child is to try to tamper with the process of the child's own development.[9]

Boys desire athletic competition, and a sound sports program will make a real contribution to their growth and development. However, it is well to remember two basic educational facts that should underlie the development of an athletic program for boys:

1. *The purpose of the school is education —not entertainment.* This does not exclude all activities which have spectator appeal but does point up the primary objective of the

[9]Jersild, Arthur T., *Child Development and The Curriculum,* Bureau of Publications, Teachers College, Columbia University, New York: 1946, pp. 2-3.

school and indicate the need for proper educational balance.

2. *The educational program at the various levels varies*—elementary, junior high school, senior high school, college. The athletic program, likewise, should be different and designed to meet the physical, social, and emotional needs of the students. This means that *the athletic program, at any level, should not be patterned on that provided for older boys.*

School athletics is a fast growing giant with a tremendous potential for making a vital contribution to the physical, social, and emotional growth of every boy who participates. However, an athletic program is not beneficial per se. Its potential for good is matched by the possibility of bad outcomes. School authorities have the responsibility for developing a program of athletics which will make a valuable contribution to all boys— the parents and patrons of our schools should see to it that the responsibility is met in full.

56. Little League baseball can hurt your boy*†

Charles A. Bucher

*Professor of Education and Director of Physical Education, School of Education,
New York University*

with Tim Cohane

Former sports editor, Look magazine

Little League baseball, played today by approximately 175,000 American kids from 8 to 12, needs revamping. The emphasis on winning, as expressed in local, state and regional tournaments that culminate in a national championship, is endangering the welfare of too many of our children.

It is encouraging social tendencies contrary to those the Little League movement, sincerely enough, always has purported to instill. By concentrating on a relatively few talented kids, Little League in many communities has seriously restricted, if not eliminated, a recreation program for other children and other age groups.

The entire Little League setup has deteriorated in many ways into a silly yet thoroughly dangerous madness that has seized not only the children but those responsible for their well-being: parents, public officials, coaches and spectators. They have come to confuse Little League with big league. As if the pennants and the world's championship were all that counted.

The drive to win is traditional in America and must be preserved. But a boy will absorb that lesson soon enough in high school. In his grammar-school years, it is more important that his recreation be guided toward other objectives: the fun of playing rather than the winning; the child rather than the game; the many rather than the few; informal activity rather than formal; the development of skills in many activities rather than specialization. Many of these desirable objectives are not accomplished in the way the Little League now works.

Consider the situation not so long ago in Port Chester, N. Y. The local Little League champions went on to win the district and state titles. They were scheduled next to contend in the regional play-offs at Schenectady, N. Y. From there, practically all of Port Chester expected, they would go on to win the Little World Series at Williamsport, Pa. Joyful fathers, mothers, uncles, aunts and other grownups saluted the boys as juvenile Genghis Khans. The Port Chester *Daily Item* rejoiced editorially: "Wonderful lads."

Then polio struck down a boy who had accompanied the team to the state finals as a rooter. There were many other local polio cases. So Dr. Bernard J. Gioffre, Port Chester health officer, recommended the trip to Schenectady be canceled. The players were brokenhearted. Dismay spread among the townspeople. A meeting was called in a church hall and attended by most of the parents of the players.

The meeting was presided over by Anthony

Posillipo, mayor of Port Chester and then Little League committee president (now a supervisor in Westchester County, N. Y.). He said he felt the question of the trip to Schenectady should be decided by the parents. They voted unanimously to disregard the recommendation of the health officer and let the boys go to the regional play-offs.

At this point, Dr. William A. Holla, Westchester County health commissioner, intervened. "There is no justification," he said, "for sending those kids on such a trip. When there are many polio cases in a community as small as Port Chester, it becomes an epidemic area. . . ."

The possibility of spreading polio was not the only danger averted by canceling the trip. Victory or defeat at Schenectady or Williamsport might well have distorted many other educational values and caused physical disturbances in the players.

There are several such case histories in the Little League. After the Stamford, Conn., champions won the 1951 World Series at Williamsport, many of them developed swelled heads. By the time they reached high-school age, some of them were serious problems.

Defeated players in a Midwestern state finals cried like babies and then further vented their grief by wrecking the lobby of their hotel. Youngsters playing in a Minnesota state tournament were affected by loss of appetite, upset stomach, insomnia, tears and homesickness. Remember, these are not professionals or semiprofessionals or even high-school competitors. They are little boys from 8 to 12.

Far more serious physical dangers than insomnia or an upset stomach exist for small boys in overorganized, overcompetitive sports. This is recognized by the highest medical authority. The American Medical Association strongly discourages even interscholastic competition below senior high-school level.

PHYSICAL STRAIN TOO GREAT

Dr. C. L. Lowman, distinguished surgeon at the Los Angeles Orthopaedic Hospital and medical consultant for Los Angeles city schools, says: "I consider the movements to encourage highly organized competitive activity for boys and girls below the high-school age to be especially dangerous because

neither skeletal growth, cartilages or joints, to say nothing of muscles, are sufficiently developed. Furthermore, the emotional pressures of practice periods before the game, followed by either victory or defeat, cannot be withstood because of immaturity."

These emotional pressures often are intensified by the attitude of parents, especially fathers. The Little League, properly conducted and understood, can foster a closer relationship between a son and father. But the relationship is impaired when a father sees in his Little League son a chance for vicarious realization of some frustrated childhood ambition of his own. This kind of father can soon lose his sense of values completely.

An extreme, yet not isolated, case was related to me by a friend. He was driving along a Southern road one night when he picked up a youngster not more than nine. My friend asked the boy how far it was to his home. "Three miles," the boy replied. "Why are you walking it this time of night?" my friend asked. "My daddy made me," the boy said, "because I muffed a fly in the Little League game today. And I won't get any supper, either."

Not only fathers but whole families have gone overboard on Little League. They plan their two weeks' vacation to coincide with the Little League World Series. The entire recreation of one family I know is circumscribed by Little League. The two sons are players, each in a different league. The father umpires. The mother attends all the games and keeps score. This goes on all week.

PARENTS BADGER COACHES

Naturally, not a few of these Little League parents are convinced their sons have bigleague potentialities. When their kid doesn't get in the game they can't understand it. Frequently, they phone the coach and ask why. Such phone calls have driven more than one coach out of Little League.

One father in my neighborhood has a son who is a pretty good Little League pitcher. The father is sure the boy will pitch in the big leagues some day. He has sold the idea to the boy and to some of the neighbors too. Perhaps this boy will make it. But the odds are about 2500 to 1 against him. When he discovers, as he probably will, that he is no budding Yankee or Dodger, it may not do his ego much good. He may even feel he has let his father down.

He may be better off, however, than the son of another of my neighbors. This kid was good enough to make a Little League squad, but not quite good enough to get to play in the games. He listened regularly to "do-or-die" pep talks, then sat it out on the bench. He continued to show up for the games and for the daily practices. These began at 5:30, so he often took dinner on the run. By the end of the season, he was highly nervous and eating poorly. His spirit was broken. Little League had lost its attraction for him.

That boy's experience emphasizes a basic weakness in Little League. It is for the few at the expense of the majority. At Bay Shore, N. Y., the town highway department brought in snow fences to enclose a Little League baseball diamond in the middle of the Fourth Avenue School's play field. The field is used spring, summer and fall. As a result, the majority of the school children are denied a full play program.

In Lynn, Mass., William F. Hines, secretary of the Board of Park Commissioners, says there are many people in his community who would turn over the whole playground system to the Little League. Gary Dunn, Southeastern Massachusetts commissioner for the Amateur Softball Association, says that in his area money is being poured into Little League to the neglect of municipal recreation programs and, consequently, nine tenths of the children who don't make a Little League team get no recreation at all.

In Brunswick, Maine, Stanton R. Curtis, director of recreation, says: "If there is a service club or industry with $1000 to donate to the community, the Brunswick Recreation Commission can professionally suggest at least fifty ways in which this $1000 could be more beneficial to the community and serve more people of all ages than a Little League program could ever hope to serve."

The exclusiveness of Little League baseball doesn't extend, unfortunately, to the men or in some cases boys who coach the teams. Most of the coaches are good men, many of them with children of their own. They are well-respected citizens with good intentions. They volunteer their efforts and

time. But all this does not qualify them to teach and train young boys.

COACHES LACK TRAINING

Leaders of young children in highly competitive sports should meet certain minimum qualifications. According to a survey conducted by New York University among 38 outstanding psychologists, educators, pediatricians and other experts in child study, these qualifications should include training in health, physical education or recreation, and knowledge of child growth and development. Such background is found in few Little League coaches. Most of them are chosen because they have a knowledge of baseball.

Quite a few concentrate on building reputations as winning strategists. Some have been known to break Little League rules about using players. Such violations in Nevada prompted the YMCA to threaten to withdraw its support. In Sayre, Pa., a manager twice broke the rule which says a boy cannot pitch on successive nights.

The professional-baseball approach is carried by some Little League managers to the extreme of cursing umpires and heckling opposing players. One coach in a game at Boston razzed the 11-year-old first baseman of the other team so unmercifully that the boy became distracted and was struck by a line drive. When the umpire warned the offending coach, the coach jeered: "What's the matter, can't the boy take it? It's all part of the game."

A heckling, profane coach in Little League doesn't lack kindred spirits among the spectators. In another game at Boston— although Boston has no monopoly on the custom—umpire Jim Wiley quit his job in the middle of a game. He felt it was unfair for the kids to have to hear the kind of language being hurled at him by coaches and spectators, including parents of players.

"Booing of officials is now a common practice," says Johnny Childs, former president of a Pennsylvania Little League. "One official, who works high-school games regularly, told me he never again wants to officiate Little League."

The partisan, unbalanced Little League fan doesn't always confine his behavior to the field. Karl Lawrence, head of physical education and former varsity basketball coach at Colgate, tells of sitting in a barber shop in a little upstate New York town. The place was crowded with waiting customers. One barber was cutting the hair of a nine-year-old boy. In a loud voice, the barber told the boy his team would have won their game the night before if he hadn't muffed that fly. There was an embarrassed silence as the kid wept.

LITTLE LEAGUE PAYS OFF

The barber's remark might have been made by the butcher, the baker or any other merchant. Many of them are in the Little League business. In Englewood, N. J., the Little League field, complete with field house and bleachers—and used solely by Little Leaguers—was financed by the Rotary Club and is maintained by the city.

Similar special facilities have been developed in many communities. Trophies, awards, prizes are bestowed on local, district, state, regional and national winners. Almost every league ends its season with a banquet or a trip. Add all this up on a country-wide basis—this year, there are approximately 11,448 teams in 2800 leagues—and it means important business for a lot of local merchants.

In return for underwriting Little League expenses, some merchants expect to have the kid's uniforms carry such messages as "Schultz's Sandwich Shop" or "Ye Old Colonial Grille." Commercialized Little League players have been aptly called "baby sandwich boards."

"Baby sandwich boards" may sound funny to some. But here is something difficult to laugh off: Len Wilbur, sports editor of the Utica, N. Y., *Observer-Dispatch,* wrote in his column of August 6, 1952, that there was gambling going on at Little League games in Utica. "Probably," he wrote, "we'll soon hear of some nine-year-old lad being offered a bribe to throw a game!"

PEEKSKILL SAYS NO

The many undesirable features of Little League are clearly recognized in many communities. In Peekskill, N. Y., the Kiwanis Club, which fostered sand-lot baseball in that city, the recreation commission and the Joint Veterans' Council all worked successfully to stop a Little League movement started by a handful of adults.

The Los Angeles Park Department opposes Little League ball on its playing fields.

In Hempstead, N. Y., Little League is restricted to determining a local champion. There are also intramural leagues for the 13-15, 16-18 and unlimited age groups. Instead of constructing expensive fields for one age group, existing softball diamonds are used by all groups.

In explaining Hempstead's stand, Le Roy L. Tintle, former director of recreation, says: "To follow the rules and regulations set forth by the Little League would be detrimental to an over-all recreation program, because it would drain the financial resources of the community. It has been my experience that the monies necessary to operate Little League can well take care of your entire baseball program from ages eight through unlimited."

The Hempstead version of Little League should be adopted nationally. It would do much to eliminate most of the prevalent abuses. Others could be eliminated by selecting coaches who think first of the welfare of each child.

But as Little League stands today, it's not for my boy. Nor yours.

Projects and thought questions for sociological foundations of physical education

1. Show how studies in the sociology of sport will affect physical education programs in the future.

2. Develop an essay concerned with increasing sports participation and at the same time reducing the trend toward spectatorism.

3. Compare Artemov's findings with similar research done in some other country relating to some aspect of the use of leisure time for physical activity.

4. What do you feel is the true place of athletics in education?

5. How would you suggest that changes be made that will bring competition of the Little League type more in line with educational objectives?

6. List at least six ways in which the physical educator can through his programs make a significant contribution to the dis-advantaged child. Make some specific recommendations under each item you have listed.

Selected readings

Anderson, J. A.: What is the best interpretation of physical education as viewed by the specialist in the growth of children and youth? Report of the National Conference on Interpretation of Physical Education, Chicago, 1962, The Athletic Institute, Inc.

Coleman, J. S.: The adolescent society: the social life of the teenager and its impact on education, New York, 1962, The Free Press.

Harris, C. W., editor: Encyclopedia of education research, New York, 1960, The Macmillan Co.

Van Huss, W.: Physical activity in modern living, Englewood Cliffs, N. J., 1960, Prentice-Hall, Inc.

Westby-Gibson, D.: Social perspectives on education: the society, the student, the school, New York, 1965, John Wiley & Sons, Inc.

Part six

Leadership in physical education

Education, and particularly physical education, is making a concerted effort to draw talented and dedicated people into the professional ranks. Lay people are more and more becoming cognizant of the fact that a teacher is more than a dispenser of information and more than just a disciplinarian.

As education is increasingly analyzed, praised, and criticized through community meetings and the news media, educators and the public they serve come to a greater understanding of just what an educator is and does. Colleges and universities that prepare educators are revising and modernizing their curriculums. Physical education especially is taking a long and hard look at the conduct of its professional preparing programs. New curriculums are being readied, new courses are being devised, new teaching methods are being tested and evaluated, and research in physical education is making new inroads in understanding.

Students in today's professional preparation programs are becoming well grounded not only in their speciality but also in general studies and the liberal arts. Their training enables them to make highly significant contributions to the entire educational community.

The readings in this division are directly concerned with the educator. A number of articles in this section explore the area of professional preparation. The remaining readings deal with the professional competencies of the teacher, with teaching itself, with the teacher's role in the community, and with the place of research in physical education.

Margery Servis Bulger and Reuben B. Frost studied a limited number of female physical education undergraduates to determine in what way personal and physical qualities might be used as predictors of success in the undergraduate professional program. The subjects in this experiment completed a variety of mental and physical tests. In addition they were rated by their peers and by faculty members. Bulger and Frost tentatively identify several mental and physical factors that could be used as predictors of success for the subjects in this study.

The problem of obtaining a corps of professional female physical educators is discussed by Waneen Wyrick. This article explains why girls often hesitate to choose a career in physical education and presents some solutions to the problem of recruiting female students. The author describes the qualities a female physical educator must possess and shows how professional programs in physical education must be altered to attract and retain the qualified individual.

A research report by Gerald S. Kenyon investigates the unique personal qualities and characteristics of men and women students in professional preparing curriculums in physical education. The qualities shown by these students were compared with those possessed by students who were not specializing in physical education. For the subjects in this study, Kenyon's results indicated that prospective physical education teachers do have certain qualities that distinguish them from nonphysical educators.

A research report by Elmo Smith Roundy identifies the problems of male secondary physical education teachers and highlights the competencies needed to overcome these problems. Roundy lists 21 problem areas and 144 competencies. In light of his findings the researcher drew implications for programs of professional preparation, for in-service training programs, and for further research.

Athletics as a part of physical education and the duties of the coach as a teacher are defined and explored in separate articles by John D. Lawther and Gayle Dawley Moore.

Lawther outlines the duties and responsibilities of the coach toward the youngsters in his charge. In addition the author shows the need for the coach to provide moral and spiritual as well as physical guidance.

Moore discusses her view of the conduct of athletic programs for girls. The writer feels that girls' programs are beginning to parallel the conduct of programs for boys and does not approve of the trend toward this value. Moore suggests that it is more important for girls to be exposed to a good basic instructional program rather than concentrate so heavily on competitive programs.

Charles A. Bucher writes on the professional preparation of athletic coaches. He describes traditional practices of certification and hiring of coaches and presents a course of action to ensure the preparation of competent and qualified personnel.

Robert N. Singer writes on the need for physical educators to sell their programs to the public. Singer delineates the qualities the physical educator needs to be a success in public relations and sets down some specific guidelines for the entire field.

Arthur S. Daniels writes that physical education is a fertile area for research and that this potential has not been exploited by the leaders of our professional or by the individual physical educator. Daniels says that if physical education is going to realize its full educational worth it is the duty of professionals in the field to become more productive scholars.

57. Qualities related to success in women's physical education professional preparation program*

Reuben B. Frost

Director, Division of Health, Physical Education, and Recreation, Springfield College

Margery Servis Bulger

School of Health, Physical Education, and Recreation, Central Michigan University

Sixty-nine physical education majors were used as subjects in an attempt to identify those personal and physical qualities of women physical education students which would most effectively predict success in the professional preparation program of physical education. The criteria of success included the cumulative academic index, a rating by the faculty, and a rating by the student's peer group. Predictive variables consisting of measures of physical fitness, general motor ability, temperament traits, mental ability, interests, and values were evaluated.

The single predictive variable yielding the highest positive relationship with success in the professional preparation program was physical fitness; the value and interest variables showed practically no relationship. The best combination of variables for predicting success was the physical fitness index, the active temperament trait score, and the mental ability score.

As enrollments in colleges and universities continue to increase, the establishment of scientifically-sound procedures for selection, guidance, and counseling becomes increasingly more important in teacher education programs. If the profession is to be assured of high-quality teaching, it becomes the responsibility of institutions preparing teachers to continually explore more effective methods of selection and retention.

PURPOSE

As in any specialized field, it is logical to assume that students preparing for a career in physical education need certain unique abilities and competencies. This study was undertaken to determine the various qualities which contribute most to probable success in physical education. From such evidence a more valid and objective selection and guidance program for undergraduate education can be developed.

REVIEW OF LITERATURE

Educators interested in improving teacher education have conducted extensive research in the areas of desirable teacher characteristics, selection and screening procedures, and the measurement and prediction of teaching success.

One of the earliest and most comprehensive studies of teacher traits was conducted by Charters and Waples (5). These authors identified 2,800 trait actions considered to be important to successful teaching. To eliminate duplication these traits were telescoped into 25 characteristics and placed in rank order of importance. The traits considered most important were: good judgment, self-control, considerateness, enthusiasm, magnetism.

In a study designed to predict success in teacher education programs, Martin (13) concluded that intelligence was the highest single factor associated with teaching ability. Rolfe (15) agreed with Martin on the importance of intelligence and concluded that personality showed little relationship to

*From Research Quarterly, Vol. 38, p. 283, May 1967. Used by permission.

teaching success. Hellfritzsh (11), however, in another investigation, reported a personality factor along with a mental ability factor, a supervisory rating factor, and an attitude factor. Hardaway (9) found that personality, combined with professional competence and academic achievement was a necessary requisite to teaching success.

Concurrent with the endeavors of general educators to determine the common traits of successful teachers, leaders in physical education focused their attention upon enlarging, extending, and analyzing these characteristics for this phase of education.

Brownell (4) proposed five factors as eligibility requirements for entrance into physical education teacher preparation: the high school record of the student, physical fitness scores, tests of social ability, tests for predicting teaching success, and personal interviews.

Graybeal (7) investigated the qualities of competent physical education teachers deemed most important by school administrators. Excellent physical condition, character, and personality were considered the most important attributes of a good teacher. A high grade of scholarship and an enriched background of academic training were thought to be of only slight importance. Blesh (3) conducted a similar study and in general his conclusions agreed with those reported by Graybeal.

Montgomery (14) concluded that the qualities specific to physical education included personality, physical skills, academic and other types of intelligence, interest in teaching, and exceptional health and vigor. Handy (8) expanded the findings of the Montgomery study and developed a predictive index for the men's physical education program at the University of California, Los Angeles. This index was found useful in the selection of teacher candidates when supplemented by guidance and counseling.

Arnsdorff (1) used the critical incident technique to identify the effective behaviors of women teachers of physical education as perceived by teachers and by high school girls. Teachers showed more concern for the planning and organizing aspects of teaching and students for behavior related to the personal qualities of the teachers.

In the above studies it is evident that there is little agreement as to what consti-

tutes a successful teacher. In general, the qualities and competencies which appear most useful for evaluating potential physical education teachers fall into the categories of personal characteristics, professional competencies, professional attitudes, and physical skills.

PROCEDURE
Subjects

All 69 women physical education majors at Central Michigan University who had completed the necessary requirements for advancement to candidacy in teacher education were included in this study.[1]

Testing instruments

Five testing instruments were used as possible predictors of success in the professional preparation program for women. Those selected were the Thurstone temperament schedule, Allport-Vernon-Lindzey study of values, Otis quick-scoring mental ability test, Scott motor ability test, and Rogers physical fitness index battery.

Criteria

The criteria of success included three independent items: academic index, faculty rating, and peer rating. The fourth criterion item was a composite of the previous three.

The faculty and peer rating scale included the 12 personal characteristics of successful teachers proposed by A. S. Barr (2) and additional professional and specialized professional competencies deemed important for successful physical educators. The 12 characteristics were: resourcefulness, intelligence, emotional stability, considerateness, buoyancy, objectivity, drive, dominance, attractiveness, refinement, cooperativeness, and reliability. The professional competencies included: communication skills, public relations, work habits, commitment to teaching, interest in children, professional growth, physical fitness, and physical performance skills. Each characteristic was clarified with descriptive and definitive terms to increase the accuracy of the scale.

To determine the relative weight of each

---

[1]Advancement to candidacy at Central Michigan University requires a minimum academic index of C, or 2.00, the completion of 90 semester hours of course work, and demonstrated competence in written and oral expression.

of the rating scale items, a questionnaire was sent to members of the physical education faculty and to the professional students at Central Michigan University. Validity of the scale was determined by rank-order correlation. The relationship between an over-all rank position of success as assigned by five faculty raters and the rank position of success as measured by the rating scale resulted in a coefficient of .94 ± .20. Reliability was determined by the test-retest method and resulted in an r of .94.

Statistical procedures

The basic multiple regression design used in this study was programed for analysis by the Esso Research and Engineering Company (6) and computed on the Dow Chemical Company electronic computer.[2] The criteria which were used to select the independent variables, and to add or remove them from the regression, were as follows:

1. If the variance contribution of a variable in the regression was nonsignificant at an F level of 2.00, this variable was removed.

[2]Appreciation is extended to John William of the Computations and Research Laboratory, Dow Chemical Company, for assistance in data analysis.

2. If the variance reduction obtained by adding a variable to the regression was significant at an F level of 2.00, this variable was entered.

If the multiple correlation coefficient between any number of independent variables was so large that most of the variability in one was related to others, this variable was not included in the regression.

RESULTS

The correlation coefficients between the predictive variables and the criteria appear in Table 1. The relationship between fitness indexes and faculty rating scores produced the highest zero-order coefficient (.68). The coefficients between the PFI and the other criterion items were also higher than any other single predictor.

The multiple correlation coefficients between the selected predictive variables and each of the criterion variables are presented in Tables 2, 3, 4, and 5. The highest obtained multiple coefficient was .76 between the composite criterion and the PFI, the active temperament trait, and mental ability. By eliminating the mental ability score from this battery, the multiple correlation was .74.

An examination of Tables 2, 3, 4, and 5

Table I. Correlations between predictive variables and criteria (N = 69)

Predictive variable	Criterion			
	Academic index	Faculty rating	Peer rating	Composite criterion
PFI	.53[a]	.68[a]	.65[a]	.67[a]
Motor ability	.45[a]	.60[a]	.60[a]	.60[a]
Mental ability	.40[a]	.37[a]	.37[a]	.41[a]
Values and interests				
Theoretical	.10	.06	.16	.11
Economic	.20	.24[b]	.23[b]	.25[b]
Aesthetic	-.13	-.12	-.21	-.17
Social	.02	.08	.07	.07
Political	.20	.17	.21	.21
Religious	.09	.10	.10	.11
Temperament traits				
Active	.53[a]	.59[a]	.61[a]	.64[a]
Vigorous	.33[a]	.56[a]	.51[a]	.51[a]
Impulsive	.08	.10	.12	.10
Dominance	.36[a]	.41[a]	.41[a]	.44[a]
Stable	-.11	.12	-.09	-.11
Social	.25[b]	.35[a]	.40[a]	.37[a]
Reflective	.13	.04	.07	.09

[a]Significant at the .01 level.
[b]Significant at the .05 level.

Table 2. Multiple correlation between selected combined predictive variables and academic index (Y_1) (N = 69)

Selected predictor	r	F Level	R	R^2	$\sigma est.Y_1$
Active temperament	.53	26.61	.53	.27	.347
PFI	.53	9.34	.59	.35	.327
Mental ability	.40	4.08	.62	.38	.320

Table 3. Multiple correlation between selected combined predictive variables and faculty rating (Y_2) (N = 69)

Selected predictor	r	F Level	R	R^2	$\sigma est.Y_2$
PFI	.68	52.43	.67	.44	29.71
Active temperament	.59	11.87	.73	.52	27.56
Motor ability	.37	3.19	.73	.54	27.11
Economic	.24	2.45	.74	.55	26.82

Table 4. Multiple correlation between selected combined predictive variables and peer rating (Y_3) (N = 69)

Selected predictor	r	F Level	R	R^2	$\sigma est.Y_3$
PFI	.65	48.58	.64	.41	31.74
Active temperament	.61	14.08	.71	.51	29.03
Motor ability	.60	4.01	.73	.53	28.39

Table 5. Multiple correlations between selected combined predictive variables and composite criterion (Y_4) (N = 69)

Selected predictor	r	F Level	R	R^2	$\sigma est.Y_3$
PFI	.67	55.42	.67	.45	10.01
Active temperament	.64	17.32	.74	.55	8.97
Mental ability	.41	3.88	.76	.57	8.79

reveals that the PFI and the active temperament trait were selected as predictive variables for all four criterion items. Mental ability was selected as a predictive variable for all criterion variables except faculty and peer ratings, motor ability as a variable for both the peer rating and faculty rating criteria, and the economic value for the faculty rating.

The regression equations which best predict the four criteria appear in Table 6. The equation with the greatest predictive value is Y_4. This equation will predict an individual's Hull score for the composite criteria of success from the results of the PFI, the Otis quick-scoring mental ability test, and the active trait of the Thurstone temperament schedule. This equation has a forecasting efficiency of 34 percent and a standard error of estimate of 8.79.

CONCLUSIONS

1. There was a significant positive relationship between success in the professional preparation program of physical education and the active, vigorous, dominant, and social temperament traits.

2. There was a significant positive rela-

Table 6. Regression equations for prediction of success in women's physical education professional preparation

Equation	$\sigma est.\ Y$	E
$Y_1 = .0064X_1 + .0012X_3 + .0038X_{10} + .2817$	.32	.21
$Y_2 = .7014X_1 + .5845X_2 + .6234X_5 + .3760X_{10} + 46.00$	26.82	.33
$Y_3 = .0620X_1 + .0654X_2 + .4760X_{10} + 69.30$	28.40	.31
$Y_4 = .2864X_1 + .3330X_3 + .1495X_{10} - 19.92$	8.79	.34

Y_1 = Academic index.
Y_2 = Faculty rating score.
Y_3 = Peer rating score.
Y_4 = Hull score of composite criterion.
X_1 = Calculated physical fitness index of the *Rogers physical fitness battery.*
X_2 = T score of Scott motor ability test for college women.
X_3 = Intelligence quotient as measured by the Otis quick-scoring mental ability test.
X_{10} = Active trait measured by the Thurstone temperament schedule.
X_5 = Economic value measured by the Allport-Vernon-Lindzey study of values.
E = Coefficient of forecasting efficiency.

tionship between mental ability and success in the professional preparation program of physical education.

3. There was a higher positive relationship between physical fitness and success in the physical education professional preparation program than between success and any other single predictive variable.

4. The value and interest variables showed practically no relationship to success in the professional program of physical education.

5. The best combination of variables for predicting success in the professional preparation program of physical education was the physical fitness index, the active temperament trait score, and the mental ability score.

6. To achieve the most efficient prediction of the composite score of success in the women's professional preparation program either of the following equations could be utilized[3]:

(a) Success (Hull score) = .2864 (PFI)
  + .3330 (mental ability)
  + .1495 (active trait)
  − 19.92.
(b) Success (Hull score) = .2875 (PFI)
  + .1824 (active trait)
  + 15.91.

DISCUSSION

Several factors were identified in this study as being related to success in a women's physical education professional preparation

---

[3]Equation (a) has a standard error of estimate of 8.79. Equation (b) has a standard error of estimate of 8.98.

program. The data analysis, however, showed that individual predictions based upon these factors alone have a high margin of error.

Departments of physical education using the formulas reported in this study for selection purposes would find it necessary to determine an appropriate cutoff point below which applicants should be extremely well-screened as their probable success in the physical education professional curriculum is being considered. Because of the relatively large standard error of estimate, an applicant's predicted success score must be interpreted with caution. This score should by no means be the single decisive factor in the selection or rejection of a candidate. In combination, however, with a student's past record of achievement, selection based upon this information will be superior to subjective judgment alone. Applicants ranking at the low end of the predicted Hull scale distribution will be a greater risk and will be more likely to be unsuccessful in the professional program than those who rank high.

RECOMMENDATIONS

1. It is recommended that similar studies be conducted at other institutions preparing physical education teachers. If the same factors are identified at other colleges and universities, it would lend support to the conclusion that these variables are truly related to success in the professional preparation program of physical education.

2. Because it is probable that other factors

are related to success in women's physical education professional preparation programs, it is recommended that additional predictors be investigated.

3. It is recommended that future research be directed toward the establishment of an operational definition of successful physical education teaching.

4. In order that future predictive studies can be more effective, it is recommended that instruments which more accurately measure teaching success in physical education be devised.

5. It is recommended that longitudinal studies be conducted which will determine the extent to which success in the physical education professional preparation program is related to later success in physical education teaching.

REFERENCES

1. Arnsdorff, Dorothy. *Perception of critical behaviors for women physical education teachers at the secondary level.* Unpublished doctoral dissertation. Stanford University, 1959.
2. Barr, A. S. Characteristics of successful teachers. *Phi Delta Kappan* 39:282-84, 1958.
3. Blesh, Erwin T. Correlations between success in student teaching and success on the job. *Res. Quart.* 13:353-99, 1942.
4. Brownell, Clifford. The preparation of teachers in health and physical education. *Amer. phys. Educ. Rev.* 33:278-80, 1929.
5. Charters, W. W., and Waples, Douglas. *The commonwealth teacher training study.* Chi-cago: The University of Chicago Press, 1929.
6. Efroymson, M. A. Multiple regression analysis. *Mathematical methods for digital computers.* Edited by Anthony Ralston and Herbert S. Wilf. New York: John Wiley and Sons, 1960.
7. Graybeal, Elizabeth. A consideration of qualities used by administrators in judging effective teachers of physical education. *Res. Quart.* 12:741-44, 1941.
8. Handy, Donald Thomas. *A predictive index as a basis for the selection of prospective teachers in physical education.* Unpublished doctoral dissertation, University of California at Los Angeles, 1952.
9. Hardaway, Charles W. Factors considered by school superintendents in the selection of beginning teachers. *Teaching in America.* Edited by Anthony C. Riccio and Frederick R. Cyphert. Columbus, Ohio: Charles E Merrill, 1962.
10. Hart, Frank W. *Teachers and teaching.* New York: The Macmillan Co., 1934.
11. Hellfritzsh, G. A factor analysis of teaching abilities. *J. exp. Educ.* 14:166-69, 1945.
12. Hunt, Herold C. The ideal teacher. *J. Educ.* 125:38, 1942.
13. Martin, Lycia O. *The prediction of success for students in teacher education.* New York: Teachers College, Columbia University Press, 1944.
14. Montgomery, Jack Ernest. *The interpretation and application of selected tests and other evaluative measures for the selective guidance and counseling of men majoring in physical education.* Unpublished doctoral dissertation, University of California at Los Angeles, 1951.
15. Rolfe, J. E. The measurement of teaching ability. *J. exp. Educ.* 14:52-75, 1945.

58. Securing professional personnel*

Waneen Wyrick

Sargent College, Boston University

Some outstanding problems we face in securing professional personnel for the role of teacher in physical education, be she generalist or specialist, are: (1) motivation of young girls to enter the physical education college degree program, (2) maintenance of high academic standards while graduating a large percentage of those who do enter the program, and (3) production of teachers from teacher education programs who have some kind of basic physical education foundation from which to enter the role of generalist and/or specialist.

This is a discussion of possible future problems in an unknown dimension, but a few brief statements about present problems are necessary to provide a background. The real problems we now face in securing professional personnel do not come at the time of application blanks and interviews in the offices of administrators and physical education supervisors all over the country during the few months prior to graduation time. The problems lie in the education of the people of the United States to the role of physical education in our way of living and the resulting lack of motivation for young girls to make this profession a part of their lives. Forty years ago, when the profession of physical education began to grow rapidly, teaching was one of very few professions in which it was socially acceptable for women to participate. Today, bright young women who feel a need to explore and produce find the fields of chemistry, physics, archaeology, psychology, and engineering more challenging—as well as socially approved—and physical education is no longer the only profession with a scientific background which they may enter. Today's interested applicant, in general, is no longer the way-above-average in intelligence, hard driving, aggressive, dedicated, dream laden, "emancipation for women" type of person. A hard look at our potential teachers will point out new problems in securing professional personnel. Tomorrow's applicant, on the whole, will be above average in intelligence, but not an intellectual giant; aggressive, but not overtly so; dedicated perhaps, but bewildered at the multiplicity of choices within our own profession to which she may be dedicated; and she will not have had a background of struggle with the idea of emancipation, for she will have been told, among other facts, that women now control in some way or other over 50% of the wealth of the United States. While some of you have watched the automobile take forty years to evolve, she will have witnessed in fifteen years an intercontinental missile develop into a manned space capsule, and it will be easy for her to see the plausibility of the soon-to-be world library which by use of satellites will videotape every book or printed material in the world for home TV sets—a library of video tapes which will be 6 cubic feet in size. So, although she may not be an intellectual giant, her store of knowledge will be greater, because the world has learned much in forty years. Because of fantastic changes in world events, the concept of physical education may change entirely and, to her, a discussion over whether she should specialize in team sports or dance will seem rather trivial and out of place. She will be oriented to a fast pace, and she will probably not understand how humans could for so many years conceive of the human in two parts—a mind and a body.

*From Selected Papers, 1964 Ruby Anniversary Workshop Report, National Association for Physical Education of College Women. Used by permission.

It has been noticeable in some teacher education programs that it is difficult to maintain high entrance requirements and high academic standards and at the same time keep a high percentage of graduating seniors in physical education. More and more in the future, as the nation's demand for physical educators grows greater and greater and more different types of job opportunities for them are opened, administrators may find the supply of teachers completely inadequate.

Briefly, a third problem which we are facing is producing teachers from teacher education programs who have some kind of basic physical education foundation from which to enter the role of teacher. There are probably fifty different concepts of what the preparation of a physical educator should be, as evidence by the teacher certification requirements of the different states. As Morehouse and Dexter have pointed out in recent research

. . . each state has its own separate guides which affect the setting of its own requirements and each state expects to procure its teachers from its own teacher-training institutions. At present it would be a curricular impossibility for one teacher-training institution in the United States to prepare its physical education graduates for certification in all 50 states.

And now to the future. In order to predict problems which may arise in securing professional personnel, as generalists or specialists, we must try to conceive what our profession will be responsible for one or two decades from today. It has been said by noted educators that due to the increased life expectancy of individuals, our nation may find that it will change from being youth oriented to being older-adult-oriented. This means to many people that it is high time physical education stops thinking of itself as a profession geared only to elementary, secondary, and college levels, and think in terms of all ages and of many different areas. For instance, one area which may open up a new need for physical educators is a proposed reconditioning center for adults. According to Wilhelm Raab, reconditioning centers for adults have been functioning very successfully in the countries of West Germany, Austria, East Germany, Czechoslovakia, Soviet Union, and Israel for some time. In the book, *Hypokinetic Disease,*

which he co-authored with Hans Kraus, Dr. Raab states:

The forgotten man in medicine is the mentally and emotionally overstrained and physically underexercised person, a candidate for early invalidism and premature death. He remains basically unattended until manifest disease requires belated remedial and rehabilitative measures at exorbitant cost. . . . Creation of such centers also in the United States is a matter of urgent necessity. It would improve general health conditions, provide substantial economic advantages for employers and employees alike, and offer vast research possibilities in the fields of preventive and physical medicine.

This is an obvious need in our country, and some members of the medical profession are trying to do something about it. The president is trying to do something about it. In the event that such reconditioning centers do materialize and are supervised by the medical profession, it seems logical that a physical educator should become a part of the medical supervisory team. This would create more job opportunities for the physical educator, and perhaps a desire for specialization in the area of preventive medicine.

In view of the comparatively recent psychosomatic concept of illness, there is still another area in which physical educators may find themselves in the future. Dr. Kennefeck of the Medfield State Mental Hospital has begun an informal type of project in which he has created a team consisting of a medical doctor, phychiatrist, community volunteer worker, and physical educator in an effort to deal with mentally ill patients. He has stated that physical movement has a very real meaning to most people, whether it be a love of movement or a total disregard for it, and types of movements can be said to have emotional connotations. As a very crude example, when we are depressed we tend to look downward, slump forward, round the shoulders, and perhaps even rest the head in the hands; whereas when we are elated, movement is almost demanded, our head is thrown upward as in laughing, sometimes our arms are flung upward or backward in extension. Dr. Kennefeck has experimented with the idea that perhaps evoking movement of this type would also evoke some kind of corresponding response emotionally, and he has stated that the physical educator more than anyone else has the kinesiological knowledge of body movement to work with the medical profession in this type of project. So here again appears to be another job opportunity for the physical educator of the future—and a type of specialization. These possibilities mean that the profession may expand into new dimensions, and the variety in this expansion may create a need for specialization within our own field. This of course will create tremendous competition among administrators for securing personnel.

Lastly, in facing problems of securing professional personnel for the role of generalist or specialist, there is the possibility of a changing concept of physical education which may alter entirely the type of person who may be a candidate for the role of physical educator. It may indicate that in the future when we speak of the generalist in physical education, we are really speaking of a physical educator whose specialty is people, and who teaches them to express themselves physically in a variety of ways. In their book, *Hypokinetic Disease,* Kraus and Raab have this to say about the role of physical education or the physical educator:

Physical education will have to reduce drastically its permissive attitude and make formal exercise, running, swimming, and other fundamental activities the backbone of its programs. But by doing so, a long step will be taken toward the other goals that are now being missed by diffusely trying for the "well-rounded" personality.

In order to accomplish this, teachers should be trained to look at their jobs as the performance of a craft rather than as a primarily intellectual activity. It will require sweat, though neither blood nor tears, and it will require discipline which should not be confused with regimentation.

It will require the stressing of controlled and organized exercise, calisthenics, running, lifting, and swimming—in other words, the more basic activities—and it will require a steady testing and retesting in order to assure that the children meet minimum standards.

We all know of the concern of the United States government for the physical fitness of our citizens, and the trend toward concern for preventive medicine and physical fitness by the medical profession. Will this urgent need enforce a different concept of physical education, and therefore will our applicants in the future have a general scientific background prepared to deal with any kind of knowledge required for movement education? Or will they be specialists in the areas of exercise and body fitness, movement activities taught in the schools, or medically oriented workers on medical teams?

We were asked to dream when planning for this panel. In a dream situation of this type, speaking of generalist or specialist in the terms of sports personnel vs. dance personnel vs. recreation personnel, etc., would be analagous to trying to determine whether a secretary should learn shorthand or speedwriting after the dictaphone had been invented. And I can't even think of an analogy which would do justice to the concept of speaking of a badminton or basketball specialist. We face the challenge of a world that is flying in intellectual development while dawdling in physical degeneration. We must try hard to look within the unknown dimension of the future, for only then can we be well prepared to cope with solving tomorrow's problems.

59. Certain psychosocial and cultural characteristics unique to prospective teachers of physical education*

Gerald S. Kenyon

Associate Professor, Department of Physical Education, School of Education, University of Wisconsin

Twenty-two years ago, Bookwalter (2) observed that physical education majors, while superior on various motor traits, were inferior to other students on the ACE Psychological Examination—an instrument designed to assess intellectual aptitude, particularly that which is prerequisite to success in college. He concluded that overemphasis on athletics in high school jeopardizes the probable success of the student in college. Other observations, both casual and careful, attesting to the intellectual inferiority of physical education students, are neither new nor novel (4, 17, 20).

In viewing nonintellectual characteristics, few would dispute the motor superiority of students attracted to physical education major programs. Moreover, these same students, insofar as they are athletes, probably possess some unique personality traits (3). Few studies have appeared in the area of attitudes, social values, and cultural characteristics of prospective teachers of physical education.

With respect to the attitudes and values of college students in general, many studies have been reported (e.g., 8, 13, 14, 16, 18), particularly since Jacob (11) concluded that the values of college students are "remarkably homogeneous" and that neither instructor, curriculum, nor teaching method "liberalizes" the student during his college career. Whether the values of college students are more homogeneous than hetero-

geneous certainly depends upon where an investigator chooses to draw the line. However, the more recent evidence, particularly that of Lehmann (14), tends to support the heterogeneity of students' values and to give credit to the college for having some influence upon their formulation. Also, Gottlieb and Hodgkins (7) have shown that when college subgroups are studied they appear to possess characteristics that are similar within, but quite different between groups. Earlier, Gottlieb (6) suggested that students with common professional goals shared common values, at least at the graduate level. He calls this phenomenon "anticipatory socialization," describing it as "a process by which the individual adopts the values of a group to which he aspires but does not yet belong." Logically, students with common professional or vocational aspirations would be expected to share values for the field in question and perhaps values in general. However, with the degree of specialization seen within most professions today, the question arises as to whether values, other than those connected with the student's particular specialty, differ among professional subgroups.

It was the purpose of this study to examine certain sociocultural characteristics of prospective members of the teaching profession. If Gottlieb's hypothesis is tenable, one would expect most teachers to attach considerable importance to education. Although subject matter interests may vary, attitudes toward education might be expected to be

*From Research Quarterly, Vol. 36, p. 105, Mar. 1965. Used by permission.

common to all prospective teachers at a given institution, particularly since they have shared many professional courses and instructors. Also, if Gottlieb's hypothesis can be generalized, prospective teachers would be expected to possess traits, other than those closely related to teaching in general or to their special field in particular, that would distinguish them from other professional groups.

To ascertain the degree of similarity between the characteristics of members of a professional subgroup and those of the profession as a whole, physical education majors were compared with other prospective teachers. Liberal arts students served as controls. Thus the research reported here represents a pilot study designed to test, in part, the following hypothesis:

The characteristics of prospective teachers of one specialty, namely, physical education, although different from those of students not anticipating to teach, are akin to those of students enrolled in other teacher preparatory curriculums.

PROCEDURE
Subjects

The subjects for this study were students enrolled in a large Midwestern university during the spring of 1962. To facilitate analyses based upon different research models, a simple random sample was drawn from each of the following populations:

1. Lower division undergraduate men enrolled in a physical education curriculum
2. Lower division undergraduate women enrolled in a physical education curriculum
3. Upper division undergraduate men enrolled in a physical education currriculum
4. Upper division undergraduate women enrolled in a physical education curriculum
5. Upper division undergraduate men enrolled in an education curriculum other than physical education
6. Upper division undergraduate men enrolled in a liberal arts curriculum
7. Male students enrolled in a graduate physical education curriculum
8. Female students enrolled in a graduate physical education curriculum
9. Male students enrolled in a graduate education curriculum other than physical education
10. Male students enrolled in a program of graduate study in the arts or sciences.

Data

The data used for this study were acquired through the use of four inventories, requiring one hour or less to complete. Special group sessions were scheduled. Those who were unable to meet for one of these were requested, by letter, to come to the office of the investigator to complete the inventories. Those who still had not responded were mailed packets containing the inventories, appropriate instructions, and a return envelope. In this manner data were obtained from 156 students out of the 175 who were originally drawn, or approximately 89 percent.

Attitudes toward education were assessed by the *Education Scale I* (ES-I), a 20-item Likert-type inventory recently developed by Kerlinger and Kaya (12). Their work has suggested two basic factors underlying attitudes toward education; "Progressivism" (A items) and "Traditionalism" (B items). The ES-I Scale provides three scores: A, B, and A-B. The latter is meant to provide an index of the "consistency of attitude structure." The degree to which students were dogmatic or authoritarian in their thinking was measured by Rokeach's *Dogmatism Scale* (19). The Allport-Vernon-Lindzey *Study of Values* (1) was used to assess social values. Social class background was estimated using Hollingshead's *Two-Factor Index of Social Position* (9, 10).

Research design

The ten populations were selected to permit analyses based upon two research designs; (a) a comparison between two educational levels and among three major fields of study (physical education, education, and liberal arts) of men only; and (b) a comparison by level and sex of physical education students only. Two-way analyses of variance were used to treat the data for each design.[3]

---

[3]Since one sample had as few as 14 subjects responding, this number was drawn at random from each of the remaining nine samples to provide equal N's in all cells in accordance with the requirements of the computer program used for this study.

Table 1. Two-way analysis of variance (level × major field) of three Kerlinger ES-I scores, social position, dogmatism, and six scores from the Allport-Vernon-Lindzey study of values (males only)

Scale	Source of variation	df (total 83)	Mean square	F	P
ES-I	Level	1	5.762	<1.0	n.s.
(progressivism)	Major	2	156.762	3.298	<.05
	L × M	2	267.762	5.634	<.01
	Error	78	47.527		
ES-I (B)	Level	1	105.190	1.985	n.s.
(traditionalism)	Major	2	272.250	5.139	<.01
	L × M	2	97.512	1.840	n.s.
	Error	78	52.982		
ES-I (A-B)	Level	1	70.583	<1.0	n.s.
(consistency)	Major	2	712.940	6.930	<.005
	L × M	2	248.083	2.411	n.s.
	Error	78	102.873		
Social position	Level	1	21.000	<1.0	n.s.
	Major	2	669.083	3.251	<.05
	L × M	2	685.964	3.334	<.05
	Error	78	205.778		
Dogmatism	Level	1	356.298	<1.0	n.s.
	Major	2	4,128.762	9.088	<.001
	L × M	2	350.333	<1.0	n.s.
	Error	78	454.332		
A-V-L	Level	1	372.964	5.851	<.025
theoretical	Major	2	287.940	4.517	<.025
	L × M	2	127.750	2.004	n.s.
	Error	78	63.744		
A-V-L	Level	1	204.298	2.888	n.s.
economic	Major	2	306.440	4.331	<.025
	L × M	2	217.726	3.078	n.s.
	Error	78	70.748		
A-V-L	Level	1	15.429	<1.0	n.s.
aesthetic	Major	2	1,002.333	9.861	<.001
	L × M	2	182.714	1.798	n.s.
	Error	78	101.646		
A-V-L	Level	1	10.012	<1.0	n.s.
social	Major	2	54.250	1.431	n.s.
	L × M	2	18.083	<1.0	n.s.
	Error	78	37.911		
A-V-L	Level	1	22.012	<1.0	n.s.
political	Major	2	118.048	3.130	<.05
	L × M	2	57.333	1.520	n.s.
	Error	78	37.717		
A-V-L	Level	1	0.048	<1.0	n.s.
religious	Major	2	709.083	6.277	<.005
	L × M	2	16.583	<1.0	n.s.
	Error	78	112.965		

RESULTS
Major field of study × level
(men only)

The results of the analyses of variance for data from male students at two levels (upper division undergraduate, and graduate) of three curricular categories for each of the variables studied are given in Table 1.[4]

Attitude toward education: progressivism. The difference between the mean progressivism score of all undergraduate students studied and that of graduate students was not significant. However, there was a significant difference among fields of study ($p <$ .05). The Scheffé test for a two-way analysis of variance (15) revealed that this difference occurred between the mean progressivism score for education students and that for liberal arts students ($p <$ .05). The major field × level interaction was significant. This is probably the result of a tendency for graduate physical education majors to be more "progressive" than undergraduate physical education majors, while the graduate education and liberal arts students tend to be somewhat less "progressive" than their undergraduate counterparts.

Attitude toward education: traditionalism. There was no significant difference in the degree of traditionalism by level, but there was a significant difference among fields of study ($p <$ .01). Although there was no significant difference between them, both physical education majors ($p <$ .05) and liberal arts students (.05 $< p <$ .10)[5] scored higher on the traditionalism scale than did education majors. The interaction was not significant.

Attitude toward education: consistency of beliefs. With respect to the difference scores or "consistency of attitude structure," again there was no difference by level but a significant difference by major field ($p <$ .01). The difference between the mean consistency score of physical education students and that of those enrolled in liberal arts curriculums was not significant. However, the mean A-B score of education majors was significantly

greater than those of the physical education group ($p <$ .05) and the liberal arts student ($p <$ .01). Again the major field × level interaction was not significant.

Social position. The difference was not significant between the mean social position of all undergraduate students studied and that of graduate students. There was a significant difference ($p <$ .05) among fields of study. A Scheffé analysis revealed no significant difference between education and liberal arts students nor between physical education and education majors, but showed physical education students to have a social class background significantly lower than liberal arts students ($p <$ .10). However, upon examining the magnitude of the scores, it would appear that the observed difference between means apparently is not of great practical significance, since both fall within the same position when scores are categorized into five divisions (9). The significant interaction suggests that undergraduate education and physical education majors tend to be from a lower class than graduate students majoring in these subjects. The converse seems to be true for liberal arts students.

Dogmatism. The difference between mean dogmatism scores was not significant by level but differences among major fields were significant ($p <$ .001). The Scheffé test showed that physical education students were considerably more dogmatic than education majors ($p <$ .01). They were also more dogmatic than liberal arts students ($p =$ .10). There was no significant interaction.

Social values. Considerable variation was evident upon examining the means for the six scales of the Allport-Vernon-Lindzey *Study of Values*. When comparing undergraduate students and graduate students of the three fields of study, the only significant difference found was with respect to "theoretical" values, with graduate students possessing the stronger attitudes ($p <$ .025). A comparison of means by major field revealed significant differences for all except the social scale. Upon closer scrutiny the physical education students were significantly lower than liberal arts students on the theoretical ($p <$ .05) and aesthetic ($p <$ .01) scales but were higher on the political ($p <$ .10) and religious ($p <$ .01) scales. When physical education majors were compared

---

[4]Descriptive statistics are available from the author upon request.
[5]Although .05 was the largest value of p justifying a rejection of the null hypothesis associated with the F tests, a $p \leq$ .10 was considered significant when the Scheffé test was used since the latter is considered somewhat conservative (5).

Table 2. Two-way analysis of variance (sex × level) of three Kerlinger ES-I scores, social position, dogmatism, and six scores from the Allport-Vernon-Lindzey study of values

Scales	Source of variation	df (total 83)	Mean square	F	P
ES-I (A)	Sex	1	72.429	1.717	n.s.
(progressivism)	Level	2	69.333	1.643	n.s.
	S × L	2	112.000	2.655	n.s.
	Error	78	42.190		
ES-I (B)	Sex	1	278.679	5.842	<.005
(traditionalism)	Level	2	63.583	1.333	n.s.
	S × L	2	36.036	< 1.0	n.s.
	Error	78	47.706		
ES-I (A-B)	Sex	1	560.583	8.568	<.005
(consistency)	Level	2	158.607	2.424	n.s.
	S × L	2	10.440	< 1.0	n.s.
	Error	78	65.431		
Social position	Sex	1	8,300.298	32.014	<.001
	Level	2	88.321	< 1.0	n.s.
	S × L	2	23.298	< 1.0	n.s.
	Error	78	259.274		
Dogmatism	Sex	1	3,510.107	8.430	<.01
	Level	2	30.250	< 1.0	n.s.
	S × L	2	305.036	< 1.0	n.s.
	Error	78	416.376		
A-V-L	Sex	1	0.048	< 1.0	n.s.
theoretical	Level	2	476.821	10.015	<.001
	S × L	2	1.655	< 1.0	n.s.
	Error	78	47.610		
A-V-L	Sex	1	1,594.714	31.448	<.001
economic	Level	2	79.321	1.564	n.s.
	S × L	2	6.464	< 1.0	n.s.
	Error	78	50.709		
A-V-L	Sex	1	3,773.440	58.272	<.001
aesthetic	Level	2	12.155	< 1.0	n.s.
	S × L	2	12.012	< 1.0	n.s.
	Error	78	64.756		
A-V-L	Sex	1	3.048	< 1.0	n.s.
social	Level	2	10.333	< 1.0	n.s.
	S × L	2	2.333	< 1.0	n.s.
	Error	78	48.879		
A-V-L	Sex	1	114.333	3.571	n.s.
political	Level	2	23.250	< 1.0	n.s.
	S × L	2	25.512	< 1.0	n.s.
	Error	78	32.018		
A-V-L	Sex	1	60.012	< 1.0	n.s.
religious	Level	2	96.083	1.104	n.s.
	S × L	2	41.583	< 1.0	n.s.
	Error	78	87.072		

with students enrolled in other teacher preparatory curriculums, their scores were higher on the economic scale (p < .05) and lower on the aesthetic scale (p < .01). There were no significant differences between education and liberal arts students.

Sex × level: physical education students

Inferential statistics for this design are given in Table 2.

Attitude toward education: progressivism. With respect to the progressivism scores of physical education students, differences between sexes and among levels were not significant. This was also true for the sex × level interaction.

Attitude toward education: traditionalism. The difference between sexes on the traditionalism score was significant (p < .01) with the males showing higher traditional scores than the females at all levels. There was no significant difference among the three levels nor with respect to the sex × level interaction.

Attitude toward education: consistency of beliefs. Regarding consistency of attitudes toward education, the female physical education students were significantly more consistent (p < .01) in their educational beliefs than the male students. Neither the difference among levels, nor the sex × level interaction was significant.

Social position. The difference between the mean social position of men and women students majoring in physical education was highly significant (p < .001). The mean for the females (three levels, N = 42) was 30.02; males, 49.90.[6] When these scores are compared with Hollingshead's five step classification system, their difference is clearly evident. Neither the differences among the three levels nor the sex × level interaction was significant.

Dogmatism. The only significant difference on the D-scale was between sexes. The males were more dogmatic than females (p < .01).

Social values. On two of the six value scales there were significant differences between sexes. Males rated economic values considerably higher than females (p < .001),

---

[6]The higher the score, the lower the social position.

while females rated aesthetic values higher than males (p < .001). Since the curriculum for women physical education teachers gives considerable attention to the aesthetics of human movement, as in modern dance, the latter observation is not a surprising one. There was a highly significant difference among levels on the theoretical scale (p < .001). Upon closer examination this was attributed to the greater importance assigned to theoretical values by graduate students as compared with undergraduates, lower or upper division. On none of the six scales was there a significant interaction.

SUMMARY AND CONCLUSIONS

College students representing teacher trainees, a subgroup of teacher trainees (physical education students), and liberal arts students were administered inventories selected or constructed to assess a variety of non-intellectual, non-physical characteristics. The data (N = 140) were treated using standard two-way analyses of variance. On the basis of the findings, it was concluded that:

1. Prospective male physical education teachers, in contrast to other prospective teachers, have a more weakly formulated, somewhat traditionalistic philosophy of education; have a slightly lower social class background, are more dogmatic and rigid in their thinking; and tend to possess different social values.

2. Prospective male physical education teachers, in contrast to prospective female physical education teachers, have a less consistent, more traditionalistic philosophy of education; have a lower social class background; are more dogmatic and authoritarian in their thinking; and possess somewhat different social values.

3. With respect to those characteristics studied, a generalized "anticipatory socialization" hypothesis is untenable when applied to those preparing to enter the teaching profession, i.e., there is considerable heterogeneity among the traits of prospective teachers. Male physical education students as a professional subgroup do not show many of the characteristics of other prospective teachers; in fact, in many respects the male physical education student is more like the student not preparing to teach.

4. For those variables studied, and within

the limits of cross-sectional data, the findings lend support to the thesis that the college environment does little to alter the values of students.

DISCUSSION

Despite the evidence presented above, it would be unwise at this time to conclude that the teaching profession has become so compartmentalized or fragmented that each subgroup is made up of members quite unlike those of another. Physical education is only one of many fields of concentration for the prospective teacher. If the characteristics of students preparing to teach social studies, or science, or English were studied there might be little or no significant heterogeneity among these subgroups outside of subject matter interests. The validity for this statement is supported somewhat by the observation that, for traits observed in this study, the variability among physical education students was far from being consistently less than the variability among other prospective teachers.

The data presented in this study suggest that prospective physical educators may have more in common with the student not planning to teach than with one who is. If the study of other subgroups, using more variables, shows prospective teachers of physical education to possess a unique value structure, it may explain, in part, the difficulty physical educators allegedly experience in gaining the acceptance of other teachers in the educational hierarchy.

REFERENCES

1. Allport, G. W., Vernon, P. E., and Lindzey, G. *Study of values.* (3rd ed.) Boston: Houghton Mifflin, 1960.
2. Bookwalter, K. W. Are high schools overemphasizing athletics? *The phys. Educ.* 1: 179-80, 1941.
3. Cofer, C. N., and Johnson, W. R. Personality dynamics in relation to exercise and sports. In W. R. Johnson (Ed.) *Science and medicine of exercise and sports.* New York: Harper & Brothers, 1960.
4. Duggan, Anne S. *Comparative study of undergraduate women majors and nonmajors in physical education with respect to certain personal traits.* Unpublished doctoral dissertation, Teachers College, Columbia University, 1936.
5. Edwards, A. L. *Experimental design in psychological research.* New York: Holt, Rinehart and Winston, 1960.
6. Gottlieb, D. American graduate students: some characteristics of aspiring teachers and researchers. *J. educ. Psychol.* 52:236-40, 1961.
7. Gottlieb, D., and Hodgkins, B. *College student subcultures: structural and characteristics.* Paper read at annual meeting of the American Educational Research Association, Chicago, February 14, 1963.
8. Heist, Paul. Diversity in college student characteristics. *J. educ. Social.* 33:279-91, 1960.
9. Hollingshead, A. B. *Two factor index of social position.* New Haven, Connecticut: Author, 1957.
10. Hollingshead, A. B., and Redlich, F. C. *Social class and mental illness: a community study.* New York: Wiley and Sons, 1958.
11. Jacob, P. E. *Changing values in college.* New York: Harper and Brothers, 1957.
12. Kerlinger, F. N., and Kaya, E. The construction and factor analytic validation of scales to measure attitudes toward education. *Educ. & psychol. Measmt* 19:13-29, 1959.
13. ————. The predictive validity of scales constructed to measure attitudes toward education. *Educ. & psychol. Measmt* 19:305-17, 1959.
14. Lehmann, I. J. Some socio-cultural differences in attitudes and values. *J. educ. Psychol.* 36: 1-9, 1962.
15. McNemar, Quinn. *Psychological statistics.* New York: Wiley and Sons, 1962.
16. Morris, Charles. *Varieties of human value.* Chicago: University of Chicago Press, 1956.
17. Mullen, G. D. *Comparative study of men physical education majors and nonmajors in their freshman year at Indiana University.* Unpublished doctoral thesis, Indiana University, 1949.
18. Riesman, D. Influence of student culture and faculty values in the American college. In Bereday, G. Z. and Lauwerys, J. A. (Eds.) *Higher Education, The Yearbook of Education* 386-404, 1959.
19. Rokeach, M. *The open and closed mind.* New York: Basic Books, 1960.
20. Wheeler, L. R., and Wheeler, Viola D. The relationship between reading ability and intelligence among university freshmen. *J. educ. Psychol.* 40:230-38, 1949.

60. Problems of and competencies needed by men physical education teachers at the secondary level*

Elmo Smith Roundy

Professor of Physical Education, College of Physical Education, Brigham Young University

The objectives of this study were: (a) to identify and to rank in order of importance the problems teachers of boys physical education at the secondary level were faced with in performing their roles as directors of learning, and (b) to identify and to rank the competencies needed by these teachers to deal more effectively with the problems. Thirty teachers and 10 administrators were interviewed in the states of California and Utah. Data from these interviews provided the basic material for the development of an inquiry form that was mailed to 526 physical education teachers and 176 administrators in California and Utah. Of the 702 forms mailed, 456 usable returns, or 65 percent were received. Twenty-one problems and 144 competencies were identified and rated. The general areas in which teachers were most often lacking competence were: (a) dealing with classes that have large enrollments, (b) grading and reporting pupil progress, (c) working in the area of adaptive physical education, and (d) evaluating the effectiveness of the physical education program. In teaching the specific activities, gymnastics and rhythms were the two areas where competency was most frequently lacking.

Many authorities have stressed that learning experiences in teacher education programs must be directed toward the development of competencies needed to solve the problems teachers are faced with in performing their professional duties (1, 3, 6). A vital step in the improvement of this curriculum is, then, the identification of these competencies. Scott and Snyder(12) have suggested a most logical approach: (a) start by discerning the problems that confront the teachers, (b) identify the competencies needed to deal effectively with these problems, and (c) delineate the learning experience that will be most effective in developing these competencies. This research involved the first two of these three steps. Although the identification of these problems and competencies must come from a number of sources, the fundamental importance of the observations made by the teachers and supervisors actually performing the professional services in the schools cannot be denied.

A variety of studies have been conducted in the general area of competencies and training experiences needed by physical education teachers (2, 4, 5, 7, 8). None, however, has employed the method used in this study. The results should be useful to those of our profession who are concerned with improving both the in-service and preparatory programs for physical education teachers at the secondary level.

PURPOSE

This study was concerned with identifying and rating the problems faced by teachers of boys physical education at the secondary level and with identifying and rating the competencies needed to deal more effectively with these problems. The investigation was limited to the role of the teacher as "director of learning activities."[1]

*From Research Quarterly, Vol. 38, p. 274, May 1967. Used by permission.

[1]Director of learning is one of the six roles of the teacher originally defined by the California Council on Teaching Education (9) and later accepted by the National Commission on Teacher Education and Professional Standards (11) as a definition of teaching for research purposes.

PROCEDURE

The investigation consisted of two main phases. First, 30 boys physical education teachers and 10 school administrators at the secondary level in the states of Utah and California were interviewed concerning the problems teachers were faced with and the competencies needed to deal more effectively with these problems. The researcher selected the interviewees randomly and employed a pretested guide in each of the interviews. From the information gathered in these interviews, an inquiry form (consisting of 21 problem areas and 144 competencies) was developed. An opportunity was provided the interviewers for free-response comments in each of the problem areas.

The inquiry form was mailed to 450 boys physical education teachers and 150 administrators in the secondary schools of California and to 76 teachers and 26 principals in the secondary schools of Utah. In each state, the population was stratified according to level (junior and senior school) and to the pupil enrollment of the schools. The educators were then randomly selected within the respective strata. Of the 702 inquiry forms mailed, 481, or 68.5 percent, were returned. Twenty-five of these 481 returns were either marked incorrectly or returned too late; thus, 456 returns, or 65 percent, were used in the analysis.

Each of the 21 problems was ranked by the respondents in terms of its importance: (a) a problem of major concern (b) a problem of minor concern, or (c) a problem of negligible concern. A weighted score for each problem was computed according to the following formula (10):

$$\text{weighted score} = \frac{2R + r}{N}$$

R = number of (a) responses
r = number of (b) responses
N = total number of responses

Through this quantitative weighting system each of the problems was ranked according to a numerical score, mean ratio, with a maximum value of 2.0 and a minimum value of 0.0.

The competencies were listed under the problem to which they applied. Each respondent indicated if the competency was needed to deal more effectively with the respective problem. They were then ranked according to the percent of respondents who identified each as being needed.

Differences between and among responses to each problem and competency of the following main groups of subpopulations were tested for statistical significance through the use of chi-square: (a) teachers vs. administrators, (b) respondents in junior high schools vs. respondents in senior high schools, (c) Utah respondents vs. California respondents, (d) teachers with five or less years of teaching vs. teachers with over twelve years of teaching experience, (e) respondents in junior high schools with pupil enrollments of less than 600 vs. respondents in junior high schools with enrollments of 600-1,200 vs. respondents in senior high schools with enrollments over 1,200, (f) respondents in senior high schools with pupil enrollments of less than 1,000 vs. respondents in senior high schools with enrollments of 1,000-2,000 vs. respondents in high schools with enrollments over 2,000.

RESULTS

Judgments of the 456 educators regarding the 21 problem areas and the 57 most significant competencies are presented in Table 1.[2] The competencies are listed under the problem to which they applied. An average of 62.3 percent of the respondents indicated that the 57 competencies were needed to deal more effectively with a specific problem.

Comparisons between and among the responses of the subpopulations in six different groupings produced substantial numbers of statistically significant differences in only one of the six divisions, administrators vs. teachers.[3] The administrators rated 14 of the 21 problems as being more serious than did the teachers and also more frequently marked 90 of the 133 competencies. The differences in response to these 14 problems and 90 competencies were significant at the 5 percent level; a chi-square value of 5.99 or

---

[2] Only 57 of the 144 competencies identified are included. Most of the other competencies were checked as being needed by a smaller percent of the respondents, or were very similar to one of the competencies listed in Table 1. A complete summary can be obtained from the author.

[3] The chi-square values are not given in this article. They may be obtained on request from the author.

Table 1. Judgments of the 456 educators regarding the 21 problems and the most significant competencies needed to deal more effectively with each problem*

| Problem and related competencies | Percent indicating problem of: | | |
	Major concern	Minor concern	Mean ratio
Dealing with classes which have large enrollment:	54.29	35.82	1.4471
1. Skill in grouping and organizing pupils for optimum control and learning. 72%			
2. Proficiency in getting student to accept responsibility for their own learning. 70.3%			
3. Skill in improvising and using activities which are suited for large classes and limited facilities. 68.7%			
4. Competence to improvise and use teaching techniques in the various activities which are adapted for large classes. 61.9%			
Working with limited facilities and equipment:	48.24	37.89	1.3436
1. Proficiency in scheduling and organizing facilities for maximum use. 71.1%			
Grading and reporting pupil progress:	47.14	34.14	1.2841
1. Ability to develop an over-all valid and objective system of grading. 76%			
2. Competence to communicate effectively with parents regarding the progress and growth of students. 58.1%			
Working in the area of adaptive physical education:	44.71	38.11	1.2753
1. Ability to recognize pupils who should be given a referral examination by a physician for placement in an adaptive program. 63%			
2. Competence to select and set up the equipment needed for an adaptive program. 58.8%			
3. Ability to work with students in implementing an adaptive program under the supervision of a physician. 57%			
Evaluating the program:	41.63	41.41	1.2467
1. Ability to summarize and organize evaluational data for meaningful interpretation. 65.2%			
2. Ability to use a variety of techniques and devices for gathering evaluational information. 64.5%			
3. Skill in the use of sound research and statistical procedures for gathering and analyzing evaluational data. 58.4%			
Dealing with the small percentage of students who do not cooperate:	41.41	39.87	1.2269
1. Ability to counsel effectively with these students in helping them meet their needs and adjust to their problems. 70.3%			
2. Proficiency in impartially and consistently enforcing the standard of conduct. 63.9%			
Providing effective and continuous motivation:	38.11	40.31	1.1652
1. Ability to help student develop correct concepts and good attitudes toward physical activity. 66.7%			
2. Skill in using teaching techniques and planning instruction so that students can be given a maximum amount of individual instruction and reinforcement as they perform. 62.8%			
3. Competence to select activities and to teach them in a manner so that each student can experience a measure of success. 60.1%			
4. Proficiency in using procedures and techniques which will keep the students continually informed of their progress. 59.3%			
5. Knowledge of a variety of instructional techniques, drills, games and materials. 54.6%			
6. Ability to provide for continuity of learning experience through developing the proper sequence of activities and the proper progression of movement patterns within an activity. 50.9%			

*Problems are in boldface; competencies are listed below the problems to which they apply. Percent indicates respondents signifying that this competency was needed to deal more effectively with the respective problem.

Continued.

Table 1. Judgments of the 456 educators regarding the 21 problems and the most significant competencies needed to deal more effectively with each problem—cont'd

Problem and related competencies	Percent indicating problem of:		
	Major concern	Minor concern	Mean ratio
Developing a broad enough curriculum to meet the needs and interests of the students: 1. Competence to teach a wide variety of activities. 61.9%	35.86	38.55	1.0991
Maintaining an orderly atmosphere without using overly rigid and militaristic methods of organization and control: 1. Skill in helping class members develop a sense of responsibility to the group. 63.9% 2. Sincere interest in helping each individual student. 55.3%	35.68	38.33	1.0969
Helping students who are having learning difficulties in class activities: 1. Skill in motivating the low achievers. 76.9% 2. Ability to develop and implement a program suited to the abilities and achievement level of the student. 65.2%	33.63	41.10	1.0837
Using tests and other devices to measure progress: 1. Ability to motivate pupils to assume an important role in evaluating their own achievement and development. 69.6% 2. Ability to devise and construct valid and objective skill tests. 68.5% 3. Knowledge of standard skill tests. 60.6% 4. Ability to devise and construct valid physical (organic) fitness tests. 60.1% 5. Skill in setting up local norms for tests. 59% 6. Knowledge of standard physical (organic) fitness tests. 58.8% 7. Proficiency in evaluating pupil progress in general attitudes and social behavior. 57.7% 8. Competence to administer tests in a valid manner. 54.8%	35.24	36.78	1.0727
Adapting instruction to the variation in growth and maturation: 1. Proficiency in teaching students of varying abilities and capacities from the slow to the gifted. 69.2%	30.31	39.34	1.0419
Teaching physical education activities to students: 1. Knowledge of proper teaching methods and drills in gymnastics. 72.9% 2. Ability to demonstrate performance skills in gymnastics. 69.6% 3. Ability to break down an activity or skill into basic movement patterns and to teach these patterns in the most effective sequence. 62.3% 4. Competence to develop effective unit and daily instructional plans. 62.3% 5. Knowledge of proper teaching methods and drills in dance and rhythm activities. 60.4% 6. Ability to demonstrate performance skills in dance and rhythm activities. 59% 7. Knowledge of proper teaching methods and progression drills in individual and dual sports. 54.6% 8. Knowledge of the principles of physical (organic) fitness and conditioning. 52%	33.41	36.92	1.0396
Helping students with their social and personal problems: 1. Skill in identifying students who have significant problems in this area. 61.9% 2. Proficiency in using procedures in class that will aid students in acquiring the special skills of effective group membership and leadership. 60.6%	29.74	44.49	1.0396
Helping students to apply knowledge and skill in non-class situations: 1. Proficiency in helping students to understand the value of physical activities. 65.9% 2. Competence to teach activities with high transfer value. 55.1%	32.38	38.77	1.0352

Table 1. Judgments of the 456 educators regarding the 21 problems and the most significant competencies needed to deal more effectively with each problem—cont'd

| | Percent indicating problem of: | | |
Problem and related competencies	Major concern	Minor concern	Mean ratio
Providing successful coeducational activities: 1. Knowledge of activities which are most successful with coeducational groups. 67.4% 2. Skill in teaching and handling coeducational groups. 67.4%	32.38	33.33	1.0308
Using good classroom teaching methodology: 1. Proficiency in using a variety of instructional materials and visual aids effectively. 61.9%	32.60	36.78	1.0198
Obtaining sufficient time for teaching and coaching: 1. Realization that teaching physical education must be given priority over coaching duties. 57% 2. Skill in planning and using time and energy more effectively. 55.7%	30.84	39.21	1.0088
Selecting activities and experiences suited to the needs and interests of students: 1. Competence in choosing activities that are suited to the needs, interests, growth and maturation level of the pupils. 59.3% 2. Knowledge of individual differences, needs, and interests of the students at this particular age level. 56.4%	32.38	35.02	0.9978
Adjusting to the many interruptions due to excusing and taking students from physical education classes: 1. Ability to implement a stringent and equitable policy regarding the acceptance of excuses for medical reasons. 66.7%	24.67	42.95	0.9229
Providing opportunities for creative experiences: 1. Skill in developing the attitude and confidence necessary for students' creative expression. 61.9% 2. Knowledge of the opportunities for creative expression in physical education. 60.4%	25.11	39.65	0.8987

greater was significant for the problems (one degree of freedom) and 3.84 or greater for the competencies (two degrees of freedom). The range for the chi-square values for the problems was 0.19 to 22.44 and for the competencies it was 0.00 to 38.99. Although these problems and competencies represented a wide variety of subjects, there were heavy concentrations in the areas of teaching methods and techniques, evaluation, counseling, transfer of learning, and motivation. Comparisons involving responses of the other five groupings produced only a few statistically significant differences.

DISCUSSION AND CONCLUSIONS

Regarding the problems and competencies, a number of useful generalizations are apparent. Large class enrollments and limited facilities are related to many of the problems identified in this study. The ideal solution would be to improve facilities and limit class enrollments to an optimum number; from a practical standpoint, however, greater competence in effectively teaching large groups of students is a must for physical education teachers in today's secondary schools. Other areas in which competence was most often lacking were evaluation, grading, and working in adaptive physical education. In the area of specific sports activities, greater competence was most frequently needed in gymnastics, in rhythms, and in individual and dual sports.

From the results of the comparisons of responses between and among the subpopulations for the six groupings, several pertinent inferences can be made. Differences in the judgments of the administrators and the teachers seemed to reflect a tendency for the administrators to be more critical, particularly in areas relating to pedagogy. The lack of statistically significant differences in the evaluation of the California and the Utah respondents indicates the results of the study, with a few exceptions, can be generalized beyond the population sampled. When the wide differences in climate, geography, and population density between the two states are considered, such generalizations appear to be valid. Size of school, experience of the teacher, and the grade level (junior or senior high school) did not appear to have any marked effect on the problems of and the competencies needed by the teachers.

RECOMMENDATIONS

1. Physical educators responsible for professional teacher preparation programs for men could profitably use the competencies identified in this study as a check list in order that important learning experiences are not slighted or overlooked. Particular attention should be given to those problems and competencies receiving the most urgent rating.

2. Educators responsible for in-service training programs could advantageously direct the learning experiences toward the more highly-rated problems and competencies identified in this study.

3. Research studies to identify learning experiences that are most effective in developing the competencies derived from this study would be beneficial.

REFERENCES

1. Athletic Institute. *Report on the 1948 national conference on undergraduate profesional preparation in physical education, health education and recreation.* Chicago: the Institute, 1949.
2. California Association for Health, Physical Education, and Recreation. *Competencies needed by men and women physical education majors.* Burlingame: The Association, 1961.
3. Conant, James B. *The education of American teachers.* New York: McGraw-Hill, 1963.
4. Coombe, Eleanor M. *Functions and competencies of physical education teachers.* Unpublished doctoral dissertation, Stanford University, 1952.
5. Curtis, James. *The training of physical education teachers.* Unpublished doctoral dissertation, University of California, Berkeley, 1948.
6. Engleman, Finnis E., and others. A symposium on teacher education. *J. Tchr. Ed.* 14:23-25, 1963.
7. Graybeal, Elizabeth. A consideration of qualities used by administrators in judging effective teachers of physical education in Minnesota. *Res. Quart.* 12:741-44, 1941.
8. Kebric, Burt M. Problems of beginning teachers of physical education in the high schools of California. *Res. Quart.* 16:42-48, 1945.
9. Kinney, Lucien. *Measures of a good teacher.* San Francisco: California Teachers Association, 1957.
10. Lundberg, George A. *Social research.* New York: Longmans—Green, 1942.
11. National Commission on Teacher Education and Professional Standards. *Measure of teacher competence*—Report of special group D at the Miami Beach conference, June 24-27, 1953. Washington, D. C.: National Education Association, 1953.
12. Snyder, Raymond A., and Scott, Harry A.: *Professional preparation in health, physical education, and recreation.* New York: McGraw-Hill, 1964.

61. The role of the coach in American education*

John D. Lawther

Former Assistant Dean, Pennsylvania State University

The late Arnold Gesell once said that it was through play and games that the child gets the "opportunity for effort, and failure and success, for judicious risks and thrills and a store of experiences which build up his morale, his capacity to endure and stand the gaff, his early learnings in sportsmanship."

Before the present generation, only England of the great civilized nations based its physical, moral, and leadership training on the lessons from the sports and games of the athletic fields. In the so-called "great public schools" of England in which the aristocracy of Great Britain were educated, the schoolmasters as well as the students spent their afternoons together on the play fields. This aspect of English education was considered an essential part of the training of Great Britain's future statesmen and military officers. The Duke of Wellington's statement that the battle of Waterloo had been won on the playing fields of Eton and Harrow has been quoted many times.

Let me quote somewhat similar opinions expressed by Thomas Wood and Clark Hetherington at the beginning of the present century. Wood said:

Very little profitable instruction in theoretical ethics can be given in the elementary or even in the high school. Children and youth get most of their moral instruction in relation to action, and many important ethical principles may be instilled in connection with the large primitive types of conduct involved in personal health problems, and in games and sports. The playground, gymnasium, and athletic field afford the best oppor-

tunity for the learning of moral lessons, sometimes even by college students.[1]

In the same year Hetherington wrote:

The fundamental character education through the guidance of conduct in play is not completed in childhood. It continues through youth, and long after moral education by intellectual inspiration may be well begun. The athletic field of the late adolescent years is as truly a laboratory of conduct as is the playfield of the child. This is the last chance age for intensive moral training by direct personal guidance and discipline. Fourteen to twenty is the critical period in which all the fundamental social traits and moral habits are formed, and they are formed in a large measure on the play side of life. . . .[2]

The athletic sports in our educational system can well be a form of recreational therapy from the grind of the academic classroom and from the anxiety neuroses of adolescence. Athletic competition motivates many youngsters to achieve undeveloped potentialities in skill, in emotional control under stress, in social development, and in strength and endurance. Athletic skills provide our youth with means for escape from the boredom and monotony of inactivity or, what is worse, from spending their energy in socially disapproved directions. Our youth use their athletic skills for social group participation in areas which they enjoy, and in which they have greater confidence in their

---

[1]Wood, Thomas D. "Physical Education." *Health and Education*. Ninth Yearbook, Part I, National Society for the Study of Education, Bloomington, Ill.: Public School Publishing Co., 1910, pp. 89-90.
[2]Hetherington, Clark W. "Fundamental Education." *American Physical Education Review* 15: 633; December 1910.

*From Journal of Health, Physical Education, and Recreation, Vol. 36, p. 65, May 1965. Used by permission.

abilities to do their part acceptably. They learn to escape from emotional upsets by physical self-expression in sports.

You, as a coach of boys' or girls' athletic teams, must remember that highly competitive activities arouse much emotional excitement and deep feeling. In this heated atmosphere your players are going to be molded in some way. Their abilities and shortcomings, their emotional reactions, their drive, energy, determination, or lack of it—in short, their personality quirks and eccentricities—will be revealed. Behavior codes and attitudes are learned rapidly under group social pressures and emotional conditioning. Under such emotional arousal, youngsters are more impressionable, more subject to change. Herein, of course, lies the absolute necessity for careful guidance. If these youngsters cannot achieve a certain amount of recognition, approval, success in activity, and therefore status, they may resort to abnormal or antisocial behavior. Unsportsmanlike conduct, breaking rules, fits of anger to cover up failure, may be expected to crop out and need correction. These youngsters' lapses from proper social codes, from complete fairness, are due to lack of understanding of how to secure success, group approval, and prestige.

You, the coach, have a closer relationship and a greater influence on youngsters than almost any other teacher. In your content area (athletics) in which physical, moral, and social behavior are of vital importance, you will have a great influence on these youngsters. Your influence is inescapable in spite of the fact that it thrusts upon you an almost fearful responsibility for directing character formation. The competitive world —in children's play, in athletics, in life—is neither gentle nor kind. You, the coach, must be both kind and firm. The youngsters *need* understanding, and *want* firm guidance by one they trust. They want the firm guidance to help them over their uncertainties and insecurities. They want to be respected adults, and they appreciate regimens requiring adoption of mature, responsible behavior.

You, the coach, can hardly help becoming a community personality, an important member of the faculty, and a focus of attention of many students. Your personal behavior will be under considerable scrutiny, hence you will have to be constantly aware of the example you set. To succeed you must be energetic, dynamic, and forceful. Sports skills are the means through which you teach, so you must become an excellent sports teacher. However, you will find the direction of interschool sports a highly interesting and unusually exciting profession. I know of no other occupation which is more rewarding in human satisfactions. All down through the ages of history, competitive sports have fulfilled such a felt need of man that neither religious edict nor royal decree has been successful in abolishing them. Cozens and Stumpf once stated:

"The exercise of physical skill, mental acumen, and spiritual courage in the field of sports and games is as old and as integral a part of the culture of mankind as the expression of these same human capacities in the fields of music and art. The rich and colorful heritage in this area of human experience is as much a part of the birthright of the children of earth as the songs that have been sung and the pictures that have been painted...."

Common interests, common loyalties, common enthusiasms, those are the great integrating factors in any culture. In America, sports have provided this common denominator in as great a degree as any other factor.[3]

---

[3]Cozens, Frederick W., and Stumpf, Florence. "American Sports from the Sidelines." *Journal of Health, Physical Education, and Recreation* 23:12; November 1952.

73. Vibrations in the ivory towers*

Samuel Baskin

President, Union for Research and Experimentation in Higher Education

Some years ago, Philip Coombs, then program director of the education division of the Fund for the Advancement of Education, asked what would happen if every institution of higher learning had on its staff an able person whose principal task was that of encouraging the development of innovative ideas—a person who, in effect, served as the college's "vice president in charge of heresy."

While more new developments have come about in higher education in the last decade than at any other time in our Nation's history, the fact remains that higher education is still badly in need of a good bit of "heresy." It is one of the major paradoxes of our times that institutions of higher learning, which should be preparing our young men and women to enter a world of social and intellectual revolution, are themselves so resistant to change.

One need only glance at the catalogs of America's colleges and universities—as they are today, and as they existed 30, 40, 50, and more years ago—to realize that the basic system for getting a higher education in America has changed little. The system is still "going to class" and "course and credit hour" requirements.

But here and there are sparks of creativity. In spite of a general ingrained conservatism and traditionalism, there is a wide range of innovation and experimentation visible in colleges and universities across the country. A few institutions are frankly experimental and, for a while at least, until the rigors of orthodoxy set in, do unusual things to try to improve the quality of student learning and to cope with the problems created by increasing enrollments and rising academic costs. The Union for Research and Experimentation in Higher Education (UREHE), a 12-college consortium consisting of Antioch, Bard, Goddard, Hofstra, Loretto Heights, Monteith, Nasson, New College at Sarasota, Illinois Teachers College—North, Sarah Lawrence, Shimer and Stephens, was formed in 1963 specifically to foster educational research experimentation. The union recently completed a series of conferences, supported by a Cooperative Research grant, stimulating new program developments and curriculum innovations in higher education.

"Experimental colleges, like Utopian colonies, grow out of dissatisfaction with reforms limited to bits and pieces," said Goodwin Watson, professor emeritus of social psychology at Teachers College, Columbia University, and distinguished service professor at Newark State College, at the first of these conferences. Dr. Watson pointed out that most experimental colleges embody certain common features since they are all responding to similar contemporary pressures. They are trying, in Clark Kerr's words, "to seem smaller as they grow larger."

"They are concerned for general, liberal education," said Watson. "They move away from a proliferation of specialized courses toward larger interdisciplinary units. They try to restore prestige to teaching to offset pressures toward research and publication. They encourage independent study and experiment with new technologies for added learning. They revise the calendar to use all the year. They cultivate campus communities but also carry students out into the field of practical affairs. They are world-minded,

*From *American Education*, Vol. 4, p. 12, Mar. 1968, Office of Education, Department of Health, Education, and Welfare. Used by permission.

327

and often provide for experience abroad.

"These new enterprises," Watson continued, "follow the New Testament injunction about the superiority of a new garment to patches on the old one. They decline to put new wine into old bottles. They seek a new design in which each part is harmoniously integrated with all the others."

Among the more familiar innovative techniques on campus today are student participation in educational planning and governance, independent study, early admissions, alteration or elimination of grades, and re-arrangements of learning-living plans.

At the New State University College at Westbury, N. Y., for instance, students and faculty have worked together in planning a new experimental college [scheduled to open in the fall of 1968]. Not having any students of his own, Harris Wofford, president of New College, went out and hired a team of student planners from Antioch, Berkeley, San Francisco State, Goddard, and the State University at Stony Brook to serve on his planning team.

At Florida Presbyterian College and New College at Sarasota, all students participate in independent study and research as a regular part of their undergraduate experience—beginning with their freshman year.

Many colleges give credit through advanced placement, examination, or early admission programs. New York State, for example, has developed a proficiency examination program under which colleges in the State provide credit in certain course areas on the basis of examinations taken by the student before or during his time at college. A similar program has been developed by the College Entrance Examination Board for use nationally.

New pass-fail systems have been introduced in a number of courses at institutions that include Yale, Ohio State, Stanford, the University of California at Berkeley, Tufts, Lehigh, Mount Holyoke, Oberlin, and Pomona College. A March 1967 report from the University of Massachusetts lists 22 colleges and universities that have adopted such pass-fail options.

In an attempt to implant new patterns of smallness within their structures—whether it be an about-to-expand small college or a large university—a number of institutions are building living-learning centers that make use of the dormitory as a center for learning as well as living. For example, Stephens College employs a house plan under which a group of 100 freshmen take all their courses from the same group of faculty members within a single residence hall. A similar, much larger effort is underway at Michigan State University, where nine residence-hall, living-learning centers, each housing about 1,200 students, have been constructed. Classroom, library, faculty offices, recreational, and in some instances, laboratory spaces have been built into the residence hall itself. The student takes the bulk of his work in his living-learning unit.

The trouble with most of the experimentation going on in higher education, however, is that it is piecemeal. Commenting on this point, Winslow R. Hatch, a program specialist at the U. S. Office of Education, says, "It is inadequate in scope, design, and pace; whereas problems are massive, multifaceted, and interdependent."

Royce S. Pitkin, president of Goddard College, agrees. "Practically every proposal has been a tinkering with what's already been done. It's like repairing a Model T when we need a jet."

One major experiment now underway which seeks to develop new forms of undergraduate education is known as the field study center or beachhead college idea. The experiment sponsored by the Union for Research and Experimentation in Higher Education is supported by grants from the U. S. Office of Education and the New World Foundation.

Under the plan, faculty, students, and local leaders in a chosen area work together in an attempt to deal with various community needs. Four such centers are to be established, each in a particular problem area: the inner city, Appalachia, an underdeveloped region, and suburbia. Depending on the particular situation, the amount of time a student will spend in the field study center will vary from six months to a year. Appropriate seminar programs, projects, and research studies are being developed in the student's center activities.

Two of these centers are already started: one on the island of Kauai, Hawaii, where a student and faculty team from several UREHE colleges are helping to establish a new community college; the other, the Appalachian Center in Pikeville, Ky., where students will help to develop various recreational and teaching programs and participate in Pikeville's new model city program.

There is, of course, much that needs to be done in evaluating the merits and effectiveness of these changes. It is likely that some of the more ambitious ventures may spread waxen wings only to watch their glistening pinions melt in the sun of practical experience. At one of the UREHE conferences, Joseph Tussman, professor of philosophy at the University of California at Berkeley, told about the frustrations experienced by Berkeley's experimental college.

The scheme was to have five professors from different disciplines prepare a program for freshmen and sophomores, using the "problems" approach—their way of avoiding the "domination of the notion of academic discipline." They would be teaching subjects they were not necessarily familiar with, so that the professors would be involved along with their students in the learning process. Faculty members agreed to take part because they believed it was a coherent attempt to involve the student in the learning process and heighten his capacity to deal intelligently with the major problems with which he is confronted today. The first semester was spent on the problem of why Greece became involved to the point of its own destruction in the Peloponnesian Wars. The second semester focused on 17th century England, the Puritan Revolution. The third and fourth semesters were to relate to America, and end with the study of one great American problem, such as race. At the end of the first year, however, the faculty wanted out— partly because such teaching was exhausting, and partly because of fundamental differences of opinion as to what a teacher is.

It is important at this juncture to make clear that no argument is being developed here for change just for the sake of change. To be productive, change must be *planned:* it must have clear objectives, appropriate support, practical means of implementation, and provisions for adequate and impartial evaluation. As Goodwin Watson points out in his essay for *Innovation in Higher Education,* "It is one thing simply to undertake change; it is quite another to seek to evaluate the effects of such a change or to try to gain, through research, a better understanding of the necessary strategies involved in the inception and adaptation of change." Watson also says many questions have to be asked,

particularly: "To what degree do the changes really seek to address themselves to the larger problems of higher education?"

James Dixon, president of Antioch College, who wrote the final essay in *Innovation in Higher Education,* says: "There is no longer a question of whether there will or should be change; the question is how the change will come about. If we regard our society as a system, how can we utilize its radical energies to produce planned, coherent, productive change? How can we avoid the wastefulness and danger of change by random processes of accommodation, timeserving, and tinkering? The world is not waiting for educators to decide whether or not they are in favor of change; it keeps moving. Whether its educational course will be in the best interest of our culture may well depend on whether we get aboard or get left behind."

It is possible that there has never been a time in America when it is more imperative for educators to establish their own educational priorities, to look to the future and determine what changes are needed and how they best can be brought about. For American education today is faced by a new and powerful force: the movement of big business into education.

The dramatic emergence of this knowledge industry (and how many people in higher education are aware of its existence?) presents the educator with a sharp challenge. His response may shape American education for generations to come. If he is not ready or able to raise himself above defensiveness and vested interest and set about revolutionizing education from within, this new force may—whether he likes it or not—do it for him, from the outside. And he may not be pleased with the results.

We live in a world in which obsolescence is the price of inertia, and destruction may very well be the price of obsolescence. So confronted, we must continually examine the means by which we educate our citizens, and when these means are found wanting we must develop better ones. Harold Howe II, U. S. Commissioner of Education, believes that by continuing to operate as they do, "American colleges run the risk of producing the oldest children in the world."

Let us ask and ponder the question: Has there ever been a time in our history when we could less afford to take that risk?

74. What will physical education be like in 1977?*

Reuben B. Frost

Director, Division of Health, Physical Education, and Recreation, Springfield College

Unidentified flying objects, Telstar, 1,000 passenger airplanes, pre-packaged babies, space platforms, soft landings on the moon, human robots, atomic power, cyber-cultural society—these, and many others, are terms which a generation ago had no meaning and yet today have become commonplace. We also read and hear about "heightened consciousness" through the use of LSD, brain-washing by means of electric needles inserted into the cerebrum, guns and missiles already aimed which can kill millions of people, the probability that the United States will have 330 million people by the year 2000, and that the average life expectancy of people will soon reach one hundred years. And only a few years ago David Sarnoff said, "The last one hundred years have been but a split second in human history. Yet they have encompassed more technological achievement than all the millennia that preceded." We understand then what is meant when it is said that is not only change that characterizes the present era, but acceleration of change.

Our society is marked by automation and mechanization, urbanization, and suburbanization, population increase and family disruption, the explosion of knowledge, an atmosphere of conflict and war, and an attitude of doubt, uncertainty, and apprehension.

On the other hand there is in most places much more freedom from drudgery and economic stress, an increasing amount of time for recreational and cultural pursuits, and many more opportunities to travel and to have fun.

We also find that health knowledge and

facilities for physical activity are much more plentiful, that the human being as a biological organism changes slowly, if at all, and that physically inferior members of our society can now not only survive but perform many of the tasks required for daily living. It is also true, however, that in such a society new ways must be found to maintain our strength, endurance, zest, and vitality.

At such a time and in such a world what are the implications for physical education, what are the problems and trends, and where do they lead us in the future? Let us try to identify some of the possibilities. The following seem to be worthy of further consideration:

1. The battle for the curricular minute, for the budget dollar, for the square foot of space, for recognition and status will continue unabated. The explosions of population and knowledge, the conflicting forces of the arts and humanities, science and technology, health, physical education, and recreation, and pedagogy will not be completely reconciled for some time to come. The demands and wants will continue to exceed the supply of dollars and things.

2. The international aspects of education will continue to advance and will be increasingly emphasized both at home and abroad. The role of health, physical education, and recreation in these programs will take on increasing importance. The image of a nation is reflected by the health and physical excellence of its people. Sports and athletics are playing a part in foreign and domestic policy. These activities serve as a means of reaching and communicating with people from other lands; they are spontaneous, expressive, and exuberant and tend to remove barriers. The

*From Journal of Health, Physical Education, and Recreation, Vol. 39, p. 34, Mar. 1968. Used by permission.

Peace Corps, Operation Crossroads Africa, American specialist program, and the various other international sports programs furnish evidence of this. The International Education Act of 1966 will give tremendous impetus to an even greater exchange of students, teachers, books, films, and programs. International conferences, play days, and even leagues will become common.

3. Related to the trend in international education will be an increased involvement in Olympic development. As the emphasis increases on assistance to the underdeveloped sports and a broader base the school physical education programs will become more and more involved. Educators will play a more important part in guiding Olympic development programs than they have in the past. Educational institutions will be asked to conduct and promote certain special programs including fencing, canoeing, cycling, luge, and equestrian activities.

4. The trend toward increased interschool competitive athletics for women will continue. Research and observation do not bear out long held fears regarding anatomical and physical weaknesses in women. The image and the role of women in our society have changed and are changing to a degree. The values of participation in competitive sports are gaining increasing acceptance, and facilities and personnel for such activities are being provided in greater quantity.

5. The role of physical education and recreation in health and fitness will be further clarified and its importance recognized. Scientific evidence and statements by the American Medical Association and other scientists are rapidly eliminating quackery and crash programs. The populace is being educated in sound principles which may guide their activity, whether as individuals or in groups. The role of exercise and its integration with other healthful practices will, therefore, receive even greater acceptance in the future. The part it plays in therapy as well as prevention will be further understood.

6. The continuously increasing amount of leisure and the growing number of opportunities for using it worthily and beneficially will change the living habits of a large segment of our population. Improvements in modes of transportation are enabling people to explore and enjoy previously inaccessible places in the mountains and wilderness areas. Increasing emphasis on the development of recreational skills and appreciations are making more people aware of the possibilities in this area. The financial support of the Federal Government in both the development and the operation of recreational areas is giving tremendous impetus to this movement. Educational institutions will keep pace.

7. The impact of vast sums of money expended by the government for education and the increasing number of grants for health and recreational purposes are and will continue to be felt throughout the nation. Some of the disparity between programs in wealthy and poor communities should gradually disappear. Special programs for the mentally retarded, the culturally and educationally deprived, and other atypical students will increase in number and quality.

8. Because of the greater emphasis on federal support, the teachers' and administrators' role in political action and other responsibilities of citizenship will be of greater significance than ever before. Action is being taken by professional associations and other educational agencies to protect teachers from possible threats and reprisals; the responsibility of teachers as examples in citizenship will receive more acceptance in the future than in the past.

9. The National Foundation for Health, Physical Education, and Recreation will have developed into a great enterprise and will have a significant effect on the profession. Research will be promoted, in-service training institutes will be encouraged, funds will be granted for pilot and experimental projects, historical documents and memorabilia will become accessible, and the profession will have come even closer to maturity.

10. Community action and community development programs will continue to include more and more elements of health, physical education, and recreation. The integration of substantive courses, community development education, pedagogical material, and health, physical education, and recreation emphases is assuming greater significance as the problems of drop-outs, juvenile delinquency, family disruption, crowded conditions, and others related to the inner city are attacked. Cooperative and coordinated programs in which the community and the schools work

together and jointly use the facilities of both will be common.

11. Professional preparation programs will change somewhat. Attention will be given to team teaching, closed-circuit television, microteaching, internships, cybernetics, and proficiency tests. A longer period of preparation, greater attention to accreditation, reciprocity, and the approved-program approach in certification, and greater autonomy and responsibility on the part of the individual institutions will be the vogue.

12. There will be more subspecializations in professional preparation programs. Students majoring in these fields may choose specialized preparation for the elementary school or the secondary school, for social agencies or community development, for recreation or for health, for coaching or for teaching, for work at home or in other countries. There will be a basic core of requirements but flexibility will be provided so that specialization is possible.

13. There will be even a greater emphasis on research, on the extension of knowledge, the deepening of scholarship, and on health, physical education, and recreation as an academic discipline. Particularly in the large universities and in graduate programs, we will see research laboratories, full-time research professors, post-doctoral fellowships, and time and resources allotted for this phase of education.

14. Physical education at the elementary and junior high school level will come into its own. There will be daily requirements, progressively planned programs, expert teaching, and careful evaluation.

15. Interschool athletics will gradually lose their place as spectator sports and will become more and more school activities. Professional football and basketball will have stolen the spotlight as far as spectators are concerned and those attending college and high school games will be mostly students, parents, and a few interested fans.

16. The athletic and sports programs will be broader and will include many more participants. School programs will normally include 10 to 15 sports and there will be more emphasis on the individual, dual, and lifetime activities. Outdoor sports such as aquatics, skiing, mountaineering, and orienteering will receive far greater emphasis than at present.

These are some of my predictions. Some of them may not materialize. The changes will generally be gradual rather than sudden. There will be new movements and new trends appearing on the horizon. The profession of health, physical education, and recreation will be more significant, fulfill more needs, and hold more promise than at any time in history.

Projects and thought questions for part seven

1. List the professional organizations in physical education that have open rather than elective membership. Select the ones that you as a professional physical educator would join, and tell why.

2. What do you feel is the function of elective membership professional organizations in physical education?

3. Write to the state certification officers of at least six states, selecting one state from each area of the country, and obtain the certification requirements for certification in physical education. Compare the standards. Determine if your professional preparation qualifies you for certification in these states.

4. Why do you feel that it is important to be certain that the professionals in a field are highly qualified in terms of meeting certification standards?

5. How would you suggest that the narrowing of the teacher shortage be best accomplished?

6. What suggestions would you make for efficient and valid nationwide standardization of teacher certification requirements?

7. Develop a report concerned with current challenges facing physical education. Cite each challenge, and give suggestions for a redefinition of each area.

8. In light of the innovations being made on the college level, prepare and deliver an oral report concerned with the future of the basic instructional program in physical education.

9. Write an article that tells how physical education can best contribute to the culturally disadvantaged child.

10. Define the role of physical education a decade from now. Show how the physical educator's role will have changed to meet the new demands that will be placed on him as a professional person.

Selected readings

Brameld, T.: Education for the emerging age, New York, 1965, Harper and Row, Publishers.

Conant, J. B.: The education of American teachers, New York, 1963, McGraw-Hill Book Co.

Dexter, J., and Morehouse, L. E.: Certification requirements between 1953 and 1959, Res. Quart. 32:20, Mar. 1961.

Great Books Foundation: Great issues in education, Chicago, 1956, The Foundation.

Koerner, J. D.: The miseducation of American teachers, Boston, 1963, Houghton Mifflin Co.

National Policies Commission of the National Education Association: Education and the disadvantaged American, Washington, D. C., 1962, The Association.

Spurr, S. H.: New degrees for college teachers. In American Association for Higher Education: In search of leaders, 1967, The Association, p. 106.

62. Professional preparation of the athletic coach*

Charles A. Bucher

Professor of Education and Director of Physical Education, School of Education, New York University

How much and what kind of preparation should the athletic coach have? The answer to this question has not been forthcoming. Yet the impact that a coach has on the lives of millions of young people means that the answer must be found. It is imperative that coaches, school administrators, physical education people, teacher training personnel, state certifying agencies, and others closely associated with this problem come to grips with the issue and determine the best course of action to be followed.

Sports play a major role in the American way of life. They have a tremendous physical and social impact on children and youth. Young boys grow up in the shadows of such heroes as Mickey Mantle, Bob Cousy, and Pete Dawkins.

The coach holds a unique position in respect to his influence on the lives of youth. What he says, how he lives, and the way he coaches play a more important part in molding character and physical fitness of American youngsters than the actions of most other teachers in the schools. In some cases, his influence is even greater than that of a father or mother. When you see a boy walk into the locker room and hear him yell, "Hiya Coach," or see the tears and hands clapping when the coach speaks at the banquet, you get a small sampling of what the boys think of their sports leader. At this time in a youngster's life his coach is the hero, the one to believe in and look to for guidance.

Such a heavy responsibility as coaching must therefore be entrusted only to individuals who are well prepared. These persons need to be well equipped to impart to youngsters the finest points of the game, set an example that can be copied, and coach in a way that best serves the interest of youth. To do otherwise is to break faith with our younger generation.

CURRENT PRACTICES

Although coaching is generally recognized as being most important to young people, there does not seem to be any consistent pattern for preparing persons for such a position. In fact, in some communities All-American mention, a file of newspaper clippings, a long winning streak, and a shelf full of trophies seem to be the important criteria for selection.

Everett L. Hebel of the State Department of Education in New Jersey conducted a survey a few years ago for the purpose of finding out what the various states did in the field of certification of athletic coaches. Executive directors of state athletic associations were sent questionnaires requesting information on this important subject. The findings, covering 43 states, showed a variety of training patterns: 37 states required coaches to be certified as teachers, 8 states had regulations beyond the certification for teaching such as work in physical education and health, and 5 states had no stipulation whatsoever as to the preparation needed to

*From Journal of Health, Physical Education, and Recreation, Vol. 30, p. 27, Sept. 1959. Used by permission.

295

be a coach. The author knows of one eastern state where until a few years ago a person could hold a job outside the school as his main occupation and coach the high school athletic team as a sort of avocation.

Others practices for hiring coaches are well known to members of our profession. Some schools have physical education majors doing all the coaching whereas others feel it is not necessary.

W. A. Healey, writing in *Progressive Education,* reveals the results of a questionnaire survey answered by 119 colleges, showing that the percentage of majors in physical education who are coaching athletics in higher education is surprisingly low.

The same condition exists in many states at the high school level. In many regions of the country there are more academic teachers handling the coaching reins than physical education majors. Some administrators encourage this practice. A committee of the National Association of Secondary School Principals, although recognizing the obvious advantages of the physical education teacher as the coach, recognize disadvantages also. This committee of educators pointed out that the instructional and intramural programs would be conducted on a much higher level if physical education teachers were relieved of coaching duties. It is common practice in private schools to have all students participating in the sports program and to require all faculty members to share the coaching responsibilities without too much thought to their special training in this area.

WHAT MAKES A GOOD COACH?

Since coaching is a form of educational endeavor there must be basic qualities that are needed to do an effective job. From personal observation and a review of the literature, I have found agreement on four essential qualities: (a) expert knowledge of the game, (b) understanding of the participant —physically, mentally, socially, and emotionally, (c) skill in the art of teaching (knowing how to get across the fundamentals and skills of the game), and (d) desirable personality and character traits.

EXPERT KNOWLEDGE OF THE GAME

A coach should be an expert in the game he supervises. This means he has knowledge of tech-

niques, strategy, rules, offenses, defenses, skills, and other information basic to the sport.

UNDERSTANDING THE PARTICIPANT

The coach needs to understand how a youth functions at his particular level of development. This implies an appreciation of such facts as: skeletal growth, muscular development, organic development, physical and emotional limitations, and social needs. It also means a personal concern for the total physical, mental, and moral welfare of youth.

SKILL IN THE ART OF TEACHING

The coach should be a master at teaching players not only the basic fundamentals of the game but also such factors as the importance of thinking clearly, making right decisions, understanding healthful and balanced living, and being a good sport. He knows the laws of learning, how to present material most effectively to the age group with which he is working, and how to apply sound psychological principles to his field of work.

DESIRABLE PERSONALITY AND CHARACTER

The coach should possess such traits as patience, understanding, kindness, courage, cheerfulness, affection, sense of humor, energy, and enthusiasm. He shoud be able to withstand pressure from forces not interested in educational athletics. His character should be beyond reproach and his example one which mothers and fathers would like to have their sons emulate.

A great many students who show exceptional skill in some interscholastic sport such as basketball, baseball, or football possess a desire to be a coach. They feel they have proved themselves as athletes in high school and therefore they will be successful in coaching. This, however, is not necessarily true. It may seem paradoxical to the layman, but there is insufficient evidence to show that exceptional skill in any activity necessarily guarantees a good teacher of that activity. Many other factors, such as personality, interest in youth, understanding the psychology of learning, intelligence, integrity, leadership qualities, and character, carry as much or more weight in coaching success.

TRAINING AND EXPERIENCE

If the above are the desirable qualities needed by the coach, the next step is to determine how such qualities can best be obtained. Training and experience are probably the two most important considerations in this regard.

Our present day is a day of increased

specialization. If a boy goes into the field of engineering, many years of training in mathematics, science, and other disciplines fundamental to this profession must be studied. Advertising, journalism, medicine, and countless other fields of work also require their special preparation.

If one desires to develop expert qualifications as a coach he also needs to receive the best training possible in the rudiments of the sport he is going to teach. In addition, thorough preparation is needed to see through Johnny and to understand his total make-up, to understand the psychology of teaching, and to appreciate one's self and one's relation to others. All are part of the education of a coach. He will be as strong as he is prepared in each of these important areas. Being weak in one will act as a deterrent factor to his optimum operating efficiency.

Although parts of a coach's training could be gained through self-study or majoring in some liberal arts area, it seems that physical education offers the most desirable and complete type of preparation for coaches.

A person who has been associated with an activity to a great extent should understand it better in all its aspects. That is why we usually want more experience in positions of increased responsibility. This is also true of coaching.

But is experience alone all that is needed? Much knowledge about the game, young people, and teaching can be gained through the trial and error method which experience provides, but many costly mistakes may occur along the way. We would not want a surgeon's preparation limited to experience through trial and error. By the same token it does not seem we should recommend such a procedure for a coach who leaves his imprint for good or bad upon youngsters.

A COURSE OF ACTION

There should be more careful screening and preparation of candidates for coaching positions. In this way we can be sure that the best interests of the young will be served. Also, it will help the coach to do his most effective job.

The job we have to do as a profession, it seems, is to delineate the specific knowledges, skills, and competencies that a coach should have. The assistance of coaches on the job, physical education personnel, school administrators, and others is needed to accomplish this task. These standards should then be translated into guides for certifying officers and school administrators in the hiring of coaches. Furthermore, it should be the responsibility of professional preparing institutions to see that such training is offered not only for the undergraduate who desires to go into coaching but also in the form of inservice preparation for coaches already in the field.

63. I'm a woman physical educator— not a coach*

Gayle Dawley Moore

Chairman, Department of Physical Education, Piedmont Hills High School, San Jose, California

Lately I have been in serious conflict with myself as to the values of physical education, and as to whether or not I am outdated in my views and beliefs.

This is my eleventh year of teaching in high school physical education and every year I enjoy it more than the previous year. However, I am seriously considering becoming an ex-physical educator. The reason is not because of the class situations, but because of extra, or co-curricula, girls' athletic activities.

Are our girls' athletic programs being patterned after the boys' programs? This appears to be becoming more true, and I haven't been pleased with the results I've seen.

To me it appears that many teachers are trying to develop a super-athlete and are demanding so much of her that she isn't the well-rounded girl.

What of our present college "majors"? I'm puzzled as to why physical education majors have so much time for extra competition and city recreation type pursuits during the school year. The college curriculum seems so demanding that I wonder where they get the time, as well as why the college isn't providing enough competitive activities for them. Too many of the majors that I have seen have shown an aggressiveness and type of sportsmanship that I would not tolerate in any students of mine. And they are our future teachers? Is it enough to claim femi-

ninity because we have been "coached" as to better grooming so as not to look like the stereotyped "P.E. Teacher," and then to participate in sports in such a manner that femininity and sportsmanship are forgotten? Possibly I am unduly concerned, but if the present trend seems to be toward a more "cut throat" competition, and the "majors" are displaying such traits, then what does the future hold?

Perhaps I'm getting too far ahead of my problem, so back to the high school level and our girls' athletics. In the past few years I have seen women teachers accuse other teachers of cheating in after-school-sports (I've even been accused of it). More and more petty arguments and hair-splitting over rules interpretations seem to be happening. Why?

I am not a coach and I don't ever hope to become a coach! Nor am I a recreation leader—I am a teacher! I teach physical education because I believe so strongly in its values. I want more than a few super-athletes; I want all girls to be interested in the benefits of sports and I want them to enjoy these benefits the rest of their lives.

In our school we may not win all of our games, but we do play to win, and we do enjoy playing. The girls display good sportsmanship and all interested girls may play in our games with other schools. Why should some girls be nothing but "bench warmers" so that we can beat another school? If a girl is interested enough to attend all practices, work hard, and to try, then she deserves to play. We practice two days a week with games scheduled either on these regular

*From Journal of the California Association for Health, Physical Education and Recreation, Vol. 30, p. 7, Nov.-Dec. 1967. Used by permission.

practice days, or on a Saturday. A high school girl has many activities, interests, and studies. She shouldn't be spending all of her energy and time in the gym. If she is, much of her personal development is being neglected and she cannot become a whole and well-rounded person.

Values learned in high school remain with our girls the rest of their lives. What type of values are girls learning if they lose and then are made to feel that they were cheated by another school? Or, if they hear their teacher yelling or arguing with an official during a game? Many teachers seem to profess a belief against such practices, but then they go out and display such traits on the field.

Why not just teach and forget about after-school-sports? I believe in the benefits of competition, and I feel that such activities are an integral part of our physical education offerings. I also feel that our main preoccupation must be with teaching, and it disturbs me to see coaching infringe on teaching time and energy.

If our women teachers are to become competitive minded coaches, I think our physical education programs will suffer. I'm idealistic perhaps, but also realistic, and tiring of an uphill struggle. What good does it do to have our girls demonstrate good sportsmanship while playing another school who plays with "no holds barred," and then lose? It probably only instills the idea that "good guys always finish last."

Is society imposing these types of competitive attitudes on our girls, or are we doing it? We are the ones who set examples for the students to follow. If we feel that it is the American way to "boo" umpires and officials, then our students will display this

trait in their lives. But if we see the need for officials, and respect them for their contribution to our sports activities, then our students will reflect this attitude.

If we are to copy the boys' programs—what are the many ramifications? Are we to start charging admission fees and encourage spectators in order to finance (and pressure) our programs? Are girls to be awarded athletic scholarships, or where do they go from high school?

We also have the problem of obtaining competent officials for our games. Here again, I feel that we have been "cutting our own throats." We are so intent on coaching our teams that we are not able to act as officials when we play against other schools. And we're so afraid that the officiating will be inferior that we won't allow our students to officiate. If we were to allow them to officiate, I'm afraid that the abuse heaped on them would soon turn them against officiating (and perhaps physical education). If we seek officials from colleges or universities and then abuse them as well as underpay them, we also are turning them away from officiating. Who is then left to act as our officials, and where can they learn to officiate?

In my experience I have never seen a good intramural program. Perhaps if we were to offer more intramural activities we could then reserve extramural activities for the more competitive type individuals. But until we do, I worry about the number of girls that we are cheating and neglecting, with regard to physical education activity offerings.

If our values have changed, then perhaps I am merely outdated, and in need of departing from the scene.

64. Communicate or perish*

Robert N. Singer

Associate Professor, Department of Health and Physical Education for Men, Illinois State University at Normal

How many physical educators feel persecuted, frustrated, misunderstood, left out, and nonimportant? Of the academic disciplines, physical education is one of the most controversial in terms of a place and function within the academic structure. Everyone outside of the field knows something about it. Many claim to be experts and will even decide our fate for us. Yet the ironical thing is that these same individuals do not really comprehend what physical education is all about.

Misconceptions and half-truths strangle our programs, their purposes, and their content. Students, other faculty members, administrators, PTA's, and communities need to know the truth. They need to know that physical education is represented by more than athletic teams and that a winning football season is not an indication of a good physical education program. They need to know that we are not interested only in the sweat and strong muscles of the student body so that our country will have a better military force. They need to know that we do not just throw out a ball and yell "Play time!"

They do have to know the truth. The most direct way for this goal to be accomplished is for physical educators to communicate what they are doing and what they hope to do, to administrators, PTA's, other faculty members, and the public in general. Communicate now! Don't sit by and think that things will take care of themselves. A good program has to be, in a sense, sold to the public. Others should be informed, by us, as to what we are doing and can do for the students in our classes.

Physical educators are notorious for viewing the world as being against them. They think that other faculty members look down upon them, that physical education is not academically acceptable. They think that the PTA is not interested in what a physical educator might have to say, and they therefore avoid any parental or community contact. They think that administrators are against them and would just as soon remove physical education from the curriculum. They think that everyone is interested in the teams they coach and not the classes they teach.

If this actually is the case in your situation, why not objectively analyze the possible reasons for it? Why not shoulder the blame? Did you do anything to further entrench these feelings in others? Did you do anything to combat such thoughts being circulated and becoming accepted?

There are many ways an industrious, intelligent, and creative physical educator can sell his program. Here are a few.

1. Meet other faculty members outside of your own profession. Have lunch with them. Socialize with them. Serve on committees with them. Learn what is happening in other disciplines, what problems are occurring. Inform others about your program, objectives, and problems. Be sympathetic, understanding, and interested in others if you expect the same treatment.

2. Communicate with administrators. Make sure they are aware of your efforts and plans. Administrators must be informed

*From Journal of Health, Physical Education, and Recreation, Vol. 39, p. 40, Feb. 1968. Used by permission.

—by you— of the role physical education plays in today's society.

3. Talk to parents at PTA meetings and take advantage of other opportunities that might arise for you to get closer to the population outside the school. These people want to see what you look like and how you sound. Disappoint them if their image of you is one of a big buffoon—inarticulate, loud, insensitive, crude, and comical.

Inform parents of what you are trying to do with their children. You may be surprised to discover that the basketball team is not of as much concern to the average parent as what his child is experiencing in your class. Athletics service a few; physical education classes service the entire student body. There are many more average kids and youngsters with some form of physical limitation than there are gifted athletic performers.

Besides your influence on their children, you are able to assist community members in answering many questions that pertain to health, physical education, and related areas. The current rage of quackery in nutrition, strength development, life expectancy, and other topics places the physical educator's knowledge at a premium. He has a role in enlightening the public in those areas in which he has been educated.

4. Explain to your students what physical education is all about and what it means to be physically educated. Don't be a molder of robots. Satisfy their inquisitiveness and explain why they should participate in various types of activities. Explain the bodily changes that will result from participation and encourage curiosity, creativeness, and reasoning to develop a sound basis for what is to be done.

If you feel you have a good cause, then inform others about it. Physical educators have taken a back seat too long. We must assume the responsibility of communicating with all those people who, in one way or another, have some relationship to the program. This will, obviously, include almost everyone within the school and surrounding community.

When this communication occurs, administrators will become more understanding and sympathetic to the physical educator's problems. Aid, in various forms, will be given to the program and for that which contributes to a good program.

Communication with the students will enable them to see beyond a push-up. They will learn to appreciate and respect skilled movement and a healthy body. Stimulation of the cognitive and affective processes will accompany physical stimulation.

Other faculty members will respect your profession, your program, and you as an individual. You will be accepted as an "equal" educator, having the same objectives as other educators except with a different means of achieving these objectives.

The public will be able to distinguish fact from fantasy with regard to physical education. These people will want to support your program, financially and/or in spirit.

Is communication not worth a try?

65. The potential of physical education as an area of research and scholarly effort*

Arthur S. Daniels†

Former Dean, School of Health, Physical Education, and Recreation, University of Indiana

It is something of a paradox that in spite of a long history in American education and support from highly respected sources, physical education must still frequently be defended as a legitimate school subject. Although millions of dollars in the form of grants and awards are available for the advancement of the natural sciences, social sciences, behavioral sciences, languages, and education, large grants to physical education are practically nonexistent. If we have failed to impress with our educational worth, it might be well to engage in a little professional introspection and seek the probable causes.

One of these is our failure to exploit the potential of physical education as an area of research and scholarly effort.

Taking what satisfaction we can from the contributions which physical education has made to American education at all school levels as a service program, there is an understandable feeling of unfulfillment in the area of scholarly effort and research. There is a widespread belief on the part of our academic colleagues and most lay persons that physical educators are primarily practitioners. Our programs in basic instruction and intramural and interschool competitive sports programs, as well as our offerings in physical recreation, provide the basis for this belief. While we have no wish to disavow these worthy utilitarian programs, the fact remains that, compared with other dis-

ciplines, there has been a paucity of scholarly effort and research.

From earliest times and with few exceptions, physical education has been a significant element of each culture. It has always been and is today a strong force in human relations. If we are to gain recognition in the academic world we must follow pathways similar to those traversed by other disciplines in achieving their progress. For us this means a greatly expanded program of scholarly activities in such areas as history of physical education and sport, the social significance of physical education and sport in our culture, motor learning, exercise physiology, biomechanics of human movement, and comparative studies indicating the contribution of physical education and sport to international understanding and cooperation. Each of these areas will be briefly explored in order to give further insight into their potential for scholarly treatment.

History of sport. Historical studies reveal the importance of physical education in each cultural epoch. The place of sport in past societies has been lightly dealt with as incidental to more thorough treatment of matters considered of greater importance. It is difficult to find an acknowledgment of sports as an important item in cultural history because sports did not function in many of the fields conventionally credited with making important contributions to history. There is a considerable amount of literature on the history of physical education and sport which, if given greater scholarly emphasis, would enable it to take its place with the history of art, history of music, history of

*From Journal of Health, Physical Education, and Recreation, Vol. 36, p. 32, Jan. 1965. Used by permission.
†Deceased.

literature, and history of science. In addition, there are innumerable opportunities for original historical research in physical education and sport.

Sport as an element of the culture. The social significance of sport in modern society has never been fully explored from the scientific and scholarly viewpoints of social psychology and cultural anthropology. David Riesman has noted, "For some strange reason students of society and social life have missed almost completely the importance of sport in their investigations, while those who teach and guide sport activities have omitted the relevance of sociology and social psychology."[1]

One interesting aspect of contemporary American sport is its interrelationship with other elements of the culture. Fred Cozens[2] noted that one cannot study the history and contemporary setting of sport in the United Sates without encountering numerous interrelationships with our major social institutions, the school, the church, government, labor and industry, channels of communication, medicine, politics, economics, the military, and national security.

A single example, communications, is selected for illustrative purposes. Approximately 400 of the 10,000 books published annually deal with sport; 300 sports magazines are published regularly. Our most popular magazines include one or more sports articles in nearly every issue; 8 to 14 percent of newspaper space is devoted to sport; some 7 to 12 percent of radio and television time is devoted to sport. Consistently the largest crowds in America are sports crowds.[3]

Biomechanics of human movement. This area of study has its base in the disciplines of physics and engineering and involves such matters as force, resistance, application of power, levers, angles, trajectories, and equilibrium. These factors may be applied to human movement in general and to skills involved in the successful performance of particular sports. In biomechanics there is integration of principles, concepts, and materials from the fields of physics, engineering, and physical education.

Exercise physiology. The primary interest here is applied physiology to provide information on such matters as what happens to individuals in the growth and development process or in changing from unfitness to fitness, functional studies of individuals ranging from average performers to world record holders, and longevity studies of the effect of fitness upon the aging process.

Motor learning. This area includes a study of some of the problems and processes involved in the learning of skills and knowledges as they relate to successful participation in physical recreation and competitive sports, with possible implications of this information for other areas of living; for example, maturation and motor learning, intelligence and motor learning, motivation and motor learning, teaching in parts and wholes, length and distribution of practice, speed and accuracy, and rate of learning.

International studies. At the international level there is recognition of the importance and values of physical education and sport in developing international understanding and cooperation. Unesco has several publications dealing with the place of sport in education. There are several international councils and federations dealing with physical education and sports. Perhaps the roots of physical education and sport which penetrate so deeply in each national group can be spread so they attain a universal dimension, thereby adding another effective medium for international cultural and scientific exchange.

Historically, sport has been a favorite literary subject. It has also been richly treated through the art forms of music, dance, painting, sculpture, and architecture. Physical education and sport link scientific, artistic, ethical, and moral aspects of our culture.

A SCHOLARLY FOCUS

There are signs that there is growing recognition of the scholarly potential in the area of physical education. At a recent meeting of departmental chairmen from a group of Midwestern universities, the feeling was expressed that perhaps we should offer two kinds of physical education programs in our colleges and universities. The first would be a continuation of the training of personnel

[1]Unpublished letter.
[2]Cozens, "Implications of Cultural Anthropology for Physical Education," in *Professional Contributions No. 1,* Washington, D. C., American Academy of Physical Education, 1951, p. 71.
[3]Adapted from an unpublished prospectus prepared by Seward C. Staley, University of Illinois.

for our service programs in elementary and secondary schools and colleges and for other physical recreation leadership roles. These are the future teachers and administrators of physical education, intramural directors, and athletic administrators. The second kind would develop scholars and researchers who would be responsible for the advancement of knowledge, the development of graduate study, and the conduct of research. An arrangement such as this should be a factor in gaining full acceptance for physical education as a legitimate branch of the sciences involved in the study of man.

To develop the scholarly type of program it will be necessary to bring into departments of physical education, where they do not already exist, faculty members with extensive backgrounds in history, social psychology, cultural anthropology, physics, physiology, and international studies. It may be necessary in some instances to encourage young doctors of philosophy in these disciplines to establish careers as sports historians, exercise physiologists, scientists in the mechanics of human movement, and social scientists specializing in sport and the forces and influences which bear upon it as an element of the culture. These scholars can then train our own qualified students who have a scholarly potential in these areas. Graduates of these advanced programs will find their places alongside the scholars of the outer disciplines in our colleges and universities.

Pursuing the idea a little further, it will be necessary to locate intellectually talented students at the undergraduate level who will follow special curriculums designed to prepare them for university teaching and research. These curriculums will be distinct from those designed to prepare teachers and leaders for service programs. They will be characterized by strong offerings in natural and social sciences, history, mathematics, and languages.

Eric A. Walker, president of Pennsylvania State University, in a thought-provoking essay,[4] supports the idea of separate and distinct types of education designed especially for those with the capacity to discover new knowledge and those who will follow and apply this knowledge for improving our ways of living and learning. Although he points out the need for designing our courses and curriculums to meet differing capacities and differing purposes, he makes it plain that a diversified system of education will work only so long as we honor all parts of it and do not stigmatize some elements as inferior to others.

In time, several important developments should occur. The first will be the development of a definitive and accepted body of knowledge in physical education. This body of knowledge will infiltrate the professional preparation programs for teachers and administrators of our service programs. This knowledge will ultimately be incorporated into the physical education curriculums in our elementary and secondary schools and colleges. It should provide scientific bases for the training and conditioning of athletes in our competitive sports programs at all levels.

Scholarly efforts are currently apparent in certain colleges and universities in the areas of history of sport, exercise physiology, and motor learning. Faculties in departments of physical education must become more involved in productive scholarship in our colleges and universities. The day is drawing to an end when respected membership in the academic community can be retained through utilitarian programs alone.

BIBLIOGRAPHY

Cozens, Fred W., and Stumpf, F. S., *Sports in American Life,* Chicago, University of Chicago Press, 366 pp., 1953.

Dulles, Foster R., *America Learns to Play,* New York, D. Appleton-Century Co., 441 pp., 1940.

Hanna, Willard A., "The Politics of Sport," *Southeast Asia Series,* New York, American Universities Field Staff (Vol. X, No. 19), 13 pp., 1962.

Holliman, Jennie, *American Sports, 1785-1835,* Durham, N. C., Seaman Press, 222 pp., 1931.

Huizinga, Johan, *Homo Ludens—A Study of the Play Element in Culture,* Boston, Beacon Press, 220 pp., 1949.

Manchester, Herbert, *Four Centuries of Sport in America,* New York, Derrydale Press, 248 pp., 1931.

Riesman, David, *Individualism Reconsidered,* Glencoe, Illinois, Free Press, 1954.

Social Changes and Sports, Washington, D. C., American Association for Health, Physical Education, and Recreation, 122 pp. 1959.

Steiner, Jess F., *Americans at Play,* New York, McGraw-Hill Book Co., 201 pp., 1933.

Stone, Gregory, "Some Meanings of American Sport," in *60th Annual Proceedings,* Washing-

[4]Walker, "Quality in Quantity," in *Vision and Purpose in Higher Education,* Washington, D. C., American Council on Education, 1962, pp. 66-79.

ton, D. C., College Physical Education Association, 1957, pp. 6-29.

Unesco, The Place of Sport in Education—A Comparative Study, Educational Studies and Documents, Paris, Unesco (No. 21), 63 pp., 1956.

Weaver, R. F., *Amusements and Sport for American Life,* Chicago, University of Chicago Press, 196 pp., 1939.

Williams, Marian, and Lissner, Herbert R., *Biomechanics of Humann Motion,* Philadelphia, W. B. Saunders Co., 194 pp., 1962.

Projects and thought questions for part six

1. What specific steps would you suggest physical education take to attract able students into professional preparation programs?

2. Write a documented report that explains the relationship of accrediting agencies to physical education professional preparing institutions.

3. Discuss in an oral report the recent trends in professional preparation in physical education. Draw implications for the future.

4. Write a brief report explaining the unique competencies needed by an activity scientist. Show how this training differs from traditional preparation.

5. If you were an administrator interviewing a candidate for a coaching position, what special preparation and qualifications would you look for? Write out a list of competencies and prepare an interview questionnaire designed to highlight these qualifications.

6. Assess your personal value structure. Compare it to the pattern suggested by Kenyon's report, and show the steps you can take to modify or change your image.

7. Design a research study that attempts to determine the predictors of success for male physical education undergraduates.

8. Interview at least ten physical educators to determine the problems they face in teaching. Rank these problems in order of frequency and suggest methods for overcoming the problems.

9. Write an editorial showing how the coach of a boys' or girls' athletic team contributes to moral, spiritual, and physical values.

10. Write an essay that either defends or opposes the conduct of interscholastic athletics for girls. Base your essay on an actual situation in some school you have visited or attended or one whose program you have observed.

11. How would you suggest that teaching styles and subject matter content be more closely aligned? Prepare an oral report on the topic and deliver it in class.

12. Assume that you are a new physical education teacher in some community selected by you. Describe the community, the forces at work in the community, the community roles taken by the teachers. Explain the role you would assume in this community and tell why.

13. Develop a unique method of convincing the parents of a hypothetical community that your physical education program is meeting the needs, interests, and abilities of their children.

14. Reread the article by Daniels. Select one area in which research is suggested and prepare an outline for a pertinent scholarly study.

Selected readings

American Association for Health, Physical Education, and Recreation: Professional preparation in health education, physical education, and recreation education, Washington, D. C., 1962, The Association.

Bruner, J.: The process of education, Cambridge, 1961, Harvard University Press.

Davis, E. C., and Wallis, E. L.: Toward better teaching in physical education, Englewood Cliffs, N. J., 1961, Prentice-Hall, Inc.

Educational Policies Commission: An essay on quality in public education, Washington, D. C., 1959, National Education Association and the American Association of School Administrators.

Larson, L. A.: Implications for the coach and recreation leader, Education 76:249, Dec. 1955.

Pape, L. A., and Means, L. E.: Toward better teaching in physical education, Englewood Cliffs, N. J., 1962, Prentice-Hall, Inc.

Pearson, G. B.: Trends in professional preparation for physical education in three districts of the AAHPER, Sixty-Seventh Proceedings, Jan. 1964, National College Physical Education Association for Men.

Woodring, P.: New directions in teacher education, New York, 1957, Fund for the Advancement of Education.

Woodruff, A.: Basic concepts of teaching, San Francisco, 1961, Chandler Publishing Co.

Part seven

The profession

The preceding divisions of this book explore the nature and scope of physical education; the philosophy of physical education as part of general education; the relationship of physical education to health, recreation, camping, and outdoor education; changing concepts of physical education; scientific foundations of physical education; and leadership in physical education. This division is concerned with a seventh dimension of physical education—the profession itself, including the growth of associated professional organizations, past and present trends in physical education, challenges facing the profession, and a vision of the future.

The origins and growth of the organization now known as the American Association for Health, Physical Education, and Recreation is the topic discussed by Charles H. Mc-Cloy. This article reveals the scope of the AAHPER as an adjunct of the National Education Association.

Rosalind Cassidy outlines the role of the American Academy of Physical Education. She reviews the philosophy of R. Tait McKenzie, which led to the founding of the Academy, and discusses the symbol of this organization and the organization's relation to the entire profession of physical education.

Maxwell L. Howell, past president of the Canadian Association for Health, Physical Education and Recreation, Inc., describes the aims, membership requirements, structure, and function of that organization. The Canadian Association, Howell explains, was founded in 1933 as a national physical education association. Growth of the organization and increased interest in it among professionals led to the addition of the fields of health and recreation in 1948.

Robert Holland's article on trends in certification in health and physical education was originally presented at the Green Meadows Conference. Holland states that certification standards vary across the nation but that several states are revising and upgrading their standards. This article highlights some of the problems raised by the lack of uniformity in certification standards.

Challenges to physical education as a profession is the topic of the articles by Ruth L. Abernathy, Charles L. Mand, and Ray O. Duncan.

An article written by Ruth Abernathy asserts that five specific areas in physical education need to be closely reexamined. Abernathy cites these crucial areas as including the primary focus of the field, professional preparation, recruitment, research, and curriculum development. She expresses the hope that the challenges presented by these five areas will be enthusiastically taken up by the members of the profession.

Charles L. Mand writes that the basic instructional programs in colleges and universities need to be examined, refined, and restructured to conform to contemporary needs. Mand's article offers seven proposals for increasing the worth of college-level programs.

Ray O. Duncan cites four problem areas challenging the physical education profession. These areas are listed as a redefinition of the purpose of physical education, the placing of physical fitness in its proper place in the curriculum, improving programs of professional preparation, and strengthening professional leadership. Duncan offers suggestions for facing each of these challenges.

Samuel Baskin writes that our colleges and universities are attempting many startling innovations in courses, curriculums, and facilities. Baskin points out that the traditional concept of a university education does not fill the needs of today's college students. This article contains many important implications for the future of the undergraduate basic instructional program in physical education as well as other phases of the physical education program. As is the case with many areas of education, we may need to change in order to keep up with the times.

The final article is concerned with the concept of physical education in 1977. Reuben B. Frost draws implications for the future and cites 16 areas of challenge to the profession that he feels will be most relevant at that time. The author makes some predictions for the course of action of the profession in each of the 16 areas.

66. The American Association for Health and Physical Education: a department of the NEA*

Charles H. McCloy†

*Former Chairman, Department of Physical Education,
State University of Iowa*

On the 28th of June [1937] the American Physical Education Association and the Department of School Health and Physical Education of the National Education Association were officially amalgamated to form the American Association for Health and Physical Education—a Department of the National Education Association. This merger marked the consummation of the efforts of many educators within and without the American Physical Education Association to bring this organization within the National Education Association, and to unite the efforts of health educators, physical educators, and leaders in school recreation under one organization.

The final terms of the merger were approved in April by the Legislative Council of the American Physical Education Association, and later by the Executive Committee of the Department of School Health and Physical Education of the NEA by mail vote. The official union of the two organizations was effected at the Annual Meeting of the NEA in Detroit in June. Thus the American Physical Education Association, as a name, goes out of existence, as does that of the Department of School Health and Physical Educa-

*From Journal of Health, Physical Education, and Recreation, Vol. 8, p. 416, Sept. 1937. Used by permission.
†Deceased.
NOTE: This article will provide the reader with historical background of the merger between the American Physical Education Association and the Department of School Health and Physical Education of the National Education Association.

tion of the NEA; and the American Association for Health and Physical Education—A Department of the NEA—arises out of the ashes.

The reorganization carried over the larger part of the organization of the American Physical Education Association, with some changes and additions. The officers elected by the APEA at the New York meeting were continued, as were the Governing Board and the Legislative Council. Three divisions were added, the Division of Health Education, the Division of Physical Education, and the Division of Recreation. . . .

The new Association will continue to publish the *Journal of Health and Physical Education* [now called the *Journal of Health, Physical Education, and Recreation*] and the *Research Quarterly*, and will carry on the work in physical education that was done in the past by the APEA. In addition, however, the American Association for Health and Physical Education assumes new and profoundly important tasks. First, the Association, through the Division of Health Education, hopes to give unity and leadership to much of the work in health education as it affects the schools. To this end— just as the APEA did and the new Association will continue to do with physical-education national professional organizations—national organizations in the field of health education that are desirous of cooperating, are invited to become affiliated organizations, to have a voice in the Legislative Council, and to participate as organizations and as individuals in our work, our

309

deliberations, our legislation, and our conventions—state, district, and national. In addition, we are hopeful that the experts in all fields of health education will co-operate with the Association in furthering the service to be rendered by the Association, without in any way lessening or limiting their services as individuals or through other professional organizations through which they have been accustomed to work. We are fortunate in beginning this new enterprise with such excellent leadership in the Health Education Division and Sections.

In the Recreation Division, the organization is not yet as complex nor as complete. This division, however, faces very important issues and opportunities in that field, especially as it affects school systems.

The merging with the National Education Association affects the Association most favorably. No limiting restrictions have been imposed. The same state, district, and national organizations and meetings will be continued and expanded to include health education and recreation in each constituent organization of the Association. In addition, the organized forces of the National Education Association will be at the service of the American Association for Health and Physical Education in every way possible. . . .

67. The American Academy: its role in the profession*

Rosalind Cassidy

Former Professor of Physical Education, University of California at Los Angeles

It is my privilege to share with the new members my remembrance of R. Tait McKenzie's words about the Academy upon the occasion similar to this one when I was elected to the Academy. It was his last meeting with us and my gratitude for that experience is so deep that I continue to feel my obligation to pass on to new members the vision of the Academy's task as he passed it on to me. It was in truth, the most moving and inspiring experience in my professional life. I hope that all of us here at this fine meeting can convey to our new members and to ourselves the quality and the meaning of our responsibility and our privilege as Academy members.

As an artist and a scholar, R. Tait McKenzie envisioned for our profession a group that would have the large over-view of our field, pushing out the frontiers to ever wider horizons. He said in his President's address at Atlanta, April 1938, just six days before his death:

The Academy should be something a little different from any other organization in physical education. Too many people are oppressed with the machinery of their work and miss the beauty of the finished product. The worker at the loom sees only the mechanics and never realizes the beauty of the completed pattern. We need a body that concerns itself with the ultimate pattern of what comes from the factory, letting others do some of the mechanical work if necessary. We need people not just to gather data and publish it, but to think through the results and their implications. We need a group that will make authoritative statements and be didactic about it. Many people will publish the results of

research, but there must be someone to see it as a whole and draw conclusions from it. We need a group which has been touched with the "divine spark" which lifts its work above the every-day level and makes of it something special. . . . Madame Curie did four years of hard physical labor to extract the ultimate milligram of radium. It is not the function of the Academy to do only hard physical labor, but it is its function to look for and recognize the ultimate milligram of truth that results from it. What physical education needs is some one ultimate discovery such as Ronald Ross's conclusion that only the mosquito could cause malaria. If we can bring about the discovery of one truth about physical education that is at all comparable to these discoveries, the Academy will not have been founded in vain. We may not be able to give material assistance to those working toward this end, but we can pay with the more valuable coin of appreciation and understanding to the workers in the field.

In 1937, Dr. McKenzie, a sculptor of note, designed and presented to the Academy its seal. You will find the seal embossed upon the parchment certificate of membership to be presented to you, our new members, at this welcoming banquet. The seal is a simple circle showing within it a torch being passed from one hand to another. Tait McKenzie thought of the role of the Academy in the profession in terms of those who speed onward carrying the sacred fire to the altar, each one moving along the light, from one to another, all working together in the sacred task, cooperating to make the total accomplishment larger than the sum of the single efforts of all. As you take your parchment, as you join this Academy group, you become one of the runners responsible for that sacred fire of knowledge, insight and vision. Together we must help move this profession to a wider, deeper frontier.

*From Professional Contributions No. 1, p. 77, Nov. 1951, American Academy of Physical Education. Used by permission.

68. The Canadian Association for Health, Physical Education and Recreation, Inc.*

Maxwell L. Howell

Professor, Faculty of Physical Education, University of Alberta

The professional association in Canada is known as the Canadian Association for Health, Physical Education and Recreation. It was initially organized as the Canadian Physical Education Association in 1933 through the joint efforts of the Quebec Physical Education Association and the Toronto Physical Education Association.

The organization of a national association was fostered and inspired by Arthur S. Lamb, Department of Physical Education, McGill University, the alma mater of R. Tait McKenzie and James Naismith.

During the period from 1931 to 1933, several local groups developed into physical education associations. Stimulated by the Quebec Association, a national physical education association was founded in 1933. The Association continued to grow as new branches were formed in nearly every province. Because the members were interested in the three fields of health, physical education, and recreation, the name was changed in 1948 to the Canadian Association for Health, Physical Education and Recreation. To coordinate the efforts in the three areas, the position of vice-president for health, physical education, and recreation was established.

In 1951, this Association became an incorporated body in order to facilitate growth and to meet the needs of and provide services for a rapidly expanding membership. The signing officers of our Association on the letters patent at this time were Iveagh Munro, Jack Lang, and Gordon Wright. . . .

*From Journal of Health, Physical Education, and Recreation, Vol. 36, p. 24, Apr. 1965. Used by permission.

AIMS

The present aims of the Association are—

To encourage the improvement of the standards of those engaged in the furtherance of health education, physical education, and recreation.

To provide such means of promotion as will secure the establishment of adequate programs under the direction of approved leadership.

To stimulate a wide, intelligent, and active interest in health education, physical education, and recreation.

To acquire and disseminate accurate information concerning it.

To cooperate with kindred interests and organizations in the furtherance of these aims.

MEMBERSHIP

CAHPER has recently changed its membership to become a more truly professional association, coinciding with similar developments in AAHPER. . . .

The following changes in membership categories [have been] in effect [since] June 1, 1965:

1. *Fellows*—individuals who have been continuous members for ten years or more and who have made a professional contribution (service on the national executive or national committees, articles published for the Journal or professional publications) to the association. Members so qualified may be eligible for election as fellows of the association.

2. *Professional members*—those indi-

viduals who have at least one under-graduate or graduate degree with a major or minor in health, physical education, or recreation.

3. *Associate members* of four types will be considered for admission: (a) persons holding degrees in allied degrees such as sociology, fine arts, social work, and psychology; or (b) those professionally qualified persons no longer engaged in one or more of the related fields of health, physical education, and recreation; or (c) those professionally qualified persons engaged in one or more of the related fields of health, physical education, and recreation in

other countries who wish to retain an association with CAHPER; or (d) those persons with an interest in the Association, but who are not engaged in any one of the related fields of health, physical education, and recreation.

GOVERNMENT OF THE ASSOCIATION

The business of the Association is conducted by the Board of Directors, the Representative Council, and the General Assembly.

The Board of Directors is elected, for a two-year period of office, by a secret ballot "mail vote."

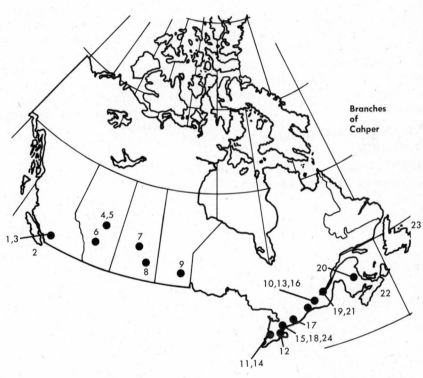

Branches of Cahper

British Columbia	1. Vancouver
	2. Victoria
	3. University of British Columbia
Alberta	4. Edmonton Men's Branch
	5. Edmonton Women's Branch
	6. Calgary Branch
Saskatchewan	7. North Saskatchewan—Saskatoon
	8. South Saskatchewan—Regina
Manitoba	9. Winnipeg
Ontario	10. Armed Forces and Civil Service Br.—Ottawa
	11. Greater London—London
	12. Hamilton and District—Hamilton
	13. Le Chapitre Hull—Ottawa—Hull and Ottawa
	14. London Br.—London
	15. Metropolitan Toronto Supervisors—Toronto

Quebec

New Brunswick, Nova Scotia Newfoundland Ontario

16. Ottawa Women's Secondary School. Health and Physical Education Association—Ottawa
17. Scarborough Men's Physical and Health Education Association—Scarborough
18. Toronto Area Association of Physical Education and Health Education—Toronto
19. Greater Montreal—Montreal
20. Le Chapitre de Quebec—Quebec City
21. Association des Diplomes en Education Physique et Recreation—Montreal
22. Atlantic Provinces—Fredericton
23. St. John's Branch—St. John's
24. North York Physical Education Association Branch—Toronto

The Representative Council is composed of the duly appointed official representatives of each branch. The Representative Council, which meets annually, is a most important body in our Association. It can: (a) effect all changes in the Constitution and By-Laws: (b) initiate any business that seems desirable; (c) exercise veto power over actions of the Board of Directors. Branches having a national membership of less than 20 are entitled to one voting delegate. Branches having a national membership of 20 to 35 members inclusive are entitled to two voting delegates. Branches having a national membership of 36 and more are entitled to three voting delegates.

The General Assembly includes all the active members of the association who elect the Board of Directors.

The basis of CAHPER is the individual member, but apart from the election of the Board of Directors the business is handled through the Board of Directors and the Representative Council. The Representative Council is made up of the representatives of the branches.

SOME DEVELOPMENTS WITHIN THE PROFESSION

CAHPER has indeed shown very rapid growth. There are now approximately 25 branches of the Association distributed throughout Canada, and there are nearly 1,000 members. A national office is now a reality at 168 Isabella Street, Toronto. We have a full-time secretary and a part time executive secretary, C. R. Blackstock. The Association prints a Journal (*The Journal of CAHPER*) six times a year dealing with all aspects of the related professions. The subscription rate for non-members is $5.00. It distributes and publishes books of professional interest and holds conferences of interest of the profession, as well as its biennial convention. It has a strong link with the Canadian Medical Association, through the activities of the CMA-CAHPER committee.

Much progress is being made in our professional association for physical education, health, and recreation personnel, and slowly but surely there has been an improvement in status and increased recognition of our three fields at the national level. Dedicated people all over Canada are working towards the betterment of their profession by devoted work through the branches and committees of CAHPER.

69. Trends in certification*

Robert Holland

Supervisor, Physical Education and Recreation, Department of Education, State of Ohio

Although several states have made changes in their certification standards in recent years, it is difficult to detect any outstanding or significant trends among the revisions which have taken place.

Below is a summary of the findings we found in reviewing the present certification standards in health and physical education of the various states of the nation:

Several states have recently made or are in the process of making revisions of their health and physical education standards. This would seem to indicate that they feel that existing standards are not adequate in light of present needs in these areas.

There seems to be no uniformity among the various states relative to certification standards in health and physical education.

Generally speaking, statements in respect to standards are general, and not specific. There seems to be a variety of ways of stating the same concept.

Many statements found in certification standards are vague and difficult to interpret.

Many states have established separate certification standards for health and physical education in addition to a combined major in health and physical education.

The norms for certification in health and physical education vary considerably in the different states. For the combined major the range is from 40 to 48 semester hours with an approximate average of 42 hours. For a teaching area in either field, the range is from 15 to 34 hours.

The present trend is to increase the number of hours required for certification, so much so that educators are predicting that within a few years a student will find it necessary to attend four and a half or five years to meet graduation requirements.

There is an increased emphasis on specific course areas like adapted physical education, recreation, outdoor education, school camping, and elementary physical education.

A few states have set up definite requirements for certification in such areas as Supervisor of Health, Physical Education and Recreation, Director of Health, Physical Education and Recreation, and Health Coordinator. These standards vary considerably in different states.

Practically all states have required courses for certification in the following areas: Anatomy and Physiology, Growth and Development, Personal Health, Safety and First Aid, etc.

*From Report of the Green Meadows Conference, 1965, p. 17. Used by permission.

70. Implications for physical education in the current re-examination of American education*

Ruth Abernathy

Professor and Chairman, Department for Women, School of Physical and Health Education, University of Washington

If current popular literature is accurate in reflecting critical opinion, crucial problems of education in the United States might well be identified as centering around *conformity, mediocrity, selfishness,* and *"softness,"* arising from political and economic pressures and consequent dichotomies. In *Quality in Public Education,*[1] the point is made that

the current debate (assessment of public education) is animated by a new spirit of urgency due to an unprecedented foreboding about the future and an unprecedented awareness of human potential for progress. Man's destiny appears to depend upon his acquisition and use of knowledge. Public concern is based, in short, upon a new sense of the relationship, between the quality of education and the future of America.

Ambivalent concerns are reflected in a variety of ways. Demands that "we do as they do but *not* believe as they believe" is only one of the improbables encountered. Gray flannel suited status seekers are viewed with alarm. Creativity and individuality are urged for the academically gifted. A committee of educators has given serious consideration to the need for a national curriculum, and Conant points out the divergencies that make it impossible to develop nation-wide standards. One speaker castigates

education because it has not changed, and there is still clamor for a "return to sound education."

The Educational Policies Commission,[2] states

Although controversy over education has been a continuing feature of the American public scene, at no time has there been serious challenge to the proposition that education must be provided. The great debates have dealt with the kinds of education to be provided, for whom, and by whom.

This picture has not changed, though critics have tended to confuse the issues and to oversimplify corrective measures. A Don Quixote tilting at a windmill labeled Dewey has in some instances been offered as a substitute for the consideration of real philosophical and moral issues.

[Dr. Abernathy discussed two areas of re-examination: purposes and organization of American education (with special reference to Trump's *Images of the Future,* see page 15) and teachers and the preparation of teachers (with special references to the recent action by several organizations, including AAHPER), that graduation from an accredited institution be a requirement for membership. She stated that much of the current re-examination of education has been enormously reassuring, some of it has been directed toward problems that educators have recognized and suffered over for some

*From Journal of Health, Physical Education, and Recreation, Vol. 32, p. 19, Jan. 1961. Used by permission.
NOTE: Dr. Abernathy's remarks are very applicable to current educational trends and crises.
[1]Educational Policies Commission, *An Essay on Quality in Public Education.* Washington, D. C.: National Education Association, 1959, p. 5.

[2]Educational Policies Commission, *National Policy and the Financing of the Public Schools.* Washington, D. C.: National Education Association, 1959, p. 5.

years, and some seem motivated by a kind of manic whimsy that could lead only to further chaos. Her talk proceeded with a listing of five specific implications of the re-examination for those in our fields of education.]

1. The primary focus of each of the fields of health education, physical education, and recreation must be re-examined and to some extent redefined. The essential purposes must be re-examined and clarified. In this connection, there are some questions as to what these fields are about. Health education does not have quite the same problem as do physical education and recreation in that it draws from the health sciences as well as from the behavioral sciences to achieve its body of knowledge. Its application is in the more traditional framework of the school; it deals, we hopefully state, with more meaningful problems to students. Recreation as a *need* has great reality, but there are some questions as to whether or not it has clearly identified the major elements of its responsibility that might be reflected in categories of needed human knowledge. Recreation has responsibilities ranging from the conservation of natural resources to a clearer recognition of its destiny as a major social institution.

If "physical education is the study of human movement in the development and maintenance of the integrity of the human organism," then more is involved than the concept of dealing with "large muscle non-vocational activities." The Graduate Subcommittee of the Physical Education Unit Curriculum study at the University of California at Los Angeles found it fascinating to rethink and regroup areas of knowledge in terms of this definition. Some tentative areas identified only by descriptive words may be provocative.

The hypothalamic, autonomic, genetic, evolutionary, cellular, muscular, and structure and function.

Movement characteristics in terms of "universalities," such as speed, timing, tempo, rhythm.

Movement patterns—from basic, developmental, survival, *fun* (joy of moving) to sports and games characteristic of the United States.

Movement in learning—from contribution to concept formation (near and far—large and small) to body image and even motor learning (which may well be a misnomer).

Movement modification and cultural and physical ecology.

Movement and "oneness with self," or the Zen level as one committeeman characterized it.

History and philosophy of human movement, derived from both the vertical and horizontal aspects of such a construction.

These are cited, not as conclusive or inclusive but rather as an indication of one approach to a most tentative, most preliminary approach to a beginning examination of theory. The purpose is to illustrate the range between a specific skill analysis, a specific sport strategy on the one hand, to the initial steps of seeking a "far out" theoretical framework for a field that many people insist is nonrational, on the other.

Excellence in activities and in technical knowledge is as essential in curriculum development, as is the knowledge of growth and development, but this must *not* mean that we postpone the stretching of horizons in another dimension as one means of clarifying focus and purpose and one means of demonstrating a discipline as contrasted with the application of a discipline. Surely there now is and must be active support for both the extension and improvement of the total continuum that should be physical education.

2. Professional preparation must needs look to breadth, depth, and specialization in both the tradition of levels of application and in the discipline itself. For example, are these disciplines with applied fields or are they only applied or vocational areas?

3. It goes without saying that the increasing competition for gifted young people may hamper critically the ultimate direction of all fields; the implication for selectivity and retention criteria in collegiate preparation is clear.

4. Research directed toward resolving questions of methods of instruction and the organization of learning experiences also must be of priority concern. For example, what objectives of each of the fields may be met more effectively in large groups, in small groups, through independent study or even through the use of teaching machines?

5. Curriculum development must be seen, too, in added dimensions. Attention to the identification of increasingly complex and sequentially arranged concepts of the meaning of human movement is essential to the achievement of appropriate activity throughout the life career.

EXCITING YEARS AHEAD

These are only some of the implications. It should be clear that the most exciting years of any one of these three fields are those immediately ahead. It is easy to slump back into the more comfortable habits and not even recognize that calluses are beginning to form. The years ahead should involve imaginative treatment of problems that we have only tried to explain away in the past. It would seem that each of the three fields, concerned as it is with basic human behavior, has some extremely important work to do to ensure that the contribution is made and the outcomes, in turn, interpreted. I wish I knew some way to make the clarion call. I wish I knew some way to identify the answers. I wish I knew some way to translate my real feeling of excitement in examining next steps, and my hope that we do not seek to find excuses, but rather to find the way in relatively unexplored areas of human experience.

71. The case for a bold, new physical education experience*

Charles L. Mand

Professor, Division for Men, School of Physical Education, The Ohio State University

The prospect of investigation and the potential elimination of the required activity program is a chronic, festering problem that afflicts college physical education. There is a broadsword inexorably poised over the program ever ready to slice academic credit or a year from the requirement or finally to decapitate the offerings entirely. Controversies relative to the maintenance of the program are joined sporadically in institution after institution, year after year. In fact, the attacks are so repetitive that many physical educators are prone to shrug, consider them common-place, and feel an intimate concern only if their program or that of a sister institution is jeopardized. These attacks are in effect considered by some an occupational hazard of the physical educator on the college level. They are embarrassing, inconvenient, and time consuming but the physical education program continues despite the repetitive nature of the dispute.

There is also a decided undercurrent that those responsible for the attacks are "academicians" and at best misguided in their efforts to change university offerings in the light of their personal educational beliefs. This fact, plus the rather superficial concern evidenced by many members of the profession over the repetitive nature of the threat, has somewhat obscured the fundamental problem, namely does the present program justify its existence at the college level? Is physical education "out of step" or the victim of current academic haste? Is there the

possibility that some of the attacks are warranted and that critics might be justified in demanding a bold, new physical education experience?

CURRENT LIMITATIONS

There are four relatively common practices which contribute to the chronic difficulty in physical education.

1. The internecine feud relative to the merits of physiological or recreational objectives eliminates consideration of much subject matter material which is integral to physical education.
2. There is a very definite reluctance to employ teaching media other than laboratory experiences in the basic instruction program.
3. The planned sequence of course experiences based on need, interest, and ability, factors representative of a curriculum, is very limited.
4. Generally, there is no comprehensive evaluation of curriculum experiences.

What is subject matter in physical education? It certainly has to do with the efficiency of people with respect to strength, flexibility, and endurance. It also has an equal concern for the behavior of people as they practice and enjoy the many activities which produce strength, flexibility, and endurance. In fact, the subject matter content in physical education includes sports information, mechanical analysis of motor movement, emotional aspects of competition, activity skills, safe and unsafe exercise patterns—in short, participation with understanding. These terms participation and understanding underline all educational efforts. One without the other is a mark of failure for the educational process. Currently in physical education this concept is being buried under a flow of verbiage "emphasizing an emphasis"

*From Journal of Health, Physical Education, and Recreation, Vol. 33, p. 39, Sept. 1962. Used by permission.

319

—either physical fitness or recreational sports participation as ends in themselves. Our students are being denied a view of the forest because of excessive concern for the trees.

Those who represent the physiological approach to physical education stoutly defend their thesis on the basis of the unique aspect of gross motor activity present in physical education but not usual in other curriculum areas. That physical education is unique in the school program with respect to motor activity is undoubtedly true. However, this factor is still not a justifiable excuse for permitting activity, even gross motor activity, without demanding understanding, without planning a curriculum that permits understanding as well as participation to occur. The music teacher represents a specific area of the curriculum but certainly on the college level requires more of students than the ability to blow a horn or strum a guitar. An even more pertinent example is in the field of art where a student's sculpture or painting is evaluated as it represents comprehension of human experience, not merely technique with the brush.

EMOTIONAL IMPACT OF COMPETITION

There is an additional factor relative to physical education activity which is equally unique as an experience in the curriculum, namely, the opportunity to participate under the emotional stimulus of competition. All who have observed youngsters and adults participate in sports and games recognize that the dynamics of the situation are quite different from the response to classroom stimuli. Success and failure in sport situations are more readily evident. The response is usually overt, often exaggerated to the point of asocial behavior. Obviously, something intrinsic is occurring in the life of each student who participates in activity with such tremendous emotional overtones. Whether the result of this participation is increased maturation or personality retardation or whether the beneficial effects are transferred to daily pursuits is a point of effort for the physical education teacher. To ignore this facet of the field, regardless of how difficult it is to measure results, is to ignore subject matter content inherent to the field of physical education.

UNDERSTANDING PERFORMANCE

The concept of participation with understanding relates directly to the second point of weakness in present instructional programs—the emphasis on laboratory experiences. The biologist, chemist, and physicist are quite involved with laboratory performance. These disciplines demand that students practice safely the theoretical basis of their respective subject matter areas. However, the "how" of chemistry, physics, or biology is inadequate; these students must also know "why." To ensure that participation with understanding is achieved in these areas, lecture and discussion classes complement the laboratory experience. There is sound cause for physical educators to review present teaching methods in an effort to discover why lectures and discussion are not central to their educational efforts as they are to other teaching fields. It must be quite difficult for the biology or physics teacher to consider seriously the impact of an area such as physical education which demands performance, as do their areas, yet provides little opportunity for understanding the performance.

The limited time available generally for the instructional program emphasizes the importance of items 3 and 4 under current limitations, the lack of a planned curriculum and comprehensive evaluation.

NEEDED—AN OVER-ALL CONCEPT OF THE PURPOSE OF PHYSICAL EDUCATION

The result of the student's courses in physical education has to reflect more than a temporary gain in physical fitness, the acquisition of recreational sports skills, or both of these objectives. The result must be greater understanding of the significance of activity. The student, at the conclusion of his experience, should have gained a concept of activity that transcends the specific factors of exercise routines, skill, sportsmanship, and other subject matter materials. Granted that this is a difficult proposition in any field, the planning of an instructional program should strive to this end. The curriculum must be designed to guide the student into personally meaningful experiences which in their sum total represent a concept rather than a series of somewhat unrelated incidents. There should be a beginning and an end to the instructional physical education curriculum.

Presently there seems to be a beginning and an end to the courses of golf, tennis, and conditioning, without relevance to the overall purposes of the physical education experience.

Evaluative techniques are necessary to distinguish and classify individual students' needs and competencies. Furthermore, evaluation not only assists in promoting developmental experiences but also is useful in determining to what extent the program has accomplished an integration of the multiple offerings inherent in any balanced program.

SUGGESTED IMPROVEMENTS

The following suggestions are offered to remedy the limitations exposed here.

1. Establish a classification profile consisting of information relative to postural and general fitness, somatotype, recreational skill level, and knowledge of and experience in sports for each student.

2. Provide each student with a personal classification profile of these factors and prescribe classes on the basis of the profile.

3. Utilize a team approach to the physical education curriculum. (One instructor should be responsible for the guidance of 100-200 students during the course of the students' physical education career. Group guidance techniques can facilitate this process and specialists can teach activity classes.)

4. Provide systematic instruction in motor analysis, scientific knowledge related to exercise physiology, and the emotional factors related to competition.

5. Utilize lecture-discussion courses and television teaching to complement laboratory experiences.

6. Establish a curriculum experience which represents the subject matter of physical education and requires specific student outcomes.

7. Evaluate each student's progress in knowledge and skills by means of a comprehensive examination at the conclusion of the physical education experience.

The institutional controversy about the value of physical education in colleges would be minimized by the adoption of these suggestions. The full impact of the potential of this field for student development would be more nearly realized.

In 1891 James Boykin made the following statement regarding physical education: "All the history of the subject shows that the conflict of systems and methods, not popular indifference has been next to the inefficiency of teachers, the most dangerous enemy with which physical education has had to contend."[1] It is time to answer the critics with action—constructive action which reflects the full potential of physical education and enriches the educational process.

[1]"Physical Training," Vol. I, p. 524. Report of the Commission of Education, 1891-92. Washington, D. C., Government Printing Office, 1894.

72. Fundamental issues in our profession*

Ray O. Duncan†

Former Dean, School of Health, Physical Education, and Recreation, University of West Virginia

The fundamental issues facing our profession involve an understanding of just what our profession entails—what is its nature and scope, what is its place in education, how can we fulfill our educational destiny and how should we prepare people to do the job? People in the field disagree about these things; that is why they become issues. This article identifies four basic problems and presents suggestions for their solution.

NATURE AND SCOPE—
PLACE IN EDUCATION

There is disagreement among the people in our profession as to the purposes of physical education. I believe the diversity of meaning is due to the efforts of physical educators to establish physical education as an integral part of general education.

Education has made tremendous advances in the United States during the past thirty years, and physical education has striven to keep pace. The educational stream has deepened and broadened into a navigable channel reaching into every city, town, and village in the nation. Physical education has been swept along this educational stream, and in an effort to remain afloat, shipshape, and serviceable, has assimilated a wide diversity of purposes and objectives; it has sailed into every tributary and inlet connected with the main stream. This attempt to measure up to all of the objectives of general education has resulted in complexity and confusion. We have been attempting to do *too much*

through physical education, we have been *too general*. It is time for us to identify the unique aspects of physical education in regard to the total educational program and to concentrate upon them.

In order to be considered an integral part of education, it is not necessary for physical education to contribute to all of the objectives of education. During the past thirty years, physical educators have claimed to develop health, strength, organic vigor, neuromuscular skills, character, citizenship, democratic concepts, cooperation, appreciations, moral values, athletic and sports skills, physical fitness, total fitness, social competence, mental health, emotional stability—to mention a few stated objectives.

If we proclaim *too much* for physical education, we weaken our claim for inclusion in the school program by suggesting duplication. Each subject area which is considered to be "essential" in the school curriculum occupies its position because of the unique contributions which it makes. For example, the primary object of English is communication reading, writing, speaking, understanding, expression. The function of mathematics is to develop the skills pertaining to arithmetic, algebra, geometry, trigonometry, calculus. These two basic areas concentrate upon their unique contributions and not upon outcomes such as character, moral values, health, safety, democratic beliefs, emotional stability, and the like which are the responsibility of *all teachers* and *all departments*.

In order for physical education to become an integral part of education at every grade level, it is essential to establish two basic principles.

1. That children need certain experiences

*From Journal of Health, Physical Education, and Recreation, Vol. 35, p. 19, May, 1964. Used by permission.
†Deceased.

322

which can only be provided through physical education.

2. That the school has the responsibility to provide these experiences. If physical educators are to be successful in this endeavor, they must concentrate upon the unique contributions which physical education can make to the education of children and youth.

There are two essential needs which must be met by the school that can only be accomplished through physical education. They are physical fitness and athletics, sports, and dance.

Physical fitness. Physical fitness is essential to effective living. Physical fitness is total body fitness, and just as health is total and represents "physical" and "mental," likewise "physical fitness" means total fitness—physical, social, emotional, mental. Physical fitness points to our unique contribution in the development of organic vigor, strength, agility, balance, flexibility, coordination, endurance, and efficient body movement. It encompasses all of the physical skills essential to body movement and manipulation. It means an understanding of the relationship of fitness to the individual's social and mental well-being, the knowledge of how to develop physical fitness, and a desire to maintain it. English, physical science, and mathematics make no contribution to these outcomes, though they do have opportunity to affect the mental and social fitness of students. This unique concept for physical education does not indicate that "mental" and "social" fitness are not important, nor that physical education does not develop them. The stated idea merely recognizes that our educational approach is through the physical, and in the development of physical fitness there will be mental and social outcomes of equal value. It may be possible for a school to develop adequate emotional stability (mental fitness) and social competence (social fitness) without physical education in the curriculum. However, it is impossible for a school to provide for the development of organic vigor, strength, endurance (physical fitness) without physical education. So let us not quibble about terminology. Physical fitness is a term which is understood by all. Physical educators should stress its development as one of the unique contributions of physical education.

Athletics, sports, dance. People recognize that play is a biological and social necessity for children. Physical educators must advance the idea that if children need to play, it necessarily follows that they must be taught *what* and *how* to play. The notion that children know how to play inherently, without instruction, guidance, and leadership, is false. This simple point is tremendously important. It is essential to convince parents that the play situation presents a real learning situation in which words and actions come from the heart. In fact, the greatest learning opportunity in the life of a child is likely to present itself during play, and the highest type of leadership and guidance should be provided. The school's acceptance of this responsibility means adequate facilities for play, scheduled time, and instruction. This is physical education.

Athletics and sports are vital parts of American culture. The Educational Policies Commission has said that "The experience of playing athletic games should be a part of the education of all children and youth who attend school in the United States."

The play need of children develops into an athletic and sports urge which becomes very strong about the eleventh or twelfth year and flourishes into adolescence. This athletic interest has resulted in school recognition and acceptance of responsibility as evidenced by the athletic programs of various types in practically all junior and senior high schools. The athletic interest is tremendous and so powerful that it occasionally disturbs the very foundations of our educational program. Yet, the public understands and supports athletics, even though there may be occasional programs which are questionable in value.

Girls have the same interest as boys in play and sports. However, at the time when boys desire an accelerated program of athletics the girls seem to favor expanded rhythms, dance, individual and recreational sports.

School administrators, parents, and patrons recognize the importance of athletics, sports, and dance in American life and will accept the school's responsibility to provide these experiences. This is a unique contribution which physical education can make to education. It requires facilities, personnel, and a place in the curriculum.

Physical education is an important phase of education for all children and youth. It provides essential learning experiences which are not provided by other curricular areas. Physical education is physical fitness, athletics, sports, dance. We must stress these essential outcomes which are unique. Social and emotional outcomes of equal importance must not be neglected, but they will evolve with the unique outcomes.

Health education, safety education, recreation, and athletics are parts of our professional responsibility. We must understand their place in our professional family and blend them into our structure in an effective manner. Health education is not synonymous with physical education; it is not the sole responsibility of the physical education teacher but a matter of concern for the entire school. The same may be said of safety education. Yet, the prevalent pattern in elementary and secondary schools is to center health education, safety education, and physical education in a single department or general curricular area with health and safety cutting across and being a part of many other school departments and areas.

Recreation includes many things done during one's leisure time and involves many areas in the school in addition to physical education. The interscholastic and intercollegiate athletic programs involve physical education activities for the physically gifted student but represent a program different from basic physical education. Yet all of these —physical education, health education, safety education, recreation, and varsity athletics—are so closely related as to be considered part of a family unit. Each is a separate entity as is father, mother, brother, sister, but the family relationship exists and we must strive to develop this concept for professional identification.

Methods of incorporating health and safety instruction into a school curriculum will vary, as will the approach to meeting recreational needs of students. However, it is imperative that our professional people understand the nature and scope of all the related areas—physical education, health education, safety education, recreation, athletics—and, most important, work cooperatively to organize an effective program within the school to meet the needs of students in all of the areas within the organizational pattern adopted to do the job.

WHAT TO DO ABOUT PHYSICAL FITNESS?

We have said that physical fitness is one of the unique contributions of physical education. We have always considered the development of physical fitness to be a general objective of physical education. However, the tremendous national interest in physical fitness has created an issue. A "part" of a program threatens to become the "whole" program. Reaction among our professional people seems to range from a complete acceptance of *physical fitness* as a new designation for our professional areas of education to a complete refusal to accept it at all. Many of our professional leaders are critical of the national development of physical fitness and look upon it as detrimental to the best interests of our profession.

I believe that there is a middle ground we must take. Physical fitness is not physical education; it is not a subject area—it is a state of being. The national interest in physical fitness has established the most favorable climate for health, physical education, and recreation that has ever existed in the history of American education. Conditions are more conducive to progress in health, physical education, and recreation at the present time than at any previous period in our professional history. I am convinced we should applaud this situation, accept it with pleasure, and set about to interpret to the pupils, parents, and patrons of our schools what physical fitness means.

We must point out that physical fitness is a state of being for all people. It is highly individual, and the desirable state of physical fitness for each person will depend upon many things. However, the development and maintenance of fitness is primarily a school responsibility. It involves many aspects of the school program, but primarily it involves physical education, health education, and recreation. It should not be difficult for us to relate physical fitness to health, physical education and recreation, and thus use the intense national interest in physical fitness to obtain support for our programs. Our job is to capitalize upon the national interest in physical fitness and utilize it to secure adequate programs of health, physical education, recreation, and safety.

PROFESSIONAL PREPARATION

How should we prepare people to do the job?

Our profession was born as physical education and centered in "gymnastics, games and athletics." Health education came into the school in an integrated manner, associated with many established curricular areas, particularly science and physical education. The prevalent pattern which developed in junior and senior high schools is to give physical educators health education responsibilities, regardless of the preparation of the teacher. Physical educators have not sought this additional responsibility, but it has been thrust upon them. As health education developed in this manner, considerable criticism has been leveled at physical education teachers for doing a poor job of teaching health. Some of the criticism is justified, for health is often a rainy day, ill-prepared program associated with physical education. However, I believe that physical education has received much undeserved criticism. Physical educators have assumed their health education responsibilities and contributed to the establishment of health education in the school curriculum. Teacher education institutions have increased health education requirements for physical education majors. Finally, of course, came the development of the health education curriculum as found today in many of our best colleges and universities preparing professional personnel in our field.

Safety education's development was similar to that of health education. In most of our professional preparation institutions, it is considered a part of health education.

The development of recreation as a profession brought many physical educators out of coaching and teaching into this new area. The athletic and sports skills of physical educators seemed to be considered sufficient preparation for recreation leadership. As it became recognized that recreation consisted of much more than athletics and sports, teacher preparation institutions added recreation to the professional preparation curriculum. In many schools recreation became

a department similar to physical education and health education.

We have come a long way since the days when the physical educator was expected to do everything in our areas of physical education, health education, and recreation. I am not suggesting a return to the former practice, but I do believe that we should not specialize to such an extent that we fail to recognize a situation which exists in our junior and senior high schools and will continue for years to come. In many communities there is no organized recreation program and whatever professional leadership may develop is likely to be centered in the high school physical education teacher or teachers. In the majority of the nation's schools, health and safety education are likely to be associated with physical education. Whether we like it or not, the prevalent pattern in secondary schools is to coordinate health and physical education, and I believe this trend will continue for some time. School administrators believe that teachers can be prepared adequately to teach physical education, health education, and safety education and give constructive recreational leadership to the school and community.

We recognize the importance of the development of separate curriculums for health education, safety education, as well as physical education in order to meet present needs. This trend will certainly continue at the college and university level. It is important that we strengthen, not weaken, the professional preparation programs in health, physical education, recreation, and safety, but let us give some consideration to the preparation of the "generalist"—namely, the physical educator who must have good preparation in health education, recreation, and safety education. The development of this concept will not interrupt the continuous growth of each member of our professional family—health education, safety education, physical education, recreation—to full maturity. It merely recognizes the fact that if all of these areas are to go forward in every community in America it is imperative that the physical educator have preparation in health safety, and recreation.

General preparation does not prevent the development of the separate curriculum in each area to its full essential strength, but assures that a physical educator will be prepared to give some essential leadership in all areas.

Colleges and universities with separate departments of health education, safety education, physical education, and recreation should continue to offer a comprehensive program in each area for students who desire this type of professional preparation.

The proposed "general program" is essential for the students who wish to prepare for the many opportunities which exist in our schools and communities to serve and give leadership in the total areas of health, physical education, and recreation. I believe that a majority of our teacher preparation programs are already of this type, although few, perhaps, are doing it satisfactorily. The important thing to bear in mind is that the physical educator must receive sufficient health, safety, and recreation for adequate preparation and this must be done without weakening preparation in physical education. The physician is prepared in general medicine before specialization in a particular area. Perhaps the same approach would be desirable for our profession, with specialization centered in the fifth year. The physical educator is really a health, safety, and physical educator, as well as a recreation leader, and his preparation should reflect this, particularly at the undergraduate level. If we can more effectively integrate the fields of health and safety education, physical education, and recreation in the undergraduate preparation, we shall take an important step toward greater unity in our profession.

IDEALS AND INDUSTRY

These three critical issues focus upon our professional people. Leadership is the key to their solution and to the continued development of our profession. There is no area of education so important to the complete well-being of children and youth as health, physical education, and recreation, yet there is probably no area which falls so short of fulfilling its opportunities and responsibilities. What is done about this situation depends upon you and me. We must realize the full significance of health, physical education, and recreation. We must have ideals and the industry to carry them out; standards and the strength to enforce them. We must have the willingness to work diligently and tirelessly in our profession.

Someone said, "I am only one, but still am one. I cannot do everything, but I still can do something; and because I cannot do everything, I will not refuse to do the something that I can do."

Multiply that by our 35,000 [now 50,000] members of AAHPER—the beginning is with us. Let us make the start "to do the something we can" to do a better job in our profession.